THE FACTORY ACTS IN IRELAND, 1802–1914

* Volumes 1–7 are published by Irish Academic Press.

The Factory Acts
in Ireland, 1802–1914

DESMOND GREER

and

JAMES W. NICOLSON

FOUR COURTS PRESS
in association with
THE IRISH LEGAL HISTORY SOCIETY

Typeset in 10 pt on 12 pt Plantin by
Carrigboy Typesetting Services, County Cork for
FOUR COURTS PRESS LTD
7 Malpas Street, Dublin 8, Ireland
e-mail: info@four-courts-press.ie
and in North America for
FOUR COURTS PRESS
c/o ISBS, 5824 N.E. Hassalo Street, Portland, OR 97213.

A catalogue record for this title is available
from the British Library.

ISBN 1–85182–583–5

Printed in England by
MPG Books, Bodmin, Cornwall

Contents

Preface

The factory acts of the first half of the nineteenth century have long held a strong fascination for political, economic, legal and social historians. They may be seen as a major example of state intervention in an age supposedly dominated by laissez faire principles; in another sense, they provide a focus for the study of labour relations and the growth of trade unionism; yet other commentators see the acts in terms of social ordering or gender politics. As a result the background to the acts, their substantive provisions and their actual operation in the period up to the 1860s have been the subject of numerous studies. Curiously, however, there has been much less interest in the much more comprehensive legislation enacted from 1878 onwards. In addition, the existing studies have been largely confined to Great Britain, even though the acts from the outset applied throughout the United Kingdom. The aim of this book is, therefore, to redress this imbalance by providing a detailed analysis of the ways in which the factory acts applied to Ireland throughout the nineteenth and early twentieth centuries, and to attempt an evaluation of the impact which successive acts, and the factory inspectors who were responsible for enforcing their provisions, had upon the working conditions of men, women and children employed in various Irish industries in the century or so leading up to the first world war.

This study is divided into four main sections. Chapters 1–4 set out, in the context of general industrial developments in Ireland, the growth of the legislation and the provision made for its enforcement from the first tentative attempt in 1802 to regulate the health and morals of a small number of apprentices in cotton factories to the comprehensive code enacted in 1901 which dealt with the working conditions of one quarter of a million men, women and children employed in all kinds of factories and workshops throughout Ireland. Chapters 5–7 concentrate on the linen industry and examine the impact of the acts on the preservation of the health and safety of women and children working in linen mills and factories, and also provide an analysis of the ways in which attempts were made by the Truck Acts to secure for these workers the fair payment of their wages. The linen industry was primarily located in the north of Ireland; accordingly, other industries, many of which were to be found throughout the island, provide the focus for Chapters 8–9, which deal in particular with three types of employment predominantly undertaken by men, and with selected 'smaller' industries, which employed both men and women. The final section of the book examines the work of the inspectors and the magistrates' courts in the enforcement of the acts, and also deals with the extent to which the standards set by the legislature were upheld by the superior courts in civil proceedings brought by or on behalf of workers killed or injured in the course of their employment.

Our aim throughout this study has been to concentrate attention on the legal history of the factory acts, on the grounds that this has been largely neglected by Irish historians. But we have endeavoured as far as possible to locate that history within its wider social and economic context. The law and its administration have much to teach us about working conditions, labour relations and social organisation, and a study of the factory acts adds another dimension to our understanding of the daily fabric of an important part of Irish society. Likewise, the social and economic context have much to teach us about the nature of law and its practical application. We have no doubt that there is much more to be said about the theoretical and philosophical issues which underlie this subject. But such an analysis could only be properly undertaken in the context of a more profound study of the factory acts throughout the United Kingdom as a whole, and we were very conscious that our work had already reached over-lengthy proportions. We can but hope that this study provides the stimulus for further work of this kind.

This book itself has a lengthy history. It originated as a Ph.D. thesis by James Nicolson undertaken at the suggestion and under the supervision of Professor J.W. Boyle of the Department of History, University of Guelph, Ontario. Some time later Dr Nicolson kindly agreed to permit his thesis to be adapted for publication by the Irish Legal History Society. Rather longer ago than he would care to remember, Desmond Greer undertook to take on this work, and it has been his task to update and extend Dr Nicolson's thesis. It is the profound hope of both authors that this unusual combination has resulted in a singular publication.

James Nicolson wishes to acknowledge the comments, criticism, patience and inspiration which he received from Professor Boyle and which went far beyond what a postgraduate student may reasonably expect from his supervisor. He is grateful to the University of Guelph and others for generous financial and other support which enabled him to undertake research in the United Kingdom and in Ireland, and he wishes to thank the staff of the Robarts Research Library, Toronto, the McLaughlin Library, University of Guelph and the Dana Porter Arts Library, University of Waterloo for their assistance.

Both authors are greatly indebted to the staff of the Public Record Office in London and the Public Record Office of Northern Ireland, the National Library of Ireland, the National Archives of Ireland and the library of the Queen's University of Belfast for their patience and expertise in answering many queries and for their general guidance and support. We are also very grateful to Four Courts Press both for their skill in the production of this work – and for their considerable forbearance while they awaited delivery of the manuscript.

Desmond Greer wishes to acknowledge his gratitude to The Queen's University of Belfast for financial assistance with respect to his researches in London and Dublin. He also wishes to record his thanks to Professor Nial Osborough, Dr Brenda Collins and Professor Leslie Clarkson for their comments and suggestions, and to the staff of the Ulster Museum, the Ulster Folk Museum and the National Photographic Library, Dublin for their help in locating the illustrations included in this book.

Last, but certainly not least, both authors wish to extend their apologies to their respective wives for long hours spent in isolation and to thank them for their continuing support and understanding over many years.

DESMOND GREER
JAMES NICOLSON

April 2002

List of Illustrations

Illustrations appear between pp. 190 and 191.

Abbreviations

AC	Law Reports, Appeal Cases (London, 1891–)
AG	Attorney GeneralBelfast
All ER	All England Law Reports (London, 1936–)
Althorp's act	Factories Act 1833 (3 & 4 Will. IV, c. 103)
B & S	Best & Smith's Reports (London, 1861–1865)
Bonner report	*Report … on the draft regulations … for the processes of spinning and weaving flax and tow* [Cd. 2851], H.C. 1906, xv, 943
Br. J. Ind. Med.	*British Journal of Industrial Medicine* (London, 1944–)
Ch	Law Reports, Chancery (London, 1891–)
Chief insp. ann. rep.	*Annual reports of the chief inspector of factories, 1878–*
CPD	Law Reports, Common Pleas Division (London, 1875–1880)
Ct Exch	Court of Exchequer
Ct Exch Ch	Court of Exchequer Chamber
Delevigne/Whitelegge report	*Report by Sir Malcolm Delevigne and Sir Arthur Whitelegge on the factory inspectorate, 1913* PRO LAB 14/182
Dublin Q.J. of Med. Science	*Dublin Quarterly Journal of Medical Science* (Dublin, 1846–1871)
Econ. Hist. Rev.	*Economic History Review* (Oxford, 1927–)
El & Bl	Ellis and Blackburn's Queen's Bench Reports (London, 1851–1858)
El & El	Ellis and Ellis Queen's Bench Reports (London, 1858–1861)
Eng Rep	English Reports, 1210–1865 (London)
Ex Div	Law Reports, Exchequer Division (London, 1875–1880)
Exch	Exchequer Reports (Welsby, Hurlstone and Gordon) (London, 1847–1856)
Freer-Smith report	*Report of the departmental committee on humidity and ventilation in flax mills and linen factories (mainly in Ireland)* [Cd. 7446], H.C. 1914, xxxvi, 1
H & C	Hurlstone & Coltman Reports (London, 1862–1866)
H & N	Hurlstone & Norman Reports (London, 1856–1862)
HC	House of Commons

HL	House of Lords
HL Cas	House of Lords Cases (London, 1847–1866)
Hansard 1, i, [etc]	*Cobbett's Parliamentary Debates, 1803–12* (London, 1804–12), continued as *The parliamentary debates from the year 1803 to the present time*, 1812–1820 (London, 1812–20)
Hansard 2, i [etc]	*The parliamentary debates ... published under the superintendence of T.C. Hansard*, new series, 1820–1830 (London, 1820–30)
Hansard 3, i [etc]	*Hansard's parliamentary debates*, third series, 1830–91 (London, 1831–91)
Hansard 4, i [etc]	*The parliamentary debates (official report)*, fourth series, 1892–1908 (London, 1892–1908)
Hansard 5 (commons), i [etc]	*The parliamentary debates (official report)*, fifth series, *house of commons*, 1909–(London, 1909–)
Hist. J.	*Historical Journal* (Cambridge, 1958–)
Hobhouse's act	Labour in cotton mills act 1831 (1 & 2 Will. IV, c. 39)
IAOS	Irish Agricultural Organisation Society
ICLR	Irish Common Law Reports (Dublin, 1849–1866)
IHS	*Irish Historical Studies* (Dublin, 1938–)
ILTR	Irish Law Times Reports (Dublin, 1867–)
ILT & SJ	*Irish Law Times and Solicitors' Journal* (Dublin, 1867–)
IR	Irish Reports (Dublin, 1894–)
Insp. half-yearly rep.	*Half-yearly reports of HM Inspectors of Factories, 1845–1877*
Insp. quart. rep.	*Quarterly reports of HM Inspectors of Factories, 1837–1844*
Insp. rep.	*Reports of HM Inspectors of Factories, 1833–1836*
Int'l J. Sociology of Law	*International Journal of the Sociology of Law* (London, 1973–)
Int'l Rev. Social History	*International Review of Social History* (Assen, Netherlands, 1955–)
Ir. Builder	*The Irish Builder and Engineer* (Dublin, 1867 –)
IR ... CL	Irish Reports, Common Law series (Dublin, 1867–78)
Ir. Eccles. Rec.	*Irish Ecclesiastical Record* (Dublin, 1864–1968)
Ir. Jur.	*Irish Jurist* (Dublin, 1966–)
Ir Jur (ns)	Irish Jurist reports (Dublin, 1849–66)
Ir WLR	Irish Weekly Law Reports (Dublin, 1895–1902)
Irish Econ. & Soc. Hist.	*Irish Economic and Social History* (Dublin and Belfast, 1974–)

Irish TUC	Irish Trades Union Congress
ITGWU	Irish Transport and General Workers' Union
J. Kildare Arch. Soc.	*Journal of the County Kildare Archaeological Society* (Kildare, 1892–)
J. Law & Econ.	*Journal of Law and Economics* (Chicago, 1958–)
J. Law & Society	*Journal of Law and Society* (Oxford, 1973–)
J. Legal Hist.	*Journal of Legal History* (London, 1980–)
JSSISI	*Journal of the Statistical and Social Inquiry Society of Ireland* (Dublin, 1863–)
KB	Law Reports, King's Bench Division (London, 1901–1952)
LC	Lord Chancellor
LCB	Lord Chief Baron
LJQB	Law Journal Reports (Queen's Bench) (London, 1831–1946)
LR Ir	Law Reports, Ireland (Dublin, 1879–93)
LR ... QB	Law Reports, Queen's Bench (London, 1865–1875)
LR ... Sc & Div	Law Reports, Scotch and Divorce Appeals (London, 1866–1875)
LT(QB)	Law Times Reports (Queen's Bench) (London, 1859–1947)
M & W	Meeson & Welsby's Exchequer Reports (London, 1836–1847)
Macq.	Macqueen's Scotch Appeal Cases (Edinburgh, 1851–1865)
Modern L. Rev.	*Modern Law Review* (London, 1937–)
NIJR	New Irish Jurist Reports (Dublin, 1900–05)
NUI	National University of Ireland
Orme-Abraham report	*Report by Miss Eliza Orme and Miss May Abraham on the conditions of work in various industries in ... Ireland* [C. 6894–XXIII], H.C. 1893–94, xxxvii (pt. 1), 545
Osborn report	*Report ... upon the conditions of work, etc. in flax mills and linen factories... in the United Kingdom* [C. 7287], H.C. 1893–94, xvii, 537.
PRO	Public Record Office, London
PRONI	Public Record Office of Northern Ireland
QB	Law Reports, Queen's Bench Division (London, 1891–1900, 1952–)
QBD	Law Reports, Queen's Bench Division (London, 1875–1890)

Report of the factory and workshop commissioners	*Report of the commissioners appointed to inquire into the working of the factory and workshop acts with a view to their consolidation and amendment* [C. 1443], H.C. 1876, xxix, 1
RI	Republic of Ireland
RIC	Royal Irish Constabulary
Sc. Hist. Rev.	*Scottish Historical Review* (Aberdeen, 1904–)
Smith report	*Report upon the conditions of work in flax and linen mills as affecting the health of the operatives employed therein* [Cd. 1997], H.C. 1904, x, 465
TLR	Times Law Reports (London, 1884–1952)
TUC	Trades Union Congress
WTUL	Women's Trade Union League
1831 act	Truck act 1831 (1 & 2 Will. IV, c. 37)
1833 act	Factories act 1833 (3 & 4 Will. IV, c. 103)
1844 act	Factories act 1844 (7 & 8 Vict., c. 15)
1856 act	Factory act 1856 (19 & 20 Vict., c. 38)
1874 act	Factory act 1874 (37 & 38 Vict., c. 44)
1878 act	Factory and workshop act 1878 (41 & 42 Vict., c. 16)
1887 act	Truck amendment act 1887 (50 & 51 Vict., c. 46)
1891 act	Factory and workshop act 1891 (54 & 55 Vict., c. 75)
1895 act	Factory and workshop act 1895 (58 & 59 Vict., c. 37)
1896 act	Truck act 1896 (59 & 60 Vict., c. 44)
1897 act	Workmen's compensation act 1897 (60 & 61 Vict., c. 37)
1901 act	Factory and workshop act 1901 (1 Edw. VII, c. 22)
1906 act	Workmen's compensation act 1906 (6 Edw. VII, c. 58)

CHAPTER ONE

Laying the foundations: 1802–40

THE STATE OF IRISH INDUSTRY IN 1800

At the close of the eighteenth century, Irish industry was 'a source of great expectations'.[1] More than one million men and women, or two-fifths of those declaring an occupation, were 'chiefly employed in trades, manu-factures or handicrafts' such as the production of woollens and silks, printing and paper-making, sugar-refining, milling, tanning, glass-making, brewing and distilling.[2] Much of this activity would now be regarded as 'proto-industry'[3] – traditional occupations undertaken in small dispersed establishments employ-ing essentially manual labour. In such conditions the relationship of master and servant was, in law, regarded as a private matter, although in some cases subject to regulation by a craft guild or other trade association. It had long been a criminal offence at common law to ill-treat or overwork an appren-tice,[4] and the Irish parliament, like its counterpart in England and Wales, occasionally intervened to prohibit grosser forms of abuse by the master.[5] But it was taken for granted that the children of poorer parents would start to work as soon as they could make a useful contribution to the family's income, and the conditions in which they worked were not in general regarded as a subject for legislative or judicial concern.

By 1800, however, the industrial revolution in Great Britain had already set in train a process of change to large-scale production in factories powered by machinery of one kind or another. In Ireland, the manufacture of textiles,

1 R.B. McDowell, *Ireland in the age of imperialism and revolution, 1760–1801* (Oxford, 1979), p. 11.
2 C. Ó Gráda, *Ireland: A new economic history 1780–1939* (Oxford, 1994), p. 274.
3 See e.g. L.A. Clarkson, 'Proto-industrialization: The first phase of industrialization?' in L.A. Clarkson (ed.), *The industrial revolution: A compendium* (Basingstoke, 1990), p. 178.
4 See e.g. Lord Eldon LC: 'If children were by over work or harsh usage injured in their health, or distorted in their limbs, as had been attributed to the severe labour of cotton factories, their parents or masters were punishable at common law for the offence ... ': *Hansard 1*, xxxix, 346 (9 Dec.1819).
5 Justices of the peace, for example, could intervene if an apprentice was subjected to 'misusage, refusal of necessary provision, cruelty or ill-treatment' by his master: Apprentices (Ire.) Act 1751, s. 3; Apprentices (Ire.) Act 1755, s. 13. In 1825, Sir John Hobhouse suggested that the Irish parliament had introduced the first 'ten hours' act in the form of the Dublin Tailors and Shipwrights Act 1772, s. 16, which set the hours of labour of journeymen shipwrights as being from 6 a.m. to 6 p.m., including one and a half hours for meals: *Hansard 2*, xiii, 644 (16 May 1825). But this legislation was designed to *extend* working hours to counteract restrictions imposed by the shipwrights' combination – see e.g. McDowell, *Ireland in the age of imperialism*, p. 23.

1

and in particular wool, cotton and linen, provided the most likely basis for a similar development. The Irish parliament had introduced protective tariffs for the benefit of the wool and cotton industries and established a Linen Board to promote the development of the linen trade.[6] With such encouragement, and the threat of increasing competition from Yorkshire and Lancashire, the Irish textile industry had slowly begun to depart from its traditional rural, domestic and manual character. As in England it was the cotton industry which led the way, the use of mechanised processes having begun in the 1770s. The new mills were set up where water power was readily available – normally in rural locations which also had the advantage, it was hoped, of removing employees 'from the temptations of urban life, including incipient trade unionism'.[7] In 1780 or thereabouts, for example, Joseph Smith of Lancaster built at Balbriggan a five-storey cotton mill which included 'a complete set of the machinery now in use in Great Britain for spinning by water ...', and in 1790 the first steam-engine in Ireland was installed in a Lisburn spinning mill.[8] These developments were part of a more general process: '[I]n the relatively short time between 1778 and 1793, cotton graduated from an insignificant domestic manufacture to a factory-based industry, on a small scale certainly, but growing rapidly.'[9] By 1811 there were more than 30 cotton mills in the Belfast area alone, directly or indirectly providing employment for 13,000 workers.[10]

Little has been found about the working conditions in these mills; but there is some evidence that they could be oppressive. One well-known example of late eighteenth-century enterprise was Robert Brooke's large cotton mill at Prosperous, Co. Kildare, and it has been said that 'he seems to have ground the faces of the poor as keenly as any of the millowners in Lancashire ...'.[11] The Irish parliament paid no particular attention to such matters; but as more extensive evidence was published of the appalling treatment of young workers in many of the mills and factories of Yorkshire and Lancashire,[12] the United Kingdom parliament was persuaded to intervene.

6   For the early history of the textile industry in Ireland see Ó Gráda, *New economic history*, pp. 274–77, 282–83 and 292–93.

7   McDowell, *Ireland in the age of imperialism*, p. 6.

8   Ibid., p. 17.

9   H.D. Gribbon, *The history of water power in Ulster* (Newton Abbot, 1969), p. 113.

10 Ó Gráda, *New economic history*, p. 276. See also C. Gill, *The rise of the Irish linen industry* (Oxford, 1925), chap. xii. Gribbon, *History of water power*, p. 113 notes that cotton 'alone received any worthwhile protection under the Act of Union'.

11 Gill, *Irish linen industry*, p. 230, citing Lord Sheffield, *Observations on the manufactures, trade and present state of Ireland* (London, 1785), p. 197: 'The pleasure of seeing children advantageously employed in these works, was greatly diminished by learning that part of them work all night, even so young as five or six years old, and the wages so low as sixpence per week ... '. According to Gill, Brooke's enterprise was strongly supported by the Irish government in order to provide employment for poor children from Dublin. But Ó Gráda, *New economic history*, p. 275 notes that 'Brooke was no businessman' and the factory soon closed. See further A.K. Longfield, 'Prosperous, 1776–1798' in *J. Kildare Arch. Soc.*, xiv (1966–67), 25.

12 See e.g. B.L. Hutchins and A. Harrison, *A history of factory legislation* (3rd ed., London, 1926), pp. 7–13. According to U.R.Q. Henriques, *Before the welfare state:*

THE HEALTH AND MORALS OF APPRENTICES ACT 1802

The mechanisation of the cotton industry had produced 'a generation of masters who asked nothing more than that they should be left to carve their way to fortune undisturbed. With a few honourable exceptions, these men were ruthless, hard, and selfish.'[13] These masters quickly found that much of the water-driven machinery could be economically worked by children – and that rural operations could be sustained by importing young boys and girls as 'apprentices' from the workhouses of London and other large cities. The lot of such children was generally not a happy one:

Forlorn and friendless, they were left entirely to the mercy of their masters, and their labour was often limited only by their exhaustion. In low, ill-ventilated rooms they were kept at their monotonous tasks sometimes for fourteen or fifteen hours a day.... Little attention was paid to their education, their morals, or their religious training, and the strain and fatigue they suffered caused ill-health and physical deformity.[14]

Conditions in Sir Robert Peel's cotton mill near Manchester were particularly harsh, and, following an epidemic in 1784, a medical report attributed the outbreak to long hours of work, filthy conditions and poor ventilation.[15] 'Other pursuits' meant that it was some time before Peel reacted to this and similar indictments, but it is to his credit that ultimately he did so by bringing in the first bill for the regulation of working conditions in the new factories.[16]

The 'Act for the preservation of the health and morals of apprentices and others employed in cotton ... mills and ... factories' was passed in 1802.[17] It applied to all cotton mills and factories throughout the United Kingdom which employed three or more apprentices or 20 or more persons. By section 2, the walls and ceilings in all such establishments were to be white-washed at least

Social administration in early industrial Britain (London, 1979), p. 66: 'it was the novelty and abuses of the factory rather than the fact of child labour [which] shocked disinterested contemporaries'.

13 M.W. Thomas, *The early factory legislation: A study in legislative and administrative evolution* (Leigh-on-Sea, Essex, 1948), p. 5.

14 Ibid., p. 7. See also H.A. Mess, *Factory legislation and its administration 1891–1924* (London, 1926), pp. 1–2: 'These wretched children were sent at an early age into what was virtually slavery; they were ill-fed, ill-housed and overworked; they were flogged when their energies failed, and they were buried without inquiry when they died.'

15 Thomas, *Early factory legislation*, p. 8. For a general assessment of the part played by concerned medical practitioners see R. Gray, *The factory question and industrial England, 1830–1860* (Cambridge, 1996), pp. 72–85.

16 'Peel rather naively gave as a reason for bringing in the Bill that he was convinced of the existence of gross mismanagement in his own factories, and having no time to set them in order himself, got an Act of Parliament passed to do it for him': Hutchins and Harrison, *History of factory legislation*, pp. 16–17. According to Henriques, *Before the welfare state*, p. 69 the act was 'an attempt ... to generalise the treatment already afforded to apprentices by the most responsible and philanthropic millowners'.

17 42 Geo. III, c. 73. The debates on the bill were not reported in Hansard, but were summarised in *The Times*, 19 May and 3 June 1802. According to Thomas, *Early factory legislation*, p. 9, there was 'surprisingly little opposition' to it.

twice a year and the number of windows was to be sufficient 'to insure a proper supply of fresh air in and through the same'. Section 4 provided that no apprentice was to work for more than 12 hours per day (exclusive of meals), and night work was to be gradually discontinued. Limited provision was also made for the general welfare, education and religious instruction of apprentices. All these provisions were to be enforced by two local 'visitors' who were 'not interested in, or in any way connected with any such mills or factories'.[18] Appointed by the local magistrates, these visitors were given 'full power and authority from time to time ... to enter into and inspect any such mill or factory, at any time of the day, or during the hours of employment, as they shall think fit', and they were to report to quarter sessions on the conditions of the mills and factories which they had visited. A factory owner in breach of the act could be fined £2 to £5 by the justices, and to encourage 'private' prosecutions, provision was made for one-half of the fine to be paid to an informer.

Despite its good intentions, the 1802 act was little more than an extension of the Elizabethan poor law relating to parish apprentices, and it is commonly regarded as having been largely, if not wholly, ineffective in improving factory conditions in the English cotton industry.[19] Although declared to be applicable throughout the United Kingdom, the act would have had little application in Ireland, where there was no poor law and no parish apprentices. But there may well have been other 'apprentices' employed in cotton mills and factories,[20] and there were by this time a number of establishments in which twenty or more persons other than apprentices were employed.[21] In 1819, however, it was reported that no visitors had even been appointed in 28 of the Irish counties and that only four mills or factories in two counties – Cork and Londonderry – had actually been visited.[22]

18 Section 9. One of the visitors was to be a justice of the peace, the other a clergyman of the established church.
19 'The inadequate system of inspection by a body of unpaid amateurs made it quite impossible to enforce the regulations': Thomas, *Early factory legislation*, pp. 12–13. *Cf.* Hutchins and Harrison, *History of factory legislation*, p. 18: 'some of [the visitors], at least, did their duty ... and endeavoured ... to control bad conditions ...'. O. MacDonagh, *Early Victorian government 1830–1870* (London, 1977), p. 23 attributes the 'fundamental weakness' of the act to 'the fact that [as] the bill had been sponsored by a private member ... no government department was responsible for its later fate'.
20 See e.g. 25 Geo. III, c. 48 (Ire.), ss. 14 and 15 (1785) (charter schools, foundling hospital and house of industry in Dublin given power 'to bind out the children under their care as apprentices to protestant tradesmen, or manufacturers'). Four hundred 'peasant' children were employed from the age of 7, and admitted as apprentices from the age of 14, in Nowlan and Shaw's wool factory at Merino, Co. Kilkenny: 'K.W.', *Sketches of the Merino factory, descriptive of its origin and progress and of its system of discipline and moral government* (Dublin, 1816–1818), pp. 8 and 42–46. See also Plate 1, below and J. O'Connor, *The workhouses of Ireland: The fate of Ireland's poor* (Dublin, 1995), chap. 3.
21 It was during the first quarter of the 19th century that the Irish cotton industry reached its peak – see Ó Gráda, *New economic history*, pp. 274–77.
22 The visitors appointed in Co. Kilkenny and Queen's Co. appear to have done nothing; in Co. Cork three mills were visited, but no report made. In Co. Londonderry, two 'inspectors' visited the cotton factory of James Forsythe & Co. in Castledawson and reported: 'Apprentices: None. The principal apartments have been regularly washed, as also the floors, with quick lime and water, oftener than by law required; and we have given

This apparent lack of concern for the health of children employed in Irish factories was confirmed in 1819, when Mr William Parnell[23] sought leave to present a bill 'for the promotion of the education and morals of children in cotton and other factories in Ireland'.[24] The bill recited that 'great depravity' arose from assembling children in such factories,[25] which should therefore be made subject to 'the inspection of benevolent individuals'.[26] Masters should also be encouraged to take greater care of the morals and education of the children; in particular, Sunday or evening schools should be established – provided such arrangements 'shall not interfere with the hours of labour'. Any master found to be 'careful of the morals and health of the children employed' was to be rewarded by exemption from the payment of certain taxes. The bill received little support, particularly when Sir George Hill[27] observed that no grounds were shown for it, no petitions had been received and there had been no returns either of the number of factories likely to be affected or of the number of children employed in such factories.[28] Although leave was given to bring in the bill, it made no progress, and it was effectively superseded by another bill, applicable to the whole of the United Kingdom, introduced in 1818 by Sir Robert Peel, supported by Robert Owen.

By this time it was becoming clear that the great expectations for the growth of Irish industry were not to be fulfilled. The exposure of Irish industry to competition from technologically-superior English industry unfettered by tariff protection, the restricted domestic market for Irish industrial goods, the lack of indigenous raw materials and shortage of capital[29] – whatever the

directions (which we will take care to have executed) to have the remaining apartments washed, though they are not generally used. There is a very good circulation of free air throughout the whole of the apartments … ': *An account of the cotton and woollen mills and factories in the United Kingdom … whereof entry has been made at the epiphany sessions in every year from the year 1803 to the last year, inclusive, in pursuance of the provisions of an act of the 42nd of the King, cap 73* … , H.L. 1819 (66), cviii, 42–43.

23 MP for Co. Wicklow 1817–21, an able but impractical independent and something of a romantic who supported a number of steps designed to alleviate the plight of the Irish poor – see R.G. Thorne (ed.), *The House of Commons 1790–1820* (London, 1986), iv, 727–28.

24 H.C. 1819 (247), i–b, 1533. The preamble to the bill added that the linen trade was *not* subject to the same problem, 'the spinning and weaving of linen yarn being carried on in the houses of the spinners and weavers themselves'.

25 The parents of young girls were 'very reluctant' to allow them to work in the Merino wool factory 'from an apprehension of that immorality which they knew to exist in the factories of a neighbouring city'; but they were persuaded to give permission by 'the efficacy of the regulations for preventing any degradation of morals': K.W., *Sketches of the Merino factory*, p. 8.

26 Any local clergyman or 'any society of benevolent individuals' should have authority to enter any cotton or other factory and make a report for the chief secretary, the Sunday School for Ireland, the Society for the Suppression of Vice in Ireland and the Society for the Promotion of the Education of the Poor.

27 MP for Co. Londonderry 1802–30, vice-treasurer and a trustee of the Linen Board.

28 *Hansard 1*, xxxix, 1479–80 (27 April 1819).

29 Clarkson, 'Proto-industrialization', p. 178, arguing that linen was the only traditional industry in Ireland to make the successful transition from proto-industry to modern, factory-based, industry.

reason, Irish industry, with the exception of parts of Ulster, failed to develop to any significant extent in the first half of the nineteenth century.[30] Accordingly, it is not surprising that the impetus for legislative regulation of working conditions was to come almost exclusively from Great Britain, and in particular from the north of England. Indeed, it would appear that Irish industrial conditions did not in any case give rise to problems which were, within the limited ambit of the early factories legislation, so unique in kind or degree as to call for distinctive legislation. As a result, Ireland was carried along in the tide of reform, on the basis of a 'parity' principle concerned less with the welfare of Irish workers than with the interests of British masters who demanded that Irish industry should not benefit from special treatment which would, or might, put it at some unfair advantage.

The advent of steam power meant that factories were now increasingly located in urban areas with easy access to coal supplies. In the new industrial towns and villages, the factory workers lived at home, with the result that young workers were now 'free' – that is, non-apprentice labour falling outside the 1802 act.[31] In the new urban factories, the work of adults and children was closely integrated; many of the children were employed directly by their parents and 'the running of the machines depended absolutely on the nimble fingers of the boys and girls'.[32] It was this interdependence of children and adults that complicated reform of working conditions, since it was often unclear whether the objective was simply to improve the working conditions of children and young persons, or to secure benefits (particularly a shorter working day) for the whole of the workforce.[33]

In any event, the Employment of Children in Cotton Mills Act 1819,[34] as amplified during the 1820s,[35] applied to all children and young persons employed in cotton mills and factories throughout the United Kingdom.

30 See e.g. Ó Gráda, *New economic history*, chap. 13; F. Geary, 'Deindustrialization in Ireland to 1851: some evidence from the census' in *Econ Hist Rev*, li (1998), 512.
31 Henriques, *Before the welfare state*, p. 69. Hutchins and Harrison, *History of factory legislation*, p. 19 explain that 'child-workers could easily be had without the trouble and responsibility of taking apprentices, who must be housed, fed and clothed at the employer's expense'; the authors also note that 'the [new] factories for the most part were much larger affairs, and much more before the eye of the public'. See also Thomas, *Early factory legislation*, chap. 2.
32 Thomas, *Early factory legislation*, p. 16. According to Henriques, *Before the welfare state*, p. 69: 'each adult required three or four children'.
33 Henriques, *Before the welfare state*, p. 67.
34 59 Geo. III, c. 66. This act, based on Owen's practice at his New Lanark mill, was preceded by two enquiries – see *Minutes of evidence taken before the select committee on the state of the children employed in the manufactories of the United Kingdom*, H.C. 1816 (397), iii, 235 and *Minutes of evidence taken before the lords committee appointed to inquire into the state and condition of children employed in cotton factories*, H.L. 1819 (24), cx, 1. Neither enquiry heard evidence of conditions in Irish factories. According to Henriques, *Before the welfare state*, p. 71, the manufacturers' lobby 'succeeded in emasculating Owen's proposals'. See further R.G. Kirby and A.E. Musson, *The voice of the people: John Doherty, 1785–1854, Trade unionist, radical and factory reformer* (Manchester, 1975), chap. x and Thomas, *Early factory legislation*, chap. 2.
35 By the Labour in cotton mills act 1820 (60 Geo III and 1 Geo IV, c. 5), the Cotton mills, etc. act 1825 (6 Geo IV, c. 63) and the Labour in cotton mills acts 1829 (10 Geo. IV, cc. 51 and 63).

Unlike Parnell's bill for Ireland, this legislation was designed 'to preserve the *health* and morals of [young] persons'.[36] No child under the age of nine was to work at all; children and young persons aged 9–16 (later extended to 18) were to work no more than 12 hours (exclusive of meal times) on a weekday and nine hours on Saturday; they were not to work at all after 8.30 or 9.00 p.m. and before 5.30 a.m. Abstracts of the act were to be posted in a prominent place in each factory or mill. But nothing was done to ensure that these provisions (once again the work of private members rather than the government) would be effectively enforced,[37] and they, too, appear to have had little practical impact in any part of the kingdom.

The legislation of the 1820s was repealed and replaced without any substantial changes by Hobhouse's act of 1831.[38] Interestingly, an attempt was made to have Scotland excluded from this act on the grounds that it had no poor law and there had been no serious complaints about working conditions there. Hobhouse conceded that Scotland was different; but he ultimately asserted that 'it would be unfair to the English manufacturers to place them under restrictions from which the Scotch were exempt ... '.[39] He then took the opportunity to confirm that the bill also extended to Ireland, presumably for the same reason. But the new act had little practical impact anywhere in the United Kingdom; it was 'seldom or never attempted to be enforced' and was 'almost completely inoperative'.[40] In 1833, for example, the manager of James Grimshawe's cotton-spinning mills in Belfast acknowledged that they worked a 72-hour week; he did not know 'whether that is more than the present Act allows' and added that he 'doesn't think any of the mills about here observe any Act at all'.[41]

36 Preamble to 1819 act (emphasis added).
37 Both Peel and Owen had argued in favour of paid and qualified inspectors – see e.g. *Hansard 1*, xxxi, 624–25 (6 June 1815). Bentham, too, was in favour of inspectors: see e.g. *First principles preparatory to a constitutional code*, ed. P. Schofield (Oxford, 1989). But Parliament, wedded to the principle of *private* enforcement, merely increased the maximum fine to £20, with one half payable to the complainant or prosecutor. Henriques, *Before the welfare state*, p. 72 explains that 'Societies for the Protection of Children in Cotton Factories' were established to bring prosecutions, but were not very successful in obtaining convictions. Informers were also 'hired' by Manchester manufacturers in a 'fairly futile' attempt to prevent overworking by competitors – see e.g. W.G. Carson, 'The conventionalization of early factory crime' in *Int'l J. Sociology of Law*, 7 (1979), 37 at pp. 40–41.
38 Labour in cotton mills act (1 & 2 Will. IV, c. 39). Sir John Hobhouse (Lord Broughton) had previously sponsored the 1825 act which had (*inter alia*) introduced the principle of a shorter (nine-hour) Saturday. Henriques, *Before the welfare state*, p. 71, categorises Hobhouse as 'a middle-class radical who ... believed in the laws of political economy and the free labour market, and was unlikely to sponsor a revolutionary measure'. J.T. Ward, *The factory movement 1830–1855* (London, 1962), p. 43 dismisses the 1831 act as 'a legislative shadow'.
39 *Hansard 3*, v, 388 (27 July 1831) and 558 (30 July 1831).
40 *First report of the central board of H.M. commissioners appointed to collect information in the manufacturing districts relative to the employment of children in factories ...* , p. 32, H.C. 1833 (450), xx, 36.
41 Ibid., *Evidence taken by Mr. Mackintosh*, p. 92. Cf. Kirby and Musson, *Voice of the people*, pp. 348–67 show that between 1829 and 1831 some 187 cases were brought by

Although largely ineffective, the earliest factory acts went a long way to establishing the *principle* of limited state intervention for the protection of children and young persons. They also settled the broad *nature* of the protection perceived to be desirable. What remained in contention was the method of enforcing such provisions, the optimum length of the working day and the much broader question whether the state should also intervene on behalf of adult workers.

THE FACTORY ACT 1833

In 1824 parliament finally removed all duties on goods passing between Ireland and Great Britain; shorn of a protective tariff and unable to compete with the highly-industrialised mills and factories of Lancashire and Yorkshire, the Irish cotton and wool industries, albeit with some notable exceptions, went into decline.[42] But the earlier *rise* of the cotton industry had left an important legacy in the north of Ireland: 'It pushed Belfast into the factory age, necessitated considerable fixed-capital formation ... and successfully developed the system of putting out mill-spun yarn to handloom weavers in Belfast and its hinterland.'[43] The beneficiary of that legacy was the linen industry. Dating back to the seventeenth century, the manufacture of linen was by tradition a rural and manual activity. Some mechanical power was applied in the bleaching process;[44] but, notwithstanding the availability of a mechanised 'dry-spinning' process from 1787 and of subsidies from the Irish linen board, flax-spinning was largely carried on by hand until the 1820s – and handloom linen weaving predominated until after the Famine.[45] By 1825 the industry, originally widespread, was concentrated in the northern part of the island, and the introduction of wet-spinning 'rapidly and

cotton workers in Lancashire; but the proceedings were largely unsuccessful due to widespread intimidation of witnesses and resort by the owners to legal technicalities.

42 See e.g. F. Geary, 'The rise and fall of the Belfast cotton industry: some problems' in *Irish Econ. & Soc. Hist.*, 8 (1981), 30 and idem, 'The Belfast cotton industry revisited' in *IHS*, 26 (1988–89), 250.

43 P. Ollerenshaw, 'Industry 1820–1914' in L. Kennedy and P. Ollerenshaw (ed.), *An economic history of Ulster 1820–1939* (Manchester, 1985), p. 66. See also E.R.R. Green, 'The beginnings of industrial revolution' in T.W. Moody and J.C. Beckett (ed.), *Ulster since 1800: A political and economic survey* (London, 1955), p. 32: 'It was cotton spinning which first brought industrial workers into Belfast in large numbers and the engineering industries of the city originated in the maintenance of machinery for the cotton mills. But it was as a model for the reorganisation of the linen industry that cotton spinning was chiefly important.'

44 Ollerenshaw, 'Industry', p. 69. See also W.A. McCutcheon, *The industrial archaeology of Northern Ireland* (Belfast, 1980), pp. 81–90.

45 Gribbon, *History of water power*, pp. 90–101 explains that dry-spinning produced only coarse or medium yarns – and the fine yarns required by Irish manufacturers could still be produced very cheaply by hand-spinning. See also McCutcheon, *Industrial archaeology*, pp. 293–95: '[T]he encouragement ... of a [mechanised] dry-spinning industry in the north was not a success ... '.

permanently changed yarn production from a domestic to a mechanised factory basis …'.[46] The new wet-spinning mills were at first small, water-powered – and therefore largely rural – affairs; but these were soon followed by 'the construction of large multi-storeyed city mills commanding the full resources of the expanding steam-engine technology'.[47] The first of these mills was that established, in somewhat fortuitous circumstances,[48] by Thomas and Andrew Mulholland in Belfast: 'The mill was completed and opened for production in the spring of 1830…. [It] was five storeys high, contained 15,300 spindles and … when in full production employed nine hundred workers …'.[49] The new mill was so successful that others quickly followed the Mulhollands' example, and by the mid-1830s Belfast had ten substantial steam-powered flax-spinning mills. Linen now replaced cotton as the most important manufacturing industry in Ireland.[50]

The wet-spinning process, by which the scutched flax was converted into yarn by passing through a complex sequence of production centred on the 'flyer and bobbin' spinning frame, dominated the Irish linen industry until well into the twentieth century.[51] Its main significance in the present context is twofold. First, 'the factory system … may be said to have entered upon the phase of maximum growth in Ulster with the large-scale adoption of the wet-spinning process … during the period 1830–1865 …'.[52] Secondly, the new process gave rise to poor working conditions – although it has been suggested that 'the evils of the factory system in Ulster, though real enough, were never so severe as in England, if only because the industrial revolution came later to the province. In this respect, at least, a late start was an advantage …'.[53] It was in this changing industrial situation in Ireland that the first effective factory act came to be enacted.

Under the leadership first of Michael Sadler, Tory MP for Newark, and then of Lord Ashley (later the earl of Shaftesbury and another Tory MP) and

---

46 'Wet spinning permitted the finest yarns to be machine-spun and was first successfully adopted in Ulster by James and William Murland whose new mill was opened, probably early in 1828, at Annsborough near Castlewellan in County Down': Ollerenshaw, 'Industry', p. 69.

47 McCutcheon, *Industrial archaeology*, p. 296, adding that 'the whole nature of the local linen industry was altered within the space of little more than a decade'.

48 The large cotton-spinning mill owned by these brothers in York Street was destroyed by fire in June 1828, and they decided that 'as the English and Scottish competition in the cotton-spinning business was so great, and as the linen trade was the natural business of Ireland, it would be advisable in rebuilding the mill to adapt it for the spinning of flax by machinery, which was accordingly done': memorandum cited by E.R.R. Green, 'Early industrial Belfast' in J.C. Beckett and R.E. Glasscock (ed.), *Belfast* (London, 1967), p. 85.

49 McCutcheon, *Industrial archaeology*, p. 297. See below, plate 2.

50 See generally Geary, 'Deindustrialization in Ireland' and the articles cited in note 42.

51 McCutcheon, *Industrial archaeology*, p. 297.

52 Ibid., p. 298.

53 R.D.C. Black, 'The progress of industrialization, 1850–1920' in Moody and Beckett (ed.), *Ulster since 1800*, pp. 57–58. For a more detailed study, see A. Takei, 'The early mechanization of the Irish linen industry, 1800–1840' (unpublished M.Litt. thesis, University of Dublin, 1990).

driven by the demands of vociferous 'short-time committees' campaigning for a shorter working day for *all* workers, the movement for factory reform in Great Britain quickened after 1830.[54] In December 1831, Sadler introduced a bill to 'restrain' the working day of all textile workers under the age of 18 to 10 hours[55] and obtained sufficient support to secure the appointment of a sympathetic select committee under his own chairmanship.[56] The committee interviewed a number of workers and local doctors who provided detailed evidence of unhealthy and unsafe conditions in the textile factories of England and Scotland – but it took no evidence of factory conditions in Ireland.[57] Before the committee could hear the employers' side of the story and compile its report, however, parliament was dissolved; but the shocking state of affairs revealed by its minutes of evidence, which were published in August 1832, 'created a profound sensation'.[58]

Sadler's bill and the select committee's *ex parte* evidence appear to have provoked much the same division of opinion in Ireland as in England, although little evidence has been found of extensive debate in this country. When Sadler presented a petition from Leeds in support of his bill, three Irish MPs – Daniel O'Connell, John Croker[59] and Sir Robert Bateson[60] – came to his aid, and O'Connell himself presented a petition from Bolton.[61] O'Connell accepted that parliament had no right to interfere with the working conditions of adults; not only were they 'masters of their own time', but the restriction of their working day would 'in consequence of the foreign

---

54 See generally Ward, *Factory movement*, chaps. 2–4; Thomas, *Early factory legislation*, chaps. 3–6; Hutchins and Harrison, *History of factory legislation*, chaps. 3–4; Gray, *Factory question*, chaps. 1–5 and P. Mandler, 'Cain and Abel: Two aristocrats and the early Victorian factory acts' in *Hist. J.*, 27 (1984), 83.

55 H.C. 1831–32 (46), ii, 1. The other notable feature of the bill was the 'draconian' level of penalties – £20 for the first offence, £40 for the second and £60 (or 3–12 months' imprisonment) for the third.

56 Henriques, *Before the welfare state*, p. 74. Henry Meynell of Lisburn (a conservative in favour of free trade) was the only one of the 37 members of the committee who represented an Irish constituency.

57 *Report from the select committee to whom the bill to regulate the labour of children in mills and factories of the United Kingdom was referred*, H.C. 1831–32 (706), xv, 1.

58 Thomas, *Early factory legislation*, p. 40.

59 Croker, a barrister and an MP from 1807 to 1832, admitted that 'Ireland had at present no such large factories as those which claimed the protection of the legislature in the present case'; but, he added, 'the day ... would probably arrive when Ireland might compete in manufactures with the other parts of the empire. It was one of the first duties of good government, to take care of those peaceable and industrious classes who were too severely occupied in earning their daily bread to have leisure to take care of themselves': *Hansard 3*, ix, 1095 (1 Feb. 1832).

60 Conservative MP for Londonderry, 1830–42. A fourth Irish MP to declare in favour of legislation was another barrister and repealer, A.G. O'Dwyer, MP for Drogheda, 1832–35 – see *Hansard 3*, xv, 1164–65 (26 Feb. 1833).

61 *Hansard 3*, x, 21 (7 Feb. 1832). There do not appear to have been any such petitions from Ireland either in 1832 or 1833. But conflicting petitions from 'the operatives of Belfast' were lodged when a later ten hours' bill was being considered in 1844 – see below, p. 33.

competition ... throw both adults and children out of employment ...'.[62] But legislative restriction was justified in the case of children: 'it might be said, that interfering between masters and their labourers violated the principles of political economy; [but] he trusted that the dogmas of that science would not be resorted to, to uphold such an inhuman arrangement as destroyed the health and morals of children, and which had inspired the well-intentioned part of the community with disgust and abhorrence'.[63] Sadler's bill was no more than an application of the traditional legal duty of the crown to protect minors. But O'Connell later intervened to correct the 'erroneous supposition' that children would receive the same wages for fewer hours' work; rather, 'it was evident that masters could only pay for the work actually done ...'.[64] In case it should be thought that parents might therefore *oppose* reform, Sir Robert Bateson was later to emphasise, as a member for a part of Ireland 'where factories were rapidly increasing', that 'he did not believe that there was any amongst them [parents] so slavish – so devoid of parental feeling – as to sacrifice the lives and morals of their children for the sake of the few shillings that they could earn by those additional hours of protracted labour'.[65] But O'Connell was more realistic: a mother exposed her child to 'the sufferings which it was said were endured in a factory ... because the suffering of hunger was still greater'. For this reason, his preferred solution was repeal of the corn laws: 'the lowering the price of a loaf a halfpenny or a penny would spare half an hour's labour to the children ...'.[66]

In the general election which followed the enactment of the Reform Act, Sadler lost his seat in the house of commons.[67] His torch passed to Ashley, who in effect re-introduced Sadler's 'ten hours' bill in March 1833 – thereby setting in train some six months of almost non-stop parliamentary and extra-parliamentary activity. Bolstered by the electoral changes which had taken place, the employers sought to establish that factory conditions were really so benign as to make legislative intervention unnecessary. They quickly persuaded parliament[68] to provide the opportunity to clear their character by appointing a royal commission chaired by Edwin Chadwick 'to collect information in the manufacturing districts, as to the employment of children in factories and as to the propriety and means of curtailing the hours of their labour'.[69] The reports

---

62 *Hansard 3*, xliii, 978 (22 June 1838) and xliv, 423–24 (20 July 1838).
63 *Hansard 3*, x, 21 (7 Feb. 1832).   64 Ibid., col. 195 (10 Feb. 1832).
65 *Hansard 3*, xliv, 410 (20 July 1838). This had also been Sadler's view – see e.g. *Hansard 3*, x, 192 (10 Feb. 1832).
66 *Hansard 3*, xliv, 424 (20 July 1838).
67 He subsequently moved to Belfast, where he died in 1835. See below, Plate 3, and J.F. Rankin, 'Michael Thomas Sadler: A forgotten member of parliament' in *Lisburn Hist. Soc. J.*, 5 (1984), 42. We owe this reference to Professor Brian Walker.
68 On 3 April 1833 the house of commons voted 74–73 in favour of setting up the commission. A number of Irish MPs, who agreed with Ashley that the commission was not necessary, voted against the proposal – but the names of those in favour is not given: *Hansard 3*, xvii, 80–114.
69 The 'central board' of the commission consisted of Chadwick, Thomas Southwood Smith and Thomas Tooke, all of whom were Benthamites committed to *laissez faire* principles which required adults, as free agents, to be free of legislative interference;

of this commission,[70] published within three months of its appointment, provide the first detailed accounts of working conditions in Irish textile mills and factories.[71]

The lowest age at which children were employed in cotton mills in Ireland was nine: 'from experience it is found that children at nine learn fully as quick, if not more so, and are better workers, than when advanced. Beside, they are learning their business at small wages at that early period, when they are nearly useless at home; and when they arrive at eleven or twelve they get good wages in place of commencing at low.' In addition, 'persons when taught young always make the best workers'.[72] Such children were primarily employed 'to get about the machines in cleaning them'.[73]

The factories generally worked 12 or 12^1/$_2$ hours per day, but sometimes for as long as 13^1/$_2$ hours to make up for lost time. In one factory, children were occasionally required to work for 15 hours a day (including one-and-a-half hours for meals);[74] but this work was not necessarily continuous: 'We do suppose upon an average such little ones have not more than from eight hours or perhaps nine per day ... they frequently pop down and sleep until they are required, which will be only for about twenty mintues at a time, and can repeat the like; a good deal depends on the operative who employs them.'[75] There was normally no night work: 'the effects of night-work [are] injurious to the habits of workers in general'.[76] Nor was it the normal practice to work children in relays: 'The first objection would be, nearly

children, however, were not free agents, and the legislature could properly impose work restrictions on their behalf and the principle of utility then required a centralised and professional administration to enforce such restrictions rigorously and effectively. See especially MacDonagh, *Early Victorian government*, pp. 34–46.

70 *Central board of His Majesty's commissioners appointed to collect information in the manufacturing districts, as to the employment of children in factories, and as to the propriety and means of curtailing the hours of their labour, with minutes of evidence and reports of district commissioners: First report*, H.C. 1833 (450), xx, 1; *Second report*, H.C. 1833 (519), xxi, 1; *Supplementary reports*, H.C. 1834 (167), xix, 253 and xx, 1.

71 Throughout the United Kingdom, 'on-the-spot' enquiries were conducted by a medical commissioner and two 'civil' district commissioners. Sir David Barry, James Stuart and Robert Mackintosh, the commissioners appointed for the 'Northern District', inspected and reported on conditions in a number of factories in the north of Ireland. Other information was obtained by means of replies to written 'queries' sent by the Central Board of Commissioners to various manufacturers.

72 *Supplementary report, part II: Answers to queries addressed by the central board of commissioners to manufacturers, A. 1: Northern District*, p. 234, H.C. 1834 (167), xx, 238 (Joseph Stevenson & Co., Belfast). According to Francis Lepper & Co., 'Lodge Road, near Belfast', 'those so very young are usually employed and paid by the operatives, and [are] most generally their own children ... ': ibid.

73 Ibid., p. 233 (John M'Cracken, Belfast). An analysis of the returns from three factories in Belfast showed that 22 per cent of the workers were aged 13 or less and 32 per cent aged 14–17: *Supplementary report, part I: Report from Dr James Mitchell*, pp. 22 and 28, H.C. 1834 (167), xix, 280 and 286 (the very small number of women aged over 30 is also noticeable).

74 Ibid., p. 237 (John Mathews, Belfast).

75 Ibid., p. 236 (Francis Lepper & Co.).

76 Ibid.

starvation of the children, having to employ two sets of hands to do one set's work; great injury to the children, in giving them idle habits; keeping them long at low wages ... and most probably never would be good workers.'[77]

The district commissioners appear to have been reasonably satisfied as to the general condition of the Irish factories. Thus, Sir David Barry, the medical commissioner, described Mulholland's new linen mill in the following terms:

The factory is situated ... in a dry, open and well-drained neighbourhood. The old mill is five stories high; the new mill four stories high. The height of the working rooms is from eleven to twelve feet.... There was no thermometer, but the temperature of the water troughs was about 90° of Fahrenheit. Squares of four panes each in every window, revolving upon an axis under the command of the workers, afford ventilation to the rooms, which are kept perfectly clean, and are free from the smell of privies. The atmosphere of the rooms is warm, but not oppressive. The flax ... emits a disagreeable odour of a peculiar nature, which is unavoidable. Two or three times a year the rooms are whitewashed....

The total number of operatives employed in this mill is 608; 319 between the ages of 9 and 15 ... 176 are males, and 432 females. 53 learners, from 11 to 15 years of age, are not included in the above total.... Married or breeding women are not employed or retained in this mill....

The work begins in summer at 5 a.m. and ends at 7 p.m; and in winter at 6 a.m. and ends at 8 p.m..... Three quarters of an hour at 9 a.m. is allowed for breakfast, and three quarters of an hour at 2 p.m. for dinner.... There is no night-work. The time required for cleaning the machinery is never deducted from the meal-hours.... Their food for breakfast generally is porridge and milk; for dinner, potatoes and some kitchen. Their general health is asserted to be as good, if not better, than that of the same class not employed in factories. Their appearance is good, and looking as if well fed. The least healthful branch of manufactory is the hackling and carding departments. Two deaths of cholera occurred among the workers in this factory. No accidents have occurred from the machinery, which is most carefully boxed off and guarded.... A surgeon employed by the firm inspects the workers twice a week, prescribes for them, and supplies medicines from the medicine chest....[78]

Much the same assessment was given of the cotton spinning and weaving factory of Francis Lepper & Co. near Belfast. However, Stuart reported that William Crossan's spinning-mill in Belfast was 'old, dirty, has narrow passages, and machinery ill-boxed; stairs steep and narrow.... The preparation-rooms dusty and without fanners. This is one of the worst specimens of the cotton-mill in point of general arrangement and management I have seen anywhere. ... Fortunately, the work is so small that its bad effects cannot reach more than eighty workers.' Boomar & Co.'s cotton and flax spinning and power-loom weaving factories were 'in many important particulars the reverse' of Crossan's. But even so, 'This work, though well regulated ... in many essential points, is not without defects; the windows cannot be opened at the top ...

77 Ibid., p. 238 (Joseph Stevenson).
78 'Medical report on the flax and tow wet-spinning factory of Messrs. T. & A. Mulholland, worked by steam ... at Belfast', in *Second report, Reports by the medical commissioners, A.3: Northern District*, pp. 74–75.

so that the rooms cannot be sufficiently ventilated. Several of the apartments to-day were far warmer than requisite. Thermometers were altogether wanting, as well as fanners in the preparation-rooms.'[79]

Reports were also made on the health of individual workers. Mary Jane Johnson, now aged 19, had worked in Stevenson's cotton-spinning mill from the age of 11:

... when she was large and fat for her age. Her ancles [sic] swelled during the first year, and were painful. Her feet became so tender and weak that her mother ... used to carry her to the mill every morning.... She was at last taken away from the mill, and remained a year off work. At present the girl looks pale and flabby, but says she is in health. Both ancles turn inwards; the right ancle most.... When she walks the foot seems to tbe turned outwards, with a kind of paralytic flap or shuffle. She is now working as a throstle-spinner, and has been for some years. She walks slowly and awkwardly. She states that she always found her feet less painful in the mill than at home and was therefore anxious to return to her work.[80]

But many other reports were quite favourable,[81] and the manager of Mulholland's mill 'does not think the question of a limitation of the hours has excited that interest in Ireland which it has done elsewhere. [He had] never heard a single individual complaint of the length of the hours as they are at present.' But one of his overlookers thought that 'the hours are too long for the children', since he had had to resort to various devices to keep them awake, such as giving them snuff.[82] In some instances at least, young children were made to get up at 4.00 or 4.30 a.m. and required to work until 8.00 p.m., with only one-and-a-half hours for meals.[83]

The Irish owners were generally opposed to further legislation. John McCracken considered 'the present [Hobhouse's] Act calculated to answer every good purpose with honest and conscientious men, and with others I fear nothing will do'; he recommended the commissioners 'to leave our trade

79 First report, Examinations by district commissioners for the northern district: A. 1: Evidence of Mr Stuart, p. 127.
80 Second report, Reports by medical commissioners, p. 76. Sally Wilson, who worked in Francis Lepper's cotton spinning mill, was 'four feet six inches high, thin, pale, and weakly. The dorsal spine is curved to the right. She is about twenty years of age.... She is still a piecer at 4s. 7½d. per week': ibid. The reports contain a number of 'case-histories' of other workers; a severe cough and swollen ankles and feet appear to have been fairly common among those working in wet-spinning conditions; the factory children were often 'more backward' in their education than other children.
81 Nancy Docherty, aged 14, had worked for three years as a piecer in cotton mills, earning 4s. 3d. per week; her health 'is perfectly good and has generally been so': First report, Evidence of Mr Stuart, p. 128.
82 First report, Evidence of Mr Mackintosh, p. 89.
83 Sarah Pollock, aged 12, who worked in Mulholland's mill, 'gets up at four o'clock sometimes, and always at half past;' but she was glad to be sent to the mill, for 'she earns her mother money': ibid., p. 90. Marcella Robinson, aged 11, who worked for John M'Cracken, 'was never tired when they worked twelve hours', for which she was paid 2s. per week. Now when they work only eight hours, she gets only 1s. 2d. per week – and 'would sooner be working twelve hours': ibid., p. 91.

as it is, and not impose restrictions on us which others are free from'.[84] Joseph Stevenson agreed that the effect of shorter hours would be 'nearly a prohibition to export of cotton-yarn and goods to the continent of Europe and the United States of America, where rapid progress is making in almost all branches of the cotton manufacture, where there are no restrictive laws to cramp industry, no import duty on the raw material, but all as free as light.'[85] And he added for good measure: 'Let manufacturers, as commerce, be free from compulsory laws, and they will work better than with all the restrictions that can be heaped on them.'[86] But Andrew Mulholland, as a member of the committee of master cotton spinners, signed the 'resolutions' adopted in June 1833 to the effect that 'if the principle of interference with free labour [had to] be admitted', there should be 'absolute exclusion up to eleven years of age, and restriction to sixty-nine hours weekly for all under twenty-one, with no system of relays'; if there was to be a relay system, children aged 10–12 should be allowed to work – but only for six hours per day. However, the committee added the following warning:

Any measures excluding or limiting the labour of their children would compel the mothers of families to work in the mills, and, the hours of labour of adults generally being extended, a more serious injury would be inflicted on the children than is now caused by working them sixty-nine hours per week, or than can by possibility accrue from the hours of labour proposed in the foregoing resolutions.[87]

It is difficult at this distance to know what to make of these reports of factory conditions in the north of Ireland which, with the exception of the length of the working day, paint a fairly benign picture. The commissioners' own assessment of this particular evidence is not recorded; but their overall conclusion was that the conditions under which children were employed in factories throughout the United Kingdom required legislative intervention on their behalf.[88] The employment of children for the same number of hours as adults not only endangered their health and physical well-being, but also deprived children of the means of obtaining adequate education. Accordingly, the commissioners recommended that no child under the age of nine should be employed in any textile factory; children aged nine to twelve should not work more that eight hours per day, and should be provided with a proper system of education. To avoid any incidental reduction in the length of the

---

84 *Supplementary report, Answers to queries*, p. 234.
85 Ibid., p. 238.
86 Ibid., p. 239.
87 *First report: Evidence taken before the central board*, p. 27. According to MacDonagh, *Early Victorian government*, pp. 43–44, this was their 'last line of defence' designed to outflank the 'ten hours' movement – and incidentally to benefit large-scale urban factories at the expense of smaller rural enterprises.
88 'Detail by detail the more sensational testimony [on behalf of the workers in Yorkshire and Lancashire] was weakened, and a slightly less inhuman picture of life in the mills began to emerge. But the evidence of overwork, ill-health and deformity was not undermined': Henriques, *Before the welfare state*, p. 85.

working day for 'adult' workers (which the commission took to be anyone over the age of 12),[89] children could be employed in shifts or relays. To enforce these provisions effectively, the government should appoint full-time inspectors of factories to reside in industrial areas and with all necessary authority to deal effectively with breaches of the law.[90]

The government acted quickly in response to the commissioners' report, which was published at the end of June 1833. Although he accepted on behalf of the government that *some* protective legislation was necessary, Althorp (the chancellor of the exchequer) opposed Ashley's 'ten hours' bill as too radical, and in July[91] it was rejected by the house of commons. On 9 August, Althorp introduced the government's own bill based on the commissioners' recommendations, albeit with some significant modifications;[92] less than three weeks later, 'An act to regulate the labour of children and young persons in the mills and factories of the United Kingdom' received the royal assent.[93]

The act applied to cotton, woollen, linen and other textile factories where steam, water or other mechanical power was used. With the exception of silk mills, no child under the age of nine was to be employed at all, and no person under the age of 18 was to employed at night.[94] No child aged between nine and thirteen was to be employed for more than nine hours a day, or 48 hours a week;[95] with some limited exceptions, no young person aged 13–18 was to be employed for more than 12 hours a day, or 69 hours a week.[96] All persons under 18 were entitled to one and a half hours for meals, and children were to attend school for two hours each day (or 12 hours per week).[97] Mill

89 On principle, because when they reach their fourteenth year, young people cease to be under the complete control of their parents and should therefore be regarded as free agents; for practical purposes, because the existence of a different limit for (say) 13–18 year olds would cause administrative inconvenience and thereby facilitate fraud and evasion: *First report*, pp. 56–57.

90 *First report*, pp. 35–36, 56–57 and 68–76. For discussion of the report, see e.g. MacDonagh, *Early Victorian government*, pp. 43–46, Gray, *Factory question*, chap. 3, Thomas, *Early factory legislation*, chap. 4.

91 *Hansard 3*, xix, 220–54 (5 July 1833) and 883–913 (18 July 1833). For the text of Ashley's bill see H.C. 1833 (48), ii, 263 and for a summary of the arguments for and against it, see e.g. Henriques, *Before the welfare state*, pp. 79–82.

92 *Hansard 3*, xx, 449–52, 528–77. The text of the bill is given in H.C. 1833 (607), ii, 281. MacDonagh, *Early Victorian government*, pp. 46–49 takes the view that 'as the bill was being debated in both houses most of its idiosyncratic and novel features were ripped away, for good and ill'.

93 3 & 4 Will IV, c. 103 ('Althorp's Act'). The extension of the act to Ireland does not appear to have been seriously contested; indeed, there does not appear to have been any active involvement of Irish MPs in the debates on the bill.

94 Section 7. Children of any age could still be employed in silk mills.

95 This provision was to come into force in stages, with the last stage due to come into force in 1836. Such children were not to be employed at all without a certificate from a surgeon as to their physical abilities; but the act did not state how or by whom the surgeons were to be appointed (a defect remedied by the 1844 act).

96 Sections 1, 2, 7 and 8. The working hours could be extended to make up for time lost as a result of an extraordinary accident or, in water-powered mills, from problems with the water supply (ss. 3–5).

97 Sections 6 and 20.

owners were required to produce certificates of age and of school attendance to prove that the law was being complied with. Parents and workers as well as factory owners were made criminally liable for breaches of the act, and alleged offences were to be tried either by a justice of the peace or by a factory inspector, who 'as regards the execution of the provisions of this Act' was given judicial powers coordinate with those of a magistrate.[98] Persons found guilty of an offence could be fined a sum 'not exceeding £20, nor less than £1'; but if the offence 'was not wilful nor grossly negligent' the justice or inspector could mitigate the penalty to less than £1 – or even 'discharge' the defendant.[99]

Many of these provisions had been foreshadowed in the legislation of 1819–31; but they were now applied to *all* textile mills and factories (and not, as previously, to the cotton industry alone) and the detailed provisions relating to the maximum number of hours for which children and young persons were to be employed and for their education were new. What made the 1833 act of even greater significance, however, was the method of enforcement which it introduced. The factory commissioners had readily accepted that the system of enforcement under the earlier factory legislation had been wholly ineffective, with the result that the law, in their view, was 'almost completely inoperative'. True to their utilitarian principles, they accepted that the effective enforcement of legislation 'not directly conducive to the immediate interests either of the master manufacturers, or of the operatives, or of any powerful class' could be achieved only by the appointment of full-time 'itinerant' inspectors with extensive rights, especially to enter all factories in which children were employed. They rejected the proposal made by a number of manufacturers that these inspectors should be appointed locally, and proposed instead that the appointments should be made by the government.[100] These recommendations were implemented by section 17 of the 1833 act, which provided for the appointment, by His Majesty and at His Majesty's pleasure, of four inspectors with extensive statutory powers. The home secretary was also authorised to appoint one or more persons 'to superintend, under the direction of any inspector, the execution of the provisions of this act'.[101]

Much has been written about the 'true' nature of the 1833 act.[102] Traditionally regarded as a major turning-point in the development of state

98 Sections 33, 34, 38 and 41.
99 Section 31. This provision was repealed in 1844, but a similar power conferred by the Dublin Police Act 1842 (5 Vict., c. 24), s. 63 was later to frustrate the inspectors in Ireland – see below, p. 308.
100 *First report*, pp. 36 and 72–73.
101 Sections 17–19. Section 32 also made it an offence, punishable by a fine of up to £10, 'knowingly and wilfully' to obstruct an inspector in the discharge of his duty.
102 See especially W.C. Lubenow, *The politics of government growth: Early Victorian attitudes to state intervention, 1833–1848* (Hamden, Conn., 1971); C. Nardinelli, *Child labor and the industrial revolution* (Indianapolis, 1990); A.P. Robson, *On higher than commercial grounds: The factory controversy, 1830–1853* (London, 1985); Gray, *Factory question*, part 1; Henriques, *Before the welfare state*, chap. 4; MacDonagh, *Early Victorian government*, chap. 3.

intervention, it has been portrayed as the product of a broad-based consensus driven, according to some, by aristocratic Tory evangelicals and according to others, by popular radicalism, while yet others have seen it as the outcome of Whig paternalism. At a more mundane (political) level, it may represent the 'revenge' of the landed class for the Reform Act – or a victory for larger factory owners over their smaller, but less scrupulous, competitors. Some feminist historians view the act as a patriarchal attempt to reinforce the 'male breadwinner' ideology. A detailed examination of these various theories would take us beyond the ambit of this study; suffice it to say that the limited evidence from Ireland tends, if at all, to support the thesis that the act had at least the implicit support of the larger textile manufacturers.

THE IMPACT OF THE 1833 ACT IN IRELAND

Notwithstanding the existence of a separate Irish adminstrative system, the 1833 act made it clear that the responsibility for its application throughout the United Kingdom rested with the home secretary and his officials in London – a principle which remained unchanged until 1920.[103] As if to underline this point, the United Kingdom was divided into four administrative divisions, each under the charge of an 'inspector of factories', and Ireland was divided into two halves which were allocated to different divisions. The northern half of the island, with Scotland and the four northern counties of England, formed Division D, under Inspector Leonard Horner;[104] the southern half joined most of Wales, Warwickshire and Gloucestershire in Division B, under Inspector Thomas Howell.[105] In 1836 Horner was transferred to another division and was replaced by James Stuart.[106] But in 1837 a general rearrange-

---

103 See generally R.B. McDowell, *The Irish administration 1801–1914* (London, 1964), chap. 1. D. Sugarman and G.R. Rubin, 'Towards a new history of law and material society in England 1750–1914' in Rubin and Sugarman (ed.), *Law, economy and society, 1750–1914: Essays in the history of English law* (Abingdon, 1984), p. 76 observe that the 1833 act represents 'one of the first instances of a special department of the central government being created for the purpose of administering a particular act'.

104 The son of a linen merchant, Horner was a distinguished geologist and scientist who had played a leading role in Whig politics in Edinburgh before his appointment as an inspector in November 1833 at the age of 48. He is generally regarded as a most able and vigorous inspector and a man of integrity who, according to Karl Marx, *Capital: A critical analysis of capitalist production*, trans. from 3rd German edition by S. Moore and E. Aveling (Moscow, 1958), i, 216, 'rendered undying service to the English working-class'. See especially B. Martin, 'Leonard Horner: A portrait of an inspector of factories' in *Int'l Rev. Social History*, xiv, (1969) 412 and P. Wusteman, 'Leonard Horner' in *HM inspectors of factories 1833–1983: Essays to commemorate 150 years of health and safety inspection* (London, 1983), pp. 9–13. See also K.M. Lyell, *Memoir of Leonard Horner* (London, 1890).

105 Formerly Judge Advocate of Gibraltar and Commissioner for West Indian Islands relief, Howell is something of a nonentity who has attracted none of the attention paid to Horner.

106 The son of a Church of Scotland minister, Stuart qualified as a writer to the signet,

ment of all four divisions with a view to achieving a more even distribution of work[107] led to the whole of Ireland being brought under Stuart's jurisdiction. The transfer of the north of England to another inspector meant that Stuart was now in charge of Scotland and Ireland,[108] and this administrative division remained in place until well after Stuart's death in 1849.

The state of the textile factories which became the responsibility of the new inspectors is summarised in Table 1:

Table 1.1: *No. of persons employed in textile factories in 1834–1835*[109]

	Cotton	Wool & worsted	Flax	Silk	Ireland total	Scotland	England and Wales	United Kingdom
No. of factories	28	36	25	1	90	425	2,667	3,182
Children (9–13)								
male	197	38	126	–	361	2,781	24,670	27,812
female	239	59	214	2	514	3,961	24,265	28,740
Young persons (13–18)								
male	477	153	399	–	1,029	4,133	38,548	43,710
female	876	223	1,308	25	2,432	11,288	51,193	64,913
Adults (over 18)								
male	879	779	463	2	2,123	8,904	76,722	87,749
female	1,532	389	1,171	20	3,112	19,113	81,176	103,401
TOTAL								
male	1,553	970	988	2	3,513	15,818	139,940	159,271
female	2,647	671	2,693	47	6,058	34,362	156,634	197,054
all	4,200	1,641	3,681	49	9,571	50,180	296,574	356,325

but never practised law. His chequered career included management of the family estates and involvement in Scottish politics as a Whig. He went bankrupt in 1825 and left the country. Returning to England in 1831, he became editor of *The Courier*, a London evening paper. Through his friend Lord Brougham, Stuart was appointed an assistant commissioner for Scotland and Ireland to make inquiries on behalf of the factory commissioners in 1833. In 1836, he was appointed a factory inspector at the age of 61 and served until his death in 1849. See generally U. Henriques, 'An early factory inspector: James Stuart of Dunearn' in *Sc. Hist. Rev.*, 50 (1971), 18 and below, Plate 4.

107 The details are given by Thomas, *Early factory legislation*, pp. 98–100 and 359–61.

108 Stuart seems to have have done well in the reorganisation; whilst the other three inspectors each became responsible for more than 1,000 factories, there were only some 600 factories in his district. See *Insp. quart. rep., Dec. 1837*, pp. 25, 28, 31 and 34.

109 *Return of the number of persons employed in the cotton, woollen, worsted, flax and silk mills and factories of the United Kingdom, distinguishing ages*, H.C. 1836 (138), xlv, 51.

This table makes it clear that the 1833 act only applied to a small number of industrial establishments and a small percentage of the workforce – and that in each respect Ireland was relatively insignificant, with less than three per cent of the factories covered by the act and a similar proportion of the 'protected' workforce. The first inspectors also found that 'a regionally-concentrated pattern of industry'[110] was already beginning to distinguish Ulster from the rest of the island. Horner reported that there were some 'considerable' cotton mills in or near Belfast, and 'recently some very large establishments for spinning flax have been erected, and more are in progress'.[111] Howell, on the other hand, reported that 'the few factories which are to be found in the south of Ireland are scattered over a very large extent of country; of these the woollen are the most numerous, and they exhibited considerable dearth of employment ...'.[112] He might have added that most of the woollen factories were small establishments which employed less than 50 workers, as compared to the average of 150 workers employed in the linen mills in the north of Ireland. Somewhat surprisingly, however, Table 1.1 suggests that cotton remained in 1835 the primary textile employer in the island as a whole.[113]

Table 1.1 further suggests that children under 13 constituted nine per cent of the textile workforce in Ireland, as compared to 13 per cent in Scotland and nearly 17 per cent in England and Wales. On the other hand, the proportion of young persons aged 13–18 employed in Ireland is somewhat higher (at 36 per cent) than in Scotland (31 per cent) and England and Wales (30 per cent). The high percentage of young workers was noted by the poor law commissioners in 1836:

The factories in Belfast are a material source of comfort and employment to the poor; they cause a decided improvement in the condition of the labourer and mechanic; in the unemployed season, in sickness, and in approaching old age, they are a resource on which a family can fall back; and many who would have been obliged to depend on charity, are supported by the exertions of their children.[114]

However, the employment pattern had changed significantly by 1837. In spite of an increase in the number of flax mills, the number of child workers decreased dramatically to less than one per cent of a workforce now estimated to be approaching 13,000.[115] The number of young persons, however,

---

110 See E.L. Almquist, 'Labour specialisation and the Irish economy in 1848 – an aggregate occupational analysis' in *Econ. Hist. Rev.*, xxxvi (1983), 506.
111 *Insp. rep., July 1834*, p. 7.
112 Ibid., p. 24.
113 In 1837 the number of workers involved in the linen industry was put at 7,810, as compared to 3,683 in cotton and 1,321 in wool: *Insp. quart. rep., Dec. 1837*, p. 50 (Stuart).
114 *Third report of the commissioners for inquiring into the condition of the poorer classes in Ireland*, App'x C, pt. I, p. 5 [43], H.C. 1836, xxx, 41.
115 *Insp. quart. rep., Sept. 1837*, p. 34; *Dec. 1837*, p. 50 (Stuart). See also *Return of mills and factories specifying ... the number of persons employed in cotton, woollen, worsted, flax*

remained much the same,[116] with the result that it was they rather than children who were the principal beneficiaries of the 1833 act in Ireland.[117] It seems that 'hands are so plentiful and labour so cheap, that the mill-owners at present have no occasion to employ any [new workers] under 13'.[118] By 1840 it was estimated that there were only eight textile mills in Ireland employing child workers[119] – and the 'abundant population' in Kilkenny even allowed six factory owners there to escape the 1833 act altogether by employing no workers under 18 years of age.[120]

The independence and autonomy of the earliest factory inspectors have been widely noted.[121] They were responsible not only for the inspection of factories and mills and the supervision of schools for the education of factory children, but also for making the rules and regulations necessary for giving effect to the 1833 act and even for deciding whether there had been a breach of the law. According to MacDonagh, the inspectors were 'in part executive officers, in part independent magistrates, and in part virtually autonomous dispensers of industrial martial law'.[122] Other commentators take a less authoritarian view of their role: 'The introduction of an external authority, free from local bias and partiality, greatly improved the administration of the law, lessened the friction between manufacturers and operatives, and provided a medium of communication between the government and the people at a time when knowledge of industrial matters was scanty in the extreme.'[123] On either view, the first factory inspectors faced considerable practical difficulties: 'they had no precedents to follow, no experience of other branches of the state service on which they could draw. They had to make the precedents and to originate the techniques of their calling.'[124]

  and silk factories of the United Kingdom … , pp. 296–97 and 334–35, H.C. 1839 (41), xlii, 296–97 and 334–35.

116 This picture of the workforce was confirmed in 1847: *Return of the total numbers of persons employed in cotton, woollen, worsted, flax and silk factories respectively, in the United Kingdom, etc.*, pp. 11 and 13, H.C.1847 (294), xlvi, 619 and 621.

117 Gray, *Factory question*, p. 32 also suggests that 'the employment of younger children was probably already diminishing [in England] by the 1830s … '.

118 *Insp. rep., July 1834*, p. 7 (Horner). Stuart later made the same point: 'In Ireland, the number of persons above 13 years old is, even in country situations, so abundant, that factory owners and occupiers hardly at all employ children not more than 13 years of age. This is the case even at Mr Malcomson's, the largest cotton factory in Ireland … at which above 1,000 workers are employed': *Insp. quart. rep., Dec. 1839*, p. 417.

119 *Fourth report of the select committee on mills and factories: Minutes of evidence*, p. 31, H.C. 1840 (334), x, 397 (Hudson).

120 Ibid.

121 See especially H.W. Arthurs, '*Without the law': Administrative justice and legal pluralism in nineteenth-century England* (Toronto, 1985), chap. 5 and other commentators discussed below, pp. 23 and 35.

122 O. MacDonagh, 'The nineteenth-century revolution in government: a reappraisal' in *Hist. J.*, 1 (1958), 51, 52. There is no evidence that the inspectors ever exercised their judicial powers in Ireland before these were formally taken away from them by the 1844 act.

123 Hutchins and Harrison, *History of factory legislation*, p. 40.

124 F.I. Taylor, 'Employment' in *Review of the work of the inspectorate 1833–1932*,

The early inspectors in Ireland, however, seem to have encountered few problems. On his first visit to Belfast in November 1833, Horner discussed the provisions of the act with the principal manufacturers. They led him to believe that there was 'no likelihood of any difficulty arising here to the carrying all the most important provisions into effect'. The number of hours worked by children could be reduced by introducing a relay system; this would lower the wages earned by children, but since they were mainly the children of well-paid spinners, the loss would in most cases 'fall upon persons well able to bear it'. The educational clauses were 'most salutary', and the employers were quite prepared to complete the necessary registers. They were, however, anxious that the remuneration paid to the new 'mill-wardens' would be 'such as to obtain the services of a person of some stature and character', and they emphasised 'the great importance, in this country, of the mill-warden being required to abstain from the expression of any decided political opinion'.[125] In the south, Howell 'found ... the same need as in England of explanation as to different clauses of the Act, the construction of which had been misunderstood; I remarked also the same willingness on the part of the masters to obey the law, and that the same objections were urged against its policy.'[126] By 1835, both inspectors felt able to report that 'with very few exceptions, the main provisions of the Factories Regulation Act are well attended to ...'.[127]

This sense of satisfaction continued under Stuart.[128] Although he visited all the factories in Ireland twice a year, he had insisted on having a superintendent resident in Ireland, and much of the actual work of inspection was undertaken by J.P. Hudson, who was based in Belfast.[129] Although a relatively

pp. 11–12, in *Annual report of the chief inspector of factories and workshops for the year 1932* (Cmd. 4377, 1933).

125 *Insp. rep., July 1834*, pp. 1–2. Joseph Stevenson, owner of the Springfield Mills in Belfast, told Horner that 'for this part of the United Kingdom at least, no legislative interference was called for'; but 'as they were to have an Act, he was very much satisfied with that which had been passed'. It was 'judiciously framed ... with every attention to the interest of the manufacturer': ibid. See also S.A. Royle, 'Industrialization, urbanization and urban society in post-Famine Ireland' in B.J. Graham and L.J. Proudfoot (ed.), *An historical geography of Ireland* (London, 1993), p. 277, observing that the entrepreneurs who set up industrial villages in the first half of the nineteenth century 'wished to improve the lot of their workers in ... moral as well as economic terms'.

126 *Insp. rep., July 1834*, p. 24. In the six months to February 1837, he visited 49 factories in the south of Ireland; 33 of these he visited twice, and 9 'thrice or oftener'. In the same period he visited 381 factories in England and Wales: *A return of the number of mills and factories ... visited by the inspectors ... between 1st August 1836 and 1st February 1837*, p. 3, H.C. 1837 (122), l, 201.

127 *Insp. rep., Aug. 1835*, p. 24.

128 See e.g. *Insp. quart. rep., Dec. 1837*, p. 51: 'the state of regulation of the factories is now ... completely in conformity with the provisions of the statute'.

129 PRO LAB 15/1, 'Minutes of half-yearly meetings of H.M. factory inspectorate', p. 77 (22 July 1837). Hudson had served as a superintendent in the north of England and south of Scotland for only five months when he was sent to Ireland in August 1837 – see *Fourth report from the select committee on the act for the regulation of mills and factories: Minutes of evidence*, pp. 27–31, H.C. 1840 (334), x, 393–97.

light work load[130] required him to spend part of his time inspecting factories in Scotland,[131] Hudson initially visited each factory in the Belfast area every three weeks – 'sixteen or seventeen times during the year' – and the factories in the rest of Ireland at least twice a year.[132] The 1833 act had not given superintendents a right of entry into any part of a factory used for manu-facturing processes,[133] but Hudson was always allowed 'to go through every part … at pleasure', and did so 'as a matter of course'. He admitted, however, that in the Belfast area, he did not make it a practice to go through a factory where no new workers had been employed since his previous visit. When it was suggested that it might be naive to rely on the word of the owner and overseer, he replied that they always suggested that he go into the mill and check for himself. In any event, the depressed state of trade was such that there was no temptation to break the law. All children and young persons had the necessary medical certificate of age; such certificates were 'generally correct'; occasionally he came across a person who appeared to be below the certified age and if he was satisfied that that was so, 'my recommendation that he should be dismissed has been uniformly complied with'. In 1840 he, too, reported that 'the law is duly observed in the factories in Ireland'.[134]

Much has been written about the prosecution policy of the early factory inspectors.[135] In particular, it has been suggested that the 1833 act had a much greater impact, and therefore imposed a much greater burden, on small, as opposed to large, firms, on rural, as opposed to urban, factories and on water-powered as opposed to steam-powered plants. Such analyses are

130 In 1837 Ireland had 112 factories with 12,814 employees, of whom less than 5,000 were children or young persons; in Scotland, there were 462 factories with 55,000 employees, including almost 22,000 protected workers – and only two superintendents: *Insp. quart. rep., Dec. 1837*, p. 50. At this time, each inspector or superintendent in the United Kingdom as a whole was, on average, responsible for 230 factories.

131 *Fourth report from select committee 1840: Minutes of evidence*, p. 33.

132 Ibid., pp. 27–36. In 1839, Hudson, travelling 2,430 miles, visited all 95 factories in Ireland, 60 of them twice, and 15 of them eight times or more: *Numbers of factories within the district of each inspector, the number of mills visited, etc.*, p. 7, H.C. 1839 (135), xlii, 507. Cf. *Final report from the select committee appointed to inquire into the operation of the act for the regulation of mills and factories*, p. 22, H.C. 1841 (56), ix, 584 reported that an inspector was expected to visit each mill three times a year, but recom-mended that this should be increased to four.

133 Section 19. Cf. on the recommendation of the select committee in 1841 (*Final report*, p. 10), the 1844 act, s. 3 provided: 'Every inspector *and sub-inspector* shall have power to enter every part of any factory at any time … when any person shall be employed therein … ' (emphasis added).

134 *Fourth report from select committee 1840: Minutes of evidence*, p. 31, adding that 'Indeed there is no inducement in Ireland to violate the law, the state of trade has been depressed; and the abundance of hands to be met with in all parts, removes every temptation'.

135 See especially H.P. Marvel, 'Factory regulation: A reinterpretation of early English experience' in *J. Law & Econ.*, xx (1977), 379, A.E. Peacock, 'The successful prosecution of the factory acts, 1833–1855' in *Econ. Hist. Rev.*, xxxvi (1984), 197, P. Bartrip, 'Success or failure? The prosecution of the early factory acts' in *Econ. Hist. Rev.*, xxxviii (1985), 423 and Gray, *Factory question*, pp. 164–89.

confined to the operation of the act in England; the tiny number of prosecutions in Ireland in the first ten years of the act's operation do not make it possible to confirm or deny how the act operated in practice in Ireland.[136] But we can confirm, and even exaggerate, one particular finding. It has been pointed out that in England and Wales 'in a ... typical year, total fines and costs amounted to slightly more than 0.001 per cent of the net value of output'.[137] In Ireland, the total fines and costs imposed in the first *ten* years of the 1833 act appear to have amounted to no more than £16!

It may indeed be that both Stuart and Hudson were somewhat complacent. We have found only one prosecution – which failed – for a breach of the 1833 act in Ireland between 1837 and 1844.[138] Like the other inspectors,[139] Stuart believed that a defaulting factory owner should be prosecuted only as a last resort:

The parties ... are far more likely to become convinced of the expediency and necessity of their co-operating in fulfilling the humane intentions of the legislature towards the children whom they employ, by persuasion, by explanations again and again repeated, and by refraining from all angry and irritating discussion and altercation, than by having recourse, except in extreme cases, to suits for penalties or coercive measures of any kind.[140]

Stuart instructed Hudson not to bring any prosecutions in Ireland without his sanction, unless he came across 'a case of decided disobedience of the Act'. Hudson agreed with this approach: 'I think an unfavourable result would have been the consequence of a different course, inasmuch as there is no temptation to violate the law; to have provoked hostility, I think, would have brought about an unfavourable result.'[141] This may have been said in support of his superior at a time when Stuart was under considerable attack.[142] But when challenged as to the desirability of uniformity in prosecution policy

---

136 We have only found details of three prosecutions (by Howell) in Dublin and one (by Stuart) in Banbridge. See further below, p. 301.

137 C. Nardinelli, 'The successful prosecution of the factory acts: A suggested explanation' in *Econ. Hist. Rev.*, xxxviii (1985), 428, 429.

138 The case against the owner of a flax-spinning factory near Banbridge was dismissed 'on the alleged ground of want of evidence': *Number and names of persons summoned for offences against the factory act ... in 1841*, p. 16, H.C. 1842 (40), xxxii, 565.

139 'Typically ... the early factory inspectorate pursued a policy in which prosecutions played little part. Not only did the enforcement problems ... dictate the necessity of such a policy, but also the establishment of a continuing working relationship between the inspectorate and manufacturers enabled the policy to develop into a workable and, we would argue, potentially effective style of regulatory enforcement': P.W.J. Bartrip and P. Fenn, 'The evolution of regulatory style in the nineteenth-century British factory inspectorate' in *J. Law & Soc.*, 10 (1983), 201, 218.

140 *Insp. rep., Dec. 1836*, p. 67.

141 *Fourth report from select committee 1840: Minutes of evidence*, p. 32.

142 See especially the criticisms expressed by Stuart's two superintendents in Scotland in *Fourth report from select committee 1840: Minutes of evidence*, pp. 62–114 (Wood) and *Fifth report from select committee: Minutes of evidence*, pp. 22–84, H.C. 1840 (419), x, 532–94 (Beal). See also Henriques, 'An early factory inspector', pp. 34–39.

between Ireland and England, Hudson replied: 'I am of opinion that what might be a good line of practice in one division, might be a bad one in another; but I should say that, under any inspectorship of Ireland and the north of England, as I found it when it belonged to me, no inspector would have directed prosecution for any infraction that came under my notice.'[143] As he went on to explain, Horner had stated his policy as follows:

Although we have power to prosecute for such disobedience of orders issued under the authority of the Act, when I find that the chief enactments in the statute itself have not been violated, and when there is no ground for suspicion that there is a disposition to evade the law, I am reluctant to institute legal proceedings for merely neglecting to make records and fix up notices; and the superintendents follow the same rule of practice. When the provisions of the Act itself have been disregarded, disobedience to the rules of the inspectors is not passed over merely with a caution to be more circumspect in those respects.[144]

In his opinion Stuart seemed 'most anxious' to enforce the act in Ireland. But he preferred to do so 'by admonitions and frequent visits, rather than by prosecutions, or the infliction of penalties'. In this respect, at least according to Hudson, Stuart had been successful.

But Stuart and Hudson may just have been too accommodating to mill owners: '[Stuart] was ... an opinionated, jealous and irascible character, tactless, difficult to work with and biased [in favour of employers].... He admininstered an act intended to protect working class children in such a way as to indicate to their parents that in the dispute between capital and labour the government was entirely on the masters' side.'[145] O'Connell appears to have taken a contrary view at the time. In 1838 he contended that the factory acts were being 'totally neglected' in Glasgow because the occupiers found Stuart 'too inconvenient' to work with.[146] Stuart vehemently

---

143 *Fourth report from select committee 1840: Minutes of evidence*, p. 36.
144 Ibid. Hudson considered that Horner would have dealt with the kinds of irregularities which transpired in Ireland 'with nothing more than remonstrance and admonition', and that the cases which Horner had prosecuted 'have not occurred in Ireland ... '.
145 Henriques, 'An early factory inspector', p. 27. Gray, *Factory question*, p. 92 also portrays Stuart as 'an apologist for employers' whose relations with the other inspectors were frequently strained. During the period 1837–46, Horner brought more than 1,900 cases in his English district, whereas Stuart brought just over 200 in Scotland and Ireland: Bartrip and Fenn, 'Evolution of regulatory style', p. 213.
146 *Hansard 3*, xliii, 978 (22 June 1838). Beal, one of Stuart's superintendents in Scotland, was particularly critical of 'the deep injury Mr. O'Connell's speech ... has occasioned to the factory cause. The workers feel that he cares nothing about them, and that he would abolish the law altogether. The mill-owners feel that it is an ungrateful return for the facility they have afforded of carrying the law into effect. The medical profession feel themselves shamefully insulted, and the superintendents most unjustly reproached; nay, it is more; it is cruel to the latter, because ... in order to carry the law into effect without prosecutions, we have worked like slaves, and our travelling expenses (enforcing the law by repeated visits) left little or no remuneration for our trouble ... ': *Fifth report from select committee 1840: Minutes of evidence*, p. 33.

denied the charges and published a lengthy defence of his actions, which included statements by a number of witnesses to the effect that the act was observed in Scotland in all its details.[147] And when Ashley presented a motion regretting that 'the law regulating the labour of children in factories, having been found imperfect and ineffective ... has been suffered to continue for so long without any amendment', O'Connell voted with the government against it.[148]

No doubt it would often have been difficult to obtain reliable evidence sufficient to support a prosecution. In some cases, however, alleged breaches of the act were reported anonymously to the inspector, who then duly investigated the complaint.[149] But on at least one occasion, which is of particular interest since it challenges the favourable picture presented by Stuart and Hudson, such a complaint was made directly to a newspaper. In the famous defamation case of *Le Fanu* v. *Malcomson*,[150] 'H' had written to the editor of *The Warder* as follows:

I beg you will say ... whether there is a law at present in force which prevents the proprietors of factories from employing their operatives by night and on Sundays; and if there is, who is supposed to enforce it. If the same tyranny is carried on in the English factories as in some of the Irish ones, the English members who opposed Lord Ashley's motion can, I think, lay very little claim to humanity. Factories being much more numerous in England than in Ireland, the English members had a much better opportunity of knowing the great hardships to which the factory labourers are exposed than the Irish members. No person, unless one who is perfectly acquainted with the working of the Irish factories, can form any but the slightest idea of the cruelties and miseries to which the Irish factory hands are subject.

I know some factories in this country; and the cruelty with which the operatives in them are used, is really incredible. The cruelties of the slave-trade or the Bastile are not equal to those practised in some of the Irish factories....

Whenever the proprietors are in a hurry to get any work done, the hands must work both by night and on Sundays until it is completed; and if one member of a

---

147 *Insp. quart. rep., Dec. 1838*, pp. 25–104. O'Connell had been a member of a select committee inquiring into combinations of workmen in Scotland. The essence of Stuart's claim was that the committee had used the inquiry as an underhand method of investigating his lack of enforcement of the factory acts. Ashley regarded Stuart's defence as a breach of the privileges of the house of commons, but O'Connell was prepared to excuse 'his hasty language': *Hansard 3*, xlv, 1164 (4 March 1839).

148 *Hansard 3*, xliv, 444 (20 July 1838). Ashley's motion was supported by a number of members for constituencies in the north of Ireland, including Sir Robert Bateson (Londonderry), the earl of Hillsborough (Co. Down) and Sir Edmund Hayes (Donegal).

149 In 1844, for example, Stuart forwarded to Hudson two anonymous complaints of the working hours having been exceeded, and of other infractions of the law having taken place, at a flax-spinning factory near Belfast: *Insp. quart. rep., June 1844*, pp. 17–18. Hudson's inquiries 'gave no reason to believe that the accusation was well-founded'; but Stuart commented that 'the difficulty of procuring testimony ... such as would warrant a conviction ... is very great, the witnesses, should their information be unfavourable to the overseer or occupier of the factory, almost always speaking with the terror of dismissal before their eyes': *Insp. quart. rep., Sept. 1844*, p. 8.

150 (1848) 1 HL Cas 637, 9 Eng Rep 910.

family refuse to work on the Sunday, the whole family are turned off on the following day. Incredible as this may appear, it is a positive fact.

I have frequently seen them on Sundays going in to work at a certain factory in the south of Ireland; and I beg, through the columns of your widely circulated paper, to call the attention of the authorities to it, in order that some measure may be taken to put a stop to such an iniquitous practice....

The Warder duly took up the matter, and on 1 June 1844 published the following editorial:

We had no notion that the abuses of the factory system were so triumphant in this country.... [I]t seems that the abuses in the county of Waterford exceed even those committed in England.... The Factory Bill must have been an United Kingdom bill ... and therefore of force in Ireland. If that be so, working on Sundays, or beyond the twelve hours limited, must be illegal.... The public must feel greatly indebted to our correspondent for his valuable communication. It is a discovery of an outrageous and tyrannical violation of the laws for the protection of the poor labourer....

Malcomsons of Portlaw[151] took this editorial as defamatory of them and sued Joseph Le Fanu, the editor of *The Warder*. The case was tried at Co. Waterford Spring Assizes in March 1845 before Lefroy J and a special jury. The defendants made no attempt to justify their comments,[152] but contended that the article was published 'without malice or gross negligence' and did not refer specifically to Malcomsons. The jury disagreed, and awarded the plaintiffs damages of £500.[153] Stuart had apparently inspected the factory during the summer of 1844, and after the case had been heard he described the Malcomsons as proprietors of a 'large and admirably conducted' factory.[154] But he pointedly contrasted the level of damages awarded by the jury with the low level of penalties imposed by magistrates for infringements of the factory act.[155]

The mixed reaction to the 1833 act in England and Wales has been extensively documented,[156] and no doubt there was a similar, if less vociferous, division of opinion in Ireland. During the phasing-in period the strength of the opposition caused both the government and the inspectors to hesitate;[157] but in 1836 the home secretary, Lord John Russell, undertook that all the

---

151 See below, Plate 5. Similar allegations were on 4 June 1844 made in *The Statesman*, another paper edited by Le Fanu.

152 In the course of a lengthy speech on Le Fanu's behalf, James Whiteside conceded that the factory system in Ireland 'is not in so bad a condition as England': *The Warder*, 8 March 1845.

153 Le Fanu's appeal to the court of exchequer chamber and then to the house of lords, was unsuccessful, and the case is still cited as a leading authority on this aspect of the law of defamation.

154 *Insp. half-yearly rep., April 1845*, p. 54.

155 Ibid. Twenty-one convictions had resulted in total fines of £68.

156 See e.g. Thomas, *Early factory legislation*, pp. 70–93 and Robson, *Higher than commercial grounds*, pp. 101–50.

157 A government bill designed to exclude 12–13-year-old children was introduced early in 1836; but was dropped when it passed its second reading with a majority of only two votes: *Hansard 3*, xxxiii, 737–90 (9 May 1836) and xxxiv, 306–07 (10 June

provisions of the act would thereafter be strictly enforced[158] and the inspectors promulgated detailed regulations for their application.[159] By the early 1840s, the tide had begun to turn in the opposite direction, as many owners realised 'that the law is not so great a hindrance, nor so difficult of observance, as they at one time believed it would be'[160] – and it came to be more generally accepted that the 1833 act did not go far enough.

1836) and Robson, *Higher than commercial grounds*, pp. 119–37. O'Connell ultimately voted with the government, ostensibly on the basis that restrictions on children brought about shorter hours, and therefore reduced wages, for all workers. But Thomas, *Early factory legislation*, p. 93n notes that the ten-hour party alleged that O'Connell, 'the sordid Judas', had succumbed to a £700 bribe.

158 *Hansard 3*, xxxiv, 840 (23 June 1836).

159 A code of rules and regulations 'uniformly applicable to all the mills in the United Kingdom' was agreed by all four inspectors and approved by the home secretary: PRO LAB 15/1, 'Minutes of half-yearly meetings of H.M. factory inspectorate', pp. 1 and 38 (Sept. and Oct. 1836) and *Insp. rep., Dec. 1836*, pp. 36–37. In the following year, Stuart supplemented these with his own 'Instructions': *Insp. quart. rep., Dec. 1837*, p. 51.

160 Quoted in Robson, *Higher than commercial grounds*, p.137.

CHAPTER TWO

Broadening the ambit of inspection: 1840–75

INTRODUCTION

Continuing agitation by the 'ten hours' lobby and other reformers[1] led in 1840 to the appointment of a select committee chaired by Ashley to examine the working of the 1833 act.[2] In the course of taking evidence from those 'who, by office or interest, were most likely to have watched, and to understand the operation of the act', the committee questioned the inspectors and seven of their superintendents at considerable length. The controversy over his performance in Scotland dominated their examination of Stuart, with the result that neither he nor his superintendent, Hudson, gave much in the way of evidence as to the operation of the act in Ireland.[3] But the experiences of the other inspectors and witnesses highlighted a number of defects which led the committee to conclude for the United Kingdom as a whole that, although 'many evils' had been removed, 'much, unquestionably, yet remains to be done'.[4]

In their report, published in February 1841, the committee claimed that their recommendations were limited to giving greater effect to the 'true spirit' of the 1833 act: 'it was not a new law that was required by the house [of commons], but the fulfilment of the intention of the existing law'.[5] But in addition to proposals designed to remedy particular defects, the committee recommended the enactment of safety provisions designed to prevent accidents and to provide some degree of compensation in the event of injury or death. They also concluded that there should be a fundamental change in the nature and powers

1 See e.g. B.L. Hutchins and A. Harrison, *A history of factory legislation* (London, 3rd ed., 1926), chap. iv; R. Gray, *The factory question and industrial England, 1830–1860* (Cambridge, 1996), chap. 1.
2 *Hansard 3*, lii, 860–61 (3 March 1840). The committee consisted of an astute balance of supporters of employers and employees. Among the former was Richard Lalor Sheil, now MP for Co. Tipperary, a barrister and associate of O'Connell who had by this time 'drifted into support for the Whig party': S.J. Connolly (ed.), *The Oxford companion to Irish history* (2nd ed., Oxford, 2002), p. 539.
3 For Stuart's evidence see especially *Select committee to inquire into the operation of the act for the regulation of mills and factories: Second report: Minutes of evidence*, pp. 75–97, H.C. 1840 (227), x, 239–61 and *Fifth report: Minutes of evidence*, pp. 85–130, H.C. 1840 (419), x, 595–640. For Hudson, see *Fourth report: Minutes of evidence*, pp. 27–38, H.C. 1840 (334), x, 393–404.
4 *Final report from the select committee appointed to inquire into the operation of the act for the regulation of mills and factories*, p. 1, H.C. 1841 (56), ix, 557.
5 Ibid. For a summary of the report, see M.W. Thomas, *The early factory legislation: A study in legislative and administrative evolution* (Leigh-on-Sea, Essex, 1948), chap. 12.

of the inspectorate. The impact of these changes went far beyond a mere 'tightening-up' of the 1833 act. Nevertheless they attracted sufficient cross-party support to ensure that when an initial attempt by the Whigs to translate them into law failed in 1841, they were adopted by Sir James Graham on behalf of the new Tory government. The new provision for the education of child workers, however, caused considerable controversy and it was not until 1844 that the committee's proposals formed the basis of a new factory act.[6]

But before we deal with this legislation, we must briefly refer to a more ambitious, but less successful, attempt to extend the ambit of the 1833 act. The factory commissioners in 1833 had frankly conceded that conditions in textile factories were probably no worse than those in many other industries – it was just that textile factories were more amenable to regulation.[7] As experience showed that the 1833 act did not have disastrous consequences for the textile trade, so calls began to be made for similar regulation of other industries. In 1840, Ashley secured the appointment of a children's employment commission to obtain evidence of the working conditions of children in mines and collieries and other 'trades and manufactures'.[8] With respect to Ireland, a small amount of evidence was given of working conditions in a number of industries, including calico printing, bleaching and dyeing, iron foundries, ship-building, rope-making, tobacco, millinery and dress-making. There was some cause for concern; in tobacco factories, for example, children were employed from the age of five, in calico-printing from the age of six, and in glass-works from the age of seven. But in general conditions were favourable. Most of the buildings attached to bleachfields, for example, were 'spacious, dry and well-ventilated', while paper-mills 'are remarkably clean and comfortable'; children employed in iron-works were 'healthy and robust', and those engaged in calico-printing 'are decidedly better fed than those who follow no occupation'.[9] The evidence from the United Kingdom as a whole, however, led the commission to report that the conditions of employment of many children fell well below the standards set by the 1833 act.[10] But as Ashley later admitted, 'the public mind was not then ripe for more comprehensive measures',[11] and, with the exception of coal-mines, the commission's findings were ignored. The Mines and Collieries Act which Ashley secured in 1842,[12] however, was of signal importance in the present

6 See e.g. Thomas, *Early factory legislation*, chap. 13; Ward, *Factory movement*, chaps. 9–14; O. MacDonagh, *Early Victorian government, 1830–1870* (London, 1977), pp. 62–66.

7 *First report from the commissioners appointed to collect information in the factory districts ... ,* p. 51, H.C. 1833 (450), xx, 51; Hutchins and Harrison, *History of factory legislation*, pp. 120–21.

8 The commission consisted of two of the factory commissioners in 1833 (Thomas Tooke and Thomas Southwood Smith) and two factory inspectors (Leonard Horner and Robert Saunders).

9 *Second report of the commission for inquiring into the employment of children in mines and manufactories: Trades and manufactures*, pp. 9, 13, 22, 23, 41, 107 and 112, H.C. 1843 (430), xiii, 307.

10 Ibid., pp. 195–99.

11 *Hansard 3*, clxxxix, 1209 (9 Aug. 1867).

12 5 & 6 Vict., c. 99. The act applied to Ireland.

context in that, as had been recommended by the commission, it added adult women to the class of 'protected' workers whose conditions of employment required legislative regulation.[13]

THE FACTORY ACT 1844[14]

Health and safety

Although the factory commissioners in 1833 had made recommendations designed to reduce the number of factory accidents, no such provision was included in the 1833 act. But the incidence of accidental death and injury revealed by the inspectors led the select committee in 1841 to recommend that there should be specific requirements with regard to the fencing of dangerous machinery, the cleaning of machinery in motion, the investigation of accidents causing injury or death and the provision of assistance to injured workers seeking compensation.[15] These recommendations were duly enacted.[16] But like their predecessors, the select committee had little to say about provisions specifically designed to protect the health of the workforce. In 1833 it appears to have been accepted that, provided children and young persons were not compelled to work excessive hours, conditions in the new factories made such provisions generally unnecessary.[17] In 1840, this approach was also followed by the select committee – with one exception of particular interest in Ireland. Appreciating the particular risks that accompanied the wet-spinning of flax (and jute), the committee proposed, and section 19 of the new act provided, that 'no child or young person shall be employed in any part of a factory in which ... wet-spinning ... is carried on, unless sufficient means shall be employed and continued for protecting the workers from being wetted, and, where hot water is used, for preventing the escape of steam into the room occupied by the workers'.[18]

Hours of employment (i) Children and young persons

There was general agreement that the minimum age for factory work should continue to be nine.[19] But the acceptance of proposals primarily designed to

---

13 *First report of the commissioners for inquiring into the employment and condition of children in mines and manufactories*, H.C. 1842 (380), xv, 1.

14 An act to amend the laws relating to labour in factories (7 & 8 Vict., c. 15). The increased detail of the legislation is reflected in the fact that the act, with 74 sections, is half as long again as the 1833 act.

15 *Final report from the select committee 1841*, pp. 23–28.

16 Sections 20–25 and 42–43. See further below, chapters 5 and 11.

17 The act did, however, include a provision (s. 26), first introduced by the 1802 act, for the limewashing of factory walls and ceilings; this was continued by section 18 of the 1844 act. But no attempt was made, either in 1833 or in 1844, to continue the ventilation requirement also enacted in 1802.

18 See further below, chapter 6.

19 *Final report from the select committee 1841*, p. 6.

facilitate education by reducing the length of the working day for children encouraged the government to think otherwise,[20] and ultimately section 29 of the 1844 act reduced the minimum age to eight. As recommended by the committee, sections 8–17 of the act tightened up the procedure for determining a young worker's age, particularly by empowering the inspectors themselves to appoint 'a sufficient number of ... certifying surgeons' to provide, after appropriate examination, a 'surgical certificate' of his or her age and fitness for employment. But the committee's primary concern was the failure of the 1833 act to ensure that children worked limited hours and received adequate education.[21] In this respect, a wholly new approach was required, and on the recommendation of the inspectors, the committee endorsed the 'half-time system', whereby children were employed (on a fortnighly or monthly rota) for up to seven hours before 1 p.m. (dinner time) or for six and a half hours after 1 p.m., the remainder of the day in each case being set aside for education.[22] The government later added the option of the 'alternate day system', whereby children were employed (for not more than ten hours a day) on alternate days, with the intermediate days set aside for education.[23] These proposals caused relatively little excitement in themselves; but considerable controversy arose as a result of the government's proposal to put the provision of education under the control of the established church.[24] The strength of the opposition forced the government to withdraw this proposal, and the 1844 act eventually required a child's parents merely to ensure that he or she received at least three hours' schooling each week day (or five hours on alternate days) from any 'fit' schoolmaster who was to provide a weekly certificate of attendance to the child's employer.[25]

As recommended by the select committee, no changes were made in the working hours for young persons aged 13–18.

Hours of employment (ii) Adult women

In a wholly new development, stimulated by the Mines and Collieries Act 1842 rather than the select committee, section 32 of the 1844 act provided that women over the age of 18 were to be governed by all provisions relating to the employment of young persons. This meant in particular that, in accordance with the 1833 act, they were not to be employed for more than

---

20 See especially *Hansard 3*, lxxiv, 757 (6 May 1844).
21 Section 9 of the 1833 act attempted to restrict the employment of children to nine hours per day, but 'the provisions of this section are frequently and grossly violated': *Final report from the select committee 1841*, p. 6.
22 Ibid.; 1844 act, s. 30.
23 1844 act, s. 31. For a particular example of education provision in Ireland, see T. Hunt, *Portlaw, County Waterford 1825–1876: Portrait of an industrial village and its cotton industry* (Dublin, 2000), pp. 32–40.
24 See especially Thomas, *Early factory legislation*, pp. 192–201.
25 Sections 38 and 39. The employer was to contribute up to two pence per week to the cost of the child's education, deductible from the wages payable to the child.

12 hours in any one day, nor for more than 69 hours in any one week. This extension of the class of 'protected' workers does not seem to have been particularly controversial at the time; the home secretary, Graham, readily conceded that it was somewhat exceptional, but contended that it was necessary for the health of those concerned, and this explanation appears to have been generally accepted.[26]

But the provision gave the ten hours' lobby another opportunity to press their case for a general reduction in the length of the working day, and the issue went to a vote in which a large number of Irish members participated with significant results.[27] In a confusing situation the house first voted by a narrow majority against a 12 hour limit, but then immediately, by a narrow margin, also rejected a 10 hour limit. The Irish members, by a majority (including O'Connell) of 21–10, voted against 12 hours, and clearly determined the outcome of that vote. But of the five who voted against twelve hours and then proceeded to vote against the shorter limit also (thus determining the outcome of the second vote), only one was an Irish MP – Capt. M. Archdale of Co. Fermanagh.[28] When the issue was again debated in May 1844, Sharman Crawford[29] said that three or four petitions presented from different bodies of operatives from the mills of Belfast to the effect that 'ten hours daily was as much labour as women and children of tender years could endure without injury' showed 'the real state of opinion among the masters and operatives of that town …'.[30] But David Ross[31] contended that Crawford's petitions did not emanate from the Belfast operatives, and that 'the majority of the working people employed in the cotton mills in that town' were against the ten hours' bill.[32] To bring to a head an issue which generated much controversy throughout the whole kingdom, Graham made it a matter of confidence and the house then came down firmly in favour of 12 hours.[33]

26 There is, however, an alternative 'male breadwinner' explanation. At a time when the employment of women was increasing rapidly, there were calls for the total exclusion of women from the workplace in order to provide more work for adult men. The less drastic step of shorter hours, it was hoped, 'would in the long run raise the wages and job security of adult men and thus decrease the dependence of family budgets on the factory earnings of children, juveniles and women': Gray, *The factory question*, p. 36.

27 See generally Thomas, *Early factory legislation*, pp. 202–08.

28 *Hansard 3*, lxxiii, 1460–63 (22 March 1844). The voting was 186–183 against a twelve-hour limitation and 188–181 against a ten-hour limitation.

29 A landowner in Co. Down and liberal MP for Dundalk 1835–37; in 1841, however, he was elected MP for Rochdale with Chartist support: see Connolly (ed.), *Oxford companion to Irish history*, p. 133.

30 *Hansard 3*, lxxiv, 637 (3 May 1844).

31 Liberal MP for Belfast 1842–47.

32 *Hansard 3*, lxxiv, 637–38 (3 May 1844). To the charge that the petitions against interfering with the hours of labour had been got up at the instigation of the masters, Ross retorted that 'the working men of Belfast were not a class of persons who would submit to the dictation of their masters, or any other persons.' He himself had earlier voted in favour of ten hours, but changed his mind when advised that 'any interference with the hours of labour would materially injure the flax trade of Belfast': ibid., col. 134 (22 April 1844).

33 *Hansard 3*, lxxiv, 1104 (13 May 1844) (majority of 297–159).

Administrative requirements

Many of the inspectors' criticisms of the 1833 act concerned the bureaucratic procedures designed to assist them in its enforcement, and the select committee accepted that in this respect the actual work of inspection had revealed a number of practical weaknesses and omissions. Accordingly, the 1844 act tightened up many of these procedures, including those governing extensions of the working day to make up for time lost as a result of accidents or the enforced stoppage of machinery 'from want of water, or too much water', the regulation of holidays and meal-times, and various formal requirements relating to factory clocks, the maintenance of factory registers and records and the posting of abstracts of the act and other notices in conspicuous places within the factory.[34]

Legal proceedings

Section 30 of the 1833 act had provided that a worker was personally liable, 'in lieu of' the employer, for any offence committed 'without the personal consent, concurrence or knowledge' of the employer. This provision was considered by the workers to be 'the source of much oppression', given that 'if the offence is thrown upon the overlooker, the overlooker admits the case rather than run the risk of losing his situation, as he expects would be the case if he were not to admit it'.[35] Stuart, for example, took the view that the unlawful employment of children was more often than not practised by workers rather than employers; it was his practice in such cases not to prosecute the employer, but to persuade him to dismiss the child – or the worker who had hired him or her.[36] The effect of this practice was to shift the burden of the legislation from owners to workers – a practice which gave rise to criticism, particularly in Scotland.[37] The select committee's solution was not to exonerate the worker entirely, but to throw the burden of proof onto the employer. Accordingly, the 1844 act provided that the employer 'shall in every case ... be deemed in the first instance to have committed the offence'; a worker should only be liable if the employer was able to show that he had used due diligence to enforce the execution of the act and that the worker had committed the offence 'without his knowledge, consent or connivance ...'.[38]

---

34 1844 act, ss. 7, 26–28 and 33–37. The select committee had been particularly critical of the provisions for time 'unavoidably lost in cases of accident' and those governing mealtimes: *Final report from the select committee 1841*, pp. 2–5.

35 Ibid., p. 16.

36 *Second report: Minutes of evidence*, p. 83. In June 1837, for example, A. M'Culloch of Bangor 'dismissed six children on my suggestion [for] working without school certificates': *Fifth report: Minutes of evidence*, p. 154.

37 See e.g. S. Field, 'Without the law? Professor Arthurs and the early factory inspectorate', in *J. Law & Society*, 17 (1990), 445 at p. 461, noting that 'the severity of such punishment when times were scarce is evident'.

38 *Final report of the select committee 1841*, p. 17; 1844 act, s. 41.

The select committee and the act also dealt with various aspects of the prosecution process in ways which were designed to assist inspectors to secure more convictions and to encourage magistrates to impose higher penalties. The process of issuing a summons was simplified and provision made for compelling the appearance of parties and witnesses and the production of evidence; changes in the rules of evidence made the inspector himself a competent witness and effectively reversed the onus of proof in relation to evidence of employment and the age of a young worker.[39] All cases were now to be heard by at least two magistrates, and no magistrate sitting in a factory case was to be 'an occupier of the factory, or ... the father, son or brother of the occupier of the factory in which the offence ... shall have been committed'.[40] If the defendant was convicted, the court was obliged to impose a minimum fine in respect of each offence.[41] A defendant who had been fined more than three pounds or convicted of any offence punishable by fine or imprisonment was given a right of appeal to quarter sessions; alternatively, he or she could proceed by way of certiorari in the court of queen's bench.[42] No right of appeal against acquittal was given to the prosecution; but the Summary Jurisdiction Act 1857 subsequently gave the prosecution – and the defendant – a general right to appeal on a point of law by way of case stated.

Status and powers of inspectorate

As we have seen, the 1833 act conferred legislative and judicial, as well as administrative, powers on the inspectors. Not only were they 'required' to make 'all rules, regulations and orders as may be necessary for the due execution of this act', but they had the same authority as a justice of the peace to hear and determine proceedings in respect of an offence.[43] Professor Arthurs sees in these provisions the potential for the development of a state regulatory agency with the kind of wide-ranging and discretionary administrative powers necessary to control powerful capitalist entrepreneurs – and presumably an increasingly radical and politicised working-class.[44] Given that the inspectors were to operate within fairly narrow parameters set by the substantive provisions of the 1833 act, this is perhaps an optimistic reading of the act. In any case, the executive and judicial authority granted to the inspectors was soon constrained in practice by government direction,[45] and

39 1844 act, ss. 44–55.
40 Ibid., ss. 45 and 71. See further below, chap. 10.
41 1844 act, ss. 56–65, as recommended by the select committee – see *Final report 1841*, pp. 18–21.
42 1844 act, ss. 69–70, discussed below, chap. 10.
43 1833 act, ss. 18 and 34.
44 H.W. Arthurs, '*Without the law*': *Administrative justice and legal pluralism in nineteenth-century England* (Toronto, 1985), especially chaps. 4 and 5.
45 The home secretary (Lord John Russell) had instructed that inspectors should hear and determine cases only in the exceptional circumstance of the magistrates of the district failing to act: see e.g. Thomas, *Early factory legislation*, pp. 250–51.

then, on the recommendation of the select committee,[46] by the 1844 act. Section 2 formally revoked the inspectors' power to act as magistrates and to make rules, regulations or orders; exclusive judicial authority was conferred on the magistrates' court, subject to review by the higher courts, and rule-making authority was transferred to the home office and parliament.

These developments may be seen as a victory for reactionary forces, particularly mill-owners keen to reduce the operational effectiveness of the inspectors by pleading the constitutional imperative of the separation of powers and the rule of law.[47] On the other hand, it has been claimed that the inspectors themselves promoted this move towards 'legalism' and a dispassionate and objective 'rule of law' in order to *increase* their effectiveness by enabling them to present their actions, not as arbitrary or personal, but as 'the non-discretionary implementation of instructions and commands contained within legal rules or political directives determined elsewhere ...'.[48] Given their somewhat precarious position in the early 1840s, we incline to the latter approach. But it is, of course, highly contentious to suggest that 'legalism' or 'the rule of law' actually secures impartiality or objectivity rather than simply replacing one set of values with another.[49] Such issues go beyond the ambit of this discussion; but the practical impact of this early example of the classic conflict between 'law' and 'discretion' may in the event have been relatively insignificant. Arthurs, for example, claims that notwithstanding the rise of legalism, the period between 1830 and 1870 was one in which 'almost the entire repertoire of modern administrative techniques ... developed' virtually unhindered by the courts. Few factory cases came before the superior courts after 1844, and although 'the magistrates ... were given ultimate power to impose sanctions, [they] could not or would not exercise it'. Accordingly, 'to the extent that obedience to the legislation took hold, credit must be given primarily to administrative intervention. Through formal regulations and orders, through increased surveillance and informal discussion, through more accurate reporting and more effective publicity, manufacturers were gradually brought into compliance.'[50]

In any event, 'the shift to closer external control of inspectoral discretion must be seen as partially real and as partially presentational, in the sense that

---

46 'These discretionary powers have been productive of much uncertainty and inconvenience to the millowners [and] ... in conformity with the opinion expressed by all parties ... should be taken away': *Final report from the select committee 1841*, p. 10.

47 See e.g. Arthurs, *Without the law*, pp. 138–50.

48 Field, 'Early factory inspectorate', p. 461. Field nevertheless accepts (at p. 454) that some leading millowners criticised the early inspectors on constitutional grounds. Hutchins and Harrison, *History of factory legislation*, p. 86 say that the power to act as a magistrate 'had proved an embarrassment to the inspectors in the exercise of their own proper functions'.

49 For example, Field, 'Early factory inspectorate', pp. 458–59 contends that the early inspectors had a highly-developed sense of political economy and were concerned to support industrial capitalism and the social relations which underpinned it.

50 Arthurs, *Without the law*, pp. 106–07 and 184–85.

it sought to disguise the still extensive discretion in enforcement'.[51] The 1844 act not only left it to the inspectors to decide whether or not to commence formal proceedings against a factory or class of factories; they also retained considerable freedom whether or not to press for further action to be taken in respect of matters not already covered by the existing law. In addition, their operational effectiveness could not but be improved by two further provisions of the 1844 act, which were quite controversial at the time. By section 3 the inspectors' assistants (upgraded from 'superintendents' to 'sub-inspectors') were given the same right as inspectors to enter *any* part of a factory at any time, and were thus entitled for the first time to enter those parts used for manufacturing processes. This extension had been opposed by owners ostensibly apprehensive of 'mill-wardens' who might well reveal trade secrets to competitors. But 'the real objection ... was that the superintendents were in a position to exercise a closer measure of control than the inspectors, since they were resident on the spot and had less ground to cover'.[52]

Their experience of administering the 1833 act also led the inspectors to call for the establishment of a central office in London. This was opposed on the grounds that such centralisation would unduly strengthen the power of the inspectorate and, even worse, would inevitably lead to the appointment of an 'inspector general'. Such an appointment had, indeed, been envisaged in 1841;[53] but it was not supported by the inspectors,[54] and was not pursued. However, the inspectors were agreed that the establishment of a central office would promote uniformity and administrative efficiency. In spite of strong opposition, the house of commons agreed with the inspectors,[55] and under section 5 of the 1844 act a central office was established in London in November 1844.[56] Somewhat ironically, the first clerk of the office was the redoubtable Alexander Redgrave, who was to become the first chief inspector of factories in 1878.

Hours of employment (iii): The normal working day

As is well known, the 1844 act did not satisfy the ten-hour lobby, and their agitation continued until victory (of a sort) was achieved in 1847.[57] The new act[58]

---

51 Field, 'Early factory inspectorate', p. 462.
52 Thomas, *Early factory legislation*, p. 102.
53 Ibid., p. 206n, noting that in 1842 the home secretary (Graham) had actually referred to Horner as 'the inspector general of factories'. See also ibid., pp. 245–47.
54 Ibid., p. 247n: 'The inspectors were determined to yield not a jot of their individual authority'.
55 *Hansard 3*, lxxiv, 337 (26 April 1844), by 157 votes to 33.
56 Thomas, *Early factory legislation*, pp. 247–50, commenting that when the office was moved to the home office building in 1847 for reasons of economy, the effect of the move 'was to identify the inspectors even more closely with the Home Office'.
57 See generally A.P. Robson, *On higher than commercial grounds: The factory controversy 1850–1853* (New York and London, 1985), chaps. 4 and 5; Gray, *Factory question*, chap. 7; Hutchins and Harrison, *History of factory legislation*, chaps. IV and VI; Thomas, *Early factory legislation*, chap. 18; Ward, *Factory movement*, chaps. 13–15.
58 An act to limit the hours of labour of young persons and females in factories (10 & 11 Vict., c. 29).

provided that from 1 May 1848 no young person or woman over the age of 18 should be employed 'for more than ten hours in any one day, nor more than fifty-eight hours in any one week ...'. By this time, of course, Ireland was in the grip of the Famine and it is hardly surprising to find that there were suggestions that the new limit should not apply.[59] But these suggestions attracted little support and the act duly applied throughout the United Kingdom.

It was not long, however, before it became obvious that the 1847 act was being seriously undermined by the use of relay systems which enabled employers to keep factories open for as much as 18 hours a day.[60] The relay (or shift) patterns were often extremely complicated, making it difficult for the inspectors to enforce the law. In Ireland and Scotland, Stuart announced that he proposed to take no action against owners who adopted a relay system, provided no young person or woman actually worked for more than 10 hours in any one day.[61] In England and Wales, however, the inspectors actively sought to restrict the use of relays, but found the magistrates largely unsympathetic to the argument that they were illegal under the 1844 act. The matter came to a head when magistrates in Lancashire threw out a test case, and the issue was brought by way of mandamus to the court of exchequer. In *Ryder* v. *Mills*,[62] Parke B, taking the view that the factory act as a penal statute must be strictly construed, held that relays were still lawful: 'we do not think that there are words in these statutes sufficiently plain and clear to render the conduct of the defendant ... liable to punishment'. Women and young persons 'are therefore at liberty to agree with the master for working [not more than ten hours] ... with any intervals of leisure that may be thought convenient'.[63]

Ashley promptly called for amending legislation to give effect to what even Parke B was prepared to 'conjecture, even strongly, ... was the intention of

59 T.M. Gibson, MP for Manchester, suggested that the effect of the bill would be to reduce by one-sixth the wages of 20,000 operatives in Ireland: *Hansard 3*, xc, 805 (3 March 1847); Mr Labouchère, MP for Taunton, observed that hand-loom weavers in Ulster were working until 2 a.m. three nights per week, and that 'it would be the greatest blessing ... if a factory mill were established there, even if they were obliged to work twelve hours a day': *Hansard 3*, xcii, 309 (3 May 1847).

60 Only three factories in Ireland used relays: *Insp. half-yearly rep., April 1849*, pp. 50 and 58 (Stuart). One of these was Malcomson's cotton factory – see T. Hunt, *Portlaw, County Waterford 1825–1876: Portrait of an industrial village and its cotton industry* (Dublin, 2000), pp. 55–56.

61 *Insp. half-yearly rep., Oct. 1848*, pp. 130–34, partly because the law was unclear and partly on the ground that banning relays would keep many young persons out of employment. Stuart's announcement provoked petitions and protests to the home secretary from Scottish workers.

62 (1849) 3 Exch 853, 154 Eng Rep 1090. Robson, *Higher than commercial grounds*, p. 260 explains Eng Rep that Mills was an owner favourable to the workers' cause who worked relays in order to get a test case into court.

63 (1849) 3 Exch 853 at pp. 869 and 872, having noted (at p. 868) that 'we are not to inquire whether the enactments are dictated by sound policy or not; that question is exclusively for the consideration of Parliament.'

the legislature ...'. The government's solution was to introduce a fixed or 'standard' working day from six a.m. to six p.m. (2 p.m. on Saturdays). No woman or young person was to be employed outside these hours; but by way of a *quid pro quo* they would only be entitled to one and a half hours for mealtimes (half an hour on Saturdays). This meant that the working week would be *increased* from 58 to 60 hours. To the horror of his supporters, Ashley accepted this as a necessary price to pay for the abolition of the relay system, and the compromise measure was duly enacted as the Factories Act 1850.[64] In the excitement, the act failed to include children – an omission put right by further legislation in 1853.[65] Thomas sums up the effect of these acts as follows:

It would be difficult to over-estimate the significance of the principle of the normal working day.... No longer were the operatives condemned to excessive and unreasonable prolongation of their hours of labour, for they were now free to leave the mill at six o'clock at night, and for the first time they were able to enjoy a period of respite on Saturday afternoon.... The institution of the normal day did not by any means preclude the possibility of evasion, but it was now a comparatively simple matter to detect overworking, and the inspectors were thus able to devote their time to other and more important aspects of their work.[66]

THE 1844 ACT IN IRELAND

One of the principal reasons for including women over 18 in the 1844 act was their increasing presence in the workplace. By this time, children had almost ceased to be employed in Irish textile factories, and it seems that they had, to a greater extent than in England and Wales but not Scotland, been replaced by women. In 1846, women over 18 represented more than 40 per cent of a workforce which now exceeded 22,000 (as compared to 35 per cent in England and Wales, and 46 per cent in Scotland).[67] Since young persons continued to constitute a further 37 per cent, the 1844 act applied in Ireland to four-fifths of those now working in textiles, predominantly in flax spinning mills.

After the Famine, the decline of the cotton and woollen industry in Ireland continued; but during the next twenty years, 'the most rapid and massive expansion [in the linen industry] took place, marked ... by ever-increasing mechanisation and centralisation'.[68] Technological developments during the 1840s and the death or emigration of many handloom weavers encouraged the mechanisation of linen weaving in the 1850s, and by 1862 there were in

64 An act to amend the acts relating to labour in factories (13 & 14 Vict., c. 54).
65 An act to regulate the employment of children in factories (16 & 17 Vict., c. 104).
66 *Early factory legislation*, p. 327.
67 *Return of the number of persons employed in cotton, woollen, worsted, flax and silk factories respectively, in the United Kingdom* ... , H.C. 1847 (294), xlvi, 609.
68 F.S.L. Lyons, *Ireland since the Famine* (London, 1971), p. 62.

Belfast more than 4,000 powered weaving looms, mainly driven by steam.[69] The increasing mechanisation of linen manufacture brought further industry in its train,[70] at a time when other great enterprises were also being established in the north of Ireland.[71]

Stuart's death in 1849 led to a reorganisation of the factory districts which now joined Ireland with the western half of England and the whole of Wales and brought Inspector Howell back to Ireland. He was particularly impressed with the expansion of the linen industry:

> ... at every place which I visited [in Ulster], and almost at every factory which I inspected in this part of the country, some extensive improvements were going on, some new machinery was being introduced, some enlargement of the existing accommodation was being made, or some new buildings were either in course of construction or about to be commenced. This remark is universally applicable in the northern parts of Ireland, where the energy, enterprise, industry and skill of the gentlemen who have embarked their capital in manufactures, are to be surpassed by no part of the United Kingdom with which I am acquainted....[72]

But the position in the south was very different. Here, the 'decay' of the factory system was 'unquestionable'; fortunately, however, it had been offset by a distinct improvement in agricultural conditions. As a result, Howell found 'a very marked improvement in the general appearance of the people' which made it 'less a subject for regret that manufactures in the south have not advanced, or even that they should have declined ...'.[73]

The textile industry was still heavily dependent upon women and young persons. Indeed, on Hudson's death in 1855, the increasing numbers of 'protected' persons – and the view that 'the factory laws had been very ill-observed in Ireland'[74] – led to the division of Ireland, once again, into two districts, with a full-time sub-inspector (Darkin) in the north and a part-time one (Steen), shared with north Wales, in the south.[75] On Howell's death in 1858, both sub-inspectors came under the supervision of Robert Baker,[76] who remained the inspector with responsibility for the whole of Ireland, as well as much of Britain, until 1878.

69 C. Ó Gráda, Ireland: *A new economic history, 1780–1939* (Oxford, 1994), p.286. See also W.A. McCutcheon, *The industrial archaeology of Northern Ireland* (Belfast, 1980), p. 305.

70 P. Ollerenshaw, 'Industry 1820–1914' in L. Kennedy and P. Ollerenshaw (ed.), *An economic history of Ulster 1820–1939* (Manchester, 1985), p. 72 notes that 'local engingeering firms responded to the great strides made by Ulster linen' and were so successful that they began to export their products about 1850.

71 E.g. the partnership of Edward Harland and Gustav Wolff was founded in 1861.

72 *Insp. half-yearly rep., Oct. 1850*, pp. 30–31.

73 Ibid., pp. 29–30.

74 Darkin to Sir George Grey (home sec.), 12 May 1862, PRO HO45/6968.

75 *Insp. half-yearly rep., April 1856*, p. 21 – 'a more convenient arrangement than that which previously existed'.

76 A surgeon in Leeds until appointed a superintendent in 1834, Baker had a wide experience of factories throughout England and Wales when promoted to inspector in

Table 2.1: Textile factories under the factory acts in 1856[77]

	Cotton	Wool/ worsted	Flax	Ireland total	Scotland	England and Wales	United Kingdom
No. of factories	12	33	110	155	530	4,432	5,117
Children (9–13)	–	1	113	114	1,348	51,010	52,472
Male young persons (13–18)	424	88	3,844	4,356	6,580	59,311	70,247
Females over 13	2,122	513	19,743	22,378	55,300	305,700	383,378
Male adults over 18	799	288	5,053	6,140	14,204	156,056	176,400
TOTAL	3,345	890	28,753	32,988	77,432	572,077	682,497

Under Howell and Baker, the sub-inspectors in Ireland continued to operate by means of exhortation rather than prosecution. Between 1850 and 1864, only six factories were on average prosecuted each year, resulting in an average fine per factory of £8 or thereabouts (or slightly in excess of £1 per information); the most common charge against employers (roughly 80 per cent of all informations) was employing women or young persons outside 'normal' hours, and these prosecutions were largely confined to three areas – Belfast and the counties of Down and Antrim, Londonderry and counties Dublin and Meath.[78]

1858 at the age of 55. He wrote two books on the factories acts: *The factory acts made easy, or How to work the law without the risk of penalties* (London, 1851) and (less optimistically) *The factory acts made as easy as possible* (London, 1867). Not unlike Horner as a 'liberal reforming zealot' (Gray, *Factory question*, p. 92), Baker took the view that 'the factory acts were enacted for the benefit of both masters and workers, and … it is our duty to hold an even hand between those that are willing to obey the law, and those who seek undue advantages by disobeying it': *Insp. half-yearly rep., April 1873*, p. 40. See generally W.R. Lee, 'Robert Baker: The first doctor in the factory department' in *Br. J. Industrial Medicine*, 21 (1964), 85 and 167.

77 *Returns of the number of cotton, woollen, worsted, flax and silk factories subject to the factories acts in each county …* , H.C. 1857 (7, sess. 1), xiv, 173. See also *Insp. half-yearly rep., Oct. 1862*, pp. 66–137 for a detailed comparison between 1839 and 1862.

78 See further below, chap. 10.

EXTENDING THE SCOPE OF THE ACTS

1. Textile-related factories

We have already seen that conditions in textile factories were probably no worse than those in many other industries. The apparent success of the 1844 act and the realisation that shorter working hours did not necessarily lead to reduced output, soon led to calls for its extension. Logically enough, the earliest extensions embraced industries allied to textiles by locality and nature of work.[79]

The poor conditions under which children worked in calico printing, where designs were applied to fabric manually or by machine, were highlighted by the children's employment commission in 1843,[80] and in 1845 Ashley chose this industry as a suitable starting point for extending the scope of regulation.[81] What he had in mind were provisions which were less stringent than those applicable to textile factories, and he accordingly proceeded by way of separate legislation rather than seeking an extension of the 1844 act. In spite of opposition based on the fact that print-works were more widely dispersed, less heavily mechanised and subject to more irregular production demands than textile factories, he was able to secure the enactment of the Print Works Act 1845.[82] But the concessions which Ashley was forced to accept, in order 'to afford the printworkers that degree of flexibility in conducting their business that the peculiar problems they had to face demanded', meant that the act imposed only 'meagre' restrictions.[83]

For the next few years, Ashley's attention was concentrated on the ten hour day. But in the early 1850s, he gave his support to a campaign by workers in bleaching and dyeing for shorter hours and successfully introduced a bill on their behalf in the house of lords.[84] In the house of commons, Isaac Butt, 'at the request of some of the workpeople', took charge of the bill[85] and secured the appointment of H.S. Tremenheere to conduct an inquiry into conditions in bleaching works throughout the United Kingdom.[86] Tremenheere's report explained the distinctive features of the

79 See generally Hutchins and Harrison, *History of factory legislation*, chap. vii.
80 *Second report on employment and condition of children in mines and manufactories 1843*, pp. 68–73.
81 See Hutchins and Harrison, *History of factory legislation*, pp. 123–31; Thomas, *Early factory legislation*, pp. 272–84.
82 8 & 9 Vict., c. 29.
83 Thomas, *Early factory legislation*, p. 276.
84 See especially *Hansard 3*, cxxxiv, 478 (22 June 1854) and 931 (30 June 1854); Hutchins and Harrison, *History of factory legislation*, pp. 131–39.
85 *Hansard 3*, cxxviii, 1277 (5 July 1853). For the text of the bill, see H.C. 1854 (226), i, 213.
86 *Report of the commissioner appointed to enquire into the expediency of extending the acts for the better regulation of mills and factories to bleaching works, etc.* [1943], H.C. 1854–55, xviii, 1; conditions in the fifty or so bleach-works in Ireland are described at pp. xxix–xxxi. According to Hutchins and Harrison, *History of factory legislation*, p. 133n, Tremenheere, a barrister and former inspector of schools, served on numerous commissions 'and was

Working conditions were also better in larger establishments. In one needlewoman's workroom in Dublin, on the other hand, a young boy had lain dying for some time, with the result that 'girls and women must have worked in what has been a permanent sick room'; another house in Grafton Street was 'very unhealthy' on account of a pool of black water in the yard.[113] The commission quickly disposed of the argument that legislation was inappropriate for such 'private' establishments:

[A]s to all essential characters, this occupation must be regarded as an industrial and commercial undertaking; it is carried on for the pecuniary profit of the employer; it demands the labour of persons who ... belong in reality to the class of work-people.... The question of the number employed has no real bearing upon the principle; and it has been clearly shown ... that among the whole industrial population, the greatest evils and the greatest oppression and suffering exist where children and young persons are employed in very limited numbers by small masters and mistresses, and still more so where engaged by workmen.[114]

Accordingly, there was no reason why millinery and dress-making should not come under legislative regulation.

Seamstresses   In 1861, nearly 62,000 seamstresses were employed in ladies' outfitters, tailors, bonnet-makers, etc. in Ireland.[115] The trade was in the process of being transformed by sewing machines, some of which were even then steam-driven, bringing about a 'tendency' towards a factory system – one of the most remarkable examples of which was shirt and collar-making in Londonderry, where 'the abundance of unemployed female labour ... afforded great facilities for the growth of such a manufacture'.[116] The leading manufacturers were Tillie and Henderson's:

Our factory ... has accommodation for 1,000 persons ... nearly all females, from 11 years of age upwards. We object, however, to employing married women with children [on the grounds that] ... they cannot attend to their work so well if they have to be thinking of their children, and absence at work prevents them from giving proper attention to their families. The work consists chiefly of cutting out the material and preparing it for the sewing machines by various kinds of hand-work, and then stitching parts by the machines, most of which are worked by steam. The shirts are then sent out into the country to be 'fitted' or put together, i.e. made up, a work which is done exclusively by persons living at their own homes.... The benefit conferred on this part of Ireland by the introduction of this manufacture is enormous.[117]

113 *Evidence collected by Mr White*, pp. 52–53.
114 *Second report*, p. lxvi. See also *Third report*, pp. xx and xxv.
115 *Second report*, pp. xlv and lxvi–lxxviii.
116 *Evidence collected by Mr White*, p. 58. The area became the leading centre for this industry in the United Kingdom, and by 1875 'the number of factories had risen to twelve, employing 4,000–5,000 workers in Derry itself and a "rural and suburban" labour force of about 15,000': Ollerenshaw, 'Industry 1820–1914', pp. 84–85. See also J. Bardon, *A history of Ulster* (Belfast, 1992), pp. 394–96.
117 *Evidence collected by Mr White*, p. 58 (evidence of Mr William Tillie).

Although there were some problems,[118] the factory was 'spacious, cheerful and airy' and the hours worked did not exceed, and frequently were less than, those required by the factory acts. The fact that such conditions already existed, concluded the commission, 'facilitated the introduction of legislative measures'.[119]

Hand-loom weaving   Although the weaving of linen was becoming increasingly power-driven, there was still a considerable amount of hand-loom weaving, particularly in Co. Armagh, since this was not only cheaper, but also more suitable for certain kinds of work.[120] But the conditions under which this work was undertaken were appalling: the following account was regarded by the commission as 'a specimen of such places':

I have four looms in my house, worked by my own family ... In summer we begin at 5 or 6 a.m. and work till dark, about 8 or 9; in winter begin at 7 or daylight and work till 11 p.m.... We are scarcely off at all for meals – I suppose not over an hour altogether.... We fetch [the children] to work just as soon as they are able – to work just like ourselves and keep one another going. My girl there, Mary Jane, aged 9 years 4 months, winds constant; another of 8 can wind for one [loom] or two.... My children did not begin weaving until they were nearly 13.... Heaps of nights we have to stop up the whole night through to get a web out, and you cannot do without a winder....

Many a one suffers severely from the wet; it's very bad for the stomach and bowels, and gives pains. In wet weather the water rises in the treadle holes, and we have to set the treadles higher, just as you regulate them for the little ones with their short legs.... The greatest loss of the business that I see is the children not getting taught. Sometimes mine go to Sunday school, sometimes they don't; they have got no proper clothes....[121]

In the face of such evidence, the case for regulation was self-evident.

These three examples formed part of the commission's overall recommendation that regulation should be extended across a wide range of non-textile trades and industries – of whatever size and extent. Larger establishments should, however, be distinguished from smaller ones – and neither class should in general be regulated as strictly as textile factories. But for the first time there should be an absolute prohibition on the employment of women

---

118 Baker had noted that the industry was mainly dependent on low-paid women workers, many of whom consumed 'vast' quantities of snuff, apparently as a stimulant to ward off 'great and vital depression ... found in the close congregation and occasional long hours of shirt-makers': *Insp. half-yearly rep., Oct. 1862*, p. 120.

119 *Second report*, p. lxvii.

120 Ibid., pp. xliii–xlv. '[S]o fine a skin (polish) cannot be put on by [a power loom] as where the hand loom is used, and the weaver keeps smoothing the surface; and also inferior and cheaper material can be worked on hand looms': *Evidence collected by Mr White*, p. 219 (evidence of Harry Cinnamon, linen manufacturer of Portadown).

121 *Evidence collected by Mr White*, p. 219 (evidence of Thomas Foy, Portadown). Evidence to the same effect was given by the medical officer of Portadown dispensary: ibid., p. 220, and see generally, pp. 220–23.

and children in a small number of particularly dangerous or unhealthy industries such as the annealing of glass and grinding in the metal trades, and the ventilation provisions of the 1864 act should be extended to 'every factory where ... any ... process is carried on by which dust is generated and inhaled by the workman to an injurious extent ...'. The government accepted these radical recommendations, and gave substantial effect to them in two complementary pieces of legislation.[122]

The first of these – the Factory Acts Extension Act 1867[123] – applied provisions similar to, but not as stringent as, the 1844 act to two categories of non-textile factories. First, a number of particular trades, such as the manufacture of machinery, tobacco and letter-press printing, were stipulated as subject to the act irrespective of the size of the workforce. Secondly, the act applied generally to all other premises, not already covered by factory legislation, which were 'in the same occupation ... and constituting one trade establishment, in, on, or within the precincts of which fifty or more persons are employed in any manufacturing process' or in manual labour. The net result, in Shaftesbury's words, was that regulation would now apply 'as nearly as possible to all the remaining branches of manufacture ...'.[124] Notwithstanding his estimate that it would embrace an additional one and a half million women, young persons and children, the bill passed into law with a minimum of fuss and controversy.

In Ireland, the 1867 act immediately brought under the jurisdiction of the factory inspectorate at least 500 additional factories, including engineering and metal works, iron and brass foundries, letter-press printing, clothing works, breweries and distilleries, and tobacco manufacturers. Although the majority of the 27,000 persons employed in these factories were adult males, 40 per cent belonged to one of the 'protected' classes.[125] As might be expected, the act had a significant impact in the north-east, where '[it] is found to work very well, and is generally approved by both employers and employed'.[126] But more than half the newly-protected persons worked outside Ulster, with the result that the factory acts now began to have a greater application in other parts of the island[127] – at least in theory: '[The act] is not popular in

---

122 'The bills were generally attacked merely on questions of detail, and not on the principle of opposing state interference': Hutchins and Harrison, *History of factory legislation*, p. 172.

123 30 & 31 Vict., c. 103. 'The list of modifications and exceptions in this Act is a long one, occupying about twice as many pages as the sections themselves ... [nullifying] half the good the regulation might have done': ibid., p. 169.

124 *Hansard 3*, clxxxix, 1209 (9 Aug. 1867).

125 See *Insp. half-yearly rep., Oct. 1868*, pp. 126–28, 258 and 266. The total of 11,204 'protected' persons consisted of 4,783 women, 5,935 young persons and 486 children.

126 *Insp. half-yearly rep., Oct. 1869*, pp. 222–23 (Cramp), adding that 'the ... Act has worked quite a revolution in the North of Ireland with regard to the hours of labour. When first enforced, the complaints were loud and general against commencing work at 6 a.m; but now that the workers have experienced the benefit of leaving off work at 6 p.m., they rejoice in the change, and are jealous of any encroachment on it ... '.

127 *Insp. half-yearly rep., Oct. 1868*, p. 126. Even in the north, 'the increase of works

this district.... [The employers] complain, especially the tobacco manufacturers, of the difficulty of introducing into the business of their trades the
regular hours which the Factory Acts make compulsory.... To them the
enforcing the Act ... appears only in the light of a novel tax on production,
and as a disadvantage arbitrarily imposed on a few selected trades, while the
great majority ... escape scot-free.'[128]

3. *Workshops*

The Children's Employment Commission took the view that it would be
wrong to restrict regulation to 'factories' and to ignore 'minor' workplaces
where a small number of children, young persons and women were or might
be employed; all workplaces, however small, should be subject to regulation.
Accordingly in 1867 a second act – the Workshop Regulation Act[129] –
extended a less restrictive form of regulation to 'workshops', that is, to 'any
room or place whatever, whether in the open air or under cover, in which any
handicraft is carried on by any child, young person or woman and to which
and over which the person by whom such child, young person or woman is
employed has the right of access and control' – and where, by implication,
less than fifty persons were employed.

The act did not extend the 1844 act to workshops, but introduced a
separate code which, by reason of many modifications and qualifications, was
less restrictive than that applicable to non-textile factories. In particular, the
concept of the normal day did not apply; the act merely provided that a child
should not be employed on any one day for more than six and a half hours
between 6 a.m. and 8 p.m., and that no young person or woman should be
employed for more than twelve hours between 5 a.m. and 9 p.m.[130] In
addition, the home secretary was given extensive powers to 'modify'
provisions of the act in respect of particular trades. As one of the factory
inspectors explained:

[The Act contained] a series of provisions ... which resembled, while they did not
coincide with, the provisions of preceding factory acts. Thus, while protected persons
might only work the same aggregate number of hours per day in both, a wider
latitude was allowed to workshops than factories in the selection of those hours....
Other relaxations of the prevalent obligations in factories followed. Surgical

        obliges me to visit towns and districts where my predecessor had no occasion to
        go ... ': ibid., p. 261 (Cramp).
128   *Insp. half-yearly rep., Oct. 1869*, p. 264 (Cooke-Taylor), who explained that 'the vast
        majority of the works ... brought under its influence are small ... and many have far
        more temptation ... to dismiss their hands altogether, and to retire from a struggling
        industry, than to overwork them in producing a supply for which there is no
        proportionate demand'.
129   30 & 31 Vict., c. 146.
130   Shaftesbury was particularly unhappy that the hours of labour should be longer than
        for factories – a provision which 'would almost render nugatory the provisions of the
        bill': *Hansard 3*, clxxxix, 1596 (16 Aug. 1867).

certificates were not required for children and young persons in workshops, nor was it compulsory to keep a register of particulars. The half-time system of education, now thoroughly established in factories, was supplanted here by a very inferior system of ten hours' schooling a week....[131]

Furthermore, the 'duty' of enforcing the act was given not to the factory inspectors but to local authorities, whose officers were forbidden to enter a workshop without the owner's permission unless authorised by a justice of the peace satisfied that there was reasonable cause for believing that the workshop was in breach of the act. A factory inspector could enter any workshop and inspect it at any time 'when any person is at work at any handicraft ...'; but he could only report any breach of the act to the responsible local authority officer.

In Ireland, the 1867 act appears to have applied to more than 3,000 workshops employing somewhere in the region of 30,000 persons. But its principal significance was geographical rather than quantitative; workshops were to be found in small towns and even villages, and with the contemporaneous enactment of the Factory Acts Extension Act, regulatory provision spread for the first time to all corners of Ireland. As in much of Great Britain, however, the local authorities proved to be generally ineffective in enforcing the provisions of the 1867 act.[132] In 1869, for example, it was reported that the act 'remains ... if not a dead letter, at least an inoperative one in the north of Ireland', for three reasons – 'the "local authority" is generally composed of employers of labour in workshops, who object to put a penal act in force against themselves.... [There is] a disinclination to incur trouble or expense ... [and] a belief that it was intended that the local authority should be passive and not active in the matter ...'.[133] The position in the south was even less satisfactory: 'The ... Act in my district is wholly inoperative. It is worse; it is a "dead letter". It is worse still; it is deliberately and wilfully ignored.'[134] The level of dissatisfaction with the performance of the local authorities became so widespread that their duties were transferred to the factory inspectorate by the Factory and Workshop Act 1871, and the position with regard to enforcement slowly improved.

4. Textile factories

The legislation of the 1860s effected a radical transformation in the ambit of industrial regulation. But before we leave this *tour d'horizon*, we must return

---

131 R.W. Cooke-Taylor, *The factory system and the factory acts* (London, 1894), p. 101. According to Shaftesbury, the act 'though far from perfect ... contained some very excellent provisions': *Hansard 3*, clxxxix, 1595 (16 Aug. 1867).

132 See Hutchins and Harrison, *History of factory legislation*, pp. 226–30.

133 *Insp. half-yearly rep., Oct. 1869*, pp. 227–32 (Cramp).

134 Ibid., p. 267 (Cooke-Taylor), for much the same reasons as those given by Cramp. But some attempt to enforce the act was made in Dublin – see *Insp. half-yearly rep., April 1870*, pp. 53–54 (Baker).

to textile factories, and in particular to the Irish linen industry, which had flourished as a result of the cotton shortage brought about by the American civil war: 'by the 1860s ... Ulster had become the largest linen-producing area in the world'.[135] Between 1857 and 1868, the number of spindles increased from 506,000 to 830,000 and the workforce almost doubled; there was then a temporary recession, but by 1875 the number of spindles (925,000) had reached its peak.[136] In the present context, one of the most noticeable features of this expansion was the *increase* in the employment of young children, who represented nearly two per cent of the workforce in 1870,[137] and six per cent in 1875.[138] By this time, too, nearly 50 per cent of the workforce were female employees over the age of 13 – a percentage which was noticeably higher than the comparable figure in Scotland (35 per cent) and England and Wales (30 per cent).

The industry had apparently come to accept the factory acts – up to a point:

Under this restriction of time [imposed by the acts] there is much work done for factory owners, and a greater amount of wages earned by operatives, than had ever been known in the days of protracted toil.... [Y]ears of experience have proved that the supervision of these concerns by government officers, and the introduction of moderate restrictions, were alike advantageous to employer and employed. There are, however, specified limits to legislation, and whenever the Crown interference between the buyers and sellers of labour exceeds certain boundaries, it frequently becomes mischievous.[139]

This warning was presumably directed against the renewed pressure for a shorter working day.[140] The immediate catalyst for 'mischievous' interference, however, appears to have been a local government report on the health of women, young persons and children in the factory districts of the United Kingdom.[141] The medical commissioners met employers' and workers' associations in a number of industrial cities, including Belfast and heard

---

135 Ollerenshaw, 'Industry 1820–1914', p. 74. See also Bardon, *History of Ulster*, pp. 327–29.

136 McCutcheon, *Industrial archaeology*, p. 298.

137 *Return of the number of manufacturing establishments in which the hours of work are regulated by act of parliament in each county of the United Kingdom, etc.*, p. 207, H.C. 1871 (440), lxii, 315. It may be noted here that an attempt by a Belfast firm in 1854 to have 300–500 boys in Irish workhouses transferred there to be apprenticed as weavers was rejected by the poor law commissioners – see *Sixth report of the commissioners for administering the laws for the relief of the poor in Ireland*, p. 79 [1645], H.C. 1852–53, l, 245.

138 D.L. Armstrong, 'Social and economic conditions in the Belfast linen industry 1850–1900' in *IHS*, 7 (1950–51), 235 at p. 241. The increase was attributed to the scarcity of older workers: *Insp. half-yearly rep., April 1871*, p. 68 (Cramp).

139 H. McCall, *Ireland – her staple manufactures: being sketches of the history and progress of the linen and cotton trades ...* (3rd ed., Belfast, 1870), p. 411.

140 See e.g. Hutchins and Harrison, *History of factory legislation*, p. 173.

141 *Report to the local government board on proposed changes in hours and ages of employment in textile factories by J.H. Bridges, MD and T Holmes* [C. 754], H.C. 1873, lv, 803.

arguments for and against a further reduction in working hours. The employers contended that there had been a 'vast improvement' in the design and construction of new mills and factories. They conceded that the speed of many machines had increased, as had the amount of machinery entrusted to each worker; but the work of tending them was said to require much less exertion on the part of the worker. Required to restrict themselves to a purely medical inquiry, the commissioners posed the issue as follows: 'Would six hours more of leisure per week promote the health of the work-people to an extent which would not be counterbalanced by a diminution ... of wages?' On the evidence they were disposed to answer in the affirmative. They took into consideration 'the unremitting and monotonous character of all labour at a machine driven by steam'. But it was not just a question of the length of the working day; the conditions of work were also relevant, and they had particular regard to the 'special evils' arising from excessive dust and the unwholesome amount of heat and steam found in cotton and flax mills, 'which together employ more than three-fifths of all protected persons in textile trades'. For these reasons, they recommended a reduction in the hours of young persons and women from 60 to 54 hours per week. The evidence – and the opinion expressed by many employers – also led them to recommend that the age at which children began to work should be progressively raised to 10, and that young persons should not start full-time work until the age of 14.[142]

The recommendation to shorten the working week by six hours aroused considerable controversy and failed to attract the support of the government. A more modest proposal in favour of a three-hour reduction was, however, introduced in 1874, at a time when the linen industry was still experiencing its temporary recession, and a determined effort was made by Irish MPs to carry an amendment excluding Ireland from the operation of the legislation. The view expressed by J.W.E. Macartney (Conservative MP for Co. Tyrone) was fairly typical: 'The one staple manufacture in [the North of Ireland] was the linen trade, which was at present in an extremely critical condition, and if a measure of this kind passed, it might deal a blow from which the trade of the North of Ireland would never recover.'[143] The *Belfast Newsletter* agreed: 'Our country is not in a position to bear this legislation. It will ruin our trade, and perhaps leave Belfast a forest of smokeless chimneys.'[144] But such pessimism was swept aside by Assheton Cross, the home secretary: 'Although ... the flax trade of Ireland might be temporarily depressed, it must be regarded as, on the whole, increasing and prosperous, and he believed that it was not likely

---

142 Ibid., pp. 3–4 and 60–62. Conditions in the linen industry are described at pp. 22–28.
143 *Hansard 3*, ccxix, 1471 (12 June 1874). T.A. Dickson (a linen manufacturer and MP for Dungannon) predicted that 'if the hours [of labour] were diminished, it would be impossible for the Irish manufacturers to compete with foreigners': *Hansard 3*, ccxx, 310 (23 June 1874).
144 1 July 1874, quoted, along with other critical observations, in Armstrong, 'Social and economic conditions', pp. 243–44. See also Bardon, *History of Ulster*, p. 333.

to suffer from being treated in the same manner as the trade of England and Scotland.'[145]

In any case, not all the Irish owners objected to the legislation. 'So far from disapproving of it, [Lawrence Brothers of Coleraine] consider that, with the alteration of eight hours in the winter and ten in the summer, it would be a great advantage to us all. The hours on cold winter mornings are too much for delicate women and children, who are the majority of hands employed in flax-spinning.'[146] But perhaps a more influential voice was that of the Belfast MP, William Johnston, who opposed the amendment 'in the interests of the working classes …'.[147] Johnston was 'the representative of the head and centre of the linen manufacture of Ireland, and if anybody was entitled to speak for the operatives of Belfast, it was [he]'.[148] Reference was also made to the poor working conditions in the linen industry, as reported by the factory inspectors[149] and by Dr Purdon,[150] the certifying surgeon in Belfast. In the event, an amendment ostensibly designed to give the Irish manufacturers an opportunity to make their case before a select committee was defeated,[151] even though it apparently had the support of no fewer than 72 Irish MPs.

The Factory Act 1874[152] accordingly reduced the working week for young persons and women in all textile mills and factories from 60 to 56$^{1}/_{2}$ hours per week by restoring the 10-hour day and reducing work on Saturday to six and a half hours.[153] No person was to work for more than four and a half hours without a meal-break. The minimum age for working was increased to nine from 1875, and to 10 from 1876, and from 1876, a person aged 13 was to be considered a child unless he or she was certified as 'having attained such standard of proficiency in reading, writing and arithmetic as may be from time to time prescribed [by the lord lieutenant]'. The act also made the alternate day system of education for children available in all textile mills and factories covered by the act.

145 *Hansard 3*, ccxx, 312–13 (23 June 1874).
146 Letter to Mr Mundella, MP for Sheffield – see *Hansard 3*, ccxviii, 1758–59 (6 May 1874).
147 *Hansard 3*, ccxx, 319 (23 June 1874). Johnston, a barrister, landlord and prominent Orange leader, was 'an independent conservative of evangelical sympathies' elected on a platform to protect the rights of Protestant working men: see J.W. Boyle, *The Irish labor movement in the 19th century* (Washington, DC, 1988), pp. 72–74 and E. O'Connor, *A labour history of Ireland 1824–1960* (Dublin, 1992), p. 39.
148 *Hansard 3*, ccxx, col. 320 (Dr Ball, A.G. for Ireland).
149 'We were told by a deputation of working men at Belfast, that their children frequently fainted from the heat of the spinning room; and this statement was confirmed by an independent and credible witness, and is, we believe, true': quotation by Mr Mundella (MP for Sheffield), *Hansard 3*, ccxviii, 1757 (6 May 1874).
150 'The flax-manufacturing operatives suffer far more from phthisis … [and] the death-rate among those employed in the preparing-rooms is exceedingly high': ibid. See further below, chap. 6.
151 *Hansard 3*, ccxx, 314–21 (23 June 1874).
152 37 & 38 Vict., c. 44.
153 'The act took half-an-hour a day off textile factories alone, leaving all others still subject to the settlement of 1850': Cooke-Taylor, *Factory system*, p. 109.

Notwithstanding the dire predictions, the act was, by 1875, working satisfactorily in the north of Ireland. In particular, many establishments moved to the alternate day system of education for child workers, a change which was 'decidedly beneficial', since 'the arrangements in the mills are thereby considerably simplified, and ... the educational improvement [of the children] has increased'.[154]

THE IMPACT OF EXTENSION IN IRELAND

The extended ambit of the factory acts in Ireland in the early 1870s is summarised in Table 2.2.

Table 2.2: Factories and workshops subject to the factory acts in 1870[155]

	No. of works	No. of children	No. of females over 13	No. of males aged 13–18	No. of males over 18	Total employed
Cotton	14	117	2,649	470	921	4,157
Wool/worsted	64	2	718	151	694	1,565
Linen[156]	271	1621	37,738	6,041	14,718	60,118
Millinery	583	67	3,764	101	227	4,159
Shirts and collars	57	24	3,639	138	355	4,156
Other textile and wearing apparel	760	218	5,537	1,239	5,415	12,409
Shipbuilding	10	6	–	392	3,288	3,686
Other metal manufactures	188	10	62	1,276	7,585	8,933
Food	85	9	121	393	4,694	5,217
Other	1,097	111	3,254	4,472	11,653	19,490
Total for Ireland	3,129	2,185	57,482	14,673	49,550	123,890
Scotland	*30,139*	*6,984*	*141,996*	*49,472*	*211,469*	*409,921*
England and Wales	*97,074*	*98,731*	*598,387*	*257,997*	*1,051,863*	*2,006,978*

154 *Insp. half-yearly rep., April 1875*, pp. 70–71 (Cameron). But the hours normally kept by the national schools (10 a.m. to 3 p.m.) meant that half-timers often failed to secure sufficient hours of education unless the mill had a private school attached to it.

155 Taken from *Report of the commissioners appointed to inquire into the working of the factory and workshop acts ...*, appendix B, pp. 5–6 [C. 1443], H.C. 1876, xxix, 135–36. Ó Gráda, *New economic history*, p. 310 explains that 'these statistics are incomplete ... the workshop details were only "partially received".... Still, the data are probably tolerably accurate for those industries coming under the provisions of the factory acts.'

156 Including hemp factories, bleaching and dyeing works and calendering and finishing works.

The steadily increasing ambit of the acts obviously required changes in the nature and organisation of the inspectorate. By 1861, the number of inspectors had been reduced by death or resignation to two (Baker and Redgrave), and the decision not to increase their number[157] marked a significant change in their perceived function: 'The original four inspectors were clearly intended personally to inspect all the factories then regulated.... [T]hey were really what their name denotes, inspectors of factories; now they are rather advisers of the Home Office in the administration of the factory law.... It is the sub-inspectors who perform the work originally confided to the inspectors.'[158] The number of sub-inspectors had gradually been increased, particularly to deal with the impact of the Factory Acts Extension Act 1867; in addition, two assistant inspectors were appointed 'who might, in subordination to [the inspectors], supervise the work of the sub-inspectors'.[159] In 1871, with the transfer to the inspectorate of responsibility for workshops, the number of assistant inspectors was increased to four and another new grade of junior sub-inspector was created.[160] By 1876, the total establishment of the inspectorate in the United Kingdom had risen to 55, namely 2 inspectors, 4 assistant inspectors, 38 sub-inspectors and 11 junior inspectors. But as Table 2.3 makes clear, the increase in the inspectorate had not kept pace with the increase in the number of establishments to be inspected, and workshops in particular failed to obtain the frequency of inspection which the inspectors felt they badly warranted to ensure obedience to the requirements of the law.[161]

Table 2.3: *Workload of factory inspectors in the United Kingdom*[162]

	Regulated establishments			Inspectorate					Approx. no. of
	Factories	Workshops	Total	Insp.	Ass't	Sub	Junior	All	establishments per inspector
1840–1844	4,200	–	4,200	4	–	14	–	18	230
1850–1855	5,000	–	5,000	4	–	15	–	19	260
1865–1867	8,000	–	8,000	2	–	25	–	27	300
1869–1871	30,000	–	30,000	2	2	39	–	43	700
1874	30,000	87,000	117,000	2	4	38	11	55	2,100

From 1858, Ireland (along with eighteen districts in Britain) remained under the overall responsibility of Inspector Baker, assisted (from 1868) by

---

157 See *Hansard 3*, clxiv, 1881 (6 Aug. 1861)(G.C. Lewis, home sec.).
158 *Report of the factory and workshop commissioners, 1876*, p. lxxxviii.
159 Ibid.
160 They were to be be attached to the sub-inspectors in the larger sub-divisions: ibid.
161 *Factory and workshop commissioners: Minutes of evidence*, p. 52 [C. 1443–I], H.C. 1876, xxx, 52 (Baker).
162 Derived from a memorandum by Redgrave showing the growth of the factory department: *Report of the factory and workshop commissioners, 1876*, appendix D, p. 187.

Joseph Ewings, an assistant inspector based in Preston.[163] Until 1869, the country remained divided into two districts, each with its own sub-inspector. The North Irish district comprised the area north of a line from Galway to Drogheda, and was supervised by a sub-inspector resident in Belfast. But in 1869, when the island was divided into three districts, the North contracted to counties Antrim, Londonderry, Tyrone, Donegal and the greater part of Down. In 1874, this area had 121 textile factories, 413 other factories and some 1,500 workshops.[164]

Until 1869, the South Ireland district was based in Dublin. When F.W. Haydon was sent there as sub-inspector in 1866, he took the view that there was no need for a separate appointment: 'There is next to nothing for him to do. There are not 100 factories in the whole district, including every description of hovels, and there are certainly no more than one-fourth of these which in point of size, importance and the numbers of persons they employ could by any ingenuity be held to rank with what we call factories in England ...'.[165] Baker disagreed, and told Haydon to get on with the job – but, perhaps not unsurprisingly, Haydon was soon replaced. In 1869, the impact of the extension act and the distances to be travelled by the sub-inspectors[166] led to an administrative reorganisation. A new Central District was created, consisting of fourteen counties and part of Co. Down; by 1874 it contained 80 textile factories, 400 other factories and about 860 workshops.[167] This left the South (or Limerick) District to consist of twelve counties containing 63 textile mills, 285 other factories and about 1,000 workshops.[168] All these changes meant that Ireland in the early 1870s had a full-time establishment of three sub-inspectors – Cameron (North), Woodgate (Central) and Monsell (South); no full-time junior inspectors were appointed for Ireland before 1878, but assistance was made available from time to time after 1871 to facilitate the inspection of workshops.[169] This meant that each inspector in Ireland was responsible for

---

163 *Insp. half-yearly rep.*, *Oct. 1868*, p. 87. Ewings was responsible for five districts.
164 *Report of the factory and workshop commissioners, 1876*, appendix C, p. 18 (Cameron).
165 Haydon to earl of Belmore (under-sec., home office), 15 Dec. 1866, PRO HO 45/7859. Nor was anything likely to change due to lack of capital and the opposition of farmers and priests – farmers because wages in factories tend to be higher, and priests because of 'the sense of independence and the freedom from control which they have heard factory workers acquire after a short acquaintance with regular employment and good wages'!
166 *Insp. half-yearly rep., April 1869*, p. 72 (Baker). The local sub-inspector (Bignold) claimed that he had 'more area than he can possibly travel over effectually', and Baker agreed that the appointment of a third sub-inspector in Ireland was 'absolutely necessary for the efficient administration of the law': Baker to G. Hardy (home sec.), 10 Nov. 1868, PRO HO45/8131.
167 *Report of the factory and workshop commissioners, 1876*, appendix C, p. 36 (Astley).
168 Ibid., p. 114 (Monsell). The central and south sub-divisions appear to have been temporarily re-amalgamated for a short period – see *Insp. half-yearly rep., Oct. 1872*, p. 29.
169 Sub-inspector Bateman 'had the supervision of the workshops' in Cameron's district for two years: *Factory and workshop commissioners, 1876: Minutes of evidence*, p. 864 (Cameron).

approximately 450 factories and 1,100 workshops, as compared to the national average of 550 factories and nearly 1,600 workshops.

Even if many of the newly-included factories employed a higher percentage of adult men, and the smaller workshops required 'but little inspection',[170] the incidence and level of inspection must have been adversely affected by the increasing workload of the inspectors.[171] In England and Wales, at any rate, the likelihood of prosecution was considerably reduced.[172] In Ireland, the incidence of prosecutions also fell after 1864 and only returned to earlier levels after 1875.[173] Most of these cases continued to arise from the over-working of women or young persons in one way or another;[174] but there was a noticeable *increase* in the number of informations concerning the unlawful employment of children[175] and failure to comply with the administrative requirements concerning the employment of young persons. During the first half of the 1870s, also, the inspectorate were also somewhat more active in charging a parent with 'not causing his [or her] child to attend school'.[176] But the transfer of responsibility for workshops from the local authorities to the factory inspectors did not bring about an immediate change in the pattern of enforcement. In 1872, for example, it was reported that pressure of work meant that 'at present the Workshop Acts are only very partially enforced in the north of Ireland'. Only one-third of the workshops had been inspected, and it seemed likely that the remaining workshop occupiers were 'in entire ignorance of their duty in this matter'. But it was hoped that three successful prosecutions in Belfast would mean that the 1867 act would now be 'tolerably well obeyed in those places in which it is most required'.[177] By 1875, with the assistance of another sub-inspector, two-thirds of the workshops

---

170 *Insp. half-yearly rep., Oct. 1874*, p. 10 (Redgrave).
171 See especially J.Pellew, *The Home Office 1848–1914: From clerks to bureaucrats* (London, 1982), pp. 123–32 and 147–49.
172 P.W.J. Bartrip and P.T. Fenn, 'The evolution of regulatory style in the nineteenth century British factory inspectorate' in *J. Law & Society*, 10 (1983), 201 at p. 206 estimate that the chance of a factory being prosecuted fell from 1:4 in 1836 to 1:40 in 1870.
173 See further below, chap. 10.
174 Informations charging an employer with the employment of women or young persons on weekdays after 6 p.m. or before 6 a.m., on Saturday afternoon or evening, or during meal-times represent two-thirds of the informations laid between 1865 and 1878.
175 See e.g *Insp. half-yearly rep., Oct. 1870*, p. 80 (Baker).
176 Ten such cases were brought between 1872 and 1874. The usual fine was five shillings (with costs of 1s. 6d.); but on some occasions it was considered that 'a reprimand from the Bench, together with the payment of costs, would meet the requirements of the case' – see e.g. *Insp. half-yearly rep., Oct. 1874*, p. 131.
177 *Insp. half-yearly rep., Oct. 1872*, pp. 125–27 (Cramp). He was particularly concerned that 'it is obviously unfair to those Belfast manufacturers who are complying with the law, that their competitors in trade, occupying smaller workshops here or similar workshops in the other towns of Ulster, should be under no compulsion to attend to its provisions.'

in the north had been visited, 'many of them several times over',[178] and a similar performance appears to have been achieved in the south.[179]

In theory, therefore, a factory act of some kind applied to a large section of those working in Irish industry in the early 1870s. But the law, now to be found in no less than fifteen separate statutes, was far from satisfactory. Textile and non-textile factories were governed by provisions which differed not only between each broad class, but also within each class – and a significantly different code applied to workshops. To the complexity of the law was added the complication of an increasing workload – and a creaking administration. The time was ripe for reform and reorganisation; the government agreed, and in 1875 a royal commission was appointed to review the whole of the factory law.

178 *Factory and workshop commissioners, 1876: Minutes of evidence,* p. 864 (Cameron).
179 By 1876, Monsell was able to claim that he had visited most of the workshops in the south – only to find that the act was not observed in the smaller workshops: ibid., p. 879.

CHAPTER THREE

Consolidation and refinement: 1875–1914

In 1875, Assheton Cross, the home secretary, persuaded that factory legislation had become 'an almost unintelligible code, scarcely understood [even] by the officers appointed to carry it out',[2] secured the appointment of a royal commission –

to inquire into the working of the factory and workshops acts with a view to their consolidation and amendment, and specially to consider whether they can be made more consistent and harmonious, and whether any of their provisions may properly be extended to other trades, industries and occupations ... and whether ... any further provisions are requisite for the improvement of the health and education of young persons and children, and whether any further provision is needed for the due enforcing of such acts ...

The commissioners took evidence from a wide range of witnesses throughout the United Kingdom, and published a comprehensive report within a year of their appointment. To learn about the operation of the acts in Ireland, the commissioners interviewed a number of witnesses in Belfast and Dublin over three days in September 1875, and, in response to a general questionnaire, received written 'answers' from all the 'Irish' inspectors, who also gave oral evidence.[3] The general picture which emerged was that the legislation was generally complied with in the larger, mainly textile, factories, but the position in the smaller, mainly non-textile, factories – and still more particularly in workshops – was much less satisfactory. According to Astley, sub-inspector

---

1 *Report of the commissioners appointed to inquire into the working of the factory and workshop acts with a view to their consolidation and amendment: vol. I, Report, appendix and index* [C. 1443], H.C. 1876, xxix, 1 [hereafter referred to as '*Report*']; *vol. II, Minutes of evidence* [C. 1443–I], H.C. 1876, xxx, 1 [hereafter referred to as '*Minutes of evidence*']. The commission was chaired by Lord Frederick Cavendish, and included The O'Conor Don, home-rule MP for Co. Roscommon.

2 *Report: Separate report by The O'Conor Don*, p. cv. Appendix H to the commissioners' report provides a 'Tabular analysis of varieties in the existing factory acts and other cognate legislation'.

3 For the oral evidence of the Irish witnesses, see *Minutes of evidence*, pp. 823–908 and 969–75. The oral evidence of the sub-inspectors may be found at pp. 864 (Cameron), 878 (Monsell), 887 (Woodgate) and 917 (Astley); their written 'answers' are mainly to be found in Appendix C to the *Report*, at pp. 18, 114, 125 and 36 respectively.

for the Central Ireland district, for example, 'additional means of enforcing the factories and workshops acts in Ireland is of the utmost necessity, and without such additional means, no permanent benefit can result to the community of workers at large, especially to that numerous class which are employed in small factories and workshops. The present failure of the law in its application to small factories and workshops is a serious matter ...'.[4] Nowhere was this more evident than in the many flax scutch mills in the northern half of the country,[5] and in dressmaking and millinery establishments in Dublin and elsewhere.[6] The primary concern of leading textile manufacturers, on the other hand, was to secure an amelioration of the law, in particular to allow greater flexibility in the hours of employment for open-air bleaching[7] and to permit water-powered mills to make up time lost as the result of an inadequate – or excessive – supply of water.[8]

The commissioners' report, containing 113 recommendations (which with one exception[9] did not make specific provision for Ireland) was published in February 1876. The commissioners took the view that the acts had been generally successful:

Some occupations are still undoubtedly unhealthy ... and in others over-work occasionally occurs.... But we are glad to state that we have reason to believe that these evils are exceptional. The improvements in the sanitary arrangements and ventilation of factories has been most marked in recent years, and the cases in which young children are employed in labour unfitted for their years, or in which young persons and women suffer physically from over-work, are now, we believe, as uncommon as formerly they were common. Much of this great improvement is undoubtedly due to factory legislation....

4 *Report: Appendix C, Answers of assistant inspectors and sub-inspectors*, p. 37. Cf. Cameron told The O'Conor Don that, with the exception of bookbinding, he did not consider that there were 'any great abuses' in the employment of persons in non-textile factories in the north of Ireland: *Minutes of evidence*, p. 868.

5 See e.g. evidence of George Walker and Robert Dempster, scutch mill owners: *Minutes of evidence*, pp. 846 and 849 and of Dr Hamilton, certifying surgeon at Cookstown, ibid., p. 857.

6 See e.g. evidence of John Keegan, secretary of Dublin United Trades Asssociation, and of Dr Mapother, sanitary officer in Dublin: ibid., pp. 902 and 890.

7 See especially evidence of R. Thompson and J. Richardson on behalf of the Bleachers' Association: ibid., p. 826. Cf. Dr Musgrave, certifying surgeon at Lisburn, emphasised the unhealthy nature of bleachworks: ibid., p. 834.

8 A deputation representing the largest owners of water-powered mills urged the commissioners to repeal section 10 of the 1874 act, which (from 1 Jan. 1876) would prohibit children, young persons and women working outside normal hours to make up lost time: *Minutes of evidence*, p. 970. But any relaxation of the law was strongly opposed by the Association of Flax Spinners and Power-loom Linen Manufacturers, who 'would be placed at a disadvantage if the users of water power were permitted to make up lost time in cases of floods or shortage of water, when the users of steam power are not permitted to make up lost time arising from any cause whatever': ibid., p. 828.

9 See *Report*, p. xcvi (recommendation, not implemented, that RIC provide assistance to check infractions of the law; see further below, p. 85). The O'Conor Don dissented from this proposal, as he did from a number of other recommendations; but his disagreement with the majority was not otherwise specific to Ireland.

We have no reason to believe that the legislation which has been productive of such marked benefit to the operatives employed, has caused any serious loss to the industries to which it has been applied. On the contrary, the progress of manufacture has apparently been entirely unimpeded by the Factory Acts; and there are but few, even among employers, who would now wish to repeal the main provisions of such Acts....[10]

The existing legislation should, indeed, be consolidated and simplified in a single act – but within limits:

[A] single set of regulations ... could not be [made] ... without offending against that legislative principle which has hitherto been followed with such excellent results in the framing of our factory and workshops acts. Only to meet proved abuses and to rectify particular evils has interference been thought justifiable. The utmost liberty of action has been left, consistent with the suppression of customs of work which could be shown to be detrimental to the health or morals of persons protected by the law. The conclusions of political economy against interference with liberty of contract, as between employers and employed, have been allowed full sway whenever they were not overruled by other considerations, founded upon established rules of hygiene or the more obvious interests of society. It has never been sought to prescribe one invariable rule ... merely for the sake of elegance in the statute book....[11]

Assimilation might be desirable to make legislation simpler and more generally understood; but the law had also to be sufficiently equitable to be capable of enforcement 'without injustice'.

The commissioners accepted that the factory acts still had no role to play in regulating the employment of adult males as such; places of employment were subject to regulation only if children, young persons or women were employed therein.[12] On the other hand, they rejected the contention of the 'women's rights movement' that legislative restrictions on the hours worked by adult women should be repealed on the ground that they inhibited employment opportunities and undermined financial independence.[13] This line of thinking had surfaced in the debates on the 1874 act,[14] and was put to the commissioners by a deputation led by Mrs Emma Paterson.[15] But the

10 *Report*, p. xi.
11 Ibid, p. xxv–xxvi. The immediate context is the regulation of the hours of employment in factories and workshops, but the principle is of general application.
12 *Report*, p. xvi. However, some provisions *did* include or permit regulation in respect of adult men. Section 28 of the Factory and Workshop Act 1895, for example, authorised the making of special rules for workshops in which men only were employed, leading B.L. Hutchins and A. Harrison, *A history of factory legislation* (3rd ed., London, 1926), p. 203 to comment: 'In these apparently unimportant provisions which at first sight read only like a trifling extension of regulations already enacted, the principle is ... implicitly granted that, cause being shown, the protection of the law can be extended to men as well as to women and children.'
13 See e.g. ibid., chap. ix.
14 It was, for example, contended that the decision as to the time spent at work, or working at all, should be left to the good sense of the workers themselves: *Hansard 3*, ccxix, 1421 (11 June 1874) (Fawcett).
15 *Minutes of evidence*, pp. 132–35. Mrs Paterson, a member of the TUC, was the

practical problem, as Isabella Tod conceded on behalf of women workers in Ireland, was that they were not yet strong enough to stand on their own:

Women have been hitherto so discouraged in doing anything directly for themselves in such matters, that they have not yet learned to combine and resent or show anything like strong displeaure with regard to the breaches of the act, or with regard to neglect of many things which should come under the act ... and therefore, perhaps, they need more protection now than would in itself be very advisable.... I look upon this as a transition period in the matter, ... and anything restrictive should be acknowledged to be in itself an injurious thing, and a thing which would be well to do with the minimum of, as far as may be.[16]

The commissioners were prepared to accept that, with respect to women, the factory acts 'constitute a chapter of legislation not necessarily permanent'; but they were not yet superfluous:

[W]hile recognising the value of the [women's rights] movement as showing a desire on the part of women to protect themselves, instead of depending for protection upon acts of parliament, and while agreeing that every new restriction ... deserves now to be more jealously watched than ever, lest the legislature should be undertaking to do that which can be accomplished by private effort, we do not think that the time is come, either for altogether rescinding this section of the factory laws, or for any serious modification of their restrictive provisions.[17]

The women's rights movement received some support from The O'Conor Don,[18] and later from Parnell,[19] among others; but it succeeded only in securing certain 'relaxations' for workshops in which women only were employed. Although the issue continued to be raised from time to time, for example over proposals in the early 1890s to limit the hours worked by women

secretary of the Women's Protective and Provident League, which assisted working women to form trades unions.

16 Ibid., p. 905. Miss Tod was 'the outstanding advocate of women's rights' from the 1860s to the 1890s: M. Luddy, 'Isabella M.S. Tod, 1836–1896' in M. Cullen and M. Luddy (ed.), *Women, power and consciousness in 19th century Ireland* (Dublin, 1995), p. 197. Cf. a spokeswoman for the factory workers said that 'the result of further restriction upon the labour of adult women would be simply disastrous ... the poorhouse, or worse' and that 'women and girls all say that overwork is better by a great deal than insufficient food': *Report: Select correspondence*, appendix D, p. 164.

17 *Report*, p. lxxvi.

18 *Report: Separate report by The O'Conor Don*, p. cxxix. See also Hutchins and Harrison, *History of factory legislation*, p. 188: 'Over and over again in committee came the amendment by Mr Fawcett, Mr Muntz, The O'Conor Don and others, to omit the word "woman" in the various clauses of the bill'.

19 To afford them 'an opportunity of attending to their household duties', married women should come within the act; but legislation 'would ... interfere unwarrantably with the right of unmarried women over the age of 21 as members of the community, who were able to judge for themselves as to whether they would work during certain hours or not. He could not see ... any good reason why they should not be allowed to make their own bargain with their employers': *Hansard 3*, ccxxxviii, 94 (21 Feb. 1878).

in commercial laundries,[20] the view that adult women should continue to be 'protected' generally prevailed during the period under consideration.

The commissioners assumed that children should continue to be employable in virtually all trades and industries, with the exception of those 'specially prejudicial to the health of workers of tender years', such as the silvering of mirrors, the annealing of glass and the dipping of lucifer matches.[21] They also recommended that the minimum age should in all cases be 10,[22] and that the provisions governing the education of children (particularly those employed in workshops) should be extended and improved. The age for starting full-time work should remain at 13.[23]

The distinction between 'factories' and 'workshops' based on the numbers employed was 'almost universally condemned' by those who gave evidence to the commissioners.[24] Factory owners, for example, objected to the 'unfair competition on the part of the smaller masters engaged in the same trade, who take advantage of the much less restrictive character of the law'; the inspectors considered the workshops regulation act to be grossly deficient, and in any event it was not in the public interest that 'such matters as the education of a child, the protection of life and limb from dangerous machinery or ... the limitation of the hours of labour ... should be deliberately made less efficient in the smaller places of work, where they are likely to be more needed'. The commissioners agreed. All premises in which mechanical power was used in a manufacturing process should be considered a 'factory' for regulatory purposes and 'workshop' should be confined to premises in which manual labour only was used.[25] But even in respect of such workshops, the 1867 act should be repealed and replaced by provisions which more closely mirrored those relating to factories and were more amenable to effective enforcement. In particular, the concept of the 'normal working day' as developed in relation to factories should now apply to workshops (albeit with certain exceptions) on the ground that 'experience has proved that the only way to enforce a law against over-work is to provide not merely a maximum

20 'The result was the miserably inadequate protection afforded by [section] 22 of the Act of 1895, which fixed the weekly limit of hours at thirty for children, sixty for young persons and women; but allowed children to work ten hours a day, young persons twelve, and women fourteen': Hutchins and Harrison, *History of factory legislation*, p. 195.
21 *Report*, p. lxxxv.
22 Ibid., pp. lviii–lix. All the inspectors, the medical and educational authorities, 'the great majority of the employers who have given evidence before us' and 'the representative witnesses of the operative class, almost without exception' were in favour.
23 The commissioners decided against an extension of the provision in the 1874 act whereby the minimum age for full-time work was raised to 14 except for those 13-year-olds who had special educational qualifications. Not more than one-third of children would satisfy these qualifications, and 'there is good reason for the apprehension, which has been expressed to us on all hands, that the operation of this provision will be a serious injury to trade': ibid., p. lxvi.
24 *Report*, pp. xiv–xv.
25 Ibid., p. xvi.

period of labour in the day, but maximum limits within which such period may be taken'.[26]

There were, however, grounds for maintaining *some* limited distinctions between textile and non-textile factories. The permitted hours of labour provided one such case:

[I]n textile factories the males above 18 years of age are under 25 per cent of the whole number employed, and 75 per cent are children, young persons and women. In [non-textile factories] ... these proportions are reversed.... The small proportion of [protected] persons employed in these trades ... both diminishes the necessity of stringent regulations against long hours of work, and also would render any such regulations hazardous to the interest of those on whose behalf they are recommended. Experience has shown that men are able to take care of themselves, and they have largely exercised that power in diminishing their hours of work. In those industries in which men form the majority of hands employed we have accordingly found few or no instances of overwork; and, therefore, as it is in general impossible to employ one part of the hands longer than the rest, further legislative restriction of hours does not seem to us to be required.[27]

In any event textile factories involved 'the unremitting and monotonous character of ... labour at a machine driven by steam' to an extent which distinguished them as a class from non-textile factories. Accordingly, 'the [existing] line of distinction between the first and second classes of factories ... should ... remain ...'.[28]

The commissioners had relatively little to say about the effects on health and safety of the working conditions in factories and workshops,[29] and we may therefore bring this brief summary of their report to an end by referring to four miscellaneous recommendations which would have been of particular interest in Ireland:

(1) The factory acts *should* apply to shipbuilding and all ropeworks, but *not* to agricultural labour, public houses or retail shops;[30]
(2) Domestic employment – more strictly, 'employment by the occupier carrying on business in a room used also for the purposes of a dwelling-house, and employing none but inmates' – should be generally exempt from regulation;[31]

---

26 *Report*, p. xvi.
27 *Report*, p. xxix. Even if this was not always so, the commissioners were concerned that 'the result of further legislative restriction would inevitably be to discourage the employment of women and young persons [in non-textile factories]'.
28 Ibid., pp. xxix–xxx.
29 *Report*, pp. lxxii–lxxv and lxxvi–lxxviii (healthy working conditions) and lxxv–lxxvi (fencing of machinery). See further below, pp. 68–70 and more generally chaps. 5 and 6.
30 *Report*, pp. xix–xxiv.
31 Although the need for regulation had been 'clearly demonstrated' by the children's employment commission in the 1860s, 'we think it desirable to interfere as little as possible with the habits and arrangements of families': *Report*, pp. xvii and xl. Cf. The O'Conor Don contended that dressmaking, tailoring, boot and shoe making, glove

(3) Limited 'relaxations' relating to the regulation of the hours and conditions of employment should be permitted to all trades subject to interruption in the process by stress of weather, including flax scutch mills, water-powered textile mills and open-air bleaching;[32]

(4) Limited 'relaxations' relating to the regulation of the hours and conditions of employment should also be permitted to all trades liable to emergency from sudden press of orders, including milliners and shirt collar makers.[33]

The largely incremental nature of the commissioners' recommendations and their generally cautious approach meant that their report gave rise to relatively little controversy, particularly in Ireland. The commissioners generally took the standards already laid down for textile factories as their starting point, and their principal concern was to decide the extent to which such standards should be extended to other factories and workshops. Those most likely to be affected by their recommendations were workshop owners who were now to be subject to the stricter regime hitherto applied to non-textile factories; but such owners do not appear to have been sufficiently organised – or to have had a sufficient degree of political support – to challenge the commissioners' general strategy.

From a legal perspective, the commissioners succeeded in bringing about a consolidation of the law; but it can hardly be said that they achieved a great deal in terms of simplification. Their concentration upon the need to rectify 'particular evils' and their readiness to accept numerous 'exceptions' or 'relaxations' with respect to particular industries or working practices implied a statutory code which would inevitably continue many of the complexities of the existing law. Nevertheless, the commissioners' report was in general accepted by the government, with the result that in 1878 there was enacted legislation – the Factory and Workshop Act – which represented by far the most extensive factory act to date. The pace of development, however, was by now such that that act remained unamended for less than five years, and within two decades further legislation had once again created 'a somewhat intricate mosaic'[34] which called out for further consolidation. This was duly effected, without the benefit of a further general inquiry, by the Factory and Workshop Act 1901, and it is this act – 'one of the longest acts ever passed'[35] – which continued to provide the legislative framework for the regulation of

---

making, etc. at home was 'to a great extent so carried on ... under conditions of labour far more injurious to the working people than if carried on in workshops': *Separate report*, p. cxi. But his solution appeared to be 'deregulation' of the ordinary workshops rather than bringing domestic workshops under greater control.

32　*Report*, pp. xliv–xlvii, acceding in particular to the concerns expressed by owners of water-powered mills in Ireland – see above, p. 61.

33　*Report*, pp. xlii–xliii.

34　*Redgrave's factory acts*, ed. J.A. Redgrave and H.S. Scrivener (7th ed., London, 1898), p. xlv.

35　Editorial, 'The factory act 1901' in *ILT & SJ*, 36 (1902), 393.

factories and workshops in Ireland as well as the rest of the United Kingdom for the remainder of the period under consideration.

THE FACTORY AND WORKSHOP ACTS, 1878–1914

As a result of the review by the commissioners, the framework of the legislation which regulated working conditions in factories and workshops in the period before the first world war continued to rest on two broad hierarchies – the classification of protected workers as 'children', 'young persons' or 'women', and the classification of industrial premises as 'textile factories', 'non-textile factories' or 'workshops'. In broad terms, all premises 'wherein ... steam, water or other mechanical power is used to move or work any machinery employed ... in manufacturing' were now 'factories', irrespective of the numbers employed;[36] 'workshops', on the other hand, were 'any premises ... not being a factory ... in which ... any *manual* labour is exercised by way of trade or for purposes of gain' in the making, repairing, finishing or adapting for sale of any article.[37] But some premises which might appear to be textile factories were 'deemed' to be non-textile factories,[38] as were some apparent workshops.[39] The general tendency over the period was to assimilate the provisions applicable to each class; but it was the textile factories which remained subject to the greatest degree of regulation, with the result that the distinction between factories and workshops tended to become less significant than the distinction between textile factories on the one hand and non-textile factories and workshops on the other.

In broad terms, once again, young persons aged 14 (or in some cases 13) to 18 were treated in much the same way as women over the age of 18. Children under the age of 14, however, were subject to greater restrictions – they could, after all, only be employed half-time – and by 1914, when only 12–14-year-olds were included, this class of worker was well on the way to extinction, a development (almost) finally achieved in 1920.[40]

This combination of different classes of workplace and of workers, together with a large number of special provisions, exceptions and modifications for particular categories or sub-categories of each, and the regular amendment of the law after 1878, make it impossible to trace the development of factory

36 1901 act, s. 149, re–enacting 1878 act, s. 93.
37 'Workshops' were in turn subdivided into ordinary workshops employing children and/or young persons, and women, 'women's workshops' (employing only women), 'men's workshops' (not employing children, young persons or women) and 'domestic workshops' (located in a private dwelling-house).
38 E.g. textile print works, bleaching and dyeing works and flax scutch mills: 1878 act, s. 93; 1901 act, s. 149(1).
39 Foundries, paper mills and tobacco factories, for example, were 'non-textile factories' whether or not they used mechanical power: 1878 act, s. 93(1) and sch. 4, pt. 1; 1901 act, s. 149(1)(a) and sch. 6, pt. 1.
40 Employment of Women, Young Persons and Children Act 1920, s. 1(1).

legislation during this period in any detail. The broad story being, however, one of incremental extension rather than radical transformation, we propose to focus our attention on the principal provisions of the Factory and Workshop Act 1901, and to outline in general terms the ways in which they developed. In so doing, we shall endeavour to pay particular attention to those provisions of greatest relevance to Irish industrial circumstances and conditions.

1. The protection of health

Sections 1–9 of the 1901 act regulated the general sanitary conditions of factories and workshops and made particular provision in respect of overcrowding, temperature, ventilation, drainage of floors and sanitary conveniences. Those relating to temperature, humidity and ventilation provide a good illustration of the growing sophistication of factory law in the years after 1878.

In what was largely a continuation of the existing law, the 'sanitary provisions' of the 1878 act required factory and workshop owners to keep their premises 'in a cleanly state' and ventilated 'in such a manner as to render harmless, so far as is practicable, all ... impurities generated in the course of the manufacturing process ... that may be injurious to health'; an inspector was empowered in appropriate cases to direct that 'a fan or other mechanical means of a proper construction' be provided 'within a reasonable time'.[41] Such provisions recognised that working conditions in certain trades could be especially unhealthy, but the general form in which they were expressed left much room for interpretation and differing standards. The need for more specific regulation was recognised with regard to white lead factories in 1883,[42] and six years later, when further steps were taken to control humidity in cotton cloth weaving factories, it was provided that 'the amount of moisture in the atmosphere ... shall not at any time be in excess of such amount as is represented by the number of grains of moisture per cubic foot of air shown ... in Schedule A ... as represents the temperature existing in such ... factory at such time'.[43] From 1891, the owner of any factory in which 'provision for the admission of fresh air is not sufficient, or ... the quantity of dust generated or inhaled ... is dangerous or injurious to health' could be required to adopt 'such special rules ... as appear ... to be reasonably practi-

---

41 1878 act, ss. 3 and 36. See also s. 33 (provision, subject to special exceptions, requiring walls and ceilings to be limewashed).

42 The Factory and Workshop Act 1883, s. 3 and sch. set out a list of conditions to be observed in such factories, in which children and young persons had already been forbidden to work by 1878 act, s. 38 and sch. 1.

43 Cotton Cloth Factories Act 1889, s. 5(1). The act also made detailed provision for the type, location and maintenance of two sets of thermometers which would show the humidity and temperature in the factory, which was to be duly recorded twice daily; the temperature, humidity, ventilation and quantity of fresh air in the factory was to be examined 'once at least in every three months' by an inspector: ss. 7 and 10. The Cotton Cloth Factories Act 1897 gave the home secretary additional powers to make regulations 'for the protection of health'.

cable and to meet the necessities of the case'.[44] This power was exercised in respect of factories engaged in various 'dangerous trades', including the linen industry, with hackling rooms, wet-spinning mills and weaving sheds being brought under special rules issued by the home secretary in 1894.[45]

All these provisions designed to secure sufficient ventilation in various categories of factory and workshop were brought together and given more general application by the 1901 act, which not only provided that 'sufficient means of ventilation shall be provided, and sufficient ventilation shall be maintained' in every factory or workshop, but empowered the home secretary to prescribe 'a standard of sufficient ventilation' for any class of factory or workshop.[46] In 1902, this power was exercised to require every textile factory in which atmospheric humidity was artificially produced to install and maintain a means of ventilation which 'shall be such as to supply during working hours not less than 600 cubic feet of fresh air per hour for each person employed'.[47] The 1901 act also extended the home secretary's power to prescribe 'dangerous trades' by providing that he could now make special regulations, which automatically applied to *every* factory or workshop in the specified class, in respect of any manufacturing process or machinery which was 'dangerous or injurious to health' or 'dangerous to life or limb', either generally or in the case of women, children or any other class of persons.[48] By 1914 many industrial processes had been certified in this way and brought under special regulations, including processes involved in letterpress printing, chemical works, the making of felt hats, wool-sorting and, of particular importance in the north of Ireland, the 'dangerous' processes of spinning and weaving flax, tow, hemp and jute.[49] In the opinion of a senior inspector of the time, 'the early years of the twentieth century saw what was unquestionably the most remarkable development that had ever yet been attempted ... in applying scientific knowledge and care to the protection of workers from industrial disease and injury'.[50]

2. *The preservation of life and limb*

Sections 10–22 of the 1901 act deal with various aspects of safety in factories and workshops. The provisions requiring the fencing of dangerous machinery and restricting the cleaning of machinery in motion (sections 10 and 13) dated back to 1844.[51] Various gaps in these provisions, including the reverse

---

44 Factory and Workshop Act 1891, s. 8. It should be noted that these rules had to be made for each separate factory or workshop.
45 Special rules for the spinning and weaving of flax 1894 – see further below, chap. 6.
46 1901 act, s. 7(1) and (2).
47 Textile Factories (Humidity) Order 1902 – see further below, chap. 6.
48 1901 act, ss. 79–86.
49 See e.g. *Redgrave's Factory Acts*, ed. J. Owner (14th ed., London, 1931), pp. 437–622. For the special regulations relating to the linen industry, see further below, chap. 6.
50 A.M. Anderson, *Women in the factory: An administrative adventure, 1893–1921* (London, 1922), p. 97. Miss Anderson was principal lady inspector from 1897 until 1921.
51 1844 act, ss. 20 and 21.

suffered in 1856, were closed by the 1878 act.[52] Every part of the mill-gearing was now required to be securely fenced 'or be in such position or of such construction as to be equally safe to every person employed in the factory as it would be if it were securely fenced'. In addition, all hoists and teagles 'near to which any *person* is liable to pass or to be employed',[53] every fly-wheel and every part of a steam engine or water wheel was to be securely fenced; the use of the word 'person', rather than (as before) 'any child, young person or woman' meant that adult men were now protected for the first time. However, the 1878 act merely continued the provision for arbitration in respect of other machinery which the inspector considered to be 'so dangerous as to be likely to cause bodily injury' and it was not until 1891 that this unwieldy procedure was repealed and replaced by the simple and straightforward requirement that 'all dangerous parts of the machinery' must be securely fenced.[54] All safety fencing was to be 'constantly maintained in an efficient state' while the parts required to be fenced were in motion or use 'for the purpose of any manufacturing process'.[55]

The 1901 act also re-enacted and extended the provision first made in 1891 for means of escape in case of fire,[56] made new provision for safer use of steam boilers and self-acting machines,[57] and re-enacted with extensions the obligation of employers, also dating back to 1844, to give the local factory inspector and/or certifying surgeon written notice of all accidents causing death or bodily injury.[58] In 1895, a magistrates' court was given power to prohibit, permanently or temporarily, the use of any machine used in a factory or workshop which was 'in such a condition that it cannot be used without danger to life or limb', and this power was continued and extended by the 1901 act to include power to prohibit the use of unsafe industrial premises.[59]

The home secretary's power, first conferred in 1891 and then extended in 1901, to make special provision in respect of 'dangerous' trades, included those which were 'dangerous to life or limb'.[60] As we have seen, a number of

---

52 1878 act, ss. 5 and 9. The Factory Act 1856 had put an end to the 'fencing controversy' by limiting the owner's duty to fence mill-gearing to those parts with which women, young persons and children were 'liable to come into contact' – see e.g. P.W.J. Bartrip and S.B. Burman, *The wounded soldiers of industry: Industrial compensation policy, 1833–1897* (Oxford, 1983), pp. 63–66 and below, p. 126.

53 This qualification was repealed by 1891 act, s. 6(1).

54 1878 act, s. 6; 1891 act, s. 6, re–enacted in 1901 act, s. 10(1)(c). The question whether machinery was 'dangerous' was now to be decided by the court, and it was this provision which led to the famous case of *Hindle* v. *Birtwhistle* [1897] 1 QB 192.

55 1895 act, s. 7(3) (and 1901 act, s. 10(1)(d)) broadened this provision somewhat by substituting the words 'except where the parts are under repair ... or are necessarily exposed for the purpose of cleaning or lubricating, or for altering ... the machine'.

56 1891 act, s. 7, as amended by 1895 act, s. 10; 1901 act, ss. 14–16.

57 1901 act, ss. 11 and 12.

58 1901 act, ss. 19–22, building on 1844 act, ss. 22–23; 1878 act, ss. 31–32 and 1895 act, ss. 18–21. These provisions did not take their final form until the enactment of the Notice of Accidents Act 1906.

59 1895 act, s. 4: 1901 act, ss. 17–18.

60 1891 act, s. 8; 1901 act, s. 79.

special rules were made under the 1891 act. But those which most directly concern us here were made under the 1901 act. In 1905, for example, the home secretary certified that self-acting mules used in the process of textile spinning were 'dangerous to life and limb', and issued regulations imposing special safety standards on employers *and* workers.[61] Similarly, special shipbuilding regulations issued in 1914 provided (*inter alia*) that 'all stages shall be securely constructed of sound and substantial material, and shall be of sufficient width, as is reasonable in all the circumstances of the case, to secure the safety of the persons working thereon', and that 'the main gangway giving access to the upper parts of the ship shall be securely protected by upper and lower hand-rails on each side ...'.[62]

3. The hours of employment:
(i) Young persons and women

By far the longest part of the 1901 act – sections 23–67 – is that dealing with the hours of employment of young persons and women, and related matters.

Until 1901, young persons and women employed in textile factories were required to work $56^1/_2$ hours per week. From Monday to Friday, they worked 10 hours per day (excluding two hours for meals) within the normal working day (6 a.m. to 6 p.m., or 7 a.m. to 7 p.m.); on Saturday, they worked for six and a half hours, normally from 6 a.m. to 1.30 p.m. (if not less than one hour allowed for meals) or from 6 a.m. to 1.00 p.m. (if less than one hour allowed for meals).[63] In 1901, however, the Saturday 'half-day' was reduced to five and a half hours, making a working week of $55^1/_2$ hours.[64] No woman or young person could be employed continuously in a textile factory for more than four-and-a-half hours without an interval of at least half an hour for a meal.

On the recommendation of the factory and workshop commissioners, women and young persons working in non-textile factories and workshops also worked within the normal working day, which could, however, also be from 8 a.m. to 8 p.m. They could be required to work 60 hours per week – ten-and-a-half hours per day from Monday to Friday (excluding one-and-a-half hours for meals) and seven-and-a-half hours on Saturday (until as late as 4 p.m.). In these establishments, no woman or young person could be employed for more than five hours without a meal break.[65]

---

61 Regulations for the process of spinning by self-acting mules (1905 No. 1103), amplifying 1901 act, s. 12. The employer was to ensure that mules 'shall be securely fenced as far as is reasonably practicable', while minders were (*inter alia*) put under a duty to take all reasonable care to ensure that no woman, young person or child worked between the fixed and traversing parts of the mule while it was in motion.

62 Regulations for the construction and repair of ships in shipbuilding yards (1914 No. 461) – see below, p. 233.

63 1878 act, s. 11, re-enacting 1874 act, ss. 4 and 5.

64 1901 act, s. 24.

65 *Report*, p. xxxv; 1878 act, ss. 13 and 15, as amended by 1895 act, s. 36; 1901 act, s. 26. Greater flexibility was allowed in respect of women-only workshops – see 1878 act, s. 15, 1891 act, s. 13(2) and 1901 act, s. 29.

In 1878, and again in 1901, however, these general provisions were either directly by statute or through powers conferred on the home secretary made subject to a bewildering number of qualifications and exceptions relating to meal-times, overtime, nightwork, holidays, etc. – and to special provisions relating to particular industries.[66] Three examples, which would have had a particular significance in Ireland, will suffice. First, the home secretary could authorise any non-textile factory or workshop to work a full day on a Saturday, when this was required by 'the customs and exigencies of the trade'.[67] This flexibility was important for many businesses in provincial towns where Saturday was market day, and was granted in particular to establishments, such as florists, in which 'any manufacturing process or handicraft is carried on in connection with a retail shop on the same premises' and to those, such as milliners and dress-makers, in which 'is carried on the making of any article of wearing apparel'.[68]

Young persons and women could also be employed outside normal hours 'so far as is necessary for the purpose only of preventing any damage which may arise … from any extraordinary atmospheric influence in the process of open-air bleaching'.[69] Although it was thought at the time that 'the work cannot be of very long duration, and in the ordinary course of events is only exceptional',[70] this was an unusual exception in that it apparently permitted the employment of young persons and women for an unlimited time. In this respect, it may be contrasted with a third exception in favour of water-mill owners. In 1878 parliament, on the recommendation of the factory and workshop commissioners prompted in part by special pleading from Ireland,[71] allowed additional time to be worked to make up for stoppages caused by drought or flood – but only in very careful terms:

Where it appears to a secretary of state that factories driven by water power are liable to be stopped by drought or flood, he may, by order … grant to such factories a special exception permitting the employment of young persons and women during a period of employment from six o'clock in the morning until seven o'clock in the afternoon, on such conditions as he may think proper, but so as that no person shall be deprived of the meal hours by this act provided, nor be so employed on Saturday; and that as regards factories liable to be stopped by drought, such special exception shall not extend to more than ninety-six days in any period of twelve months, and as

---

66 See in particular the special exceptions as to hours of work, holidays, overtime and nightwork in 1878 act, ss. 42–60, substantially reenacted in 1901 act, ss. 36–56.
67 1878 act, s 46; 1901 act, s 43. This was effected by substituting another day for the Saturday half-holiday – a power first conferred by the 1867 act.
68 See Order of December 1882, set out in *Redgrave's Factory Acts* (7th ed., 1898), p. 63. See further the case of *Snape* v. *Alexander*, discussed below, p. 327.
69 1878 act, s. 55; 1901 act, s. 53. This provision was first introduced in 1870, when bleaching and dyeing were brought more directly under the factory acts – see 1870 act, s. 4 and sch. 1, para. 6, and above, p. 44.
70 *Redgrave's Factory Acts* (7th ed., 1898), p. 78.
71 *Report*, pp. xliv–xlvii, and see above, p. 61.

regards factories liable to be stopped by floods, such special exception shall not extend to more that forty-eight days in any period of twelve months....[72]

Such changes as occurred in the working hours of women and young children between 1878 and 1914 were restricted to matters of detail, such as those summarised above. The more ambitious campaign for an eight hour-day, which began in the 1880s,[73] made no progress in legislative terms.

(ii) Children

As recommended by the factory and workshop commissioners in 1876, the 1878 act laid down a general rule that 'a child under the age of ten years shall not be employed in a factory or workshop'.[74] Following a resolution adopted at the Berlin International Labour Conference in 1890, the minimum age for the employment of children was in 1891 raised to 11,[75] and then in 1901 to 12.[76] Contrary to the recommendation of the commissioners,[77] the normal upper age limit was set at the age of 14; but a child aged 13 who had attained a prescribed educational standard was allowed to work full-time.[78] There were, however, certain factories and workshops, such as those making white lead, carrying on dry metal grinding or the dipping of lucifer matches, in which no child could be employed at all.[79] A child (or young person under 16) could not be employed for more than a week in any factory unless he or she had been certified as fit for employment in that factory by the certifying surgeon for the district; but in the case of workshops, an owner was merely authorised, not required, to obtain such a certificate.[80]

---

72 1878 act, s. 57, re-enacted in 1901 act, s. 52. The exception, granted by Order issued in Dec. 1882, applied to mills and factories in which only water power was used, and was made subject to additional requirements, including the giving of notice to the inspector of the time lost and its cause, and of the 'recovery' of that time – see *Redgrave's Factory Acts*, p. 80.

73 See e.g. *Reports of the First Irish Trades Congress* (Dublin, 1894), p. 105 and *Thirteenth Irish Trades Union Congress* (Athlone, 1906), pp. 45–46; A. Hinsley, 'The hours of labour' in *Ir. Eccles. Rec.*, xiii (1892), 911.

74 *Report*, pp. lviii–lx; 1878 act, s. 20.

75 1891 act, s. 18. 'I cannot report that the raising of the age will cause very much inconvenience to the masters. I find the inconvenience, if any exists, is more on the part of the parents or their children, who are anxious for employment as soon as they are old enough to present themselves to the certifying surgeon to be passed': *Chief insp. ann. rep. 1892*, p. 113 (Woodgate).

76 1901 act, s. 62.

77 *Report*, pp. lxv–lxvii, on the grounds that the higher age diminished the supply of labour, causing 'a serious injury to trade', without any corresponding educational advantage to the children concerned.

78 1878 act, ss. 26 and 96; 1901 act, s. 156. The education test had been introduced for textile factories only by the 1874 act, s. 12, and was dismissed by the commissioners as a 'dislocation'. But parliament disagreed and extended the provision to all factories and workshops.

79 1878 act, s. 38 and sch. 1: 1901 act, s. 77.

80 1878 act, ss. 27–30; 1901 act, ss. 63–67. But by s. 66 of the 1901 act, the home

Children continued to be employed on a 'half-time' basis, which allowed them to work in morning or afternoon sets, or for the whole day on alternate days only, and this system was for the first time extended to children employed in workshops. A different provision had applied to workshops prior to 1878, but it was 'universally condemned' by those giving evidence to the factory and workshop commissioners. The commissioners considered that employment in morning or afternoon sets was, on balance, educationally preferable to the alternate day system, which should, therefore, only be used with the permission of the home secretary.[81] But the chief inspector of schools in Ireland and a schoolmistress from Belfast both thought that children learnt more by the alternate day system, and The O'Conor Don accordingly proposed that the choice of system should be left with employer and workers.[82] As a result of the 1874 act, the pattern of half-time work was already entirely a matter of choice in textile factories, and this continued to be the position after 1878.[83] But in non-textile factories and workshops, it was provided that the alternate day system could only be used where the owner voluntarily worked a 10-hour day,[84] which was seldom the case. In either case, the other 'half' of the child's time was, as before, largely taken up with attendance at a 'recognised efficient school', for which more elaborate provision was made in an attempt to ensure that he or she received a sufficient education.[85]

4. Women's workshops and domestic workshops

As the result of 'an amiable, if oddly directed, respect for the freedom of the "small master" and the "'home industry'"',[86] workshops employing only women[87] and workshops in private dwellings[88] were excepted from a number of the provisions applicable to 'ordinary' workshops.[89] In particular, they

secretary was given power in special circumstances to require certificates of fitness for employment in certain workshops. The surgeon had to certify that he was satisfied, by production of a birth certificate or other sufficient evidence, of the age of the child, and that the child 'is not incapacitated by disease or bodily infirmity for working daily for the time allowed by law in the factory named in the certificate'.

81 *Report*, pp. lx–lxv.
82 *Minutes of evidence*, pp. 873 and 859; *Separate report*, p. cxxvii.
83 1874 act, s. 6; 1878 act, s. 12; 1901 act, s. 25.
84 1878 act, s. 14; 1901 act, s. 27.
85 1878 act, ss. 23–26; 1901 act, ss. 68–72.
86 Hutchins and Harrison, *History of factory legislation*, p. 201.
87 More strictly, any workshop 'conducted on the system of not employing therein either children or young persons' and duly notified as such to the inspector: 1878 act, s. 93; 1901 act, s. 29.
88 More strictly, 'where ... a private house ... though used as a dwelling, is by reason of the work carried on there a ... workshop within the meaning of this Act ... in which the only persons employed are members of the same family dwelling there': 1878 act, s. 16; 1901 act, s. 115.
89 1878 act, s. 16 and 61; 1901 act, ss. 29 and 111(4). But, as pointed out in *Redgrave's Factory Acts* (7th ed., 1898), pp. 86–87, with regard to cleanliness, overcrowding and

were not subject to the normal working day, but could work for up to $10^{1/2}$ hours at any time(s) between 6 a.m. and 9 p.m., 'in spite of the many years' experience which showed the impossibility of effectively enforcing [limited hours] within this wide margin'.[90] In 1888–89, however, the evidence given to an inquiry into the sweating system[91] clearly showed the need for stricter regulation of women's workshops at least, and in 1891 it was provided that the period of employment was no longer to be at the employer's pleasure, but must be 'a specified period' of twelve hours between 6 a.m. and 10 p.m. during the week, and of eight hours between 6 a.m. and 4 p.m on Saturday.[92] The hours of work in domestic workshops, however, remained under a 'wide margin' for the remainder of the period under consideration.[93]

Perhaps more importantly for our purposes, the home secretary was in 1891 given power to require every occupier of a factory or workshop to maintain lists of outworkers[94] and the places where they were employed, and these lists were made available to the factory inspector (and the local sanitary authority).[95] During the next twenty years, this power was exercised with respect to many different classes of work; indeed, by 1901, the regulation of 'home work' was considered sufficiently important to warrant its own part (vi) of the factories act. The occupier of a factory was now, for example, prohibited from giving out work to be done in any domestic workshop where conditions were 'injurious or dangerous to the health of the persons employed therein', and district councils were empowered to prohibit work being given to any workshop where any 'inmate' was suffering from a prescribed infectious disease.[96] All these provisions applied (*inter alia*) to the many domestic workshops in Ireland engaged in 'the making ... altering, finishing and repairing of wearing apparel' or 'the making-up ... of table linen, bed linen or other household linen'.[97]

5. *The fair payment of wages*

From the outset, the factory acts did not attempt to regulate the level of wages payable to industrial workers. But two developments which occurred

ventilation, regulations 'of equal force' were applicable under the public health legislation.
90 Hutchins and Harrison, *History of factory legislation*, p. 183.
91 See *Fifth report from the select committee of the house of lords on the sweating system in the United Kingdom*, H.L. 1890 (169), xvii, 1, which focused in particular on small workshops in the east end of London. For a summary, see Hutchins and Harrison, *History of factory legislation*, pp. 211–16.
92 1891 act, s. 13, re-enacted in 1901 act, s. 29.
93 See especially 1901 act, s. 111.
94 More strictly, 'all persons directly employed by [the occupier of a factory or workshop or any contractor employed by him in the business], either as workman or as contractor, in the business of the factory or workshop, outside the factory or workshop ... ': 1891 act, s. 27; 1901 act, s. 107.
95 Ibid.
96 1901 act, ss. 108–10.
97 See *Redgrave's Factory Acts* (14th ed., 1931), pp. 142–45 and 147.

during this period indirectly derogated from this general principle. In 1831, the Truck Act had attempted (once again) to prohibit the payment of wages in certain trades 'in goods or otherwise than in the current coin of the realm'. Enforcement of this act, which unusually did *not* apply to Ireland, was a matter for the individual worker, and so it remained for the next fifty years. The question whether responsibility for enforcement should be taken over by the factory inspectorate was briefly considered by the factory and workshop commissioners in 1876, but they 'cannot recommend that the factory inspectors should be authorised to interfere in a matter of wages'.[98] Nevertheless, Truck Amendment Acts of 1887 and 1896 not only extended the ambit of the provisions of the 1831 act *and* applied them to Ireland, but transferred to the factory inspectorate throughout the United Kingdom the 'duty' of enforcing them.[99]

Secondly, the 'particulars' clause introduced in 1891 required the occupier of a factory or workshop to furnish in writing particulars of the rates payable to each piece-rate worker, so that he or she could ascertain the amount of wages to which he or she was entitled.[100] This provision at first applied only to certain classes of workers in textile factories; but in 1895 it was extended to *all* textile workers and could, by order, be made applicable to any class of non-textile factories and workshops.[101] These provisions were consolidated by section 116 of the 1901 act, which confirmed that outworkers were also covered, and were then applied to a wide variety of trades and occupations carried on in Ireland, including the preparing or finishing of any process in the manufacture of wool or linen, the making-up of wearing apparel and the manufacture of tobacco.[102]

6. Concluding observations

This summary of the legislation enacted from 1878 onwards has been designed to show that, by 1914, the factory acts had, in terms of coverage and refinement, developed to a degree undreamed of in 1833. Years of constant testing and probing by owners and workers, the factory inspectorate, official inquiries, legislators and others had resulted in a code which applied increasingly specific and detailed regulation to a wide range of industrial activity.[103] In later chapters we attempt to examine in greater depth how this legislation applied to selected trades and industries in Ireland. But first we must deal with the general organisation of those primarily responsible for ensuring that the requirements of this code were complied with in the factories and workshops which came within their jurisdiction.

---

98 *Report*, p. xxv. In any event, 'in most cases, it is adult males in respect to whom protection is desired'.
99 See further below, chap. 7.
100 1891 act, s. 24.
101 1895 act, s. 40.
102 For further details see *Redgrave's Factory Acts* (14th ed., 1931), pp. 155–84, and below, chap. 7.
103 'We might describe the evolution of Factory Act regulations as starting from a

THE FACTORY INSPECTORATE, 1878–1914

In spite of the radical expansion in the ambit of the factory acts which had taken place in the previous decade, the factory and workshop commissioners saw no need for any fundamental changes in the nature or organisation of the factory inspectorate. Constitutionally, they were to remain a United Kingdom service under the home office, with headquarters in London and inspectors resident in their respective districts. But it was now 'in the highest degree expedient' that the inspectorate should have a single 'principal' responsible to the home secretary for the administration of the law, and acting under his direction.[104] The 1878 act so provided, and in December 1878 Sir Alexander Redgrave was formally appointed 'Her Majesty's Chief Inspector of Factories and Workshops'.[105] It was now his sole responsibility to supervise the administration of the factory acts, to allocate inspectors to districts and supervise their performance, to identify working conditions which called for special investigation and to advise the home secretary in all matters of factory law, and in particular on the need for further reforms. Redgrave presided over 'a period of conservatism' until 1891; after two short-term appointments, Dr (later Sir) Arthur Whitelegge provided the inspectorate with 'capable leadership and continuity' from 1896 until 1917.[106]

But if there was need for a single chief executive, there was also need for greater decentralisation. As we have seen, the post of assistant inspector had been created in 1868 to lighten the duties of the inspectors and to provide more adequate supervision of the sub-inspectors;[107] but they had not been allowed to fulfil their intended role. The commissioners recommended that they should be given 'real power and authority' with a view to achieving not only a greater degree of consistency in the application of the law, but also a higher degree of efficiency through more active supervision of the work of the inspectors:

The duties of the assistant inspectors should include ... first, his standing to the subordinate inspectors in the place of their official head, and the substitution of his discretion for that of the inspector in all cases where, by laying down a general rule, and entrusting it to the administration of an experienced official, sufficient security

---

vaguely benevolent and general type of enactment ... and becoming constantly more particular, more detailed, and more scientifically directed as time goes on': Hutchins and Harrison, *History of factory legislation*, p. 201.

104 For some time prior to 1876, responsibility for the inspectorate had been equally divided between the two remaining inspectors, Redgrave and Baker. They were 'two co-ordinate heads' residing in different cities and with 'all concert between them ... limited to the bare necessities of their official duty'; this arrangement had not worked satisfactorily in practice and 'never could have commended itself by way of an intentional experiment in administration': *Report*, pp. xxix and lxxxvii–lxxxix.

105 1878 act, s. 67; *London Gazette*, 24 Dec. 1878.

106 J. Pellew, *The Home Office 1848–1914: From clerks to bureaucrats* (London, 1982), pp. 151 and 157–58.

107 *Report*, p. lxxxix.

may be obtained against irregularities. Thus we consider that, subject to a few general directions, he might be given power, in all ordinary cases, to sanction prosecutions. The right to direct the work of the sub-inspectors, and the disposal of their official time, should also, subject to the general control of the [central] office, be reposed in their hands.[108]

This recommendation was duly put into effect by the appointment of five 'superintending inspectors of factories and workshops', each of whom was made responsible for a 'division' consisting of a number of the 39 districts into which the United Kingdom was divided.

The district, administered by an officer now raised to the rank of 'Her Majesty's inspector of factories and workshops',[109] remained the basic 'unit of inspection'. Following a competitive examination,[110] inspectors were appointed by the home secretary and assigned to a district by the chief inspector. Their powers and duties were set out as follows:

(1) To enter, inspect and examine at all reasonable times [any] factory or workshop ...;
(2) To take ... a constable into a factory in which he has reasonable cause to apprehend any serious obstruction in the execution of his duty;
(3) To require the production of the registers, certificates, notices and documents kept in pursuance of [the acts] and to inspect, examine and copy the same;
(4) To make such examination and inquiry as may be necessary to ascertain whether the enactments ... relating to public health and ... of this act are complied with ...;
(5) To enter any school in which he has reasonable cause to believe that children employed in a factory or workshop are ... being educated;
(6) To examine ... with respect to matters under this act, every person whom he finds in a factory or workshop ... and to require such person to be so examined and to sign a declaration of the truth of the matters respecting which he is so examined;
(7) To exercise such other powers as may be necessary for carrying this act into effect.[111]

In 1867 it had been stated that an inspector should be a man with 'general intelligence, faculty of observation, discretion, tact and firmness, united to a sufficient amount of bodily vigour and activity'.[112] The average age of the 40

---

108   Ibid.
109   'The title of inspector ... correctly expresses the character of their duties' and the 'honorary prefix' was designed to distinguish factory inspectors (like school inspectors) from local officials with lesser duties and lower qualifications: *Report*, p. xci. Inspectors were paid £300-£500 per annum depending on seniority.
110   The nature of this examination varied considerably over the years. At one time a knowledge of factory law was necessary for appointment; but that was dropped – 'one of the great improvements that have been made', and the inspector was expected to learn on the job. He was then examined in factory law at the end of his two-year probation period: *Royal commission on the civil service: second report: Minutes of evidence*, p. 122 [Cd. 6535], H.C. 1912–13, xv, 384 (Sir Edward Troup, permanent under-sec., home office).
111   1878 act, s. 68, re-enacted by 1901 act, s. 119.
112   'Treasury-Home Office report, 9 Dec. 1867', PRO T1 6833/19090, p. 2, cited Pellew, *Home Office*, p. 128.

or so inspectors appointed in the course of the next decade was 31; they came from a wide variety of backgrounds, but 'only three had any apparent connection with manufacturing'.[113] The inspection of a factory or workshop involved (*inter alia*) checking that all abstracts (of the acts, special rules, etc.) and statutory notices were prominently displayed; all registers (of children and young persons, accidents, etc.) were properly kept; dangerous machinery was securely fenced and safety provisions regularly observed, and the factory or workshop kept in a sanitary state, properly limewashed and ventilated. The inspector had to ensure that the permitted hours of employment were observed in all their various particulars, inquire into any accidents which had occurred, review the school attendance records of child workers and check that the proper medical certificates had been obtained. The discovery of any significant breach of the law could result in the inspector bringing proceedings in the local magistrates' court.

In the busiest districts, inspectors might be given the assistance of a junior inspector. Appointments to this post – essentially a traineeship[114] – had begun in 1872, when responsibility for workshops was transferred from local authorities to the factory inspectorate. It was the workshops which, according to the factory and workshop commissioners in 1876, posed the greatest operational problems for the inspectorate, who 'have as yet not been able even to visit all their workshops'; indeed, 'so great is the number in some districts, and so widely are they scattered in some, that it is difficult to fix a date at which the first visit will have been paid at all'. To make matters worse:

Nor must it be supposed that a single visit by the inspector is in all cases enough to secure the future observance of the law. The occupiers of workshops, who are disposed to infringe it, derive safety from their number and obscurity, and while they are at least as slow as were the old factory occupiers to accept the interference of government in their concerns, they are much slower to see the reason and benefits of regulation. Thus it happens that, with this class of employers, evasions of the law are more frequent, and detection more difficult.[115]

The commissioners hoped that their proposals for amending the regulatory provisions governing workshops, such as the introduction of the normal working day, would substitute 'conditions of efficient inspection' for the 'inefficient nature' of the Workshop Regulation Act. But they also accepted the need for additional personnel and, drawing on the experience of the few local authorities which had made a real effort to enforce the 1867 act, they proposed the creation, at least temporarily, of a new inferior grade of

---

113 Pellew, *Home Office*, p. 128, citing *Return of the names, ages and previous occupations or professions of the inspectors ... appointed since 1 Jan. 1867*, H.C. 1880 (371), xl, 335. Much the same position was confirmed by *Return showing the names, dates of appointment, and present salaries of Her Majesty's inspectors of factories, etc.*, H.C. 1887 (305), lxvi, 459.
114 *Report*, p. lxxxviii.
115 Ibid., p. xciii.

assistant, 'of the standing, for instance, of inspectors of nuisances', to visit workshops under the immediate direction of the local factory inspector.[116] But Redgrave disapproved, 'in terms we think far too sweeping',[117] and this recommendation was not immediately implemented.

There matters rested until the early 1890s – and Redgrave's retirement. By then, factory inspection was beginning to enter a new phase:

The work of inspection, and generally of the administration of the acts, becomes steadily more complex and difficult.... The comparatively simple question of hours of employment, age and education of children, and the like, still, of course, require careful watching – calling for a large amount of routine inspection, both during and after working hours.... But the more difficult work [of inspecting machinery, investigating accidents and exposing truck, etc.] now forms much the larger proportion of the duties of an inspector.[118]

The response to the increasing complexity of the factory acts was reflected in a number of changes which occurred from 1890 onwards. A number of specialist officers were appointed to provide 'scientific' supervision and assistance throughout the United Kingdom.[119] Perhaps a more noticeable change was the substantial increase in the very number of inspectors – from 50 or so during the 1880s, to 152 by 1902 and 205 by 1912. This enlarged inspectorate also became more specialised, as they increasingly came from an engineering or scientific background, with the result that by 1911 'a large proportion of the inspectors have had a previous training as engineers; some have been chemists or analysts; some have been managers of business firms; some have been sanitary inspectors; [only] a few have had a purely academic training'.[120] From 1893, a small number of lady inspectors were appointed to pay particular attention to the specific needs of women and children.[121] At much the same time, the home secretary (Asquith), encouraged by the Trades Union Congress,[122] revived the idea of a new grade of low-paid

116 Ibid., pp. xciv–xcvi.
117 Ibid. Redgrave continued his opposition when the idea was raised some ten years later – see *Chief insp. ann. rep., 1879*, pp. 96–97.
118 'Report of the factory staff committee 1907', p. 3, PRO LAB 14/182.
119 Of particular importance was the appointment of Dr T.M. Legge as Medical Inspector of Factories in 1898. He conducted scientific and medical research on such industrial hazards as chemical poisoning and silicosis, and was in charge of the appointment and supervision of certifying surgeons.
120 *Report of the departmental committee on accidents in places under the factory and workshop acts*, p. 49 [Cd. 5535], H.C. 1911, xxiii, 50. See also *Return of the names and previous occupations or professions of the inspectors, the inspectors' assistants and the lady inspectors, who are now serving, etc.*, pp. 1–3, H.C. 1907 (172), lxxvi 321–23 and Pellew, *Home Office*, pp. 158–60.
121 See further below, chap. 4.
122 During the 1880s, Congress had called for the appointment as inspectors of working men with practical experience in industry, and ten were appointed as junior inspectors: 'That was the time when we got the very worst specimens of factory inspectors we have ever had': *Royal commission on the civil service: second report:*

assistants – 'a set of energetic, quick-sighted, practical men, knowing the actual conditions of factory and workshop life ... but not necessarily equal to the educational tests which are at present imposed',[123] whose principal function, as 'inspectors' assistants', was the inspection of workshops.[124] Finally, the overall administration of this new, enlarged, inspectorate was strengthened by the appointment in 1899 of a deputy chief inspector, and a second such post was created in 1908.

A 'snapshot' of the inspectorate in 1912 reveals the changes which had occurred since 1890.[125] The chief inspector was assisted by two deputy chief inspectors, a principal lady inspector and six inspectors attached to the central office in London. The six divisions of the United Kingdom,[126] each with its own superintending inspector, were sub-divided into 52 districts manned by 111 inspectors and 53 inspectors' assistants. A senior lady inspector was also assigned to each division, and there were a further 11 lady inspectors to assist them. These inspectors were also supported by nine peripatetic 'technical' officers – two medical inspectors (the first appointed in 1898, the second in 1908), an electrical inspector (first appointed in 1902), an inspector for dangerous trades (first appointed in 1899) and an examiner and four assistant examiners of textile particulars (dating from 1892). This team of just over 200 inspectors was responsible for more than 110,000 factories and 150,000 workshops employing more than five million workers, and they cost the taxpayer £99,000 (compared to £29,000 in 1892).[127] Their work during 1912 is summarised in an annual report by the chief inspector which ran to 235 pages and 30 appendices.

In spite of these developments, a regular and comprehensive system of full inspection was seldom, if ever, achieved. Nor was it necessarily desirable:

[I have] no intention ... of introducing the notion that the state undertakes by means of its inspectors to supervise the manufacturers of this country. Any such attempt would be futile ... for it would relieve employers of the responsibility which now attaches to them and which they alone are capable of fulfilling. The most important function of inspectors is by their active influence to bring about a co-operation of employers and employed in the observation of the law. The utmost that inspection can accomplish ... is to render it dangerous for an employer to break the law.[128]

Minutes of evidence, p. 122 (Sir Edward Troup). See also Pellew, *Home Office*, pp. 151–52.

123 'Memorandum of Dec. 1892', quoted Pellew, *Home Office*, p. 156.

124 Fifteen persons, 'all of them working men', were appointed: *Chief insp. ann. rep., 1893*, p. 18. By 1907, their number had increased to forty. The post is considered to have been largely unsuccessful, partly on account of 'deficiencies' in education and partly due to an apparent lack of tact and diplomacy – see e.g. H.A. Mess, *Factory legislation and its administration 1891–1924* (London, 1926), p. 149.

125 See *Chief insp. ann. rep., 1912*, pp. 236–39.

126 Northern, Northeastern, Northwestern, Midland, Southeastern and Southwestern. The sixth division resulted from a general reorganisation carried out in 1908.

127 *Chief insp. ann. rep., 1902*, pt. II, p. 55 and *1912*, p. 265.

128 'Memorandum by Sir Henry Matthews,' 8 Aug. 1892, quoted Pellew, *Home Office*, p. 154. See also 'Report by Sir Malcolm Delevigne and Sir Arthur Whitelegge, dated

A return made in 1886 suggests that on average an inspector visited each factory in his district once a year, and each workshop every 17 months.[129] The standard of one inspection per year was in 1898 considered 'fair' for ordinary cases, but inadequate for establishments known to be badly managed or dangerous.[130] Accordingly, it became the aim of the inspectors to visit each place under the act at least once a year, and works under special rules or regulations four times.[131] It was thought that an inspector working in a 'concentrated' district should be able, on an average day, to visit 10 or 12 factories or 20 workshops; but not all the visits could take the form of a full inspection: 'As the department is constituted, inspection can only be by sample, and an inspector must use his discretion and experience of the district in selecting the details for attention'.[132] This might indeed mean that some irregularities escaped notice – in 1906, for example, it was reported that nearly one quarter of the factories, and more than one quarter of the workshops, had not been visited at all.[133] On the other hand, less frequent, but more thorough, inspections lessened the need for an annual inspection.[134] Given the resources available, the verdict in 1907 was that 'we find nothing to suggest that the system as such is ineffective to secure the general observance of the acts'.[135] But in spite of regular additions to the establishment over the next six years, the home office continued to be concerned about the frequency of inspections and in 1913 warned that without another substantial increase the reduction in standards could expose the government to severe criticism:

16 January 1913, and subsequent correspondence with the Treasury', p. 12, PRO LAB 14/182 (hereafter '*Delevigne/Whitelegge report, 1913*'): 'constant' supervision tends 'to transfer the responsibility for the safety and health conditions from the occupier to the inspector'.

129 *Return showing the names, etc. of HM inspectors of factories 1887*, p. 5.
130 'Report of the factory staff committee 1898', p. 5, PRO LAB 15/5. The committee considered that that there should be no less than 1.8 visits per factory and 1.6 visits per workshop each year.
131 *Chief insp. ann. rep., 1902*, pt. I, p. iv. See also *Departmental committee on the truck acts, vol. II: Minutes of evidence (days 1–37)*, pp. 18–19 and 31 [Cd. 4443], H.C. 1908, lix, pp. 168–69 and 181 (Whitelegge).
132 'Report of the factory staff committee 1907', p. 7. Smaller factories in rural areas required less inspection – 'when once the machinery is properly found there remains little for the inspector to do'.
133 Ibid., p. 4. By 1911 the percentage of factories *not* visited during the year had decreased from 23% to 21%, and of workshops from 27% to 22% – see *Delevigne/ Whitelegge report 1913*, p. 1.
134 *Delevigne/Whitelegge report 1913*, p. 9: 'If a thorough inspection of all important works could be carried out once, say, in every five, seven, or even ten years, an appreciable advance on the present standard would be made.'
135 'Report of the factory staff committee 1907', p. 7. For a description of a fairly typical year, see B.C.D. Hopkinson, 'Factory inspection in 1908', in *H.M. inspectors of factories, 1833–1983: Essays to commemorate 150 years of health and safety inspection* (London, 1983), p. 14.

Of course, factory inspection can be worked perfectly well on a lower standard ... if Parliament is content to have it so. The frequent inspection of dangerous works and badly managed establishments is more important than the routine visiting of every place that comes within the acts; but unless the routine visiting is kept up to a certain standard, there is always the danger that certain bad cases will escape attention for a long time. If the standard [of visits] is lowered from a year to eighteen months, that risk is increased.[136]

The Treasury's response to this warning was 'unhelpful' – and so the arguments over adequate means of enforcement continued.

THE FACTORY INSPECTORATE IN IRELAND, 1878–1914

During the forty years or so prior to the outbreak of the first world war, there was 'some *increase* in aggregate [industrial] output in Ireland ... with the progress of textiles (notably linen), shipbuilding, brewing and distilling more than matching the decline in other sectors'.[137] Nevertheless, the overall picture is one of relative industrial *decline* in comparison with Great Britain: 'While Irish output held its own over these decades, United Kingdom industrial output quadrupled'.[138] The continuing decrease in the general population of Ireland meant, however, that the percentage of that population covered by the factory acts significantly *increased*. The distribution of the industrial workforce was, however, wholly uneven. In 1907, for example, five counties (Down, Armagh, Tyrone, Londonderry and Antrim) contained almost one-half of the factories and workshops, and employed more than two-thirds of the workers. At the other end of the scale, there were eighteen counties, mainly in the south and west, where less than one per cent of the population worked in factories or workshops. Taken as a whole, the number of workers in Ireland covered by the factory acts in 1907 (the latest date for which figures are available) represented just under five per cent of the total workforce required to be supervised by the factory inspectorate – a percentage which, on account of the increases which had also taken place in Great Britain, remained much the same as that in 1870.

136 *Delevigne/Whitelegge report 1913*, p. 10. See also Pellew, *Home Office*, pp. 163–64.
137 Ó Gráda, *New economic history*, p. 309.
138 Ibid.

Table 3.1: Scope of the factory acts, 1870 and 1907[139]

	1870		1907	
	No. of plants	No of workers	No. of plants	No. of workers
Ireland	3,129	123, 890	11,987	240,003
Scotland	30,139	409, 921	26,464	660,056
England/ Wales	97,074	2,006,978	200,277	4,227, 050
United Kingdom	130, 342	2,540,789	238,728	5,127,109

The composition of this workforce in terms of 'protected' workers is summarised in Table 3.2.

Table 3.2: Composition of industrial workforce in Ireland, 1907[140]

	Children	Young persons	Adult women	Adult men	Total
Textile factories	4,075	15,262	38,886	17,469	75,692
Non-textile factories	62	18,779	36,813	82,471	138,125
Workshops	58	6,074	12,836	7,218	26,186
TOTAL	4,195	40,115	88,535	107,158	240,003
1870	*2,185*	*nk*	*57,482*	*49,550*	*123,890*

---

139 The figures for 1870 are derived from *Statistical abstract for the United Kingdom, 1860–1874*, p. 119 [C. 1268], H.C. 1875, lxxix, 119 and *Return of the number of manufacturing establishments in which the hours of work are regulated by Act of Parliament ...*, pp. 206–07, H.C. 1871 (440), lxii, 314–15; those for 1907 are from *Statistical abstract for the United Kingdom, 1895–1909*, p. 361 [Cd. 5296], H.C. 1910, civ, 369 and *Summary of returns of persons employed in 1907 in textile factories* [Cd. 4692], H.C. 1909, lxxix, 851; ... *in non-textile factories* [Cd. 5398] H.C. 1910, lxxxiii, 789, and ... *in workshops* [Cd. 5883], H.C. 1911, lxxix, 1.

140 Ibid. Pease note that the figure for adult women in 1870 is a combined figure for 'females above 13 years of age'.

The employment of children in textile factories *increased* after 1870, and in 1907 children still represented more than five per cent of textile factory workers – a higher proportion than in England and Wales (just over three per cent) and Scotland (less than one per cent).[141] There was also a significant increase in the *aggregate* number of adult women workers who, by 1907, represented just over one-half of textile workers and more than one-third of the total workforce – once again, a higher ratio than elsewhere in the United Kingdom. We may note finally that whereas 'protected' workers predominated in the textile factories and in workshops, they were in the minority in non-textile factories – much the same pattern as in England and Wales and Scotland.

In Ireland, as elsewhere, it was the workshops, not the factories, which presented the inspectors with their greatest difficulties. The solution which they put to the factory and workshop commissioners was that they should be given the assistance of the Royal Irish Constabulary,[142] a suggestion adopted by the commissioners: 'We do not propose that such officers ... should undertake the work of visitation or inspection ... but that they should be directed to take notice of such apparent infringements of the law as the presence in or departure of women and children from workshops at late hours, and the resort to workshops of children of tender age, to prove which is often difficult ...'.[143] But this recommendation faltered in the face of strong opposition from Sir John Wood, inspector-general of the Royal Irish Constabulary,[144] and The O'Conor Don, who could 'imagine hardly anything more calculated to make the whole system of factory legislation hateful in the eyes of the Irish people than placing the every-day actions of the working classes in carrying on their trades under minute police supervision ...'.[145]

The failure of the 1878 act to make any additional provision for inspection in Ireland meant that the matter remained a cause for concern. In 1894, for example, the first Irish Trades Congress was of opinion that 'the present number of factory inspectors is totally inadequate for a proper carrying-out of the duties of the position ... it being physically impossible for them to visit and thoroughly inspect even once a year the several factories and workshops placed under their charge'.[146] This view was repeated at regular intervals during the next twenty years.[147] But it was not just a question of numbers.

141 *Summary of returns of persons ... employed in textile factories*, p. 5.
142 *Minutes of evidence*, pp. 879–80 (Monsell), 888 (Woodgate) and 921 (Astley).
143 *Report*, p. xcvi.
144 *Minutes of evidence*, pp. 882–83, on the grounds that such duties would draw the police away from their 'legitimate duties' of upholding the law and preserving public peace, and that the unpopularity of the work would make it more difficult to procure information when a 'real' crime occurred.
145 *Separate report*, p. cxxviii.
146 *Report of the first Irish Trades Congress* (Dublin, 1894), pp. 19–21.
147 See e.g. *Report of the sixth Irish Trades Congress* (Londonderry, 1899), pp. 50–51; *Report of the sixteenth Irish Trades Union Congress* (Limerick, 1909), pp. 8 and 31.

Congress also took the view that the appointment of more persons with 'practical knowledge' of working conditions in factories and workshops was particularly desirable in Ireland if the existing 'evils' were to be brought to an end.[148] More women inspectors were also required, particularly in the north, 'where so many females are employed ... and [where] even a greatly increased number of male inspectors could not deal so effectively with many of their causes of complaint'.[149] And there would also be more respect for the inspectors if more Irish persons were appointed.[150] As we show in chapter 4, there was a positive, if limited, response to the plea for the appointment of lady inspectors. The number of inspectors was also increased; we know relatively little about their background, but it would appear that 'working class' appointments were limited to the ranks of the inspectors' assistants. We do know that some of the inspectors were born or educated in Ireland,[151] but their appointment does not appear to have been a matter of deliberate policy.[152] A small degree of local devolution was achieved by the setting up of 'permanent' offices in Belfast and Dublin in 1893; but the appointment, allocation and duties of the inspectors in Ireland remained a responsibility of central government – the Irish administration 'have no knowledge of their proceedings, which are regulated entirely by the Home Office'.[153]

At this time Ireland may be said to have consisted of two distinct economic and industrial districts. One, which we shall call simply 'the north', contained a number of factories (many of which were large) and a wide variety of workshops, all of which were concentrated within a relatively small geographical area; this type of industrial district was common in Great Britain and therefore quite familiar to the factory inspectors. The other district, which we call 'the rest of Ireland', was quite different – a much larger, predominantly agricultural, area containing many small and widely-dispersed industrial units. Although the precise boundaries between these two districts adopted for the purposes of administering the factory acts changed from time to time, their essential nature did not, and it is therefore convenient to use them as the basis for looking more closely at the organisation of the inspectorate in Ireland after 1878.

---

148 Ibid. See also *Hansard 4*, cviii, 1017–18 (30 May 1902)(Sir Charles Dilke).
149 *Report of the fifth Irish Trades Congress* (Belfast, 1898), pp. 32 and 50. See further below, chap. 4.
150 *Report of the fifteenth Irish Trades Union Congress* (Belfast, 1908), p. 7.
151 W.J. Neely, a graduate of Trinity, was an inspector in Dublin from 1896 to 1900 and from 1903 to 1908; W.J. McCaghey, an inspector in Belfast 1906–12, had worked in the linen trade in Co. Down before his appointment.
152 'Factory inspectors are liable to serve in any part of the United Kingdom ... and the question of nationality is not considered in connection with their appointment': *Hansard 4*, cli, 598 (8 Aug. 1905)(A. Akers-Douglas, home sec.). Cf. 'In the appointment of inspectors ... in Wales ... among candidates otherwise equally qualified, persons having a knowledge of the Welsh language shall be preferred': 1878 act, s. 23: 1901 act, s. 118(2).
153 *Fourth report of the royal commission on the civil service: Minutes of evidence*, p. 183 [Cd. 7338], H.C. 1914, xvi, 183 (Sir James Dougherty, under sec. for Ireland).

The north

In the 1890s and early 1900s, linen still dominated industrial activity in the north of Ireland, giving employment to almost one-half of the industrial workforce. The industry went through some difficult times, due to declining prices for flax and linen goods, competition from European linen and British cotton and a trend towards the protection of foreign (non-Empire) markets,[154] and some of the linen magnates took the view that they were hampered by the restrictions imposed by the factory acts. R.H. Reade, a director of York St. Flax Spinning Co., for example, took the view that the strength of competition derived not just from the lower wages paid, but also from the longer hours worked, in foreign mills.[155] A decline in spinning was, however, offset by an increase in weaving. All in all, business was good, and the linen industry may be said to have reached its peak just before the outbreak of the first world war.

For the linen workers, the period was marked by a general rise in their standard of living: '[A]lthough the factory system brought many hardships for the workers, it was not without its compensations. Wages and working conditions did improve very considerably ... in fact, real wages in the linen industry rose by more than 200 per cent between 1850 and 1900.'[156] But not all the workers benefitted equally – 'only a small minority of the labour force, primarily skilled men and overlookers, could have consistently earned enough to support a family of four at a "minimum comfort" level.... The wages of women workers, girls and juveniles – the bulk of the workforce – were still pitiably low at the beginning of the twentieth century.'[157] Out-workers in the 'making-up' trades, working 'in the poorest and most unhealthy of our dwellings' suffered in particular: 'in some streets one could hardly enter a

154 P. Ollerenshaw, 'Industry 1820–1914' in L. Kennedy and P. Ollerenshaw (ed.), *An economic history of Ulster 1820–1939* (Manchester, 1985), p. 79.
155 *Report from the select committee on industries (Ireland): Minutes of evidence*, p. 640, H.C. 1884–85 (288), ix. 642. See also Bardon, *History of Ulster*, pp. 390–91.
156 R.D.C. Black, 'The progress of industrialisation, 1840–1920' in T.W. Moody and J.C. Beckett (ed.), *Ulster since 1800: A political and economic survey* (London, 1955), pp. 57–58. The author goes on to note, however, that the wages of outworkers were often considerably lower than those of factory workers: 'As recently as 1910 there were women employed as outworkers in the making-up of linen, who found it hard to earn a penny an hour.'
157 H. Patterson, 'Industrial labour and the labour movement, 1820–1914' in Kennedy and Ollerenshaw (ed.), *Economic history of Ulster*, pp. 165–66, citing E. Boyle, 'The economic development of the Irish linen industry' (unpublished Ph.D. thesis, Queen's University Belfast, 1979), p. 166. In September 1906, the average weekly wage in linen mills and factories in Belfast was 26s. 2d. for adult men as compared to 10s. 10d. for adult women; young persons averaged between 7s. 11d. (if girls) and 8s. 11d. (if boys), and half-timers were paid 3s. 8d. Compared with 1886, average wages for males had risen by 13–18 per cent, and by 21–24 per cent for females. All Belfast workers were paid slightly more than the United Kingdom average, and often considerably more than their counterparts outside the city: *Report of an inquiry by the Board of Trade into the earnings and hours of labour of workpeople of the United Kingdom, I: Textile trades in 1906*, p. xxi [Cd. 4545], H.C. 1909, lxxx, 22.

house without seeing 2, 3, 4 or more children, varying in age from 6 to 12 years sitting around a table all intensely busy trying to earn a miserable pittance ...'.[158] But those who worked in linen mills and factories also faced an unhealthy combination of heat, humidity and dust and the risk of death or injury from the rapidly moving machinery. The poor state of working conditions in the industry led to no less than four official enquiries within a 20-year period.[159] One reason for this relative lack of improvement in working conditions and rates of pay was the weakness of the linen workers, especially the women. Many of the male workers had become unionised after the 1870s, but the majority of workers were much slower to become organised:

From 1889 until 1893 Belfast, like many other industrial centres in the United Kingdom, experienced the upsurge of trade union organisation among hitherto unorganised groups. This was the 'new unionism'. A result of this brief period of militancy was an attempt by the local trades council to organise a mass of female workers in linen. A union, the Textile Operatives Society of Ireland, was established, but by 1910 it had only managed to unionise a small section of potential recruits, and in 1914 only about 10 per cent of the labour force in linen was organised.[160]

The other major industrial developments in the north of Ireland during this period were associated with various metal trades – particularly ship-building and engineering works. By 1880, Harland and Wolff employed some 5,000 persons; but with the rapid expansion which took place after that date, and the opening of a second shipyard by Workman and Clark, the numbers quickly increased. By 1914, the total labour force had grown to 20,000. This massive increase in shipbuilding brought other industrial developments in its train. Marine engineering flourished, and by 1902, the Belfast ropeworks, with a workforce of 3,000, 'had become the largest single works of its kind'.[161] One of the chief characteristics of all these industries was that they employed large numbers of skilled and relatively well-paid – and mainly adult male – workers, with relatively high levels of trade union organisation.[162] But such employment was particularly subject to the vagaries of the market: 'These

---

158 *Chief insp. ann. rep., 1906,* p. 417.
159 *Reports made ... by E.H. Osborn, esq., one of H.M. inspectors of factories, upon the conditions of work, etc. in flax mills and linen factories in the United Kingdom* [C. 7287], H.C. 1893–94, xvii, 537; *Report upon the conditions of work in flax and linen mills as affecting the health of operatives employed therein* [Cd. 1997], H.C. 1904, x, 1: *Report of the committee of enquiry into the conditions of employment in the linen and other making-up trades of the north of Ireland* [Cd. 6509], H.C. 1912–1913, xxiv, v and *Report of the departmental committee on humidity and ventilation in flax mills and linen factories* [Cd. 7433], H.C. 1914, xxxvi, 1.
160 Patterson, 'Industrial labour', pp. 173–74, suggesting five explanatory factors. See also J.P. Hamill, 'A study of female textile operatives in the Belfast linen industry, 1890–1939' (unpublished Ph.D. thesis, Queen's University Belfast, 1999), pp. 60–79 and D.W. Bleakley, 'Trade union beginnings in Belfast and district' (unpublished M.A. thesis, Queen's University Belfast, 1955).
161 Ollerenshaw, 'Industry', p. 92.
162 See e.g. Patterson, 'Industrial labour', pp. 166–67 and 176, stating that in 1886

high earnings have to be evened out over periods of lower rates, under-employment and unemployment. Thus skilled workers' overall earnings may not have been significantly greater than those of unskilled workers ...'.[163]

While the linen industry and shipbuilding and engineering may be said to have dominated industrial development in the north of Ireland, other industries also played their part in the expanding economy of the region. Indeed, these developments have led one commentator to observe that 'between 1870 and 1914 the relative significance of linen in the economy of the Belfast region declined as the growth of other industries, shipbuilding, marine and mechanical engineering, food processing, tobacco manufacture and drink, including whiskey distilling and aerated waters, combined to diversify, strengthen and balance the regional economic base.'[164] In factory act terms, those employed in non-textile factories in 1907 outnumbered those employed in textile factories by 82,896 to 68,777 (with a further 11,145 employed in workshops of all kinds).[165] The net result of all these developments was that 'The nature of industrialisation in north-east Ulster was such that this region did compare and co-operate far more closely with industrial regions in Britain, notably west-central Scotland and north-west England, than it did with other parts of Ireland.'[166]

Table 3.3: Principal industrial occupations in Ireland, 1907[167]

Industry	Ulster	Rest of Ireland	Ireland Total
Linen	77,121	2,911	80,032
Other textiles	4,583	5,212	9,795
Clothing	32,823	13,466	46,289
Machines, tools, etc	22,766	8,405	31,171
Food and drink	7,718	23,290	31,008
Paper printing, stationery	3,499	6,373	9,872
Wood	2,341	3,787	6,128
Laundries	2,317	2,663	4,980
Furniture	1,544	1,818	3,362
Chemicals	1,261	2,015	3,276
Other	6,845	7,245	14,090
TOTAL	162,818	77,185	240,003

skilled workers in shipbuilding and engineering in Belfast earned between 27s. and 30s. per week, while unskilled workers earned only 13s. per week.

163 A. Reid, 'Skilled workers in the shipbuilding industry, 1880–1920' in A. Morgan and R. Purdie (ed.), *Ireland: Divided nation, divided class* (London 1980), pp. 117–18.
164 Ollerenshaw, 'Industry', p. 86.
165 Figures derived from *Summary of returns of persons employed in 1907 in textile factories, in non-textile factories and in workshops* – see above, n. 139.
166 See e.g. Ollerenshaw, 'Industry', p. 62.
167 The 'rest of Ireland' figures given are the combined totals for the Dublin and Cork districts as recorded in *Summary of returns of persons employed in 1907 in textile factories, in non-textile factories and in workshops*.

In order to achieve an equal division of work in Ireland, the north of Ireland district continued during the 1880s to comprise only that part of Ulster north east of a line from Newry to Letterkenny; this district was 'small in area but full of manufacturing life'.[168] In 1895, however, the district was extended,[169] and by 1900 covered the whole province. In 1898, responsibility for both Irish districts had been transferred from Manchester to Glasgow; in 1902 this division was renamed the 'Scotland-Ireland' division. A further reorganisation took place in 1907, when Ulster was divided into two districts, Belfast and Londonderry. Apparently in recognition of the similarity between Scotland and Ulster, the two districts remained in what was now called the Northern Division, still based in Glasgow.

Table 3.4: Composition of the workforce in the north of Ireland, 1870–1907[170]

	1870	1895	1907 Belfast	1907 Derry	Total
Children	1,859	4,958	3,926	157	4,083
Young persons	9,697	25,503	25,095	3,231	28,326
Adult women	44,542	61,690	58,180	8,909	67,089
Adult men	27,533	58,106	56,739	6,581	63,320
TOTAL	83,631	150,257	143,940	18,878	162,818

Although the precise percentages changed from time to time, these figures illustrate two of the features of the north of Ireland from the factory acts perspective – a relatively large number of child workers,[171] and a high percentage of adult women workers.[172] The number of factories and workshops in which these workers were employed varied quite considerably; in 1895, for example, there were said to be 1,968 factories and 2,174 workshops; by 1914, these numbers had grown to 3,484 factories and 3,154 workshops.

Until 1893, the inspection of 4,000 or so factories and workshops was the responsibility of a single inspector. In that year, one of the newly appointed 'inspectors' assistants' was assigned to assist with the inspection of workshops,

168 *Chief insp. ann. rep., 1887*, p. 19 (Redgrave).
169 *Chief insp. ann. rep., 1897*, p. 326 (Counties Antrim, Down, Londonderry, Donegal and Tyrone, and parts of counties Fermanagh, Monaghan and Armagh).
170 Figures derived from 1870, 1895 and 1907 returns – see above, n. 139 and *Chief insp. ann. rep., 1896*, pp. 168, 225 and 287. Note that for 1870, the 'young persons' figure includes only males, while 'women' includes all females over 13.
171 The figure for child workers in 1907 represents 2.5% of the total workforce in the north of Ireland; the comparable figures for Scotland and England/Wales were 0.1% and 0.8% respectively. Of course, the total number of persons employed in these two countries meant that the absolute number of children employed there was higher than in Ireland.
172 41% in the north of Ireland, as compared to 27% in Scotland and 25% in England and Wales.

and the 'resident' inspector also received assistance from time to time from one of the new lady inspectors. In 1896, a second (junior) inspector was appointed, and in 1900, a third. By 1904 the decision had been taken to assign a lady inspector 'chiefly for work in Ireland' and based in Belfast.[173] When these arrangements came to be reviewed in 1907, it was decided that Ulster should be sub-divided into two districts – Belfast and Londonderry,[174] and that the 'difficult and responsible post' of resident lady inspector should carry senior rank. The implementation of these recommendations in 1908 meant that the inspectorate for the remainder of the period under consideration consisted of four male inspectors and one inspector's assistant (all full-time), a peripatetic male inspector (three-quarters time) and a senior lady inspector and a peripatetic lady inspector (part-time).[175] An official assessment of these arrangements in 1912 was not very reassuring:

The extent of the factory districts in the north of Ireland and the smallness of the inspecting staff appear to us to render it difficult for the factory inspectors to carry out their numerous duties as completely as could be wished. In ordinary circumstances the district staff can only pay one visit a year to each factory and workshop, and, even when they have had to call an employer's attention to some defect, it appears usually to be six months or so before they can find time to ascertain, by a second personal visit, whether such defect has been properly remedied.[176]

The rest of Ireland

Although, as we have seen, the division of Ireland for factory act purposes was not made on strictly provincial lines until 1900, it is convenient to regard the area outside Ulster as constituting the 'rest of Ireland' from 1878. In geographical terms (an important factor for itinerant inspectors), it was an 'enormous district', with an area almost three times the size of Ulster;[177] but the number of factories and workshops to be inspected was roughly the same.

173 'Report of the factory staff committee 1904', p. 13, PRO LAB 15/5. She was to spend about eight months of the year in Ireland; although her duties extended over the island as a whole, it was expected that much of her time would be spent in the north.

174 'The area to be covered is large and the work heavy. Complaints are numerous; the flax and tow works call for special attention in connection with the enforcement of the new regulations; questions of truck are numerous, and generally the conditions in many of the factories call for close inspection. The figures show a shortage of factory visits equivalent to the time of a junior inspector... . We recommend the creation of a new one-man district with its centre in Londonderry, to include Co. Donegal and parts of the counties of Londonderry and Tyrone': 'Report of the factory staff committee 1907', p. 21. Additional assistance would be provided by a new peripatetic inspector for Ireland who would spend three months in the new district, six months in Belfast and three months in the new Cork district.

175 Ibid., pp. 10, 13–14 and 21.

176 *Report of the committee on the conditions of employment in the linen and other making-up trades of the north of Ireland*, p. xix [Cd. 6509], H.C. 1912–13, xxxiv, 385.

177 24,006 square miles to Ulster's 8,581 square miles. The description is that of sub-inspector Monsell, in his evidence to the factory and workshop commissioners in

Table 3.5: Factories and workshops in the two Irish districts

| | North of Ireland | | | Rest of Ireland | | |
	Factories	Workshops	Total	Factories	Workshops	Total
1895	1,968	2,174	6,142	2,762	3,596	6,358
1907	3,484	3,154	6,638	3,189	3,738	6,927

The primary industry was agriculture. The figures recorded by the factory inspectorate in 1870 had confirmed that 'though the factory system had effectively substituted for traditional industry in the north-east, throughout most of the south, west and east hardly anything of significance remained'.[178] This may have been an unduly pessimistic assessment; but in any event the period after 1870 was one of increasing productivity and a rising standard of living. This was reflected in the continuation or development of a small number of textile factories[179] and a much larger number of small factories and workshops engaged in agriculture-related activities such as grain-milling, bacon-curing, dairy produce and brewing and distilling.[180] Indeed, Lyons has pointed out that in 1907 the most important industry in Ireland in terms of the value of gross output was the food and drinks industry, reflecting the overwhelming importance of agriculture throughout the island as a whole.[181] And as the standard of living rose, so did the demand for what we would now call consumer goods and services, many of which were manufactured or provided locally – clothing and millinery, boots and shoes, furniture, dyeing and cleaning, etc. Nevertheless, by 1907, the rest of Ireland gave employment only to one-third of the workers coming under the factory acts – and an even lower percentage of the 'protected' workers.[182] In Ulster, just over nine per cent of the population worked in establishments covered by the factory acts; in the rest of Ireland, that figure fell to two per cent – as compared to 11.5 per cent in England and Wales and 13.9 per cent in Scotland.[183]

1876: *Minutes of evidence*, p. 879. In 1893, for example, Woodgate (based in Dublin) travelled just over 19,000 miles during the year, while Taylor (Limerick) travelled almost 16,000 miles; by way of contrast, Snape (Belfast) covered just over 4,000 miles: *Chief insp. ann rep., 1893*, pp. 336–38.

178 Ó Gráda, *New economic history*, p. 310.

179 In 1895, 7,073 were employed in textile factories in the south of Ireland, by 1907, the number had fallen to 6,915. For one notable example, see below Plate 6.

180 In 1895, 40,685 were employed in non-textile factories and 14,778 in workshops; by 1907, these numbers had risen to 55,229 and 15,041 respectively:

181 *Ireland since the famine*, p. 67. See also the table of gross industrial output in Ireland in Ó Gráda, *New economic history*, p. 312, which suggests that the output from agriculture-related industries in the 26 counties which later formed the Irish Free State amounted in 1912 to almost £21.5 million, as compared with the figure (for the island as a whole in 1907) of £16.5 million for textiles and £6 million for shipbuilding and engineering.

182 *Chief insp. ann. rep., 1896*, p. 155 (general summary of persons employed in factories and workshops).

183 Ibid. If we exclude the three least industrialised counties of Ulster (Fermanagh,

Table 3.6: Composition of the industrial workforce in the south of Ireland[184]

	1870	1895	Dublin	1907 Cork	Total
Children	326	290	50	62	112
Young persons	4,976	9,683	8,359	3,430	11,789
Adult women	12,940	15,157	15,144	6,301	21,446
Adult men	22,017	37,400	30,607	13,231	43,838
TOTAL	40,259	62,530	54,160	23,025	77,185

From 1869 until 1887 this area (including parts of Ulster) was formally divided into two factory districts – Central (based in Dublin) and Southwestern (based in Limerick).[185] In 1887, however, these two districts were amalgamated to form the South of Ireland; as Redgrave explained, a resident inspector was no longer required in the south-west:

It has been for some considerable time evident that there was a manifest decrease of manufacturing industries in the south and south-west of Ireland, and when this fact is taken into consideration with other facts, that in such parts children ... are rarely employed in factories and workshops, and that the young persons ... bear a much less proportion to the number of persons employed, than in the north of Ireland and in England, it will be evident that although the area to be covered is large, there are comparatively much fewer regulations to be enforced than in other parts of the kingdom.[186]

The chief inspector did allow, however, that if the inspector (Woodgate) required assistance because of the large size of the district, a junior inspector could be sent from England 'as may be from time to time desirable and necessary'.[187] Woodgate was not long in calling for assistance. His expanded district still had a total of 1,625 factories and more than 2,000 known workshops, and there were many more unknown because they were not registered with the home office.[188] In 1888 a resurgence in trade caused him

Monaghan and Cavan) the figure for the north rises to 11%. The overall figure for Ireland as a whole was 4.5%.

184 See above, n. 170.
185 *Chief insp. ann. rep., 1878*, p. 8.
186 *Chief insp. ann. rep., 1887*, p. 5. The local inspector (Woodgate) agreed that industrial prospects in 1887 looked bleak: 'There does not appear to be any tendency to start any new industries ... if I except butter and condensed milk'. This assessment was quickly confirmed when an inspection of 625 factories in south and south-west Ireland found that 155 'were not at work' (ibid).
187 Ibid., p. 6. Indeed, Redgrave acknowledged that experience might show that the reduced staff was 'not sufficient to secure an uniform observance of the factory regulations'; if this proved to be the case, 'I shall not hesitate to make a representation upon the subject'.
188 *Chief insp. ann. rep., 1887*, pp. 6–7.

to report that in Dublin the number of factories alone rose from 290 to 302, which did not include the expansion of existing buildings.[189] By 1892 it was clearly demonstrated that Woodgate needed assistance[190] and a junior inspector (Taylor) was sent temporarily to Limerick, the administrative centre for the old southwestern district.[191]

The reorganisation of the factory districts in 1902 formally recognised that the 'South Ireland' district consisted of Leinster, Connaught and Munster.[192] But a *de facto* subdivision was achieved by reinstating the practice of stationing a junior inspector at Limerick.[193] This position was formally recognised in 1907,[194] with the subdivision into two districts – Dublin and Cork.

The division of the south into two districts meant that there were two inspectors there on a regular basis until 1887; and this remained the position even after its reduction to a single district. In 1893–94, the inspectors were assigned one of the newly appointed inspectors' assistants,[195] and a second assistant appears to have been available for two or three years prior to 1897; a third inspector was added in 1902. Notwithstanding the redivision of the district in 1907, this establishment of three inspectors and one assistant remained in place until 1914. From 1893, however, these inspectors had part-time assistance from one or more lady inspectors, and from 1907 from the peripatetic male inspector, one quarter of whose time was to be spent in Cork.

The differing nature of the new districts from those in the north was recognised by the transfer of Dublin and Cork from the Northern division to

189 *Chief insp. ann. rep., 1889*, p. 37.
190 "Owing to the very large area comprised in this district and to the difficulties of reaching many of the far distant towns … ': *Chief insp. ann. rep., 1892*, p. 111.
191 'His time has been chiefly occupied in visiting outlying corn, scutch, and saw mills which have not been visited for some time, and enforcing the requirements of the act … as regards guarding machinery, etc.': *Chief insp. ann. rep., 1893*, p. 28.
192 *Chief insp. ann. rep., 1902*, pt. I, p. 125.
193 Given that the south of Ireland was 'the largest in area in the United Kingdom', the home office accepted that the work of inspection could not be adequately undertaken by the existing staff. The new inspector would be able to give special attention to the rapidly-developing creamery industry throughout the south-west, and to the factories and workshops in the Cork area 'which are at a very great distance from the headquarters in Dublin': 'Report of the factory staff committee 1902', PRO LAB 15/5.
194 'We think the time has now come when this large district … should be sub-divided… [I]t will conduce to efficient and economical administration to create a new one-man district in the south-west … , to include the counties of Cork, Kerry, Limerick, Clare and Tipperary': 'Report of the factory staff committee 1907', p. 14. The work of inspecting 1,164 factories and 1,211 workshops would be too much for one man, who should therefore be assisted during the summer, 'when the creameries need special inspection', by a new peripatetic inspector for Ireland who would spend the rest of the year in the north.
195 A Mr Ryan, who was stationed in Cork 'with a view to carrying out and enforcing the provisions of the act … in all workshops, such as dress-makers, tailors, bootmakers, saddlers, and all places where no steam, water, or gas power is used …': *Chief insp. ann. rep., 1893*, p. 28.

the newly-formed Southwestern Division, based in Bristol.[196] This arrangement may have been logical in industrial terms; but the division of Ireland into two divisions must have created administrative difficulties. Two superintending inspectors were now required to liaise not only with the home office, but also with the Irish government departments at Dublin Castle; and developments in the island were now reported in two different sections of the chief inspector's annual report

The overall picture at the close of the period under consideration may be summarised as follows:

Table 3.7: Factories and workshops in Ireland in 1914[197]

	No. of factories	No. of workshops	No. of workers	No. of inspectors	Approx. no. of plants per inspector
North Ireland					
– Belfast district	2,532	2,320	143,940	6	970
– L'Derry district	952	834	18,878	1	1,200
South Ireland					
– Dublin district	1,925	2,123	54,160	3	1,150
– Cork district	1,269	1,615	23,025	1	2,250
IRELAND	6,678	6,894	240,003	11	1,200
SCOTLAND	12,535	14,966	660,056	19	1,400
ENGLAND and WALES	103,845	131,937	4,227,050	175	1,300
UNITED KINGDOM	123,058	153,797	5,127,109	205	1,350

The position with regard to factory inspection in Ireland, as elsewhere throughout the United Kingdom, was still not satisfactory. The workload of the inspectors, whether in terms of the number of establishments, or the number of workers, for which they were responsible, was still too heavy: 'All of [the Irish districts] show considerable arrears of inspection'.[198] But the prospect of home rule[199] – and then the onset of the world war – meant that no immediate action would be taken to remedy the situation.

196 'Report of the factory staff committee 1907'; *Chief insp. ann. rep., 1908*, pp. xx–xxiii and 214–17.
197 The numbers of factories and workshops are taken from *Chief insp. ann. rep., 1914*, p.123; the numbers of workers are from the 1907 returns, since later information is not available.
198 *Delevigne/Whitelegge report 1913*, p. 13.
199 Administration of the factory acts was set to become an 'Irish service' under the Government of Ireland Act 1914, s. 4(6).

CHAPTER FOUR

The special role of the lady inspectors, 1893–1914

THE ADMINISTRATIVE 'ADVENTURE'

Although the factory acts were primarily designed to protect the health and welfare of women, as well as young persons and children of both sexes, it was long assumed that they should be administered and enforced by an inspectorate which was exclusively male. Thus it was in 1876 that the factory and workshop commissioners gave no consideration to the appointment of lady inspectors,[1] even on the narrow ground that women over the age of 13 then constituted almost one-third of industrial workers in the United Kingdom.[2] In 1878, however, Emma Paterson, founder of the Women's Protective and Provident League (later the Women's Trade Union League), persuaded the Trades Union Congress to amend one of its regular resolutions so as to call for the appointment of 'practical working men *and women*' as factory inspectors.[3] But the notion was immediately rejected by the chief inspector, Alexander Redgrave:

I doubt very much whether the office of factory inspector is one suitable for women .... The general and multifarious duties of an inspector of factories would really be incompatible with the gentle and home-loving character of a woman .... Factory inspecting requires activity and acumen and the stern authority of a man to enforce obedience to his interrogatories. It is not an agreeable duty for a man, but I cannot conceive that such functions would commend themselves to a woman, or that she could successfully discharge them .... It has been urged that where women are employed some enquiries could be more appropriately made by women ... but it is seldom necessary to put a single question to a female [worker], and I do not see how the services of ladies could be made available to render the administration of the laws more effective. Possibly some details, here and there, might be superintended by a female inspector, but, looking at what is required at the hands of an inspector, I fail to see the advantages likely to arise from her ministrations in a factory or a workshop, so opposite to the sphere of her good work in the hospital, the school or the home.[4]

1 These inspectors were called variously 'female', 'lady' and 'women' inspectors; in accordance with the leading study of their work, M.D. McFeely, *Lady inspectors: The campaign for a better workplace 1893–1921* (New York and Oxford, 1988), we use the designation 'lady inspectors'.
2 The issue had been raised in evidence – see e.g. *Factory and workshop commissioners: Minutes of evidence*, p. 642 [C. 1443–I], H.C. 1876, xxx, 642 (evidence of Miss Wilson, representing women workers in Leeds).
3 See e.g. N.C. Soldon, *Women in British trade unions, 1874–1976* (Dublin, 1978), chap. 1.
4 *Chief insp. ann. rep., 1879*, pp. 97–100.

Such reasoning failed to satisfy Paterson and her supporters, but she was unable to make any progress.[5] On her death in 1886, the issue was taken up by Emilia Dilke,[6] the new leader of the Women's Trade Union League, and her assistant, May Abraham.[7] The campaign for the appointment of lady inspectors received a significant boost from the notable contribution made by the four women assistant commissioners appointed in 1891 by the royal commission on labour to report on the condition of working women,[8] and by evidence given to the commission to the effect that 'women workers themselves tendered practically none of the complaints that the [men] inspectors were there to remedy and to which they looked for clues in exercising their protective functions'.[9] In spite of continuing opposition from the home office and from the inspectors themselves,[10] the idea that 'women ought to be inspected by women'[11] attracted increasingly widespread support.

Redgrave retired in 1891, and was replaced by a more sympathetic chief inspector (Sprague Oram).[12] In August 1892, the Liberals won the general

5 In 1883, for example, Sir Charles Dilke suggested the appointment of women inspectors, but the home secretary (Harcourt) would have none of it – see G.M. Tuckwell, *A short life of Sir Charles W. Dilke* (London, 1925), pp. 224–25.

6 See generally B. Askwith, *Lady Dilke: A biography* (London, 1969), pp. 57–59 and Soldon, *Women in British trade unions*, chap. 2.

7 Born in Dublin, the daughter of a solicitor, May Abraham became Emilia Dilke's secretary in 1888 and treasurer of the Women's Trade Union League. She was actively involved in attempts to improve working conditions for women, and as an assistant commissioner, investigated conditions in English textile factories and the Irish linen factories for the royal commission on labour in 1891–92. As we shall see, she became one of the first lady factory inspectors in 1893. See generally V.R. Markham, *May Tennant: A portrait* (London, 1949), and below, Plate 7.

8 McFeely, *Lady inspectors*, pp. 8–12. S. Yeandle, *Women of courage* (London, 1993), p. 5 notes that three of the first lady inspectors were associated with the royal commission and that its significance in this context 'cannot be over-estimated'. The commission did not report until 1894, when it noted the appointment of lady inspectors 'with satisfaction': *Fifth and final report of the royal commission on labour*, p. 109 [Cd. 7421], H.C. 1894, xxxv, 117.

9 A.M. Anderson, *Women in the factory: An administrative adventure, 1893 to 1921* (London, 1922), p. 3.

10 See e.g. J. Pellew, *The Home Office 1848–1914: From clerks to bureaucrats* (London, 1982), pp. 154–55, who explains that although objections were articulated on grounds of 'administration, economy and practicability', the real reason for opposition 'may have been the conservative prejudice of a department where, as yet, there were no other female officers'. Cf. 'the majority of the inspectors considered that the advantages of their appointment were over-estimated, and the difficulties under-estimated': Royal Commission on Labour, *Summary of the evidence received by Group C*, p. 248 [Cd. 7421–I], H.C. 1894, xxxv, 516.

11 *Hansard 4*, v, 643 (9 June 1892)(Dr Tanner, MP for Co. Cork). According to the secretary to the royal commission on labour, the majority of witnesses who gave evidence to the commission supported the notion that 'where a large number of women were employed, a staff of female inspectors should be appointed because, in the first place, they would know where to go and what to look for, and in the second place, women will make statements to one of their own which they would not make to men': *Summary of the evidence received by Group C*, p. 248.

12 According to H. Jones, 'Women health workers: The case of the first women factory

election, and the new home secretary (Asquith) also proved more receptive than his predecessor. In January 1893, Asquith promised 'to do something – it will not be much – to gratify the desire of our lady friends for female inspection',[13] and within a couple of months appointed May Abraham[14] and Mary Paterson[15] to begin work as inspectors in May 1893. Their immediate success[16] led to the making of two further appointments early in 1894,[17] and of a fifth in January 1896.[18] Further appointments followed, and by 1914 the number of lady inspectors had risen to twenty-one.

In broader social and political terms, the appointment of women to the factory inspectorate marked 'a great advance' in that 'for the first time the government had given women highly responsible jobs'.[19] In our narrower

inspectors in Britain' in *Social History of Medicine*, 1(2) (1988), 165 at p. 170, 'the change of heart in the Home Office was due to more than an alteration in personnel. The 1890s was the age of the "new woman". Gradual developments in middle-class women's educational facilities, and various changes in the law which improved their job opportunities, meant that there were suitably qualified women to appoint, while the employment of women in other areas of government service made the concept less novel.'

13 Speech to National Liberal Federation, *The Times*, 25 Jan. 1893, as quoted in McFeely, *Lady inspectors*, pp. 13–14.

14 'Conspicuously successful at the conduct of prosecutions, she combined a power of lucid expression with a moderation and a sense of fairness that won approval from the Bench and compliments from her professional opponents': *The Times*, 12 July 1946. She was also the author of *The law relating to factories and workshops* (London, 1896).

15 A native of Glasgow, where her father was in the boot trade, Paterson was a graduate of Queen Margaret College and had been active in charitable social work with working women and girls in Scotland before her appointment, at the age of 31. She was assigned to Scotland, where she spent most of her working life until appointed deputy principal lady inspector in 1908. She resigned in 1911 when appointed a national health insurance commissioner. See e.g. McFeely, *Lady inspectors*, pp. 15–18 and *Glasgow Herald*, 11 June 1941.

16 For a description of the work which they undertook in the second half of 1893, see *Chief insp. ann. rep.*, 1893, pp. 10–17 and Yeandle, *Women of courage*, p. 8.

17 Lucy Deane, a member of WTUL, had trained as a nurse and lecturer in public health, and worked as a sanitary inspector in London prior to her appointment; she resigned from the inspectorate in 1908 on grounds of ill-health. Adelaide Anderson had studied moral sciences at Girton College Cambridge, lectured for the Women's Co-operative Guild, and was a member of the staff of the royal commission on labour prior to her appointment at the age of 31. Promoted to principal lady inspector in 1897, she remained in that post until 1921. See generally Anderson, *Women in the factory*.

18 Rose Squire, the daughter of a Harley St. doctor, had worked with Lucy Deane as a sanitary inspector in London and lectured on public health. Appointed an inspector at the age of 35, she went on to become a senior lady inspector in 1908, and deputy principal lady inspector in 1912. Following a period of secondment to other ministries in 1918–1920, she returned briefly to the inspectorate; but on the disbandment of the separate women's branch in 1921, she became a principal officer in the home office and retired in 1926. See generally, R.E. Squire, *Thirty years in the public service: An industrial retrospect* (London, 1927) and especially chap. vi dealing with her work in Ireland.

19 S. Boston, *Women workers and the trade unions* (London, 1980), p. 36. See also H. Martindale, *Women servants of the state, 1870–1938: A history of women in the civil service* (London, 1938), pp. 53–54: '[Asquith] realised that, when opening a new career to women, the future would depend on the choice of the first women to fill the

context, however, the appointments posed a number of practical problems. For a start, what qualifications were to be required for appointment? Women were, of course, obliged to pass the civil service examinations set for men inspectors.[20] But, contrary to the view of Emma Paterson, Asquith decided to appoint educated middle-class women rather than 'practical working women', whom he thought would lack not just the necessary initiative and capacity to assume responsibility, but also experience in office work and the ability to write articulate reports.[21] In all these respects, the lady inspector had to be at least the equal of her male colleagues.[22] But she also had to possess other qualities:

We need quiet, well-mannered women in this service.... A woman as a factory inspector, in an industrial district away from her own family and social surroundings, as well as her women colleagues, can find no normal associates in, or through her own work. Her work compels her to lead a life that is quite different from that of other women, and the slightest deviation from extreme caution and prejudice may subject her to injurious criticism. She must be ready to go anywhere at any hour of the day or night where her work calls her. She cannot, like a medical woman called out at night, count on going into a house where she is desired and welcomed, she may also have to request an entrance against the will of the occupier.[23]

And she had to be relatively young:

[O]ur average age at first was twenty-seven years, and this was almost imperative as the nature of the work made great demands. Long hours of standing in a factory followed often by a long walk to the next factory ... coupled with a call on one's mental powers which the enforcement of a complicated body of legislation entailed, and again the effort needed at times to meet opposition and obstruction made demands on the physical, mental and nervous sides of an inspector which probably could best be met by someone with the idealizing powers of youth.[24]

How were the new inspectors to be absorbed into a department with a fixed hierarchical and decentralised structure? Asquith adopted the principle

posts, and he chose well. Indeed, he had done something to establish what proved, as the years went on, to be one of the greatest public services rendered by women.'

20 See McFeely, *Lady inspectors*, pp. 25–26; Squire, *Thirty years in the public service*, pp. 31–32.

21 Yeandle, *Women of courage*, p. 2 explains that Paterson sought the appointment not of 'ladies', but of 'practical working women'. This distinction is emphasised by Jones, 'Women health workers', pp. 167–69.

22 McFeely, *Lady inspectors*, p. 14. Cf. 'With regard to women inspectors, in the making of the appointments the general fitness of the candidate had to be considered, and amongst the qualifications to be considered was certainly acquaintance with the life of the working classes. The lady should also be able to extend her sympathies to those whom she was appointed to protect and the class with whom they worked': *Hansard* 4, cxxxix, 1044 (4 Aug. 1904)(A. Akers-Douglas, home sec.).

23 A.M. Anderson, 'On the reasons against unqualified mobility of residence for women inspectors': Memorandum of 15 Sept. 1905, PRO, HO45/10327/132951.

24 Anderson, *Women in the factory*, p. 1.

of 'separate but equal'.[25] The first lady inspectors were given the same powers as their male colleagues, but were appointed on a peripatetic basis, 'not being attached to any fixed districts' and responsible only to the chief inspector.[26] To give 'official recognition' to the women's branch, however, the early inspectors sought and obtained 'the appointment of a single person in authority' who would be answerable to the chief inspector.[27] In March 1896, May Abraham was appointed 'superintending lady inspector' – a title designed to signify a status equal to that of the (male) inspectors responsible for each of the five factory divisions.[28] On her resignation in May 1897, Abraham was replaced by Adelaide Anderson; but her designation as 'principal lady inspector' was perceived as a reduction in status.[29] The salary was, indeed, 'considerably less' than that of a superintending inspector; nevertheless, it was later asserted that the new post corresponded in rank 'partly to a deputy chief inspector and partly to a superintending inspector'.[30] Miss (later Dame) Adelaide Anderson remained in this post until 1921.[31]

The principal advantage of the initial organisation of the lady inspectors was that it facilitated a 'concentration of the women inspectors in a team-work that could be applied in any area or centre, or to any particular problem in any industry ...'.[32] But the success of three exceptions to the peripatetic approach,[33] the time taken up by travel from London to remoter parts of the United Kingdom, the shortage of local clerical assistance and the gradual increase in the number of lady inspectors during the early years of the new century prompted a reconsideration of these arrangements in 1907.[34] It was

25   But not entirely – each of the lady inspectors was paid a salary of £200 per annum, at a time when men inspectors earned between £300 and £320 per annum.
26   *Chief insp. ann. rep., 1893*, p. 10. Paterson was based in Glasgow; all the other lady inspectors worked from London.
27   McFeely, *Lady inspectors*, pp. 44–46.
28   Ibid., pp. 46–47.
29   The title 'suggested a leading position in a comic opera rather than in a government department': May Abraham, 'The women's factory department' in *Fortnightly Review*, (July 1898), 151.
30   *Second report of the royal commission on the civil service: Minutes of evidence*, p. 117 [Cd. 6535], H.C. 1912–13, xv, 379 (Sir Edward Troup, permanent under-sec., home office) – 'but they have a much smaller staff under them'. A salary review in 1907 still left the lady inspectors a 'notch' below the men – see McFeely, *Lady inspectors*, p. 114.
31   Hilda Martindale later wrote: 'For the women inspectors of factories and the women in industry it was indeed fortunate that they were led in those early days by a pioneer and a whole-hearted feminist, for those were hard and strenuous days and much opposition had to be met from all sides; and if the head of their branch had been lacking in courage, in determination and fighting qualities the result would have been very different, and we should certainly not have the comprehensive body of factory legislation and the first-class inspectorate of both men and women which we have to-day': *Women servants of the state*, p. 55.
32   Anderson, *Women in the factory*, p. 53.
33   In 1899 a 'resident' lady inspector (Deane) was assigned to West London, an area which contained over 4,000 women's workplaces: *Chief insp. ann. rep., 1899*, p. 238; in 1904, Martindale was 'stationed' in the Potteries, and the following year in Ireland – see below, p. 108.
34   'Report of the factory staff committee 1907', p. 24, PRO LAB 14/182; McFeely, *Lady*

accepted that they should remain an autonomous branch of the inspectorate; but the majority of the lady inspectors, like their male colleagues, should now have divisional responsibilities, and work from a local office with resident staff.[35] Accordingly, a 'senior lady inspector' and one or more lady inspectors were assigned to four regional centres across the United Kingdom.[36] The senior lady inspector was to reside in the principal town of the division, establish and supervise the organisation of an office, and 'direct the work of a staff of women who inspected in different parts of the division wherever she felt they were especially needed …'.[37] Five lady inspectors continued to be based in London, for special assignment by the principal lady inspector.[38]

One of the new senior lady inspectors summed up these new arrangements as follows: 'The women inspectors, while remaining a separate branch, were to fit in with the organised system of inspection by the men's staff … We four senior lady inspectors were provided each with an office and staff in the division to which we were allotted, and we and our juniors removed with our goods and chattels and took up residence in the central town of our sphere of labour.'[39] The changes proved to be successful:

Concrete results, such as a reduction in the number of accidents in laundries and improved safety in workshops in institutions, could be seen. On another level, the resident inspectors were becoming familiar with the people of their communities. In their first year, they had already done much to develop friendly relations with all kinds of associations and representative persons interested in improvement of the life of the industrial worker.[40]

By 1914, Asquith, now prime minister, could be rightly pleased with the success of his experiment: 'I think we should look towards the extension of the women inspectorate as one of the best securities for a healthy condition of things.'[41] But it should, perhaps, be recalled that the percentage of lady inspectors (roughly ten per cent of the inspectorate) fell considerably short

inspectors, pp. 113–15.

35   'Report of the factory staff committee 1907', pp. 24–26. McFeely, *Lady inspectors*, p. 116 suggests that this change was opposed by Anderson on the grounds that the establishment of regional centres would undermine the authority of the principal lady inspector.

36   Belfast, Glasgow, Manchester and Birmingham.

37   Martindale, *From one generation to another*, p. 148.

38   'Report of the factory staff committee 1907', p. 26; *Chief insp. ann. rep., 1908*, pp. xx and 120. A new post of deputy principal lady inspector was filled by Paterson, on promotion from Scotland.

39   *Thirty years in the public service*, pp. 131–32.

40   *Chief insp. ann. rep., 1909*, p. 120 (Anderson). Five years later, the chief inspector (Whitelegge) considered that the reorganisation had been so successful that a further three lady inspectors should be appointed: 'Report on the question of an increase in staff of the factory department by Sir Malcolm Delevigne and Sir Arthur Whitelegge', p. 15, PRO LAB 14/182.

41   Quoted in home office memorandum, 17 Jan. 1914, cited McFeely, *Lady inspectors*, p. 124.

of the percentage of women over the age of 13 coming within the factory acts (almost 36 per cent of all workers).[42] By this time, however, support for the 'separate but equal' principle was on the wane, as the lady inspectors came to be seen as a more integral part of a single inspectorate – and indeed the process of amalgamation into a unitary organisation began almost as soon as the first world war was over.[43]

THE ROLE OF THE LADY INSPECTORS

The lady inspectors were appointed to deal with the particular problems faced by women, and 'Mr Asquith … gave them a liberal starting-point and a wide field of activity'.[44] But there was an obvious administrative difficulty of defining their duties in such a way as to avoid conflict with, or unnecessary duplication of, the work undertaken by the male inspectors. Some attempts were, indeed, made to identify areas of exclusive interest. Thus, it was generally understood that the lady inspectors had a distinctive responsibility for questions of general hygiene (cleanliness, sanitary conveniences, etc.). On the other hand, they initially made a point of referring fencing matters to the men, at least until they had gained sufficient experience from their inspection of clothing factories and laundries.[45] But it was with the appointment of senior lady inspectors in 1908 to work 'in concert' with the superintending inspectors of divisions that a determined effort was made to assign the former a number of 'definite' duties:

[I]nvestigation of (a) accidents to women and girls in laundries and clothing factories, and (b) industrial poisoning cases among women and girls; district charge of some of the institution factories and workshops … ; special responsibility for routine inspection once a year of all works in which women and girls work under special regulations … ; strengthened responsibility for administration of the [law] prohibiting employment of women within one month of childbirth, and of provisions relating to child-labour, and suitability of sanitary accommodation.[46]

The notion of 'women inspectors for women's work', however, could not but include *some* responsibility for such matters as hours of employment, health and safety, truck and particulars, and it seems that a more comprehensive demarcation was never attempted. This inevitably meant that there was a certain amount of overlapping, at least in theory; in practice, however, 'elaborate' arrangements were made 'to make the two classes of inspectors work consistently', and it was claimed that these worked 'extremely well'.[47]

---

42   Figure (for 1907) derived from table in *Chief insp. ann. rep., 1911*, p. 289.
43   See McFeely, *Lady inspectors*, chap. 18.
44   Martindale, *Women servants of the state*, p. 53.
45   Anderson, *Women in the factory*, p. 12; Jones, 'Women health workers', p. 172.
46   *Chief insp. ann. rep., 1908*, pp. xx and 120.
47   See especially *Royal commission on the civil service, Second report: Minutes of evidence,*

Nevertheless, it is not surprising that the women initially met with some opposition from their male colleagues.[48]

Abraham and Deane ascribed this hostility to the fact that the latter had been 'lax in their work thro'', probably, want of enthusiasm and thro' having been appointed merely as a livelihood ... they are angry at what virtually amounts to an inspection of their inspecting work'.[49] A more recent assessment agrees:

Stationed in cities far from London headquarters, these men had settled down with their families and fallen into friendly relationships with the local establishment, including the employers it was their duty to regulate. The lady inspectors, with their confident reformers' zeal for strict enforcement of the law and their determination to prove themselves, were likely to disturb this quiet coexistence of management and guardians of the law.... Small wonder that some of the district inspectors felt threatened by this encroachment on their territory.[50]

No doubt there is some truth in this generalisation; but it is difficult, if not impossible, to test its validity by reference to objective evidence. Perhaps a more realistic assessment was given by Rose Squire:

Looking back on the system [of men and women inspectors] I think that, broadly speaking, it occasioned in the minds of the majority of the men a sense of irritation that a set of inspectors not subject to their direction and control (and *women* at that!) should be circulating in their districts; to the women it caused at times a galling sense of limitation of function and of isolation from the main current of departmental practice and policy vested in the men's organisation.[51]

The lady inspectors tended to make more thorough inspections,[52] but 'I think a man inspector covers more ground – inspects more factories in a given time ...'.[53] As argued by way of justification for their appointment, the

pp. 117 and 128 (Troup) and *Fourth report: Minutes of evidence*, pp. 97–98 [Cd. 7338], H.C. 1914, xvi, 460–61 (J. Leishman and M. Paterson). The small number of women inspectors also reduced the scope for overlapping.

48 McFeely, *Lady inspectors*, pp. 27–31; Jones, 'Women health workers', pp. 173–74.
49 *Diary of Lucy Deane*, quoted in McFeely, *Lady inspectors*, p. 26.
50 McFeely, *Lady inspectors*, p. 29. See also Markham, *May Tennant*, p. 27: 'It is impossible to read these early reports of the women inspectors ... and not to ask oneself what ... the men inspectors had been doing. Apparently they were preoccupied by technical questions and those concerned with mechanical equipment. If not the blind eye, at least there was a strange lack of perception about some of the human aspects of industry ... '.
51 Squire, *Thirty years*, p. 133. Jones, 'Women health workers', pp. 171–74 emphasises that the lady inspectors had a positive perception of themselves as '*pioneers* ... doing something of great importance ... [with] something peculiar to women to contribute ... ' (emphasis in original).
52 'Report of the factory staff committee, 1907', p. 32. Several MPs had earlier voiced a similar opinion: 'The average work done by the female inspector is higher than that done by male inspectors': *Hansard 4*, lxiii, 516 (29 July 1898) (R. McKenna (Monmouth, N.)); 'Relatively, the female inspectors did infinitely better work than the male inspectors' *Hansard 4*, cxxxix, 1022 (4 Aug. 1904) (J. Burns (Battersea)).
53 *Second report of the royal commission on the civil service: Minutes of evidence*, p. 115 (Troup). Cf. Anderson's policy, when special duties permitted, was to allot routine inspection according to the proportion of women and girls in a particular industry; thus, almost

lady inspectors tended to get more information from women workers, often by way of complaints;[54] in addition, 'employers employing a large number of women made very great demands on us for advice and suggestions'.[55]

The authority to sanction prosecutions was one of the most important powers given to the principal lady inspector,[56] and the fact that the lady inspectors were authorised to conduct proceedings in magistrates' courts at a time when women were regarded as unfit to qualify as solicitors or barristers[57] has rightly been regarded as particularly remarkable.[58] Between 1898 and 1914, the lady inspectors prosecuted nearly 2,000 occupiers in respect of nearly 5,000 offences.[59] This annual average of nearly 300 cases is roughly in proportion to the number brought by the men inspectors,[60] and the conviction rate which the lady inspectors achieved is also much the same as the men.[61] The broad nature of the offences in question is summarised in Table 4.1:

Table 4.1: Percentage distribution of prosecutions by general
nature of offence, 1898–1914[62]

	Lady inspectors	Men inspectors	All inspectors
Forms	17.4	13.1	13.4
Sanitation	2.8	2.7	2.7
Safety	1.5	6.9	6.4
Hours of employment			
– Women	34.0	35.7	35.6
– Young persons	33.8	36.8	36.5
– Children	3.7	2.6	2.7
Particulars	2.4	1.2	1.3
Truck	3.7	0.7	0.9
Other	0.6	0.4	0.5

one-half of the lady inspectors' time would have been taken up with textiles, a quarter with clothing trades, and so on: *Chief insp. ann. rep., 1912*, pp. 142–44.

54 'I fancy the lady inspectors ... undertake a larger number of special inquiries on complaint, as distinguished from the regular routine examination of factories': *Second report of the royal commission on the civil service: Minutes of evidence*, p. 117 (Troup).

55 *Fourth report of the royal commission on the civil service: Minutes of evidence*, p. 98 (J. Leishman and M.M. Paterson).

56 McFeely, *Lady inspectors*, p. 47; Anderson, *Women in the factory*, p. 200. Though granted to Abraham in 1896, it appears to have been 'lost' between 1898 and 1903, when the decision to prosecute was once again left to the principal lady inspector. See further below, chap. 10.

57 This restriction was only removed by the Sex Disqualification (Removal) Act 1919.

58 S. Boston, *Women workers and the trade unions* (London, 1980), p. 37. They apparently received little training – Anderson records that she conducted her first prosecution within a 'few weeks' of her appointment, 'never having previously entered a police court': Anderson, *Women in the factory*, pp. 201–02.

59 *Women in the factory*, p 209, adding that 'the years of greatest activity in the courts were between 1901 and 1911'.

60 The average number of cases brought by the men inspectors during this period was in the region of 3,000 per annum – see below, chap. 10.

61 Anderson's figures suggest a conviction rate of 95 per cent, as compared to the 97 per cent achieved by the men; once again, see below, chap. 10.

62 Derived from tables published in the annual reports of the chief inspector.

These figures suggest that lady inspectors were more keen than men inspectors that occupiers should comply with the various formal requirements of the factory acts; they were also more likely to bring proceedings in relation to particulars and truck – but less likely to bring 'safety' prosecutions. Both men and women, however, most frequently prosecuted in respect of failure by occupiers to abide by the laws regulating hours of employment. Even if, as seems doubtful, the seriousness of the offences for which convictions were obtained can be gauged from the level of fine imposed by the court, it does not appear possible to suggest that the cases brought by lady inspectors were more – or less – serious than those brought by the men; there is just no consistent pattern. In 1901, for example, the average fine in cases brought by lady inspectors was 17s.1d, as compared with an overall average fine of 18s. 11d., whereas in 1907 the comparable figures were £1 4s. 6d. and 19s. 8d. respectively.[63]

It has been pointed out 'there were very few [lady] inspectors, [and] common sense tells us that their impact must have been extremely limited'.[64] Indeed, the inspectors themselves recognised that there were still 'a great number and variety of deplorable contraventions of the actual requirements and spirit of the law and an amount of apparently preventable suffering and overstrain and injury to life, limb and health'.[65] Nevertheless, the first lady inspectors were, on balance, a success: 'In carrying out their duties, the early women inspectors displayed dedication and enormous energy, often working to the limits of what was humanly possible, and to the cost of their own health. They were motivated by considerations of social justice, compassion and human dignity.'[66] The annual reports of the principal lady inspector, which describe their work from 1896 onwards in considerable detail, show that they carried out not only routine inspections of factories and workshops throughout the United Kingdom, but also conducted special inquiries on particular industrial problems affecting women and children.[67] In 1897, for example, lady inspectors conducted inquiries into unhealthy or dangerous conditions in earthenware works, lucifer match factories, white lead factories, woolcombing sheds, cotton mills, silk mills and laundries; they investigated problems arising from the lifting of heavy weights, excessive vibration of machinery, injury to eyesight from defective lighting, defective fencing and meal-time working, and they looked in some detail at the working of the truck acts.[68] In 1908, their work also included the investigation of lead and

---

63 See *Chief insp. ann. rep., 1901*, pt. I, p. xi; *1902*, pt. II, p. 193 and *1907*, p. 201.

64 Jones, 'Women health workers', p. 180.

65 *Chief insp. ann. rep., 1913*, p. 70 (Anderson).

66 Yeandle, *Women of courage*, p. 13. See to the same effect Hutchins and Harrison, *History of factory legislation*, p. 249, Martindale, *Women servants of the state*, pp. 51–63 and 182–86, and T.K. Djang, *Factory inspection in Great Britain* (London, 1942), pp. 61–64.

67 For a general survey, see Yeandle, *Women of courage*, pp. 13–43; Anderson, *Women in the factory*, chap. vi.

68 See 'Annual report on the work of Her Majesty's women inspectors during 1897' in *Chief insp. ann. rep., 1897*, p. 89.

mercury poisoning and diseases arising from dusty processes in the china and clay industries.[69] On a number of occasions, inquiries such as these were supported by comparative studies of French, German or Austrian law designed to demonstrate weaknesses in the law of the United Kingdom.[70] Many of the reports giving details of these inquiries led to improvements in working conditions either voluntarily or as a result of changes in the law.[71] And in the wider field of social development, the lady inspectors played a considerable part 'in establishing a professional field for women'.[72]

THE LADY INSPECTORS IN IRELAND

Within months of her appointment in 1893, Abraham returned to Ireland to inspect millinery and dressmaking workshops, assess the use being made of respirators in flax spinning mills, investigate complaints of truck act infringements and extend her special enquiry into the laundry and lucifer match trades.[73] She was followed by the other lady inspectors, who (*inter alia*) made inquiries into home-work in the Londonderry shirt and collar industry, working practices in commercial and 'convent' laundries, piece-work particulars, fines and other deductions from wages and fish-curing in Co. Donegal.[74] But the greatest test of the skill and determination of no less than four of the then seven lady inspectors came during the period 1897 to 1900 with their attempts, which were ultimately unsuccessful, to enforce the truck acts in Co. Donegal.[75]

After 1900, the lady inspectors continued to visit Ireland on a part-time basis. In 1903, for example, Squire spent much of her time, in Ireland as well as in England, continuing a special inquiry into the need for the particulars clause to be extended to the making-up of wearing apparel such as handkerchiefs, shirts and collars, etc., in the course of which she visited 'all the agents and a number of outworkers engaged in the fancy sewing and embroidery of handkerchiefs and bed and table linen in a large district of County Down'.[76] The case for extension was so strong that the appropriate Order was made

69   See 'Report of the principal lady inspector of factories' in *Chief insp. ann. rep., 1908,* pp. 119 and 141.
70   See e.g. *Chief insp. ann. rep., 1894,* p. 33 (protection of health and safety in France); *1895,* pp. 136 and 188 (German and Austrian industrial codes); *1902,* pt. 1, p. 194 (regulation of laundries in France, Belgium and Germany).
71   See e.g. Jones, 'Women health workers'. pp. 177–80; McFeely, *Lady inspectors,* pp. 172–73.
72   McFeely, *Lady inspectors,* p. 173.
73   *Chief insp. ann. rep., 1893,* pp. 10–14; *1894,* pp. 11–19 and *1895,* pp. 99–100.
74   See e.g. *Chief insp. ann. rep., 1895,* p. 98 and *1896,* pp. 56–73, and below, chaps.7, 9 and 10.
75   See especially Squire, *Thirty years,* chap. vi; McFeely, *Lady inspectors,* chaps. 10–11; D. Greer, '*Middling hard on coin*': *Truck in Donegal in the 1890s* (Dublin, 2000), pp. 13–31, and below, chap. 7.
76   *Chief insp. ann. rep., 1903,* pt. I, pp. 194 and 233–34.

by the home secretary at the end of the year.[77] Squire also engaged in 'prolonged efforts' to persuade 'several large works' to institute proper heating arrangements and an efficient system of exhaust ventilation for the removal of fumes and dust, and made enquiries concerning the health of women and girls in tobacco factories.[78]

But by this time Anderson, as principal lady inspector, acknowledged the need for some additional provision:

Though some very valuable work has been done [by lady inspectors in Ireland] from time to time on particular subjects, e.g. truck among outworkers in north Ireland, Ireland has received much less attention than it would seem entitled to, having regard to the number of women employed; and we think that the representations that have been made to the secretary of state from several quarters for further inspection there, are to a great extent justified.[79]

Those 'representations' had in fact begun not long after the first lady inspectors were appointed. In 1894, the Belfast United Trades Council and the Textile Operatives Society of Ireland claimed that the appointment of a lady inspector based in the north of Ireland was 'absolutely essential', given the employment of about 50,000 females in the linen industry. The home secretary, Asquith, taking a line which was to be repeated on frequent occasions over the next ten years, replied that he could see no prospect of more than four or five lady inspectors for the whole of the United Kingdom, and he could not 'undertake that any one of them should be permanently resident in any one centre of industry'.[80] But he was prepared to 'take care that there was no neglect' in their deployment in the Belfast area.[81] The issue was then taken up by the Irish Trades Congress, which at its inaugural meeting in 1894 adopted a resolution calling for the appointment of additional factory inspectors, both men and women, 'with practical experience of factories and workshops in Ireland'.[82] Similar resolutions were passed annually for the next decade or more,[83] with the rider, added in 1898 at the instigation of Mary Galway, secretary of the Textile Operatives Society, that 'the time has arrived for the government to appoint *permanently* for the north of Ireland a female factory inspector'.[84]

---

77 See further below, chap. 6.
78 *Chief insp. ann. rep., 1903*, pt. I, p. 194.
79 'Report of the factory staff committee 1904', p. 13, PRO LAB 15/5.
80 *Hansard 4*, xx, 1336–37 (11 Jan. 1894). The matter was raised by T. Sexton, MP for North Kerry, but formerly MP for Belfast N.
81 *Hansard 4*, xxxii, 31–32 (25 March 1895).
82 *Report of the first Irish Trades Congress* (Dublin, 1894), pp. 19–21.
83 See e.g. *Report of the fifth Irish Trades Union Congress* (Belfast, 1898), p. 50; *ninth Congress* (Cork, 1902), p. 13 and *eleventh Congress* (Kilkenny, 1904), pp. 42–43.
84 *Report of the fifth Irish Trades Union Congress* (Belfast, 1898), p. 50. Galway was supported by Richard Wortley, President of the Belfast Trades Council, on the basis that 'even a greatly increased number of male inspectors could not deal so effectively with many of [the women workers'] causes of complaint': ibid., p. 32.

When the issue was raised in the house of commons,[85] the home secretary (C.T. Ritchie) continued to insist that 'the organisation of the staff of lady inspectors is not regulated according to geographical divisions, and would not, therefore, admit of a lady inspector being stationed permanently in Ireland'. He pointed out that 'Ireland absorbs a considerable proportion of their attention', and intimated that the solution lay in the appointment of additional lady inspectors.[86] Much the same attitude had been taken to calls for a lady inspector to be stationed in the Potteries;[87] but in 1904 the home office relented and a lady inspector was 'attached' to that district. The principle having been breached, and the case for additional provision being readily accepted by the principal lady inspector, it was not long before Ireland followed suit.

In 1904, a working party proposed that an additional lady inspector should be appointed 'chiefly for work in Ireland', and be stationed there for approximately eight months each year.[88] The home secretary, encouraged by the Irish TUC, finally accepted the 'justice' of this recommendation.[89] Although Anderson would have preferred to follow the Scottish precedent and appoint an Irish woman 'who, like Paterson [in Glasgow], would be on home ground', there was no such person on the existing staff.[90] Accordingly, it was decided to transfer to Ireland the inspector already stationed in the Potteries, Hilda Martindale.[91]

85 By J.P. Nannetti, nationalist/labour MP for Dublin (College Green). Nannetti, who had been a foreman printer and active in the Dublin Trades Council, was elected lord mayor of Dublin in 1906 and 1907.

86 *Hansard 4*, xcviii, 1333–34 (5 Aug. 1901) and 1445–46 (6 Aug. 1901). Nannetti was later advised that 'there is already a staff of "permanent female factory inspectors" whose services are available in Ireland not less than in other parts of the United Kingdom': *Hansard 4*, cviii, 1548 (5 June 1902) (Ritchie, home sec., who refused to find out the number of inspections carried out by lady inspectors in Ireland: *Hansard 4*, cix, 700–01 (16 June 1902), and then fell back on the party line: 'It was far better that the staff should be a central one, available for work in any particular district': *Hansard 4*, cxxxix, 1009 (4 Aug. 1904)).

87 'The staff of lady inspectors could be best turned to account by sending members of it where their services were most needed from time to time. Under that system, the Potteries had received their fair share of attention': *Hansard 4*, cxxiv, 604 (25 June 1903) (Akers-Douglas, home sec.).

88 Since the other four months were to be spent in the Potteries, it seems that the committee had a good idea of who should be given the job: 'Report of the factory staff committee 1904', p. 13.

89 *Report of the twelfth Irish Trades Union Congress* (Wexford, 1905), p. 9. The home secretary's decision was attributed to 'the prompt and persistent action of the Congress committee, backed by the united voice of the organised workers of Ireland'. But the home secretary quickly rejected the suggestion that he should appoint a second resident lady inspector who was also an Irishwoman: *Hansard 4*, cli, 360 (7 Aug. 1905).

90 McFeely, *Lady inspectors*, pp. 98–99.

91 The daughter of social worker and suffragist mother, Martindale had studied hygiene and sanitary science at Bedford College for Women and then gained practical experience by visiting poor law and other institutions for children. She was appointed an inspector, initially on a temporary basis, in 1901 at the age of 26. In 1907 she was

The first permanent lady inspector in Ireland took up residence on St Patrick's Day 1905 and stayed for seven years – 'a lengthier spell than was usual for an inspector to stay in one place'.[92] When first appointed to the inspectorate in 1902, she had felt somewhat less than qualified:

No one could have known less about industrial conditions, the intricacies of machinery, factory workers and the factory acts. I could claim to know something about the technique of inspection. I had learnt to observe, to register facts in my mind, to note them accurately on paper, and to make a thorough investigation. I had learnt to deal with people and had realized the need for meeting opposition in an impersonal way; that was really all I had to offer to the factory department.[93]

By 1905, however, she had gained considerable experience, particularly in west London and the Potteries.[94] One of her first tasks in Ireland was to put her appointment on a more satisfactory footing: 'For three and a half years I travelled from hotel to hotel, without an office or clerk ...'.[95] Matters came to a head in June 1907, when Martindale pressed for an increased salary and proper secretarial assistance.[96] Anderson supported her claims:

Miss Martindale's ... present salary is quite inadequate for her suitable maintenance in her solitary position there, with its exacting responsibilities and its undoubted risks .... The valuable work that Miss Martindale has been doing especially within the last six months – at such cost to herself – shows me that she is one of the women that I would personally choose for exceptional service of this kind. I earnestly beg that ... [the home secretary] will take into consideration the cost that it means to an English woman to successfully hold her own with all the Irish difficulties added to those that are inseparable from the work of a factory inspector.[97]

Whitelegge, the chief inspector, agreed:

        promoted to senior lady inspector, and became deputy chief inspector in 1925. She
        retired in 1933. See generally H. Martindale, *From one generation to another, 1839–1944*
        (London, 1944).
92   Ibid., p. 90.
93   Ibid., pp. 73–74. Five days after her appointment she was inspecting workshops in
        West London on her own, and soon after that she was conducting prosecutions in Bow
        St. magistrates' court.
94   See *Chief insp. ann. rep., 1904*, pt. I, p. 144.
95   *From one generation to another*, pp. 91–93.
96   Martindale to Anderson, 4 June 1907, PRO HO 45/10327/132951. She received some
        support from Mary Galway, who was at the same time calling for more lady inspectors
        'with a head office in Ireland to which complaints could be made, as the present
        arrangement caused a good deal of delay': *Report of the fifteenth Irish Trades Union
        Congress* (Belfast, 1908), pp. 7, 11 and 14.
97   Anderson to Whitelegge, 7 June 1907, PRO HO 45/10327/132951, adding that 'the
        work is strenuous and fatiguing and leaves little time for seeking out new
        acquaintances, particularly in a locality where the society available for the woman
        inspector lies chiefly among the wives and daughters of manufacturers, whom official
        duty may compel her to offend'.

Miss Martindale has done excellent work in Ireland, as elsewhere, and her reports ...
have been most valuable. Her position in Ireland is comparable to that of Miss Paterson
in Scotland, but with material differences in that she was not stationed there at her own
request, that she has no home or friends there, and that she has at present none of the
advantages ... which have for some years past been given to Miss Paterson.[98]

The home secretary (Herbert Gladstone) duly accepted that 'the position
of lady factory inspector in Ireland ... should become a full-time appointment of senior rank with a higher salary, clerical assistance and office
facilities', and in December 1907, Martindale was promoted to a senior lady
inspector and set up her office in Donegall St., Belfast.[99] Her promotion has
been seen as serving to reinforce the fundamental role of the lady inspectors
and as 'a prototype for a new organisation of the women's branch'. Martindale's
experience in Ireland, together with that of two other lady inspectors assigned
to 'special districts' in Britain, demonstrated the value of having them, like
their male counterparts, permanently on the scene: 'the inspector's constant
and vigilant presence helped to discourage dangerous and illegal practices,
and even, occasionally, to persuade some employers that they could improve
working conditions and efficiency at the same time'. And 'a concentrated
presence' was necessary if the lady inspectors were to play a more active role
in improving the working conditions of women and children.[100]

Be that as it may, Martindale, with occasional assistance from other lady
inspectors,[101] embarked upon a wide range of activity which could involve
her travelling 10,000 miles in a year.[102] In so doing, she does not appear to
have experienced any particular problems from working 'in concert' with the
men inspectors in Ireland. Although they were to a certain extent covering
the same ground, 'my men colleagues more or less appeared to welcome my
inspections in their districts and put no difficulties in my way'.[103] This was
particularly the case with regard to the south of Ireland:

It could not have been altogether easy for the district inspector ... to have a woman
inspector with perhaps different standards come into his domain, and while she was
there leave the jurisdiction of the acts in certain factories in her hands. [But] Mr
Bellhouse ... seemed to take my advent calmly and without any fuss, and ... made a
long list of factories which he thought it would be very useful if I would visit.... I
found him a pleasant change after some of the district inspectors with whom I had
been obliged to deal and I felt he knew how to play the game.[104]

---

98 Whitelegge to Sir Mackenzie Chalmers (permanent under-sec., home office), 1 July
    1907: ibid.
99 'Report of the factory staff committee 1907', p. 26.
100 McFeely, *Lady inspectors*, pp. 109–11.
101 See e.g. *Chief insp. ann. rep., 1909*, pp. 157 (assistance from Anderson in connection
    with a prosecution 'of some importance') and 177 (Paterson); *1910*, pp. 133–34
    (Whitlock).
102 See e.g. *Chief insp. ann. rep., 1911*, p. 128.
103 Martindale, *From one generation to another*, p. 92.
104 H. Martindale, *Some Victorian portraits and others* (London, 1948), pp. 42–43.

Her working relationships in the north also appeared to be satisfactory:

[C]ertain accidents I do not investigate. I hand them over to the lady inspectors, together with questions relating to children employed half-time. Again, if any complaints were made relating to sanitary accommodation for women or to the employment of women within a month of giving birth ... I should hand them over to the lady inspectors. Otherwise we both deal with everything.... There is undoubtedly overlapping ... but we try to avoid [meeting in the same factory]. The lady inspector notifies me beforehand of the places that she intends to visit, and she also notifies me now of places that she has completed. Unless something very important arises, I generally wait about a month after she has finished an inspection, before I do any further inspection at any given factory or workshop.[105]

But Martindale did encounter a number of difficulties when it came to enforcing the factory acts. Although she had no doubt that the law should be strictly observed in the north, she was not quite so certain about the rest of the island:

According to the requirements of the factory acts no employment should be carried on in a textile factory such as a woollen mill after 1 p.m. on Saturdays. This day being the market day in the town of Galway, the villagers from the neighbouring district came on that day in their little donkey carts in order to do their weekly shopping, and used the opportunity to bring their wool to the mills for carding. It was the custom on arriving to go straight to the mill and leave the wool, and then to return for it during the course of the late afternoon; hence Saturday was a busy day in these mills. It was, of course, my duty to give instructions that this illegal employment much cease; the occupier was very disinclined to make any alterations, and I was left wondering whether the English factory act drawn up to deal with conditions of employment in, for example, a Lancashire cotton mill, quite fitted a little woollen mill in the west of Ireland.[106]

She considered Irish workers to be 'reticent about giving definite information to an inspector, although they were very conscious of grievances'. As word of her work in Ireland spread, however, the number of complaints, at least in the north, 'rose by leaps and bounds'.[107] Many of these complaints were anonymous, for obvious reasons, for they gave graphic descriptions of poor working conditions:

You are defending the outworkers but what about the smoothers and laundry hands that work in some of the laundries in 1st class houses are not fit to work in. I have been working for some time in — smoothing room & it is not fit for any girls to spend their day in the pay is alright but the air is awful no proper ventilation & the foul gas that comes from the irons is terrible.... Spend 10 minutes in this laundry & sweating will not be the word you will use....

105 *Committee of inquiry into the conditions of employment in the linen and other making-up trades of the north of Ireland: Minutes of evidence*, p. 52 [Cd. 6509], H.C. 1912–13, xxiv, 444 (Eraut).
106 *From one generation to another*, pp. 102–03.
107 Ibid., p. 96.

It would do you and the poor workers of this town of B— good if you would kindly give us a call unawares and see for yourself the awful black holes of workrooms we have to try and work in with scarcely any light the very luk of the dungeon would set one blind to say nothing of working in it…. Please say nothing when coming about receiving this letter….

I think you are neglecting your Bussiness do you allowe wemen in there confinement to stand and hold an iron in there hand untill 3 minutes before there time and then go out and come back in the snow in 10 Days as that has been done in Mr. S's….

It would open your eyes to go up there any day at the dinner hour and see the shirt workers and turner outs working away for dear life and carrying big parcels home with them to earn a mere pittance.[108]

Martindale was somewhat nonplussed by the reception given to her by some workers and their employers:

I soon realized that the Irish employer and worker were very different from those to whom I had become accustomed in the Potteries. A government official from England was certainly not regarded in Ireland as a missionary of the state. To many of the employers she was somebody to be received pleasantly, and with a certain amount of blarney; but, if it appeared advisable, misled. To many of the workers she was a person to be treated with some apprehension, since a reputation as an informer was something to be avoided at all costs.[109]

Not surprisingly, she often found it difficult to obtain the evidence necessary for bringing a prosecution:

My arrival at a town or village was at once noted and the news quickly spread. Many of the factories in the country places stood in isolated positions so that my approach was easily watched. Added to the fear of answering the inspector's questions, so often exhibited by the workers, the custom was prevalent among foremen and forewomen of going to a worker soon after I had left, and enquiring as to my questions and the replies given. I was often obliged to speak seriously to those in charge about this as it naturally intimidated the workers.[110]

Nonetheless, she was convinced of the educative value of prosecutions:

In spite of the difficulty of collecting evidence and of making certain that it would be reliable and dependable, I felt that prosecutions helped more than any other method

---

108 Ibid., pp. 98–100 (spelling and grammar as in original). She had earlier reported that 'the fact that thirty-three of the eighty-nine complaints received [in the last year] came from the officers of trades unions, local authorities and philanthropic societies, is … a hopeful sign that public opinion in Ireland is being gradually enlightened, and the importance of industrial legislation is being realised': *Chief insp. ann. rep., 1908*, p. 127.

109 *From one generation to another*, p. 91. Her experience in the Potteries had led her to agree with a newspaper's observation (quoted ibid., p. 86) that 'The woman factory inspector is not a spy, nor a wanton disturber of trade. She is a missionary of the state whose business it is to see that, in the pressure and rush of industry, the human element is not driven to the wall.'

110 Ibid., pp. 106–07.

to stir up public opinion on the need for the provisions of the factory and truck acts. Owing to the number of local newpapers published and read ... and the publicity given in them to the cases taken before the petty sessions, prosecutions certainly helped to spread knowledge of the law.[111]

Like many of the other inspectors in Ireland, she found the outcome of many cases 'disappointing' and 'it was difficult not to be depressed'; but she could still appreciate the peculiar character of summary justice in Ireland:

I am inclined to the opinion that there there were few places [in the early 1900s] ... where such real humour and wit were displayed as in an Irish [magistrates'] court. Meeting once a month in a bare little room, usually in a small townland or country place, they took the place of the present-day cinema as a means of amusement and interest. They were usually crowded, people coming from far and near and making a day of it.[112]

The presence of a lady inspector added to the occasion. One chairman of a 'little country court', having found that the defendant had 'seriously infringed' the law – and then imposed a fine of one shilling – addressed the court as follows: 'Gentlemen, the presence, gentlemen, of a lady in court has given in my opinion a tone to our proceedings'. Martindale records that 'his remark was received with applause and all that was left for me to do was to bow and leave the court with all the dignity I could muster'.[113]

We discuss elsewhere some of Martindale's most pressing concerns as a lady inspector in Ireland, namely ventilation in linen factories and scutch mills, truck, deductions from wages and piece-work particulars and convent laundries.[114] We deal here with two other issues to which she attached particular importance.

TWO PARTICULAR CONCERNS

1. Employment and welfare of children

Given her opinion that 'the illegal employment of children is one of the most pressing matters in Ireland',[115] it is not surprising that their working conditions were a regular feature of Martindale's reports.[116] In 1907, there

---

111 Ibid., pp. 108–09. She herself received praise as a prosecutor: '[She] proved herself a most capable and convincing advocate with a charm of manner sufficient to upset any but the most hardened of solicitors opposed to her': *Lurgan Times*, quoted ibid., p. 109. Cf. McFeely, *Lady inspectors*, p. 106 characterises her approach as 'objective and remote' and 'professional', in contrast to the 'deep personal involvement' of Deane and Squire.

112 *From one generation to another*, p. 109.

113 Ibid. See further below, chap. 10.

114 See below, chaps. 6, 7 and 9 respectively.

115 *Chief insp. ann. rep., 1910*, p. 134.

116 See especially *Chief insp. ann. rep., 1906*, pp. 230–31, *1907*, pp. 178–80 and *1908*, pp. 154–55, summarised in *From one generation to another*, pp. 110–18. The employment of children also concerned the men inspectors – see e.g *Chief insp. ann. rep., 1907*, pp. 131 (Williams) and 132 (McCaghey).

were still 4,075 children employed in textile factories (mainly linen), and a further 120 in non-textile factories and workshops – a higher percentage of the total workforce in Ireland (1.7 per cent) than in England and Wales (0.8 per cent) or Scotland (0.1 per cent).[117]

The debilitating combination of poor housing, inadequate diet and working mothers, compounded by the ill-effects of work from an early age, had been well-documented prior to Martindale's arrival in Ireland.[118] She found that little had changed. Economic circumstances compelled many married women to work, with the result that 'the child was often deprived of a mother's care at a very early age'; the standard of feeding in any case was 'deplorably low'.[119] Accordingly:

[T]he majority of the children came to the mills in a handicapped condition.... Ill-nurtured and insufficiently fed, [they] entered the mill at 12 years of age. The majority of the half-timers, both girls and boys, were employed in the spinning-mills as doffers and cagers. They worked under a doffing mistress whose duty it was, when the bobbins on a spinning frame were full, to blow a whistle, then the spinner stood aside from the frame, and a bevy of little boys and girls rushed to the frame and as rapidly as possible took off the full bobbins, replacing them with empty ones. Their duty then was to place the full bobbins on pins in flat boxes and remove them to a place of safety.[120]

This work was undertaken in rooms where the temperature was between 70° and 80° and the atmosphere saturated with moisture; the noise of the spinning frames was also considerable. These conditions, and the length of the working day,[121] took a significant toll on already vulnerable children,[122] and

---

117 See *Summary of returns of persons employed in 1907 in textile factories*, p. 5 [Cd. 4692], H.C. 1909, lxxix, 856, *in non-textile factories*, p. 10 [Cd. 5398], H.C. 1910, lxxxiii, 799, and *in workshops*, p. 8 [Cd. 5833], H.C. 1911, lxxix, 9. According to Anderson, *Women in the factory*, p. 174: 'Ireland, and particularly Belfast, exceeded all other parts of the United Kingdom in what must be described as exploitation of child labour'.

118 See especially H.S. Purdon, 'Flax and linen' in T. Oliver (ed.), *Dangerous trades: The historical, social and legal aspects of industrial occupations as affecting health, by a number of experts* (London, 1902), pp. 696–701. Dr Purdon had been certifying surgeon for Belfast since 1883. See also P. Horn, *Children's work and welfare, 1780–1880s* (Basingstoke, 1994).

119 *From one generation to another*, pp. 110–11. 'The child during her infancy is put into the charge of an old woman, who "minds" her and feeds her for 2s. 6d. to 3s. 6d. per week. As soon as possible she is sent to school ... [E]ven if the mother returns home for dinner, which I believe in many instances is not the rule, the dinner hours for the mothers and children do not coincide. The natural result is that the child takes "a piece in her hand" to school': *Chief insp. ann. rep., 1906*, p. 230.

120 *From one generation to another*, p. 110. See also D.L. Armstrong, *The growth of industry in Northern Ireland: The story of the golden age of industrial development, 1850–1900* (Long Hanborough, Oxford, 1999), pp. 332–35.

121 'In Belfast the half timers are usually employed on the alternate day system, the hours being 6.30 a.m. to 6 p.m., with three-quarters of an hour for breakfast and dinner. In view of these conditions, it is not surprising to find that the Belfast half-timer is delicate and undersized': *Chief insp. ann. rep., 1906*, p. 230.

122 'Commencing [work] as they do just at the time when all their physical powers are needed for the merging of childhood into adolescence, the strain of the long day in

may have contributed to the fact that the death rate for those aged 5–20 was higher in Belfast than in Manchester.[123] A head teacher, 'who had worked in connection with a half-timers' school for many years ... pathetically remarked to me, as we were standing in a classroom where there were sixty of these children, that, from her previous experience, she would say that comparatively few of them would live to over thirty years of age.'[124]

By law, no child was to be employed in a factory without a 'fitness certificate' from the certifying surgeon for the district to the effect that he was satisfied of the child's age, that he had personally examined the child and that he or she was 'not incapacitated by disease or bodily infirmity for working daily for the time allowed by law in the factory named in the certificate'.[125] An inspector could 'overrule' a certifying surgeon if he or she had 'reasonable cause to believe' that the real age of the child was less than that certified or that the child was incapacitated for work.[126] The procedure for issuing a fitness certificate, which dated back to 1833, had recently been tightened up;[127] nevertheless, few children were rejected by certifying surgeons.[128] Although it had earlier been

the hot and noisy mill or factory leaves them without the reserve of strength necessary to support growth of mind and body': Mrs Dickie, Local Government Board inspector of boarded-out children, quoted by Martindale in *Chief insp. ann. rep., 1908*, p. 154.

123 Belfast Health Commission, *Report to the local government board for Ireland*, p. 2 [Cd. 4128], H.C. 1908, xxxi, 723, quoted by Martindale in *Chief insp. ann. rep., 1908*, p. 154. The death rate for children under five was lower in Belfast. According to Paterson, in *Chief insp. ann. rep., 1907*, p. 178, 'the heat [in the Belfast flax mills] is not so great as in the ring spinning rooms in Lancashire, but the atmosphere is more oppressive and the work seems heavier'.

124 *From one generation to another*, p. 112. But Martindale also observed that 'some of the Belfast schools, with their often small, ill-ventilated, overcrowded, and insufficiently-warmed rooms ... must [be] an important factor in the cause of the high death-rate': *Chief insp. ann. rep., 1908*, p. 154. A separate inquiry cited a school inspector as having stated that 'no other city in the world of the wealth and enterprise of Belfast would tolerate such primitive and unsanitary houses as are many of the Belfast schools': Belfast Health Commission, *Report to the local government board for Ireland 1908*, p. 89.

125 1901 act, s. 64(4). This certificate was not generally required for workshops, but the home secretary could make it obligatory where it appeared 'by reason of special circumstances ... expedient for protecting the health of ... children employed therein': 1901 act, ss. 63 and 66. Where this power was not exercised, there was nothing to stop a child who had been rejected for factory work from finding employment in a workshop.

126 1901 act, ss. 64(4), (9) and 67. In such a case, the child was not to be employed unless or until the certifying surgeon issued a fresh certificate. By s. 122(5), the home secretary could direct a certifying surgeon to re-examine any child.

127 1895 act, s. 46; 1901 act, s. 64.

128 Between 1895 and 1910, the 'rejection' rate in the United Kingdom never exceeded three per cent, and that for Ireland alone tended to be lower. In 1907, for example, 1.7 per cent of the 40,000 children examined by certifying surgeons in England and Wales were rejected, as compared to 1.2 per cent of 5,011 Irish children, while the corresponding figures for 1910 were 3.1 and 1.9 per cent respectively: see *Chief insp. ann. rep., 1900*, p. 520; *1907*, p. 306 and *1910*, p. 226. It seems that the number of under-age children presented for certification had considerably diminished – in

suspected that the medical examination was often 'perfunctory', by 1913 at least, the system of personal examination by certifying surgeons was thought to work satisfactorily in the majority of cases.[129]

Although Martindale occasionally invoked the statutory power to have a child re-examined,[130] her primary concern was the reaction of many parents when a certificate was refused:

> I found that little real care is taken by the mothers of the children rejected to ensure that the ailments for which the children are rejected should have proper treatment. In many cases the mothers send the children to other factories in the blind hope that they may escape detection, and be taken on; or else they make an effort to 'patch up' the children just sufficiently, so that they may pass the examination of the certifying surgeon, and directly this has been done they discontinue any further treatment, feeling that the child is now safely at work, and that they need take no further trouble.[131]

She agreed with Dr Purdon, the certifying surgeon for Belfast, that the certifying surgeon should inspect working children (and young persons) every three months, 'to see what the effect of the work is upon the constitution of those employed. If there are signs of suffering they should cease work'.[132]

Martindale also found that the alternate day system for half-timers was not working satisfactorily.[133] Children employed on this system often performed poorly in school: they 'seemed always tired', 'made little progress' and many left at 14 'still in the third or fourth standard'; conditions in many of the schools were very poor, and the poor quality of much of the teaching blighted the potential of children who were 'naturally quick and intelligent'.[134] But the fundamental problem with child labour was that many parents, as well as employers, encouraged them to work. There was little public

1876, Dr Purdon, certifying surgeon for Belfast, testified that in one six-month period he had rejected nearly two-thirds of the children seen by him: *Factory and workshop commissioners 1876: Minutes of evidence*, p. 841.

129   *Chief insp. ann. rep.*, *1913*, p. 98. Cf. frequent complaints of 'diversity of practice' had been made to the factory and workshop commissioners in 1876 – see *Report*, p. lxix.

130   Normally as a result of her own observations – see *Chief insp. ann. rep.*, *1906*, p. 231. But one particular surgeon apparently certified 'doubtful' children and then informed Martindale so that she could, 'after a few months, if it seems necessary', require them to be re-examined: *Chief insp. ann. rep.*, *1907*, p. 178.

131   *Chief insp. ann. rep.*, *1906*, p. 231. See also *1907*, p. 180.

132   'Flax and linen', p. 700. Purdon was also in favour of restricting the employment of half-timers in machine shops and prohibiting the morning employment of half-timers who 'according to the certifying surgeon appear weakly or not well-developed for their age ... '.

133   This had been the view of the factory and workshop commissioners in 1876: 'the disadvantage of [the alternate day system] is that children are employed at work on the alternate days for a length of time unsuited to their strength, which is not compensated by the comparative rest of the school day... ': *Report*, p. lxi. According to Anderson, *Women in the factory*, p. 165, the whole half-time system 'had begun to be more than suspected as an evil in itself'.

134   *Chief insp. ann. rep.*, *1906*, p. 230 and *1907*, pp. 179–80. See also the similar views expressed by Paterson in *Chief insp. ann. rep.*, *1907*, p. 178 and *1908*, p. 154.

opposition to the practice, and public opinion in Ireland lagged 'far behind' that in Great Britain.[135]

Employers used child labour not just because it was less expensive: 'I became accustomed to being told that it would be useless to employ girls of 17 and 18 years who had not previously worked in a spinning mill as doffers, as they would not put up with the heat and damp, whereas children were eager to work and quick at it, and did not complain of the conditions. They [the employers] maintained that it would ruin the trade if children could not be employed.'[136] Parents sent their children out to work primarily as a result of economic necessity: 'parents, when speaking of a child, dwelt immediately on her earning capacity, as if that were the most important point to be considered'.[137] One of the worst cases she came across was that of a girl aged 12, the eldest child of an unemployed labourer and a sick mother who was unable to work. Although the girl had suffered from abdominal tuberculosis for some three years, she was 'quite anxious to help out' and sought work as a half-timer; when examined by the certifying surgeon, she was found to be 'emaciated, temperature 102 degrees, cough', and was rejected. She died a few weeks later.[138] But the employment of children was 'by no means found only in homes where the family income from other ways is especially low'.[139] Martindale was also concerned about 'the alarming amount spent in drink in some of the homes'; one survey of 43 families showed that there were 23 in which one or both parents were reported as drinkers, and 'it is very unlikely that the money thus spent is less than the wages of the half-timer'.[140]

Such attitudes made it difficult to enforce the law, particularly in country districts.[141] Parents altered birth certificates or produced other false 'proof' that a child had reached the age of 12; baptismal 'certificates', for example, were often written on a sheet of notepaper and signed by a person whose official capacity was not recorded or a genuine certificate for one child might be used for a younger sibling.[142] In one case, Martindale went to court with six certificates – all showing a different age.[143] A prosecution was unusual,

135 *Chief insp. ann. rep., 1908*, p. 154, where she recounts that when she prosecuted a firm in Co. Donegal for employing three girls full-time from the age of 9 or 10, 'it is impossible for me to describe the antagonism aroused in the whole district ... Everyone was against me, and the case was dismissed on a small technical point'.
136 *From one generation to another*, p. 115.
137 Ibid. Martindale explains that 'the wages the children could earn were so high, in proportion to those earned by the women, that the temptation to send their children into the mills was great.'
138 *Chief insp. ann. rep., 1910*, pp. 133–34.
139 *Chief insp. ann. rep., 1907*, p. 179.
140 Ibid. In one case, Martindale was told that the wages of a half-timer 'just paid for her father's tobacco and porter': *Chief insp. ann. rep., 1908*, p. 153.
141 'If a factory is opened in a country district every kind of subterfuge is resorted to so that the children may as young as possible, certainly under the age of 12 or 13 years, be employed full time': *Chief insp. ann. rep., 1907*, p. 179.
142 See *Chief insp. ann. rep., 1907*, p. 180; *1909*, p. 157 and *1910*, p. 133. The charge for a false certificate apparently ranged from 6*d.* to 2*s.* 6*d.*
143 *From one generation to another*, p. 116. The case, which arose from the employment of

however, for Martindale normally preferred to caution the parents 'seriously' and make them destroy the false certificate in her presence. But proceedings were sometimes necessary 'in order to ventilate the matter'.[144]

Martindale concluded that 'until public opinion is roused the children of the Irish industrial classes will remain weakly and undersized, the high death-rate will continue, and the children will grow up as illiterate as their innate brightness and cleverness will allow'.[145] Before she left Ireland, however, she saw some hopeful signs of a change of attitude[146] – and she was later to feel that the information which she had collected on child labour was taken into consideration when the Employment of Women, Young Persons and Children Act 1920 made it unlawful to employ any child under the age of fourteen. When she returned to what was now Northern Ireland in 1924, she found that 'the processes on which I had been repeatedly told only young children could be employed were now being satisfactorily carried on by older workers, and that the trade had not suffered in consequence as had been gloomily foretold'.[147]

2. Women returning to work after childbirth

In 1873, Dr C.D. Purdon, certifying surgeon for Belfast, reported that many working mothers returned to the mill almost immediately after a child was born. His primary concern was not the effect this might have on the mother, but on the newly-born child, and it was for this reason that 'each mother ought not to be allowed to resume work for at least two months after the birth of her child ...'.[148] This opinion was shared by another medical report in the same year which concluded that 'it does not appear to us impracticable, and if practicable, it certainly appears desirable to make some arrangements by which mothers of young infants shall either be employed for half-time, or be excluded for a time from the factories altogether'.[149] But the factory and workshop commissioners, while not wishing to understate the 'evil', considered

    young children in the making of carpets in Co. Donegal, is the one which aroused the antagonism of the whole district – see above, n. 135.
144 Ibid., p. 118.
145 *Chief insp. ann. rep., 1908*, p. 155.
146 In 1909, for example, the General Assembly of the Presbyterian Church 'feel deeply the obligation for the safe-guarding of child life, especially in manufacturing districts [and] recommend that ministers and members of this Church ... endeavour to arouse public opinion in favour of enforcing the law, with a view to the protection both of the children and of the law-abiding employer' – quoted by Martindale in *Chief insp. ann. rep., 1909*, p. 156. Nevertheless, her successors continued to find illegal practices – see e.g. *Chief insp. ann. rep., 1912*, p. 149 and *1913*, p. 98 (Slocock).
147 *From one generation to another*, pp. 118 and 145.
148 *The mortality of flax mill and factory workers* (Belfast, 1873), pp. 8–9. See also M. Neill, 'Women at work in Ulster, 1845–1911' (unpublished Ph.D. thesis, Queen's University Belfast, 1996), pp. 122–30.
149 *Report to the local government board on proposed changes in hours and ages of employment in textile factories, by J.H. Bridges and T. Holmes*, p. 61 [C. 754], H.C. 1873, lv, 863.

a legal prohibition to be impracticable: 'the objections to making the employer responsible appear ... to be insuperable' and it was 'out of the question' to require the factory inspectors to undertake a 'periodic inspection' of adult women. The remedy, they suggested, lay in the provision of 'public nurseries' in factory towns.[150]

Accordingly, no legislative action was forthcoming in the United Kingdom until the matter was taken up at the International Labour Conference in Berlin in 1890.[151] Following a resolution adopted at that conference, the Factory and Workshop Act 1891 provided that 'an occupier of a factory or workshop shall not knowingly allow a woman to be employed therein within four weeks after she has given birth to a child'.[152] Although medical opinion was subsequently in favour of extending this period to three, or even six, months, this was again considered impracticable:

An obvious objection to such further legislation, however desirable it may otherwise be, is that in very numerous cases the existence of very young children makes the earning of wages of vital importance to a mother, even although she often has to pay a considerable part of them to caretakers, who look after babies in a very inadequate manner.... [But] it is, perhaps, possible that the injurious effects of this state of things might to some extent be diminished by the better organisation of a system of creches, or other institution where very small children could be looked after.[153]

'Social and administrative difficulties' were again cited as the reason for retaining the existing law in 1904,[154] and in spite of further calls for extension,[155] four weeks remained the statutory period until well after 1914.

It was natural that enforcement of the new law should be allocated to the newly-appointed lady inspectors, and the home secretary instructed that all communications received by men inspectors on this matter were to be referred to the relevant senior lady inspector for investigation and action.[156] They soon found that 'cases of employment within four weeks of childbirth

---

150 *Report*, pp. lxvii–lxviii. The commissioners were also concerned that a legislative restriction would add 'a new and very powerful motive for concealment of birth ...'.

151 See Hutchins and Harrison, *History of factory legislation*, pp. 270–71.

152 Section 17, re-enacted as section 61 of the 1901 act.

153 *Fifth and final report of the royal commission on labour (pt. 1)*, p. 102 [C. 7421], H.C. 1894, xxxv, 111. By 1902, 'owing to the efforts of Lady Henderson', two creches had been opened in Belfast: see Purdon, 'Flax and linen', p. 701.

154 *Report of the inter-departmental committee on physical deterioration*, pp. 47–50 [Cd. 2175], H.C. 1904, xxxii, 53–56. The committee did not doubt that the employment of mothers 'is attended by evil consequences both to themselves and their children', but concluded that the four-week period could not be extended 'without counter-balancing disadvantages'. The better approach was to strengthen the existing law by reversing the onus of proof on the employer.

155 The National Conference upon Infant Mortality in 1906, for example, recommended extension of the period of absence to three months, and suggested that a medical certificate of fitness should be required for employment during pregnancy – see *Chief insp. ann. rep., 1907*, p. x.

156 See *Chief insp. ann. rep., 1909*, p. 158.

were frequent'[157] – and not least in the north of Ireland, where a legal prohibition introduced with the best of intentions clashed with the harsh reality of poverty which drove mothers, 'torn between their natural duty and the demands of an unnatural and short-sighted system', back into the mills and factories at a time when 'it is desirable that they should ... be freed in favour of an infinitely greater task'.[158]

On her arrival in Ireland, Martindale, who had encountered a similar problem when she worked in the Potteries,[159] found that the employment of married women, particularly in Belfast, was 'rapidly on the increase', largely on account of the lower wages which they were paid.[160] The law was difficult to enforce,[161] in part on account of the fact that many employers took no steps to ensure that it was followed: 'A woman who leaves the factory for a time is re-engaged without any question being asked, and no attempt is made by making use of outside agencies to hear of infringements. In fact it would almost appear as if many employers are not desirous to *know* whether [the law] is observed in their works.'[162] In any event, if the employer did 'know', and was prosecuted, he might well react by summarily dismissing the mother from her employment.[163] Then there was the attitude of many of the women themselves. In one particular case:

The woman ... stoutly denied having any children. On a subsequent visit to her home, I found that she had five children under six years of age.... The woman's husband was a painter by trade, but had been out of work for seven months; thus the woman was practically obliged to work up to the night of her confinement, and,

157 Anderson, *Women in the factory*, p. 152.
158 *Chief insp. ann. rep.*, *1906*, p. 233 (Deane). See generally Anderson, *Women in the factory*, pp. 152–63. Poor law relief, in a workhouse infirmary or otherwise, was available in some cases – see e.g. *Chief insp. ann. rep.*, *1909*, p. 159 (relief in money and kind) – but only for a maximum of fourteen days after the birth.
159 See *Report of the committee on physical deterioration*, appendix V, pp. 47–49 and 'Memorandum [by Anderson] on the employment of mothers in factories and workshops', ibid., pp. 118–29. However, Martindale (quoted ibid.) was impressed by 'the universal preference amongst the women for factory over domestic life, and how depressed and out of health they became if they were obliged to remain at home'.
160 *Chief insp. ann. rep.*, *1906*, p. 235. Other reasons were the high rate of adult male unemployment and the fact that, having worked in mills and factories from an early age, many women were 'entirely unfamiliar' with cooking, housework and the rearing of children.
161 It appears that only six prosecutions were brought during the period 1891–1904 – see *Report of the committee on physical deterioration: Anderson memorandum*, pp. 116–17.
162 *From one generation to another*, p. 120. Cf. 'section 17 [of the 1891 act], although of so great importance to the community no less than the individual, must remain for the most part a dead letter owing to the difficulty of proving the employer's knowledge of all the circumstances': *Chief insp. ann. rep.*, *1897*, p. 107 (Squire).
163 The first prosecution under the 1891 act, which was not brought until 1897, concerned a Yorkshire employer who sent for an unmarried mother to return to work, even though he knew that her child was only nine days old; the employer was convicted – and promptly dismissed the mother. Fortunately, she obtained employment soon afterwards from one of the magistrates who heard the case: *Chief insp. ann. rep.*, *1897*, p. 96 (Squire).

although she was aware of the law, she returned to work at the end of two weeks, in spite of being weak and unfit for work, rather than see her children starve.[164]

In spite of Martindale's sympathy for such women – 'With no maternity benefit available in those days, could she have done anything else?' – the law had still to be enforced. But how was she to obtain the necessary evidence on a systematic basis? One obvious source, the local maternity hospitals, proved uncooperative: 'I have received from matrons of hospitals and officials in public and private institutions much valuable information with regard to the ill-health resulting from such illegal employment, and all have deplored the prevalence of it, and yet a reluctance has been shown in giving me actual data – names and addresses of women or names of the factories where the infringements occur.'[165] Accordingly she was compelled to rely mainly on complaints from sympathetic persons and anonymous informers – and on voluntary action by more benevolent employers.

What was really required was action on a more general scale. In 1908 the Belfast Health Commission had suggested that 'it would be a great advantage if employers could facilitate the provision of assistance during the forced period of unemployment in such cases by means of organised sick funds or loans repaid by small instalments from wages'[166] – but there is no evidence that any such arrangements were made. Some 'modest' maternity relief was provided by the National Insurance Act 1911;[167] but more generous financial and other support for working mothers was not achieved until much later.

ENVOI

At the end of her period in Ireland, Martindale felt that there had undoubtedly been 'an onward move to greater industrial well-being'; many improvements in the working conditions of women and children had been made, and there was an evident desire to see this trend continue. Nevertheless, she felt obliged to list a number of 'voluntary' welfare measures, above and beyond the existing requirements of the factory acts, which some progressive factories had already taken and which she hoped 'would be imitated and carried out in the Irish industries'[168] – the introduction of an eight-hour day, regular chemical analyses of workroom air, the appointment of an inspector

---

164 *From one generation to another*, pp. 119–20. See also *Chief insp. ann. rep., 1906*, p. 236 (mother of new-born child absent from work for only four days).

165 *Chief insp. ann. rep., 1906*, p. 236. The position should have improved after the Notification of Births Act 1907, which enabled local authorities to require births to be reported to the medical officer of health.

166 *Report to the local government board for Ireland 1908*, p. 96. See also *Chief insp. ann. rep., 1909*, p. 159 (Anderson).

167 *From one generation to another*, p. 121.

168 Ibid., pp. 140 and 143–44.

of machinery guards, daily visits to the factory by a medical practitioner, the formation of sick clubs and the appointment of 'an educated and highly trained woman' as labour manager. She was even able to cite a precedent:

It was cheering ... after a close inspection of a mill where over 1,500 women and children were employed, to receive a visit from the managing director, and to learn from him that he had been so impressed by the various irregularities which my visit had brought to light, that he had decided to appoint an educated woman, trained in hygiene and health questions, to give her whole time to seeing that the requirements of the factory act were carried out in his works in every respect.[169]

But this was an unusual experience, and it is more realistic to suggest that her achievements, while not insignificant, were nonetheless fairly modest:

In the best progressive spirit, [Martindale] based her optimism on a sense that people had become conscious of industrial problems and their social cost. Yet the record suggests that even when cases were prosecuted successfully, the fines were too small to offer real dissuasive power, and the impossibility of maintaining frequent, recurring inspections and enforcement reduced the effectiveness of the law substantially. Determined employers simply wrote off the fines as an inevitable business expense, which in the long run proved to be cheaper than meeting legal requirements. The end results of Martindale's dramatic and vigorous court-room activity largely repeated the ambivalent achievements of Deane's and Squire's often frustrating efforts.[170]

169 Ibid., p. 120. This appears to refer to the 'interesting experiment' reported in *Chief insp. ann. rep., 1907*, p. 188, where Martindale explains that the woman's duties were 'to supervise the health conditions under which the work was carried on, namely ventilation, temperature, humidity, cleanliness, etc.; to undertake also the registration of all home office requirements, the passing of the children by the certifying surgeon, the supervision of dining room and catering arrangements and occasional visiting of cases of distress.' A similar arrangement had also been made in another large factory.
170 McFeely, *Lady inspectors*, p. 106.

CHAPTER FIVE

The safety of linen workers

THE DEVELOPMENT OF THE LAW PRIOR TO 1878

As early as 1833 it was accepted that the danger of accidental injury or death was 'one of the great evils to which people employed in [textile] factories are exposed'.[1] Although the early linen mills in Ireland do not appear to have been particularly dangerous places,[2] the mechanisation of the spinning process in the 1820s and of weaving in the 1850s undoubtedly increased the risk to workers of all ages, particularly as technological developments produced more complex machinery operating at higher speeds.[3] Other industrial workers, and not just those in textile factories, found themselves in much the same position, with the result that safety provisions designed to prevent – or at least to reduce the incidence of – industrial accidents became an increasingly important aspect of the factory acts. It is with the development and application of these provisions in the context of the linen industry in Ireland that this chapter is primarily concerned.

The first factory commissioners accepted that some accidents were the result of 'culpable heedlessness or temerity' by the workers themselves; but most were not. The problem was essentially one of good management, advised and directed by the factory inspectors. But 'we apprehend that no inspector would probably be so fully conversant with all the uses of every variety of machinery as to be acquainted with all the dangers which may be provided against', and in any case 'there is much that could not be made entirely safe without the reconstruction of whole manufactories'. Accordingly, it was also desirable to encourage higher standards by imposing 'pecuniary consequences' if the employers failed to take all necessary precautions:

---

1 *First report of the central board of His Majesty's commissioners appointed to collect information in the manufacturing districts, relative to the employment of children in factories ...*, p. 31, H.C. 1833 (450), xx, 31. See further D.S. Greer, '"A false, mawkish and mongrel sense of humanity"? The early history of employers' liability in Ireland', in O. Breen, J. Casey and A. Kerr (ed.), *Liber memorialis Professor James C. Brady* (Dublin, 2001), p. 227.

2 Ten mills employing more than 3,000 workers had apparently experienced only one fatal accident and a few serious injuries in recent years: ibid., *Appendix A.1: Reports of examinations taken before Mr Stuart*, pp. 127–34, and *Appendix A.2: Evidence taken by Mr Mackintosh*, pp. 89–93. Cf. P.W.J. Bartrip and S.B.Burman, *The wounded soldiers of industry: Industrial compensation policy 1833–1897* (Oxford, 1983), p. 14, referring to the cotton industry in England, say that 'the available data are capable of manipulation to demonstrate that industrial injury constituted either a major or minor hazard'.

3 See e.g. W.A. McCutcheon, *The industrial archaeology of Northern Ireland* (Belfast, 1980), pp. 296–317 and below Plates 8 and 9.

It is ... the proprietor of the machinery who has the most effectual means of guarding against the dangers attendant upon its use.... [He] is necessarily the person who can best foresee all the consequences incidental to its use, and can best guard against them. By throwing upon him a portion of the pecuniary responsibility for those mischiefs, we combine interest with duty, and add to the efficiency of both.[4]

To this end, the factory owners should be obliged to pay compensation, to the extent of medical expenses and half wages during the period of incapacity, to children under 14 in the case of all accidental injuries, and to adults in the case of injuries which did not result from their own 'culpable temerity'.[5]

Such thinking, which in the twentieth century led market economists to propound a theory of 'general deterrence' for the prevention of accidents,[6] was far too radical for the government of the day, which claimed that the employer's liability at common law was adequate security against carelessness on his part. Although this was an exceedingly optimistic interpretation of the common law,[7] the bill which became the Factories Act 1833 contained no safety or compensation provision of any kind. The newly-appointed factory inspectors nevertheless drew attention to the number and severity of accidents in the factories which they inspected,[8] and as a result, the matter was again considered in 1840. A select committee chaired by Lord Ashley, largely eschewing a 'pecuniary consequences' approach, now recommended the enactment of a number of specific 'safety' provisions to be enforced by the inspectorate.[9] These recommendations were duly implemented by the Factories Act 1844, which set the pattern of statutory provision for the next seventy years or more.[10]

The act first required the fencing of certain 'dangerous' machinery. Every part of a steam engine or water wheel, every fly-wheel 'directly connected with the steam engine or ... other mechanical power', every hoist or teagle 'near to which children or young persons are liable to pass or be employed'

---

4 *First report of the factory commissioners 1833*, p. 73.
5 Ibid., on the grounds that 'an allowance of full wages would occasion considerable fraud in the protraction of that period [of incapacity], especially in the cases of accidents of a less serious nature'.
6 See e.g. G. Calabresi, *The costs of accidents* (New Haven, Conn., 1970), as explained and criticised in P.S. Atiyah, *Accidents, compensation and the law*, ed. P. Cane (6th ed., London, 1999), pp. 374–92.
7 See e.g. Greer, 'Early history of employers' liability in Ireland', pp. 229–34.
8 See *Special reports of inspectors of factories on the practicability of legislative interference to diminish the frequency of accidents to children and young persons employed in factories, arising from machinery being cleaned when in motion, and from being left unguarded*, H.C. 1841 (311), x, 199.
9 *Final report from the select committee appointed to inquire into the operation of the act for the regulation of mills and factories*, pp. 25–28, H.C. 1841 (56), ix, 587–90. With reference to the controversy which arose in the 1850s (see below, p. 126), it should be noted that the committee specifically recommended that shafts and gearing should be fenced or boxed off 'to the height of at least seven feet from the floor'.
10 For a useful summary, see W.B. Lauder, 'Safety', in 'Review of the work of the inspectorate, 1833–1932', published in *Chief insp. ann. rep., 1933*, p. 26.

and all parts of the mill-gearing 'shall be securely fenced', and that fencing 'shall not be removed while the parts required to be fenced are in motion ... for any manufacturing process'.[11] Where an inspector considered that any other unfenced machinery was likely to cause bodily injury to a worker, he could give written notice to the employer requiring him to erect appropriate fencing. The employer could either agree to do so, or 'appeal' to two arbitrators 'skilled in the construction of [that] kind of machinery'. If they were of the opinion that it was 'unnecessary or impossible' to fence the machinery, the inspector cancelled the notice; but if they agreed with the inspector, the employer was bound to fence the machinery in question.[12]

The second form of safety provision in the act imposed restrictions on the cleaning of certain machinery: 'No child or young person shall be allowed to clean any part of the mill-gearing in a factory while the same is in motion for the purpose of propelling any part of the manufacturing machinery ...'.[13] The third and final strategy was to require the occupier of a factory to report to the certifying surgeon within twenty-four hours any accident which caused any bodily injury sufficient to prevent the injured worker from returning to work before 9 a.m. on the morning after the accident. The certifying surgeon was to notify the local factory inspector and 'with the least possible delay' conduct a 'full investigation' into the cause of the accident and the nature of the injury. The results of this investigation were given to the inspector, not just for general consideration, but also to decide whether he should seek the home secretary's authority to bring a civil action for the recovery of damages 'in the name and on behalf of' the injured person.[14]

Breach of these safety provisions made the factory owner liable to a fine in the ordinary way.[15] But if a worker suffered injury as a result of the employer's failure to fence a dangerous machine, special provision was made for 'penal compensation' in the form of an enhanced fine of not less than £10 and not more than £100, 'the whole or any part of [which] ... may be applied for the benefit of the injured person, or otherwise as the Secretary of State shall determine'.[16]

By the early 1850s, accidents of one kind or another would have been fairly common in the Irish linen mills, particularly in the machine hackling and carding rooms.[17] But it was accidents caused by overhead horizontal shafts which became the focus for the fencing 'controversy' which arose at

11 Section 21.
12 Section 43.
13 Section 20. Nor was a child or young person to work 'between the fixed and traversing part of any self-acting machine while [it] is in motion ...'.
14 Sections 22–25.
15 The maximum fine for not fencing dangerous machinery was £20: section 59.
16 Section 60. Such compensation was not payable in a case of instantaneous death – see Bartrip and Burman, *Wounded soldiers of industry*, p. 60.
17 See especially D.L. Armstrong, 'Social and economic conditions in the Belfast linen industry, 1850–1900' in *IHS*, 7 (1950–51), 235 at p. 254.

this time.[18] As we have seen, the 1844 act provided that 'all' parts of the mill-gearing were to be securely fenced. The inspectors, however, initially required employers to fence only those parts of the mill-gearing which were within reach of the workers – that is, within seven feet of the factory floor.[19] In January 1854, however, the inspectors changed course – apparently under pressure from a home secretary (Palmerston) concerned by the high number of factory accidents – and issued a circular requiring all overhead shafts to be fenced.[20] The occupiers demurred, contending that it was not necessary to fence shafts which were normally out of the reach of the operatives. The inspectors replied that many accidents had been caused by unfenced over-head shafts in the course of whitewashing walls or ceilings or when oiling coupling or gearing. But a deputation (which included three Irish MPs)[21] representing the textile owners persuaded Palmerston that the inspectors had gone too far, and an amended circular was issued in March 1854.

It was at this point that the issue came before the courts in Ireland. In *Darkin v. Herdman's of Sion Mills*[22] the owners had failed to ensure that a horizontal shaft (part of the mill-gearing) more than seven feet above the floor was securely fenced. There was a ladder up to the shaft 'which was left there for the purpose of bringing [certain workers] within arm range to adjust the straps and oil the journals'. In the summer of 1854 a boy worker aged 13 climbed the ladder and was injured by the unfenced shaft. The owners were prosecuted by sub-inspector Darkin, convicted and fined £10. But the conviction was reversed on appeal, when a number of prosecution witnesses (including the injured boy himself) patently changed their testimony in the owner's favour.[23] Nevertheless, the prosecution seems to have been successful in the longer run: 'since the decision all the shafts in the factory have been fenced'.[24]

The controversy over the true scope of the 1844 act continued in 1855, particularly when the court of queen's bench in England, in the well-known case of *Doel v. Sheppard and Others*,[25] came down in favour of the inspectors.

18 See generally *Insp. half-yearly rep., April 1854*, p. 48; *April 1855*, p. 48; *Oct. 1855*, p. 106 and *April 1856*, p. 3; H. Martineau, *The factory controversy* (Nat'l Ass'n of Factory Occupiers, Manchester, 1855); Bartrip and Burman, *Wounded soldiers of industry*, pp. 63–66; R. Dickson, 'Legal aspects of the Factory Act of 1856', in *J. Legal Hist.*, 2 (1981), 276.
19 See *Insp. half-yearly rep., April 1854*, p. 50.
20 Reproduced ibid., p. 55. See also 'Memorandum to the home office on fencing securely horizontal shafts in factories, 24 Feb. 1854', PRO HO45/5209.
21 J.J. Richardson (MP for Lisburn and a member of a well-known linen family), W. Kirk (MP for Newry and a linen merchant) and V. Scully (Liberal member for Cork and a QC).
22 A full report of the case is given in *Insp. half-yearly rep., Oct. 1854*, pp. 29–39.
23 The injured boy was one of seven members of the same family employed by Herdman's and, as counsel for Darkin observed, 'A manager can easily discharge factory operatives ...'. At one stage in the proceedings, the assistant barrister is reported to have said: 'I will commit these boys to bridewell: it is a disgusting exhibition': ibid., pp. 33 and 36.
24 Ibid, p. 39 (Howell).
25 (1856) 5 El & Bl 856, 119 Eng Rep 700.

The textile employers had by now formed the National Association of Factory Occupiers to campaign against this particular fencing requirement – and the factory acts in general. In March 1855, the linen manufacturers of Belfast joined this association,[26] which proceeded to promote a bill designed to limit the scope of the 1844 act. This bill was, not unexpectedly, supported by several Irish MPs on behalf of the linen owners;[27] it was strongly opposed by (amongst others) Col. F.P. Dunne (MP for Portarlington), who believed 'the measure to be the prelude to an attempt to get rid of the factory laws altogether …'.[28] But, crucially perhaps, it met with the 'entire approbation' of Lord Campbell CJ[29] and, perhaps for this reason, ultimately excited relatively little political interest. The Factory Act 1856,[30] which represents the only serious 'reverse' in the onward march of factory legislation, overruled *Doel* v. *Sheppard* by restricting the obligation to fence mill-gearing to such parts 'with which children and young persons and women are liable to come in contact, either in passing or in their ordinary occupation'.[31] Other transmission machinery was to be fenced only if the inspector gave notice of danger to the employer, who could then take the matter to arbitration under the 1844 act.

The inspectors were disappointed that 'protection has been withdrawn from those who may be obliged, in the execution of special orders, … to place themselves in positions of danger, of the existence of which they are not conscious, and from which, by reason of their ignorance, they are unable to protect themselves'.[32] They were also critical of the arbitration provisions of the act, as was exemplified by their reaction to the Irish case of *MacCracken* v. *Dargan and Haughton*,[33] in which a plaintiff, injured while putting a belt on an unfenced shaft situated some nine feet above the floor, was awarded damages of £200:

26 Armstrong, 'Social and economic conditions', p. 257, citing *Belfast News-Letter*, 19 March 1855.
27 Including two of the MPs in the owners' deputation which met Palmerston in 1854 – see *Hansard 3*, cxl, 1673 (3 March 1856) (Kirk) and cxli, 444 (Richardson). Richardson even went so far as to suggest that the bill 'would give increased security to the operatives'.
28 *Hansard 3*, cxli, 377 and 443 (3 and 4 April 1856).
29 *Hansard 3*, cxlii, 1671 (19 June 1856). The judge, who had presided in *Doel* v. *Sheppard*, explained that he did not believe that the interpretation of section 21 given by the court 'was the meaning of the framers of the [1844] act'.
30 19 & 20 Vict., c 38.
31 1856 act, s. 4. Section 21 of the 1844 act had always contained this qualification with respect to steam-engines, water wheels, hoists and teagles.
32 *Insp. half-yearly rep., Oct. 1856*, pp. 5–7. Although the arbitrator was to be 'skilled in the construction of the kind of machinery' in question, the inspectors had no confidence that he would have personal knowledge of the ways in which accidents occurred: 'This is in reality a question which requires for its solution, not the opinion of professional engineers, but the evidence of intelligent and observant men who are daily employed in factories'. The engineers employed as arbitrators were also likely to be biased in favour of the occupiers, 'who are their customers'.
33 Ibid., p. 3.

If an inspector should unwarily give rise to an arbitration under the Factory Act of 1856, and if the arbitrators ... should be of opinion that [the machinery] was from its position harmless ... and need not be fenced, and if a young person should afterwards ... suffer a similar injury to that of the plaintiff MacCracken ... from such machinery remaining unfenced ... we apprehend that the formal though extra-judicial award of two arbitrators ... would materially damage the plaintiff's case before a jury, if not destroy his right of action altogether.[34]

As a result of this apprehension, the inspectors 'refrained' from sending 'danger' notices to wayward employers,[35] leaving themselves in turn open to the justified criticism that if they 'purposely abstained' from giving notice that machinery was dangerous and an accident then occurred, 'it might be not unreasonably argued on behalf of the defendant that it was not deemed to be dangerous by the inspector'.[36]

The adverse impact of the 1856 act should not, however, be exaggerated; women, young persons and children, who in Ireland as in England accounted for the large majority of those working in textile factories, were still generally protected.[37] Perhaps because of this, Howell was able to report considerable progress in 1857:

I am happy to be able to state that in the important manufacturing district of the north of Ireland ... considerable progress has been willingly made in fencing horizontal shafts for the prevention of accidents to workpeople.... Mr Darkin reports that of 96 factories recently visited by him, 42 are either completely fenced (by which is meant that all the shafts are guarded in some way or other, mostly by rectangular hooks), or are promised to be completely fenced, and the fencing is in progress; 53 have the shafts in the spinning rooms fenced, and in some few cases there are partial attempts at fencing elsewhere than in the spinning rooms; and in one case only is the occupier indisposed to add to the three rectangular hooks already fixed in his factory. This forms an instructive commentary on the objections of some factory occupiers in other districts.[38]

But just how dangerous were the mills and factories of mid-Victorian Ireland? From 1845, the factory inspectors' reports included a summary of the accidents reported to them by the certifying surgeons. Unfortunately, these returns do not give separate figures for Ireland, and the best we can do is to assume that the rate of reported accidents in proportion to the working population was at that time roughly similar throughout the United Kingdom (and that the inaccuracies in the reporting of the number of 'protected' workers were equally consistent). On this tenuous basis, Table 5.1 provides

34   Ibid., p. 4.
35   Ibid., p. 7.
36   H. Waddington (under-sec., home office) to HM factory inspectors, 31 Jan. 1857, PRO LAB 15/4.
37   Bartrip and Burman, *Wounded soldiers of industry*, p. 66, note that the act of 1856 only meant a return to the practice followed between 1844 and 1853, and that the number killed or injured by overhead shafts was 'relatively small'.
38   *Insp. half-yearly rep., April 1857*, p. 47.

an estimate of the position before and after the ambit of the factory acts was extended beyond textile factories in the 1860s.

Table 5.1: *Estimated number of accidents in textile factories in Ireland, 1856 and 1870*[39]

	1856	1870
No. of workers		
– United Kingdom	682,497	2,540,789
– Ireland	32,988	123,890
– Ireland as % of UK	4.8%	4.9%
No. of reported accidents in United Kingdom causing		
– death	50	373
– amputation of limb	536	1,470
– other injury	3,343	16,744
– total	3,929	18,587
Estimated no. of accidents in Ireland causing		
– death	2–3	18
– amputation of limb	26	72
– other injury	160	821
– total	189	911

The earlier figure roughly tallies with Baker's estimate in 1860 that the accident rate during the past six months had been one for every 389 workers in flax, which suggests that the 28,753 workers in the Irish flax factories in 1856 would have sustained about 150 accidents during the course of that year.[40] If these figures seem somewhat lower than might have been expected, it should be remembered that many accidents were probably not reported; nevertheless, it may still be the case that the factories of this period were not as dangerous as they are sometimes portrayed.

Were women and children at particular risk of accidental injury? Once again we do not have separate figures for Ireland, but the answer for the

39   The number of workers is taken from *Returns of the number of cotton, woollen, worsted, flax and silk factories, etc.*, H.C. 1857 (7, sess. 1), xiv, 173 and *Return of the number of manufacturing establishments … regulated by act of parliament, etc.*, H.C. 1871 (440), lxii, 105; the number of accidents is derived from *Insp. half-yearly rep., Apr. 1856*, p. 6 and *Oct. 1856*, p. 21 and *Apr. 1870*, p. 4 and *Oct. 1870*, p. 4. 'Other injury' consists of a fracture or injuries to the head or face, lacerations, contusions and other minor injuries.

40   See *Insp. half-yearly rep., Apr. 1860*, p. 53. The equivalent rate for cotton was 1:261 and for wool 1:348, making flax the safest of the three. It should, however, be noted that these figures relate to his whole district, and not just to Ireland.

United Kingdom as a whole would appear to be 'no' in the case of women, and 'possibly' in the case of children. It appears to have been young male workers who were at greatest risk proportionate to their percentage of the workforce.

Table 5.2: *Death and injury rates in United Kingdom*
textile factories, c. 1856[41]

	Males over 18	*Males 13–18*	*Females over 13*	*Children under 13*
% of workforce	25.8	10.3	56.2	7.7
% of deaths	46	25	22	8
% of amputations	18	26	47	10
% of other injuries	19	26	46	9

The factory inspectors in Ireland apparently did not consider that the incidence of accidental death and injury required strong action in terms of prosecutions under the 1844 act. The first 'safety' prosecution in Ireland does not appear to have been taken until 1854,[42] and between then and 1878, there appear to have been only three other prosecutions for failure to fence mill-gearing or other machinery,[43] one for allowing a young person to clean a machine while in motion[44] and only six for failing to report an accident.[45] The number of prosecutions seems unreasonably low and suggests that the 1844 act was not adequately enforced in Ireland.[46] But the

41 Figures derived from returns cited above, n. 39. Seperate figures are not given for females aged 13–18.

42 *Darkin v. Herdman's of Sion Mills* – see above, p. 126.

43 *Darkin v. James Kennedy & Son* (Belfast flax-spinners), *Insp. half-yearly rep., Apr. 1856*, p. 28 (failing to fence horizontal shaft nine feet above floor, whereby young person lost his arm; case dismissed on grounds that summons not preferred within two months as required by 1844 act, s. 44); *Steen v. Nicholas Kenny* (mill-owner, Carrick-on-Suir), *Insp. half-yearly rep., Apr. 1859*, p. 48 (failing to fence mill-gearing, whereby young person injured; fined £10); *Cramp v. Robert Rowan & Co.* (hemp-spinners, Belfast), *Insp. half-yearly rep., Oct. 1873*, p. 146 (failing to fence fly-wheel and other parts of steam-engine – fined £5).

44 *Steen v. Bridget Jordan* (operative mule spinner, Greenmount Cotton Co., Dublin), *Insp. half-yearly rep., Oct. 1856*, p. 62 (allowing young person to work between fixed and traversing parts of self-acting machine negligently set in motion by the defendant, killing the young person; fined £2).

45 *Darkin v. Francis Ritchie & Sons* (felt manufacturer, Belfast), *Insp. half-yearly rep., Oct. 1856*, p. 59 (case dismissed – premises not a 'factory'); *Darkin v. Foster Connor* (power loom weaver, Belfast), *Insp. half-yearly rep., Apr. 1857*, p. 59 (fined £2); *Darkin v. Francis Ritchie & Sons*, ibid., p. 60 (case dismissed – still not a 'factory'); *Darkin v. James Kennedy & Sons* (flax-spinners, Belfast), *Insp. half-yearly rep., Apr. 1858*, p. 31 (fined £2); *Darkin v. Brookfield & Doagh Spinning Co., Insp. half-yearly rep., Oct. 1858*, p. 73 (fined £2); *Bignold v. James Haigh* (Dublin ironfounder), *Insp. half-yearly rep., Apr. 1870*, p. 87 (fined £2).

46 Cf. Darkin claimed to have succeeded 'in obtaining the fencing of machinery without resorting to penalties to an extent which is unknown elsewhere': Darkin to Sir George Grey (home sec.), 12 May 1862 (PRO HO45/6968).

inspectors may, of course, have achieved many necessary improvements by encouragement and advice, or by the threat of prosecution. And it may be that prosecutions in Ireland were infrequent as a result of the practical difficulties encountered by sub-inspector Darkin in his proceedings against Herdman's of Sion Mills.[47]

THE DEVELOPMENT OF THE LAW, 1878–1914

In their review of the law in 1876, the factory and workshop commissioners devoted less than one page to the question of safety.[48] The provisions of the 1844 act had worked well, and 'in view of the frightful number of accidents reported every year, it cannot be said that they are too stringent'. On the contrary, the restrictions which had been enacted twenty years earlier were inappropriate, given the ample evidence that 'the danger, even to young persons and children, is not limited to those parts of the machinery with which they may be thought ... "liable to come in contact". We conceive that the principle of protection against accident ... may be considered to extend to all dangerous machinery, and that the limitation contained in the act of 1856 ought therefore to be repealed'.

Section 5(3) of the 1878 act, however, provided only that 'every part of the mill-gearing shall either be securely fenced or be in such position or of such construction as to be equally safe to every person employed in the factory as it would be if it were securely fenced.'[49] An employer could still argue that unfenced machinery was safe because it was out of normal reach of the workforce, or because he had given safety instructions to his workers or put up warning notices.

With regard to other dangerous machinery, the act continued the cumbersome 'notice and arbitration' procedure,[50] which does not appear ever to have been invoked in Ireland. It was finally superseded in 1891, when 'other' dangerous machinery was brought within section 5(3) of the 1878 act, so that 'all [other] dangerous parts of the machinery', as well as 'every part of the mill gearing' were now to be securely fenced, or at least to be in such position or of such construction as to be equally safe as if securely fenced.[51] The question whether machinery other than mill-gearing was 'dangerous' now became a matter for the courts and, somewhat surprisingly,

47 See above, p. 126.
48 *Report of the commissioners appointed to inquire into the working of the factory and workshops acts with a view to their consolidation and amendment*, pp. lxxv–lxxvi [C. 1443], H.C. 1876, xxix, 75–76.
49 Mill-gearing is defined in s. 96 as meaning 'every shaft, whether upright, oblique, or horizontal, and every wheel, drum, or pulley by which the motion of the first moving power is communicated to any machine appertaining to a manufacturing process'.
50 1878 act, s. 6.
51 1891 act, s. 6(2). This general fencing provision, as amended, was re-enacted as section 10(1)(c) of the 1901 act.

the courts responded generously from the workers' point of view. In particular the queen's bench division in England held in *Hindle v. Birtwhistle*[52] that the requirement to fence applied to all machinery from which, in the ordinary course of working, danger might reasonably be anticipated. In the Irish case of *Bermingham v. O'Reilly*,[53] a young girl employed in a box factory in Dublin was awarded damages of £50 when injured by the blade of a cutting knife operated by a treadle; neither the blade nor the treadle was protected in any way, and Kenny J. held that both were 'dangerous parts' which should have been 'securely' fenced.

During the 1890s, the safety provisions of the factory acts were considerably extended in other ways. In particular, the home secretary was given the power to certify that any machinery in a particular factory or workshop was 'dangerous or injurious to health or dangerous to life or limb, either generally or in the case of women, children or any other class of persons ...'; in such cases, he could require the adoption of such special rules or measures as appeared to the chief inspector to be reasonably practicable and to meet the exigencies of the situation.[54] This power was subject to arbitration – and was initially limited to individual factories and workshops. But in 1901 the provision was extended to enable the home secretary to issue special regulations to be observed in specified classes of factory or workshop. As we shall see in the following chapter, this power was specifically used to safeguard the health of linen workers. But in respect of their safety, the only use of the power appears to have been to supplement the requirement, first introduced in 1895 in response to a large number of 'melancholy' accidents,[55] that in all new factories 'the traversing carriage of any self-acting machine shall not be allowed to run out within a distance of 18 inches from any fixed structure not being part of the machine, if the space over which it so runs is a space over which a person is liable to pass, whether in the course of his employment or otherwise'.[56] In 1905, the home secretary certified that these self-acting mules were dangerous to life and limb, and issued regulations which provided (*inter alia*) that six specified parts of such machinery 'shall be securely fenced as far as is reasonably practicable' – unless, again, it could be shown that by their position or construction they were 'equally safe to every person employed as they would be if securely fenced'.[57]

---

52 [1897] 1 QB 192 – see further below, p. 155. See also *Redgrave v. Lloyd* [1895] 1 QB 95 ('machinery' includes all the operative machinery in a factory).

53 (1903) 3 NIJR 116.

54 1891 act, ss. 8–11.

55 *Hansard 4*, xxxi, 169 (1 March 1895)(Asquith, home sec.).

56 1895 act, s. 9, which also provided that no worker was allowed to be in the space between the fixed and the traversing portions of such machinery 'unless the machine is stopped with the transverse portion on the outward run ...'. This provision was substantially re-enacted as section 12 of the 1901 act – but with exceptions in the case of cotton or woollen spinning machines.

57 Regulations for the process of spinning by self-acting mules (1905 No. 1103), reg. 3. By reg. 4, the minder of a self-acting mule was required to take all reasonable care,

From 1895 a magistrates' court which, on complaint by an inspector, was satisfied that any manufacturing process or handicraft could not be carried on without danger to health or to life or limb, was authorised to prohibit all or part of a place from being used as a factory or workshop until such works had been executed as were in the opinion of the court necessary to remove the danger.[58] In addition, 'on being satisfied that any machine ... is in such a condition that it cannot be used without danger to life or limb', the court could prohibit a particular machine from being used at all, or until it was duly repaired or altered.[59] Indeed, where satisfied that the use of a machine involved *imminent* danger to life, the court on application by an inspector could make an interim order prohibiting either absolutely or subject to conditions the use of that machine until the earliest opportunity for hearing and determining the complaint. All these provisions were substantially re-enacted in 1901, but appear to have been seldom invoked in practice.[60]

Finally we may note briefly that the prohibition on the cleaning of machinery in motion introduced by the 1844 act was gradually extended in 1878 and thereafter.[61] The most extensive prohibition applied to children – in its final form,[62] no child was allowed to clean any part of any machinery or, with the exception of overhead mill-gearing, any place under any machinery, while it was in motion. Less extensive protection was afforded young persons and women; no young person was allowed to clean any *dangerous* part of machinery while it was in motion, and no woman or young person was allowed to clean mill-gearing while it was in motion for the purpose of propelling any part of the manufacturing machinery.[63]

THE GENERAL OPERATION OF THE SAFETY PROVISIONS IN IRELAND

In Ireland, as elsewhere in the United Kingdom, the single most common cause of all industrial accidents was machinery moved by mechanical power.[64] Accordingly, as the linen industry became ever more mechanised, so the risk of accidental death and injury likewise increased:

while the machine was in motion, to ensure that no child cleaned it and that no woman, young person, or child worked between its fixed and traversing parts.

58 1895 act, s. 2; 1901 act, s. 18. After 1891, all new factories were also to be provided with 'such means of escape in case of fire ... as can reasonably be required under the circumstances of each case': 1891 act, s. 7; 1901 act, s.14.

59 1895 act, s. 4; 1901 act, s. 17.

60 But see *Chief insp. ann. rep., 1907*, p. 318 (two factories in Ireland required by court to fence machinery).

61 1878 act, s. 9; 1895 act, s. 8.

62 1901 act, s. 13(1).

63 1901 act, s. 13(2)-(4). But for this purpose, 'such parts of the machinery shall, unless the contrary is proved, be presumed to be dangerous as are so notified by an inspector to the occupier of the factory': ibid.

64 See e.g. *Chief insp. ann. rep., 1900*, pp. 546–47 (responsible for 38 per cent of reported

Where machinery is extensive the risk of mutilation and sudden death must always be present to a greater or lesser degree; and apart from roughing and sorting the processes of linen manufacture were fully mechanised. The dangers to the lives and limbs of the workers at these processes were great owing to the manifold number of moving parts, some of which travelled at [increasingly] high speeds ...[65]

The ideal solution from the inspectors' point of view was to have machinery supplied by the maker with 'secure' fencing already attached, so that neither employer nor worker had any real choice in the matter. But the factory acts did not address machinery manufacturers, and attempts to persuade them to be more safety conscious apparently met with limited success.[66] The position with regard to textile machinery used in the north of Ireland, however, appears to have been rather more satisfactory: 'In the new machines supplied in this industry it is seldom necessary to suggest any additional safeguards. The guards supplied are neat, effective and easily removable for repairing and cleaning purposes.... The engineering firms which supply these machines have evidently found it to be to their interest to have all fencing complete and of a satisfactory nature.'[67] Although the position appears to have been at least as satisfactory after 1900,[68] there were still plenty of unfenced machines to be found throughout the industry.

The 1878 act may have added little to the inspectors' formal powers with regard to safety, but the new regime had an encouraging start in Ireland. Cameron reported from Belfast that the gearing of spinning frames was now 'securely fenced, and it is seldom that an accident, which was of common occurrence, is now reported, viz., the laceration of fingers and hands of the children and young persons working in the spinning rooms, rendering necessary amputation ...'.[69] He was also optimistic about the guarding of

accidents in Ireland, 33 per cent in Scotland and 29 per cent in England and Wales). The table does not give a specific figure for the linen industry.

65 Armstrong, 'Social and economic conditions', p. 253.
66 'The attention of makers of machinery and appliances used in factories is invited to the importance of adequately fencing the dangerous parts in the process of construction and fitting.... It is unsatisfactory to find that new machines, in other respects improved, are still sent out by the makers without due regard to this essential point, and that precautions which are taken as a matter of course in the case of those made for export, are often omitted in the construction of the like machinery intended for use in the United Kingdom': 'Memorandum addressed to makers of machinery', issued by the chief inspector and reproduced in *Chief insp. ann. rep., 1900*, p. 107. A similar circular was issued in 1907: *Chief insp. ann. rep., 1907*, p. xv.
67 *Chief insp. ann. rep., 1901*, pt. I, p. 135 (Young). See also *Chief insp. ann. rep., 1911*, p. 115 (Eraut): 'the local textile machinery makers have been giving great attention to the fencing of dangerous parts of new machines, and ... this is leading to a gradual diminution of cleaning accidents ...'.
68 'Year by year, we find more, and better thought-out attention being given by the makers of machinery to the application of suitable guards before supplying their goods to customers': *Chief insp. ann. rep., 1906*, p. 159 (J.S. Maitland, superintending inspector for Scotland and Ireland division).
69 *Chief insp. ann. rep., 1879*, pp. 62–63. For evidence that fencing of horizontal shafts was not always properly maintained, see e.g. *Chief insp. ann. rep., 1886*, p. 52.

weaving looms, in particular to reduce the incidence of accidents caused by flying shuttles.[70] Safety was high on his list of priorities:

I consider that of recent years, and owing no doubt to recent legislation, the whole subject of secure fencing has attained increased importance in the eyes of occupiers. Much, I am happy to recognise, is done, and readily done, for the sake of humanity; and where the higher motive may, perhaps, halt a little, a possibility of legal contingencies renders some assistance. I, myself, regard the subject as second in importance to none of the many which come under our notice as inspectors of factories; and albeit that employees themselves are frequently the most difficult to convince, and the slowest to appreciate protection, if it in any way interfere with an acquired routine, yet immunity from accident is a boon which very certainly obtains in the end both recognition and gratitude, and as certainly yields an abiding satisfaction to all concerned in its creation.[71]

The principal strategy for the prevention of industrial accidents continued for some time to depend upon the employers' response to the factory acts. The Irish factory inspectors used the carrot, not the stick. During the 1880s and early 1890s, they brought on average only two prosecutions per year against occupiers who failed to fence dangerous machinery.[72] With the notable exception of scutch mills,[73] few of these proceedings involved the linen industry. Perhaps the most significant case in this regard was the prosecution in 1894 of the Bessbrook Spinning Company for failing to fence securely the friction plate and transverse shaft of a winding frame, as a result of which a young girl was injured.[74] The company was fined £2. 10s. 0d. and ordered to pay 7s. costs; by the standards of the time, this was quite a heavy fine.[75]

Proceeding by way of advice and encouragement, rather than by way of prosecution, did not involve lower standards:

70 *Chief insp. ann. rep., 1879*, p. 63.
71 *Chief insp. ann. rep., 1886*, p. 52. The chief inspector (Redgrave) also acknowledged the readiness of the principal manufacturers in the north of Ireland 'where the strict factory regulations might interfere with old customs', to cooperate with the inspectors 'in a spirit of frankness and cordiality': *Chief insp. ann. rep., 1879*, p. 63.
72 Details of all prosecutions brought by Irish inspectors are given in the annual reports of the chief inspector until 1900.
73 See further below, p. 142. The frequency with which corn and saw mills were prosecuted is also noticeable.
74 *Chief insp. ann. rep., 1894*, p. 272. As it happens, this was a year in which the Irish inspectors brought an unprecedented number of prosecutions for all kinds of factory act offences – see ibid., pp. 264–84.
75 Most of the fines were for ten shillings or less. But a woollen mill in Dublin was fined £5 for failing to fence a fly-wheel: *Chief insp. ann. rep., 1890*, p. 133 and a Belfast foundry which caused the death of a young boy by failing to provide secure fencing was fined £10 by way of penal compensation: ibid., p. 126 (compensation of £32 – 'a small sum' – had already been paid to the deceased boy's father). By way of contrast, a Cork saw mill operator who failed to fence mill-gearing with the result that a young person was killed was fined only £1: *Chief insp. ann. rep., 1895*, p. 23 (no reference to any payment of compensation).

I have, on more than one occasion, been told when inspecting factories that I was too strict, too exacting, and too particular (and this in some of the largest works) in requiring the smaller parts of machinery to be securely guarded. In all cases I have insisted on having the increased guarding carried out, and I find after all has been done that masters and managers admit that it is far more satisfactory than running any unnecessary risk of loss of life or limb to any worker. HM inspectors of factories necessarily gain a great deal of experience in going over all classes of works inspecting machinery, inquiring into accidents, attending inquests, and giving evidence in law courts as regards machinery after any accident has happened. These facts I find masters and managers are not slow to recognise.[76]

In some cases, 'firmness and determination' on the part of the inspectors was called for.[77] But in general they were confident – even possibly a bit complacent – that their general strategy was succeeding in reducing the overall number of industrial accidents in Ireland. In 1889, for example, Cameron reported from Belfast 'a marked diminution in the reports of accidents from mill machinery';[78] two years later, Woodgate reported from Dublin that there had been 'a considerable falling off in the number of accidents in the various factories'.[79]

Unfortunately, we have no way of verifying this assessment prior to 1900, when the first industrial accident statistics for Ireland were published. By this time the importance attached to the reduction of industrial accidents in the United Kingdom as a whole was reflected not only in the legislative developments of the 1890s, but also in the attention given in the annual reports of the chief inspector to accidents and to the statutory requirement for the reporting of accidents. With regard to the latter, which dated from 1844, there were two underlying principles. All fatal accidents had to be reported to the certifying surgeon and the factory inspector, and accidents which did not result in any 'bodily injury' did not have to be reported at all. What changed from time to time was the scope of the requirement to report accidents in which a worker was injured. By 1895 this category was divided into two classes. Class A accidents were those which resulted from certain specified causes – in particular, the operation of machinery moved by mechanical power; these had to be reported to the certifying surgeon of the district. Class B accidents were all other injury accidents which prevented a

---

76 *Chief insp. ann. rep., 1892*, p. 112 (Woodgate).
77 'Some [occupiers] argue, as they have never had an accident, they do not see why they should trouble to put up guards, but with the exercise of firmness and determination I have found them all amenable': *Chief insp. ann. rep., 1893*, p. 241 (Woodgate).
78 *Chief insp. ann. rep., 1889*, p. 35.
79 *Chief insp. ann. rep., 1892*, p. 112. This assessment was endorsed by Woodgate's successor – see *Chief insp. ann. rep., 1895*, p. 81 (Bellhouse). But the junior inspector (Shuter) was less content: 'The greater portion of the irregularities that exist arise from the neglect to keep all dangerous machinery securely fenced; and it certainly is surprising to find occupiers, who, generally speaking, appear desirous to fulfil every obligation towards their employees, and are yet so blind to their own interests, as to neglect this most important branch of factory legislation': ibid.

worker from returning to work within three days;[80] these had to be reported only to the factory inspector.[81] In 1906, however, the scope of Class A was *extended* by adding additional causes (especially accidents 'due to electricity'), but also *reduced* by introducing a requirement that the resulting injury caused a worker 'to be absent throughout at least one whole day from his ordinary work'; the scope of Class B accidents was also reduced by increasing the prescribed period of incapacity caused by the accident from three to 'more than seven' days.[82]

In 1900, when the number of Irish workers covered by the factory acts was almost 220,000, the number of reported accidents was 1,588, giving an overall rate of 7.3 per 1,000 workers – less than one-half of that in England and Wales (18.7) and Scotland (14.8).

Table 5.3: Number of reported accidents, 1900 and 1910[83]

	No. of workers under Factory Acts	No. of reported accidents			
				Injury	
		Fatal	Class A	Class B	Total
1900					
England and Wales	3,664,355	864	22,606	45,036	68,506
Scotland	602,719	160	3,408	5,358	8,926
Ireland	216,726	21	645	922	1,588
United Kingdom	4,483,800	1,045	26,659	51,316	79,020
1910					
England and Wales	4,227,050	854	35,936	72,577	109,367
Scotland	660,056	170	5,567	10,795	16,532
Ireland	240,003	56	1,211	2,384	3,651
United Kingdom	5,127,109	1,080	42,714	85,756	129,550

The workers most at risk in Ireland, as throughout the United Kingdom, were still young men aged 13–18, and now also men over 18; but even for them, as for women and children, the risk of accident was *less* than their counterparts in Scotland or in England and Wales:

---

80 More strictly, where the injury was such as to prevent the injured worker 'on any one of the three working days next after the occurrence of the acccident from being employed for five hours on his ordinary work': 1895 act, s. 18(1)(b). The 1878 act had prescribed a period of 48 hours, but this was increased to three days by the 1891 act, s. 22(1).
81 1895 act, s. 18; 1901 act, s. 19.
82 Notice of Accidents Act 1906, s. 4.
83 The figures for the number of workers are taken from *Chief insp. ann. rep., 1898*, pt. I, p. 210 and *1911*, p. 289 (returns for 1907); the numbers of reported accidents are taken from *Chief insp. ann. rep., 1900*, Table 18 and *1910*, Table 2.

Table 5.4: Rate of reported accidents per 1,000 workers in 1900[84]

	Ireland	Scotland	England and Wales
Adults			
Male	11.7	21.2	26.2
Female	1.5	2.5	2.6
Young persons			
Male	15.4	24.4	27.3
Female	3.5	4.9	4.6
Children			
Male	3.8	4.6	8.8
Female	0.3	1.2	1.9
All	7.3	14.8	18.7

On the other hand, an analysis of the Class A accidents suggests that Irish workers, if injured, were more likely to suffer the amputation of a limb.[85]

In comparison with other Irish industries, the linen factories had a relatively good safety record:

Table 5.5: Estimate of accident rates in selected Irish factories in 1900

Industry	No of reported accidents[86]	No of persons employed	Accident rate per 1,000 employed[87]
Linen	310	81,432	3.8
Other textile	32	4,805	6.7
Wood	92	4,914	18.7
Machinery/engineering	250	24,556	10.2
Food and drink	252	23,338	10.8
Paper, printing, etc.	69	9,421	7.3

84 Derived from figures given in *Chief insp. ann. rep., 1900*, p. 548 (number of reported accidents by age and sex).

85 See *Chief insp. ann. rep., 1900*, p. 543, where just over 20 per cent of these accidents in Ireland resulted in an amputation, as compared to 14 per cent in Scotland and just under 10 per cent in England and Wales. But it must be remembered that Class A injury accidents represented only one-third of the total number of reported accidents.

86 Ibid., pp. 544–45.

87 Based on figures returned for 1898 in respect of factories only: ibid., pp. 7 and 20–21. The figure for linen includes scutch-mills and bleaching and dyeing.

The relative safety of linen factories and mills, which is borne out by other statistics relating to the textile industry as a whole,[88] apparently benefitted all categories of workers, and in particular female workers.

Table 5.6: Injury accident rates per 1,000 employed
in the textile industry, 1895[89]

	Children		Young persons		Adults	
	Male	*Female*	*Male*	*Female*	*Male*	*Female*
Flax	4.2	0.9	6.1	1.4	2.1	0.8
Wool	5.5	2.0	7.9	4.4	2.7	1.5
Cotton	7.8	2.9	8.7	4.5	4.3	1.8
All	6.3	2.3	8.0	3.9	3.6	1.5

The lower rate of accidents to female workers was explained at the time as follows:

[Women] as a rule have fixed workplaces, and the work prescribed for them is usually of a definite and limited range at the floor level, in which the same operations are repeated *ad infinitum*. In such cases almost all the risks can be met by attention to the statutory safeguards. In the case of males, however, ... the area of risk is much extended, both male young persons and male children being engaged at more dangerous operations than females of the corresponding age; while men ... have to approach prime movers, mill gearing and other machinery in motion and require to perform difficult and dangerous tasks on ladders, narrow platforms and temporary staging.[90]

All these findings tend to support the optimism shown earlier by Cameron and Woodgate. But as the number of reported accidents began to increase, their successors found more scope for criticism of employers and workers. In 1901, for example, Young reported from Belfast that some employers were

88 In 1904, for example, the accident rate for all textile factories in the United Kingdom per 1,000 employed was 11.0 for males and 3.8 for females – as compared with 76.9 and 10.2 respectively in shipbuilding: *Chief insp. ann. rep., 1907*, p. xxxiv and *Report of the departmental committee on accidents in places under the factory and workshop acts*, Table IV, p. 5 [Cd. 5535], H.C. 1911, xxiii, p. 11. In 1911, workmen's compensation in the textile industry cost employers from 1*s*. 5*d*. to 2*s*. 3*d*. per person employed, as compared to an average for all factories of 4*s*. 3*d*.: *Statistics of compensation and of proceedings under the workmen's compensation acts ... during the year 1911*, p. 6 [Cd. 6493], H.C. 1912–13, lxxv, 783.

89 *Chief insp. ann. rep., 1896*, p. 8, but 'it must be remembered that the hours of work [of children] ... are much shorter [than for adults and young persons]. The result would be different ... if the accident rate were calculated per hour or per 1,000 hours of actual work.' For a detailed analysis of accidents in the Irish linen industry in 1908 and 1910, see *Chief insp. ann. rep., 1908*, p. 109 and *1910*, p. 97.

90 J. Calder, *The prevention of factory accidents* (London, 1899), pp. 19–22.

much more willing to admit that a machine was dangerous *after* an accident had occurred. Fate had smiled on him in one such case. An occupier denied that some spur wheels were dangerous and asserted that they did not require to be fenced; with that, his coat was caught and 'severely damaged' by an unfenced wheel – 'a practical and emphatic contradiction of his argument and he himself frankly admitted his mistake and had the wheels securely fenced'.[91] But there were other occupiers in the north of Ireland who continued to take the view that 'no fencing should be done till it is pointed out by the inspector'[92] – and in 1906 an inspector in the south of Ireland reported that one-third of the non-fatal accidents which he had investigated arose as a result of fencing which was 'wanting or defective'.[93]

Workers, too, came in for criticism. In many cases, accidents were simply inevitable – 'such as are likely to occur in all industrial centres, and in which the experience and caution of the workers and the safeguarding of the machinery are powerless to entirely prevent'.[94] But some workers were found to have 'deeply rooted prejudices' against certain types of fencing, especially if they had worked at a particular machine for some time without injury; a suggestion that the machine should be fenced was taken as 'an imputation on their skill and an interference with their liberties'.[95] In some cases, too, workers were killed or injured as a result of their 'excessive zeal', carelessness or even 'extreme rashness'.[96]

The more critical attitude of the inspectors was reflected in the number of 'safety' prosecutions[97] brought in Ireland after 1900. Although detailed figures are not available, the number of such prosecutions in Ireland during the first decade of the twentieth century averaged 25 per year, as compared to 10 in Scotland and 215 in England and Wales (and this at a time when, as shown by Table 5.7, the number of reported accidents in Ireland was very much lower than that in Scotland and amounted to no more than three per cent of the number in England and Wales). The most dramatic year in this respect was 1907, when safety prosecutions in Ireland amounted to almost one-fifth of the total for the United Kingdom.[98] On conviction, the occupier could expect a 'small' fine; but in many cases 'the magistrates content themselves with making an order to fence under section 135 [of the 1901

---

91 *Chief insp. ann. rep., 1901*, pt. II, p. 135.
92 Ibid. (Kirkwood).
93 *Chief insp. ann. rep., 1906*, p. 157 (Jackson). See also to the same effect his report in *Chief insp. ann. rep., 1907*, p. 119.
94 *Chief insp. ann. rep., 1901*, pt. II, p. 135 (Jackson) and *1904*, pt. I, p. 186 (Snape).
95 *Chief insp. ann. rep., 1901*, pt. II, p. 135 (Young).
96 *Chief insp. ann. rep., 1904*, pt. I, p. 186 (Bellhouse).
97 This collective term included the failure to report an accident and the failure to fence dangerous machinery; these offences accounted for most 'safety' prosecutions. But also included were other offences such as failure to keep an accident register and allowing children, young persons and women to clean machinery in motion.
98 *Chief insp. ann. rep., 1907*, p. 316 (47 out of a total of 254). In particular, the number of prosecutions for failing to fence dangerous machinery (18) was double the number of such prosecutions in Scotland: ibid., p. 134.

act] and requiring the firm to pay costs ...'.[99] It seems that the inspectors received little support from the Irish magistrates.

This increased activity may reflect the fact that there was at this time, in Ireland as throughout the United Kingdom, a steady increase in the number of reported accidents.

Table 5.7: *Number of reported accidents 1900–1913 (selected years)*[100]

	1900	*1905*	*1910*	*1913*
Ireland	1,588	2,552	3,651	4,192
Scotland	8,926	11,587	16,362	23,325
England and Wales	68,506	86,470	109,537	150,644
United Kingdom	79,020	100,609	129,550	178,161

The apparent increase in the number of accidents gave rise to such concern that in June 1908 the home secretary appointed a departmental committee to consider the question.[101] Most of the evidence came from Great Britain, and no reference was made to any particular problem in Ireland. The committee found that the rise in the number of accidents was mainly confined to minor accidents.[102] Most of the 'increase' was due to the fuller reporting of minor accidents under the Notice of Accidents Act 1906, improved inspection and the effect of the workmen's compensation acts. Other factors included (i) a steady enlargement in the area of accident risk due to the gradual growth of trade during the last twenty years, (ii) the increased use of machinery, and (iii) the increased speed of much of that machinery and the fact that much work was being done under greater pressure, often as a result of payment by piece-work. But these factors had been counteracted by improved inspection, better fencing of machinery and greater care by employers anxious to keep down the cost of workmen's compensation. Accordingly, the committee's overall conclusion was that, during the past decade, the real risk of accidental injury had probably remained 'almost constant'.[103]

Mary Galway, secretary of the Textile Operatives Society of Ireland, tended to agree with this assessment. The number of accidents involving members of the society had increased 'a little bit these last few years owing to the workers having learned that they can claim compensation and also the

---

99 *Chief insp. ann. rep.*, *1905*, p. 212 (Jackson).
100 Taken from *Chief insp. ann. rep.*, *1913*, p. 162.
101 See *Report of the departmental committee on accidents in places under the factory and workshop acts* [Cd. 5535], H.C. 1911, xxiii, 1.
102 Ibid., p. 9. The number of fatal accidents in the United Kingdom had actually decreased (from 1,045 in 1900 to 946 in 1909) and the number of accidents involving loss of a limb or part of a limb had only slightly increased (from 2,958 in 1900 to 3,394 in 1909).
103 Ibid., pp. 9–21.

employers having insured their workpeople'; but this increase was due to better reporting rather than a real increase in the number of accidents.[104] By 1910,[105] the fatal accident rate was much the same throughout the United Kingdom; but the relative number of injuries (of either class) remained significantly lower in Ireland.[106] Nevertheless, the inspectors' reports continued to reveal the personal toll taken by accidents and the limited effect of safety legislation. Overhead shafts still remained unfenced in many instances: 'despite the attention given to this subject for years, there still lingers a great degree of apathy to, or ignorance of, the dangers of overhead shafting'.[107] The heavy rollers used in shirt and collar glossing machines and linen laundering calenders also caused horrific accidents, often to young workers.[108] And in spite of the statutory prohibition, children and young persons were still required to clean machinery in motion, often with serious consequences.[109]

We now examine in greater detail the impact of the safety provisions in two particular cases – the dangers faced by workers in scutch mills, and from flying shuttles in weaving sheds.

ACCIDENTS IN SCUTCH MILLS

Flax scutch mills presented a problem with regard to the fencing of machinery which was almost exclusively confined to Ireland. At the scutch mill, the retted flax was first 'bruised' by grooved or fluted rollers made of wood or iron and driven by water wheel or steam engine; the crushed and softened stems were then 'scutched' by being held against rapidly revolving wooden blades (or 'fliers') set on a power-driven spindle. This process knocked off the unwanted pith and skin and left the flax fibres relatively clean, ready for hackling, preparing and spinning.[110]

Machine scutching was well-established in Ireland by the 1830s, when there were more than 500 scutch mills, predominantly in Ulster and virtually

---

104 *Report of the departmental committee on accidents: Minutes of evidence*, p. 246 [Cd. 5540], H.C. 1911, xxiii, 322. In *Chief insp. ann. rep., 1906*, p. 156, one of the inspectors (Williams) also attributed the rise in the number of accidents to better reporting of accidents and 'the improved state of trade'.

105 The overall number of reported accidents per 1,000 workers was 15.2 in Ireland, 25.0 in Scotland and 25.9 in England and Wales.

106 The number of fatal accidents per 1,000 workers was 0.23 in Ireland, 0.26 in Scotland and 0.20 in England and Wales; for injuries, the numbers were 15.0, 24.8 and 25.7 respectively.

107 *Chief insp. ann. rep., 1912*, p. 105 (Eraut). The slightest contact with such a shaft could bring about serious injury or death – see e.g. *Chief insp. ann. rep., 1909*, p. 111 (girl killed when hair caught in shaft).

108 *Chief insp. ann. rep., 1909*, p. 111 (Eraut) and *1913*, p. 85 (Slocock).

109 See e.g. *Chief insp. ann. rep., 1901*, pt. II, p. 34 and *1911*, pp. 113 and 115 (Eraut).

110 McCutcheon, *Industrial archaeology*, pp. 240–41. See also Armstrong, *Growth of industry*, pp. 379–89 and 402–03, H.D. Gribbon, *The history of water power in Ulster* (Newton Abbot, 1969), pp. 103–07 and below, Plate 10.

all driven by water-power. With the growth of a linen industry largely dependent on locally-grown flax, the number of scutch mills increased, reaching a peak in the late 1860s, when there were more than 1,500 throughout the island.[111] The number of mills declined after 1870, as the industry increasingly relied upon imported flax; by the end of the century, scutching was 'a decaying industry',[112] and by 1914 the number of mills had been reduced to 608.[113]

Many of the scutch mills were situated 'in country places, on small waterfalls, and in isolated spots'.[114] They were generally small affairs, 'managed by men of the working class' and normally employing no more than ten persons, 'the sons, wives and daughters of the small farmers'.[115] Although some mills were modern and well-run,[116] most were – and remained – housed in buildings which were old, decrepit and dirty. Indeed, the scutching process traditionally employed in Ireland was frequently criticised as inefficient both as to the quantity and quality of the product, which compared unfavourably with that produced by more modern systems operated 'under expert supervision' on the continent, particularly in Belgium.[117] But it was the working conditions in these mills which became a primary concern of the factory inspectorate:

As a rule the Irish scutching mills are ill-built, ill-kept, unhealthy sheds, packed with dangerous machinery, unfenced, revolving rapidly, and liable to entangle and perhaps destroy any person coming within its reach.... Accidents are frequent, and loss of life or limb invariably takes place whenever an accident occurs. In most of these mills,

111   *The agricultural statistics of Ireland for the year 1868*, p. xxii [C. 3], H.C. 1870, lxviii, 459. Of the 1,542 mills, 1,420 were in Ulster; more than 80 per cent of all the mills were water-driven.

112   *Chief insp. ann. rep., 1899*, p. 231, explaining that great quantities of scutched flax were being imported from abroad, especially Belgium and Russia.

113   *The agricultural statistics of Ireland for the year 1914*, p. 19 [Cd. 8266], H.C. 1916, xxxii, 659. All but six were in Ulster; more than three-quarters were still water-driven. For a typical example see below Plate 11.

114   *Fifth report of the commissioners on the employment of children and young persons in trades and manufactures not already regulated by law*, p. xiv [3678], H.C. 1866, xxiv, 15.

115   Ibid., p. xv. In 1895, returns from just over 700 mills showed a total workforce of 6,654: *Chief insp. ann. rep., 1895*, p. 203. By 1907, the number had fallen to 4,073: *Summary of returns ... of persons employed in 1907 in non-textile factories*, p. 5 [Cd. 5398], H.C. 1910, lxxxiii, 793. In both cases, the figures were based on incomplete returns.

116   A large new scutching mill near Buncrana, for example, contained all necessary safety arrangements: *Fifth report of the children's employment commission 1866*, p. 124 (Darkin). Scutch mills attached to spinning and weaving factories were generally better – see e.g. *Report of the commissioners appointed to inquire into the working of the factory and workshop acts: Minutes of evidence*, pp. 846–47 [C. 1443–I], H.C. 1876, xxx, 846–47 (Mr Walker, owner of such premises in Newtownards, stated that he had 'a great deal' more fencing than smaller mills, and had had only one accident in nine years).

117   See e.g. *Insp. half-yearly rep., Oct. 1862*, p. 119, where Baker refers to the 'careless and inefficient manner' in which flax was scutched. In *Chief insp. ann. rep., 1885*, pp. 7–8, Woodgate reported that 'a large amount of the flax crop [is] wasted owing in a great measure to inexperienced workmanship in the scutching', and in 1897 Snape reported that 'there is no doubt that the Belgians are far ahead of us in Ireland in the treatment of flax': *Chief insp. ann. rep., 1897*, pp. 43–45.

men and women, boys and girls, work from daylight usually till 9 and 10 and frequently till 12 p.m. The atmosphere in which they work is one thick constant cloud of dust and fine particles of straw and flax. From September to February and March is the period of work, and girls and boys leave other employment for the sake of the overtime and higher wages made in the scutch mills.[118]

Although this assessment was made in 1862, the condition of many of the mills did not significantly improve over the next fifty years or so.[119]

The women, young persons and children who worked in these mills were mainly employed to bruise the flax. At first, this work was carried out by 'a primitive vertical ... roller consisting of three massive corrugated wooden cylinders ...'.[120] From the 1850s, however, these wooden rollers were being replaced by the MacAdam rolling frame consisting of a horizontal series of metal cylinders arranged in pairs. The problem in both cases was that the flax stems had to be fed manually into the mechanically-driven cylinders, exposing the operator to the risk of having a hand, and then an arm, caught in the machine and crushed. In this respect, the new MacAdam roller was thought to be safer:

The worst source of injury and loss of life has been the use of the old wooden rollers, through which the flax has to pass several times; they are served from a narrow table, to which the flax is returned after passing through, and from which it is again started, so that the hands of the operative serving them are in frequent and close proximity to danger. The patent [MacAdam] rollers used in most new mills are much smaller, capable of being completely covered, served from a table of over three feet long, and the flax has only to pass through once, and is delivered at the opposite end to its entrance, so that the operative serving them need never be in danger....[121]

This was an overly optimistic assessment; according to McCutcheon, the MacAdam frame was 'particularly dangerous', especially in the dim and dusty atmosphere of many of the scutch mills.[122] In an attempt to keep the

---

118 *Insp. half-yearly rep.*, Oct. 1862, p. 119 (Haydon). See also *Fifth report of the children's employment commission*, pp. 122–23, where the point is made that 'every season, in autumn and winter, persons wholly unaccustomed to machinery are taken from field labour to feed these rollers; and as the machinery is entirely unprotected, and the persons quite unacquainted with the dangers they incur, the accidents are, in number and kind, wholly unexampled in the history of machinery'.

119 In 1890, it was still being said that 'the occupiers of the majority [of scutch mills] are comparatively poor; the mills are, as a rule, very small and a great number of them are in a very dilapidated condition': *Chief insp. ann. rep., 1890*, p. 37. In 1907, two lady inspectors (Martindale and Whitworth) reported that 'the mills ... were in many cases little more than barns ... and often in a dilapidated condition .... In almost every case the mills were in an excessively dirty condition ...': *Chief insp. ann. rep., 1907*, p. 211.

120 McCutcheon, *Industrial archaeology*, p. 241.

121 J.K. Maconchy, 'A comparison between the accidents which have occurred in scutch mills, and in factories subject to government inspection, as they have come to my notice during the eight years of my connexion with the county Down infirmary', in *Dublin Q.J. of Med. Science*, 43 (1867), 65. For an earlier study, see W. Moore, 'A notice of some cases of injuries produced by the machinery of flax scutch mills', in *Dublin Q.J. of Med. Science*, 17(1854), 60.

122 McCutcheon, *Industrial archaeology*, p. 243.

operator at a safe distance from the rollers, he or she was sometimes 'harnessed' to the wall or floor of the mill;[123] but the value of this practice was doubted:

Those who feed the rollers with the flax are accustomed to stand close to them, and are in danger of being drawn in between the teeth of the machinery, either through misjudging their distance, or from their wrists becoming entangled in the flax. The usual precaution adopted is the clumsy one of a sort of harness or strait-jacket, which prevents the feeder from moving beyond a certain point in the direction of the machinery. As in the case of ... all other precautions which depend upon the will of the individual worker for their application, this device is constantly being neglected, and with very lamentable results.[124]

An alternative precaution, which does not appear to have been widely adopted, was to install a pair of false rollers to provide a warning when the operator's hand came too close to the machinery. Greater safety was also promised by various technological developments which took place from time to time;[125] but it appears that there was prior to the first world war little change in the machinery used in most of the mills.[126]

Safety in scutch mills was a cause for official concern from the 1850s. In 1861, for example, Thomas MacDonnell, a fourteen-year-old boy, was killed in an accident at a mill near Portadown; at the subsequent inquest, the coroner's jury returned a verdict of manslaughter against the owner of the mill. Asked to give evidence at the trial, sub-inspector Darkin testified that the machinery in the mill was unfenced, and that the accident could have been prevented 'by a very trifling outlay'; he brought the case to the attention of the home secretary, with a recommendation for action.[127] Shortly after this, two eminent medical practitioners emphasised the disproportionate number – and severity – of accidents in scutch mills as compared with spinning and weaving factories.[128] Thus, Dr. Maconchy estimated that in his

123 See e.g. *Factory and workshop commissioners 1876: Minutes of evidence, appendix D*, p. 165, where Dr Hamilton suggests that 'a band passing over the shoulders of the person rolling and attached to a hook behind them would prevent them from being pulled forward into the rollers'.

124 *Report of the factory and workshop commissioners 1876*, p. lxxvi. In his evidence to the commissioners, Mr Walker, a scutch mill owner, had referred to workers being 'chained with large straps, almost as if they were lunatics ...': *Minutes of evidence*, p. 847. The inspectors were later advised that the practice was 'exceedingly dangerous and liable to bring on enlargement of the heart': *Chief insp. ann. rep., 1895*, p. 80 (Bellhouse).

125 See e.g the 'Cardon' scutching machine so enthusiastically welcomed by Cameron – only to be dismissed the following year: *Chief insp. ann. rep., 1886*, pp. 6–7 and *1887*, p. 22. Another machine, invented by a Mr Johnston of the Kiltonga Bleach Works in Newtownards, was 'so constructed as to be almost impossible for an accident to happen'; but it was not widely adopted: *Chief insp. ann. rep., 1887*, p. 25.

126 See e.g. *Chief insp. ann. rep., 1907*, pp. 211–12.

127 W.S. Darkin to Sir George Grey (home sec.), 9 May 1862, PRO HO 45/6968. The scutch mill owner was acquitted by direction of the trial judge.

128 Maconchy, 'Comparison between accidents in scutch mills and factories' and T. H. Babington (of Londonderry infirmary), 'Flax mills – their machinery: accidents occurring therein, with suggestions for their prevention', in *Dublin Q.J. of Med.*

part of Co. Down spinning and weaving employed four times as many workers as scutching; yet 'during the [past] eight years the factories have occasioned the loss of two forearms and seriously impaired three arms, whereas, in the same time, the scutch mills have killed six people, seven survive minus a limb, and [three] others with seriously impaired arms.'[129] In 1866, Darkin told the Children's Employment Commission that he was convinced that '*serious* accidents from very simple machinery in scutching mills (proportionably to the number of persons employed) are infinitely more numerous than those which occur in factories under inspection, though the latter are filled with complicated machinery, and crowded with workpeople.'[130]

But unfenced machinery was not always to blame. Many of those who worked in scutch mills were 'wholly unaccustomed to machinery' and 'quite unacquainted with the dangers they incur'.[131] Scutchers were often paid by the quantity of flax cleaned and 'their eagerness to earn large wages makes them reckless and hastily careless'.[132] 'Intemperance and drinking' were also 'frequent', leading to 'carelessness, indifference and accidents'.[133]

The problem about taking action in the face of such reports was that scutch mills did not yet come within the factory acts. Although section 1 of the 1833 act had referred to 'any ... flax ... [or] linen ... mill or factory, wherein steam or water ... power is ... used to propel or work the machinery ... either in scutching ... spinning ... or weaving of ... flax', scutch mills were not considered textile 'factories'.[134] and, as early as 1854, Darkin was advised that 'it was not expedient to interfere with them'.[135] Scutching was not an industrial process, but 'an agricultural operation' analogous to threshing.[136] More

---

Science, 43 (1866), 392, reproduced in full in *Insp. half-yearly rep.*, *Oct. 1867*, pp. 61–64.

129 At least three of the fatal accidents and one of the amputations involved young men (aged 15–17), and two of the amputees were women (one a girl aged 15). The contrast between accident rates in factories and scutch mills was also a common theme in medical evidence presented by Darkin in 1866 – see *Fifth report of the children's employment commission*, pp. 124–26.

130 Ibid., p. 123. In a scutch mill at Kildinan in Cork, for example, six deaths and about sixty mutilations had occurred between 1852 and 1856, during which time there had not been a single accident at the local factory.

131 Ibid. (Darkin).

132 Babington, 'Flax mills', p. 395, recommending that scutchers be paid 'proper daily wages'. By 1907, some scutch mill workers were being paid a set weekly wage in an attempt to encourage slower and more thorough scutching, as in Belgium: *Chief insp. ann. rep., 1907*, p. 211 (Martindale).

133 Scutchers were 'proverbial' for hard drinking, and 'it is a common phrase to say "as thirsty as a scutcher"': *Factory and workshop commissioners, 1876: Minutes of evidence*, p. 858 (Dr Hamilton).

134 Baker's opinion to the contrary 'has been overruled': *Insp. half-yearly rep.*, *Oct.1867*, p. 61.

135 *Fifth report of the children's employment commission 1866*, p. 122.

136 Memorandum by A. Redgrave, 19 Nov. 1860, PRO HO 45/6968. Cf. Baker extolled the virtues of scutch mills 'for more readily and economically converting the produce [flax] into money' and produced figures to show their profitability in an attempt to encourage their development in England: *Insp. half-yearly rep.*, *Oct.1864*, pp. 42–43.

pragmatically, Darkin suggested that 'possibly their number ..., their difficulty of access, the illiterate character of most of the occupiers, and the great
expense which must have been incurred by a regular system of inspection,
may have deterred the then authorities from interfering'.[137] Even at this early
date, the factory acts assumed a degree of organisation and managerial
capacity not to be found in many scutch mills: 'The elaborate provisions of
the various factory acts are wholly inapplicable to mills managed by illiterate
peasants, alike destitute of writing materials and ability to use them ...'.[138]
What was required instead was 'a short special Act for Ireland', which would
simply require the machinery in scutch mills to be fenced. This new law
could be enforced by a 'registrar' conversant with machinery and assisted by
the police, to whom would be given 'powers [of inspection and prosecution]
similar to those given by the Factory Act to inspectors ...'; the entire cost of
administering the act would be met from the savings in parochial allowances
to widows, orphans and maimed workers brought about by the reduced
number of accidents and the increased compensation payable by scutch mill
owners for breach of the new statutory duty to fence.[139]

Although the children's employment commission supported this sensible
suggestion for 'a simple legislative measure',[140] none was enacted. The
general provisions of the Factory Acts Extension Act 1867 may have brought
scutch mills within the definition of 'factories', but this is not at all clear.[141]
However, further evidence of the disproportionate number and severity of
accidents occurring in these mills[142] led the factory and workshop commissioners in 1876 to recommend that the matter be put beyond doubt.[143] This
recommendation was opposed by some of the linen barons on the grounds
that it would be 'almost fatal' to the growth of flax in Ireland if scutch mills
were brought within the employment provisions of the acts:

137 Letter of 21 Dec. 1865, in *Fifth report of the children's employment commission 1866*,
     p. 122.
138 Ibid., p. 123, adding that the machinery used in scutch mills 'though highly
     dangerous, is so simple and can be so easily fenced, as not to call for the scientific
     arbitration provided by the factory act ...'.
139 Darkin was aware that 'the common law already affords a remedy', but he had 'never
     yet heard of any compensation whatever having been given for any scutch mill
     accident ... so that, owing to the poverty and ignorance of the sufferers, the present
     legal remedy is practically inoperative ...': ibid., p. 124.
140 *Fifth report, 1866*, p. xv.
141 *Chief insp. ann. rep., 1879*, p. 65 (Redgrave). But in 1876 Cameron had told the
     factory and workshop commissioners that scutch mills 'hitherto have not been
     placed under any legislative restriction ...': *Report, appendix C*, p. 20.
142 'The person feeding the rollers, often a woman, is hourly in danger of her arms being
     dragged into the rollers from a portion of the flax straw getting warped on the fingers
     or hand, or by a portion of the dress dragging the hand into the rollers, the injury
     thus inflicted frequently necessitating amputation of the arm, owing to the dreadfully
     torn and comminuted state of the limb': *Report of the factory and workshop commissioners
     1876, appendix D*, p. 165 (Dr Hamilton, certifying surgeon for Cookstown). See also
     Minutes of evidence, pp. 838 (Dr Musgrave) and 857 (Dr Hamilton).
143 *Report*, p. lxxvi.

If they are to be restricted in their hours of labour during those few months that they work, it will very materially interfere with the growth of flax, because they are all small concerns ... and it would increase their cost amazingly if they were either restricted to working the factory hours or precluded from employing different members of a family for the daylight work....[144]

Support for this view in parliament[145] led to a compromise. Under the Factory and Workshop Act 1878, scutch mills were classified as 'non-textile factories' and therefore subject, in particular, to the safety provisions of the act.[146] But it was also provided that 'the regulations of this Act with respect to the employment of women shall not apply to flax scutch mills which are conducted on the system of not employing either children or young persons therein, and which are worked intermittently, and for periods only which do not exceed in the whole six months in any year'.[147] This exemption was re-enacted in 1901;[148] but in 1907 it had to be repealed in order to bring United Kingdom law into conformity with the requirements of the Berne Convention of 1906.[149]

The debates on the 1878 act had revealed the underlying problem of enforcement: given that these small mills were scattered all over the country, 'it would require an army of inspectors to watch them'.[150] The notices returned by the scutch mill occupiers after 1878 revealed that only 15 per cent or so of the 1,200 mills then in operation worked more than six months in the year and employed children or young persons.[151] This, it was hoped,

144 See especially *Factory and workshop commissioners 1876: Minutes of evidence*, p. 829 (Thomas Valentine (Northern Spinning Co.), James Hind (Durham St. Mill) and Finlay M'Cance (Ulster Spinning Co.)). Cf. Mr George Walker, owner of a spinning, weaving and scutching factory at Newtownards, appeared to have no problems operating a scutch mill 'under the same hours as the factory hours': ibid., p. 846, while another owner of a combined mill at Newry (R. Dempster) thought that requiring scutch mills to work shorter hours would create work for the mills which were currently idle: ibid., p. 851.

145 'If any obstacle were put in the way of the growth of flax in Ireland the farmers would cease its cultivation, and the only manufacture which had ever taken root in that country would be destroyed': *Hansard 3*, ccxxviii, 503 (28 Feb. 1878) (Mulholland). Cf. 'If the factory act should protect women at all, it should certainly include one of the most unhealthy of all occupations': ibid., col. 595 (1 March 1878)(Dr Ward, MP for Galway). Parnell not only agreed with Ward (ibid., cols. 590–91), but wanted the employment of children and young persons in scutch mills to be made unlawful: ibid., col. 877 (7 March 1878).

146 Section 93 and sch. 4, pt. 1(19), replicated in 1901 act, s. 149 and sch. 6, pt. 1 (19).

147 Section 62, adding that 'a flax scutch mill shall not be deemed to be conducted on the system of not employing therein either children or young persons until the occupier has served on an inspector notice of his intention to conduct such mill on that system'.

148 1901 act, s. 57.

149 See Employment of Women Act 1907, s. 1. Scutch mills were the only 'factories' in respect of which repealing legislation was required.

150 *Hansard 3*, ccxxxviii, 601 (1 March 1878) (Assheton Cross, home sec.).

151 *Chief insp. ann. rep., 1879*, p. 66. Returns from 726 mills in 1895 indicated a workforce of 6,654 which consisted of one per cent children, 10 per cent young persons,

would ease the problem of enforcement;[152] but every mill had still to be inspected to determine if the machinery was properly fenced. Both Irish inspectors immediately set to work, and produced lengthy assessments of the impact of the new law. According to Cameron, the inspector for the north of Ireland:

In some few of the mills which I have visited, all the fencing possible has already been provided, with the exception of the outside water-wheel univerally unprotected. But in very many I have found rollers uncovered, their gearing naked or insecurely fenced, and, although less common, the feeding-tray of the rollers not sufficiently long to be an effectual protection.... [However] I have found the occupiers to be quite alive to the necessity for protecting their employees, and ready to promise willingly to carry out all instructions.... I do not question the entire possibility of effecting a very great improvement ... and I conceive that this may be brought about by a quiet insistence, and the gradual recognition by the occupiers that the requirements specified *must* be fulfilled.[153]

Woodgate found much the same in the rest of the island:

[The occupiers] seem to think that as they have already 'wrought' so long without an accident, there is no reason to think that they ever will be visited with one, and it will be time enough to guard after the accident has happened. After talking the matter over with them ... they have nearly all seen the great necessity for fencing the dangerous parts, and have promised me, before leaving the mill, that they will at once attend to all instructions....[154]

These assessments led the chief inspector to conclude that 'the manner in which the legislature decided to deal with flax scutch mills has proved to be a very successful modification of the factory regulations, amply sufficient to protect persons from injury, and ... calculated to enlist the co-operation of the proprietors, which is an element most essential to insure a cordial observance of the law.'[155]

It is difficult to determine just how successful the inspectors were. On the one hand, the scattered nature of the mills must have hindered efficient

30 per cent women over 18 and 59 per cent men over 18: *Chief insp. ann. rep., 1896*, p. 203. In 1907, inspectors Martindale and Whitworth were surprised to find 'a fair number of young persons' working in scutch mills, generally without the necessary fitness certificate from the certifying surgeon: *Chief insp. ann. rep., 1907*, p. 212. The returns for that year suggest a reduction in the employment of children, but otherwise little change in the make-up of the workforce: *Summary of returns of persons employed in 1907 in non-textile factories*, p. 5.

152 *Chief insp. ann. rep., 1879*, pp. 66 and 73, where Redgrave hoped that 'the boon offered to proprietors of working unrestrictedly with women' would do away altogether with the employment of children and young persons. But Cameron was doubtful, since he had found children carrying stricks of flax in a number of 'adult-only' mills and was told 'lightly' that 'these are only the "bit weans" of some farmer who has on that day brought his flax to be scutched': ibid., pp. 68–69.
153 Ibid., pp. 69–70 (Cameron).
154 Ibid., pp. 70–71.
155 Ibid., p. 73.

inspection and enforcement,[156] and the poverty of many of the occupiers meant that they were often unable or reluctant to incur additional expense in making improvements. But the efforts made by the inspectors nevertheless seem to have had achieved some beneficial results, even if only temporarily. In 1882 Cameron visited 'numerous' scutch mills, and was 'struck in many instances with the prompt and intelligent manner in which proprietors have complied with instructions given on the occasion of former visits as to the fencing of the very dangerous machinery used in these small works.... Since secure fencing has been so universally observed, there has been a marked decrease in the number of their accidents.'[157] Four years later he was able to confirm that 'the requirements of the act with regard to the fencing of ... machinery have been complied with – I may say satisfactorily', with the result that 'serious accidents ... have materially decreased'.[158] But he felt constrained to admit that in some cases improvements were often only temporary: 'A mill perfectly fenced and leaving nothing to be desired ... [on] a subsequent visit reveals a state of things almost as in the old time ... before fencing was heard of.'[159] This may explain why in 1896 one of his successors reported that the fencing in scutch mills was 'in a very dilapidated condition, a very small proportion of the machinery being securely fenced'.[160]

Many scutch mills in Co. Donegal, for example, were found to be in a particularly poor condition. In 1885, Woodgate reported that he had found 'a large amount of most dangerous machinery ... all unguarded', and expressed the view that 'very few of this class of millowners seemed to realise in the least the great danger of running machinery in such exposed and dangerous states, and if any person was killed or maimed the invariable reply would be it was the person's own fault or carelessness'.[161] In an effort to change this attitude, he prosecuted three owners in Newtowncunningham for their failure to guard dangerous machinery. These were the first such prosecutions in the neighbourhood, and when the owners stated in court that the machinery was now properly fenced, Woodgate simply 'asked the Bench to withdraw the summons on payment of costs'.[162] He then felt able to report that 'the proper and secure guarding of dangerous machinery [is now

---

156 See especially Woodgate's description of his travels in Co. Donegal: ibid., pp. 67–68.
157 *Chief insp. ann. rep., 1882*, p. 6.
158 *Chief insp. ann. rep., 1886*, p. 50. He admitted, however, that there were still some 'incidents' arising from 'practically an utter disregard' of safety considerations.
159 Ibid. Cameron continued: 'There is, however, always a pleased demand that "your Honor" should admit that things were alright before, and a deprecating smile greets the query as to whether aught has happened to render the existing machinery innocuous'. Fortunately, 'these are but incidents' which were 'not very general'.
160 *Chief insp. ann. rep., 1896*, p. 18 (Kellett).
161 *Chief insp. ann. rep., 1885*, p. 10. In 1895, there were two fatal accidents caused by scutch mill rollers provided with 'perfectly suitable feeding-boards'; both accidents were attributed to gross carelessness on the part of the feeder: *Chief insp. ann. rep., 1895*, p. 80 (Bellhouse).
162 *Chief insp. ann. rep., 1883*, p. 158. The costs in each case were 1*s*. 6*d*.

observed] in nearly all the mills in this district'.[163] By 1895, 'frequent' visits by the inspectors to mills throughout the county had apparently brought about a situation in which 'almost all the machinery that is possible of being guarded is now securely fenced'.[164]

Although five scutch mill owners were convicted and fined in 1899,[165] it is tempting to suggest that by 1900, when only eight accidents were reported,[166] the inspectors considered that the problem of accidents in scutch mills had been largely resolved.[167] It is certainly the case that they gave the matter little attention in their reports after that date. It may be, as the Flax Supply Association itself had hoped, that, as the number of mills declined, 'the oldest and perhaps the poorest class of mills will give up most readily ... [giving] rise to a better class of mills in both structure and working'.[168] Given the continuing concern of the inspectors about excessive dust and the lack of adequate ventilation,[169] however, this does not appear to have occurred to any significant extent. It may also be that the number of accidents, particularly those resulting in death or injury to women, did decline as safety practices improved[170] – but the inspectors themselves admitted that many scutch mill accidents were probably not reported.[171] What seems most likely, therefore, is that scutch mills continued to give rise to accidents on a regular basis, but, as their numbers continued to decline, they no longer did so to an extent sufficient to make their prevention a priority for inspectors with other, more pressing, problems.

163 *Chief insp. ann. rep., 1885*, p. 10.
164 *Chief insp. ann. rep., 1895*, p. 81 (Shuter).
165 Two mill owners in Coleraine were each fined five shillings (plus 4*s.* 6*d.* costs), and another owner in Co. Derry was fined £1 (with 6*s.* costs); in Co. Monaghan, one owner was fined 10*s.* (and costs of 1*s.* 6*d.*), while another was fined 2*s.* 6*d.* (with 2*s.* costs) and was ordered by the court to carry out the fencing within a week: *Chief insp. ann. rep., 1899*, pp. 402 and 406. Details of prosecutions after 1900 are not available.
166 *Chief insp. ann. rep., 1900*, p. 544. None of these accidents resulted in death.
167 In 1899 Woodgate reported that 'accidents in scutch mills ... have been reduced to a minimum, only one bad accident at the rollers having come under my notice this season. I have found the scutch millowners on the whole careful to carry out instructions as to guarding dangerous machinery': *Chief insp. ann. rep., 1899*, p. 37.
168 Quoted in *Chief insp. ann. rep., 1894*, p. 102. Woodgate concurred: 'It would be no loss to the country if many of the small scutch mills scattered about in the north and north-west with the very rude and antiquated machinery, were to go out of use'.
169 See below, p. 166.
170 In 1912, Eraut noted 'the steady improvement in the fitting of wider and safer feed delivery boards at the patent rollers and at the old-fashioned wooden rollers': *Chief insp. ann. rep., 1912*, p. 105. Cf. only five years earlier, Martindale and Whitworth 'found too often that these rollers were situated in a dark part of the barn and in a crowded corner, and it is difficult not to feel that absence of light and space, conditions often prevailing in these barns, adds considerably to the danger': *Chief insp. ann. rep., 1907*, p. 212.
171 As reported by Martindale and Whitworth in *Chief insp. ann. rep., 1907*, p. 212. Cf. Snape attributed the apparent increase in the number of scutch mill accidents to *improved* reporting: *Chief insp. ann. rep., 1905*, p. 197.

ACCIDENTS CAUSED BY FLYING SHUTTLES

The scutch mills may have represented the linen industry at its technological worst; but even in the more advanced spinning and weaving mills the workers faced a number of dangers, including one which for many years occupied the inspectors – the risk of serious injury, or even death, from being struck by a 'flying' shuttle.

The process of weaving linen, cotton and wool involved the 'firing', at considerable speed, of thread housed in a wooden shuttle with a sharpened metal point through the warp and weft threads. This shuttle was intended to take a predetermined path and be 'caught' at the end of its journey by the shuttle box. But on occasions the shuttle flew out of the loom at such speed and at such an angle that if, as was quite likely, it struck a worker it could cause considerable injury, often resulting in the loss of an eye, facial disfigurement or brain damage. The danger was recognised as early as 1858: 'When the shuttle is flying across the raceboard of the loom with great speed, a very slight interrupting body will cause it to leave its bed at such an angle as to make it almost certain to reach the eye or temple of a neighbouring worker.'[172]

Prevention was better than cure,[173] but the need for some kind of guard was evident from an early date. If the loom was not 'securely fenced', an inspector could for many years only invoke the cumbersome 'notice' procedure of the 1844 and 1878 acts, under which arbitrators were appointed to determine whether it was 'necessary and possible' to fence the loom.[174] There is no evidence that this was ever done in Ireland; instead, the inspectors preferred to proceed on a voluntary basis. They do not appear to have succeeded in persuading the manufacturers to incorporate guards into the design of looms.[175] But they do appear to have had some success in persuading the owners of mills and factories to install guards themselves. In 1879, for example, Cameron reported from the north of Ireland that 'guards have been placed on all the looms in my district, though indeed in some few factories they have always been adopted, and shuttle accidents are now very few and far between'.[176] In this respect, Ireland was even held out by the inspectors as an exemplar for the rest of the country.[177]

172   *Insp. half-yearly rep., Oct. 1858*, p. 64 (Baker).
173   'The best security against such accidents ... is to keep the loom in thorough good order ...': *Chief insp. ann. rep., 1883*, p. 23.
174   See above, pp. 125 and 127.
175   The loom manufacturers could readily supply looms already fitted with shuttle-guards – the additional expense was 'of a very trifling nature' (*Chief insp. ann. rep., 1883*, p. 22) and a major loom manufacturer in Lancashire 'never' sent a loom to the continent 'unprovided with shuttle-guards' (*Chief insp. ann. rep., 1888*, p. 16). In 1900, the chief inspector issued a general circular to 'the makers of machinery' emphasising 'the importance of adequately fencing the dangerous parts in the process of construction and fitting': *Chief insp. ann. rep., 1900*, p. 107.
176   *Chief insp. ann. rep., 1879*, p. 63 and *1883*, p. 22.
177   'The time has arrived when the system so successfully carried out in Ireland by the voluntary action of the manufacturers there should be required to be adopted

There were two main types of shuttle guard. The bar guard was a fixed or moving iron rod or bar[178] close to or following the course taken by the shuttle and designed to stop it from flying out of control or at least to deflect it downwards. More advanced versions of this guard consisted of two or more parallel bars which could be raised to facillitate access to the loom when the weaver wished to handle the thread.[179] The wing guard was a piece of wood or wire netting attached to the side of the loom; such a guard might be fitted on one or both sides of the loom and it could be fixed in place or hinged. Both forms of guard were used in Ireland; but Cameron, who paid special attention to the matter, preferred the bar guard:

I believe [the wing guard], if of sufficient size and attached in a proper position, to be effective;[180] but the [bar guard] has many advantages in economy of space and in neatness, in addition to being at least as efficacious. It cannot be so easily removed by the worker, and even though a shuttle should escape, striking the guard, its ascent is diverted, and it rarely rises so high as the faces of the workers at adjacent looms.... [A]fter careful consideration I can confidently recommend the bar guard, although I am aware that it is not absolutely perfect. But a perfect guard, one at the same time combining all essentials, has I believe yet to be invented....[181]

Many of the owners also preferred the bar guard, 'owing to its advantages in economy of space and neatness, and when properly placed, it is effective and economical, can be made by the factory mechanics, and ... put up at an outside cost of 2s. 6d. per loom'.[182] In England, many of the workers appear to have objected to the bar guard on the grounds that it interfered with their work,[183] but this does not appear to have been a problem in Ireland.[184] A moveable bar guard was obviously preferable,[185] but it was often left out of

absolutely in the other parts of the Kingdom': *Chief insp. ann. rep., 1888*, p. 43 (Redgrave, chief inspector).

178 A cruder version used a length of cable or wire instead of an iron bar.

179 See especially Webster's guard, which consisted of *three* parallel bars: *Chief insp. ann. rep., 1883*, p. 23.

180 'They are effective if care be taken that their position be accurately retained; this is not always so. The supporting bar is, not infrequently, bent down by the weight of shawls placed on it, and from general use and wear. Thus the position of the guard is made too low': *Chief insp. ann. rep., 1888*, p. 38 (Cameron).

181 *Chief insp. ann. rep., 1883*, pp. 24–25, quoting the manager of the York Street Flax Spinning Co. , who adds: 'our shuttle accidents are now fewer for 1,000 looms than when we had old wing guards and only about 600 looms'.

182 *Chief insp. ann. rep., 1888*, p. 38 (Cameron). Redgrave noted that 'a simple rod of iron can by fixed for sixpence ...': ibid., p. 43.

183 See e.g. *Chief insp. ann. rep., 1884*, pp. 14–15.

184 '[A]lthough on the first introduction of these bars they are always found fault with by the workers, in a very short time these latter become accustomed to them, and experience no hindrance to their work': *Chief insp. ann. rep., 1879*, p. 63 (Cameron). Woodgate went further: 'Many of the mill owners and managers tell me that the workers have got so much accustomed to work with shuttle guards that they do not feel safe working at looms without them': *Chief insp. ann. rep., 1883*, p. 26.

185 The inspectors regularly reported details of 'improved' guards – see e.g. *Chief insp. ann. rep., 1884*, pp. 14–16.

position when the loom was restarted; in addition, some weavers objected to the loss of time (and wages) involved in frequently lifting and lowering the bar guard. A modification which automatically raised and lowered the bar guard was available, but was often considered too expensive by the owners.[186]

Although bar guards might be installed, they were not always kept in working condition.[187] In this context, Cameron considered that the Employers' Liability Act 1880 provided employers with an additional incentive: 'undoubtedly, the provisions of the Employers' Liability Act are of service in illustrating the importance of fencing and of keeping efficient the guards which have been put up. I think that the penalties under the Act may probably secure a more perfect system of general supervision, and a more prompt replacement of any guard which has broken or become inefficient.'[188] An award of damages in an action brought under the Act could certainly 'penalise' a negligent employer. In *Leech* v. *J.H. Gartside & Co.*, for example, the owners of a cotton factory in England were held liable when a shuttle flew from an unguarded loom and struck the plaintiff, causing him to lose the sight in one eye; he was awarded damages of £225.[189] As we shall see in chapter 11, however, the use made of the act in Ireland was quite limited, and it seems more likely that it had relatively little impact on the practices of employers by way of general deterrence.[190]

As a result of the employers' actions and the inspectors' efforts, we might have expected that, at least in Ireland, the problem of shuttle accidents had been satisfactorily resolved by the 1880s. Unfortunately, however, that is not the case, and the story of the next thirty years or so is essentially one of failure by the factory owners – and the inspectors – to maintain the satisfactory state of affairs which had apparently been achieved.[191] This is all the

---

186 See e.g. *Chief insp. ann. rep., 1888*, p. 14 (Redgrave). Cameron came across a new form of bar guard patented by Mr Robert Smythe of Co. Armagh, which 'recedes when the loom is stopped, allowing the worker perfect freedom for manipulation, and reverting to its position when the loom is started'. The 'drawback' was that this guard cost 7s. 6d. 'exclusive of 1s. 3d. royalty': ibid., pp. 38–39.

187 In 1881 two serious accidents occurred because a loom was worked 'for a few days' with a broken guard: *Chief insp. ann. rep., 1881*, p. 12 (Cameron).

188 Ibid. This view was shared by a number of the inspectors in England, including the chief inspector (Redgrave), who took the view that where employers were reluctant to fence, 'the Employers' Liability Act serves most usefully as an auxiliary force': ibid., p. 4.

189 *Chief insp. ann. rep., 1884*, pp. 11–12, leading Redgrave to observe that 'assuming that there were in the factory ... about 1,000 looms, the expense of fitting a satisfactory guard to each at 2s. 6d. per guard would be £125. They would thus have actually saved money, and the unfortunate sufferer would have saved his eye.' See also *Sutton* v. *John Coupe & Son*, *Chief insp. ann. rep., 1888*, pp. 15–16 (weaver in Lancashire awarded £125 for loss of eye) and *Rowland* v. *J Leech & Sons*, *Chief insp. ann. rep., 1889*, pp. 39–40 (damages of £172 for loss of one eye and damage to the other).

190 'Business was able to settle down and continue, little affected by the new liability rules': Bartrip and Burman, *Wounded soldiers of industry*, p. 189.

191 In 1879, six linen workers were injured by flying shuttles; in 1885, the number was 17, and in 1890, it was seven. All the injuries were suffered by women over the age of 13. In 1890, there was one injury for every 7,000 looms, as compared to one

more surprising given that the cumbersome notice and arbitration procedure was replaced in 1891 by the much more straightforward requirement that '*all* dangerous parts of the machinery' were to be 'securely fenced'.[192] The inspectors could now proceed directly against a recalcitrant employer who failed to provide an effective guard against flying shuttles – or so it seemed.

In *Hindle* v. *Birtwhistle*,[193] however, cotton weavers in Lancashire contended that the obligation to fence only applied to machinery which was in itself dangerous in the ordinary course of careful working. In that case, a shuttle had flown out of an unfenced shuttle-race and seriously injured a weaver. The defendants argued that this was a rare occurrence – there had been in the past five years only four such accidents in a shed of 1,400 looms. They also pointed out that the accident in question resulted from the injured weaver's own negligence in fastening the picking band too tightly. In short, the loom, when properly operated, was not 'dangerous'. The local justices rejected these arguments and convicted; but on appeal the recorder of Blackburn found in the defendants' favour. On further appeal, the queen's bench division held that the unfenced loom might well be dangerous: 'machinery or parts of machinery is and are dangerous if in the ordinary course of human affairs danger may be reasonably anticipated from the use of them without protection'. This was 'entirely a matter of degree', depending upon 'the frequency with which that contingency is likely to arise' – and any such consideration must include 'the contingency of carelessness on the part of the workman in charge of [the machinery]' in addition to all other relevant factors.[194] The case was therefore remitted to the recorder, who now agreed that the loom in question was indeed 'dangerous'.[195]

There is no evidence that this important decision led to a significant increase in the number of prosecutions brought in Ireland, though it must at least have strengthened the persuasive powers of the inspectors. But the decision also cleared the way for injured workers to claim damages for breach of statutory duty – and it was this development which was to lead to an important victory for Irish linen workers in *Scott* v. *Brookfield Linen Co. Ltd*.[196] The plaintiff, a weaver in the defendants' factory, was working at her loom while a mechanic repaired an adjoining box-loom. Many of the looms in the factory were apparently fitted with two wing-guards, or 'screens', one on each side of the loom. But the loom in question had only one screen, as was common when looms closely adjoined each other. In the course of

injury per 9,500 looms in the cotton industry: see *Return of the number of accidents to men, women, young persons and children by shuttles flying from power looms, which have occurred in the cotton, woollen, worsted, flax and silk trades in … 1879, 1885 and 1890*, p. 3, H.C. 1890–91 (197), lxxvii, 345.

192 1891 act, s. 6(2)(emphasis added) – a provision re-enacted by the 1901 act, s. 10(1)(c).
193 [1897] 1 QB 192.
194 Ibid., pp. 195–96, per Wills J.
195 *Chief insp. ann. rep., 1896*, pp. 15–16.
196 [1910] 2 IR 509. See also below, Plate 12.

repairing the loom, the mechanic operated it manually, a shuttle flew out of the unguarded side of the loom and struck the plaintiff in the eye, causing serious injury.

She claimed damages on the grounds of negligence and breach of statutory duty. At the trial, the jury found that the defendants had been negligent in failing to take adequate safety precautions[197] and awarded the plaintiff damages of £450. On appeal by the defendants, Palles CB upheld the verdict on the grounds that the defendants were in breach of their statutory duty to fence under the Factory and Workshop Act 1901.[198] The defendants had admitted that the loom was 'dangerous' and not 'securely' fenced; but they contended that there was no duty to fence machinery while it was being repaired. This defence required the court to look very closely as section 10(1)(d) of the 1901 act, which provided that 'All fencing must be constantly maintained in an efficient state while the parts required to be fenced are in motion or use, *except where they are under repair or under examination in connexion with repair* …'. Palles CB first emphasised that this provision was subject to the general duty to fence, since the passive wording of section 10(1)(c) – 'all dangerous parts … must … be securely fenced' – refers to 'an habitual and continuing state and condition of the machinery'. The obligation to fence therefore continues even during periods of repair unless it is not reasonably practicable, having regard to the exigencies of such repair, to keep all or part of that fencing in place. If the defendants could show that they had originally provided 'secure' guards, and that these had to be removed to enable the repairs to be carried out, they would not be liable. But the fact that the single wing-guard provided in this case *had not* been removed suggested[199] that if a second guard had been fitted to the other side of the loom, it too would have been left in place while the repairs were being carried out. This meant that the real cause of the plaintiff's injury was *not* the failure to maintain the requisite fencing, but the failure to provide it in the first instance.

In spite of these developments, the number of reported shuttle accidents in Ireland generally increased after 1900 or thereabouts. In 1904, for example, 24 accidents were reported; in 1907, 35 and in 1910, 69.[200] Part of

197 In particular, the jury found that the loom was dangerous, that it was not securely fenced and that it was not in such a position or of such construction as to be as safe as it would have been if securely fenced.

198 The chief baron accordingly found it unnecessary to deal with the question of the defendants' liability for negligence. Nor was it necessary to deal with the alternative defence of *volenti non fit injuria*, 'as it was admitted that this doctrine does not apply to the cause of action dependent on statutory liability …': ibid., p. 515. See further below, chap. 11.

199 'The mode in which the screens were attached to the looms was not proved; but … as a removal of the screen during the work of repair would, undoubtedly, have been dangerous, … we ought not to assume that, had the screen been provided, [the repairer], contrary to his duty to his fellow-servants, would have knowingly exposed them to unnecessary danger, by the removal of the screen': ibid., p. 518.

200 *Chief insp. ann. rep., 1904*, pt. II, p. 22; *1907*, p. 122 and *1910*, p. 97.

this increase may have been due simply to the better reporting of accidents. There was also a higher risk of injury from the faster-moving looms[201] – and some evidence of continuing carelessness on the part of the workers.[202] But in most cases, the problem was the failure to provide an adequate guard – not a lack of fencing,[203] but a lack of 'secure' fencing. In 1903, Mary Galway, leader of the Textile Operatives Society, persuaded the Irish Trades Union Congress to resolve that, in light of the 'huge' number of shuttle accidents, all factory owners should be compelled to adopt 'whatever shuttle guard is considered best'.[204] There was still no perfect solution, but the inspectors had a strong preference for some kind of automatic bar guard. Many owners and workers, however, continued for a variety of reasons to prefer wing guards,[205] and in 1911 inspector Eraut felt obliged to concede that automatic bar guards had not been widely adopted; all that he had managed to secure was the better design and care of wing guards.[206] At the behest of the Textile Operatives Society, the Irish Trades Union Congress still sought to have the factory acts amended 'so as to empower the factory inspectors to compel the adoption of any improvements in fencing approved by the Board of Trade'.[207] But this plea fell on deaf ears as the number of shuttle accidents in Ireland showed no sign of declining.[208]

201 See e.g. *Chief insp. ann. rep., 1910*, p. 100 (Eraut).
202 See e.g. ibid. (alleged carelessness in tenting of looms).
203 Cf. as late as 1908, there were still some flax weaving sheds where no guards were in use: *Chief insp. ann. rep., 1908*, p. 111 (Eraut). Damask looms, in particular, were often unguarded – as were woollen looms – on the questionable ground that 'this class of loom works so slowly that there is no danger': *Chief insp. ann. rep., 1898*, pt. II, pp. 39–40 (Kellett) and *1906*, p. 159 (Jackson).
204 *Tenth report of the Irish Trades Union Congress* (Newry, 1903), p. 14.
205 *Chief insp. ann. rep., 1898*, pt. II, p. 39. In 30 of the 35 accidents reported in 1907, wing guards were in use: *Chief insp. ann. rep., 1907*, p. 122 (Williams).
206 *Chief insp. ann. rep., 1911*, pp. 111 and 119.
207 *Seventeenth report of the Irish Trades Union Congress* (Dundalk, 1910), p. 33. Similar resolutions were adopted in 1911, 1912 and 1913 – see e.g *Twentieth report of the Irish Trades Union Congress* (Cork, 1913), pp. 54–55.
208 Although no separate figures are given for 1913, there were in that year 80 non-fatal shuttle accidents in flax weaving sheds; the vast majority of these would have been in Ireland: *Chief insp. ann. rep., 1913*, p. 172.

CHAPTER SIX

The health of linen workers

THE GENERAL DEVELOPMENT OF THE LAW

The production of linen may be reduced to four broad stages – scutching, preparation, spinning and weaving. The scutching of flax was not only dangerous to life and limb; it also exposed scutchers working in a confined space to large quantities of dust. So, too, did the preliminary processes of roughing, hackling and carding to which the scutched flax was subjected in the spinning mills. The flax then passed to the preparing rooms, where further, finer, dust was generated as the fibre passed through a series of stages – spreading, drawing and doubling, and roving – until it was ready for spinning. The wet-spinning process which prevailed in Ireland from 1828 onwards was designed to soften the fibre and to increase its flexibility and tensile strength so that it could be drawn out and spun into fine yarn. For this purpose it passed through a trough containing hot water before reaching the drawing rollers and spindles. During the spinning, which took place at high speed, the water flew off the yarn, thread and spindles in a fine mist or spray. The heat and humidity generated by the very nature of wet-spinning was also to be found, albeit generally to a lesser degree, in the weaving sheds.[1] In short, every stage in the manufacture of linen involved processes which in one way or another were liable to endanger the health of the workers concerned.

Early commentators on conditions in the textile industry were primarily concerned with the *general* effect of factory work, and in particular the length of the working day, on the health – and morals – of the workers, particularly women and children.[2] It was this view which dominated the thinking of the factory commissioners in 1833, although they did acknowledge that 'excessive fatigue, privation of sleep, pain in various parts of the body, and swelling of the feet experienced by the young workers, coupled with the constant standing, the peculiar attitudes of the body, and the peculiar motions of the limbs required in the labour of the factory, together with the elevated

---

1 See generally W.A. McCutcheon, *The industrial archaeology of Northern Ireland* (Belfast, 1980), pp. 241, 299–300 and 307–12 and Dr H.S. Purdon, 'Flax and linen' in T. Oliver (ed.), *Dangerous trades: The historical, social and legal aspects of industrial occupations as affecting health, by a number of experts* (London, 1902), p. 691. Further details on each stage of the manufacturing process are to be found in the various reports discussed below.

2 See e.g. J.P. Kay, *The moral and physical condition of the working classes employed in the cotton manufacture in Manchester* (London, 1832) and P. Gaskell, *The manufacturing population of England, its moral, social and physical condition* (London, 1833).

temperature and the impure atmosphere in which that labour is often carried on, do sometimes ultimately terminate in the production of serious, permanent, and incurable disease …'.[3] By this time, there was some medical concern about *specific* health hazards. Working with flax, for example, was known to cause respiratory problems,[4] and the use of exhaust ventilation in factories was being recommended 'for removing the dust of all manufactures which affect the lungs by mechanical irritation'.[5] The dangers of exposing children to the conditions in flax spinning-mills was also recognised. One report prepared for the factory commissioners, for example, characterised the wet-spinning process as 'by far the worst feature in the whole system', and continued:

It cannot be permitted that [young children] should continue their work for twelve or thirteen hours in the state in which I have witnessed some, from the spray which the spindles throw off upon their chests, while their bare feet rest upon the wet floor. With all possible precautions, such as waterproof clothing, the occupation would still be much to be lamented for any age; but I think a too general disregard must be confessed to exist on the part of the proprietors of factories … of all means to alleviate this great grievance.[6]

Although the 1833 and 1844 acts generally ignored the question of safe working conditions, the one noticeable exception was a provision specifically designed for the protection of children and young persons in flax spinning mills.[7]

Further medical studies were undertaken from time to time, before the 'canker' of industrial diseases was brought firmly to public attention by John Simon, medical officer to the privy council, in the 1850s and early 1860s. One of his many studies of factory conditions suggested that about three-quarters of flax-workers had severe bronchial disorders, and that others had stomach or eye problems caused by the fine dust. Simon also drew attention to the hazards encountered from working in an overheated and humid atmosphere.[8] As a result of his endeavours, the annual meeting of the Social

---

3 *First report from the central board of H.M. commissioners appointed to collect information in the manufacturing districts, as to the employment of children in factories* … , p. 29, H.C. 1833 (450), xx, 33.

4 See B. Ramazzini, *De morbis artificium diatriba* (1705), trans. R. James (London and York, 1746) and other early work cited in E. Tuypens, 'Byssinosis among cotton workers in Belgium' in *Br. J. Indust. Med.*, 18 (1961), 117.

5 C.T. Thackrah, *The effects of the principal arts, trades and professions, and of civic states and habits of living, on health and longevity* (London, 1831), p. 109.

6 *First report from the factory commissioners: Examinations by district commissioners for the northern district, A.2: Evidence of Mr Mackintosh*, p. 94, H.C. 1833 (450), xx, 94. For example, Catharine Mullens, a spinner aged 16 employed by Boomar & Co. in Belfast, stated that 'although she is protected in some degree by an oil-cloth petticoat, she is very wet about the legs and feet, and has a severe cough at present, and her feet and ancles swell': ibid., A1: *Evidence of Mr. Stuart*, p. 129.

7 1844 act, s. 19. See further below, p. 175. Section 18 of the act continued a general provision for the periodical limewashing of interior walls and ceilings first introduced in 1802.

8 See especially *Third annual report of the medical officer of the committee of council on the state of the public health*, pp.145–52, H.C. 1861 (161), xvi, 487–94 (report by Dr

Science Association held in London in 1862 was devoted to the effects of occupation upon health, and concluded with the passing of a resolution for the extension of the factory acts to cover industrial diseases and unhealthy working conditions.[9] Two years later, the factory acts were extended to non-textile factories of a particularly unhealthy nature, and provision was expressly made for their ventilation 'in such a manner as to render harmless so far as is practicable any ... dust or other impurities generated in the process of manufacture that may be injurious to health'.[10] The further extension of the acts in 1867 to all non-textile factories in which 50 or more persons were employed in *any* manufacturing process also brought with it a general provision relating to the installation of fans, where a grinding, glazing, polishing or any other process generated dust which was inhaled by the workers 'to an injurious extent'. An inspector who considered that such inhalation could be prevented by the installation of a fan or other mechanical means could now direct the factory occupier to provide such means within a reasonable time.[11]

Neither of these provisions applied to textile factories. But the particular effect of working conditions on the health of linen workers in Ireland came under particular scrutiny from 1867 onwards,[12] largely as a result of the initiative of Dr C. D. Purdon, certifying surgeon for the Belfast District.[13] He described the effect of dust inhalation as follows:

> Greenhow on lung diseases in the linen district of Yorkshire) and *Fourth annual report*, pp. 12–32, H.C. 1862 (179), xxii, 476–96, especially p. 18: 'In flax factories, the production of disease is terribly great ... [T]he deaths from unboxed machinery ... probably count as nothing in comparison with those which the unventilatedness of factories occasions.' These reports are confined to England and Wales.

9   *Transactions of the national association for the promotion of social science* (London, 1862), p. 670.
10 Factory Acts Extension Act 1864, s. 4. To prevent this requirement from being infringed by 'the wilful misconduct or wilful negligence of the workmen', a factory owner was authorised (by s. 5) to make special rules, subject to the approval of the home secretary, breach of which could lead to 'a penalty not exceeding one pound'. The act applied only to the manufacture of earthenware, lucifer matches, percussion caps and cartridges and to factories in which paper-staining and fustian-cutting was carried on.
11 Factory Acts Extension Act 1867, s. 9.
12 The earliest work appears to be that of Dr J. Moore, 'On the influence of flax spinning on the health of the mill workers of Belfast', in *Transactions of the National Association for the Promotion of Social Sciences meeting in Belfast, 1867* (Linenhall Lib., N 13668), reproduced in P. Brooke (ed.), *Problems of a growing city: Belfast 1780–1870* (Belfast, 1973), p. 176.
13 See especially *The mortality of flax mill and factory workers as compared with other classes of the community, the diseases they labour under and the causes that render the death-rate from phthisis, etc. so high* (Belfast, 1873); *Longevity of flax mill and factory operatives* (Belfast, 1875) and *The sanitary state of the Belfast factory district during ten years (1864 to 1873 inclusive) under various aspects* (Belfast, 1877). See also Dr Purdon's evidence in *Report to the local government board on proposed changes in hours and ages of employment in textile factories by J. H. Bridges, M.D. and T. Holmes*, p. 22 [C. 754], H.C. 1873, lv, 827 and in *Report of the factory and workshop commissioners: Minutes of evidence*, p. 839 [C. 1443–I], H.C. 1876, xxi, 838, and the summary by his son, Dr H.S. Purdon, 'Flax and linen' in Oliver, *Dangerous trades*, p. 691.

The irritating quality of the dust is felt on the throat, which soon becomes dry. This irritation gradually creeps into the lungs, and produces chronic inflammation of the lining membrane, which soon manifests its presence by the worker being attacked each morning with a paroxysm of dyspnoea and coughing: the dyspnoea is sometimes so great that he takes hold of the table of the machine in order to enable him to get over the attack more easily; this state is so well known that when a worker is seen suffering so, he is said to be 'poucey'.[14] Those employed in the roughing, sorting, hackling and preparing of flax suffer from this affection, and in the great majority of cases die from phthisis, etc.[15]

Purdon's analysis showed that flax workers, with 'nearly three-fifths of those that die annually being taken off by diseases of the respiratory organ', suffered 'far more' from phthisis than the general working population, only two-fifths of whom died from such causes.[16] In the preparing and hackling rooms, 'the atmosphere is constantly loaded with the flax dust'. The death rate of those employed in preparing rooms was 'exceedingly high' at 31 per thousand; few of the workers – mainly adult men – 'live beyond sixty years', and 'the greatest number die before forty-five years'.[17] Next came the hacklers, with a death rate of 11.1 per thousand; in their case, illness was compounded by alcohol: 'When they begin to suffer from the effect of the dust, they commence to drink and go on using alcoholic stimulants till at last they die from the effects of the drink, or hasten the advance of chest affections [*sic*] by its inordinate consumption'. But the workers who suffered most from inhaling the dust were those, mainly females, who worked in the preparing and carding departments: 'These suffer in the same manner as the males, but in a far more aggravated degree.... And it is not surprising that in this department the death rate from chest affections is very high, exceeding that of the entire district from all diseases.' If a carder began work under the age of 18, 'she very rarely, if constantly employed at it, lives beyond 30 years'. The rate of mortality among spinners and weavers was 'also very great' due to 'the constant inhaling of the damp air in a room where the temperature is kept rather high'. In addition, 'a good deal of disease is generated by their garments being wetted by the spray from the spindles, which so saturates them that in going out into the cold air in the evening the wet clothes give

14 From the French *poussière*, dust.
15 *Mortality of flax mill and factory workers*, p. 7.
16 Ibid., p. 4. Further details are given in *Sanitary state*, which also includes (at pp. 43–48) an 'address to millworkers' by Dr R.H. Newett, medical officer at Ligoniel, which concluded: 'You owe it as a duty to yourselves, to your country, and above all, to the generations which are to come, to directly aid the state in its efforts to conserve your health. Provide for your families a nutritious, wholesome diet.... In your clothing, have regard to health, comfort and neatness. In your persons, clothing, and houses practice cleanliness.... Read good and profitable books; banish from your houses the villainous trash issued in cheap numbers which sets forth as heroes, the highwaymen and other vile characters ...'.
17 *Sanitary state*, p. 13, adding that 'this affection of the lungs, that flax dressers suffer so much from, is so well known to the army surgeons that they have forbidden the recruiting sergeants to enlist any from this department'.

them bronchitis, almost invariably'. But notwithstanding these dangers, spinning was not as dangerous to health as carding and hackling.[18]

Dust and humidity were not the only dangers faced by textile workers, who were also exposed to 'long standing and a drooping posture in the spinning and doubling department; monotony of work; continuous strain upon the attention, and excessive noise with vibration of machinery. To these must be added vitiated air from excessive consumption of gas, from overcrowding, and general defects of ventilation.'[19] For some time, however, the extent to which poor working conditions were responsible for the undoubted unhealthy state of many workers remained in some doubt. In 1867, for example, Dr John Moore agreed that 'a large amount of sickness' prevailed among the mill-working population of Belfast; but he concluded that this was due not to 'the nature of the occupation', but to the lack of 'good, nutritious and well-cooked food'.[20] But Dr Purdon took the more balanced view that working conditions were not *solely* to blame for high mortality:

The great mortality from chest affections, in certain departments, is caused chiefly by the unhealthiness of the employment, commencing to work in unhealthy departments at too early an age, in being employed at work that is unsuited to the physical capacity (either through age or physical development), neglect of sanitary laws [with regard to domestic houses], insufficient or improper diet, unhealthy parentage, and insufficient clothing.[21]

As with safety, the protection of health occupied only a small part of the factory and workshop commissioners' attention in 1876. They briefly acknowledged the problems caused by dust in the carding and hackling of flax and by splashing in the process of wet-spinning; but they contented themselves with a call for the better enforcement of the existing law and an exhortation to the inspectors to encourage 'such measures of relief as have been ascertained to be practicable'.[22] The 1878 act gave effect to these recommendations by extending to all factories and workshops the ventilation provision in the 1864 act and the inspector's authority to direct the installation of a fan or other mechanical means where dust was generated by grinding, glazing, polishing 'or any process' to an 'injurious' extent.[23]

It will be noted that up to this point the health provisions of the factory acts, such as they were, tended to be very general both as regards the standards to be applied and the range of industries which they covered. This approach may be attributed in part to other priorities, and in part to a lack

18   Ibid., pp. 5–7 and 13–14.
19   J.T. Arlidge, *The hygiene, diseases and mortality of occupations* (London, 1892), p. 73. See also A.S. Wohl, *Endangered lives: Public health in Victorian Britain* (London, 1983), chap. 10.
20   'On the influence of flax spinning on the health of the mill workers of Belfast', p. 4.
21   *Sanitary state*, p. 10.
22   *Report of the commissioners appointed to inquire into the working of the factory and workshop acts*, pp. lxxii–lxxv [C. 1443], H.C. 1876, xxix, 72–75.
23   1878 act, ss. 3 and 36.

of scientific and particularly medical expertise on the part of the inspectorate.[24] All this changed in the last decade or so of the nineteenth century. As before, it was cotton which led the way. As a result of medical findings and, it should be said, of trade union pressure, parliament passed the Cotton Cloth Factories Act, the first major industrial health legislation, in 1889.[25] This was followed by the 'dangerous trades' provision of the Factory and Workshop Act 1891, which authorised the home secretary to certify *any* industrial process as 'dangerous or injurious to health' and thereupon to require the occupier of a particular factory to adopt 'such special measures as appear to the chief inspector to be reasonably practicable and to meet the necessities of the case'.[26] This enactment was followed by a number of special inquiries into various industries considered to be 'dangerous', and by 1896, factories engaged in twenty or so processes were subject to special health or safety rules.[27] This process of specialisation was facilitated after 1895 by a growing expertise on the part of the inspectorate. In 1896, a medical doctor (Whitelegge) was appointed chief inspector; two years later, the first medical inspector of factories (Dr Legge) was appointed, to be followed in 1899 by the appointment of an engineering adviser.[28]

It was in this general context that the causal connection between working conditions in the manufacture of linen and the ill-health of many linen workers was put beyond reasonable doubt.[29] In 1891, an inquiry into the mortality of linen workers in Belfast with particular reference to their conditions of work was conducted by E.H. Osborn, the inspector responsible for enforcing the special

24 'Looking back over 100 years of the history of the factory department the most striking feature seems to be the long period that elapsed before the science of medicine was considered necessary as an aid to improving working conditions in industry': J.C. Bridge, 'Health' in 'Review of the work of the inspectorate 1833–1932', in *Chief insp. ann. rep.*, *1932*, p. 41.

25 See *Hansard 3*, cccxl, 91 (22 Aug. 1889).

26 Section 8. For a general survey see e.g. H.A. Mess, *Factory legislation and its administration 1891–1924* (London, 1926), chaps. III–V and B. Harrison, 'Suffer the working day: Women in the "dangerous trades", 1880–1914', in *Women's Studies Int'l Forum*, 13 (1990), 79.

27 See e.g. *Redgrave's Factory Acts*, ed. J.A. Redgrave and H.S. Scrivener (7th ed., London, 1898), pp. 192–93. Each set of rules applied only to a particular factory, a restriction which meant that factories carrying on a similar 'dangerous' process could be subject to different rules.

28 See e.g. Mess, *Factory legislation*, p. 215: 'The period from 1891 ... is marked by great advances in factory legislation.... Medical and chemical science were applied to problems of industrial hygiene. The greatest improvements were in the ... unhealthy trades.'

29 But not *all* doubt: 'Since ... Belfast's [general] record as regards phthisis is not exceptional for Ireland ... and also since the incidence of that mortality on age and sex in Belfast is broadly similar to that in Ireland as a whole, it might fairly be contended that it is not likely that industrial causes have played a very important part in conducing to the disease in Belfast.... [But] it may be that industrial causes have operated to conduce to the exceptional female phthisis mortality [in Belfast] at the ages of 25–35, and 35–45': Belfast Health Commission, *Report to the local government board for Ireland*, pp. 36–37 [Cd. 4128], H.C. 1908, xxxi, 746–47.

provisions now applicable to cotton cloth factories.[30] In his report, published in 1893,[31] Osborn drew upon an extensive experience of the cotton industry thereby inaugurating a process which over the next twenty years or so was to enable linen workers indirectly to benefit from regulatory developments designed to provide healthier working conditions which the more powerful cotton workers were able to secure from time to time.

Osborn's findings generally corroborated those of Dr Purdon. The mortality rate for linen workers was higher than for the general population and this fact clearly pointed to the effect of 'special conditions' to which they were subject, which Osborn summarised as 'dust, damp, heat and imperfect ventilation'. In general, the inhalation of dust was more dangerous to health than exposure to heat and humidity, but both were harmful. Hacklers and roughers among the males, and carders among the females, were particularly liable to suffer from phthisis, bronchitis and asthma.[32] Spinning and weaving involved a level of humidity which Osborn characterised as 'oppressive' and 'unwholesome', and worse than anything which he had found in England or Scotland.[33]

These findings led the home secretary in January 1894 to certify that the processes carried on in flax mills and linen factories were among those which were 'dangerous or injurious to health', and the industry was to retain this status for the remainder of the period under consideration. Accordingly, from 1894 the only issue was the nature of the 'special measures' required to meet 'the necessities of the case'. The first set of special rules, based on Osborn's own recommendations, was published in July 1894 and amended in April 1896. But these rules were soon subjected to criticism, and in 1902 a second inquiry was undertaken by a superintending inspector of factories, Commander H.P. Smith,[34] who concluded that greater medical knowledge and experience, together with the effects of new technology, now required further, and in particular more detailed, provisions for safeguarding the health of linen

---

30 Osborn joined the inspectorate in 1868 and spent most of the next twenty years based in Lancashire. He was cotton cloth factories inspector from 1889 to 1899, and engineering adviser from 1899 to 1903, when he retired. In 1883 he had carried out a special study of the mortality of cotton weavers in Blackburn – see *Report on the effects of heavy sizing in cotton weaving upon the health of the operatives employed* [C. 3861], H.C. 1884, lxxii, 169.

31 *Report of an inquiry into the conditions of work in the Belfast flax mills and linen factories, and into the mortality among textile operatives, etc., in the city of Belfast during 1891* [C.7287], H.C. 1893–94, xvii, 537.

32 Ibid., pp. 6–8. In particular, women aged 15–29 were disproportionately liable to die from phthisis if they worked in the linen industry.

33 Ibid., pp. 3–5 and 15–18. Most of the doctors who wrote to Osborn agreed with his general analysis – but not all. Thus, Dr Taylor of Tandragee wrote that 'in my experience, extending over fourteen years, I have never noticed any special ailment attributable to employment at the flax industries here among those employed at them': ibid., p. 20.

34 A former Royal Navy officer, Smith joined the factory inspectorate in 1875, assigned to Sheffield; he was a member of the dangerous trades committee during the 1890s, and was superintending inspector with special duties connected with dangerous trades and dangerous machinery from 1903 until 1906.

workers.[35] Accordingly, a new set of regulations was adopted in March 1906,[36] and these remained in force until 1914.

Danger to health arising from excessive humidity, however, remained of paramount concern to the cotton workers of Yorkshire and Lancashire, and in 1909 they secured the appointment of a further committee of inquiry, which in due course led to more stringent regulation.[37] These developments led in turn to a third inquiry into working conditions in the linen industry, with particular reference to the unhealthy nature of excessive humidity. Following extensive investigations of, and experiments relating to, conditions in spinning rooms and weaving sheds, a committee of experts under the chairmanship of Commander Smith (now Sir Hamilton Freer-Smith) concluded that further provision was also required in linen, as in cotton.[38] But the first world war intervened before any action could be taken.

Although various aspects of their working conditions adversely affected the health of linen workers,[39] we concentrate in this chapter on the attempts to alleviate the problems caused by excessive dust and humidity.

ALLEVIATING THE DANGER TO HEALTH CAUSED BY EXCESSIVE DUST

Legislative attempts to relieve linen workers from the adverse effect of inhaling excessive quantities of flax dust involved the inspectorate in two quite different exercises. In relation to scutch mills they were normally dealing with a traditional and technologically-backward aspect of linen manufacture organised in poorly-maintained premises controlled by impecunious and part-time operators; but when it came to the spinning mills and factories, they were in general dealing with highly organised, large-scale and technologically-advanced establishments run by highly successful entrepreneurs. In both cases,

35 *Report upon the conditions of work in flax and linen mills as affecting the health of the operatives employed therein* [Cd. 1997], H.C. 1904, x, 465. See also *Report of the departmental committee on compensation for industrial diseases*, p. 15 [Cd. 3495], H.C. 1907, xxxiv, 1065 (fibroid phthisis accepted as an industrial disease specific to employment in flax mills – see especially evidence of Professor James A. Lindsay at p. 229).

36 These regulations were governed by the Factory and Workshop Act 1901, s. 79 and therefore applied automatically to *every* factory and workshop of the specified class.

37 *Report of the departmental committee on humidity and ventilation of cotton weaving sheds* [Cd. 4484], H.C. 1909, xv, 635. The recommendations made in this report led to the Factory and Workshop (Cotton Cloth Factories) Act 1911 – see further below, p. 185.

38 *Report of the departmental committee on humidity and ventilation in flax mills and linen factories* [Cd. 7433], H.C. 1914, xxxvi, 1. It may be noted that the nucleus of this committee consisted of members of the departmental committee which had examined the cotton weaving sheds in 1909. The linen industry was represented by G.H. Ewart (of William Ewart & Sons, Belfast) and H. Cummins (President of the Lurgan Weavers' Association).

39 For a general study, see J.P. Hamill, 'A study of female textile operatives in the Belfast linen industry, 1890–1939' (unpublished Ph.D. thesis, Queen's University Belfast, 1999), chap. 3.

however, the inspectors were also required to have regard to the attitude of workers often torn between safeguarding their health and safety and preserving their earnings and ultimately their jobs. When we add to these competing tensions the need to master the developing technology of exhaust ventilation,[40] we begin to understand the complexity of the task facing the inspectorate.

1. Scutch mills

The inspectors' initial concern may have been the safety of those working in the scutch mills; but they quickly appreciated the additional danger to health arising from the vast quantities of dust generated by the scutching process. As with other factories, these mills were supposed to be 'ventilated in such a manner as to render harmless, so far as is practicable, all the ... dust or other impurities generated in the course of the manufacturing process ... that may be injurious to health'; it was also open to an inspector, if he considered it appropriate, to direct a scutch mill owner to provide a fan or other mechanical means of ventilation within a reasonable time.[41] When Redgrave visited Ireland in 1878, however, he was less than optimistic about bringing the scutch mills into line with these provisions:

The dust clings to walls and roofs, and the heavier particles lie on the mud floor knee deep; even the approach is frequently over heaps of dust and broken flax straw. I am not as sanguine of immediate improvement in cleanliness as I am in the precautions that will be taken to prevent accidents.... I visited several flax scutch mills with the special object of examining the machinery, and the condition of the interiors as to ventilation and cleanliness, and I am strongly impressed with the difficulty of dealing with the question of ventilation and cleanliness satisfactorily.[42]

The local inspectors were equally pessimistic:

All of [these mills] are greatly in need of improved ventilation, though to remedy this last state of things would be very difficult. The occupiers are in very many instances poor men who live from hand to mouth, and who would, if called on for any considerable expenditure in the way of improvements, simply abandon the business, and close the scutching mill. Apart from this is the fact that the nature of the work entails an atmosphere thick with flax dust; and where, as in the majority of instances, the building is low roofed, and the accommodation of a most limited description, to

---

40   See especially *Departmental committee appointed to inquire into the ventilation of factories and workshops: First report* [Cd. 1302], H.C. 1902, xii, 467 (includes 'a general account of the conditions of efficient ventilation') and *Second report* [Cd. 3552], H.C. 1907, x, 449 (effectiveness of low pressure and high pressure fans, arrangement of inlets and outlets, etc.); *Illustrations of methods of dust extraction in factories and workshops compiled by Commander Sir Hamilton Freer-Smith RN* [Cd. 3223], H.C. 1906, cx, 125.

41   1878 act, ss. 3 and 36; 1901 act, ss. 1(1)(d) and 74. In *Hoare* v. *Ritchie* [1901] 1 QB 434 it was held necessary to show only that the dust existed in such quantity as must necessarily be injurious to health in the long run; no evidence of actual injury to health was required.

42   *Chief insp. ann. rep., 1879*, p. 71.

effect any real improvement it would become necessary to pull down the whole structure and erect a new building.[43]

The inspectors' attempts to persuade mill owners to adopt the most obvious solution – the installation of an appropriate fan – only brought about further frustration:

Over and over again the occupiers of the wretched sheds ... have been enjoined to erect fans ... and over and over again they have evaded this duty under one excuse or other. Either the occupier is too poor, or the fan has been ordered, but has not yet arrived, or the scutching season is nearly over, and it is not worth while doing anything till the next one – anything, in short, rather than what is required. Sometimes indeed the fan has come, after years of effort, and is promptly put up in the wrong place, where its action does more harm than good; often, whether put up in the right or wrong one, it is not properly looked after, becomes clogged with dirt and worse than useless.[44]

Little progress was made until the 1890s.[45] Snape, the new inspector for the north of Ireland, saw 'reason' in the argument that the harmful effect of dust in large quantities was offset to some extent by the fact that scutchers only worked for four or five months each year and, when working, frequently stepped outside for a breath of fresh air.[46] He was satisfied, nevertheless, that conditions could – and should – be improved, particularly when he discovered that a locally-made fan had been installed in a scutch mill near Coleraine with good results.[47] Accordingly, when another scutch mill owner in that area refused to instal a fan, Snape brought what turned out to be an important test case. In *Snape* v. *Young*,[48] the court held that the dust generated in Young's mill had been inhaled by the workers to an injurious extent; he was fined one guinea – but, more importantly, the court further ordered that his mill should not be worked next season unless a fan or other mechanical means of ventilation had been installed. Both the fine and the order were upheld when Young appealed to Coleraine quarter sessions.

Encouraged by this decision, Snape brought proceedings against other recalcitrant scutch mill owners.[49] His arm was further strengthened in 1900,

43 Ibid. (Cameron). See also Woodgate at p. 79.
44 *Chief insp. ann. rep.*, *1901*, pt. I, p. 140 (Whitelegge). There was also opposition from the male scutchers themselves, on the basis that fans caused 'an unpleasant draught', and 'there is [already] quite enough ventilation, especially in stormy weather': *Chief insp. ann. rep.*, *1900*, p. 335 (Kirkwood).
45 The inspectors 'have not taken very vigorous action against owners of scutch mills from the passing of [the 1878 Act] until the present time ...': *Chief insp. ann. rep.*, *1899*, p. 35 (Snape).
46 As reported in *Chief insp. ann. rep.*, *1907*, p. 37.
47 *Chief insp. ann. rep.*, *1895*, p. 134, where the point is also made that the scattered nature of the scutch mills meant that neither owners nor workers had the opportunity to obtain the kind of technical education 'readily obtained on the continent and which is so essential to the success of ... the textile trade'.
48 *Chief insp. ann. rep.*, *1899*, p. 34. See further below, p. 323.
49 In 1901, he brought proceedings against eight owners for failure to install fans and

with the appearance of a new fan, 'on the Belgian principle', which was not only more efficient and safer than any other then in use, but also cheaper.[50] The mill owners no longer had any justification for failing to comply with the law, and Snape's more aggressive approach met with further success: 'during the present season we have had more fans erected than in any former season'.[51] But his 'earnest endeavour' to complete this work was unduly optimistic. As he himself admitted, many mill owners still could not afford a fan of any description – and many of those who could preferred to use a make which was not only 'comparatively useless' when new, but which was also inadequately maintained in many instances.[52]

His realism proved to be only too well founded. When the Employment of Women Act 1907 repealed the exemption which hitherto had applied to the hours of employment of women in scutch mills,[53] two of the lady inspectors (Martindale and Whitworth) undertook a special inquiry into their general working conditions. Having agreed with Snape that ventilation was 'the most important matter requiring attention', they reported that in those mills in which a fan had been installed, 'the fan was often too small and situated very high up and entirely clogged by dust and dirt, and we became accustomed to the workers complaining that it was of little use and had to be incessantly cleaned'. They found that a 'Belgian' fan had been installed in only a few mills – and in any case, 'in our opinion ... this does not prove to be an efficient method of carrying away the dust'.[54]

It was clear that little had changed – and so it remained. In 1908, it was observed that 'the millers are in nearly all cases ... men without any idea of the first principles of exhaust ventilation, to whom a fan is a fan no matter what the type, where placed or how driven, and such details as inlets and outlets and short circuiting receive little or no consideration'.[55] The difficulties to be overcome were so 'enormous' that 'little or no progress has been made in spite of constant attention on the part of the inspectors'.[56] In 1913 it was

secured a conviction in each case. In two of the cases, a small fine was imposed; in the other six, 'orders were given by the magistrates to erect the fans before a given date, and, when after these decisions, five of the occupiers neglected to obey these, the defendants in each case were fined in penalties from 15s. to 20s.': *Chief insp. ann. rep., 1901*, pt. I, p. 141 and *1902*, pt. I, p. 140 – leaving Snape to wonder if it was all worth the effort.

50   A type of fan which was attached to the main shaft, so that it was bound to be in motion whenever the mill was working. Although the original was made and designed in Belgium, replicas could be made in Ireland by an ordinary village carpenter at a cost of not more than £4 – although one fan was required between every second and third stock, so that a six-stock mill, for example, would require three fans: *Chief insp. ann. rep., 1900*, p. 334.

51   *Chief insp. ann. rep., 1902*, pt. I, pp. 141–42.

52   Ibid.

53   See above, p. 148.

54   *Chief insp. ann. rep., 1907*, p. 213.

55   *Chief insp. ann. rep., 1908*, p. 104 (Eraut). See also *Chief insp. ann. rep., 1912*, p. 101, where Bennett reported that little had changed – fans, when installed, were generally ineffective, on account of 'crude design, want of regular cleaning, and ignorant use'.

56   *Chief insp. ann. rep., 1909*, p. 104 (Graves, superintending inspector for the Northern

openly conceded that the problem had 'baffled' most of the inspectors – and yet, in the face of the usual litany of failure, came a resolute shaft of optimism: 'The outlook at the present time is distinctly hopeful for the future.'[57]

2. The preparation rooms of flax spinning mills

Parliament was slow to respond to the growing medical evidence of the dangers to health posed by the working conditions typically found in textile mills and factories. Its first, somewhat tentative, step in this direction was a further reduction in the length of the working day:

Our report has indicated the existence of specially unfavourable conditions in two manufactures which together employ more than three-fifths of all protected persons in textile trades, viz., the cotton and the flax manufactures. Some of these evils admit of entire removal, and all probably of mitigation, were sanitary inspection of factories rendered more efficient than in the present state of the law it is. Meantime their principal bearing on the specific object of our inquiry is, that if an atmosphere is bad, it is better and safer to work in it for nine hours than for ten.[58]

The Factory Act 1874 – 'an act to make better provision for improving the health of women, young persons, and children employed in manufactures ...' – duly reduced the working week for women and young persons, albeit only from 60 hours to 56½ hours, and also raised the minimum working age for children from 9 to 10.[59] These changes were effected in the face of predictions by the employers of their dire consequences for the Irish linen industry, and it may be that the strength of this opposition tempered for some time the movement for further 'mitigation' of the working conditions in the industry. But as Baker clearly showed through his development of a 'respirator' for use by hacklers,[60] the way was still open for the 'voluntary' adoption of more healthy practices.

The particularly unhealthy conditions associated with carding and hackling flax were, as we have seen, acknowledged by the factory and workshop commissioners in 1876; but the 1878 act included only a general requirement (in section 3) that all factories should be ventilated 'so far as is practicable'. In

---

Division), adding that 'it is a pity that something cannot be done on the lines of the co-operative dairies to foster [scutching] and improve its conditions'.

57 *Chief insp. ann. rep., 1913*, p. 14 (Bennett). In 1914 the principal lady inspector (Anderson) took part in discussions with the Irish Department of Agriculture and Technical Instruction with a view to concerted action to deal with the problem of ventilation in scutch mills; but the war intervened before any action could be taken: A.M. Anderson, *Women in the factory: An administrative adventure, 1893 to 1921* (London, 1922), pp. 109–10.

58 *Report on proposed changes in hours and ages of employment in textile factories 1873*, p. 60.

59 1874 act, ss. 4–5 and 13.

60 See e.g. C.D. Purdon, *Sanitary state*, p. 39. This respirator was worn 'for a time ... as [some workers] derived much benefit from it. Many of the men, however, would not wear it, as it prevented them from expectorating when chewing tobacco': H.S. Purdon, 'Flax and linen', p. 696.

sharp contrast to their experience with scutch mills, however, the inspectors in Ireland were at first favourably impressed by the efforts made by the owners of flax spinning mills. In 1879, for example, Cameron reported that 'much has been done ... to prevent, as far as possible, the issuing of dust from the varied machinery, and to improve ventilation in the mills ...'.[61] He was, apparently, 'very successful in persuading the occupiers of numerous factories to erect fans both in the preparing and spinning rooms, thus reducing to a large extent the collection of dust'.[62] But he met with much less success in his efforts to persuade the workers to use mouth and nose respirators; like many inspectors before and after him, Cameron was unable to overcome the 'prejudice' of the workers against the use of such safeguards.[63]

In spite of Cameron's apparent success, the working conditions in flax mills and factories remained a matter of concern, and in 1891 came under the detailed scrutiny of E.H. Osborn, the cotton cloth factories inspector. He examined the conditions of work in flax mills and linen factories throughout Ireland and received evidence from a number of doctors practising in various parts of Ulster.[64] His findings were sufficiently serious to persuade the home secretary in January 1894 to certify the linen industry as involving processes which were 'dangerous or injurious to health' for the purposes of the 1891 act.[65] Osborn himself drafted a set of special rules to deal with the questions of dust and humidity, which he then discussed with the Irish Flax Association and the Linen Merchants' Association as representatives of the linen employers.[66] They found his proposals in general to be 'fair', but they also managed to secure some modifications. The rules were then promulgated in July 1894 by the home secretary as 'Special rules for the spinning and weaving of flax'.[67]

Osborn had found that many roughers and sorters worked in 'a continual cloud of dust', but that the York Street Flax Spinning Co.'s mill had a more effective system of ventilation by which the dust was drawn forward and down from the face of the worker. This he thought was the 'best arrangement' and should become the rule, 'unless some other arrangement

---

61 *Chief insp. ann. rep., 1879*, p. 63.

62 *Chief insp. ann. rep., 1890*, pp. 38–39 (Snape).

63 *Chief insp. ann. rep., 1886*, p. 62 (Cramp). Cf. 'The repugnance that the operatives in the dusty and consumption-engendering departments of flax mills have to the wearing of these life preservers is remarkable ... They tacitly agree not to show their frailty – thus making its assertion more inevitable – by subjecting themselves to any precautionary measure whatever': L.C. Marshall, *The practical flax spinner* (London, 1885), p. 118.

64 This evidence is summarised in *Chief insp. ann. rep., 1893*, pp. 211–13.

65 *London Gazette*, 5 Jan. 1894.

66 He does not appear to have consulted any workers' representatives, even though concern about 'the hackling shops in Belfast and elsewhere' was expressed at the inaugural meeting of the ITUC – see *Report of the first Irish Trades Congress* (Dublin, 1894), p. 35.

67 These rules, reproduced in *Chief insp. ann. rep., 1893*, p. 214, were amended in 1896 in relation to humidity, but not in relation to dust. Osborn explained that this 'special

shall be found equally effective, to the satisfaction of the inspector'.[68] In the machine hackling rooms, the most effective system of ventilation was to have fans 'provided on the side of the room where the machines are, and inlets provided from 6–7 feet from the ground on the opposite side' – once again, unless some other arrangement 'shall be found equally effective' by the inspector. In all rooms, 'respirators shall be provided for the use of ... children or young persons, and be worn by them at work'. But Osborn was advised that it was 'pointless' to include adults in this last rule: 'It was stated that men and women would not wear [respirators], the former chiefly because they are generally in the habit of chewing tobacco while at work. The opinions upon this point were practically unanimous, and I think have reasonable grounds ...'.[69] The penalty for contravention of any special rule was a fine not exceeding £2, and provision was made for the promulgation of all such rules 'in legible characters in conspicuous places in the factory ... where they may be conveniently read by the persons employed'.[70]

Not unnaturally, Osborn was given the 'superintendence' of the new rules in Scotland and Ireland.[71] He reported an immediate improvement in working conditions in roughing and sorting rooms, and observed that 'the [new] system for drawing the dust ... straight away from the hackles where it is made has amply answered expectations, and quite revolutionised the working conditions of these rooms to the satisfaction both of employers and of employed'.[72] He did, however, concede that it was proving difficult to devise a system for preventing the dust escaping into the air in the first place. But he found enough workers wearing respirators to lead him, 'with perseverance', to anticipate success in overcoming any remaining prejudice against them.[73]

In 1900, however, the new cotton cloth factories inspector (Williams) was much less sanguine. The special rules had, no doubt, been effective in improving standards in a number of instances; but there were still considerable variations both in the means of ventilation and in the results attained. In particular, 'inlets were frequently so utterly inadequate or unsuitable as to seriously cripple the efficiency of the exhaust fans provided [in roughing, sorting and machine hackling rooms] in accordance with the Rules', and 'the condition

rule' procedure was preferable to an act, 'in the passage of which, under present conditions of legislation, less satisfactory restriction might be imposed ...': ibid., p. 201.
68 1894 rules, r. 3. See below, Plate 13.
69 He hoped, nevertheless, that as a result of the use of respirators by children and young persons 'the custom of wearing respirators might take root ...'; since a certain amount of dust was unavoidable, it seemed only 'right and reasonable that the workpeople themselves should exercise a contributory care of their own health, and take such precaution on their own behalf as lies within their power': *Chief insp. ann. rep., 1893*, pp. 202 and 213.
70 1891 act, ss. 9 and 11.
71 *Chief insp. ann. rep., 1894*, p. 95.
72 Ibid., p. 96. He added later that 'under the old conditions the men were often subject to chronic ailments caused by the cloud of dust in which they worked, so that many could only work a portion of the day, and others not at all from October to March ... Now they can work all the year round the whole week ...': *Chief insp. ann. rep., 1896*, p. 79.
73 *Chief insp. ann. rep., 1896*, p. 79.

of the bulk of the carding rooms … was extremely bad'.[74] The problem lay not
with the rules as such, but with the way in which they were implemented in
practice: 'Elaborate plans and systems of ventilation have often failed owing to
bad workmanship or to simply carrying out the letter of the law without the
exercise of intelligent thought.'[75] Indeed, some arrangements simply made
conditions worse: 'I have seen fans erected quite as required, not simply doing
no good, but doing positive harm, drawing the dust right from under the
carding machines into the operatives' faces and dispersing it throughout the
work room. The law has been complied with, but complied with ignorantly.'[76]
A further inquiry was, therefore, necessary with a view to the introduction of 'a
more exact standard than is at present laid down'.[77]

The resulting inquiry was conducted by Commander Smith, a superintending inspector with special duties relating to 'dangerous' trades.[78] He
concluded that recent technological developments meant that, 'without
causing serious inconvenience or excessive cost to the manufacturers', more
could now be done to bring about improvements in working conditions
'which I have no hesitation in saying are seriously, and in some cases
dangerously, affecting the health of the persons employed'.[79] In some cases
'considerable good' had been achieved in roughing and sorting rooms – once
again, the York Street Mill was held up as an exemplar of good practice, as
illustrated below in Plate 14. But in many other cases the ventilation
arrangements were 'practically useless':

In many instances the fans were placed at such distances from the exhaust that the
current at the far end was inappreciable. In others, the ducts were of the wrong
size.… In others again, greater efficiency might have been obtained without increased
cost by having several fans … instead of one.… In many of the rooms visited the
current of air was practically inappreciable, and means intended to carry away dust
were not doing what was required.[80]

What was clearly required were more detailed standards, in particular with
regard to the size of exhaust openings and air velocity.

74 *Chief insp. ann. rep., 1900*, p. 425. Indeed, 'the atmosphere breathed by the [card]
    operatives [mainly women] was so highly charged with fine dust as to warrant the
    conclusion that healthy and vigorous life under such conditions could not be
    expected.' See to the same effect *Chief insp. ann. rep., 1902*, pt. I, p. 127 (Snape).
75 *Chief insp. ann. rep., 1903*, pt. I, p. 163 (Snape).
76 Ibid., p. 12 (Cooke-Taylor, superintending inspector for the Scotland-Ireland division).
77 *Chief insp. ann. rep., 1900*, p. 425 (Williams). There was, apparently, no official interest
    in the resolution adopted by the ITUC in 1898 that 'no boy under 18 years of age
    should be permitted to engage in flax roughing, as the average boy under that age is
    not sufficiently developed to stand the great physical strain required in this
    employment without engendering lung disease in some form or creating other
    complications in his system that tend to shorten life or make his years miserable':
    Report of the fifth Irish Trades Union Congress (Belfast, 1898), p. 44.
78 *Report upon the conditions of work in flax and linen mills as affecting the health of the
    operatives employed therein* [Cd. 1997], H.C. 1904, x, 465 [hereafter referred to as
    'Smith report, 1904'].
79 Ibid., p. 5.
80 Ibid., p. 11.

The main problem in the machine hackling and carding rooms was the failure to install appropriate fans as near as possible to the point at which the dust was generated. The difficulty here was practical – indeed, a Belgian expert had recently concluded 'after exhaustive enquiry' that 'there is great difficulty in rendering machine hackling rooms healthy, and that no efficient solution had come to his knowledge'.[81] But with the assistance of some local manufacturers,[82] Smith felt able to conclude that the difficulties 'are not insurmountable'. Accordingly, he recommended the same detailed standards of local exhaust ventilation as for roughing and sorting rooms.[83]

Notwithstanding the 1894 rules, Smith found 'no single instance' of a worker wearing a respirator. He accepted that 'this is an old difficulty not confined to this industry', and attributed most of the prejudice against respirators to the fact that they were not 'properly' made and maintained: 'A dirty respirator means inhalation through a vitiated medium, and is a source not only of discomfort but of danger; but if respiration can be performed with comfort through a clean medium, objections would largely cease.' Although convinced that several types of 'proper' respirator were already available,[84] Smith bowed to experience and concluded that it was undesirable to lay down an absolute rule 'which cannot be enforced'. The employers should be required to supply 'suitable and efficient' respirators, but the workers, whether children or adults, should not be required to wear them.[85]

Smith's recommendations were set out in the form of draft regulations to be made by the home secretary under the Factory and Workshop Act 1901. There followed a lengthy process of consultation with interested parties, in the course of which the linen trade managed to water down some of Smith's proposals.[86] When the regulations were finally promulgated in 1906,[87] detailed standards were specified only in respect of rooms in which roughing, sorting and hand-hackling was carried on. In such rooms, 'the exhaust ventilation ... shall not be deemed to be efficient if the exhaust opening at the back of the hackling pins measures less than 4 inches across in any direction, or has a sectional area of less that 50 square inches or if the linear velocity of the

---

81   *Rapport d'enquête présenté à M. le Ministre de l'Industrie et du Travail par le Dr D Glibert, Inspecteur-Medicin du Travail à l'administration centrale* (Brussels, 1902), p. 400.

82   See e.g. the method of extracting dust from a carding machine adopted by J. & T.M. Greeves Ltd., Belfast, as set out in *Smith report, 1904*, appendix 15, and in Plate 15, below.

83   *Smith report, 1904*, pp. 13–15. See also below, Plate 16.

84   And that the Society of Arts had offered a prize for a new dust-arresting respirator: ibid., p. 12.

85   Ibid., pp. 11–12.

86   But not so as to undermine the principle that ventilation should be as near as possible to the place where dust was generated: 'I have no hesitation in reporting that it is most important for the health of the workers that local exhaust ventilation ... should be made compulsory': *Report to Her Majesty's Secretary of State for the Home Department on the draft regulations ... for the processes of spinning and weaving flax and tow, and the processes incidental thereto*, pp. 5–6 [Cd. 2851], H.C.1906, xv, 947–48.

87   Regulations for the processes of spinning and weaving flax and tow and the processes incidental thereto (1906 No. 177).

draught passing through it is less than 400 feet per minute at any point within a sectional area of 50 square inches.'[88] In respect of machine-hackling, carding or preparing rooms, on the other hand, the occupier was only obliged to provide 'efficient exhaust and inlet ventilation ... to secure that the dust is drawn away from the workers at, or as near as reasonably possible to, the point at which it is generated'.[89]

As Smith had recommended, workers were put under a duty not to interfere 'in any way ... without the concurrence of the occupier or manager, with the means and appliances provided for ventilation, or for the removal of dust ...'.[90] But they were *not* obliged to wear the 'suitable and efficient' respirators which the employers were now requred to provide – a decision ratified by a departmental committee on ventilation:

Experience has ... shown that it is extremely difficult to enforce the use of respirators, as they are all more or less uncomfortable and inconvenient, besides being unsightly. It is also very difficult to keep respirators in working order and closely applied to the face. Often enough it is found that most of the air breathed by a person wearing a respirator leaks in between the face and the respirator, and is consequently unfiltered. ... Except, therefore, where dust is definitely dangerous and cannot be dealt with by exhaustion ... or in other ways, we are unable to recommend the use of respirators as an alternative to keeping the air clear of dust.[91]

The immediate implementation of the new regulations was 'often retarded by the neglect of occupiers to consult experts when installing the exhaust, or to keep it in good order when fitted'.[92] But examples of well-planned installations for dust removal were published in booklet form from 1907 and brought to the notice of occupiers.[93] 'Experimental work' also produced some very satisfactory results, particularly in carding rooms.[94] Hackling machines still gave rise to problems,[95] but the engineering industry appeared to have found a solution in two mills by boxing in the whole machine and

88 1906 regulations, reg. 2. Smith had originally recommended a much larger exhaust opening (120 square inches) and a draught velocity of 450 feet per minute: *Smith report, 1904*, p. 11.

89 Ibid. Smith had recommended that the fans be 'as near as possible', not 'as near as is *reasonably* possible'.

90 1906 regulations, reg. 14. Apparently, some workers blocked inlet or exhaust access, or dismantled or vandalised the fans in an attempt to prevent 'draughts' which they considered unhealthy.

91 *Second report of the departmental committee appointed to enquire into the ventilation of factories and workshops*, p. 11 [Cd. 3552], H.C. 1907, x, 459.

92 *Chief insp. ann. rep., 1906*, p. x. In 1908 it was reported that 'little progress ... seems to have been made in reducing the excessive dust to which the feeders are exposed in the process of carding tow': Belfast Health Commission, *Report to the local government board for Ireland*, p. 96 [Cd. 4128], H.C. 1908, xxxi, 808.

93 *Illustrations of methods of dust extraction in factories and workshops compiled by Commander Sir Hamilton Freer-Smith RN* [Cd. 3223], H.C. 1906, cx, 125.

94 See *Second report of departmental committee on ventilation, appendix*; *Chief insp. ann. rep., 1907*, p. 128 (Williams) and Plate 17, below.

95 *Chief insp. ann. rep., 1908*, p. 115.

putting an extractor fan on top. The system proved to be effective in controlling the dust and it was hoped that it would be widely adopted.[96]

In short, the inspectors who were 'baffled' by the dusty conditions of the scutch mills clearly felt that considerable improvements had been achieved in the preparation rooms of the flax spinning mills. In 1912, William Williams, who as cotton cloth factory inspector had inspected the flax mills and linen factories in 1900, and who had later returned to Ireland as an inspector in the Belfast district from 1906 to 1908, stated that there had been an 'absolute revolution in the condition of the dust departments', which he explained in the following terms:

I can well remember in many of these rooms – the carding room in particular, and even the roughing and sorting rooms – if the room was at all long you could not clearly see the end of the room, as there was such an absolute fog of dust. Take roughing rooms when I went in in my younger days as inspector. There was an absolute continuous bark of coughs going around the room. Now frequently you can go into a roughing room, and you may stay in it for five minutes without hearing a single cough. There is not the faintest doubt that the conditions have been wonderfully improved. I think the generosity of the manufacturers here in dealing with dust has been remarkable. I know of nothing to compare with it in the whole of my experience of factory inspection.[97]

But it should not be thought that all the problems had been satisfactorily resolved by 1914.[98]

REDUCING EXPOSURE TO EXCESSIVE HUMIDITY

As we have seen, it was the exposure of children to the wet conditions in flax spinning mills, 'by far the worst feature in the whole system', which led to the first legislative provision specifically relating to the health of linen workers.[99] Section 19 of the Factory Act 1844 provided that children and young persons should not work in a wet spinning room 'unless sufficient means shall be employed and continued for protecting [them] from being wetted, and, where hot water is used, for preventing the escape of steam into the room occupied by the workers'. But this provision, which remained in force

---

96   *Chief insp. ann. rep., 1909*, pp. 115–16. This new system 'has now been adopted by six firms': *Chief insp. ann. rep., 1910*, p. 104 (Eraut).

97   *Departmental committee on humidity and ventilation in flax mills and linen factories: Minutes of evidence*, p. 80 [Cd. 7446], H.C. 1914, xxxvi, 190. The committee itself commented that 'In the matters of general ventilation ... in the dry processes of the flax trade ... the flax manufacturers in Ireland have met the existing Regulations in a spirit calling for the highest commendation': *Report*, p. 8 [Cd. 7433], H.C. 1914, xxxvi, 8.

98   See e.g. G.C.R. Carey, P.C. Elwood, J.D. Merrett and J. Pemberton, *Byssinosis in flax workers in Northern Ireland: A report to the Minister of Labour and National Insurance* (Belfast, 1965).

99   See above, p. 159.

for the remainder of the period under consideration,[100] was exceptional, and it was another fifty years before the enactment of further legislative safeguards designed to protect linen workers from the harmful effects of heat and humidity. Nor was section 19 particularly effective. Two means of protection were available – splash-boards and aprons. But splash-boards were seldom used in Irish mills – 'there is a prejudice against them on the part of the workers who think that they are in the way, and render it more awkward to reach over to the frame and piece the ends'.[101] The use of aprons was common, but these typically offered little protection. In 1876 the factory and workshop commissioners concluded that the section had not been 'duly' enforced; they considered that it should be – and they recommended the introduction of properly-designed splash boards.[102] But, in the face of the mounting medical evidence,[103] that was all that they had to say on the matter, and no new 'humidity' safeguards were introduced by the 1878 Act.

During the 1880s, Cameron reported some improvements in the use of splash-boards and the design of water-proof aprons.[104] But, mindful perhaps of legislative developments in relation to the cotton industry, he noted that much remained to be done in the way of improving the working conditions in spinning rooms and weaving sheds. In 1889, the Cotton Cloth Factories Act, a private member's act, laid down in respect of cotton weaving sheds maximum limits of humidity at given temperatures, and made detailed provisions for recording the actual humidity in every shed by means of two sets of standardised wet and dry bulb thermometers.[105] This act applied directly to the remnants of the cotton industry in Ireland. But more importantly, the similarity of the machinery and processes in cotton and linen meant that the act could – and did – provide the basis for an increasingly scientific approach to the regulation of flax spinning and weaving. It also set in train a process in which the problems caused by humid working conditions in the linen industry came under detailed scrutiny on three occasions within a 20-year period.

The implementation of the 1889 act throughout the United Kingdom was overseen by a peripatetic inspector, E.H. Osborn, and, as we have already noted, it was he who was asked by the home secretary in 1891 to conduct the first official inquiry into the Irish linen industry.[106] For this purpose Osborn

---

100 See 1878 act, s. 37 (extended to include women); 1901 act, s. 76.
101 *Report on proposed changes in hours and ages of employment in textile factories 1873*, p. 25.
102 *Report of the factory and workshop commissioners 1876*, p. lxxiv.
103 See above, pp. 159–61.
104 *Chief insp. ann. rep., 1890*, pp. 35–36. In his annual report for the previous year, Redgrave (at pp. 6–7) had provided details of 'Neill's patent improved system for moistening air in weaving factories'.
105 The terms of the act were said to be 'entirely agreed upon between the operatives and workmen engaged on this class of business and their employers', and the bill gave rise to little discussion: see *Hansard 3*, cccxl, 92 (22 Aug.1889).
106 *Reports … upon the conditions of work, etc. in flax mills and linen factories in the United Kingdom* [C. 7287], H.C. 1893–94, xvii, 537. The principal report deals with mills and factories in Belfast [hereafter '*Osborn report, 1893*'], and a supplementary report

inspected a large number of wet-spinning rooms and weaving sheds, in the course of which he took detailed 'hygrometrical' readings. All the evidence pointed towards levels of heat and humidity which went beyond anything necessary for the production of fine linens,[107] were 'unwholesome' and harmful to the health of the workers, particularly women and children,[108] and were not monitored on any regular basis. The north of Ireland could clearly learn from Yorkshire and Lancashire,[109] and to this end Osborn proposed to follow the strategy already adopted in the 1889 act of setting down a statutory standard for a maximum permitted level of humidity. This would be achieved by a twofold process; the amount of humidity generated in the first place would be *reduced* by various measures, and the amount carried away would be *increased* by more effective ventilation. The effectiveness of the measures taken in any particular factory would be monitored by daily thermometer readings.

Osborn set out his proposals in the form of special rules, which he then discussed with leading representatives of the linen industry.[110] Given that his analysis was often supported by evidence from individual linen employers themselves or based on his experience of cotton factories in Lancashire, most of his recommendations raised no insuperable objections. Nevertheless, they did not become law until 1894.

During working hours, spinning rooms and weaving sheds were to be kept at a difference of at least two degrees between the 'dry' temperature and the 'wet' temperature.[111] To reduce the basic level of humidity, all steam pipes 'shall be jacketed with non-conducting composition to the satisfaction of the

(at p. 14) deals with the rest of Ireland and Great Britain. Both reports were reproduced in *Chief insp. ann. rep., 1893*, p. 189.

107　Humidity in weaving rooms in Belfast in the early summer of 1891 often reached 85–100 per cent, as opposed to an average 'outside' humidity of 63 per cent. In a memorable comment, Osborn characterised the system in the weaving sheds as 'unreasonable and wasteful, resembling nothing so much as the Chinese extravagance immortalised by Elia, of burning a house to roast a pig ...': *Osborn report, 1893*, pp. 5 and 12.

108　Osborn paid particular attention to the doffers, whose work in the spinning mills made them particularly vulnerable to being saturated above the waist, giving rise to 'the danger of developing lung diseases at an early age where the constitution is weak or predisposed'. Although the majority 'appeared ... in fairly good health', many were 'of evidently poor stamina, and inferior in growth to children of the same age in Lancashire': ibid., p. 6.

109　A suggestion explicitly adopted in the *Fifth and final report of the royal commission on labour*, p. 95 [C. 7421], H.C. 1894, xxxv, 103.

110　See *Chief insp. ann. rep., 1893*, pp. 201–03 and 214–16, where the 'Special rules for the spinning and weaving of flax 1894' are set out. The *Belfast Evening Telegraph*, 15 May 1894 was not impressed: 'Mr Osborn shows that the mill and factory operatives are subject to every disease provided for in the Medical Encyclopaedia ... What lively places these mills and factories must be! St. Thomas' Hospital would not be a patch on any manufactory with such a variety of patients.'

111　'This avoids the necessity for a complex schedule [as in the 1889 act], and allows adequate humidity for practical purposes': *Osborn report, 1893*, p. 5.

inspector'.[112] In spinning rooms, the lids of the hot-water troughs were to be kept 'in perfect repair' so as to minimise the escape of steam, and the floors 'shall be kept in sound condition so as to prevent retention or accumulation of water'. To increase ventilation in weaving sheds, an 'efficient 14-inch extracting fan' was to be provided for every 2,500 square feet of floor surface, arranged 'to the satisfaction of the inspector' and kept in operation during working hours. In every spinning room and weaving shed there were to be 'provided, maintained, and kept in correct working order' two sets of standardised wet and dry bulb thermometers; these were to be read twice a day and the readings recorded on a prescribed form, one copy of which was to be sent to the inspector at the end of every month.

Osborn also attempted to breathe new life into section 19 of the 1844 act. Splashboards 'shall be provided' on any spinning frame with a clearance, from the adjoining frame, of 4 feet 6 inches or more. In all other cases, 'waterproof overalls or aprons shall be provided by the occupier for all the workers ... [and] to be sufficient to cover the chest in the case of children and young persons'.[113] The employers had claimed that the workers would 'decidedly' object to wear overalls or aprons, and Osborn had deferred to them in some respects, since he was really pinning his hopes on the 'undoubted superiority' of splashboards, the introduction of which 'will completely revolutionise the aspect of Irish wet-spinning'.[114]

Osborn's experience of the 'initial difficulties' with the 1889 act in Lancashire led him to warn that 'considerable patience' and 'great forbearance' would be required to bring the linen industry into line with the rules which imposed restrictions which were 'so entirely new'. For this reason he intended to circulate 'a few diagrams of satisfactory methods of dealing with some points of ventilation, etc., and with splashboards'[115] – indeed, it is very noticeable how much the success of the rules depended upon his technical expertise. Even so, he was quickly forced to make a concession in respect of splash-boards. Complaints were made that they could not always be fitted so as to prevent the escape of spray, and that many workers strongly objected to them 'as impeding them in their work, and so lessening the wages earned, and that the pressure against them ... caused much bodily discomfort'. A conference with the associated employers in Belfast led to the rule being amended to allow employers to choose between splashguards and 'efficient waterproofs', but with the addition of a new rule which required that water should not be allowed to accumulate on the floor. These amendments were approved by the

112 'Economy and efficiency alike dictate that ... steam-jets ... should be so arranged as not to impinge upon the workers, the pipes should be covered with non-conducting composition, and the steam injected at low pressure, which also means a lower temperature for the room': ibid.

113 1894 rules – see *Chief insp. ann. rep., 1893*, p. 215.

114 Ibid., pp. 201 and 203 (report of meeting between Osborn and Linen Merchants' Association).

115 Ibid., p. 202. These diagrams, which included illustrations of techniques used in France and Germany, appeared as a supplement to his report.

home secretary, and an amended set of rules was promulgated in April 1896.[116]

It is hardly surprising that Osborn reported optimistically – and somewhat prematurely – on the beneficial effect of the new rules in reducing humidity, so that the atmosphere in spinning rooms and weaving sheds was 'very noticeably improved'.[117] But this assessment was quickly shown to be mistaken – or, at least, to have been made without reference to the higher standards now being set for the cotton industry. In 1900, Osborn's successor as cotton cloth factory inspector (W. Williams) was much less complimentary; the 1894/96 rules may have had led to some 'great improvements', but conditions in many of the mills 'seemed to me so dangerous to health as to call for serious consideration'.[118] Four years later, the superintending inspector of dangerous trades (Commander Smith) agreed with Williams: 'The 1896 Rules have done much to secure more healthy conditions for the workers ... [but] new methods have [since] been discovered with the result that greater efficiency can be attained, and improvements may yet be made which will reduce to a minimum conditions which ... are seriously, and in some cases dangerously, affecting the health of the persons employed.'[119] Since the analysis in these two reports also coincides to a considerable degree, we shall take the two together.

The most general problem was the unsatisfactory standard of ventilation, both in weaving sheds and spinning rooms. The 1894/96 rules did not apply to spinning rooms at all. In the weaving sheds, which were covered, Williams found 'considerable variations in efficiency of output [of fans], which did not always reach a very high standard'.[120] The problem here was that the rules had used a standard based on floor area – an approach, derived from the 'air space' tests set out in the Cotton Cloth Factory Act 1889[121] and the Factory and Workshop Act 1895,[122] which had since been found unreliable and impractical.[123] In 1898, the standard of ventilation for cotton weaving sheds

---

116 See *Chief insp. ann. rep., 1896*, p. 78, where Osborn claimed that the amended rule 'really will enable us to secure better conditions than the original rule, which only applied when the passes between the machines were of not less than a specified width, which practically excluded the older mills in many cases'.

117 *Chief insp. ann. rep., 1894*, pp. 95–96 and *1896*, p. 78.

118 *Chief insp. ann. rep., 1900*, pp. 423–24 [hereafter referred to as '*Williams report, 1900*'].

119 *Report upon the conditions of work in flax and linen mills as affecting the health of the operatives employed therein*, p. 5 [Cd. 1997], H.C. 1904, x, 465 [hereafter referred to as '*Smith report, 1904*'].

120 *Williams report, 1900*, p. 424.

121 By section 9, 600 cubic feet of fresh air per worker per hour had to be admitted during working hours.

122 A factory or workshop was deemed to be so overcrowded as to be dangerous or injurious to health if there was less than 250 cubic feet of space per person in any room: 1895 act, s. 1(1).

123 'It is difficult to measure with accuracy the amount of air that is passing into a weaving shed, and even when it is approximately known ... it by no means follows that every part of the shed is properly ventilated': *Smith report, 1904*, p. 6. 'The existence of a certain cubic air-space per person affords no reliable guarantee of

had been raised by reference to the proportion of carbonic acid (carbon dioxide) in any room during working hours. As Table 6.1 suggests, the new standard of no more than 9 volumes of carbon dioxide per 10,000 volumes of air[124] was considerably higher than before.

Table 6.1: Standards of ventilation[125]

Proportion of CO_2 per 10,000 volumes of air	Fresh air delivery (cubic feet per head per hour)
8	1,500
9	1,200
10	1,000
12	750
14	600

In 1902, a departmental committee on ventilation agreed that the carbon dioxide standard was 'the best objective criterion of sufficiency of ventilation'.[126] Practical difficulties had been encountered in the collection of a sufficient air sample and the making of a sufficiently accurate analysis, but these had now been overcome.[127] The committee considered the standard set for cotton weaving sheds to be 'somewhat stringent' for general use, and recommended a level of 12 volumes of carbon dioxide per 10,000 volumes of air for all classes of factories and workshops not otherwise specially provided for.[128]

Commander Smith found, however, that the carbon dioxide level in ten flax spinning rooms averaged 6.4:10,000, and in eight weaving sheds the average level was 7.5: 10,000 – in other words, the air quality was generally *above* the proposed new standard. He acknowledged that these tests were taken 'in exceptionally fine weather, generally speaking with a light breeze and when practically every window was wide open'. Even with these advantages, however, the condition of the air in some places was 'much below what is

reasonably sufficient ventilation …': *First report of the departmental committee appointed to inquire into the ventilation of factories and workshops*, p. 3 [Cd. 1302] H.C. 1902, xii, 469.

124 See *Report of a committee appointed to inquire into the working of the Cotton Cloth Factories Act 1889* [C. 8348 and 8349], H.C. 1897, xiii, 61, and Factory and Workshop (Cotton Cloth Factory) Regulations 1898, r. 5, re-enacted as 1901 act, s. 94(3).

125 Taken from *Chief insp. ann. rep., 1907*, p. xii.

126 *First report of the departmental committee on ventilation, 1902*, p. 3.

127 Cf. 'The way I make the test is: I fill small bottles with the air from the room and send four or five of these to the Home Office, and there they are analysed by an independent analyst, who does not know the room or the place from which the air comes or anything about it': *Departmental committee on humidity and ventilation 1914: Minutes of evidence*, p. 2 (Eraut).

128 *First report of the departmental committee on ventilation 1902*, p. 5.

considered normal'. After due consideration, he recommended the adoption not of an absolute standard, but one which was relative to the outside air; the level of carbonic acid in any room during working hours, he suggested, should not exceed that in the air outside by more than five volumes of carbon dioxide per 10,000 volumes of air.[129] This standard should apply to all spinning rooms and weaving sheds, 'whether artificial humidity is produced or not'.[130]

With regard to the working conditions in spinning rooms, Williams and Smith were agreed that these 'frequently appeared ... to be deplorable'.[131] We may consider their recommendations for remedying this situation under three main headings.

(i) Protection from wet working conditions   The 1894/96 rules relating to splash-guards and waterproof aprons failed to prevent many of the workers, particularly children, from being soaked. Smith found that splashboards, when provided, were generally effective in keeping the workers – and floors – dry; but they were not always provided – and the objections to their use of workers, who generally worked in their bare feet, 'are probably as strong' as ever.[132] In the absence of splashboards, the rules stipulated only that waterproof aprons should be *provided*; they did not oblige the workers to wear them. Since a waterproof covering impaired 'the free perspiration necessary to minimise the distressing effect of a high temperature', many workers did not wear the aprons, with the result that children in particular had their clothes wet through by the spray of water from the spinning frames.[133] It was clear that the rules had to be tightened up:

Seeing that splash boards produce useful results; that they are found in many of the best conducted works in the country; and that by adopting modern methods of construction many of the objections primarily raised can be removed, I am of opinion that they should again be required, but not in all spinning rooms. It is in spinning low counts [i.e. coarser yarn] that moisture in large quantities is given off in the form of spray from the frames, as the rove is much thicker and absorbs more water when passing through the troughs. I propose that where counts of 50 or less are spun that the use of splash boards should be compulsory. Where the counts are higher the requirement might remain as at present, but amended so that where splash boards are not in use overalls and aprons made of water-proof or of some suitable absorbent material should be provided by the occupier and worn by the workers.[134]

129   The proportion of carbon dioxide in the open air was generally assumed to be four per 10,000, although 'it is usually less and may occasionally be more': *Chief insp. ann. rep., 1907*, p. xii. The relative standard recommended by Smith, in other words, might often in practice be higher (say 5+3) than the absolute standard (9) then set for cotton weaving sheds.
130   *Smith report, 1904*, pp. 6–7.
131   *Williams report, 1900*, p. 424; *Smith report, 1904*, p. 9.
132   *Smith report, 1904*, p. 9.
133   *Williams report, 1900*, p. 424; *Smith report, 1904*, p. 9.
134   *Smith report, 1904*, pp. 9–10. The distinction between finer and coarser yarns could also be expressed in terms of the width of the 'pitch'; the coarser the yarn, the wider the pitch. As we shall see, it was this approach which was preferred when the regulations came to be drafted.

Another strategy, already adopted for cotton cloth factories, was to require 'sufficient and suitable cloak-room accommodation' to be provided so that workers could change their clothes before setting off for home.[135] The need for such a facility in flax spinning rooms 'is not less', given that it was 'distinctly dangerous' for women and young persons, particularly in winter, to leave hot and damp rooms and walk home in wet clothes.[136]

(ii) Reduction in level of humidity   No difficulty had, apparently, arisen from the general requirement to maintain a difference of at least two degrees between the wet and dry bulb readings. Given assurances from 'reliable' sources that 'the range at present allowed is necessary for manufacturing purposes', this standard should be left unchanged. But more could be done to reduce the escape of steam from the spinning troughs and to insulate steam pipes – and once again the tighter regulations imposed on cotton weaving sheds pointed the way forward.[137]

(iii) Protection from use of impure water in spinning troughs   Both Williams and Smith accepted that serious injury to health could result from the use of 'impure' water in the spinning troughs.[138] The need for 'pure' water having already been recognised in respect of cotton,[139] it comes as no surprise to find a similar regulation being proposed for linen.

The 1906 regulations

The process by which these recommendations were translated into binding regulations provides an interesting insight into the making of delegated legislation in the early twentieth century. On 11 May 1905 the processes of spinning and weaving flax and tow were duly certified by the home secretary to be 'dangerous' trades for the purposes of the 1901 act, and draft regulations designed to give effect to the Williams/Smith recommendations were, as required by the act,[140] sent to all persons likely to be affected by them. Objections were received from four representative bodies (including the Flax Spinners' Association) and 18 individual firms (including 13 in the north of Ireland). Some of these objections were withdrawn following informal discussions between the home office and the chief representatives of the flax spinning industry, which led to some changes, particularly with respect to the

135   But only in respect of factories erected after February 1898 – see Cotton Cloth Factory regulations 1898, r. 7, re-enacted as Factory and Workshop Act 1901, s. 94(5).
136   *Smith report, 1904*, p. 10.
137   Ibid., pp. 8–9 and 10. See especially Cotton Cloth Factory Regulations 1898, r. 4, re-enacted as Factory and Workshop Act 1901, s. 94(2).
138   *Williams report, 1900*, p. 424; *Smith report, 1904*, p. 8. Snape had made much the same point ten years earlier: *Chief insp. ann. rep., 1890*, p. 39.
139   Cotton Cloth Factory Regulations 1898, r. 3, Factory and Workshop Act 1901, s. 94(1).
140   1901 act, s. 80(1).

carbon dioxide standard for measuring ventilation[141] and the use of splash-boards.[142] But agreement could not be reached on all points, and accordingly the home secretary was obliged to appoint 'a competent person' to conduct a public inquiry.[143] This was held in Belfast and Dundee in November 1905 before Mr G.A. Bonner (a barrister). His report, published in January 1906, rejected all the remaining objections to the humidity provisions, and recommended only two minor amendments to the regulations as previously agreed.[144] The regulations were then laid before parliament under the negative resolution procedure.[145] No such resolution having been passed within forty days, the regulations were finally promulgated in March 1906 and generally came into force in February 1907.[146]

Insofar as they dealt with the questions of ventilation and humidity, the regulations finally provided as follows:

Regulations for the processes of spinning and weaving flax and tow and the processes incidental thereto

Duties of occupiers

1. In every room in which persons are employed the arrangements shall be such that during working hours the proportion of carbonic acid in the air of the room shall not exceed 20 volumes per 10,000 volumes of air at any time when gas or oil is used for lighting ... or 12 volumes per 10,000 when electric lighting is used ... or 9 volumes per 10,000 at any other time.

Provided that it shall be a sufficient compliance with this Regulation if the proportion of carbonic acid in the air of the room does not exceed that of the open air outside by more than 5 volumes per 10,000 volumes of air....

4. In every room in which wet-spinning is carried on, or in which artificial humidity of air is produced in aid of manufacture a set of standardised wet and dry bulb thermometers shall be kept affixed in the centre of the room or in such other position as may be directed by the inspector ... by notice in writing, and shall be maintained in correct working order.

141 The basic standard was now to be identical to that set for cotton weaving sheds, namely nine volumes of carbon dioxide per 10,000 volumes of air; but this standard was 'deemed' to be met if the air satisfied the standard recommended by Commander Smith, namely that the proportion of carbon dioxide in the room did not exceed that of the outside air by more than five volumes per 10,000.

142 The home office agreed to relax the rule requiring the use of splashboards by increasing the width of the 'pitch' which brought it into operation from $2^{1}/_{2}$ to $2^{3}/_{4}$ inches, and to add a proviso under which the regulation might be suspended altogether under certain conditions: *Report to His Majesty's Secretary of State for the Home Department on the draft regulations ... for the processes of spinning and weaving flax and tow, and the processes incidental thereto, by G.A. Bonner, barrister-at-law*, p. 8 [Cd. 2851], H.C. 1906, xv, 950 [hereafter '*Bonner report, 1906*']. No application for suspension was received before 1914.

143 1901 act, ss. 80(4) and 81.

144 *Bonner report, 1906*, p. 8.

145 1901 act, s. 84.

146 *Regulations for the processes of spinning and weaving flax and tow and the processes incidental thereto* (1906 No. 177).

Each of the above thermometers shall be read between 10 and 11 am on every day that any person is employed in the room, and again between 3 and 4 pm on every day that any person is employed in the room after 1 pm, and each reading shall be at once entered on the prescribed form.

The form shall be hung up near the thermometers to which it relates, and shall be forwarded, duly filled in, at the end of each calendar month to the inspector....

5. The humidity of the atmosphere of any room to which Regulation 4 applies shall not at any time be such that the difference between the readings of the wet and dry bulb thermometers is less than 2 degrees.

6. No water shall be used for producing humidity of the air, or in wet spinning troughs, which is liable to cause injury to the health of the persons employed or to yield effluvia; and for the purpose of this Regulation, any water which absorbs from acid solution of permanganate of potash in four hours at 60 degrees more than 0.5 grain of oxygen per gallon of water shall be deemed to be liable to cause injury to the health of the persons employed.

7. Efficient means shall be adopted to prevent the escape of steam from wet-spinning troughs.

8. The pipes used for the introduction of steam into any room in which the temperature exceeds 70 degrees, or for heating the water in any wet-spinning trough, shall, so far as they are within the room and not covered by water, be as small in diameter and as limited in length as is reasonably practicable and shall be effectively covered with non-conducting material.

9. Efficient splash guards shall be provided and maintained on all wet-spinning frames of $2^3/4$-inch pitch and over, and on all other wet-spinning frames unless waterproof skirts, and bibs of suitable material, are provided by the occupier and worn by the workers.

Provided that if the Chief Inspector is satisfied with regard to premises in use prior to 30th June 1905, that the structural conditions are such that splash guards cannot conveniently be used, he may suspend the requirement as to splash guards....

10. The floor of every wet-spinning room shall be kept in sound condition, and drained so as to prevent retention or accumulation of water.

11. There shall be provided for all persons employed in any room in which wet-spinning is carried on, or in which artificial humidity of air is produced in aid of manufacture, suitable and convenient accommodation in which to keep the clothing taken off before starting work, and in the case of a building erected after 30th June 1905, in which the difference between the readings of the wet and dry bulb thermometers is at any time less that 4 degrees, such accommodation shall be provided in cloak-rooms ventilated and kept at a suitable temperature and situated in or near the workrooms in question....

Duties of persons employed

13. All persons employed on wet-spinning frames without efficient splash guards shall wear the skirts and bibs provided by the occupier in pursuance of Regulation 9.

14. No person shall in any way interfere, without the concurrence of the occupier or manager, with the means and appliances provided for ventilation ... or for the other purposes of these Regulations.

These regulations, which were the product of a lengthy process informed by experience gained from the regulation of the cotton industry, appeared to have a beneficial effect on working conditions in the linen industry: 'The supervision exercised under the factory acts by His Majesty's inspectors and the official regulations as to temperature and humidity, have ... done much to mitigate the evil conditions of weaving sheds and wet spinning rooms, while various modifications in spinning frames have been introduced with the object of preventing, as far as possible, the scattering of water and the escape of steam ...'.[147] But they had only just come into force when trades union pressure in England forced another inquiry into conditions in cotton weaving sheds which in due course led in 1911 to the adoption of yet more stringent standards.[148] This development put the linen industry under a certain amount of pressure to follow suit, and in 1912 the government appointed a departmental committee[149] to consider what amendments (if any) to the 1906 regulations were 'expedient' in view of the changes made in relation to cotton, 'or on other grounds'. The committee's report, published in 1914,[150] showed that there had in fact been little improvement – and that the 1906 regulations were indeed inadequate.

We cannot hope in the present context to do justice to the most detailed and scientific inquiry yet into this aspect of working conditions in the Irish linen industry, and we content ourselves with some of the committee's principal findings and recommendations.

Spinning rooms

The 1906 regulations had 'done much' to improve working conditions in some spinning mills; but in many others there was 'ample room for improvement', which could be made without detriment to the process of

---

147 Belfast Health Commission, *Report to the local government board 1908*, p. 95.
148 See *Reports of the departmental committee on humidity and ventilation in cotton weaving sheds* [Cd. 4484], H.C. 1909, xv, 635 and [Cd. 5566], H.C. 1911, xxiii, 807; Factory and Workshop (Cotton Cloth Factories) Act 1911 and Cotton Cloth Factories Regulations 1911 (No. 1259). Both the act and the regulations applied to cotton factories in Ireland.
149 Under the chairmanship of Sir Hamilton Freer-Smith, who (as Commander Smith) had chaired the inquiry which led to the 1906 regulations and who had served on the cotton committee which reported in 1909. Two other members of the 1912 committee had also served on the cotton committee, and, as previously noted (above, n. 38), the linen interest was represented by G.H. Ewart and H. Cummins.
150 *Departmental committee on humidity and ventilation in flax mills and linen factories (mainly in Ireland): Report* [Cd. 7433], H.C. 1914, xxxvi, 1 [hereafter 'Freer-Smith report, 1914'] and *Minutes of evidence* [Cd. 7446], H.C. 1914, xxxvi, 107.

manufacture. Crucial to this conclusion was the finding that a difference of only 2° between the wet-bulb and dry-bulb temperatures was *not* necessary: 'only one mill in twenty works on an average at the legal limit, all the others being normally considerably drier'.[151] The spinning process, in other words, allowed for a greater degree of flexibility which ought to be reflected in the regulations.

The essence of the problem was that flax-spinning 'necessitates the introduction of large quantities of heat into a relatively limited space'.[152] Almost half the heat introduced into spinning rooms came from the spinning troughs, which therefore should be much more efficiently insulated. But this was more a matter of encouraging best practice in respect of lagging and the use of automatic steam valves than of more detailed regulation. Steam pipes were another cause of humidity, and here the answer did lie in adopting the more stringent regulations as to insulation now in force for cotton weaving sheds. Where the wet bulb temperature nevertheless exceeded 75°, 'the point at which according to medical evidence bodily discomfort begins',[153] more could also be done by way of regulation to increase the amount of heat carried away by ventilation. This could be done by requiring appropriate means to be taken so as 'to introduce 1,000 cubic feet of air per hour for every linear foot of trough installed in the room'.[154]

With regard to the better protection of the workers from being soaked, the 1906 regulations had been largely unsuccessful: 'generally speaking, the condition of the wet spinning rooms ... must be described as unsatisfactory. The floors are not kept as clean or as dry as they should be, and extensive accumulations of dirty water are not uncommon.' Largely on account of opposition from the workers, the installation and use of splashguards was still unsatisfactory; but more could and should be done to compel their use. Nor had the regulations overcome the workers' objections to the wearing of protective overalls: 'The wearing of the bibs, which are intended for the protection of the chest, ... is almost wholly disregarded.' Regulations should either be strictly observed or, 'if the objections are sound', altered accordingly; the objections to this particular regulation were *not* 'sound'. Splashguards should therefore be required on all frames of 2¼ inch pitch and over, unless (i) the size and speed of the spindles made the process of 'laying on' dangerous or

151 *Freer-Smith report, 1914,* pp. 10–11.
152 'Compared with a weaving shed of the same capacity, the heat produced [in a spinning room] is approximately ten times as great': ibid.
153 The committee had collected extensive data on temperature and humidity, and commissioned scientific and medical experiments on working conditions – see especially appendices ix (report on body temperature of linen workers by Dr Legge, medical inspector of factories) and x (report on experimental work in spinning mills and weaving sheds by Professor Petavel and others).
154 *Freer-Smith report, 1914,* pp. 11–13, on the basis that the amount of heat generated depended not on the size of the room but on the amount of machinery in it. The committee also recommended specific standards for the construction of new rooms, with particular reference to the height of the room, the size of the windows and the layout of the machinery.

difficult (a concession to the workers which was not to apply if they failed to wear waterproof skirts and bibs), or (ii) there was less than four and a half feet between the frames (a concession to the occupiers).[55]

'Very little' had been done to provide 'suitable and convenient accommodation' in which to keep dry clothing for use when walking home after work. Once again, the workers themselves were apparently to blame: 'if accommodation is provided it will not be used by the workers' on account of the inconvenience and loss of time involved. But Martindale had found that where 'suitable' accommodation was provided and 'managers ... have been insistent on the subject', the workers *did* make good use of it.[156] The whole purpose of the regulation was, however, effectively undermined by the Irish high court in *Eraut* v. *Ross Bros. Ltd.*[157] In their weaving room, the defendants had provided pegs on a wall sheeted with wood on which the workers could hang their 'walking-home' clothes. They contended that the pegs amounted to 'suitable accommodation' in that clothes hung on them were dry at the end of the day's work, and they called four other factory occupiers who provided similar facilities on the basis that they were the most suitable and convenient in practice. The Belfast magistrates found as a fact that the pegs satisfied the requirements of the regulations, but stated a case for the opinion of the high court. Gibson J held that the question of what was 'suitable and convenient accommodation' being a matter of fact, the court could not disturb the finding of the magistrates. He did not expressly refer to, but by implication rejected, Eraut's argument that the accommodation must be of such a character that the words 'in which' will aptly apply. But he did, however, point out that any insufficiency in the wording of the regulation could be remedied by 'the responsible authority'.[158]

The departmental committee, however, took the view that the provision of separate cloakrooms, while desirable in theory, was not practicable in most wet spinning rooms: 'These rooms are situated on storeys one above another, and are approached by stair cases, so that the provision of cloakrooms on each floor is in almost every instance impossible.' Accordingly, they recommended only that each employer should adopt whatever means he thought fit, subject to the condition that the clothing should not be exposed to spray or condensed moisture, and that it should not be in contact with the wall or other damp surface.[159]

---

155 Ibid., p. 13. See also *Freer-Smith report, 1914: Minutes of evidence*, pp. 4 and 72 (workers will use splash boards once they become accustomed to them – Eraut and Martindale); Cf. pp. 10–11 (splash boards 'awfully in the way' and 'awkward to use' according to Mary Galway, secretary, Textile Operatives Society).

156 *Chief insp. ann. rep., 1909*, pp. 145–46. Cf. Mary Galway explained that 'there is only three-quarters of an hour to gather up their clothes and get home to dinner and get back': *Freer-Smith report, 1914: Minutes of evidence*, p. 10.

157 [1910] 2 IR 591.

158 Ibid., pp. 599–600. The decision was, in effect, upheld in *Second report of the departmental committee on humidity and ventilation in cotton weaving sheds*, pp. xvii–xviii [Cd. 5566], H.C. 1911, xxiii, 823–24.

159 *Freer-Smith report, 1914*, p. 14.

Weaving sheds

Working conditions in the weaving sheds also remained dangerous to health in spite of the 1906 regulations. But there was not the same scope for improvement, given the conclusion from the scientific experiments conducted for the committee that 'for the manufacture of fine linens ... a difference of about two degrees between the dry and wet bulb temperatures must be maintained, even at high temperatures'. Accordingly, it was not possible to give to linen weavers the full measure of 'relief' recently granted to the cotton weavers:[160] '[U]nless an important industry is interfered with in such a way as to risk loss of trade and its transference to other countries in which no special regulations for flax are in force ... work in a limited number of factories must continue under conditions causing bodily discomfort and possibly in the long run injury to health ...'. But a compromise *was* possible:

> We ... recommend that all artificial humidity ... shall cease when the wet bulb temperature reaches 80° Fahrenheit. In recommending this limit, we fully recognise that for a limited number of hours during the hot days of summer, weaving of cambric and other fine materials may be carried on under difficulty with a possibility of a less satisfactory output, but we feel that this should be accepted by the trade rather than that work should be continued under conditions causing great discomfort and probably loss of health.

In addition, every possible effort should be made to keep the wet bulb temperature under 75° by adopting methods advocated for cotton weaving sheds – namely, the use of double or insulated roofs, the spraying of roofs with cold water, the whitewashing of roofs, the introduction of air for ventilating purposes from as cool a source as possible, and the covering of steam pipes.[161]

The monitoring of working conditions

By way of a final comment on the deficiencies of the 1906 regulations we may note that their success depended to a considerable extent on the daily monitoring of actual working conditions in spinning rooms and weaving sheds. Readings were apparently taken as prescribed on a regular basis and returned monthly to the home office for scrutiny. But the system does not appear to have worked as intended. For a start, there were considerable reservations as to the value of the readings: 'There is a great deal of romanticism in the Irish nature, and I am perfectly certain some of them are not strictly accurate. One of my early experiences when I came here was the

160   The cotton weavers had long campaigned for a total abolition of artificial humidity, but in 1911 settled for its prohibition when the wet-bulb temperature exceeded 75°: *Second report of the departmental committee on humidity and ventilation in cotton weaving sheds,* p. xiii and Cotton Cloth Factory Regulations 1911, regs. 1 and 9.
161   *Freer-Smith report, 1914,* p. 17; *Second report of the departmental committee on humidity and ventilation in cotton weaving sheds,* pp. xviii–xx.

discovery of a man entering them up a week in advance.'[162] The incidence of excessive humidity revealed by the returns was miniscule: in 1911, for example, there were for every 10,000 readings only 12.1 reported instances of excessive humidity in flax spinning mills and 9.8 in linen weaving sheds.[163] Little or no good was derived from sending in a large number of reports 'saying everything is right'.[164] And given the huge number of readings prepared, forwarded and examined annually, the sheer size of the exercise in administrative terms was enormous.

The obvious remedy was the 'self-inspection' system which had been adopted in cotton weaving sheds, whereby the readings were made jointly by two persons representing the employer and the workers respectively, with records being sent to the inspector only when an irregularity was discovered. But the inspectors in Ireland were not at all happy with this suggestion; it would 'trench' on the internal discipline of the mill, and would be 'entirely subversive of the whole principle of factory legislation'. It was doubtful whether any infringements would be admitted, and in any case the workers' representative in Ireland 'would just be the spinning master or foreman'. For these reasons, 'the checking of hygrometers can only be done satisfactorily by inspection'.[165]

Strangely, the committee did not refer at all to these concerns, and for some unexplained reason adopted a curious compromise. There should be no change with regard to the spinning mills – except that the daily number of readings should be *increased* from two to three. But the system of joint inspection should be adopted in the linen weaving sheds. It was acknowledged that workers might be unwilling to give up work-time, and therefore earnings, to undertake such readings, or (more convincingly) to run the risk of incurring the wrath of their employers. Rather naively, the committee considered that both these objections could be overcome. But in any event they stressed the optional nature of the arrangement, and blithely commented that 'if the workers ... fail to take advantage of requirements framed for their benefit, the responsibility rests with them alone'.[166]

Even though they were the recent product of an informed consultative process, the 1906 regulations were, in short, defective and should be amended and extended in a number of important respects. We may suggest four interrelated reasons for this disappointing lack of progress. First, as compared to the dangers arising from excessive dust, less attention had been

162 *Freer-Smith report, 1914: Minutes of evidence*, p. 80 (Williams).
163 *Chief insp. ann. rep.*, *1911*, p. 291. Since many of the reported instances of excessive humidity were attributed to neglect of hygrometers or to reading or recording errors, more detailed regulations for the construction and use of hygrometers were recommended in *Freer-Smith report, 1914*, pp. 21–22.
164 *Freer-Smith report, 1914: Minutes of evidence*, p. 7 (Eraut).
165 Ibid., pp. 6–7 (Eraut) and 71 (Martindale).
166 *Freer-Smith report, 1914*, pp. 13–14 and 19–20. In particular, 'we find it difficult to believe that a manufacturer ... would find fault with a worker for fulfilling a legal obligation'.

paid in Ireland, at least until relatively late in the day, to the health problems arising from humidity: 'although the excessive heat and humidity in the wet spinning rooms and weaving sheds come in for frequent notice and criticism, the special rules and regulations were ... aimed chiefly at the elimination of dust in the dry processes ...'.[167] Secondly, there was less informed pressure from the workers, who 'are less completely organised than [the cotton workers] in Lancashire' and did not properly understand 'the question of humidity'.[168] Nor was this lack of understanding confined to the workers: 'such provisions [in the 1894 and 1906 regulations] as concern the humid rooms relate to efficient ventilation and protection of the operatives from actual moisture rather than to the physiological aspect of the question, the effect on health and comfort of work in a warm moist atmosphere'.[169] Thirdly, there appears to have been something of a mystique about the need for a high level of humidity in the spinning and weaving of fine linen, which withstood 'scientific' investigation and inhibited change. And, finally, many of the mills and factories were housed in older buildings which just did not lend themselves readily or at all to the kinds of physical changes required to effect significant improvements. There were, of course, some 'good' employers who embraced change willingly or with a little prompting; but in many cases the inspectors were simply unable to bring intransigent factory owners into compliance with the new legal standards.[170]

Implementation of the committee's recommendations would have provided a real test of the efficacy of the factory acts in the early twentieth century. But their report was published only months before Archduke Franz Ferdinand was assassinated in Sarajevo, and any legislation response was indefinitely postponed.[171]

167 Ibid., p. 7.
168 Ibid., pp. 7–8, explaining that when they received petitions from weavers and tenters *opposing* any reduction in 'the present allowance of moisture' which would only add to the difficulty of weaving and a corresponding loss of wages (see appendix v), the committee circulated an explanatory memorandum designed to deal with the 'considerable misapprehension' of the workers.
169 *Freer-Smith report, 1914*, p. 3.
170 Few prosecutions were in fact brought under the 1906 regulations. In 1907, for example, 12 Irish firms were convicted of breaches of the regulations and fined an average of less that 10s.: *Chief insp. ann. rep., 1907*, pp. 134–35. In 1908 there were only two convictions: *Chief insp. ann. rep., 1908*, p. 118.
171 The 1906 regulations were still in force in 1931 – see *Redgrave's Factory Acts*, ed. Joseph Owner (14th ed., London, 1931), p. 519.

1 Cotton factory at Merino, Co. Kilkenny, founded in 1810 by Messrs. Nowlan and Shaw for the manufacture of superfine cloth.

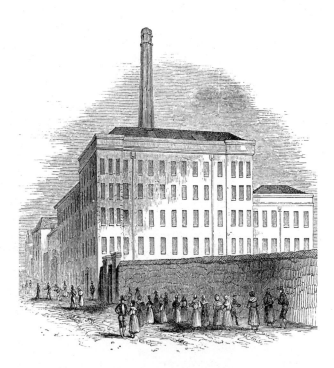

2 Thomas and Andrew Mulholland's flax-spinning mill, York Street, Belfast in 1842.

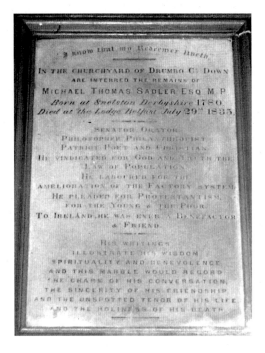

'In the churchyard of Drumbo,
Co. Down are interred the remains
of Michael Thomas Sadler, Esq.
M.P. Born at Snelston, Derbyshire
1780. Died at The Lodge, Belfast,
July 29 1835. Senator, Orator,
Philosopher, Poet and Christian.
He vindicated for God and Truth
the Law of Population. He
laboured for the amelioration of
the Factory system. He pleaded
for Protestantism, for the Young
and the Poor. To Ireland, he was
ever a Benefactor and Friend. His
writings illustrate his wisdom,
spirituality and benevolence, and
this marble would record the
charm of his conversation, the
sincerity of his friendship and the
unspotted tenor of his life and the
holiness of his death.'

3 Memorial tablet to Michael Sadler, M.P.

4 James Stuart of Dunearn.

5   The Mayfield Spinning Mill, Portlaw, Co. Waterford between 1880 and 1900.

6 Gleeson, Smith & Co., Shannon and Burnbrook Woollen Mills, Athlone, Co. Westmeath.

'In every matter of mechanical equipment and labour-saving device, this large establishment founded in the year 1859 has been brought up to the highest modern standard of completeness and efficiency, and its working organisation leaves nothing to be desired in any department.'

7 May Abraham

8 Spinning room, Bessbrook Mills, *c.*1900.

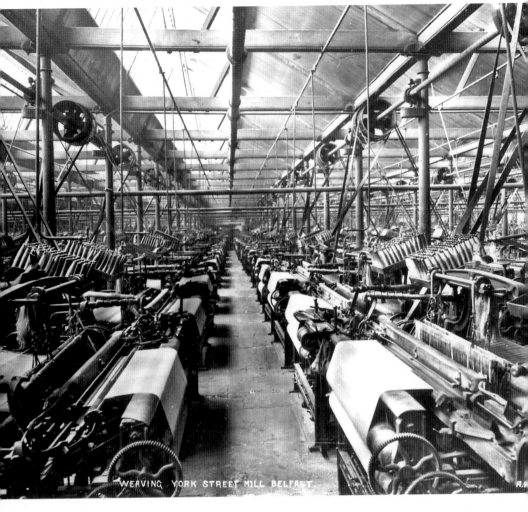

WEAVING YORK STREET MILL BELFAST.

9   Weaving room, York St Flax Spinning and Weaving Co. Ltd, Belfast.

10 Scutch mill, Bryansford, Co. Down, *c.*1910.

INTERIOR OF SCUTCH MILL, SHOWING BACK... ...OLES, TOOME, W.A.G. 1020

11 Scutch mill interior.

12 Plain weaving, Brookfield Linen Co., Crumlin Road, Belfast, 1911.

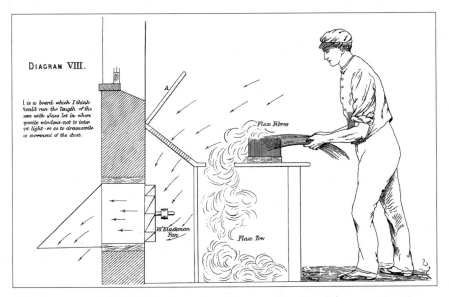

13 Arrangement of 18" Blackman fans for removing dust from roughing shops, New Northern Co., Belfast, *c*.1893

14 Hackling flax by hand: method of extracting dust, York Street Flax Spinning and Weaving Co., Belfast, *c*.1904.

'The system is to have a hood H of the shape shown immediately in front of the worker's comb. At the base of this hood is a grid G through which dust is drawn in the direction of the arrows A downwards into a main exhaust duct DD, which in its turn leads towards a powerful propeller fan F, and thence to a properly arranged discharge. The duct itself is simply placed between the wall and the row of tow boxes and covered in by a lean-to wooden roof as shown.'

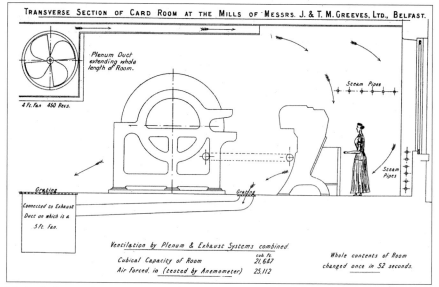

Plenum Duct
extending whole
length of Room.

4 Ft. Fan 450 Revs.

Steam Pipes

Steam
Pipes

Grating

Grating

Connected to Exhaust
Duct on which is a
5 Ft. Fan.

Ventilation by Plenum & Exhaust Systems combined.

Cubical Capacity of Room — 21,647 cub. ft.
Air forced in (tested by Anemometer) — 25,112

Whole contents of Room
changed once in 52 seconds.

15   Method of extracting dust from carding machine, Messrs. J. & T.M. Greeves Ltd, Belfast, c.1904

'The drawings and descriptions forwarded by Messrs. Greeves … indicate another efficient system … of ventilation. … The inlet currents are over the heads of the workers feeding the machines, and the dust is drawn downwards. … Messrs. Greeves say … "we have extended the fresh air inlet ducts over the cards … and we have also increased the capacity of the exhaust fan. The rooms are now much cleaner."'

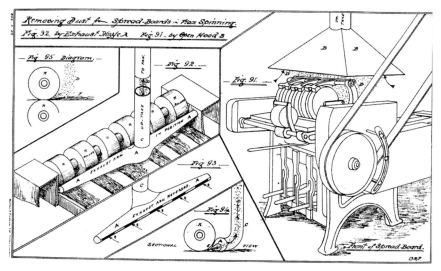

16   Removing dust from spread boards in flax spinning, c.1904: Open hoods v. close nozzles.

'The removal of dust from machines which cannot well be thoroughly encased is often attempted by means of a large hood placed immediately over the machine with a vertical uptake, such as is shown at BB at Fig. 91. This method is seldom successful, especially when accidental drafts or currents of air are blown across between the hood and the machine, thus dispersing the dust before it can be collected into the upward stream attracted by the fan. … Obviously, if this dust can be snatched up by some closely applied exhaust nozzle before it has a chance to disperse … its removal will be much more effectually accomplished. … Fig. 92 gives a general view of the exhaust arm A as applied in front of the rollers of a machine similar to that shown in Fig. 91. … This appliance is neater and more compact, less obstructive in light and far more effective, at much less expenditure of fan power than any other system tried for the purpose.'

A CARDING ROOM, BELFAST. R.W. 1223.

17 Carding room, Linfield Mill, Ulster Spinning Co. Ltd, Belfast, 1909.

*Witness: 5 Blucher St.
Londonderry*

INFORMATION.

a. Inspector's name in full.

The Information and Complaint of ⁴ Samuel Robert Bennett of Londonderry.

one of His Majesty's Inspectors of Factories and Workshops, Home Office, enforcing the provisions of the Truck Acts 1831 to 1896 so far as respects the undermentioned and other factories situate in the district of the said Inspector who saith that on and inspected by the him. day of who saith that on Friday the sixteenth day of

b. Year in words.

January   in the year One Thousand Nine Hundred and ⁵ fourteen

c. Defendant's name in full, or usual title of firm.

⁶ Messrs Welch, Margetson & Co.Ld

S. 146 1901.

d. "Was Occupier" or "Were Occupiers."
e. Factory, Workshop, Laundry, &c.

ᵈ were occupiers   of a certainᶠ   factory

within the meaning of the Factory and Workshop Acts, 1901 and 1907,

f. Address of works.

atᶠ Carlisle Rd., Londonderry

in the Parish of

and County of City of Londonderry   and that on the said date the said occupiers being the employers of one Nellie Frances Doherty, a workman within the meaning of the said Truck Acts, employed in the said factory, did unlawfully make a deduction, to wit the sum of nineteen shillings and ninepence from the sum contracted to be paid as wages by the said employer to the said workman, for or in respect of bad or negligent work on or about January 6th or 7th 1914, contrary to section 2 (2) (a) of the Truck Act 1896 in for that such deduction was not made in pursuance of and in accordance with such a contract as is required by section 2 (1) of the Truck Act 1896, the amount of the deduction not being fair and reasonable having regard to all the circumstances of the case.

Given under my hand this *twentieth*

day of *February* 1914

Samuel R Bennett

H.M. Inspector of Factories and Workshops.

264305—W. & S. Ltd.—6394—2,500—5-08.

18 Information in *Bennett* v. *Welch, Margetson & Co. Ltd.*

19 SS *Titanic* and *Olympic* under construction in stocks, Harland & Wolff Ltd, Belfast, 1910.

20 Cantrell & Cochrane Ltd, Belfast and Dublin.

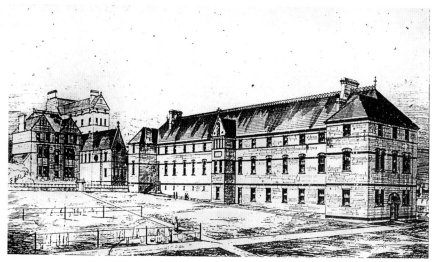

21 New Magdalen Asylum and Laundry, and proposed convent and chapel, Kingstown, for the Sisters of Mercy.

'The laundry occupies the principal floor, and will be fitted up with every modern appliance and requirement for a steam laundry.'

Date.	Names, Addresses, and Occupations of Persons summoned.	Court at which the Charges were heard.	Description of Offence.	Amount of Penalty.	Amount of Costs.	Special Remarks.
1895.			*In the Belfast District—cont.*	£ s. d.	£ s. d.	
pr. 16	Mathers and Bunting, hand-kerchief manufacturers, Mary Street, Lurgan.	Lurgan Police Court -	Failure to keep prescribed register of over-time.	0 2 6	0 1 6	
"	" "	" " -	Failure to enter overtime on prescribed Form No. 12.	0 2 6	0 1 6	
" 25	James Clarke, dressmakers, 20, Frances Street, Newton-ards.	Newtonards Police Court	Failure to enter overtime on prescribed form	0 2 6	0 6 6	
" 30	William Woodside, tailor, 312, Shankhill Road, Belfast.	Belfast Police Court -	Employing one young person at a meal time -	0 2 6	0 2 6	
"	Northern Cloth Co., tailors, Bridge End, Belfast.	" " -	Employing one woman at a meal time -	0 2 6	0 2 6	
"	J. Boyle, machine hackler of flax, Weir Street, Belfast.	Petty Sessions, Belfast Town Hall.	Failure to observe special rules by not wear-ing respirators provided.	0 0 6	0 1 6	It was explained to the Court that these proceedings were taken as a caution that the special rule as to respirators must be obeyed, and that a nominal penalty or discharge on payment of costs with a warning would suffice, and the cases were thus dealt with.
"	S. McFarland, machine hack-ler of flax, Loftus Street, Belfast.	" "	Failure to observe special rules by not wear-ing respirators provided.	0 0 6	0 1 6	
"	D. McCudden, machine hack-ler of flax, 7, Park View Street, Belfast.	" "	Failure to observe special rules by not wear-ing respirators provided.	0 0 6	0 1 6	
"	Pat. M'Laughten, machine hackler of flax, 30, Sultan Street, Belfast.	" "	Failure to observe special rules by not wear-ing respirators provided.	0 0 6	0 1 6	
ct. 8	James Foster, baker, 6, Main Street, Larne.	Larne Petty Sessions -	Employing young persons after legal hour on Saturday.	0 2 0	0 6 0	Although it was stated more than once that these firms had been cautioned a short time before, the Chairman spoke of the offences as being of a technical nature.
"	George Baine, baker, Point Street, Larne.	" " -	Employing young persons after legal hours on Saturday.	0 3 0	0 9 0	

22   Extract from list of prosecutions in North Ireland district in *Chief insp. ann. rep. 1895*, pp. 70 and 78.

Date.	Names, Addresses, and Occupations of Persons summoned.	Court at which the Charges were heard.	Description of Offence.	Amount of Penalty.	Amount of Costs.	Special Remarks.
1895.			*In the Dublin District—cont.*	£ s. d.	£ s. d.	
ug. 9	E. Deevy & Co., dressmakers, 1 and 2. Michael Street, Waterford.	Petty Sessions Court, Water-ford.	Employing three women after legal hour -	0 3 0	0 7 6	
"	" "	" "	Failure to specify on notice the period of employment.	0 1 0	0 1 6	
" 14	Mrs. E. O'Looney, dress-maker, Ennistymon, co. Clare.	Ennistymon Petty Sessions Court.	Employing three young persons beyond the legal hour.	0 1 6	0 7 6	
" 20	B. Hyam, tailor, 29 and 30, Dame Street, Dublin.	Dublin Police Court -	Employing three young persons after legal hours.	- - -	- - -	Cases dismissed. The three females swore that the work upon which they were engaged was for them-selves; the Magistrate said it certainly was a strange story, and cautioned occupier.
"	Patrick McCourt, confectioner, 14, Fownes's Street, Dublin.	" " -	Employing a young person after legal hour on Saturday, 20th July 1895.	1 0 0	0 4 6	
pt. 13	James Lacey, bookbinder, Dame Court, Dublin.	" " -	Employing two young persons under 16 years of age without certificates of fitness, 13th July 1895.	0 10 0	0 4 0	
" 20	P. Faulkner and Son, paper bag manufacturers, Mount Brown, Dublin.	" " -	Employing two women after 4 p.m. on Satur-day, 13th July 1895.	4 0 0	0 6 0	Adjourned from 13th September 1895.
" 27	Michael Sullivan, aërated water manufacturer, High Street, Waterford.	Waterford Petty Sessions Court.	Employing two young persons more than seven days without obtaining certificates of fitness.	0 5 0	0 5 0	
t. 7	M. Clocan and Sons, flour mills, Nun's Island, Gal-way.	Galway Petty Sessions Court -	Neglecting to fence mill-gearing -	0 10 0	0 2 6	Magistrates decided to affix a small penalty as this was the first case that had been heard in Galway for a long time.

23   Extract from list of prosecutions in South Ireland district in *Chief insp. ann. rep. 1895*, p. 84.

24 Poster advertising William Ewart & Son Ltd, Belfast, *c.*1888.

CHAPTER SEVEN

The fair payment of wages

INTRODUCTION

The dearth of alternative employment opportunities, a ready supply of labour, a workforce consisting mainly of women, young persons and children and a traditionally low level of trade union membership combined to bring about an average weekly wage in the Irish linen industry which consistently fell below the cost of maintaining a minimum standard of comfort.[1] Orthodox economic theory in the nineteenth century, however, ordained that the state had no right or interest in regulating wage rates. But public concern as to the *manner* in which those wages were paid or calculated did bring about legislative intervention, with the result that from 1887 onwards the work of the factory inspectors took on a wholly new dimension as they were called upon to suppress or regulate a number of practices which, in Ireland as elsewhere in the United Kingdom, unfairly reduced the real value of whatever wages were otherwise payable by an employer.

The earliest of these was 'truck' – the payment of wages in goods rather than in cash. Workers might be 'paid' wholly or partly in the employer's own products or, more commonly, by 'tickets' or 'tokens' redeemable only in the employer's shop.[2] The practice of truck generally, though not invariably, reduced the value of the wages received by the worker:

[Truck], if honestly and reasonably carried out, is not necessarily detrimental to the workman, for a large employer of labour can buy in the wholesale market, and if the articles bought are retailed at cost price the workman will get better bargains than he could possibly do at a retail shop.... [But] since the workman was bound to take articles supplied by his master at the price put upon them by the master, there was nothing to prevent an unscrupulous employer from supplying articles of inferior quality and putting an exorbitant price upon them; and this actually happened in very many instances. The commonest way of working this system was by means of the 'tommy shop' ... belonging to the employer where were kept food, clothes, crockery, ironmongery and other articles required by workmen, usually of the most inferior quality. The men's wages were paid wholly or partly in orders upon this shop.[3]

1 See especially E.J. Boyle, 'The economic development of the Irish linen industry 1825–1913' (unpublished Ph.D. thesis, Queen's University of Belfast, 1977), chap. 7.
2 G.W. Hilton, *The truck system* (Cambridge, 1960), p. 1. This leading study focuses on nail-making, coal-mining and iron works and unfortunately makes little reference to Ireland.
3 *Redgrave's factory, truck and shop acts*, ed. C.F. Lloyd (12th ed., London, 1916), p. 412. As P.S. Atiyah, *The rise and fall of freedom of contract* (Oxford, 1979), pp. 533–34 points out, the position of many workers was exacerbated by the fact that they were often paid at irregular intervals and had to buy on credit while they waited for their wages.

Legislation prohibiting this practice dated from the fifteenth century; but its enforcement was long regarded as the private responsibility of the aggrieved worker. It was not until the Truck (Amendment) Act 1887 that the government's resolution to abolish the last vestiges of truck led it to accept the need for public intervention in the form of enforcement of the law by the factory inspectorate.

A more recent development was the practice of linking wages more closely to output by means of 'piece-work' payments. This practice, which Marx described as 'the form of wages most in harmony with the capitalist mode of production',[4] provided 'a genuine incentive for the worker to intensify his labour and thus raise his productivity, a guarantee against slacking [and] an automatic device for reducing the wage-bill in times of depression ...'.[5] Payment by piece-work could be abused by unscrupulous employers who obscured or even concealed the methods by which each 'piece' was measured or paid. Some of these cases could be caught by existing legislation.[6] But in 1891 parliament was prevailed upon to enact a 'particulars' clause – section 24 of the Factory and Workshop Act 1891 – whereby an employer was generally obliged to supply any worker 'paid by the piece' with 'sufficient particulars to enable him to ascertain the rate of wages at which he is entitled to be paid for the work'. Enforcement of this provision was from the outset entrusted to the factory inspectorate.

Two other employment practices which also came under parliamentary scrutiny about this time were the 'fining' of workers for disciplinary 'offences' and the imposition of deductions from wages in respect of working facilities supplied to, or materials damaged by, workers. Reasonable fines and deductions for such matters were considered justifiable, for example, to encourage good time-keeping or to discourage poor or careless workmanship. But legislation in the form of the Truck Act 1896 was considered necessary to enable the factory inspectors to control unscrupulous employers who might abuse otherwise acceptable practices by imposing excessive fines or making unfair or unreasonable deductions.

While all these unfair employment practices were found throughout the United Kingdom, Ireland achieved a disproportionate degree of notoriety on account of the extent to which some employers, particularly in the linen industry, took advantage of these methods to deprive 'protected' workers of what often amounted to a significant portion of their already low wages.

---

4 *Capital: A critical analysis of capitalist production*, trans. from 3rd German edition by S. Moore and E. Aveling (Moscow, 1958), i, 556.

5 E. Hobsbawm, *The age of capital 1848–1875* (London, 1975), p. 219. For a contemporary summary of the arguments for and against piece-work, see *Fifth and final report of the royal commission on labour*, pp. 11–12 [C. 7421], H.C. 1894, xxxv, 19–20.

6 For example, the Factory and Workshop Act 1878, s. 80, which applied weights and measures legislation to factories and workshops, was used for the benefit of hemstitchers of handkerchiefs paid by the 'inch' – see *Chief insp. ann. rep., 1885*, pp. 21–22.

TRUCK

The Truck Act 1831

Legislative intervention in the *method* of paying wages began as early as 1464, when the first Truck Act[7] was passed by the English parliament. The act, which soon came to apply to Ireland,[8] recited that men and women had been 'discouraged' from working at woollen cloth-making as a result of being 'driven to take a great part of their wages in pins, girdles, and other unprofitable wares'; accordingly, they should now be paid 'lawful money for all their lawful wages ...'. Over the next three hundred years or so, parliament from time to time restated this principle and extended it to various other trades and occupations. In 1725, for example, woollen manufacturers in England and Wales were required to pay their employees 'in good and lawful money' and not 'in goods or by way of truck',[9] and in 1748, this requirement was extended to all persons employed 'in or about any of the manufactures of silk ... hemp, flax, linen, cotton ... iron or leather ...'.[10]

Neither of these later acts applied to Ireland prior to the Union. During the eighteenth century, however, the Irish parliament, 'true to mercantile principles', passed a number of enactments 'aimed at regulating the working conditions and wages of craftsmen'.[11] In particular, the Unlawful Combinations Act 1729[12] required 'every person ... concerned in employing any artificer, work-men, servants or labourers in any of the trades or manufactures of this kingdom' to pay all their workers 'the full wages or other price agreed on in good and lawful money of this kingdom, and shall not pay the said wages ... or any part thereof in goods, or by way of truck, or in any other manner than in money ...'. This legislation formed part of a more general attempt to regulate wage-levels in a number of trades and occupations, and tends to support the view that the early truck acts were designed not for the protection of workers, but of employers, by preventing their competitors from circumventing a standard wage set by collective bargaining or otherwise.[13] Although there is little evidence to go on, it would seem, however, that this legislation was largely ineffective:

A manufacturer generally keeps a shop of dry goods, the poor workman is paid in full at one counter, but he is obliged to go to the other, (by a private understanding, that

---

7   4 Edw. IV, c. 1, s. 5.
8   And was not formally repealed in Ireland until the Statute Law (Ire.) Revision Act 1872.
9   12 Geo. I, c. 34, s. 3.
10   22 Geo. II, c. 27. See further Hilton, *Truck system*, pp. 71–87.
11   J.W. Boyle, *The Irish labor movement in the nineteenth century* (Washington, DC, 1988), p. 8. See also J.D. Clarkson, *Labour and nationalism in Ireland* (New York, 1925), pp. 35–38 and F.A. D'Arcy, 'Dublin artisan activity, opinion and organisation, 1820–1850' (unpublished MA thesis, NUI, 1968).
12   3 Geo. II, c. 14 (Ire.), s. 8 – a provision similar to that in the English act of 1725, but not apparently limited to the woollen industry.
13   This explanation, advanced by Sidney and Beatrice Webb, *Industrial democracy* (London, 1902), pp. 317–18 is supported, with some reservations, by Hilton, *Truck system*, pp. 40–45 and 101–05.

if he does not he will not be employed) where he receives a shawl, or a gown-piece, or a coat, or something that is useless to him, and at one-third more than he could buy it for, with his money at another shop; what he receives, he takes to the pawn-office immediately, and pledges for half the amount he was obliged to give for it, and most probably he never afterwards redeems it – he being ground down in his weekly pittance of subsistence money for his family, by the present low price of labour, on account of the great depression of trade. If he complains to a magistrate, he gets no more employment from the person complained against, nor will others trust him; thus, he must patiently suffer the robbery, or starve.[14]

By 1830 the law relating to truck had become excessively complicated; but proposals to consolidate and simplify the law were opposed by classical economists who viewed the prohibition of truck as an unwarranted interference with freedom of contract: 'If it should be more convenient or profitable for a workman to receive payment for his labour partly or wholly in goods, why should he be prevented from doing so? For if such a practice is inconvenient or injurious to any man, he will not work a second time for the master who pays him in that manner.'[15] But a more pragmatic defence of truck was that, by reducing real wages, it operated to maintain levels of employment during periods of recession.[16] Both of these arguments were supported by O'Connell, who regarded the proposed legislation as 'destructive to Ireland',[17] and a futile attempt to interfere with freedom of labour. Truck was 'the result and the proof of the existence of poverty and distress in the country; and this was not the way to remedy such a state of things. The way to do that was to increase the market for labour, and to increase the competition amongst the masters.'[18] Indeed, 'in the present state of Ireland [the bill] might do great evil, for although some inconvenience might arise from the truck-system near Belfast, it was not to be compared to the injury which would be done in the south, by throwing many hands out of employment.'[19]

14   *Hansard 2*, xxiv, 327–28 (3 May 1830)(R.H. King, 4th earl of Kingston and MP for Cork Co., on the basis of information supplied privately by a Bandon magistrate). A more benign system was practised at Malcomson's factory in Portlaw – see T. Hunt, *Portlaw, County Waterford 1825–1876: Portrait of an industrial village and its cotton industry* (Dublin, 2000), p. 29. See also W.J. Davis and A.W. Waters, *Tickets and passes of Great Britain and Ireland* (Leamington Spa, 1922).

15   *Hansard 1*, xxiii, 1175–76 (21 July 1812) (Joseph Hume MP – the principal opponent of the 1831 act).

16   See e.g. the contention of Robert Torrens that 'the abolition of truck would diminish the demand for labour, and throw operatives out of work' unless the profits of trade could be increased by 'cheap food and low taxes'; any attempt to abolish truck 'while the corn-laws and high taxes continued' would, accordingly, 'do little to mitigate the evils': *Hansard 3*, vi, 1361–62 (12 Sept. 1831).

17   *Hansard 2*, xxv, 947 (5 July 1830). Cf. Sir R. Bateson (Conservative MP for Co. Londonderry) initially argued that it was important that the provisions of the bill *should* extend to Ireland: *Hansard 3*, iii, 1256 (12 April 1831), but on 12 September 1831 he voted against the bill (ibid., vi, 1362), as did a number of Irish MPs.

18   *Hansard 3*, iii, 1258 (12 April 1831).

19   *Hansard 3*, vi, 1359 (12 Sept. 1831). Indeed, it was suggested by Nicholas Leader (MP for Kilkenny City) that 'a considerable manufactory in Ireland had been totally ruined in consequence of such interference …': ibid., col. 1362.

The opposition of O'Connell and other Irish MPs ensured that the new legislation did not apply to Ireland; but neither they nor the economists persuaded the government on the general issue. Accordingly, the Truck Act 1831[20] reiterated that 'the entire amount of the wages' of any 'artificer' in certain designated trades[21] must be paid in 'the current coin of the realm' and not in kind, and added that no employment contract might contain any direct or indirect restrictions as to how and where all or any of the wages shall be spent. An employer who infringed these provisions was liable on summary conviction to a fine ranging from a minimum of £5 and a maximum of £10 for a first offence, to a maximum of £100 for a third offence. Further, an employer was debarred from bringing a civil action against a worker for the cost of any goods supplied 'as or on account of his wages ... or for or in respect of any goods supplied ... at any shop ... kept by or belonging to such employer, or in the profits of which such employer shall have any share or interest'.

O'Connell appears to have overstated the potential significance for Ireland of the 1831 act. Its enforcement remained primarily a matter for the individual worker; and it would have been a brave – or desperate – man or woman who would have taken an employer to court in the virtual certainty of losing his or her job.[22] In any case, it is not at all clear how the repeal of earlier truck legislation, designed to make way for the new act, affected the application of that legislation in Ireland[23] – and the truck provisions of earlier Irish acts, particularly that of 1729, still remained in force. But it may well be that these acts were of no practical significance – certainly, there is little or no evidence that they were enforced *after* 1831. In 1846, for example, it was considered necessary to make it unlawful for any person undertaking public works in an Irish county 'to persuade or induce any labourer ... to take goods in lieu of ... wages, or to expend his wages in any particular shop ...'.[24] Four years later, a bill proposed by the solicitor general for Ireland (John Hatchell) and Sir William Somerville (MP for Drogheda) would have enacted for Ireland legislation similar to the 1831 act; but the bill failed to progress beyond a

---

20 1 & 2 Will. IV, c. 37. For further details, see Hilton, *Truck system*, chap. VI.

21 By s. 19, the act applied (*inter alia*) to the knitting and cloth trades and to lace making, but not otherwise to the textile industry.

22 According to Atiyah, *Rise and fall of freedom of contract*, pp. 535–36, there was 'a spate of prosecutions' immediately after the act came into force; by 1838, however, 'it was said to be a dead letter, though this was certainly an exaggeration'. Some prosecutions were brought on behalf of employers by anti-truck societies whose 'primary purpose was to prevent concealed wage reductions in the form of truck, usually when depressions were forcing down prices'.

23 There is nothing in the Truck Acts Repeal Act 1831 (1 & 2 Will. IV, c. 36) to exclude its application to Ireland; but the principal act clearly did *not* apply, and therefore such a limitation may be implicit.

24 County Works (Ire.) Act 1846 (9 & 10 Vict., c. 2), s. 20.

25 Money Payment of Wages (Ire.) Bill, H.C. 1850 (76), iv, 567. The bill appears to have succumbed to the general antagonism which defeated the strenuous efforts being made at this time to extend the protection afforded by the 1831 act in England and Wales – see Hilton, *Truck system*, pp. 122–31.

first reading.[25] There the matter largely rested for the next thirty-seven years, notwithstanding the fact that resort to truck in Ireland appears to have grown rapidly from the early 1860s,[26] and that such practices, at least in England and Wales, gave rise to public concern from time to time.[27]

The Truck (Amendment) Act 1887

By the 1860s, the relationship between employer and worker was beginning to change:

Increasingly ... the wage-relationship was transformed into a pure market-relationship, a cash nexus.... British capitalism in the 1860s abandoned non-economic compulsion of labour (such as the Master and Servant Acts which punished breaches of contract by workers with jail), long-term hiring contracts ... and truck payments, while the average length of hiring was shortened, the average period of payment gradually reduced to a week ... thus making the market bargain more sensitive and flexible.[28]

Other factors were also at work:

Various causes, such as the rapid development of new industries, the constant tendency of these towards centralisation in large groups, easy communication between large centres of work, the demand for workers skilled in any particular trade or manufacture, the interlocking of towns with villages by railway, the transfer of any given class of work from one district to another have had a remarkable effect in doing away with the 'truck system'. To these may be added the spread of education and of general knowledge. While last, but by no means least, we must take the action of the trades unions.[29]

Truck may, for these reasons, have been in decline, particularly in the urban industrial areas;[30] but it persisted, particularly in rural areas, at an unacceptable level.

26 See W.A. Seaby, 'Employers' truck tickets and food vouchers issued in Ulster during the latter half of the 19th century and the early part of the 20th century', in *Numismatic Society of Ireland Occasional Papers*, nos. 5–9 (1969), 11, where the author quotes the manager of the Blackstaff Flax Spinning & Weaving Co. as stating that 'there is no doubt that prior to the Truck Act [1887] there were many abuses and workers were literally forced to take groceries, etc. in lieu of wages ... and employers recovered a considerable percentage of their outgoings through profits made in the so-called "shops".'
27 See especially *Report of the commissioners appointed by the Truck Commission Act 1870 for the purpose of inquiring into the operation of the [Truck Act 1831] and upon the operation of all other acts or provisions of acts prohibiting the truck system* [C. 326], H.C. 1871, xxxvi, 1. The commissioners' remit did not extend to Ireland, which is particularly unfortunate given that their report, according to Hilton, *Truck system*, p. 132, is 'one of the most comprehensive and intelligent social inquiries of the Victorian period'.
28 Hobsbawm, *Age of capital*, pp. 218–19.
29 *Chief insp. ann. rep., 1890*, p. 51 (Gould).
30 In 1877, for example, the TUC regarded truck payments 'as a grievance not important enough to include in its legislative programme': S. and B. Webb, *History of trade unionism, 1666–1920* (London, 1920), p. 371.

One element of the continuing problem was that some workers were still being paid at lengthy intervals, driving them to buy food and other supplies on credit which may only have been available from a tommy-shop. Accordingly, the principal recommendation of a report published in 1871 was that employers should be compelled to pay wages weekly.[31] But it was also accepted that the 1831 act could be more effectively enforced:

It is complained that the expense of prosecution [under the 1831 act] is too great, that the duty is not one which can be fairly expected to be undertaken by a workman with the certainty of losing his employment, and no small probability of being unfavourably considered by other masters.... These complaints are well founded; the duty and cost of such prosecutions must, in this case, if the law is to be effectual, be considered as of a public nature ... and, if possible, the institution of prosecutions should be entrusted to some public officer. It is, however, probable that a system of inspection, at least in the districts where truck is of the more petty kind, would be even more effectual, because more constant and general in operation, than merely penal provisions.[32]

A bill introduced in 1872 to give effect to these recommendations proposed to give the factory inspectorate some responsibility for enforcing the 1831 act, but it received little support and was quickly withdrawn.[33] Specific provisions dealing with the particular problem of excessive charges for the use of equipment supplied by employers in the hosiery trade commanded more general support and were duly enacted in 1874.[34] But enforcement of the Hosiery Manufacture (Wages) Act 1874, which made frame rents and charges 'illegal, null and void',[35] remained the responsibility of the aggrieved worker.

In 1876, the factory and workshop commissioners were opposed in principle to the inspectorate being authorised to 'interfere' in the matter of wages:

We are convinced that it would be a bad precedent for future social legislation, if the necessary check which is afforded by the difficulty of enforcing an Act were to come to be made light of, through the easy resource of keeping in reserve a gigantic staff of inspectors, ready for and capable of any kind of work, and to whom the enforcement of all perilous experiments in legislation might be entrusted, in a form that would leave them a large amount of discretion, and with the expectation that they would in general use their powers discreetly.[36]

31 *Report of the truck commissioners 1871*, p. 45.
32 Ibid., p. 46.
33 Master and Servant (Wages) Bill, H.C. 1872 (65), iii, 13 (which did not extend to Ireland) – see *Hansard 3*, ccx, 214 (18 March 1872); according to Hilton, *Truck system*, p. 135: 'On the third occasion in four decades, rising prices and growing prosperity had caused an apathy towards truck legislation'.
34 This legislation, primarily the work of Mr Mundella, MP for Sheffield and a leading stocking manufacturer, was 'the culmination of decades of effort in the framework knitting trade': Hilton, *Truck system*, p. 136.
35 Thus, the act was later invoked in Donegal against employers who charged a rent for knitting-machines supplied to home-workers.
36 *Report of the commissioners appointed to inquire into the working of the factory and workshop acts ...* , p. xxv [C. 1443], H.C. 1876, xxix, 28.

In any case, truck primarily affected adult males, not the 'protected' classes of women, young persons and children. But this backward-looking attempt to limit the role of the inspectorate to their 'proper' duties foundered in the face of a continuing depression which duly brought truck practices once more to public attention. The need to obtain 'trustworthy and untainted evidence'[37] for the purpose of enforcing the law now persuaded parliament to accept the proposal for public supervision and prosecution by the factory inspectorate.[38] Indeed, this aspect of the Truck (Amendment) Bill 1887 did not give rise to any significant controversy. Nor did the proposal that the legislation should extend to Ireland.[39]

What did give rise to concern, particularly in Ireland, was the government's rejection of the earlier recommendation that all workers should be paid weekly. In 1886, Harland & Wolff Ltd. had departed from previous practice and began to pay their workers fortnightly rather than weekly.[40] Growing resentment at the change led to six thousand shipyard workers going on strike in May 1887. Their case was that the payment of wages fortnightly 'plunges the men into a system of credit, and the effect is to produce a system of truck – a very bad system of truck, because it obliges them to resort to certain shops and to put up with certain terms which, having regard to the price and quality of the goods, they would not accept had they their wages in their hands every week'.[41] The men were persuaded to return to work by a promise of legislative action[42] and, indeed, the house of commons duly accepted an amendment to the Truck (Amendment) Bill to the effect that a worker employed in Ireland for wages calculated by time must be paid weekly.[43] This amendment was, however, rejected by the house of lords, which stuck to its guns in the face of pressure from the lower house.[44]

37   *Chief insp. ann. rep., 1890*, p. 53.

38   Hilton, *Truck system*, p. 140 ascribes parliament's receptivity to the fact that in England and Scotland 'the period from 1873 to 1887 was one of almost unremitting deflation'.

39   The bill was welcomed by T.M. Healy (Longford N.) as 'an excellent measure': *Hansard 3*, ccxiv, 306 (28 April 1887).

40   Workers in Ireland other than agricultural labourers were at this time normally paid weekly. This had been the practice in Harland & Woolf; but it was claimed that the complexities of payment on a piecework basis had made this impractical.

41   *Hansard 3*, cccxix, 1240 (19 Aug. 1887) (Thomas Sexton, Belfast W.). Cf. '[T]ruck in the coal and iron trades is but one form of the wide evils caused by long pays, and … cannot be effectually prevented except by the abolition of long pays …': *Report of the truck commisioners 1871*, pp. 45–46.

42   See *Hansard 3*, cccxvi, 1310 (30 June 1887)(Sexton).

43   *Hansard 3*, cccxvii, 611–25 (12 July 1887). The amendment was proposed by a number of nationalist MPs, including Patrick Chance (Kilkenny S.) and Arthur O'Connor (Donegal E.); it was opposed on the grounds that 'the shipbuilding trade in Belfast is [already] sufficiently handicapped' and that fortnightly payments of wages were 'universal' in other shipyards – see ibid., col. 613 (T.W. Russell (S. Tyrone)) and *Hansard 3*, cccxix, 1245 (19 Aug.1887) (Sir James Corry (Mid-Armagh)). Acceptance of the amendment was seen as an unwarrantable concession to the Parnellites – see *Belfast Newsletter*, 14 July 1887.

44   An obligation to pay wages at different periods in different parts of the United Kingdom is undesirable, and a provision for regulating the time for the payment of

Accordingly, the government, eager to save the remainder of the bill, fell back on its original compromise proposal that any payments on account of wages paid fortnightly must be paid in money, and that no deductions from wages (for example, by way of interest) should be made in consequence of such payments.[45]

The Truck (Amendment) Act 1887 applied to Ireland not only the provisions of that act, but also the 1831 act 'so far as it is not hereby repealed'.[46] By section 2, the prohibition on the use of truck in Ireland now extended to all industrial workers who came within the definition of 'workman' set out in section 10 of the Employers and Workmen Act 1875, namely, 'any person other than a domestic or menial servant who, being a labourer ... journeyman, artificer, handicraftsman, miner or otherwise engaged in manual labour ... has entered into or works under a contract with an employer, whether the contract ... be a contract of service or a contract personally to execute any work or labour ...'. Section 6 of the act clarified the range of practices which were prohibited:

No employer shall, directly or indirectly ... impose as a condition, express or implied, in or for the employment of any workman any terms as to the place at which, or the manner in which, or the person with whom, any wages ... paid to the workman are ... to be expended, and no employer shall ... dismiss any workman from his employment for or on account of the place at which, or the manner in which, or the person with whom, any wages ... paid by the employer to such workman are ... expended or fail to be expended.

Finally, section 13(2) made it the 'duty' of the factory inspectorate throughout the United Kingdom to enforce both the 1831 and 1887 acts, and gave to them the same powers and authority for doing so as they had for the purpose of enforcing the factory acts. However, a worker could still bring a civil action against his or her employer for non-payment of wages, and in such a case, the employer could not set off the value of any goods supplied to the worker.[47]

wages is not germane to a truck bill: see *Hansard 3*, cccxix, 1239 (19 Aug. 1887) and cccxxi, 447–48 (12 Sept. 1887). Sexton was disgusted: 'this clause, after being debated in this house at length, was disposed of in a few seconds by about twenty peers, not one of whom has any real knowledge of Ireland': *Hansard 3*, cccxix, 1241.

45 *Hansard 3*, cccxxi, 444–55 (12 Sept.1887). This provision became section 3 of the 1887 act.

46 1887 act, s. 18. A particular problem arose as to the penalty for breach of the act in Ireland. The 1831 act, s. 9 had stipulated a minimum penalty of £5, but this particular provision had been repealed for England and Wales in 1884; the Statute Law Revision Act 1891 then repealed the relevant part of s. 9 'except as to Ireland'. In 1897, it was held in *Snape* v. *Belfast Flax Spinning & Weaving Co.* that the minimum fine provision still applied in Ireland, and the law officers agreed: PRO HO 45/9929/B25591 (opinion dated 24 Jan. 1898).

47 See e.g. *Glasgow* v. *Irish Independent Printing Co.* [1901] 2 IR 278, where some workers had agreed, at a time of financial difficulty, to take part of their wages in shares of the company. When the plaintiff later claimed that this was in breach of the truck acts, the court of appeal agreed and ordered the defendant to make good the cash deficit.

Truck in Ireland

The introduction of the factory inspectors did not result in a large number
of truck prosecutions in Ireland or elsewhere in the United Kingdom. For
some time after 1887, the male inspectors clearly continued to give priority
to working conditions, no more than two truck convictions having been
obtained by 1896.[48] The appointment of lady inspectors from 1893, however,
brought about a change of emphasis, as they gradually acquired experience
of 'the human results of uncertain and low wages, peculiarly oppressive to
women and girls, by their investigation of complaints, by long drawn-out
inquiries into homework and into payment of wages in over-valued groceries
and other goods instead of money'.[49] Although they appear to have encouraged their male counterparts to greater activity,[50] all the inspectors preferred,
where possible, to proceed by accepting undertakings from employers to
abide by the law coupled, where appropriate, with (re)payments to the
aggrieved workers. This practice may explain the fact that during the period
1897–1913 an average of only six cases per year were brought throughout the
United Kingdom; convictions were obtained in two-thirds of these cases, but
were rewarded by fines averaging £2–£3 – significantly higher than the level
of fine normally imposed for breaches of the factory acts.[51] The relatively low
rate of conviction was explained as follows:

> The act itself was none too clear, and intimidation, both direct and indirect, made the
> finding of good witnesses in cases of prosecution difficult. Neither were the
> inspectors' powers clearly known. They had right of entry into shops on factory
> premises, but only doubtfully into 'tommy' shops elsewhere, or to shops kept not by
> factory owners, but by a middleman or contractor, who gave out home-work for
> which he gave payment in goods from his shop. The difficulties were experienced to
> the full by the inspectors working in Ireland....[52]

The difficulties in Ireland mainly arose from the increasing number of
women undertaking 'making-up' work in their own homes.[53] In the urban

48 See *Departmental committee on the truck acts, vol iv: Precis and appendices*, p. 136 [Cd.
    4568], H.C. 1909, xlix, 318.
49 A.M. Anderson, *Women in the factory: An administrative adventure, 1893 to 1921*
    (London, 1922), p. 59.
50 See e.g. *Chief insp. ann. rep., 1907*, p. 133 and *1908*, p. 117 (McCaghey, on truck
    practices in dress-making workrooms, a dyeworks factory, and a corn and saw mill);
    Chief insp. ann. rep., 1908, p. 35 and *1910*, p. 33 (Allhusen's attempts to prevent the
    'well-rooted practice, almost hoary with age' of paying bakehouse workers partly in
    kind), and *Chief insp. ann. rep., 1910*, p. 107 ('extensive inquiry' by Eraut among
    scutch mills in Co. Antrim 'without ... bringing much to light').
51 See especially *Departmental committee on the truck acts 1908*, iv, 134–36 and 145
    (which show, incidentally, that between 1897 and 1905 at least, some two-thirds of
    the cases were brought by lady inspectors). The average fine for factory act offences
    during this period was less than £1 – see further below, chap. 10.
52 H. Martindale, 'Truck', in 'Review of the work of the inspectorate, 1833–1932',
    published in *Chief insp. ann. rep., 1932*, p. 66.
53 See e.g. E. Boyle, *The Irish flowerers* (Holywood, Co. Down, 1971); B. Collins, 'The

areas, outwork was essentially an extension of the factory; work was taken home to be prepared or finished by factory workers or their neighbours either to avoid the restrictions on the hours of factory work or to maximise the use of machinery by avoiding the loss of time spent on incidental (non-machine) processes.[54] Truck in its traditional sense does not appear to have been widespread; the problem which these outworkers faced in many cases was the very low level of wages, frequently exacerbated by failure to provide them with piece-work particulars.[55]

But in the countryside, and particularly in counties Down and Donegal, outwork was undertaken by the wives and daughters of small farmers and agricultural labourers when they were not working on the land.[56] Manufacturers and businesses in Belfast, Londonderry and other industrial centres appointed local shopkeepers as agents to distribute knitting and sewing 'home-work'. The low commission rates typically paid to such agents[57] – or their own simple greed – encouraged them to increase their income by forcing the outworkers, who typically earned less than one shilling per day,[58] to accept payment in goods rather than in cash:

In Donegal the worker … takes wool out from the agents' shops in the towns to her own cabin … and knits it up into socks and stockings, and at week-ends carries back to the towns the week's work, say two dozen of socks…. Instead, however, of being paid by the

organisation of sewing outwork in late nineteenth-century Ulster' in M. Berg (ed.), *Markets and manufacture in early industrial Europe* (London, 1991), p. 139 and M. Neill, 'Homeworkers in Ulster, 1850–1911' in J. Holmes and D. Urquhart, *Coming into the light: The work, politics and religion of women in Ulster, 1840–1940* (Belfast, 1994), chap. 1. Another industry redolent with truck was road construction in the west of Ireland – see *Royal commission appointed to inquire and report upon the operation of the acts dealing with congestion in Ireland: Appendix to the Tenth Report*, pp. 16–17 [Cd. 4007], H.C. 1908, xlii, 114–15 (Father Flatley).

54 *Chief insp. ann. rep., 1901*, pt. I, p. 145 (Snape). Beatrice Webb criticised 'the employer who, to escape the factory acts, gives work out to be done at home, [and therefore] was not liable for the age, health, education and hours of the protected classes …': 'Women and the factory acts', in S. and B. Webb (ed.), *Problems in modern industry* (London, 1902), pp. 140–50.

55 See especially *Committee of inquiry into the conditions of employment in the linen and other making-up trades of the north of Ireland: Report and evidence*, pp. vii–xviii [Cd. 6509], H.C. 1912–13, xxxiv, 371–82.

56 See especially H. Martindale, 'Truck and gombeening in Donegal', in *Departmental committee on the truck acts, vol. iii: Minutes of evidence (days 38–66)*, p. 248 [Cd. 4444], H.C. 1908, lix, 786 and in *Chief insp. ann. rep., 1907*, p. 214.

57 The commission paid to the shopkeeper agent was 'so miserably low [that] the agent, if he is to make any profit at all, must make it out of the unfortunate workers': *Chief insp. ann. rep., 1899*, p. 277 (Squire).

58 'We found that 1s. was considered to be a good day's wage; and we were informed that the usual wage was 9*d.* a day, and many old women can earn only 3*d.* to 6*d.* a day': Martindale, 'Truck and gombeening in Donegal', p. 249, who explains that the problem was part of a wider system of buying goods on credit brought about by 'the scarcity of ready money during most of the year'. For a more general study of this problem, see e.g. *Report of the departmental committee on agricultural credit in Ireland* [Cd. 7375], H.C. 1914, xiii, 1.

truck master the 2s. 6d. or 3s. a week which is due to her, she is paid in goods, mostly in small packets of tea, which ... was priced at a high figure [of] ... 3s. 6d. per lb. They may also get some other article of diet, such as brown sugar or maize....[59]

The practical disadvantages of this practice were obvious:

The expenses which should be met by money extend beyond the cost of the tea and sugar and flour; there is rent, there are implements, there is help that the women need in getting in their crops when the men are away; there are seeds and necessaries for the ground and garden; there are the household goods to be renewed, and there is the clothing. The truck masters prefer to give tea to any other thing, because I presume their profit upon it is greater, and the women drink a great deal more tea than is good for them.[60]

Such 'payment' in goods was clearly contrary to the principle of the truck acts; but the enforcement of these acts in a depressed area such as the west of Ireland was not a straightforward matter. In an attempt to encourage economic development, the congested districts board had been set up in 1891, and as O'Connell had earlier pointed out, truck was perhaps a price worth paying for the opportunity of gainful employment. But the lady inspectors took the opposite view:

The frequent evasions and infringements of these [truck] acts ... encourage the shiftlessness and the poverty which are so deplorable, and form a real obstacle to the efforts of those public-spirited persons who are endeavouring to ameliorate the lot of the peasantry in those parts. Self-respect and proper independence are almost impossible in the circumstances and under the conditions produced by a wide-spread disregard of the right of the worker to the free control of her own earnings unhampered by any condition as to where and how they should be spent.[61]

In spite of a possible clash with the congested districts board, the inspectors, led by their principal, embarked in 1897 upon a sustained campaign to put a stop to truck practices in county Donegal.[62] To begin with, all went quite well. A determined effort in the southern part of the county led to *Deane* v. *Boyle*,[63] one of the first successful prosecutions in Ireland under the 1887

---

59 *Report of the departmental committee on the truck acts, 1908*, p. 11.
60 *Departmental committee on the truck acts, vol. ii: Minutes of evidence (days 1–37)*, p. 80 [Cd. 4443], H.C. 1908, lix, 230 (Squire). To make matters worse, 'heavy deductions' were often made for work damaged or spoiled: ibid., p. 81.
61 *Chief. insp. ann. rep., 1900*, p. 403 (Deane).
62 See especially Anderson, *Women in the factory*, chap. III; R. Squire, *Thirty years in the public service: An industrial retrospect* (London, 1927), chap. VI; Martindale, 'Truck and gombeening in Donegal'; M.D. McFeely, *Lady inspectors: The campaign for a better workplace, 1893–1921* (Oxford, 1988), chaps. 10 and 11, and D.S. Greer, '"Middling hard on coin":Truck in Donegal in the 1890s' (Irish Legal History Society, Dublin, 2000).
63 See *Chief insp. ann. rep., 1897*, pp. 90–96, 108–09 and 282n; *Departmental committee on the truck acts 1908*, ii, 103 (Deane); McFeely, *Lady inspectors*, pp. 78–82 and Greer, 'Truck in Donegal', pp. 13–16.

act.[64] In December 1897, a 'truckmaster' in Ardara was convicted on four charges of truck and fined £40 in the hope that 'the prosecution would act as a warning to similar offenders'.[65] Three further convictions, based on evidence obtained by inspectors Deane and Squire in west Donegal, followed at Dungloe petty sessions in November and December 1899,[66] and the inspectors received further encouragement in January 1900, when the queen's bench division in *Squire* v. *Sweeney (No. 1)*[67] gave a helpful ruling on their powers to enter premises in connection with truck enquiries.

But Deane and Squire then ran into a legal minefield, as 'every artifice which the Irishman's wit could devise was employed to prolong and complicate legal proceedings and to avoid conviction'.[68] A charge of truck against the 'chief offender', Mr John Sweeney, was dismissed on dubious grounds by a majority of the Dungloe magistrates and taken by way of case stated to the queen's bench division. In *Squire* v. *Sweeney (No. 2)*[69] it was shown that Mary McGeoghegan, who had taken from Sweeney wool which she had knitted into socks, received in exchange a ticket with the sum of 2*s*. 3*d*. marked on it. She then used this ticket to 'purchase' groceries from Sweeney's shop – an apparently clear case of payment otherwise than in current coin contrary to section 3 of the 1831 act. Sweeney, however, argued that the truck acts simply did not apply to this kind of case – and Palles CB for the queen's bench division agreed.

The principal problem was that Mrs McGeoghegan was not a 'workman' since she had not entered into 'a contract of service or a contract personally

64 The first case appears to have been *Snape* v. *Belfast Flax Spinning & Weaving Co.*, 26 Nov. 1897 – see *Chief insp. ann. rep., 1897*, p. 282 (and see above, n. 46).

65 Ibid., pp. 96 and 282n. The congested districts board made no reference to this case when it later claimed the credit for the reduction of truck in this area: *Ninth report of the Congested Districts Board for Ireland for the year ending 31 March 1900*, p. 40 [Cd. 239], H.C. 1900, lxviii, 223.

66 Patrick O'Donnell, a hosiery agent, was fined £5 for one offence (a second case was withdrawn when a witness failed to appear); Maurice Boyle, a shirt agent, was fined £5 for one offence (six other cases were withdrawn 'in deference to the magistrates') and Charles Kennedy, another hosiery agent, was fined £15 for two offences: *Chief insp. ann. rep., 1899*, p. 405. In July 1899, Andrew Jamison, a shirt, apron and blouse manufacturer of Belfast, was also fined £5 for two truck offences: ibid.

67 (1900) 6 Ir WLR 30, 34 ILTR 26. In order to ascertain whether the law was being complied with, the Factory and Workshop Act 1878, s. 68(4) gave an inspector power to enter '*the factory or workshop* [in question]' (emphasis added). A truck offence had allegedly been committed in one part of Sweeney's premises, but Squire was attempting to question him in another part of those premises when she was obstructed. Sweeney claimed that her power of entry was limited to the actual place where the offence had occurred, but Palles CB for the court held that there was nothing in section 68(4) to restrict its operation in this way.

68 Squire, *Thirty years*, p. 89.

69 Unreported, QBD, 27 June 1900, but see *Report of the departmental committee on the truck acts 1908*, p. 111, and *Minutes of evidence*, ii, 79 (Squire) and iii, 18 (Sweeney). According to Squire, the truck issue 'became almost lost sight of, [as the affair] developed gradually into a prolonged struggle for the vindication of law and order …': *Chief insp. ann. rep., 1899*, p. 248. For further details of this struggle, see especially Greer, 'Truck in Donegal', pp. 16–31.

to execute any work or labour' as required by section 10 of the Employers and Workmen Act 1875.[70] There was no contract of service, since the contract was not for a definite period of time. Nor had Mrs McGeoghegan contracted 'personally to execute the work', since she was not bound to knit the socks herself. According to the learned chief baron, 'By the contract as disclosed upon the evidence, she was not bound to perform the work of knitting personally or any part of it. Her contract ... would have been performed had she had the work done either in whole or in part by others or wholly by herself.' It made no difference that the work in question was in fact performed wholly by Mrs McGeoghegan.[71] Accordingly, the truck acts did not apply to her case.

In reaching this decision, Palles CB regarded himself as bound by previous decisions as to the ambit of section 10 of the 1875 act.[72] The limitations imposed by these earlier decisions had, indeed, been recognised in 1871, when it was recommended that outworkers should be brought within the truck acts by *excluding* 'contractors who engage to supply the result of other persons' labour on a large scale', but *including* cases where 'it is consistent with the contract that the person should give his personal labour, and ... he has in fact done so to a substantial extent ...'.[73] But for no apparent reason this distinction had not been made in the 1887 act, and the obvious explanation was that parliament intended to adopt the definition of 'workman' as then understood. This may be an unduly legalistic interpretation – but in 1905 it was 'upheld' by the king's bench division in England in *Squire* v. *Midland Lace Co.*[74]

The court in *Squire* v. *Sweeney (No. 2)* also held that 'manual labour' for the purposes of the 1875 act, once again as interpreted in earlier cases,[75] required work which 'tests the muscles and the sinews'. The knitting of socks

---

70 The definition had given rise to much litigation – see e.g. *Redgrave's Factory Acts*, ed. J. Owner (14th ed., London, 1931), pp. 359–61.
71 Squire was aware that there might be a problem in this regard, and had deliberately 'selected the case of a woman who herself did the work so that there might be no flaw': *Departmental committee on the truck acts 1908*, ii, 91.
72 *Sleeman* v. *Barrett* (1864) 2 H & C 934, 159 Eng Rep 386 (Exch) and *Ingram* v. *Barnes* (1857) 7 El & Bl 115, 119 Eng Rep 1190 (Exch Ch) – cases which might have been distinguished on the grounds that they were decided under the 1831 act and that the 1887 act provided a different statutory context.
73 *Report of the truck commissioners, 1871*, p. xlvii.
74 [1905] 2 KB 448, where the court (without referring to *Sweeney*) also held itself bound by *Ingram* v. *Barnes* to hold that a Nottingham lace clipper was not a 'workman' for the purposes of the truck acts. Kennedy J (at p. 455) dismissed the appeal 'with some reluctance', given that, by reason of the nature of their employment as 'wage-earning manual labourers, and not "contractors" in the ordinary and popular sense', the clippers belonged to a class of workers 'practically indistinguishable' from those already within the protection of the truck acts.
75 *Yarmouth* v. *France* (1887) 19 QBD 647, 651, *per* Lord Esher MR, followed in *R (Hollywood)* v. *Louth JJ* [1900] 2 IR 714, 716, where Palles CB had held that 'the ordinary occupation of a hairdresser, although manual work, does not require such expenditure of physical energy as is necessary to render it manual "labour" within the meaning of the section.'

might be manual *work*; but it 'does not require that amount of physical energy to bring it within the words "manual labour" as [so] ... construed'. There was to be no subsequent support for such a narrow construction of this part of the act.[76]

The decision in *Squire* v. *Sweeney (No. 2)* not only cost several witnesses their livelihood,[77] but effectively put outworkers in county Donegal – and the rest of Ireland – outside the protection of the truck acts.[78] Squire nevertheless hoped that 'the truck system had ... received a serious check from the publicity given to [the case], and workers, emboldened to ask for money payment, [now] obtained it'.[79] The principal lady inspector was less sanguine: the effect of the decision could be overcome by outworkers strong enough to insist on cash, or even on contractual terms which made them 'workmen', but 'the peasant women in congested districts of Ireland are not in the position to impose their will upon any would-be employer'.[80] And so it proved to be. In 1908, it was reported that, although conditions in Donegal had improved in some respects, 'no real change' had taken place:

The prices charged for the tea and other articles may be less exorbitant, but the evil still exists.... [T]he Truck Acts may be nominally observed by handing actual coin to the worker. But, as a general rule, no work is to be obtained, at any rate not the best work, unless the wages are left at the shop; or else the workers are allowed, or even induced, to get heavily into debt, to be wiped off subsequently by out-work.... [T]hough ... the workers [complain] as to the difficulty of obtaining coin, it seems to be almost instinctive with them that it would be an ungenerous act to take their wages from the shop.[81]

---

76 Cf. 'Knitting was included in the trades to which the Act of 1831 applied; it is one of the industries included in section 10 of the Act of 1887; and the decision is inconsistent with decisions of the English courts as to the meaning of the same phrase in the Factory Acts (compare *Hoare* v. *Robert Green Ltd* [1907] 2 KB 315)': *Report of the departmental committee on the truck acts, 1908*, p. 19. However, the court in *Hoare* expressly stated that the meaning of 'manual labour' for the purposes of the factory acts was not necessarily the same as in the different context of the 1875 act, and section 10 of the 1887 act was (presumably deliberately) limited to cases where homework was bought by a shopkeeper in the way of trade.

77 See *Chief insp. ann. rep., 1899*, pp. 250 (Deane) and 277 (Squire).

78 For example, conditions 'very similar' to those in Co. Donegal existed amongst the linen outworkers in Co. Down, except that 'the houses were perhaps not so poor ...': *Chief insp. ann. rep., 1903*, pt. I, pp. 233–34 (Squire). But some protection was given to outworkers when the 'particulars' clause was extended in 1903 to those engaged in making-up wearing apparel – see below, pp. 209–10.

79 *Thirty years*, p. 97. She explained that 'the High Court decision ... did not seem to have impressed them so much as the convictions actually in their own neighbourhood': *Departmental committee on the truck acts 1908*, ii, 95.

80 *Chief insp. ann. rep., 1900*, p. 359 (Anderson).

81 *Report of the departmental committee on the truck acts 1908*, p. 11, a conclusion based on Martindale's report on 'Truck and gombeening in Donegal'. Further inquiries in 1911 led Martindale to conclude that the position was still 'much the same' – see *Committee of inquiry into the linen and other making-up trades, 1912: Minutes of evidence*, p. 60.

Similar practices still occurred in other parts of Ireland also,[82] and even in cases which did come within the truck acts, the inspectors found it extremely difficult to secure convictions. In one notorious case, a truck prosecution in the west of Ireland was dismissed when the witnesses 'went back entirely' on their written statements – only for Martindale to be told 'on good authority' that 'Mr X had paid wages in goods from "time immemorial" and that everyone in the court knew it'. She was clearly dejected: 'With such an object lesson it is impossible not to feel somewhat hopeless about ever being able to lessen this truck evil in Ireland, although, undoubtedly, a prosecution of this kind does quicken public opinion.'[83]

The amendment of the truck acts to include outworkers was again recommended in 1908 as 'the first step to the introduction of a better system [of payment]'; it might not 'immediately or entirely remedy the conditions prevailing in these remote districts' and might even be 'for a short period distasteful both to employers and employed', but it would in time prove 'a substantial gain'.[84] This modest recommendation, following upon the widespread dissatisfaction produced by *Sweeney* and *Midland Lace*, nevertheless proved insufficient to galvanise the government into action[85] – primarily because these problems 'prevail most largely in remote parts of the United Kingdom where little publicity attends them and where the workers have no trades unions or organisation to voice their grievances or promote any attempt at legislative remedy'.[86] Attempts to persuade the principal manufacturers to appoint full-time salaried agents, who would be less likely to resort to truck practices, also met with little success.[87] Fortunately, other developments, such as the growth of cooperatives and agricultural credit societies and the efforts of the congested districts board, were by now helping to improve the lot of the rural outworkers.[88]

---

82   In 1912, for example, Co. Down was described as 'a notorious centre' for truck: *Committee of inquiry into the linen and other making-up trades, 1912: Minutes of evidence*, p. 15 (McCaghey).
83   *Chief insp. ann. rep., 1908*, p. 159. In *From one generation to another*, pp. 135–37, Martindale explains how a sympathetic priest and a gold sovereign enabled her to influence public opinion by securing a full and detailed report of the case in a local newspaper.
84   *Report of the departmental committee on the truck acts 1908*, p. 13.
85   The issue was raised on a number of occasions, and as late as July 1914, the home secretary was declaring that he hoped to introduce a bill 'very shortly' – see *Hansard 5 (commons)*, lxiv, 2106–07 (16 July 1914). But nothing had even been done by the time Squire published her memoirs in 1927: *Thirty years*, p. 98.
86   *Report of the departmental committee on the truck acts, 1908*, pp. 10–11.
87   The *Report of the committee of inquiry into the linen and other making-up trades, 1912*, p. xviii called for 'concerted action' by the firms to employ 'agents paid by salary, exclusively employed as such, and directly responsible to the firms'. Although a number of such agents were appointed, there was no 'concerted' response – see *Chief insp. ann. rep., 1913*, p. 106 (Slocock).
88   See Martindale, 'Truck and gombeening in Donegal', p. 252 and *From one generation to another*, pp. 134–38. See also P. Bolger, *The Irish cooperative movement: its history and development* (Dublin, 1977), chaps. 12 and 13.

THE 'PARTICULARS' CLAUSE

The practice of linking wages more closely to output by adopting a system of 'piece-work' payments gave rise to public concern when it became clear that some employers were deliberately failing to make clear to workers how various 'pieces' were measured, thus making it difficult, if not impossible, for the workers to determine if they were being underpaid – and, incidentally, once again enabling 'bad' employers to undercut 'good' ones.[89] Pressure for legislative intervention seems to have come mainly from Lancashire, where the wages payable to cotton weavers were dependent on the width of the loom, the width of the cloth, the numbers of ends per inch, the number of picks per quarter inch, the thickness of the warp and a number of other 'particulars'. But legislation was opposed by a number of employers on the dubious ground that a written statement of piece-work rates would reveal commercial information likely to be of assistance to their (foreign) competitors.[90]

Parliament finally obliged by enacting the 'particulars clause' – section 24 of the Factory and Workshop Act 1891 – which required a worker 'paid by the piece' to be supplied with 'sufficient particulars to enable him to ascertain the rate of wages at which he is entitled to be paid for the work', coupled with a provision designed to meet employers' concerns about the disclosure of sensitive information.[91] This provision initially applied only to cotton, woollen, linen and jute weavers and to cotton winders and reelers; but in 1895 it was extended to all piece-rate textile factory workers.[92] The 1895 act also gave the home secretary power to apply the particulars clause, 'subject to such modifications as may in his opinion be necessary', to any appropriate class of non-textile factories or of workshops,[93] a power which was almost immediately exercised in the case of textile workshops[94] and

---

89 See especially *Hansard 4*, cl, 1377 (2 Aug. 1905)(D.J. Shackleton, MP for Clitheroe, Lancs.).

90 E.J. Holmes, 'Piecework particulars', in 'Review of the work of the inspectorate, 1833 to 1932', in *Chief insp. ann. rep., 1932*, pp. 68–70.

91 It was made an offence for a worker to disclose, or for any person to solicit or procure a worker to disclose, such particulars 'with a fraudulent object or for the purpose of gain'. This appears to have been nothing more than a sop to the employers, whose contention was a 'myth', since 'any of their competitors, by examining a few inches of the cloth (which is always obtainable in the market), can not only tell how it is made, but also the yarns used and the number of threads ...': *Chief insp. ann. rep., 1893*, p. 222 and *1897*, p. 86 (Birtwhistle).

92 Factory and Workshop Act 1895, s. 40(1). The worker concerned was to be given the particulars of the rate of wages applicable to the work to be done by him or her in writing when the work was given out; such particulars were also to be 'exhibited on a placard ... posted in a position where it is easily legible'. It remained an offence for the worker to disclose such particulars 'for the purpose of divulging a trade secret'.

93 1895 act, s. 40(6).

94 Textile Workshops (Particulars) Order 1898 – see *Chief insp. ann. rep., 1898*, pt. II, p. 100 (replacing an earlier Order made in 1897 which applied to factories and workshops making handkerchiefs, aprons, pinafores and blouses). In 1900, there were only 41 textile workshops in Ireland which paid their workers on a piecework basis

which over the next twenty years or so led to the addition of a large number of non-textile trades and processes.[95]

It quickly became obvious that effective enforcement of the particulars clause required expert technical knowledge of the textile trades, and in June 1892 Thomas Birtwhistle, secretary of the North-Eastern Lancashire Weavers' Association, was appointed Examiner [later Inspector] of Textile Particulars 'to superintend the bringing into operation' of the clause throughout the United Kingdom.[96] This specialised department was gradually increased to a total of five inspectors;[97] but its duties were limited to the textile trade, principally in Lancashire and Yorkshire. The enforcement of the clause in non-textile trades remained the responsibility of the 'ordinary' inspectors – both male and female.

By this time, most of the linen and other textile factories in Ireland paid their workers wholly or partly on a piece-work basis,[98] with the result that the particulars clause had a major impact in this country. As in many other matters, however, it is difficult to gauge the extent of compliance with the new law.[99] During the period 1892–1905, for example, there were on average only 30 convictions per year throughout the kingdom as a whole, and the conviction rate with regard to textile factories thereafter declined.[100] Few of these convictions were obtained in Ireland.[101] It appears, nonetheless, that the particulars required by law were not always given to factory workers in Ireland. In 1905, for example, Martindale reported:

It is not the usual custom in these factories to exhibit particulars of the rate of wages on a placard.... Hence, the workers have to depend on being furnished with a written

---

    – as compared to 279 textile factories: *Chief insp. ann. rep., 1900*, pp. 406–07; by 1911, these numbers had increased to 73 and 303 respectively: *Chief insp. ann. rep., 1911*, p. 168.

95 By 1907, the particulars clause covered 'all but one of the really large industries in which women and girls are employed': *Chief insp. ann. rep., 1907*, p. 192 (Anderson). The one exception was the laundry trade.

96 *Chief insp. ann. rep., 1892*, pp. 80–81. This was an astute move, given that many of the weavers worked in Lancashire, and most of their employers 'were personally well known to me previously': ibid.

97 See e.g *Chief insp. ann. rep., 1902*, pt. II, p. 5.

98 In 1897, it was reported that 96 per cent of Irish textile factories paid their workers wholly or partly by piece; the equivalent figure for Great Britain was 91 per cent: *Chief insp. ann. rep., 1897*, pp. 86–87.

99 Although Irish employers 'showed remarkable readiness to comply with the provisions of the clause, immediately their attention was drawn thereto' and the particulars which they supplied to their weavers 'seem ... substantially correct', in Irish factories *not* previously inspected, 'the particulars supplied were invariably insufficient': *Chief insp. ann. rep., 1893*, p. 222 and *1895*, p. 135 (Birtwhistle).

100 Figures extrapolated from tables in chief inspector's annual reports. The average fine, in the region of 12–13s., was regarded as too low: 'Unless employers looked upon appearance in a police court as a source of degradation, such penalties would never act as a deterrent': *Hansard 4*, cl, 1377 (2 Aug. 1905) (Shackleton).

101 No more than fourteen convictions in Ireland have been traced for the period 1900–1913.

or printed statement of such particulars when the work is given out. In many cases it was found that these particulars were not given until the work was returned, when the necessary entries were made in the worker's book; in this way the whole object of the provisions was frustrated.[102]

Problems also arose when particulars *were* given out in advance:

The custom in many of the Irish factories is to attach written particulars to the work; the work with these particulars goes round from worker to worker; each doing her small part of it, but in no case retaining the particulars.... The workers received work many times a day and the prices they receive vary considerably and as they are often paid only once a fortnight they complain that, as they have no particulars to retain, they are unable to compute the amount of their earnings.[103]

Particular problems once again arose in the case of outworkers. Although the 1895 act had attempted to curtail the practice of giving out factory work to be finished at home,[104] it did not require the requisite particulars to be given when such work was lawfully undertaken. In 1901, however, when the particulars clause was re-enacted in section 116 of the Factory and Workshops Act of that year, the home secretary was given power to extend its application to outworkers. This new power was exercised in 1903 to require piece-work particulars to be given to outworkers employed in the making, altering, ornamenting or finishing of wearing apparel (including handkerchiefs).[105] This order, together with the statutory restrictions on homework by factory workers, should have put at end to difficulties in urban areas.[106] But the problem remained sufficiently serious for Inspector Williams to issue a circular to all employers in 1907, pointing out that the inspectors had noted instances of workers being employed 'late at night (far beyond the period of employment of the factory) on work which they had brought home from the factory' and hoping that all employers would take 'effective steps' to see that

102 *Chief insp. ann. rep., 1905*, p. 323.
103 *Chief insp. ann. rep., 1907*, p. 193. In some cases, however, a metal token was given to the worker and in others she could see the details of the work which she had done being entered in a ledger.
104 1895 act, s. 16. For an unsuccessful attempt by shirt and collar manufacturers in the north of Ireland to secure exemption from this provision on the grounds of 'the customs or exigencies of the trade', as allowed by s. 16(6), see PRO HO 45/9900/B19144 (March 1896).
105 Wearing Apparel (Particulars) Order 1903, reproduced in *Chief insp. ann. rep., 1903*, pt. I, p. 328. An 'outworker' was defined as 'any person employed in the business of a factory or workshop outside the factory or workshop, whether directly by the occupier thereof or by any contractor employed by him, and also any person employed by the occupier of any place from which work is given out, or by a contractor employed by him ...'. This Order was later repealed and replaced by a similar Order of 14 September 1909 – see below, p. 211.
106 'Whether in Belfast, Dublin, Bristol, Nottingham ... or other cities, I have found that the difficulties anticipated by occupiers [concerning the Wearing Apparel Order] have not arisen, and that the giving of the particulars is easily arranged and is most certainly appreciated by the workers': *Chief insp. ann. rep., 1904*, pt. I, p. 279 (Squire).

the law was obeyed. Williams went on to say that the provisions of the 'wearing apparel' order were not complied with in many instances; in some cases written particulars were not provided at all, and in others the particulars were given 'in such a form as to be unintelligible, except to an experienced worker'. He called for an end to such irregularities.[107] Many employers apparently took notice of the circular, and by 1912, although there were still some 'instances of neglect', factory workers in the making-up trades were thought to be 'generally' supplied with the particulars required by law.[108] But McCaghey was not so sure: although he had found few irregularities, 'inspection ... is necessarily by sample [and] time will not permit of more than one or two workers' books [containing particulars] being examined in one factory, or of more than one or two workers being questioned, and very often it happens that the books, picked up at random, are in order and that factory would for that occasion be regarded as regular in this respect.' Accordingly, the particulars clause might be 'much more seriously disregarded' than was generally thought. On the other hand, the Irish factory worker was now sufficiently aware of piece-work rates so as not to be, as a result of any failure to obtain particulars, 'at any greater disadvantage than the English worker'.[109]

As with truck, the principal problem lay with rural outworkers. The earlier investigations had revealed that outworkers in counties Donegal and Down, for example, frequently did not even know the price which the manufacturers were prepared to pay for the work given out on their behalf by shopkeeper-agents.[110] Even if these agents passed on the information, outworkers 'are often obliged to send for their work and cannot personally fetch it, and they should not, therefore, have to depend on word of mouth, to know the prices they are to receive'.[111] In this respect, the 'wearing apparel' order of 1903 was a partial – and apparently successful – legislative response to the decision in *Squire* v. *Sweeney (No. 2)*.[112] But when Martindale investigated under-clothing outworkers in the north of Ireland in 1907, she found that in many cases they still had no written particulars or other information of the price to

---

107 *Committee of inquiry into the linen and other making-up trades, 1912: Minutes of evidence*, pp. 37–38, where the terms of the circular are set out in full. According to McCaghey, the circular led to a prosecution which resulted in conviction – and a fine of five shillings!: *Chief insp. ann. rep., 1907*, pp. 132–34.

108 *Report of the committee of inquiry into the linen and other making-up trades, 1912*, p. xvii. See to the same effect *Chief insp. ann. rep., 1911*, p. 124 (Eraut) and *1913*, p. 103 (Anderson).

109 *Committee of inquiry into the linen and other making-up trades, 1912: Minutes of evidence*, pp. 13–14.

110 See e.g. *Departmental committee on the truck acts 1908*, ii, 81 and 82, where Squire stated that during the 1890s outworkers in Donegal were not given particulars as to prices – a practice which was not then unlawful.

111 *Chief insp. ann. rep., 1906*, p. 238 (Martindale), adding that 'mistakes may arise which cannot be so easily rectified by workers living long distances from their employers, and everything should be done by written statements to minimise this risk'.

112 In 1908, Martindale (somewhat inconsistently) reported that outworkers *had* 'usually' received verbal particulars: 'Truck and gombeening in Donegal', p. 248.

be paid 'although these wages were the principal means of support of the family'.[113] Part of the problem was the limited scope of the order: 'the majority of the agents give out both handkerchiefs and household and fancy linens, and whereas they are obliged to give particulars when giving out handkerchiefs to be embroidered or stitched, they are not required by law to do so when handing a worker a doyley or tray cloth which requires the same work as the handkerchief'.[114] A revised 'wearing apparel' order issued by the home secretary in 1909[115] failed to end this confusion, and the matter was only dealt with effectively when the particulars clause was further extended in 1911 to include factories, workshops and outworkers employed in the making-up, ornamenting, finishing or repairing of household linen and any processes incidental thereto.[116]

But, as in the case of truck violations, the principal problem was the attitude of the shopkeeper-agents who gave out the work. In 1909, for example, both Eraut and McCaghey reported that the agents frequently did not pass on the particulars of the price to be paid for work, giving rise to a widespread suspicion that they did not pay the prices set by the firms.[117] As McCaghey was later to explain: 'This irregularity in the case of an outworker is much more serious than it is likely to be in a factory. In the latter, labour is more or less in the mass, and therefore more ready to make grievances of this kind articulate. The outworker, on the other hand, is isolated ... and, without an observance of the terms of the Particulars Order, is at the mercy of an agent.'[118] By 1912, it was still 'not uncommon' for full particulars *not* to be given to outworkers, and it was the agents who were especially lax in this regard.[119] The obvious solution was for the employers to stamp the necessary details on the goods before they were sent out – a course 'already adopted by many firms', but clearly not by all.[120]

---

113 *Chief insp. ann. rep., 1907,* p. 193. She cautioned a number of firms, and was later obliged to prosecute two of them. McCaghey also reported that many isolated country outworkers had complained that 'they did not know the rate of pay for the work in hand': ibid., p. 132.

114 *Chief insp. ann. rep., 1908,* pp. 157–58 (Martindale) and Martindale, *From one generation to another,* p. 125.

115 Reproduced in *Redgrave's Factory Acts,* ed. J. Owner (14th ed., London, 1931), pp. 164–65.

116 See ibid., pp. 170–71.

117 *Chief insp. ann. rep., 1909,* p. 118.

118 *Committee of inquiry into the linen and other making-up trades, 1912: Minutes of evidence,* p.14.

119 *Report of the committee of inquiry into the linen and other making-up trades, 1912,* p. xvii. 'The manufacturer or merchant supplies the agent with an invoice, showing the price to be paid for each grade ..., but the [agent], either through ignorance or other causes, seldom furnishes written particulars ... with the small quantity of goods handed to each worker': ibid., *Minutes of evidence,* p. 15 (McCaghey). Martindale agreed: ibid., pp. 58–60.

120 *Report of the committee of inquiry into the linen and other making–up trades, 1912,* p. xviii. Cf. the practice of stamping the price and any necessary instructions onto embroidery work 'has been largely extended recently', a development which had

FINES AND DEDUCTIONS

In a number of industries,[121] employers traditionally supplied workers with materials, tools or other facilities for the purpose of doing their work, and charged for such facilities by making deductions from wages. Some employers also made deductions from wages for spoilt or damaged work or materials and imposed 'fines' for breaches of factory discipline such as coming late to work, using bad language, behaving inappropriately, etc. Such penalties were primarily designed to foster good working habits rather than subsidise labour costs;[122] but their effect was to reduce the payment received by a worker, often to a significant extent.[123] The Truck Act 1831 had expressly provided for limited exceptions, by way of stoppages or deductions, to the general principle that wages were to be paid in the current coin of the realm;[124] but the courts were soon to hold that certain charges for workframes and other materials traditionally supplied to workers in the hosiery trade did not contravene the act.[125] The charging of excessive frame rents led to these particular decisions being reversed in 1874, when the Hosiery Manufacture (Wages) Act provided that no deduction or stoppage 'of any description whatever' shall be lawful, 'except for bad and disputed workmanship'.[126] But in 1889 the legality of fines and deductions in other industries was confirmed in *Redgrave v. Kelly*,[127] on the grounds that the 1831 act was directed against the payment of wages by way of goods, not the use of fines or deductions to determine the amount of those wages. Faced with increasing evidence of

simplified 'enormously' the administration of the particulars clause: *Chief insp. ann. rep., 1913*, p. 103 (Slocock).

121   'The most important examples occurred in poorly paid, weakly organised trades, and especially in trades largely practised by women': Hilton, *Truck system*, p. 147.

122   The fines and deductions might be repaid to good workers by way of a bonus, or donated to charitable or other public purposes – see e.g. *Chief insp. ann. rep., 1907*, p. 133 (McCaghey); Hunt, *Portlaw, County Waterford 1825–1876*, p. 56. But some employers simply put the money in their own pockets.

123   Some fines and deductions were so substantial that they had to be paid by instalments over several weeks.

124   1831 act, ss. 1, 23 and 24.

125   *Chawner v. Cummings* (1846) 8 QB 311, 115 Eng Rep 893; *Archer v. James* (1859) 2 B & S 61, 121 Eng Rep 996, on the basis that the frames, etc. were supplied not as a *reward* for labour but as a *means* of labour; the worker's 'wage', therefore, was the *net* amount payable to him or her, all of which was paid in coin.

126   Section 1. In an attempt to preempt another *Archer*, s. 7 provided that 'any money … contracted to be paid … for any labour … shall be deemed … to be the wages of such labour'.

127   (1889) 5 TLR 477. This legalistic approach was queried in *Hewlett v. Allen & Sons* [1892] 2 QB 662 – and ultimately rejected when the House of Lords in *Williams v. North's Navigation Collieries (1889) Ltd* [1906] AC 136 held that an employer could lawfully make only those deductions expressly sanctioned by the 1831 Act. As Goff LJ was later to point out, 'it is a matter of some speculation whether, if *Williams'* case had been decided before 1896, Parliament would have thought it necessary to enact section 1, or indeed section 2, of the 1896 Act': *Bristow v. City Petroleum Ltd.* [1985] 3 All ER 463, 470.

excessive fines and unfair deductions in various industries,[128] however, the government was in 1896 persuaded to take further action. On this occasion, regulation was preferred to prohibition[129] – a strategy which does not appear to have given rise to any significant controversy in parliament,[130] since the Truck Act 1896 was passed with a minimum of debate.

By section 1, no worker was to be fined unless (i) he had previously been given full particulars of all 'offences', and the fines payable in respect of them, either by way of a written notice prominently and constantly displayed at the workplace or by a contract in writing signed by him or her; (ii) the fine was in respect of an act or omission causing or likely to cause damage or loss to the employer or interruption or hindrance to his business; (iii) the amount of the fine was fair and reasonable having regard to all the circumstances of the case, and (iv) when a fine was imposed, written particulars of the fine and the reasons for it were supplied to the worker. By sections 2 and 3, similar but less stringent conditions attached to the making of deductions, from 'the sum contracted to be paid by the employer',[131] in respect of 'bad' or 'negligent' work, or damage to the employer's property or materials, or for tools or other facilities supplied by the employer;[132] once again, any deduction had to be fair and reasonable, having regard to all the circumstances, but with the added requirement that it must not exceed 'the actual or estimated damage or loss occasioned to the employer ...'. An employer was obliged, on demand in writing, to provide a factory inspector with a copy of the prescribed notice or contract setting out the relevant details.[133]

---

128 'The [Royal Commission on] Labour ... have drawn attention to various deductions on payment of wages, but the decisions of the higher courts are so embarrassing to magistrates that Her Majesty's inspectors are often uncertain as to the proper course to adopt': *Chief insp. ann. rep., 1893*, p. 327. Details of deductions made in some factories are to be found in *Chief insp. ann. rep., 1895*, pp. 120–21.

129 Cf. the Trades Union Congress had, as early as 1872, advocated the complete abolition of *all* fines and deductions from wages – see Hilton, *Truck system*, p. 147. In 1896, its Irish counterpart adopted the same stance – see *Report of the third Irish Trades Congress* (Limerick, 1896), p. 41.

130 The opposition came mainly from Lancashire weavers ostensibly concerned that 'the attention of employers would be called by a new Act to powers which in many trades were unused and scarcely known to exist': H.A. Mess, *Factory legislation and its administration 1891–1924* (London, 1926), p. 28. Cotton weavers in Lancashire, Cheshire and Yorkshire were in fact granted exemption from the Act, but not the shirt and collar industry in Londonderry – see *Chief insp. ann. rep., 1897*, pp. 73 and 90 (Deane).

131 See above, n. 126.

132 'The contract does not have to specify any act or omission. It merely has to provide for the right to make a deduction for bad or negligent work or injury to the materials. ... The nature of the bad or negligent work does not have to be identified ... [and] no scale of deduction has to be specified ...': *Bristow v. City Petroleum Ltd* [1987] 2 All ER 45, 52, *per* Lord Ackner. But all relevant particulars had to be given to the worker when a deduction was made – see ss. 2(2) and 3(2).

133 Section 6(1). Section 6(3) also required an employer to maintain a register of fines (but not deductions) 'at all times open to inspection' by a factory inspector.

The inspectors were initially optimistic: 'armed with powers under the new act, [they] have been able to put a stop to many unreasonable fines, the arbitrary character of which became apparent under the compulsory publicity which the act demands'.[134] But it was not long before they began to run into difficulties, at least in Ireland:

[A]lthough the provisions of the Truck Act, 1896, are now understood and carried out a little better than formerly, a great deal of the willingness on the part of the employers to comply with it is due to the minimum penalty being £5[135].... [W]ith the exception of a few cases, the contract notice would not be exhibited until an inspector had visited the establishment and explained the requirements of the acts. Many of the employers look upon the supplying of the 'particulars in writing' as a great deal of unnecessary work. Until I insisted upon further particulars being supplied, it was the general custom to simply mark in the workers' wages books the amount of their wages, without any statement showing the acts or omissions in respect of which the deductions or payments were made. When I have called attention to the particulars not being sufficiently explicit, I have invariably received the reply that 'the workers know what it means'. It has only been by insisting that the provisions of the Truck Acts be further complied with, and pointing out what the minimum penalty was ... that has made many of the employers carry out my instructions.[136]

Various problems arose from the vagueness of the requirement that any fine or deduction must be 'fair and reasonable'.[137] In particular, the courts were reluctant to have regard to the amount of the worker's wages,[138] and in the case of deductions, the inspectors often found it 'very difficult' to determine the loss to the employer.[139] The legislation also applied more readily to cases where high individual fines were imposed than to those involving a series of smaller fines; in the case of the latter, 'it is difficult to select one as being unfair and unreasonable, it is rather the whole system that is radically wrong'.[140] And in 1901 the decision in *Squire v. Bayer & Co.*,[141] that an

---

134   *Chief insp. ann. rep., 1897*, p. 73 (Chief inspector Whitelegge). Some employers even stopped imposing fines to avoid the bother of complying with the requirements of the act.

135   See above, n. 46.

136   *Chief insp. ann. rep., 1898*, pt. II, pp. 75–76 (Kellett). As Hilton, *Truck system*, p.148 notes, several unsuccessful attempts were made during the period 1896–1900 to make all fines and deductions unlawful – see e.g. the private member's bill introduced in 1900: H.C. 1900 (116), v, 523.

137   'There is nothing in the Act itself to guide a court of law in coming to a conclusion in regard to this point, and different magistrates have often taken quite different views of what is fair and reasonable': *Report of the departmental committee on the truck acts, 1908*, p. 20.

138   'The real difficulty ... is ... getting the magistrates always to see that fines may be oppressive and deductions unfair having regard to the low wages of operatives': *Departmental committee on the truck acts 1908*, ii, 6 (Sir Henry Cunynghame, legal ass't under-sec., home office). For a particular example arising from damask weaving, see *Chief insp. ann. rep., 1907*, p. 133 (McCaghey).

139   *Departmental committee on the truck acts 1908*, ii, 23 (Whitelegge).

140   *Chief insp. ann. rep., 1913*, p. 155 (Slocock).

141   [1901] 2 KB 299. Some girls were fined for dancing during their dinner-hour, the

employer was entitled to fine a worker for breach of a rule requiring workers simply to observe 'good order and decorum', opened the door to abuse 'for under such a general rule all kinds of petty offences against discipline may be made the subject of a fine'.[142] Accordingly, it is hardly surprising that many of the prosecutions under the 1896 act were unsuccessful.[143]

Table 7.1: *Prosecutions for excessive fines and deductions in the United Kingdom*[144]

	No. of prosecutions	No. of convictions	Average fine
1896–1905			
– fines	59	44	16s. 6d.
– deductions	235	178	19s. 4d.
– other	25	21	18s. 0d.
1906–1913			
– fines	61	35	£1 9s. 0d.
– deductions	182	155	£1 0s. 1d.

Although few of these prosecutions were brought in Ireland,[145] fines and deductions were common throughout the island,[146] and were in particular

magistrates having found that dust created by the dancing might have caused damage to machinery and materials. The court upheld the fine; although the contract did not specify particular acts or omissions, the reference to the need for 'good order and decorum' was a sufficient compliance with the requirements of the act.

142 *Report of the departmental committee on the truck acts 1908*, p. 19. Indeed, the prosecution backfired in the sense that it operated to 'advertise' this form of contract: ibid., ii, 65 (Anderson).

143 'The number of cases we lost is ... much larger than the proportion under the Factory Acts, but that ... is only natural, because the Truck Act ... deals largely with matters of opinion as to whether a given charge [comes] ... under a more or less vague definition included in the notice, whether it is reasonable in the circumstances of the case, and what circumstances should be taken into account': *Departmental committee on the truck acts 1908*, ii, 19 (Whitelegge).

144 The figures for 1897–1905 are derived from the table by Whitelegge in *Departmental committee on the truck acts 1908*, iv, 134–35; those for 1906–1913 are from the tables of prosecutions in the chief inspector's annual reports.

145 Between 1895 and 1914 there were on average only two convictions per annum in Ireland for *all* 'truck' offences – that is, for payment of wages in goods as well as for excessive fines and deductions; all but seven of the 42 convictions occurred in Ulster.

146 See e.g. the case where an old woman, employed as a sweeper in Dublin at 6s. per week, was fined one shilling for being late: 'The magistrate agreed ... that the wages were to be regarded as a charitable dole to which the firm attached the condition of punctuality, and as this had not been fulfilled ... they were entitled to make this fine, and it was, in the circumstances, not unfair or unreasonable': *Departmental committee on the truck acts 1908*, ii, 94 (Squire).

extensively imposed in the linen industry.[147] Two of the problems which the
inspectors regularly encountered were (i) the 'bonus' system, and (ii) unfair
deductions for spoiled or damaged work.

The 'bonus' system

In many Irish textile factories, a 'bonus' for consistent punctuality and/or
good work was paid at the end of the working week, even to children working
half-time.[148] The amount of the bonus varied from sixpence to two shillings
per week, but 'in the majority of cases the bonus is 1*s*.'. There was little
correlation between the amount of the bonus and the rate of pay – a bonus
of one shilling was as often paid to a person earning 6*s*. a week as to a person
earning 9*s*. In some cases, a worker could earn a double bonus – carders in one
particular spinning mill, for example, were paid a weekly bonus of one shilling
and a further bonus of 10*s*. to 12*s*. 6*d*. per quarter for 'careful' work.[149]

This system had originally been introduced to deal with a shortage of
women workers – the bonus being designed to induce them to remain in
their employment. It had then been retained as a means of dealing with poor
time-keeping, when employers found that 'it was a difficult matter to ensure
the workers came regularly'; the factory machinery had to be kept running:
'spinning frames and weaving looms should not stand idle'. Martindale
found this explanation 'curious', given that in Ireland 'there has always been
rather a dearth of employment than of employees'.[150] But her primary
concern was that the bonus system often operated unfairly:

In some mills [tardy] workers are allowed entrance to the mill five or ten minutes
after the time of beginning work, and at the end of meal-hours, by paying a fine of 1*d*.
or 2*d*. After that hour they are shut out from the factory until the next meal-hour and
lose, in addition to the wages for the amount of time lost, their bonus. In other mills,
and these are in the majority, the workers who are not punctually at the mill at the
exact commencement of the period of employment and after meal-hours, are closed
out until the next meal-time, and again lose the wages for the amount of time which

---

147 See e.g. *Chief insp. ann. rep., 1904*, pt. I, p. 201 (female cutter fined £3. 15*s*. for
     spoiling work and paying fine by instalments of 2*s*. per week; employer convicted of
     failing to stipulate details in contract notice and fined £5); *1905*, p. 209 (eight cases
     investigated by Snape resulted in refund by employers); *1908*, p. 117 ('many
     instances of apparently unreasonable deductions for material supplied'; fines and
     deductions imposed in linen industry 'with a want of uniformity which makes one
     sceptical of the whole system').
148 *Chief insp. ann. rep., 1901*, pt. I, pp. 147–48 (Snape) and *1906*, p. 240 (Martindale).
149   In some weaving factories, a weaver might receive a 'time bonus on a cut' of 1*d*. per
     hour saved by completing the work in less time than normal, or a 'time bonus on a
     beam' for saving time on each cut; alternatively, the bonus might be linked to the
     amount of wages earned; on every 5*s*. earned, for example, a bonus of 6*d*. might be
     paid, on 6*s*. earned, the bonus was 7*d*., and so on: *Chief insp. ann. rep., 1906*, pp.
     240–43 (Martindale).
150 Ibid., p. 243. See also *Departmental committee on the truck acts 1908*, ii, 85–86 (Squire)
     and 107 (Deane).

they have been forced to lose, and in addition, the entire bonus, or half of it for the first offence and the whole of it for two offences.[151]

In other words, the loss of the bonus was in reality an additional 'fine' for poor time-keeping which was often excessive, and in such cases the bonus system appeared to circumvent the restrictions on fines imposed by the 1896 act.

A suitable test case was provided by Abraham Wilson & Co., the occupiers of a spinning factory in Newry. In *Deane* v. *Wilson*,[152] it was established that if Theresa Dixon worked a full week of 55½ hours, she qualified for a bonus of 2*s.*, which brought her total 'wages' for the week to 10*s*. One day in February 1906, however, she was more than three hours late for work, and as a result lost not only 4*d.* (one quarter of the daily wage of 1*s*. 4*d.*), but also the whole of her weekly bonus. The employers were fully entitled to deduct the sum of 4*d.*; but Deane contended that the bonus constituted part of 'the sum contracted to be paid' to Dixon and that the failure to pay it therefore constituted a fine contrary to section 1 of the 1896 act.

Both the magistrates' court and the king's bench division[153] disagreed. Andrews J stated:

I am unable to hold that the non-payment of the 2*s.*, which was not earned, and never became due, was a *deduction* from the *sum contracted to be paid* to the worker. There was no contract to pay it unless it was earned.... Further, even if this non-payment of the 2*s.* ... could be possibly held to be a deduction from the sum contracted to be paid to her, it could not, in my opinion, be held to be a deduction for, or in respect of, a *fine*. The non-payment took nothing from her to which, in any view, she had become entitled, or to which, when the week ended, she could have ever become entitled. It was simply withholding payment of what she had not earned, and never could earn.[154]

There was nothing unfair or unreasonable in a contract which gave a workman, at the end of the week, an additional sum in consideration for his uninterrupted work. On the contrary, 'such a contract is beneficial to both the employer and the employed. Under it the worker gets an additional payment to which he would not otherwise be entitled, and the employer gets, what may be very important for him, uninterrupted work.'[155] Kenny J emphasised this latter point:

---

151 *Chief insp. ann. rep., 1906*, pp. 241–42.
152 [1906] 2 IR 405. See also *Chief insp. ann. rep., 1906*, p. 240 and *Irish Times*, 28 June 1906.
153 When the case was dismissed on the merits at Newry petty sessions, the home secretary (H.J. Gladstone) himself instructed an appeal to be taken by way of case stated: *Hansard 4*, clx, 1339 (16 July 1906).
154 [1906] 2 IR 405, 409 (emphasis in original). Cf. '[W]hen the language of s. 1 is considered as a whole and in the context of the mischief which it was designed to cure, "fine" means a financial loss agreed on in the case of the non-fulfilment of some contractual obligation': *Bristow* v. *City Petroleum Ltd* [1987] 2 All ER 45, 51, *per* Lord Ackner.
155 [1906] 2 IR 405 at p. 410.

[T]he great north of Ireland factories ... are dependent for their regular and continuous working and the amount of manufactured stuff they can turn out on the absolute co-ordination of all the departments. I can well understand that position, and fully appreciate the dislocation that would ensue and the effect which the stoppage of the machines for want of a sufficient number of operatives or any other reason might have upon the output of the factory.... I believe the offer of a bonus in the present case for punctual and regular attendance to be a perfectly *bona fide* effort on the part of the company to ensure the latter [and] that it in no respect savours of a device or contrivance to evade the conditions of the Truck Acts....[156]

The inspectors begged to differ; in their opinion, both employers and workers regarded the bonus as part of the wages:

For example, in one large factory in Belfast, the managing director in quoting to me the sums he had contracted to pay his workers, always included the bonus.... In another factory the manager spoke of the bonus as being part of the 'standard wage', and said that it would be impossible to get workers, if they paid the wages minus the bonus.... [A]lmost invariably in stating to me their wages, the workers included the bonus, and many of them were unable to tell me how much of it was given in the shape of bonus; they knew merely the total sum they received.[157]

But the matter was not quite so simple and straightforward. There could be no doubt that 'the system is obviously open to grave abuse, and from the evidence placed before us we believe it is abused'.[158] Nevertheless, a *bona fide* bonus intended as a stimulus to good attendance and as a real addition to the wage was advantageous to both employer and worker, 'and is adopted [as such] by many of the best employers'. The problem was to distinguish between a 'true' and a 'false' bonus; this could only be achieved by giving a court 'power to decide after considering all the circumstances of the case whether or not the bonus was a bona fide addition to the current wage'.[159] But even this modest proposal, which would not have altered the decision in *Deane* v. *Wilson*,[160] was not accepted by the government – no doubt on the basis that it would present a court with a very difficult, if not impossible, decision – and the 1896 act remained unamended. The inspectors had to content themselves with attempts to make parliament and the general public more aware of the injustice of the practice, and to persuade factory occupiers that it was in their own interests to make alternative arrangements.[161]

156 Ibid., p. 414.
157 *Chief insp. ann. rep., 1906*, p. 241 (Martindale).
158 *Report of the departmental committee on the truck acts 1908*, p. 28.
159 Ibid. Two members of the committee (Mrs Tennant and Stephen Walsh, a Labour MP) dissented on the basis that this proposal would still allow employers to evade the act's restrictions on fines; in their view, both should be prohibited: 'the bonus is as unnecessary in order to procure a high standard of work or conduct, as is the fine': ibid., p. 88.
160 Anderson, *Women in the factory*, p. 77.
161 See e.g. *Departmental committee on the truck acts 1908*, ii, 86 (Squire). See also *Chief insp. ann. rep., 1913*, p. 107, where Slocock explains how she convinced the owner of

Something certainly persuaded the linen industry to change its ways, for when Martindale returned to Northern Ireland in 1924, she found that the bonus system had been 'entirely swept away'.[162]

Unfair deductions for spoiled or damaged work

In 1902 Squire found 'the workers, both inside and outside the Irish factories, both north and south, to be subject to heavy deductions for work soiled or not done as well as it might have been ...'.[163] Irish employers were also prone to making excessive deductions from their workers' wages for damaged goods.[164] But there was a considerable amount of inconsistency;[165] some factory owners rarely resorted to deductions, while others did so to such an extent that Martindale was led to wonder whether 'a standard of work is being required from workers who are incapable of giving it'.[166] Where a deduction had been made which the inspectors considered unlawful, the inspectors normally contented themselves with a caution and reimbursement of the worker; but if the employer 'refused to accept the Home Office view of what was fair and reasonable', proceedings were usually taken.[167]

Three cases may be used to illustrate particular practices exposed by the inspectors.

The County Down outworkers. 'Women doing beautiful fine handkerchiefs, fancy embroidery and sewing linens ... for a wage that appears ridiculous when compared with the sum charged to the customer, are liable at any time, for some difference in pattern or quality to that of the pattern shown them, to be fined an amount which represents to them half a week's wages or more.'[168]

McBride v. Williams.[169] A girl was paid for making handkerchiefs at the rate of $^3/_4d$. per dozen; if she spoiled one handkerchief, she was fined $4^1/_2d$. The

a woollen mill in Dublin that his system of fines actually encouraged workers to be late for work and he substituted an alternative disciplinary procedure.

162 *From one generation to another*, pp. 145–46.
163 *Chief insp. ann. rep., 1903*, pt. I, p. 194. 'Fines ... for defective work are prevalent in the flax-weaving industry, and give rise to many complaints ...': *Chief insp. ann. rep., 1907*, p. 133 (McCaghey).
164 See e.g. *Report of the departmental committee on the truck acts, 1908*, pp. 35–36 (evidence of 'heavy' deductions from outworkers in the clothing trade in Belfast) and *Chief insp. ann. rep., 1909*, p. 164 ('owing to a comparatively slight defect', employers required worker to purchase two dozen overalls for 30*s*.; some months later, 'she was still 24*s*. in debt to her employers, with little chance of being able to reduce it').
165 See e.g. *Chief insp. ann. rep., 1907*, p. 133 (McCaghey).
166 *Chief insp. ann. rep., 1910*, p. 141.
167 See e.g. *Chief insp. ann. rep., 1901*, pt. I, p. 148 (Snape) and *1903*, pt. I, p. 194 (Squire).
168 *Chief insp. ann. rep., 1903*, pt. I, p. 234 (Squire). 'Heavy' deductions for damaged work were also imposed on outworkers in Co. Donegal – see *Departmental committee on the truck acts 1908*, ii, 81 (Squire).
169 *Departmental committee on the truck acts 1908*, ii, 93 (Squire). This was one of three

handkerchiefs in question were a common type which had to be passed rapidly through a machine, and the level of wages 'would not allow of very great care being taken'. She was fined 1s. 5¹/2d. for soiling four dozen handkerchiefs, even though there was no evidence that she was responsible for the soil; the factory apparently operated the rule that 'work which had passed through a particular set of hands was reckoned to that worker if not found satisfactory'. The court refused to find the deduction unfair, 'because it had been made by instalments and did not exceed the damage or loss to the employer'.[170]

Bennett v. *Welch Margetson & Co. Ltd.*[171] The defendants, shirtmakers in Londonderry, employed 'stampers' to stamp names or figures on shirt collars; when collars were stamped with the wrong name or figure, deductions were made from the stampers' wages.[172] These deductions were entered in wage books which at all times remained in the defendants' custody. No particulars of the deductions were given directly to the stampers, but the wage books were shown to them every fortnight prior to the payment of their wages. Inspector Bennett contended that the entries in four wage books were not 'particulars in writing' for the purposes of section 2(2)(b) of the Truck Act 1896, and in any event were not given to the workers *before* the deductions were made. The Londonderry justices (by a majority) disagreed and dismissed all four cases; but the king's bench division held that the defendants were in breach of the 1896 act, and they were fined £20.[173]

THE ISSUES REVIEWED

Although the 1896 act enabled the inspectors to check 'the worst abuses',[174] the provisions relating to fines and deductions were clearly defective, and

'Belfast' cases used, with other examples from England and Scotland, by Sir Charles Dilke to show that 'it is necessary to put an end to fines and deductions from wages' – see *Hansard 4*, clii, 1076 (27 Feb. 1906).

170 For a similar case see *Departmental committee on the truck acts 1908*, ii, 105 (Deane)(girl in Belfast shirt factory earning 5s. 2³/4d. a week had 2s. 1¹/2d. deducted for damage to a shirt, for being five minutes late one morning and for the provision of needles and thread).

171 Unreported, KBD, 12 June 1914, noted in *Chief insp. ann. rep., 1914*, pp. 30 and 118. The proceedings at the magistrates' court are reported in *Derry Standard*, 27 Feb. 1914 and *Londonderry Sentinel*, 28 Feb. 1914. See also above, Plate 18.

172 For example, one girl had 19s. 9d. deducted from her fortnight's earnings of 22s. 11¹/2d. for inadvertently stitching a large lot of collars in the wrong place, while another earning about five shillings per week had 19s. 10¹/2d. deducted at the rate of sixpence a week for stamping the wrong depth on a large bundle of collars.

173 The court directed that the defendants be convicted on one count only; the other counts were withdrawn with the consent of the solicitor general, who represented Bennett: PRONI D1583/23.

174 *Departmental committee on the truck acts 1908*, ii, 20 (Whitelegge).

even the government accepted that, in this respect at least, the act 'has failed in its purpose'.[175] Calls for reform of the law were, however, countered by the argument that making all fines and deductions unlawful might simply lead employers 'to dismiss workpeople for small and trivial offences'.[176] The question was therefore referred to a departmental committee for detailed consideration.

Extract from typical contract in textile factory in Belfast under Truck Act 1896[177]

Regulations and Conditions of Work

Any worker may on request obtain from the employer, free of charge, a copy of these regulations and conditions....

2. All workers must be in their places in the workroom at 8.30 a.m. Any worker not in her place in the workroom before 8.35 a.m. shall be liable to a fine of 1*d*. Any worker arriving after 8.45 a.m. shall not be allowed to work during that half day.

3. After dinner hour every worker must be in her place in the workroom at 2 p.m. Any worker not in her place in the workroom before 2.05 p.m. shall be liable to a fine of 1*d*. Any worker arriving after 2.15 p.m. shall not be allowed to work during the remainder of the day.

4. Any worker preparing to leave his or her place of work before the bell sounds shall be liable to a fine of 2*d*; or, in case of frequent breaches of this regulation, to instant dismissal....

10. Any worker injuring any materials or property of the employer, or doing work in a bad or negligent manner, shall be liable to a deduction from her wages in respect of such injury or defect of a sum not exceeding the actual or estimated damage or loss occasioned to the employer. Every worker against whom such a claim shall be made shall be required to sign a note of the said actual or estimated damage or loss, and shall be given a copy of such claim. In case of refusal to sign such note, the worker shall be liable to instant dismissal.

11. All workers shall observe good order and decorum while in the factory, and shall not do anything which shall interfere with the proper and orderly conduct thereof or of any department. A fine of 3*d*. (or less, at the discretion of the employer) shall be paid by each worker guilty of any infringement of this rule.

---

175 *Hansard 4*, clii, 1093–94 (27 Feb. 1906). At the behest of Mary Galway, secretary of the Textile Operatives Society of Ireland, the Irish TUC resolved that fines and deductions should be abolished on the grounds that 'the girls were barefacedly robbed by reason of the system in vogue in big factories': see e.g. *Irish Trades Union Congress: Twelfth report* (Wexford, 1905), p. 43 and *Fourteenth report* (Dublin, 1907), p. 53.

176 *Hansard 4*, clii, 1097–1100. Anderson, on the other hand, considered that outright prohibition would lead to 'such wholesale evasions ... that it would be found necessary to obtain power for inspectors to investigate and review the alternative methods of discipline which would be adopted by the less desirable sort of employers': *Departmental committee on the truck acts 1908*, ii, 70.

177 *Departmental committee on the truck acts 1908*, iv, 163. Cf. 'The contract ... has been found to be defective in many respects, and ... it is to be hoped that a new and less elaborate, and yet legal, contract will shortly be substituted ...': *Chief insp. ann. rep., 1909*, p. 163 (Martindale).

The committee praised the 'unsparing interest' of the inspectors, which had gone 'far beyond the mere scope of regulation duty'.[178] Trades unions had also done much to check abuses and to 'articulate the grievances of those who would otherwise have silently suffered contraventions of the law' – to such effect that many employers had been brought into 'a regular system of loyalty' to the law.[179] As a result, the 1896 act had indeed been 'productive of a large amount of good'. But the imposition of excessive fines and deductions still caused hardship and injustice, particularly in the 'unorganised' trades.[180] The committee were agreed that the fining of young persons aged 16 or under should be totally prohibited, as should deductions for the supply of materials.[181] But they could not agree on what should be done in other cases. The majority were in favour only of tighter regulation; in particular, 'unreasonable and extortionate' fines could be prevented by imposing a ceiling of five per cent of the worker's wages for that week and the price to be paid for inferior grades of work should be set down in advance rather than allowing the employer 'when the work is completed, in his own discretion [to] make a deduction the amount of which the worker has no means of forecasting and in the fixing of which he has no voice'.[182] But two members of the committee (Mrs Tennant and Stephen Walsh, a Labour MP) considered that *all* fines and deductions should be made unlawful:

In our opinion, disciplinary fines fail in their purpose. We believe them to be not merely negative in good but active in harm, inasmuch as they maintain and even create the very situation they are designed to destroy. Irritating in their imposition and ineffective in their result, they occupy in the organisation of industry, where they exist, the place that should be held by supervision.[183]

This inability to present a unanimous report probably contributed to the absence of any amending legislation before 1914.[184]

It was therefore left to the inspectors to try to bring about improvements on a voluntary basis. In 1911, Anderson and Martindale tackled a particular problem in the south of Ireland, where weavers – and particularly trainees – suffered severe deductions for producing poor cloth. At one mill in Dublin, for example, almost two-thirds of the weavers had been fined an average of

178 *Report of the departmental committee on the truck acts 1908*, p. 9.
179 Ibid.
180 Ibid., pp. 17 and 21. Trades unions were generally able to protect their members against excessive fines.
181 Ibid., pp. 30 and 40.
182 Ibid., pp. 29 and 37–38.
183 Ibid., pp. 84–85. Stricter regulation would remove many of the abuses, but 'the sense of injustice, the irritation that is the essence of the system, the friction, the substantial grievance of the loss … all this would remain'.
184 Reform of the truck acts was 'a hardy annual' in parliament, but any 'gentle reminder' to the home secretary fell on stony ground – see especially the debate on a private member's bill to prohibit all fines and deductions in *Hansard 5 (commons)*, lvi, 551–54 (30 July 1913). Both that bill (H.C. 1913 (289), v, 907) and another introduced in 1914 (H.C. 1914 (260), vi, 521) failed to progress beyond a first reading.

$8^3/_4d$. in one week, and $7^1/_2d$. in another, the highest gross weekly wage being
$7s$. $2^3/_4d$.[185] The mill was making 'little or no profit', and Anderson observed
that she 'never had so strong an illustration of the truth that thriving
manufacture cannot be built up on the labour of depressed and half-starved
workers'. The manager of the mill promised to cut back the number of fines for
an experimental period and to introduce a better system of training – with the
result that productivity increased, as did the supply of good weavers.[186]

In the north of Ireland negotiations with the Linen Manufacturers'
Association produced 'meagre results' when a new standard 'contract' for the
purposes of the 1896 act was introduced in most of the flax spinning and
weaving factories in October 1911.[187] Although the contract notice purported to be issued for the purposes of the act, the employers took the
opportunity to include a number of other disciplinary provisions.[188] Adverse
trading conditions, which forced many of these factories on to short time,
and widespread labour unrest in Belfast, meant that it was not long before
some of the mill-workers went on strike, citing the truck acts as one of their
grievances. But even with the support of James Connolly they were quickly
forced to return to work. Connolly advised them to act collectively: 'If one
girl is checked for singing, let the whole room start singing at once; if you are
checked for laughing, let the whole room laugh at once, and if anyone is
dismissed, all put on your shawls and come out in a body.'[189] But much of
the heat was taken out of the situation when a number of employers
withdrew the worst of the new rules.[190] The factory inspectors nevertheless
engaged in 'systematic visits to a large number of weaving sheds ... in order
to investigate and take records of the actual operation of these contracts,
particularly on the side of deductions for flaws and damages in woven
cloth'.[191] They found that 'while in some factories there are no fines at all, in
others doing exactly the same class of work the fines are so numerous and
excessive as to amount to a permanent reduction of wages'.[192]

No doubt the truck acts and the work of the inspectors in Ireland helped
to ameliorate unfair practices in the methods of paying workers. But the
failure to deal with the admitted deficiencies of the 1887 and 1896 acts,
compounded by judicial interpretation and magisterial application generally
unsympathetic to workers, meant that the law had less impact on the varieties

185 *Chief insp. ann. rep., 1911*, p. 162.
186 *Chief insp. ann. rep., 1912*, p. 154 and Anderson, *Women in the factory*, pp. 71–72. For
     another example, see *Chief insp. ann. rep., 1913*, p. 108 (Slocock).
187 *Chief insp. ann. rep., 1911*, p. 162; Anderson, *Women in the factory*, p. 75.
188 *Chief insp. ann. rep., 1911*, p. 162. The need to keep truck notices free of non-truck
     matters had been emphasised in the *Report of the departmental committee on the truck
     acts 1908*, pp. 17–18.
189 *Irish Worker*, 1(24) (28 Oct. 1911), 1, quoted in W.K. Anderson, *James Connolly and
     the Irish left* (Dublin, 1994), p. 18.
190 C.D. Greaves, *The life and times of James Connolly* (London, 1961), pp. 219–20. See
     also *Belfast Newsletter*, 3–17 Oct. 1911.
191 *Chief insp. ann. rep., 1912*, p. 154 (Anderson).
192 Ibid., p. 155 (Slocock).

of truck practised in Ireland than might otherwise have been the case.[193] The
relative weakness of the law might have been offset by trades union pressure;
but in spite of the efforts of Mary Galway, and later of James Connolly, this
was not forthcoming in the case of the linen workers prior to 1914. However,
a number of employers were by then finding that fines and deductions did
not significantly reduce the incidence of bad time-keeping or produce better
work, and that such objectives could much more readily be attained by a
proper system of training and supervision.[194] It was becoming clear that the
real problem was not unfair pay practices, but low rates of pay – and this was
something on which the Liberal government was prepared to legislate.

The evils of 'sweating' had first been exposed in the 1880s;[195] but little
had been done by 1906, when a board of trade inquiry confirmed that rates
of pay in certain trades, including linen spinning and weaving, were excessively low.[196] In Belfast, for example, the average weekly earnings of a woman
working full-time in a linen factory was 10s. 10d., or about 2¹/₂d. per hour.[197]
Following further investigations, not least by the departmental committee on
the truck acts, the government brought in the Trade Boards Act 1909, which
provided for the setting up of a trade board in appropriate cases to set a
statutory minimum wage for particular trades. A separate trade board could be
set up in respect of any trade carried on 'to any substantial extent' in Ireland.

The act had a mixed reception in Ireland. Members of parliament from
urban constituencies, and the trades unions, were generally enthusiastic;
indeed, Sir Charles Dilke pointed out that 'the agitation for this Bill came

193 In 1912, 'complaints were received of harsh or arbitrary reductions for damaged
     work ... by some employers': *Report of the committee of inquiry into the linen and other
     making-up trades 1912*, p. xviii. According to Martindale: 'In the weaving there are
     a great many deductions. There are not perhaps so many of them in the making-up,
     but when they are made they are very heavy': ibid., p. 58, while McCaghey reported
     that proper contract notices were 'seldom encountered': ibid., p. 14. Cf. Eraut
     suggested that although there were still 'the usual technical irregularities', there were
     only 'a few definite breaches of the law which are ... seldom wilful and are corrected
     after attention is drawn to them': *Chief insp. ann. rep., 1911*, p. 124.
194 See e.g. the 'cheering' news that a laundry and a paper box factory in Dublin had
     discontinued the making of fines and deductions without any deterioration in working
     standards, and the 'practical abolition' of deductions for bad work in linen factories at
     Drogheda: *Chief insp. ann. rep., 1911*, pp. 161–62 (Martindale) and *1912*, pp. 30–31
     (May). By 1924, deductions from wages and fines were 'seldom imposed', since 'many
     occupiers and managers had come to realize that fines and deductions did not have the
     desired effect, that it was often the same worker who was repeatedly fined, and that
     therefore it was a wiser policy to discharge her than continue the irritating system of
     making deductions from wages. The unfairness of fining for an occasional lapse had
     also been realized': Martindale, *From one generation to another*, pp. 145–46.
195 *Fifth report from the select committee of the House of Lords on the sweating system*, H.L.
     1890 (169), xvii, 257.
196 *Report of an inquiry by the Board of Trade into the earnings and hours of labour of
     workpeople of the United Kingdom, I: Textile trades in 1906* [Cd. 4545], H.C. 1909, lxxx, 1.
197 Ibid., p. xxi. The comparable figure for adult men was 26s. 2d. Rates of pay outside
     Belfast were slightly lower. Both men and women working in Belfast earned slightly
     more than the United Kingdom average for linen workers.

first of all from Ireland',[198] and the Belfast Trades Council claimed that 'the need for such boards was greater in Ireland than in any other part of the three kingdoms'.[199] On the other hand, Mr John Hayden (MP for South Roscommon) contended that the application of the act to the west of Ireland would mean that 'industries, built up amongst the poorest portion of the people of Ireland, will be crushed out of existence' and he stressed 'the necessity of excluding Ireland absolutely from the provisions of this bill'.[200] *The Irish Times* agreed:

In Ireland the shirt and underclothing-making industry is carried on in rural districts at low rates, but under conditions which are not otherwise undesirable. It is most important that a wages board at Westminster should not be able artificially to raise the cost of production in Ireland because sweating exists in London. Not that there is the least objection to Irish peasants getting the full value of a rise in wages, if it is natural.... It is better for our country people to make additions to their income, however small, by such industries than to be deprived of the opportunity through a well-meant effort to assist them.[201]

The government replied simply that this was 'quite clearly impossible'; but it seems clear that they accepted the special position of the 'cottage' industries and were in any event resolved to proceed slowly and cautiously.[202]

The act initially applied only to four trades – chain-making, machine-made lace and net finishing, paper-box making and bespoke tailoring; but it could be extended to any other trade where the rate of pay was exceptionally low and the other circumstances of the trade were such 'as to render the application of this Act ... expedient'.[203] Further evidence of the low wages paid in the linen and other making-up trades of the north of Ireland led to a strong recommendation that the act should be applied to some at least of the making-up trades.[204] Somewhat surprisingly, the employers were amenable

198 *Hansard 5 (commons)*, iv, 380–82 (28 April 1909), adding that it was 'the Irish Trades Congress and the Irish tailoring trade [who] were the first and strongest supporters of this Bill ...' and that 'any rough and ready plan of cutting Ireland out from the general field of labour legislation will be fatal to the efficiency of Irish labour and the prosperity of Ireland'.

199 Ibid., cols. 1442–43 (10 May 1909)(J. Devlin, MP for W. Belfast). J.P. Nannetti, MP for Dublin (College Green), 'speaking as a representative of the working men of Ireland' was prepared 'to see Irish industries languish rather than that people engaged in them should be exploited ...': ibid., cols. 396–97.

200 Ibid., cols. 378–79. Hugh Law (MP for Donegal W.) later quoted the chief inspector of industries for the congested districts board as having testified that 'while favourable to anything which would tend to raise the level of wages', he had 'the gravest apprehension' as to what might happen if the act were to apply to trades in the west of Ireland: *Hansard 5 (commons)*, vii, 2454 (16 July 1909).

201 *Irish Times*, 27 March 1909, p. 6.

202 In 1911, for example, the government rejected a petition requesting the extension of the act to the linen and cognate trades in Belfast: *Hansard 5 (commons)*, xxv, 1195 (10 May 1911).

203 Section 1(2), subject to the approval of parliament.

204 *Committee of inquiry into the linen and other making-up trades, 1912*, p. xv. Connolly was demanding a trade board for the whole linen industry – see e.g. A. Morgan, *James Connolly: A political biography* (Manchester, 1988), p. 99.

to this proposal – provided that it applied equally to their competitors in the rest of the United Kingdom. This concession was not as generous as it might seem, since the employers 'believed ... that if a trade board was established it would have a difficult, if not impossible, task, in view of the facts that minimum wages would presumably have to be fixed with some regard to wages in other trades and occupations, and that these differ widely in the north of Ireland, as well as in the south and west, and in England and Scotland'.[205] By June 1914, however, a minimum wage had been set only in relation to the paper-box making and bespoke tailoring trades in Ireland.[206] A shirtmaking trade board for Ireland was set up in 1914; but it was not until 1916 that a minimum rate of $3^{1}/_{4}d$. per hour 'clear of all deductions' was set for female workers (including homeworkers).[207] A board for the linen and cotton embroidery trade in Ireland followed in 1916, under which minimum rates ranging from $2^{1}/_{2}d$. to $3^{1}/_{4}d$ per hour were set in December 1917.[208] With the extension of the legislation by the Trade Boards Act 1918, there were by 1921 some 19 trade boards in Ireland, and the problem of low pay was at last being directly addressed.[209]

205 *Committee of inquiry into the linen and other making-up trades, 1912*, pp. xv–xvi.
206 A trade board had also been established for the sugar, confectionery and food-preserving trades, but no minimum rate of pay had been determined – see *Hansard 5 (commons)*, lxiv, 11 (29 June 1914), where various teething difficulties are discussed.
207 See Shirt-making Trade (Ire.) Female Workers Order (1916, No. 363), which also set out minimum piece-rates in considerable detail.
208 See Linen and Cotton Embroidery Trade (Ire.) Order 1917 (1917 No. 1238).
209 See generally *Report of the advisory committee on trade boards* [Cmd. (N.I.) 7] (1922), pp. 4–7 and 33; *Report of the committee of enquiry into the working and effects of the Trade Boards Act* [Cmd. 1645, 1922], pp. 5–7; J. Harris, 'Working and effects of trade boards in the linen industry' (unpublished Ph.D. thesis, Queen's University, Belfast, 1924) and B.M. Browne, 'Trade boards in Northern Ireland, 1909–1945' (unpublished Ph.D. thesis, Q.U.B., 1989).

CHAPTER EIGHT

The regulation of men's employment

Although the primary focus of the factory acts was the regulation of trades and industries in which the workforce consisted largely or mainly of women, young persons and children, occupations traditionally dominated by men were not entirely ignored. During our period, the state had no great concern with the length of the working day in these industries, nor with the general conditions of employment; the development of trades unions meant that these tended in practice to be left to regulation by collective agreement, 'supervised' by trades union officials.[1] Much of the work was skilled, leading to relatively high wages; but this was not the case in all predominantly male occupations – a point underlined by the contrast between two examples of men's employment – shipbuilding and dock labour – which form the primary focus for this chapter.[2] Both, however, illustrate the state's concern, particularly in relation to 'dangerous' trades, for safe working conditions, even for adult males – a concern which was noticeably absent when it came to minimising the dangers arising from the steam boilers which were used extensively in Irish industrial establishments of the later nineteenth and early twentieth centuries.

SHIPBUILDING

There is a long history of ship and boat-building in Ireland.[3] But in spite of an early interest in steam power and diversification from wood to iron in the 1840s, the industry prior to the 1870s was a small one by United Kingdom

---

1 See e.g. W.E. Coe, *The engineering industry of the north of Ireland* (Newton Abbot, 1969), pp. 171–74 and 177–78.
2 The extension of the factory acts to shipbuilding, dock labour and other male occupations led to the hope that 'this beneficent process will cause the whole question of labour regulation to be re-studied on larger issues, and will help to rob the opposition to special regulations for women of its bitterness': B.L. Hutchins and A. Harrison, *A history of factory legislation* (London, 1903), p. 209.
3 See generally M. Moss, 'Shipbuilding in Ireland in the nineteenth century', in S. Ville (ed.), *Shipbuilding in the United Kingdom in the nineteenth century: A regional approach* (St. John's, Newfoundland, 1993), p. 177; D.L. Armstrong, *The growth of industry in Northern Ireland: The story of the golden age of industrial development, 1850–1900* (Long Hanborough, Oxford, 1999), chap. 14 and P. Ollerenshaw, 'Industry, 1820–1914', in L. Kennedy and P. Ollerenshaw (ed.), *An economic history of Ulster, 1820–1940* (Manchester, 1985), p. 87.

standards. In 1853, for example, only 24 ships with a total tonnage of 2,695 tons were built in Ireland. Although shipbuilding of one kind or another was carried on in Cork, Dublin, Waterford, Londonderry and elsewhere, it was the opening of an iron shipyard on Queen's Island in Belfast which paved the way for the unprecedented developments which shortly followed.[4] By 1875, Harland & Wolff Ltd, with six slipways, dominated shipbuilding in Ireland, and in 1879 another shipbuilding yard (which was to become Workman Clark & Co.)[5] was established on the north side of the river Lagan. By the 1890s, these two yards were responsible for well over 90 per cent of all tonnage constructed in Ireland and some 10 per cent of total United Kingdom tonnage.[6] Between 1890 and 1894 Harland & Wolff built more vessels than any other shipyard in the United Kingdom, and after 1893, when Workman Clark took over the shipbuilding yard and engine works on Queen's Island owned by McIlwaine and MacColl, their production expanded to such an extent that they even overtook Harland & Wolff on the eve of the first world war.[7]

Between the 1850s and 1912, Harland & Wolff grew from a site of three acres employing 48 men, to one of 80 acres with a workforce of 15,000 or so.[8] By 1902, Workman Clark employed 7,000 on a fifty-acre site.[9] Most of this workforce were adult males, for whom the shipyards represented a major source of employment. Some two-thirds of these were skilled or semi-skilled workers, who were comparatively well paid, many averaging close to 30s. per week; but at least one-third were labourers earning less than half that amount.[10] The higher pay of many of the workers contrasted with the generally low rates of pay in the linen industry, although skilled male workers in that industry were, of course, better paid than the majority of women workers. In addition:

4   See especially S. Pollard and P. Robertson, *The British shipbuilding industry, 1870–1914* (London, 1979), pp. 66–67. For a general history of the company, see e.g. D. Rebbeck, 'The history of iron shipbuilding on Queen's Island up to 1874' (unpublished Ph.D. thesis, Queen's University Belfast, 1950), J.G. Peirson, *Great shipbuilders: The rise of Harland and Wolff* (Belfast, 1935) and M. Moss and J. Hume, *Shipbuilders to the world – 125 years of Harland and Wolff* (Belfast, 1986).
5   See Workman Clark (1928) Ltd., *Shipbuilding at Belfast* (Belfast, 1934).
6   See e.g. the figures given in *Chief insp. ann. rep., 1902*, pt. I, p. 322.
7   Moss, 'Shipbuilding in Ireland', pp. 192–93. The expansion of shipbuilding was paralleled by the development of engineering works – see e.g. Coe, *Engineering industry* and W.P. Coyne (ed.), *Ireland: Industrial and agricultural* (2nd ed., Dublin, 1902), pp. 446–501.
8   Pollard and Robertson, *British shipbuilding industry*, p. 110.
9   H. Patterson, 'Industrial labour and the labour movement, 1820–1914', in Kennedy and Ollerenshaw (ed.), *An economic history of Ulster, 1820–1940*, p. 16. See also H. Patterson, *Class conflict and sectarianism* (Belfast, 1980), p. 88.
10 See e.g. Patterson, 'Industrial labour and the labour movement', p. 166 and *Report on the wages of the manual labour class in the United Kingdom, with tables of the average rates of wages and hours of labour of persons employed in several of the principal trades in 1886 and 1891*, pp. 20–24 and 74–76 [C. 6889], H.C. 1893–4, lxxxii (pt. II), pp. 20–24, 74–76. Cf. 'These high earnings have to be evened out over periods of lower rates, under-employment and unemployment. Thus skilled workers' overall earnings may not have been significantly greater than those of unskilled workers, as has normally

In contrast to linen, shipbuilding and engineering had a labour force with large groups of workers in categories with relatively high levels of trade union organisation throughout the United Kingdom. Metal workers had been unionised from the first half of the century; the iron moulders had a branch from 1826; the boilermakers from 1841, and when the Amalgamated Society of Engineers was established in 1851, there were already branches of its constituent unions in Belfast.[11]

Skilled shipyard workers were also more mobile:

Workers in the linen trade were interchangeable, lacked any choice of work technique, were subject to constant work pressure and were forbidden free physical movement. For employment opportunities they were entirely dependent on local conditions.... [Shipyard workers, on the other hand], possessing trade qualifications as they did, ... were generally free from reliance upon conditions of purely local prosperity to find work.... They were not tied to the mechanical indefinite repetition of the same task, but had a fair discretion of job selection, freedom of movement and could work more or less in their own time.[12]

But, as we shall see, the shipyard workers faced a considerably higher risk of accidental death or injury.

Shipbuilding first came under the factory acts in 1867, when the Factory Acts Extension Act, which applied generally to blast furnaces, iron mills and foundries, the making of machinery and the like, made particular provision in respect of 'any premises in which steam, water or other mechanical power is used for moving machinery employed ... in the manufacture of any article of metal ...'. Inspector Baker considered that this wording was apt to include shipbuilding,[13] but the courts were not convinced. In *Palmer's Shipbuilding & Iron Co.* v. *Chaytor*,[14] shipbuilders in Jarrow were convicted of employing a boy under the age of 11 for more than the statutory maximum of six and a half hours per day and were fined 20s. The court of queen's bench upheld the fine, but only on the particular facts of the case. The child in question was employed as a rivet boy in a department in which steam machinery was used for cutting and shaping iron plates. The defendants argued that a ship was not an 'article', and Cockburn CJ was inclined to agree: 'I cannot bring myself to think that such a process as the ... building of a ship was intended by [the word] ... "*article*" ... and I should hesitate very much before I could hold that a boy was employed in a "factory" merely because he was

been assumed': A. Reid, 'Skilled workers in the shiphuilding industry, 1880–1920', in A. Morgan and B. Purdie (ed.), *Ireland: Divided nation, divided class* (London, 1980), pp. 117–18.

11   Patterson, 'Industrial labour and the labour movement', p. 176. According to E. O'Connor, *A labour history of Ireland, 1824–1960* (Dublin, 1992), p. 37, 'By the end of the [nineteenth] century, the proportion of unionized men in the northern shipbuilding and engineering trades exceeded the United Kingdom average'.

12   P. Gibbon, *The origins of Ulster unionism: the formation of popular protestant politics and ideology in nineteenth century Ireland* (Manchester, 1975), pp. 83–85.

13   *Insp. half-yearly rep., Oct. 1868*, pp. 175–81.

14   (1869) LR 4 QB 209.

employed in some department of shipbuilding.' But there was no need to decide the point, for an iron plate was clearly an 'article' even when used in shipbuilding, and the cutting and shaping of the plate was part of the process of manufacture.

The limited nature of this decision does not appear to have deterred the inspectors and, in 1870, Harland & Wolff felt obliged to apply for a modification of the employment provisions of the 1844 act. During the winter they could employ their 1,200 hands for only nine hours per day (i.e. less than the statutory maximum), and they claimed that they should therefore be allowed to work extra hours on Saturdays all the year round in order to make up the 'lost' time. This would, during the summer months, bring them above the statutory maximum for the week, and sub-inspector Cramp commented tersely that 'this of course is illegal'. He was not unsympathetic: 'I think it a real grievance, inasmuch as they pay the same wages for a day's work during the short days of winter as they do in summer'; but all he could offer was the hope that the workers 'will make up the loss to their employers by redoubled energy and exertion'.[15]

In 1876, the factory and workshop commissioners took the view that the decision in *Palmer* had 'less substantive effect than might have been anticipated, since it appears that although a ship is not an "article", each part of it, taken separately, is …'.[16] But any remaining doubt should be settled in favour of regulation, with the result that the Factory and Workshop Act 1878 expressly provided that 'any premises in which any ships, boats or vessels used in navigation are made, finished or repaired' were non-textile factories for all purposes of the act.[17]

In spite of this development, it was conceded in 1884 that 'the frequent inspection of shipbuilding yards, in which the normal hours of work are considerably within the limits laid down in the Factory Act, and in which the proportionate number of lads to male adults is small, is not as necessary as it is in textile factories, where the bulk of the persons employed are children and women'.[18] Nevertheless, all yards were inspected from time to time, with particular reference to safety: 'every endeavour has been made to suggest careful fencing of dangerous parts, which suggestions are almost invariably attended to at once'.[19] One problem faced by the inspectors, however, was that the only accidents occurring in non-textile factories which had to be

15 *Insp. half-yearly rep.*, Oct. 1869, p. 222.
16 *Report of the commissioners appointed to inquire into the working of the factory and workshop acts*, p. xx [C. 1443], H.C. 1876, xxix, 25.
17 1878 act, s. 93 and sch. 4, pt. II, re-enacted as Factory and Workshop Act 1901, s. 149 and sch. 6, pt. II. In the unlikely event that no mechanical power was used, a shipyard qualified as a workshop.
18 *Chief insp. ann. rep., 1884*, p. 39 (Redgrave). In 1895, for example, there were in the United Kingdom only five convictions in shipbuilding, out of a total workforce of just over 125,000 – a conviction rate of 0.4% per 10,000 employed; the equivalent rate for the linen industry was 3.9%: *Chief insp. ann. rep., 1896*, p. 51.
19 *Chief insp. ann. rep., 1884*, p. 39.

reported to them were fatal accidents and injuries caused by machinery; given that 'the greater portion of accidents which occur in shipbuilding yards are caused by men falling from the stages upon which they are at work or down the holds of the vessels', the inspectors 'know nothing of these unless they are fatal'.[20] In addition, it appears that many trades union representatives took some time to appreciate that the factory acts now clearly applied to shipbuilding.[21]

There is, however, some evidence of official concern about safety in the Belfast shipyards. In 1890 McIlwaine & MacColl were convicted of having neglected to send notice of an accident to the factory inspector and to the certifying surgeon – an offence for which they were fined five shillings![22] In 1897, Workman Clark were fined £2. 10s. for failure to fence dangerous machinery.[23] These details were underlined by the graphic description of a visitor to a Belfast shipyard:

Men rush about with great plates of steel on hardcarts; there is the creaking of cranes as the plates are swung through the air into place, the clang of hammers reverberating again and again. Every vessel is surrounded by a network of scaffolding, and inclined wooden ways are built to the top of the ship. Chains, pieces of iron, heaps of bolts and blocks of wood litter the ground, and you shudder as the casual remark is made to keep out of the way of falling bolts.... On the average a baker's dozen of men are killed in the course of a year.[24]

In 1899, Inspector Young reported from Belfast that shipbuilding and engineering were responsible for 'perhaps the greatest number' of industrial accidents in the north of Ireland. However, he continued:

I had occasion to investigate a complaint regarding the adequacy of the stages used in the two Belfast shipyards, but I am bound to say – after having made a careful inspection of the stages in use – that the Belfast shipyards would compare very favourably with any of the Clyde yards with regard to the working stages. The occupiers are fully alive to their own advantage in providing ample and safe working space for those engaged in building the vessels.[25]

20 Ibid. 'I know of many cases where the base of the skull has been fractured ... yet no medical report is made.... There must be a surprisingly large number of men who are permanently incapacitated from injuries thus produced': *Chief insp. ann. rep., 1902*, pt. I, pp. 323–24 (Wilson).

21 *Chief insp. ann. rep., 1884*, p. 38.

22 *Chief insp. ann. rep., 1890*, p. 215.

23 *Chief insp. ann. rep., 1897*, p. 281. Workman Clark had previously been fined £1. 10s. for employing six male young persons on St Patrick's Day, a compulsory holiday: *Chief insp. ann. rep., 1884*, p. 141. These three cases appear to be the only 'shipbuilding' convictions in Ireland during the period 1880–1900. Details of cases after 1900 are not available.

24 *Belfast Evening Telegraph*, 14 Jan. 1899, quoted in J. Bardon, *A history of Ulster* (Belfast, 1992), p. 393.

25 *Chief insp. ann. rep., 1901*, pt. I, pp. 134–35. Cf. 'The union [Amalgamated Society of Engineers] complained of poor safety practices, lighting and sanitation in the shipyards ...': O'Connor, *Labour history of Ireland*, p. 38.

The inspectors' concern with safety was, nonetheless, confirmed in 1902 by the findings of a special inquiry into shipbuilding accidents in the north-east of England,[26] and by two subsequent reports in 1907[27] and 1913.[28] All three reports confirmed the dangers of working in a shipyard; indeed, given that many injuries from falls were not reported, these figures undoubtedly understate the general position.[29] Unfortunately, the reports do not provide separate figures for the Belfast shipyards;[30] but it was later stated that 'in Belfast we have probably one of the best managed shipbuilding yards in the Kingdom ... [and] I have no doubt that this has had a great effect in reducing accidents'.[31]

Table 8.1: *Accident rates in shipbuilding and other industries in 1902*[32]

	Deaths from all causes per 1,000 employed	Injuries from all causes per 1,000 employed
Shipbuilding	0.7	71.3
Dock labour	1.4	57.0
Textile factories		
– males	0.1	6.2
– females	–	2.7

26 *Special report by Mr H.J. Wilson, HM inspector of factories, on shipbuilding accidents,* reproduced in *Chief insp. ann. rep., 1902,* pt. I, p. 322 [hereafter *Report on shipbuilding accidents, 1902*].

27 *Special report by H.M. Robinson (HM superintending inspector of factories for Scotland and Ireland Division) and H.J. Wilson (HM inspector of factories for Glasgow) on shipbuilding accidents,* reproduced in *Chief insp. ann. rep., 1907,* p. 272 [hereafter *Report on shipbuilding accidents, 1907*].

28 *Report to the secretary of state for the home department on accidents occurring in shipbuilding yards, by H.M. Robinson (HM deputy chief inspector of factories) and H.J. Wilson (HM inspector of factories, Glasgow)* [Cd. 7046], H.C. 1913, lx, 115 [hereafter *Report on shipbuilding accidents, 1913*].

29 'One of the largest insurance companies in the country informs me ... that they hold shipbuilding and ship-repairing equivalent to dock-labouring in point of danger ...': *Report on shipbuilding accidents 1902,* p. 323.

30 Cf. *Report on shipbuilding accidents 1907,* p. 277 states that in 1906, there were 10 fatal and 36 non-fatal accidents in Belfast, as compared to 26 and 329 in Glasgow; but it must be remembered that the tonnage produced on the Clyde was roughly three times that of the Lagan.

31 *Report on shipbuilding accidents 1902,* p. 323, as amended by *Report on shipbuilding accidents 1907,* p. 272. Much depends, of course, on the basis on which such figures were compiled; but it is noticeable that the much higher ratio of accidents in shipbuilding, as compared with textile factories, was confirmed by the *Report of the departmental committee on accidents in places under the factory and workshop acts,* pp. 5–6 [Cd. 5535], H.C. 1911, xxiii, 11–12.

32 *Departmental committee on accidents: Evidence,* p. 80 [Cd. 5540], H.C. 1911, xxiii, 156 (Williams). Robinson agreed that the both shipyards were 'well managed', and,

Death or injury was almost wholly due to falling from a height or being struck by a falling tool, plank or other object.[33] The most frequent causes of such accidents included (i) the use of narrow, unsecured or defective planks in the staging used on the outside of the vessel; (ii) the practice inside the vessel of slinging staging from chains or ropes; (iii) the use of open boarding on outside and inside staging which allowed objects to fall onto men below; (iv) the failure to provide handrails on gangways; (v) the placing of loose planks – or nothing at all – across open hatchways in the deck plating, and (vi) an inadequate system of lighting, especially in the vicinity of bunker hatchways or holes in decks temporarily left uncovered.[34] As ships became longer, wider and deeper, the number of accidents – and their severity – increased.[35] Yet many of these defects, being the result of inadequate supervision, the inappropriate use of unskilled workmen or simple carelessness, could be avoided by the adoption of practicable and affordable measures.[36]

In his first report, Inspector Wilson, 'with a view to rendering shipbuilding less dangerous as a calling', made twelve 'suggestions' for dealing with the principal causes of accidents. These suggestions, which reflected precautions 'adopted by some of the best shipbuilders' and which were reiterated in 1907, were given 'considerable attention' by some shipbuilders, but not by others. Two calls for voluntary action having failed to produce a sufficient response, the inspectors set out their third list of recommendations in the form of draft regulations, and in 1914 these became law when the home secretary, acting under section 79 of the 1901 act, certified the building and repairing of ships exceeding 150 feet in length as a 'dangerous trade'.[37]

---

although he was unable to make a detailed comparison between Belfast and Glasgow, 'I should be very much surprised ... if it does not turn out that the Belfast serious accidents are fewer': ibid., p. 62.

33 *Chief insp. ann. rep., 1901*, pt. I, p. 134 (Young). In 1907, falls killed two men and injured 189 in Belfast, as compared to 15 and 558 respectively in Glasgow; two men were killed and 403 injured in Belfast by falling articles, as compared to 6 and 505 in Glasgow: *Chief insp. ann. rep., 1907*, p. 119.

34 *Report on shipbuilding accidents 1902*, pp. 324–28 (where the 'general principles' of shipbuilding are explained); *Report on shipbuilding accidents 1907*, pp. 273–74.

35 *Report on shipbuilding accidents 1907*, p. 272. Cf. 'a practice recently resorted to in Belfast in the construction of very large vessels, namely, the plating of the decks immediately the framing permitted ... greatly increased the safety of inside work by doing away with much internal staging': *Chief insp. ann rep., 1910*, p. 98 (Eraut). But a Harland & Wolff spokesman later explained that when large ships such as the *Titanic* and the *Olympic* were in skeleton form, 'there is a larger percentage of risk, particularly of serious accidents ...': *Departmental committee on the system of compensation for injuries to workmen: Minutes of evidence*, ii, 289 [Cmd. 909], H.C. 1920, xxvi, 894 (Mr Robertson, accident and compensation department, Harland & Wolff). See above, Plate 19.

36 Cf. 'many accidents [in Belfast shipyards] may be attributed to circumstances which could not be foreseen, and others to errors of judgment on the part of the injured persons': *Chief insp. ann. rep., 1908*, p. 112 (Eraut). McCaghey, another Belfast inspector, thought that 'there can be no doubt whatever that the men do contribute largely to their own accidents': ibid.

37 *Regulations for the construction and repair of ships in shipbuilding yards* (1914 No. 461), reproduced in *Redgrave's Factory Acts*, ed. J. Owner (14th ed., London, 1931), pp.

These regulations imposed a number of duties on the employers; given that safety depended to a large extent on the cooperation of the workers, however, certain duties were also laid upon them to assist their employers in the adoption and maintenance of safety standards.

From the outset, the inspectors had argued strongly in favour of better supervision, particularly in relation to the construction and rigging of staging: 'supervision lies at the root of the whole question, and it is entirely due to the lack of it that many casualties occur ...'.[38] In some instances, staging was erected by sub-contractors outside the control of the shipbuilder. In others, it was erected by the riveters or platers themselves, and a lack of supervision was compounded by the fact that they were paid by the piece, so that 'all time spent in erecting or moving stages is unremunerative, with the result that such work is hurriedly done, as few planks as possible are used and scant attention is given to securing them'.[39] The inspectors recommended that 'the whole of the staging, both outside and inside the vessel, should be put up by skilled men (shipwrights) with a sufficient number of labourers, all employed direct by the firm, and ... these men should exercise systematic supervision over the erection and maintenance of all staging ... during the whole time the vessel is on the stocks'.[40] The subsequent negotiations with employers and workers reduced this to a duty to ensure that staging was erected 'by competent persons specially but not necessarily exclusively employed for that purpose by the occupier', a duty which did not apply to 'such adjustment or shifting of the staging ... as may be necessary ...'.

Most of the other regulations were based on common sense. The staging, for example, was to be constructed of 'sound and substantial material' and wide enough 'to secure the safety of the persons working thereon'; gangways and ladders were also to be of sound construction and properly secured, so as to provide 'safe means of access' to all working areas. For their part, the workers were under a duty not to leave articles or materials lying about 'in any place from which they may fall on persons working or passing' and they were not to throw tools, planks or other materials from staging without taking adequate safety precautions. The 'dangerous' parts of openings in decks were to be provided with temporary covers or other sufficient protection, and all parts of the ship in which work was being carried on were to be 'efficiently lighted in such manner as is reasonable in all the

603–05. The number of accidents in yards in which small boats, yachts or barges were built 'are very infrequent and seldom of a serious nature' and did not justify the application of the regulations: *Report on shipbuilding accidents 1913*, p. 5.

38 *Report on shipbuilding accidents 1907*, p. 273.

39 Ibid., p. 274. The Belfast inspectors considered that the quality of staging and supervision was 'above the average', but that the piece–work system 'has a lot to answer for in being an incentive to recklessness on the part of the men': *Chief insp. ann. rep., 1908*, p. 112 (Eraut and McCaghey). See also *Report by Sir Ernest Hatch as to the methods of applying the 'particulars' section of the Factory and Workshop Act 1901 to sundry industries*, pp. 16–18 [Cd. 4842], H.C. 1909, xxi, 724–26.

40 *Report on shipbuilding accidents 1907*, pp. 273 and 275.

circumstances of the case to secure the safety of the persons employed'. Finally, the employer's duties included the appointment of 'a competent person or persons' to enforce the observance of the regulations.[41]

A particular problem was the disproportionate number of accidents to boys aged 14 to 16: 'young and inexperienced, they are often set to do the most hazardous work, that is "heating" rivets and "catching" or passing them when heated to the riveters'.[42] In 1902, it seemed that the only solution was to prohibit all young persons under 16 from working on board ships under construction. Action by the state was required for the simple reason that 'these lads leave few dependants, and consequently cost employers comparatively little [if they are killed]'.[43] But it was also the case that apprenticeships were a matter of grave concern to the shipbuilding trades unions. Not only did these unions restrict the number of apprentices in order to maintain wage levels for journeymen; but they insisted that apprentices learn their trade by observing and assisting experienced workmen. But perhaps what bothered them most was that a prohibition of this kind would encourage employers to bring in semi-skilled adults as apprentices and thereby decrease wages.[44] The inspectors bowed reluctantly to this opposition, although they hoped nevertheless that 'it might be possible to come to some agreement whereby young persons ... would be prohibited from doing certain of the more dangerous operations'.[45] But the employment of young boys – and the number of accidents to them – did not decrease, and eventually the inspectors were forced to admit defeat:

The prohibition or restriction of their employment is no doubt a difficult matter, and ... the feeling in the trade, especially on the part of the workmen, would be against such a restriction. Still it is with considerable hesitation that we have refrained from recommending a rule prohibiting the employment in the meantime of those under fifteen, and we have only done so because we think that if the Regulations we have submitted are fully observed by both employers and workers, and greater care and supervision is exercised, the risk of accident will be appreciably diminished. Otherwise we think that the employment of those under 16 on a vessel in course of construction or repair will have to be entirely prohibited.[46]

41 One noticeable omission from the regulations was any provision for the wearing of goggles by riveters, caulkers and the like. The inspectors were told that goggles tended to obscure vision, especially in warm or damp weather, and that many workers refused to wear them for this reason. They conceded that 'there is, no doubt, a certain amount of truth in this', and therefore did not recommend that the provision of goggles should be made compulsory. Nevertheless, they hoped that employers would continue to supply goggles to workers who wished to wear them: *Report on shipbuilding accidents 1913*, p. 4.

42 *Report on shipbuilding accidents 1902*, p. 329. During the years 1901–07, at least 87 young persons were killed in shipyard accidents – some 12 per cent of all fatalities: *Report on shipbuilding accidents 1907*, p. 276.

43 *Report on shipbuilding accidents 1902*, p. 329. But if only injured, the employer might have to pay a fair amount of compensation – see below, p. 364.

44 *Report on shipbuilding accidents 1913*, p. 3; Coe, *Engineering industry*, p. 175.

45 *Report on shipbuilding accidents 1907*, p. 275.

46 *Report on shipbuilding accidents 1913*, p. 4.

As the inspectors themselves acknowledged, safety measures could also be encouraged by the desire to reduce the cost of accidents either directly or by way of minimising insurance premiums. Although shipbuilders might, in theory, incur liability at common law for negligence or breach of statutory duty, their principal concern was the payment of compensation under the Workmen's Compensation Acts of 1897 and 1906. This was particularly the case with Harland & Wolff, who did not take out insurance cover, but were self-insurers – a practice which 'encourages the avoidance of accidents and the taking of precautions'.[47]

The combined effect of all these factors on the accident rate at least at Harland & Wolff appears to have been quite beneficial. During the years 1907 to 1914, the average annual number of accidents was 740,[48] representing a rate of 65 accidents per 1,000 workers, considerably lower than the national average suggested by Table 8.1 above, although still amongst the highest – if not the highest – in Ireland. But although the cost of providing compensation in respect of those accidents never exceeded 1.2 per cent of the total wage bill, the average annual cost to the firm of workmen's compensation per worker appears to have been slightly higher than the national average.[49]

DOCK LABOUR

Dock labour was an unlikely subject for inclusion under the factory acts for three reasons – the workforce consisted solely of adult men, there was no obvious manufacturing process and, until at least the turn of the century, the dockers had insufficient political support to bring about the necessary extension of the acts.[50] In any event, the complex relationship of dock authorities, shipowners, cargo owners and stevedores made it difficult to identify a responsible 'occupier'. The turning point proved to be the appalling record of death and injury produced by the dangerous nature of the work and exacerbated by the pressures under which it was performed.

47　*Departmental committee on compensation for injuries to workmen, 1920: Minutes of evidence*, ii, 292 (Robertson).

48　Ibid., p. 289. This figure appears to be higher than that reported by the inspectors. Thus Robertson gives the number of accidents in Harland & Wolff in 1908 as 670, whereas the inspectors reported a total for 696 accidents for *both* shipyards: *Chief insp. ann. rep., 1908*, p. 108. As already explained, the inspectors' figure would not have included a large number of non-fatal falls.

49　Robertson (at p. 289) suggests that the annual cost of compensation to Harland & Wolff in the years 1907–1914 averaged 13s. 9½d. per employee per annum, while in the United Kingdom as a whole, the average annual cost per employee in 'engine and shipbuilding' during the years 1908–1914 was 13s. 2d., according to the annual *Statistics of compensation and of proceedings under the Workmen's Compensation Act 1906 and the Employers' Liability Act 1880*. See further below, p. 372.

50　See generally E. Taplin, *The dockers' union* (Leicester, 1985); A. Morgan, *Labour and partition: The Belfast working class 1905–1923* (London, 1991), chap. 5.

Dock labour was essentially casual employment which lent itself to exploitation through the system of hiring in gangs.[51] The ganger (or foreman), acting as a middleman for the shipowner or stevedore, chose the men and paid them on an hourly basis. The foreman was paid by the shipowner or stevedore according to the tonnage of the vessel, and he in turn divided the wages among the men in his gang.[52] In an attempt to secure further employment, the men were usually obliged to provide the foreman with a 'sweetener'. In some cases, the foreman simply kept part of the men's wages for himself; in others, the men were paid in a public house so that they could buy rounds of drink for the foreman.[53] There might even be an 'agreement' between the ganger, who gave the publican custom by paying the wages in his public house, and the publican, who in return extended credit to the men while they were waiting to be paid. This was a problem throughout the ports of the United Kingdom; but it had particular repercussions in Dublin, where many public houses also sold groceries in violation of the truck act.[54] Even Larkin was unable to put an end to the practice in Dublin,[55] and attempts in Belfast led by the Reverend J. B. Wallace were equally unsuccessful.[56]

Although some earlier provision had been made under local legislation,[57] it was not until 1895 that a home secretary (Asquith) could be persuaded to

51 E. Larkin, *James Larkin, Irish labour leader 1876–1947* (London, 1968), p. 19n.
52 The tonnage was fixed on the word of the employer; the ganger had no legal right to see a bill of lading or any other documentary proof. J.P. Nannetti (MP for Dublin, College Green) argued that dockers and coal porters should have tally-men, as did the textile workers: *Hansard 4*, xcv, 643 (11 June 1901). But the matter remained unresolved, and, indeed, Sexton, the general secretary of the National Union of Dock Labourers, suggested that it was a dispute over tonnage which was the immediate occasion of the Belfast dock strike of 1907: *Report of the departmental committee on the checking of piecework wages in dock labour*, p. 2 [Cd. 4380], H.C. 1908, xxxiv, 474.
53 Larkin, *James Larkin*, pp. 10–20. See also *Report of the departmental committee on the checking of piecework wages in dock labour*; both Larkin and James Sexton, general secretary of the National Union of Dock Labourers, sat on this committee.
54 See *Minutes of the Dublin Trades Council*, 30 Aug. 1897 and Larkin, *James Larkin*, pp. 20–21.
55 'More than one drunk docker went head first down the steps of Liberty Hall with Larkin the propelling force ...': Larkin, *James Larkin*, p. 161. In 1911, as secretary of the ITGWU, Larkin led a delegation to see the home secretary (Winston Churchill) 'concerning the engagement and payment of dock labourers in public houses throughout Ireland'; Churchill merely referred the matter to the Irish administration, in the mistaken belief that it was outside home office jurisdiction: Sir Henry Cunynghame (legal ass't undersec., home office) to Sir James Dougherty (undersec., Dublin Castle), 24 March 1911 (PRO, HO 152/28/165656/8).
56 See especially *Brotherhood*, 5 April 1890. We owe this reference to Professor J.W. Boyle. This newspaper was edited by the Revd Wallace, a Congregational minister who lived and worked in Belfast from 1880 to 1890. His efforts to publicise the harmful effects of the payment of wages in public houses led in 1889 to a libel action by Francis and Daniel Burns, stevedores who also owned a public house known as the White Star. Wallace was found liable and ordered to pay damages of £40 and costs.
57 See e.g. the by-law, relating to gangways used in discharging coal-boats, made under the Dublin Port and Harbour Act (Ire.) 1786 (26 Geo. III, c. 19), which was used in an unsuccessful attempt to found a claim for damages for breach of statutory duty in *Norton* v. *Kearon* (1871) IR 6 CL 126.

take general action to deal with the accident problem on the docks.[58] Notwithstanding opposition from politicians of both parties representing the shipping interest,[59] section 23(1) of the Factory and Workshops Act 1895 extended the power to make special provision for 'dangerous' trades, and the requirement to give notice of accidents, to 'every dock, wharf, quay and warehouse, and, so far as relates to the process of loading or unloading therefrom or thereto, all machinery and plant used in that process'. Conscious of the departure from the traditional basis for state intervention, parliament took the odd step of treating docks as if they were factories and dock machinery as if it was used for a manufacturing process. The need to provide an extensive definition of 'occupier' further complicated a provision which, when incorporated into the Workmen's Compensation Act 1897, was to lead to prolific litigation in which some 'very fine distinctions' were drawn by the courts.[60]

The limited nature of section 23(1) meant that although the inspectors could now investigate dock accidents, they had no basis for bringing a prosecution, since the substantive provisions of the factory acts did not apply.[61] But their reports quickly made it clear that dock labour was a very dangerous occupation.[62] Accordingly, Asquith's successor (Sir Matthew Ridley) felt obliged to appoint J.S. Maitland and Sydney Eraut, two inspectors with special experience of docks, to inquire into the causes of dock accidents and the means for preventing them. In the course of this inquiry, the inspectors visited Belfast and all the other important ports of the United

58 *Hansard 4*, xxxi, 176 and 202 (1 March 1895), where the government explained that only a limited application of the acts was necessary, given that no women or young children were employed in the docks.

59 See e.g. *Hansard 4*, xxxv, 149 (3 July 1895), where an amendment to exclude the loading or unloading of ships was moved on the grounds that the bill 'proposed to add another army of inspectors to that of the Board of Trade'. Sir Edward Harland, in support of the amendment, commented that 'it was very probable that many of the ordinary factory or workshop inspectors would lose their lives whilst inspecting ships already passed by the Board of Trade surveyors'. The amendment was withdrawn when the home secretary agreed that 'it was undesirable to bring ships, as ships, within the scope of the factory acts' and accordingly changed the wording of the bill to emphasise the process of loading and unloading: ibid., cols. 151 and 160–61. See also *Chief insp. ann. rep., 1895*, pp. 20–23.

60 *Redgrave's Factory Acts*, ed. J. Owner (14th ed., London, 1931), pp. 130–31. Thus, the act provided no definition of 'dock', 'wharf' or 'machinery' – see e.g. *Hanlon* v. *North City Milling Co.* [1903] 2 IR 163 ('dock' includes a wet dock) and *Fogarty* v. *Wallis & Co.* [1903] 2 IR 522 (shed on wharf temporarily used by Post Office was a 'factory' of which the Post Office was the occupier).

61 Until 1905, enforcement of statutory requirements relating to docks rested with local harbour commissioners and county councils: see e.g. Coyne (ed.), *Ireland: industrial and agricultural*, pp. 258–60.

62 With no little prompting from James Sexton, general secretary of the National Union of Dock Labourers, who drew attention to the large number of dock accidents and implored employers 'to have a little more consideration for the lives and limbs of the men whose precarious employment at the docks compels them to take any and every risk to earn a living': *Chief insp. ann. rep., 1895*, p. 23.

Kingdom. Their report, published in 1899,[63] described the various methods used for loading and discharging vessels and explained that the most common causes of accidents were (i) falls (e.g. into the hold of a ship or into the water, or the fall of goods being hoisted); (ii) machinery in motion (e.g. clothing catching in cog-wheels or winches, the breakage of chains or ropes, overloading of cranes); (iii) shunting accidents from the use of locomotives; (iv) fatigue due to excessive hours of work, and (v) the handling of dangerous materials. In 1898, such activities had led to 89 fatal, and 4,070 non-fatal, accidents in United Kingdom docks. These accidents were largely the result of defective gear, inadequate lighting or improper supervision and were therefore preventible if those concerned took suitable precautions, which were set out in a series of recommendations.

On receipt of the report, Ridley announced that 'the matter cannot be allowed to remain in its present position, and that further and more systematic precautions are necessary to safeguard the persons engaged in this occupation'.[64] The first step was to clarify the scope of the legislation, and this was achieved, to a limited extent only, by section 104 of the Factory and Workshop Act 1901, which extended cover to 'all machinery or plant used in the process of loading or unloading or coaling any ship in any dock, harbour or canal'. But the fact that the inspectors still had power only to report led to criticism by several MPs representing dock labourers.[65] In particular, J.P Nannetti, MP for Dublin (College Green), argued that 'it should be in the power of the inspector, who could only now report, to order the removal of any defective tackle, defective planks or defective gangways ...'.[66]

In 1902, Maitland and Eraut presented a second report,[67] from which it appeared that although 'speaking generally, the occupiers appear to recognise that in the past there has been a want of sufficient precautionary measures', they were only willing to carry out some recommendations 'provided they can do so at small outlay'. A new home secretary (Akers-Douglas) promptly certified 'the processes of loading, unloading, moving and handling goods in, on or at any dock, wharf or quay and the processes of loading, unloading and coaling any ship in any dock, harbour or canal' to be 'dangerous',[68] and in

---

63 *Special report upon the causation and prevention of accidents at docks, wharves and quays,* reproduced in *Chief insp. ann. rep.,* 1899, p. 74.

64 See *Circular letter addressed to occupiers and others,* reproduced in *Chief insp. ann. rep.,* 1902, pt. I, p. 111.

65 'The docker at present had practically no protection under the factory acts.... There was a considerable amount of insufficient, worn-out and dangerous plant and machinery used by the dockers ... and what the docker wanted was ... prevention from danger in the performance of his work': *Hansard 4,* xcv, 142 (11 June 1901)(T.P. O'Connor (Liverpool)).

66 Ibid., col. 642. Asquith, now in opposition, pointed out that the apprehension of the shipowners in 1895 had been shown to be 'quire unfounded', and urged the home secretary to consider 'the expediency of enlarging the dock clause': ibid., col. 632.

67 *Accidents in docks: Further special report by Mr J.S. Maitland and Mr Sydney Eraut, HM inspectors of factories,* reproduced in *Chief insp. ann. rep.,* 1901, pt. I, p. 262.

68 *Chief insp. ann. rep.,* 1902, pt. I, pp. 346–47. The Registrar-General's tables for

September 1902 issued draft regulations based on the Maitland-Eraut recommendations.[69] These regulations provoked a number of objections from both sides of the industry, including the National Union of Dock Labourers, the harbour commissioners in Belfast, Londonderry and Sligo and the Irish Commissioner for Public Works. Accordingly, in June 1904, the home secretary appointed a barrister, Mr Chester Jones, to hold an inquiry into the draft regulations.[70] In the course of this inquiry Jones inspected many docks and quays, including those in Belfast and Dublin; he held a number of hearings (including one in Belfast) at which many of the objectors were legally represented. After eighteen sittings over a period of three months, most of the interested parties asked for an adjournment to allow informal discussions to take place under home office supervision, 'with the result that substantial agreement was secured on many points at issue'.[71] This left only a few matters for Jones to resolve, which he was quickly able to do. The final form of the regulations appeared in October 1904, and for the most part came into force on 1 January 1905.[72]

The twenty-five regulations required (*inter alia*) that all dangerous parts of a dock, wharf or quay and its machinery were to be securely fenced 'as far as is practicable'; 'properly secured and fenced' gangways or other safe means of access to a ship and its hold were to be provided; all staging was to be 'substantially and firmly constructed and adequately supported': hoisting machinery and chains were to be periodically tested and marked with 'safe-load' limits, and life-saving appliances were to be provided, as was 'efficient' lighting at night. The duty to comply with these requirements was variously imposed on (i) the person having the general management and control of the dock; (ii) the owner or officer in charge of a ship; (iii) the owner of machinery or plant used in loading or unloading, or (iv) 'every person who by himself, his agents or workmen, carries on the [relevant] processes ...'. Breach of the regulations was punishable by fine, so that the inspectors were at last given full enforcement powers.

In Ireland, the regulations soon applied to more than two hundred docks, wharves or quays.[73] As recommended by Jones, however, the home secretary

1881–1890 'show that (with the exception of seamen and bargemen) the occupation of dock labourer is more exposed to fatal accidents than any other. The "comparative mortality figure" from accidents, which is 56 for all occupied males, 80 for factory workers, and 141 for miners, rises in the case of dock labourers to 162': 'Circular letter of July 1903', reproduced in *Chief insp. ann. rep., 1903*, pt. 1, p. 188.

69   *Chief insp. ann. rep., 1903*, pt. I, p. 186.

70   See *Report to His Majesty's secretary of state for the home department on the draft regulations relating to docks, wharves and quays* [Cd. 2284], H.C. 1904, lxxii, 515.

71   *Chief insp. ann. rep., 1904*, pt. I, p. 209 (Eraut).

72   Regulations dated October 24, 1904, in respect of the processes of loading, unloading, moving or handling goods in, or at any dock, wharf or quay, and the processes of loading, unloading or coaling any ship in any dock, harbour or canal (1904 No. 1617), reproduced in *Chief insp. ann. rep., 1904*, pt. I, p. 340.

73   *Chief insp. ann. rep., 1905*, p. 426, suggesting that 54 of these were in the north of Ireland district, and 156 in the south.

was given power to exempt from all or any of these regulations 'any docks, wharves or quays in respect of which application for such exemption shall have been made to him by the Department of Agriculture and Technical Instruction for Ireland or by the Congested Districts Board for Ireland'. This provision was intended to apply only to some small wharves and quays, mainly in the west of Ireland, and then only subject to conditions; but it is noticeable that a similar power was not given in respect of any other parts of the United Kingdom. As it was, the inspectors were to find a significant difference between the smaller and larger docks. In particular, county councils in charge of smaller facilities were prone to ignore the regulations or provide the bare minimum.[74] A particular problem arose when Cork County Council refused to implement necessary safety measures at Courtmacsherry Pier on the grounds that they were not the occupiers – and in any event they had no authority to raise the money to pay for the work.[75] A writ of mandamus was obtained to require the council to comply with the regulations: but when they continued in default and the case came before the king's bench division in 1910, the court ruled in their favour.[76]

Inspection of docks and quays was for many inspectors 'the most constant' of their duties: 'Dock inspection is so many sided, and the docks themselves are of such differing and complex characters, as regards their ownership, subownership, purposes and uses that any consolidated report as to observance of the regulations in them as a class is well-nigh impossible.'[77] In 1907, an inspectors' assistant (Burns) was transferred to Belfast specifically to assist with the inspection of docks and vessels,[78] and in 1909, the inspectors paid 913 visits to docks, and 734 visits to ships in the Belfast district.[79] They encountered problems which seldom arose from the inspection of factories and workshops: 'What with stevedores, agents, etc. it has not always been a simple matter in these cases to get hold of the responsible party at the time the offence is being committed.'[80]

In spite of such difficulties, the inspectors in Ireland were reasonably optimistic. In the north, the verdict was that 'the regulations have been fairly well attended to'.[81] In the south, 'upon the whole, the attitude of those concerned is favourable to the regulations and where irregularities still exist, they

74 *Chief insp. ann. rep., 1906*, p. 168 (Neely). Two particular problems were lighting (particularly where there was no gas supply) and the provision of life-saving appliances – see *Chief insp. ann. rep., 1907*, p. 126 (Jackson and Burns) and *1909*, p. 114 (Young).
75 'I have only met with serious difficulty in places controlled by Cork County Council': *Chief insp. ann. rep., 1907*, p. 126 (Jackson).
76 See *R. (Jackson) v. Cork CC* [1911] 2 IR 206 and *Chief insp. ann. rep., 1909*, pp. xx–xxi and 32.
77 *Chief insp. ann. rep., 1906*, pp. 166–67.
78 *Chief insp. ann. rep., 1907*, p. 112.
79 *Chief insp. ann. rep., 1909*, p. 114.
80 *Chief insp. ann. rep., 1906*, p. 168 (Brothers).
81 *Chief insp. ann. rep., 1905*, p. 204 (Snape).

are due either to want of knowledge of the regulations or to some difficulty to which a solution has not been found, rather than to a wish to evade them'.[82] It appears, too, that 'remarkably few accidents' were due to any breaches which did occur.[83] But these hopeful assessments were undermined by more specific reports. All the inspectors in Ireland reported a dearth of properly fenced gangways;[84] defective ladders aboard ship were common, particularly on small cargo boats and coal-carrying ships;[85] hatch covers were customarily used for staging;[86] inadequate chain-testing facilities led to some dubious practices,[87] and dockside cranes were frequently overloaded.[88] The inspectors' overall optimism is also difficult to reconcile with the cost of workmen's compensation; not only was the cost per docker significantly higher than the cost per shipyard worker, but it consistently rose in the years leading up to the great war.[89]

STEAM BOILER OPERATIVES

The development of steam as a means of driving machinery meant that by 1870 some 100,000 steam boilers were in use throughout the United Kingdom,[90] and, although concentrated in industrial areas, they could be found in all parts of Ireland.[91] From time to time a steam boiler would explode, sometimes with

82 Ibid., p. 205 (Jackson).
83 *Chief insp. ann. rep., 1911*, p. 121 (Graves, superintending inspector for Northern Division).
84 Ibid.
85 See e.g. *Chief insp. ann. rep., 1907*, pp. 126–27 (Burns and Jackson) and *1909*, p. 114 (Burns). The invention of a special ship's ladder by an Irish engineering firm, and the adoption of non-slip shoes and supports for ladders promised some improvements: *Chief insp. ann. rep., 1911*, pp. 31 and 121.
86 See e.g. *Chief insp. ann. rep., 1905*, p. 204 (Snape) and *1908*, p. 25 (Allhusen). For the prosecution of a stevedore in Londonderry, where this practice was 'persistent', see *Chief insp. ann. rep., 1910*, p. 103. See also *Eraut* v. *McCaughey*, *Northern Whig*, 1 Aug. 1911.
87 See e.g. *Chief insp. ann. rep., 1906*, p. 169 (Warren), *1907*, p. 127 (Jackson) and *1909*, p. 114 (Burns).
88 See e.g. *Chief insp. ann. rep., 1911*, p. 121 (Burns) and *Burns* v. *Symington*, *Northern Whig*, 27 Jan. 1911. In 1908, cranes and lifting tackle caused twenty of the 85 accidents in docks in the north of Ireland: *Chief insp. ann. rep., 1908*, p. 107. See also *M'Cartan* v. *Belfast Harbour Commissioners* [1911] 2 IR 143, where a craneman was held liable in damages for negligently lowering a bucket into a ship, seriously injuring a seaman engaged in unloading the ship; an attempt by the defendants to rely on the defence of common employment was rejected by the house of lords.
89 During the years 1909–1914, the average annual cost of workmen's compensation per docker was £1 1s. 7d., as compared to 13s. 4d. for shipyard workers: figures derived from the annual *Statistics of compensation and of proceedings under the Workmen's Compensation Act 1906*.
90 *Report from the select committee appointed to inquire into the cause of steam boiler explosions, and as to the best means of preventing them*, p. 1, H.C. 1871 (298), xii, 267. This estimate was exclusive of boilers in railway engines and steam-ships and those in domestic use.
91 Most were apparently made in Great Britain. According to Coe, *Engineering industry*,

devastating effect to life and limb; during the period 1865–75, for example, an average of 61 explosions occurred annually in the United Kingdom, causing on average 68 deaths and many injuries.[92] Although many of these explosions occurred in factories and workshops, it was not until 1901 that the inspectorate came to have a formal role in the regulation of boiler use, and the reasons for this delay cast an interesting light on the development of state inspection during the later part of the nineteenth century.

Prior to 1882, there was no provision for *state* regulation of any kind.[93] In theory, a boiler manufacturer or factory owner could be liable at common law for an injury or death caused by an explosion. But as a series of Irish cases confirmed, a claim for damages usually encountered considerable, if not insurmountable, difficulties. In *Murphy v. Pollock*[94] the plaintiff's son, who was employed in the defendants' rope factory to operate a steam-engine, was killed when the boiler exploded. The essence of the claim was that the defendants' foreman had negligently failed to take appropriate precautions when advised that there was an unusual amount of steam in the boiler; but to avoid the defence of common employment, the plaintiff alleged that the defendants had knowingly employed an incompetent foreman.[95] This was denied by the defendants, who also contended (*inter alia*) that the steam-engine had at all relevant times been under the sole and exclusive control of the deceased. The jury at Cork city assizes awarded damages of £30, but on appeal it was held that judgment should have been entered for the defendants on the grounds that there was no evidence to show that the defendants knew that their foreman was incompetent.[96]

In *Barnett v. Lucas*,[97] the defendant was the manufacturer of a boiler which exploded, killing the owner of a flax mill and one of his employees.

p. 41 there were a number of steam-engine makers in the Belfast area by the 1850s, but most of these had gone out of business by 1905, 'leaving the Falls Foundry as the only maker of large steam engines in the north of Ireland, apart from the marine engineering firms'.

92 Separate figures are not given for Ireland, but in one two-year period (1875–76) there were two fatal accidents, one in Co. Armagh (1 person killed), the other in a scutch mill in Co. Down (8 persons killed): *Return of all fatal accidents from boiler explosions in the United Kingdom in the years 1875 and 1876 ...* , p. 4, H.C. 1877 (361), lxviii, 376. This tally of two fatal accidents causing nine deaths may be compared with five accidents and twelve deaths in Scotland and 42 accidents and 131 deaths in England and Wales.

93 Deaths caused by boiler explosions were, of course, subject to a coroner's inquest; but such inquests were generally considered to be inadequate: 'The chief object of the witnesses seems to be to conceal as much as possible all important facts, and screen the culpable – no difficult matter where, as in most cases, both coroner and jury are totally ignorant of everything relating to boilers, or their working': W.H. Chaloner, *Vulcan: The history of one hundred years of engineering and insurance, 1859–1959* (Manchester, 1959), p. 24.

94 (1864) 15 ICLR 224.

95 See further below, p. 344.

96 (1864) 15 ICLR 224, at p. 238. The court of exchequer was equally divided on this point, but the court of exchequer chamber unanimously held in favour of the defendants.

97 (1872) IR 6 CL 247.

The boiler was shown to be defective and, since the manufacturer had sold it directly to the millowner, he was liable for breach of contract – or even in tort – to the owner's family.[98] The jury awarded them damages of £500 in respect of the death; the widow, as administratrix, was also entitled to damages, assessed at £161, for damage to the mill. But in *Corry v. Lucas*,[99] a claim by the widow of the deceased employee was rejected. Any warranty of quality or fitness for purpose extended only to a party to the contract; the 'privity of contract' policy established by cases such as *Langridge v. Levy*[100] and *Winterbottom v. Wright*[101] meant that the second widow was entitled to damages only if she could show that the defendant had knowingly made a false representation concerning the boiler which he knew, at the time of making the representation, would be communicated to the injured party.[102]

It seems likely, therefore, that few workers or their dependants recovered damages for injury or death caused by boiler explosions. But another form of private regulation developed with the growth of voluntary steam-users' associations[103] and of boiler insurance.[104] As a measure of 'public safety' and in the interests of their members, the users' associations and the insurers conducted, or at least encouraged, periodical inspections of boilers by competent engineers.[105] By 1870, however, the limited nature of voluntary inspection had generated sufficient public support[106] for more effective regulation to bring about the appointment of a select committee to enquire

98   Ibid., pp. 249–50, per Fitzgerald J.
99   (1868) IR 3 CL 208.
100 (1837) 2 M & W 519, 150 Eng Rep 863.
101 (1842) 10 M & W 109, 152 Eng Rep 402, as explained by P.S. Atiyah, *The rise and fall of freedom of contract* (Oxford, 1979), pp. 498–99.
102 Cf. *Thompson v. Belfast Harbour Commissioners* (1889) 23 ILTR 48, where the court held that an employer was bound to see that machinery does not cease to be fit for its purpose, and is under an obligation to test it from time to time and, if necessary, repair it; in default of such testing, he may be liable to an employee injured in consequence of a defective condition brought about by reasonable wear.
103 In particular, the Manchester Steam Users' Association which, in spite of its name, operated throughout the United Kingdom; by 1870, it was sending inspectors all over the country, including Cork and Bantry Bay: *Select committee appointed to inquire into the cause of steam boiler explosions: Minutes of evidence*, p. 27, H.C. 1870 (370), x, 493.
104 Several companies were formed in the late 1850s. The best known was the company which became the Vulcan Boiler and General Insurance Co.; by 1860, this company had an agent in Belfast, and a resident inspector for the north of Ireland was appointed in 1864: Chaloner, *Vulcan*, pp. 11–12. By 1884, the Boiler Insurance and Steam Power Co. Ltd. of Manchester also had a resident inspector in Belfast – see *First report on the working of the Boiler Explosions Act 1882*, p. 60 [C. 3903], H.C. 1884, xvii, 446.
105 Cf. 'The natural working of such companies is to make money at the least possible cost, and to enlarge their dividends at the cost of a comparatively limited number of inspectors': *Select committee on steam boiler explosions, 1870: Minutes of evidence*, p. 2 (Sir William Fairbairn, chairman of the Manchester Steam Users' Association, contending that the leading insurance company employed only ten men to inspect some 10,000 boilers, as compared to the seven inspectors employed by the association to examine 2,000 boilers).
106 In the form of a private member's bill (H.C. 1868–69 (64), v, 223) which provided for the registration, periodical inspection and testing of steam boilers by Board of

into the causes of steam boiler explosions and the best means of preventing them.[107]

The committee agreed that there was a considerable risk of death or serious injury. Many of the boilers were 'situated in much frequented parts of towns and cities, under pavements in crowded thoroughfares ... and in the midst of crowded dwellings', and the boilers were often 'faulty in construction, are frequently so placed that inspection without removal is impossible, ... have exposed safety valves, whereby the pressure can be increased to a dangerous extent by anyone having access to the boiler, and are too often worked by men who are ignorant of almost everything connected with a steam boiler beyond the mere act of keeping up a fire'. Any one of these defects could lead to an explosion.[108]

The problem was whether inspection should be compulsory (as already in the case of passenger steamships[109]) or remain voluntary. While accepting that voluntary inspection had a limited effect,[110] the committee were not prepared to recommend the adoption of any system 'founded upon the theory of compulsory periodical inspection'. Most explosions arose from causes 'independent of ... anything that could be prevented by periodical inspection'; more importantly, compulsory inspection would tend to 'lessen the responsibility of the users, who are best able to ascertain the condition of their boilers, and the competency of the men employed to work them'. A better remedy was to be found in the 'pecuniary consequences' principle, which could be achieved by making it easier for an injured worker, or the dependants of a deceased worker, to sue the employer for damages.[111] The position could also be more effectively monitored if a coroner, assisted by a Board of Trade boiler surveyor, was obliged to inquire into all explosions (whether or not anyone was killed) and report the results of his investigation to the home secretary for presentation to parliament.

In July 1871, these recommendations were embodied in a bill which declared that 'every steam-user shall be deemed responsible for the efficiency

Trade officials. The bill was withdrawn after a first reading, but reintroduced in 1870 (H.C. 1870 (58), iv, 547) and 1871 (H.C. 1871 (56), vi, 199).

107 The committee was appointed in May 1870, and included Sir Thomas McClure (Liberal MP for Belfast).

108 *Report from the select committee on steam boiler explosions*, p. iii, H.C. 1871 (298), xii, 269.

109 Under the Merchant Shipping Acts 1854 and 1862 every boiler on a passenger steamship had to be examined and certified by a Board of Trade engineer before the vessel put to sea, and subsequently from time to time.

110 It seems that something like one-fifth of all boilers were 'independently' inspected by users' associations or insurers: *Select committee on steam boiler explosions, 1870: Minutes of evidence*, p. 35 (C. Thompson, chairman, National Boiler Ins. Co.).

111 *Report*, p. iv. Boiler insurance was also opposed on much the same ground; by relieving the user of the liability to pay compensation, 'the insurance principle does not tend to the prevention, but directly to the promotion, of steam boiler explosions': *Minutes of evidence*, p. 28 (L.E. Fletcher, chief engineer, Manchester Steam Users' Ass'n). For an earlier (and equally unsuccessful) attempt to apply the 'pecuniary consequences' principle to textile factories, see above, p. 123.

of all boilers employed by him ... and for the employment of competent persons to work such boilers'.[112] If a boiler exploded, killing or injuring a worker, 'the burden of proof of the efficiency of such steam boiler ... shall be on such steam-user; and in order to raise a prima facie case of negligence it shall be sufficient that the person injured ... shall show that such steam boiler was at the time the explosion occurred under the management, care, control or custody of such steam-user or his servant, or other person employed by such steam-user'. The user could escape liability by proving that the explosion arose from some cause beyond his power or control, and that it did not arise from want of reasonable care or forethought by himself or his servants; in the latter case, the defence of common employment was to be excluded.

As might be expected, such a radical proposal received little support and the bill was withdrawn.[113] But for the next forty years or so, and on an almost annual basis, there was continuing parliamentary agitation for some degree of *state* regulation. At its highest, this took the form of proposals for compulsory registration and inspection of all steam boilers.[114] But successive governments, while prepared to concede that factory inspection had been successful, generally refused to accept that there was a case for state intervention with regard to boilers.[115] Matters came to a head in 1900, when no fewer than three private members' bills were introduced[116] and the issue was once again referred to a select committee.[117] This committee found that although boilers were now, in general, better designed, better made and better managed, explosions still occurred, more frequently in boilers which had not been inspected. But they again disagreed with the almost unanimous opinion of their witnesses that compulsory periodical inspection by government inspectors was highly desirable. It was still the case that 'inspection, however efficient, could not prevent such explosions'. And it would be 'a grave mistake' to give a government department control over the inspection of boilers. It was still 'of the greatest importance' that the boiler owner should be directly responsible for the condition and safety of the boiler; the appointment of government inspectors would mean that the owner would 'shelter himself behind the inspector'. In

112   H.C. 1871 (273), vi, 201.
113   The debates on the bill were not reported. It was reintroduced the following year (see H.C. 1872 (80), v, 603), but suffered a similar fate.
114   See e.g. Compulsory examination of steam boilers bill, H.C. 1889 (126), viii, 129 (boilers to be registered with government department and inspected periodically by person appointed by boiler user); Boilers (registration and inspection) bill, H.C. 1898 (86), i, 207 (all boilers to be registered with Board of Trade, and to be examined by duly qualified inspector).
115   The issues are rehearsed in *Memoranda on the registry and inspection of land boilers prepared for the consideration of the right honourable the president of the Board of Trade* [C. 5375], H.C. 1888, lxxx, 519.
116   See H.C.1900 (1), i, 147; (88), i, 155, and (107), i, 171.
117   *Report from the select committee appointed to inquire into and report on the advisability of legislation to insure the systematic and regular inspection of boilers, with the object of diminishing the risk to life and property arising from boiler explosions*, H.C. 1900 (294), vi, 285.

addition, 'inspectors under a government department would work upon inelastic lines' – a practice which would undoubtedly 'hamper the development of boiler improvement'.[118] The fact that all these arguments had long been disproved and rejected in relation to factories and workshops seems to have been simply ignored.

An alternative strategy was the regulation of boiler operatives.[119] As early as 1879, Thomas Burt (Liberal MP for Morpeth and one of the first trade unionists to be elected to the house of commons) moved 'that in the opinion of this house it is desirable that enginemen should undergo an examination as to their fitness before they are placed in charge of engines and boilers ...'.[120] This apparently common-sense motion ran into trouble once it was realised that it was motivated only in part by a desire for greater safety: 'the men actually in charge of engines and boilers wished in addition to restrict their numbers by seeing to it that no one was allowed to work at the trade without obtaining from the government a certificate of competence'.[121] The government therefore demurred; most of those in charge of boilers were not incompetent, most explosions were caused by defective construction or overuse rather than by faulty supervision, and in any case the need for a certificate of competence would cause considerable inconvenience to – and have 'unforeseen consequences' for – the Board of Trade.[122] Nevertheless, the Trades Union Congress in 1881 resolved that 'no person should be allowed to take charge either of a steam engine or boiler until he has been examined by a properly constituted Board of Examiners and obtained a certificate of competency ...',[123] and their campaign in favour of legislation along these lines was to continue into the twentieth century.[124]

From 1894 onwards, the 'certification' principle attracted the continuing support of the Irish Trades Union Congress.[125] But it also provoked the

---

118 Ibid., p. iii.
119 Another approach derived from the Merchant Shipping Acts 1854 and 1862, which provided that all steamships must carry at least one (and in some cases at least two) certificated engineers.
120 *Hansard 3*, ccxlv, 1404–26 (29 April 1879).
121 Chaloner, *Vulcan*, p. 28.
122 *Hansard 3*, cclxvii, 561–70 (9 March 1882).
123 See *Board of Trade memoranda on the registry and inspection of land boilers, 1888*, p. 18, where it is also pointed out (at pp. 10–11) that 'legislation on the subject has been consistently urged for years by the public press ... and again and again coroner's jurors have called attention to the necessity for action'.
124 Steam engines and boilers (certificates) bills were introduced at regular intervals in the period 1890–1910 – see e.g. H.C. 1890 (98), ix, 23; H.C. 1895 (7–sess.I), vi, 283; H.C. 1901 (18), iv, 249; H.C. 1905 (26), v, 149, and H.C. 1910 (106), i, 631.
125 See e.g. *Report of the third Irish Trades Congress* (Limerick, 1896), p. 37, referring to the 'urgent necessity' for legislation since 'much personal injury and loss of life and property occur through the incompetency of the attendants'. A motion in favour of legislation was passed on an annual basis – see *Select committee to whom the steam engines and boilers (persons in charge) bill was referred: Minutes of evidence*, p. 107, H.C. 1901 (278), viii, 123 (evidence of Effingham Richardson, secretary to ITUC Parliamentary Committee). The campaign continued after 1901 – see e.g. *Report of*

opposition of some influential Irish industrialists. In 1895, for example, Sir Edward Harland (then MP for Belfast North) attacked a certification bill as likely to have 'the effect of seriously injuring the industries of this country'; if boilers could only be used by certificated engineers, 'a tremendous tax would be put upon industry'. In any case, the certificate would be practically useless, in that it would only 'require that something should be driven into the heads of such men merely for the purpose of passing an examination to be all forgotten in a month' – and it would serve to discourage 'youths who, starting with a donkey engine, rose gradually by steps until they ultimately became thoroughly well-trained engine drivers'.[126] Two years later, Mr Gustav Wolff (then MP for Belfast East) argued that the promoters of a similar bill had adduced no evidence that a certificate requirement would diminish the number of explosions: 'All those things happened, if not through defects of construction, [then] through the negligence of the men, and the fact of a man having passed an examination would not make any difference'. Such legislation 'was not wanted, would very much interfere with trade, and the sooner it was given up the better'.[127]

Any prospect of legislation was dashed in 1901 when a select committee[128] concluded that the number of accidents 'arising from ignorance on the part of the persons in charge [of boilers]' was small,[129] a fact corroborated by evidence which indicated that 'great care appears to be taken in the selection of capable, trustworthy and qualified persons to take charge of engines and boilers'. As a matter of principle, 'absolute responsibility' should in any event continue to be placed on the boiler owner. From a more practical perspective, there was the problem of conducting a proper examination of a large number of men[130] – and the fact that a certificate system 'would unduly restrict the opportunities of selection, especially in outlying localities'.[131]

the *Twelfth Irish Trades Union Congress* (Wexford, 1905), p. 49 and *Nineteenth report* (Clonmel, 1912), p. 62.

126 *Hansard 4*, xxxii, 841–43 (3 April 1895).

127 *Hansard 4*, xlvi, 630–31 (17 Feb.1897) – remarks which were accompanied by 'Cheers'.

128 *Report from the select committee to whom the steam engines and boilers (persons in charge) bill was referred*, pp. iv–v, H.C. 1901 (278), viii, 4–5.

129 Between 1890 and 1895, for example, just under one-third of the boiler explosions investigated under the 1882 act were attributed to such a cause, and this figure fell to less than one-sixth in the period 1896–1900.

130 '[S]uch examination, if it were to be any real test of efficiency, would need to include practical demonstration before experienced examiners, and certificates when granted would require to show the special class of engines or boilers which the holder of the certificate was qualified to work.... Moreover, the ... examination ... would be limited to technical qualifications. The certificate of efficiency in the more essential matters of steadiness, nerve and sobriety, could only be based on second-hand evidence derived from the persons by whom the candidate for the certificate had been employed ...': *Report from the select committee on the steam engines ... bill, 1901*, pp. iv–v.

131 The Dublin Port and Docks Board, for example, stated that if only certificated men could be legally employed, 'great embarrassment would frequently result when vacancies from ill-health or other causes occurred, and no spare certificated man was

These arguments defeated all further attempts to introduce a statutory qualification for boiler operators.[132]

So it was that a Board of Trade official could write in 1888 that 'a steam user can submit his boiler to any inspection he chooses, or to none. He can entrust its management to any person he likes, however ignorant such person may be of boilers and their management. A very large number of boilers are never inspected at all [and] some are worked by men who have no knowledge of their business, and this being so, it can scarcely be wondered at that explosions happen and lives are lost ...'.[133] The rejection of general deterrence based on extended tort liability and of state regulation by way of inspection or certification left the way open for more in the way of voluntary action. In 1881, the Manchester Steam-Users' Association, through its president, Hugh Mason (MP for Ashton-under-Lyme), had introduced a bill designed to encourage more boiler users to enrol in voluntary associations and to ensure a more systematic investigation when an explosion occurred.[134] The government gave their support to this modest proposal,[135] which ultimately became the Boiler Explosions Act 1882.[136]

When a boiler exploded, the owner or user was now to notify the Board of Trade within twenty-four hours; the board, 'if it thinks fit' (as it invariably did), could then order a preliminary enquiry by a competent and independent engineer. The report of the preliminary inquiry was sent to the owner – and to other interested parties such as newspapers, insurance companies and guarantee societies. However, if the preliminary inquiry made it appear 'expedient', there was then to be a formal investigation by a 'court' of not less than two commissioners.[137] The court was to make a 'full and clear' report of the circumstances and causes of the explosion, 'adding thereto any observations ... on any matters arising out of the investigation which they think right to make ...'. This report was likewise published and widely disseminated. But the court was not given any power to fine a blameworthy owner or user, although it could order the costs and expenses of an inquiry to be paid by any person summoned to give evidence.[138]

---

available': *Select committee on the steam engines ... bill, 1901: Minutes of evidence*, p. 213.

132 See e.g. Steam engines and boilers (persons in charge) bill, H.C. 1909 (116), ii, 239 (rejected at second reading).

133 *Board of Trade memoranda on the registry and inspection of land boilers, 1888*, p. 11.

134 See H.C. 1881 (39), i, 379.

135 'Not a very strong or radical measure', according to Chamberlain: *Hansard 3*, cclxvi, 1352 (23 Feb.1882).

136 45 & 46 Vict., c. 22. The act was administered by the marine department of the Board of Trade.

137 To include a 'competent' lawyer and a 'competent and practical engineer specially conversant with the manufacture and working of steam boilers'. No formal inquiries were held until 1888, when it became the practice to order a formal investigation in any case where a preliminary inquiry pointed to serious neglect or mismanagement on the part of any person, or when the loss of life appeared to call for a fuller and more through inquiry: *Select committee on the systematic and regular inspection of boilers, 1900: Minutes of evidence*, pp. 1–2.

138 'The object [of the 1882 act] is enquiry, and not punishment': *Board of Trade*

From 1884 the Board of Trade published an annual report on the working of the act. During the 1880s, some 54 boiler explosions per annum caused, on average, 29 deaths and 61 injuries in the United Kingdom; less than five per cent of these explosions – and resulting casualties – occurred in Ireland.[139] During the 1890s, the number of explosions increased (to an average of 80 per annum in the United Kingdom), but the casualty rate remained much the same. By 1900, 517 persons had been killed, and 1,078 injured, in explosions investigated under the 1882 act.[140] This steady toll of death and injury may have failed to overcome the arguments against direct regulation by the state; but it was sufficient to lead a select committee in 1900 to recommend an *indirect* method of increasing the incidence and effectiveness of inspection.

The committee accepted that explosions occurred more frequently in boilers which had not been inspected by a competent person, and that inspection 'would tend to diminish the risk of explosion'. Although the need to maintain the individual responsibility of the boiler owner for the condition and safety of the boiler ruled out a system of *compulsory* inspection by a government department, a boiler owner or user could still be required to produce, to a government official, written evidence that the boiler had been recently inspected by a competent person. In the case of boilers in factories and workshops, that official could be a factory inspector; in other cases, the authority should be vested in the police.

When the first part of this recommendation was included in the Factory and Workshop Bill 1901, an issue arose as to the required frequency of inspections. Attempts to require an inspection to have been undertaken within the past three months were opposed by many owners and users, who considered twelve or fifteen months to be more appropriate.[141] There was also the question of the competency of the person who inspected the boiler:

---

memoranda on the registry and inspection of land boilers, 1888, p. 9. Cf. the select committee considered that a court set up under the 1882 act should be empowered to inflict a heavy penalty on (i) the user of a boiler who had failed to have it properly inspected or failed to work it in accordance with the inspector's recommendations, and (ii) an inspector who had carelessly or insufficiently carried out an inspection: *Report of the select committee on the systematic and regular inspection of boilers, 1900*, p. iv. This recommendation was not implemented.

139 The first preliminary inquiry in Ireland arose from the explosion of the boiler of a steam crane at Wicklow Harbour in Sept. 1882, when two workers were killed: *First report on the working of the Boiler Explosions Act 1882*, pp. 21–22 [C. 3903], H.C. 1884, xvii, 353–54. The most serious incident was the explosion of a wrought-iron kier at a paper mill in Ballyclare, in which three persons were killed and four injured: *Seventh report on the working of the Boiler Explosions Act 1882*, p. 6 [C. 5855], H.C. 1889, xviii, 124.

140 *Select committee on the systematic and regular inspection of boilers, 1900: Minutes of evidence*, p. 2.

141 See e.g. the letter of protest from the Dublin Chamber of Commerce: M. Goodbody (honorary secretary) to Sir Matthew Ridley (home secretary), 15 May 1900 (PRO HO 45/9950, B31418E). Mr Stromeyer, Chief Engineer of the Manchester Steam Users' Association, also objected to a three-month inspection period – ibid.

'I think that as in other professions the certificates of competency should be given by the body representing the profession, not by a secretary of state. The Institute of Civil Engineers and the Institute of Mechanical Engineers should grant certificates of competency in the same way as the General Medical Council that examines and registers qualified medical practitioners.'[142] In the event, section 11(1) of the Factory and Workshops Act 1901 provided that every steam boiler used for generating steam[143] must be examined thoroughly by a competent person (who might be an inspector for a boiler insurance company or users' association) at least once in every *fourteen* months. A report of the examination must, within fourteen days, be entered into the factory register, where it could be checked by the factory inspector. In addition, every steam boiler used for generating steam must have attached to it a proper safety valve and safety gauges, all of which were to be maintained 'in proper condition'. The factory inspector could then use his general power under section 17(1) of the 1901 act to complain to a court of summary jurisdiction that a steam boiler was in such a condition that it could not be used without danger to life or limb, and the court, if satisfied, could prohibit its use – or, if satisfied that it was capable of repair or alteration, prohibit its use until it was duly repaired or altered.

The government's view was that these provisions would deal with the cause of most boiler explosions without infringing 'the very best principle' of placing primary responsibility upon the employer.[144] And it does appear to be the case that there was, after 1901, a small reduction in the overall number and severity of boiler explosions in the United Kingdom.[145] Just how much part the 1901 act played in this improvement is impossible to say; but it would seem that in Ireland, as elsewhere in the United Kingdom, most of the explosions which occurred after 1901 continued to arise from boilers which had neither been inspected nor insured.[146] Although the number of explosions in Irish factories and workshops appears to have been small,[147] the prosecution figures for

142 Sir Edward Troup (under-sec., home office) to Sir Matthew Ridley (home secretary), 4 April 1900 (PRO HO 45/9950, B31418E/4).
143 It was later pointed out that the definition of 'boiler' in the Boiler Explosions Act included vessels in which steam was not generated, such as kiers, ovens, boiling pans, etc., and it was suggested that the 1901 act should be extended 'to all vessels into which steam is liable to be introduced under such pressure as might render them dangerous': *Report of the departmental committee on accidents, 1911*, p. 58.
144 See e.g. *Hansard 4*, xciii, 374–79 (1 May 1901).
145 See *Report to the secretary of the board of trade upon the working of the Boiler Explosions Acts 1882 and 1890 for 1913–1914*, p. 17 [Cd. 7797], H.C. 1914–16, xxi, 129. Separate figures are not given for Ireland.
146 The worst year in Ireland appears to be 1909, when there were five explosions, all in the north; fortunately only four persons were injured: *Annual report to the secretary of the board of trade upon the working of the Boiler Explosions Acts 1882 and 1890 for 1909–10*, pp. 3–5 [Cd. 5730], H.C. 1911, xxii, 143–45.
147 It appears that between 1901 and 1914, there were some 33 reported explosions, which resulted in 14 deaths and 33 injuries; not all these explosions occurred in premises which came within the factory acts.

1906–08 suggest that there were a disproportionate number of section 11 offences in Ireland.[148]

The factory inspectors in Ireland seem to have exercised their new powers with some enthusiasm, but to little effect. In the south, Bellhouse found that ninety per cent of the boilers were insured and regularly examined by insurance company inspectors. Some uncertainty as to who was 'competent' to undertake an inspection for the purposes of section 11 had 'caused ... considerable increase in the number of boilers that are insured, a result which is, in my opinion, desirable from every point of view'.[149] But *not* one which guaranteed an effective inspection:

At a recent prosecution, the question was raised by the defendant as to what was a thorough examination. He produced a report from an insurance company, which, as the boiler was not properly prepared, gave no permissible working pressure, and he contended that a thorough examination had been made. The magistrates accepted this as such. It would appear reasonable to hold that no examination was a 'thorough' one which did not enable the person making it to certify the pressure at which the boiler could be safely worked during the following fourteen months.[150]

Boilers had to be cooled and emptied prior to inspection, and this could cause difficulties if the owner was given insufficient notice: 'if the boiler inspector arrives and finds steam up he is unable to find any alternative work in the neighbourhood and so has to pass on to his next place of call'.[151] In the case of boilers which were not insured, the inspections were frequently undertaken by persons describing themselves as 'fitters'; while many of them were 'competent', 'many I am sure are not'.[152] Accordingly there remained a large number of boilers which had received 'scant attention',[153] and Bellhouse thought it remarkable that they had not given rise to more explosions, 'left as they frequently are ... in the hands of men who have no pretence to any knowledge of boilers at all, and even in some cases in the charge of quite young boys'.[154]

In the north, the 1901 act was 'fairly well observed' in the towns, but not in the outlying districts.[155] Although encouraged to insure, 'as it is a most

---

148 In 1906–08, for example, 92 of the 162 prosecutions were brought in Ireland – see *Chief insp. ann. rep., 1906*, p. 174, *1907*, p. 134 and *1908*, p. 118.

149 *Chief insp. ann. rep., 1903*, pt. I, p. 142.

150 *Chief insp. ann. rep., 1905*, p. 198.

151 *Chief insp. ann. rep., 1906*, p.163.

152 *Chief insp. ann. rep., 1904*, pt. I, p. 191 and *1906*, p. 163 ('it was obvious from the state of the boiler either that [the fitters] had made no examination or knew nothing about boilers').

153 See e.g. *Chief insp. ann. rep., 1902*, pt. I, p. 133 (boiler with defective pressure gauge and safety valve adjusted by a thumb screw; the owner 'expressed surprise to be told that it was dangerous') and *1903*, pt. I, p. 142 (two boilers with wedges designed to keep down the safety-valve levers).

154 *Chief insp. ann. rep., 1902*, pt. I, p. 133.

155 *Chief insp. ann. rep., 1903*, pt. I, p. 142 (Snape).

difficult matter in out of the way places to find a person sufficiently expert to carry out the requirements of the act', there remained 'a slight prejudice' against insurance, 'whether it is the expense or that the small occupiers do not consider it necessary'.[156] As ever, there was a particular problem with boilers in scutch mills, which were 'specially liable to neglect' and seldom insured.[157] 'Numerous' cases could be cited 'of country mills in Ireland where ... some of the boilers seem to be kept in use, not because they will still hold water and get up steam, but because *they do not leak too fast*. Many of those which do receive any care are entirely dependent on the ministrations of the local smith.'[158] But as in the south, 'where thorough examinations are purported to have been made, instances have been discovered where the apparently satisfactory report is based upon an entirely insufficient examination'.[159]

The inspectors might have been more effective had they been more enthusiastically supported by the courts. As in many other instances, the inspectors appear to have been able to secure convictions, only to be dismayed by the imposition of fines which they considered wholly inadequate. In 1908, for example, the Currahoe Cooperative and Dairy Society (a creamery) was fined 10*s*. for failure to have its boiler inspected,[160] while in the Belfast district, 'where there seems great difficulty in getting steam users to take any precaution at all', fifteen prosecutions resulted in an average fine of 17*s*. 4*d*., which Eraut considered 'not a sufficient deterrent'.[161] In the following year, an occupier was fined 2*s*. 6*d*. for working a boiler which was later 'totally condemned', and in another case a boiler tube exploded and injured an employee shortly after the occupier had been convicted and fined one penny for neglecting to have the boiler examined within the statutory period.[162] In such a case, however, the power to order a party to pay all or some of the costs of a formal investigation under the 1882 act could result in a much heavier penalty. In 1903, for example, the uninsured boiler of a steam press in a hosiery factory in Newtownards exploded, killing one person and injuring two others; the formal investigation blamed one of the owners, his manager and a mechanical engineer who advised them, and ordered them to

156 *Chief insp. ann. rep., 1905*, p. 197, where Snape adds that many occupiers 'seem to have the idea that any wheelwright or ordinary smith is a competent person to undertake the thorough examination required by the statute'.
157 *Chief insp. ann. rep., 1906*, p. 163 (Brothers). Four of the six prosecutions under section 11 of the 1901 act brought in his district in 1906 involved boilers in scutch mills.
158 *Chief insp. ann. rep., 1908*, pp. 112–13. One boiler working at 50 pounds psi had never been examined 'within the memory of anyone on the place'; another working at 76 pounds psi had last been examined at the time of purchase when an insurance company declared it unsuitable for any pressure higher than 36 pounds psi and recommended that it was not purchased: 'It was bought nevertheless.'
159 *Chief insp. ann. rep., 1906*, p. 163.
160 *Impartial Reporter and Farmers' Journal, 24 Sept. 1908*, p. 6 and 1 Oct. 1908, p. 6.
161 *Chief insp. ann. rep., 1908*, p. 112.
162 *Chief insp. ann. rep., 1909*, p. 112.

pay £45 towards the costs of the investigation.[163] This power even extended to 'fining' insurance companies in cases where their inspection of the boiler had been inadequate.[164] But it is difficult not to conclude that a proper system of inspection in the first place would have been much more successful in reducing the incidence of death and injury.

163 The steam press had been bought second-hand in 1900; it had not been properly examined at that time, and no measures had since been taken to ascertain the pressure at which it could safely be worked. Neither the owner nor his manager had any special knowledge of machinery, and instead of employing a skilled engineer, they relied on the advice of a local mechanic, who was consulted as occasion required: *Report upon the working of the Boiler Explosions Acts … for 1903–04*, pp. 7 and 17 [Cd. 2513], H.C. 1905, ix, 897 and 907. For an English case in which the owners were ordered to pay costs of £150, see *Report … for 1900–01*, p. 15 [Cd. 733], H.C. 1901, ix, 583.
164 In the English case mentioned in the previous footnote, for example, the boiler insurers were ordered to pay costs of £50 as a result of the 'neglect' of their inspector.

CHAPTER NINE

Miscellaneous small trades and industries

Earlier chapters have largely been devoted to working conditions in the manufacturing industries which formed the major components of the Irish economy before 1914 and which were concentrated in the north of Ireland. But it was the many smaller trades and industries which brought the factories acts to the island as a whole. In this chapter we examine just a few of these smaller establishments with a view to illustrating the wide variety of other problems encountered by the factory inspectors in Ireland. Given the predominance of agriculture, many of these smaller industrial establishments were in some way connected with food or drink; but many other 'small' trades and industries collectively employed a considerable proportion of the industrial workforce.[1]

BAKEHOUSES

The importance of bread as part of the staple diet brought it under legal control from the thirteenth century, when the assize of bread first sought to regulate its price and quality. This regulation did not always result in good bread at the right price[2] – and it also created something of a monopoly. In 1815 it was suggested that 'if the trade was thrown open by the repeal of the assize laws, it would have the effect of gradually drawing persons with capital into it [and] of diminishing the waste of labour ...'.[3] This step was taken for England and Wales in 1836[4] and, having been found 'beneficial to the public as well as to the bakers', was extended to Ireland two years later.[5] But the legislation did not have the intended effect: 'There is probably no branch of

---

1 See above, chap. 3, table 3.3.
2 A number of acts 'for the better regulation of the baking trade', particularly in Dublin, were passed by the Irish parliament in the eighteenth century – see J. Swift, *A history of the Dublin bakers* (Dublin, 1948), pp. 246–50.
3 *Report from the committee to inquire into the state of the laws which regulate the manufacture and sale of bread*, p. 10, H.C. 1814–15 (186), v, 1350.
4 Sale of Bread Act (6 & 7 Will. IV, c. 37).
5 Bread (Ire.) Act 1838 (1 & 2 Vict., c. 28). E. O'Connor, *A labour history of Ireland, 1824–1960* (Dublin, 1992), p. 31 explains that the price of bread in Ireland had risen to its highest level since the famine of 1817, leading to attacks on bakeries and bread carts in the summer of 1837; but food prices had declined by the time the 1838 act was passed.

trade supplying a vast and constant demand which has so completely remained in its primitive condition of ministering to that demand from a multitude of small and insulated sources, as the baking trade.'[6]

Many of these 'insulated sources' in Ireland were dirty and insanitary. The bakers also worked long and unsociable hours, although Sunday work was, to a large extent, prohibited by the 1838 act.[7] In 1842 the Dublin bakers initiated a campaign to end night-work; but although this campaign spread to the rest of the country, it was largely ineffective.[8] As the demand for bread increased after 1850, the hours of labour became even longer. The Dublin bakers, following the example of their counterparts in London, returned to the fray in 1859,[9] and a national campaign against 'the oppressive and slavish system of working' began the following year. In 1862, the government appointed Mr Seymour Tremenheere to investigate the grievances of the London bakers,[10] and in the following year the inquiry was extended to encompass the remainder of the kingdom.

Tremenheere, who had been inspector of mines since 1842, had little sympathy for the bakers, although he did recommend that young persons under the age of 18 should not be required to work between 9.00 p.m. and 5.00 a.m.[11] The protection of public health was a higher priority, and all bakehouses should, therefore, be required to meet minimum standards of ventilation, cleanliness, etc., enforceable by a system of inspection. These recommendations were 'entirely approved' by the bakers in Ireland.[12] But the Association for the Abolition of Sunday-work and Night-work in the Baking Trade (whose secretary was the indefatigable Dr W. Neilson Hancock)[13] wanted Tremenheere to do more to reduce the hours of employment. First, the standard for textile factories set by the factory acts – a maximum of ten hours' work per day – should apply to all young persons working in bakehouses. Although the association were supported by similar demands from England and Scotland, Tremenheere was dismissive:

6   First report to the home secretary relative to the grievances complained of by the journeymen bakers, p. xiii [C. 3027], H.C. 1862, xlvii, 13.
7   Section 13. In theory, of course, *all* Sunday work was prohibited by the Lord's Day Observance Act (Ire.) 1695 (7 Will. III, c. 17), s. 1.
8   O'Connor, *Labour history*, p. 19; Swift, *History of Dublin bakers*, p. 230.
9   See *Papers relating to the case of the journeymen bakers, published for the information of the clergymen, merchants and citizens, who have joined in the requisition to the Lord Mayor of Dublin to convene a meeting to consider their case* (Dublin, 1860). Extracts from these papers are given in Swift, *History of Dublin bakers*, pp. 236–39.
10   First report on grievances of journeymen bakers, 1862.
11   Second report to the home secretary relative to the grievances complained of by the journeyman bakers, p.xiii [3091], H.C. 1863, xxviii, 335. The employment of young persons in bakeries had first given rise to concern in the 1840s – see e.g. the report on Miss M'Creedy's bakery in Belfast in *Appendix to the second report of the children's employment commissioners*, pt. II, p. N44, H.C. 1843 (432), xv, 496.
12   Second report on grievances of journeymen bakers, 1863, p. vi.
13   See J. McEldowney, 'W. Neilson Hancock' in *Ir. Jur.*, 20 (1985), 378.

It cannot be truly urged, that such work as would fall to the lot of youths under 18 in the baking tade, between five in the morning and nine at night, is likely to be physically injurious to any number of them, or in any degree that would justify the interference of the legislature in their behalf. In the worst cases the severe portions of the labour are necessarily separated from each other by periods of comparatively easy work. In a large proportion of the trade the youths are out of the bakehouse delivering bread, or assisting in the shop, during a considerable part of the day. In those cases where they are more confined to the bakehouse, the provisions for securing better ventilation and cleanliness in bakehouses will deprive such confinement of much of its present ill-effects.... The analogy of factory labour ... does not hold good in this case, as factory labour is severe, uniform and continuous.[14]

In any case, 'the machinery of the factory acts is inapplicable to such a case as that of a number of small insulated places of work, such as bakehouses, in any one of which it would be rare to find more than one youth under 18'.[15]

The Bakers' Association also called for the law against Sunday work to be made 'more effectual and be systematically enforced' by increasing the penalties for breach and by giving the police a right of entry to check whether the law was being broken. Their argument was part of a more general case for a 12-hour day:

The Committee believe that the hours of labour are limited by natural laws which cannot be violated with impunity. That any constant work beyond twelve hours a day encroaches on the domestic and private life of the working man, and so leads to disastrous moral results, interfering with each man's home and the discharge of his family duties as a son, a brother, a husband and a father. That work beyond twelve hours has a tendency to undermine the health of the working man, and so leads to premature old age and death, to the great injury of families of working men thus deprived of the care and support of the head of the family when most required.[16]

Once again Tremenheere disagreed. The existing law was thought adequate in England and Scotland; conditions of work were getting better in Ireland – night-work having been partially or entirely abolished in a number of towns, and where bakehouse owners were in breach of the law, they could be prosecuted, as had several of the leading master-bakers in Dublin. In any case, 'the regulation of adult labour is altogether beyond ... the limits to which legislation could be carried with the view to remove existing grievances'.[17] Tremenheere hoped, however, that 'the result of again drawing public attention to the unnatural hours of labour ... may be to create such an amount of public opinion against the present practice as to oblige the master bakers to adopt hours of work more consistent with the health, morals and comfort of the journeymen'.

14 *Second report on grievances of journeymen bakers, 1863*, pp. vi–vii.
15 Ibid., p. x.
16 Ibid., pp. vii and xii.
17 Ibid., p. xiii.

The upshot of Tremenheere's inquiries was the Bakehouses (Regulation) Act 1863,[18] which applied to 'any place in which are baked bread, biscuits or confectionery, from the baking or selling of which a profit is derived'.[19] As was to be expected, the act had little to say about working conditions;[20] but it did set the pattern for the next fifty years and more in respect of public health provision. Every bakehouse was to be kept in a cleanly state, provided with proper ventilation and be free from effluvia arising from any drain, privy or other nuisance. A bakehouse in a city or town with a population over 5,000 was to be either painted in oil every seven years and washed every six months, or lime-washed every six months. No room was to be used as a sleeping place, unless 'effectually separated' from the bakehouse and properly ventilated. All these provisions were to be enforced by appropriate officials appointed by the local authority.

The 1863 act fell 'lamentably below what is really and imperatively demanded'[21] and was not a success in many parts of the United Kingdom.[22] It may have been 'zealously' applied in Dublin, where many of the defects previously found in bakehouses 'have been remedied' by regular inspections; but the picture elsewhere was very different. In 1866, only six cities or towns in Ireland had even bothered to reply to a request for information, and all six suggested that the act was a dead letter.[23] It was later explained that it had been enacted at a time of grave public disquiet arising from the unhealthy conditions under which bread was baked – but that 'temporary alarm' had quickly subsided.[24] And even though steam-power was by now used in some bakehouses in which women and young persons were employed,[25] the trade was not brought within the factories acts when their ambit was considerably broadened by the Factory Acts Extension Act 1867 – an anomaly aggravated in 1871, when responsibility for the supervision of workshops was transferred to the factory inspectorate because the local authorities had also failed to perform their duties under the Workshop Regulation Act 1867.[26]

18   26 & 27 Vict., c. 40 (applied to Ireland).
19   This definition applied throughout the period under consideration – see 1878 act, sch. 4, pt. II, para. 22; 1901 act, sch 6, pt. II, para. 23.
20   As recommended by Tremenheere, young persons were now permitted to work only between 5 a.m. and 9 p.m.
21   *Chief insp. ann. rep., 1882*, p. 15 (Redgrave), setting out five criticisms of the act.
22   See especially *Reports made to the secretary of state by Mr Tremenheere on the operation of the Bakehouses Regulation Act*, H.C. 1866 (394), lxvi, 373. In 1876, the factory and workshop commissioners confirmed that 'it is only here and there that any active steps have been taken by the local authorities to carry out the provisions of the Bakehouse Act': *Report of the commissioners appointed to inquire into the working of the factory and workshop acts*, p xviii [C. 1443], H.C. 1876, xxix, 21.
23   *Reports on the operation of the Bakehouses Regulation Act*, p. 21 – see e.g. Cork ('no officer ... acting under this statute') and Newtownards ('no inspection under the act').
24   *Report of the factory and workshop commissioners 1876*, p. xviii.
25   See e.g. Swift, *History of Dublin bakers*, pp. 242–43. The most dangerous machines appear to have been the dough brakes (mixers) – see *Chief insp. ann. rep., 1911*, p. 112.
26   See above, p. 51.

In 1876, however, the factory and workshop commissioners were 'clearly of opinion' that the baking trade should be placed under the general law.[27] The 1863 act was, accordingly, repealed and the Factory and Workshop Act 1878 provided instead that bakehouses using mechanical power were to be subject to the general provisions relating to non-textile factories; all other bakehouses were to be treated as workshops.[28] But in order to reduce this considerable addition to the workload of the factory inspectors a further distinction was made between wholesale and retail bakehouses by the Factory and Workshop Act 1883.[29] The inspectors were solely responsible for enforcing the law in all wholesale establishments, and (from 1891) in other bakehouses which qualified as non-textile factories; but in respect of retail bakehouses which were 'workshops' for the purposes of the 1878 act, they were relieved, by local authority inspectors, of the responsibility for sanitary conditions.

The 1878 act for the first time regulated the employment of women and children in bakehouses and extended the provisions of the 1863 act with regard to the employment of young persons. In general, the hours of employment were now to be the same as those worked in other non-textile factories or workshops; but these general requirements could be disapplied in certain cases. In particular, young male persons over the age of 16 could be employed, for a maximum of nine hours, between 5.00 a.m. and 9.00 p.m.,[30] and all young persons as well as women and children could be obliged to work up to thirty minutes' overtime if baking was 'in an incomplete state' at the end of the normal period of employment.[31]

The factory inspectors found that these provisions were frequently ignored. During the 1890s, for example, more than thirty bakehouse owners in Ireland were convicted of employment offences involving young persons, mainly by employing them at night.[32] But the magistrates do not appear to have been entirely supportive of the inspectors. The average fine was less than ten shillings, and when Mr F. Merain, a Waterford baker, was prosecuted for employing a young person at night, he was fined only one shilling

27 *Report of the factory and workshop commissioners 1876*, p. xviii. The inspectors in Ireland had so recommended – see especially ibid., appendix C, p. 37 (Astley).

28 Section 93 and sch. 4, pt. 2., which took the unusual step of including bakehouses in which only adult males were employed; in general, such workshops were not regulated by the act. These provisions were continued by 1901 act, s. 149.

29 Factory and Workshop Act 1883, s. 17, re-enacted as 1901 act, s. 102.

30 1878 act, s. 45; 1901 act, s. 38.

31 1878 act, s. 54; 1901 act, s. 51 – a general provision extended by order of the home secretary in 1882 to 'non-textile factories and workshops ... in which is carried on the process of baking of bread or biscuits' – see *Redgrave's Factory Acts*, ed. J.A. Redgrave and H.S. Scrivener (7th ed., London, 1898), p. 159. By 1878 act, s. 53 and sch. 3 and 1901 act, s. 49 and sch. 2, young persons and women were allowed to work additional time on a limited number of days in the making of biscuits, as one of a number of trades 'where the business is liable to sudden press of orders arising from unforeseen events'.

32 See in particular *Chief insp. ann. rep., 1895*, pp. 69–86, giving details of the prosecution of ten bakeries, some of them more than once.

on the grounds that when baking was only carried on at night, it was a
hardship that a boy should not be given an opportunity of learning his trade
before he was 18 years old.[33]

But the major bone of contention with the 1878 act in terms of working
conditions was that it did nothing to prohibit the employment of adult men
during the night or on Sundays.[34] Baking at night was common in the larger
cities:

> In Ireland, as in Scotland, large bakeries predominate. In Belfast, the bakers supply
> not only to Belfast, but … inland to towns and places up to 150 miles distant.…The
> bulk of the bread sold in [Ulster] … is supplied mainly from Belfast and partly from
> Londonderry.… In many towns and villages, local baking capacity is so small that the
> demand upon the [city] trade has continually grown and has to be met daily. Most of
> the baking factories are working night and day.… Under the night-work system the
> country retail distributors are supplied with bread twenty-four hours old; if night
> work is prohibited they would be supplied with bread forty-eight hours old.[35]

Although they received no support from the factory inspectors, the Irish
bakers, following their English counterparts, took up this issue in the 1890s.
In 1890 an unsuccessful attempt was made to amend the law relating to
work on Sundays.[36] In 1892–1893, strong representations were made to the
royal commission on labour,[37] and in 1895 the Irish Congress of Trades
Unions adopted the first of many motions calling for the total abolition of
night work in bakeries.[38] This was in line with TUC policy in Great Britain,

---

33 *Chief insp. ann. rep., 1896*, p. 368. In the same year, Inglis & Co. of Belfast were fined
    2s. 6d. for employing a young person without a certificate of fitness, and Ogilvie &
    Moore, wholesale confectioners of Cork, 15s. for three similar offences: ibid., pp. 365
    and 368.

34 Although Irish bakers had become organised on a local basis at a fairly early date, 'no
    national organisation was attempted until … 1889, [when] Murray Davis, the
    principal figure in the Belfast Bakers' Society and a leading member of the Belfast
    Trades Council, formed the Bakers' Federal Union of Ireland': A.J. Boyle, *The Irish
    labour movement in the nineteenth century* (Washington, DC, 1988), p. 98.

35 *Report of the committee of inquiry into night work in the bread-baking and flour
    confectionery trade*, p. 22 [Cmd. 246], H.C. 1919, xxvi, 506. An agreement for day
    work only had been reached in Dublin, but 'it would appear … that the system is
    causing inconvenience to the public outside Dublin'. Cf. the 'day work system' had
    been practised in Limerick 'with satisfactory results': *Report of the Sixth Irish Trades
    Congress* (Londonderry, 1899), p. 46.

36 The bill, which was not printed, was brought in by Col. J.P. Nolan (Galway N.),
    Arthur O'Connor (Donegal E.) and P. O'Brien (Monaghan) – see *Hansard 3*, cccxli,
    173 (12 Feb. 1890).

37 See especially *Evidence taken before Group C of the Royal Commission on Labour, vol. iii*,
    pp. 326–38 [C. 6894–XII], H.C. 1893–94, xxxiv, 340–52 (evidence of J. Lawlor
    (Bakers' Society of Dublin), J. O'Connor (Bakers' Society of Cork) and M. Davis
    (Irish National Bakers' Federation).

38 See *Report of the Second Irish Trades Congress* (Cork, 1895), p 22 (Lawlor and
    O'Connor). Similar motions were, for example, adopted in 1898, 1905 and 1909 –
    see respectively *Reports of the Fifth Congress* (Belfast, 1898), p. 49, *Twelfth Congress*
    (Wexford, 1905), p. 46 and *Sixteenth Congress* (Limerick, 1909), p. 33.

which saw to it that bills to restrict labour in bakehouses to 48 hours per week were introduced in the house of commons on almost an annual basis.[39] But all this pressure to change the law was to no avail[40] – and attempts to enforce even the existing law proved largely unsuccessful.[41] It was to take an International Labour Organisation convention – and further agitation – before legislation prohibiting night-work was finally enacted in the 1930s.[42]

In the period under consideration, what more immediately concerned the factory inspectors – and parliament – was the continuing insanitary state of many bakehouses.[43] The 1878 act had in this respect added little to the 1863 act, but steps were regularly taken to put this right. By 1901 the sanitary regulations applicable to bakehouses formed a special section (part V(iii)) of the factories act, with new requirements as to their use and construction. In addition to the limewashing or painting, and regular washing, of all interior surfaces,[44] there was a general duty not to allow any workroom to be 'in such a state as to be on sanitary grounds unfit for use or occupation as a bakehouse'.[45] As to construction, the 1901 act replicated the original restrictions on sleeping places,[46] prohibited the creation of new underground bakehouses,[47] and provided that no place was to be let or allowed to be occupied as a bakehouse unless it complied with specific requirements relating to sanitary conveniences.[48]

39 See e.g 1897 (152), i, 109 and 1911 (87), ii, 607, summarised in *Report of the committee on the bread-baking and flour confectionery trade, 1919*, pp. 7–8.
40 The problem was the perceived needs of customers – and the lack of compelling circumstances; as late as 1919 it was stated that there was no evidence that night work was 'unduly detrimental to health': ibid., p. 30.
41 A conviction under the Lord's Day Observance Act was, apparently, secured in Belfast during the 1880s, but a similar case in Newry was dismissed: *Evidence taken before Group C of the Royal Commission on Labour, 1893*, iii, 328 (M. Davis). In 1905 or thereabouts, three 'test' cases under the 1838 act were brought in Waterford and Limerick; the case in Waterford was dismissed, as was one in Limerick; but in a second Limerick case, the defendant was convicted and fined five shillings: see *Report of the 13th Irish Trades Union Congress* (Athlone, 1906), p. 11.
42 Baking Industry (Hours of Work) Act 1938 [UK] and Night-Work (Bakeries) Act 1936 [IFS] – and even this legislation was subject to 'special exceptions'.
43 Initial attempts to enforce the 1878 act, and the belief that there was only a 'very slender chance of any real and effectual amelioration taking place in the making and baking of bread without the interposition of authority', led Redgrave to call for further legislation: *Chief insp. ann. rep., 1882*, p. 22. Parliament responded in 1883, 1891 and 1895.
44 Section 99, replicating 1863 act, s. 5 and 1878 act, s. 34.
45 1901 act, s. 98, re-enacting 1883 act, s. 16. Provisions on much the same lines had been enacted in the 1863 act, s. 4, and were included in the general sanitary provisions of the 1878 act, s. 3.
46 1901 act, s. 100, replicating 1863 act, s. 5 and 1878 act, s. 35.
47 1901 act, s. 101, extending 1895 act, s. 27(3) (no room with floor more than three feet below street level to be used as bakehouse unless so used before 1895, and even in such case not to be used after 1904 unless certified by district council to be suitable for that purpose). The 'unwholesome' nature of underground bakehouses had long been stressed by Redgrave – see e.g *Chief insp. ann. rep., 1882*, p. 23.
48 1901 act, s. 97, replicating 1883 act, s. 15 (no water-closet to be within or communicate directly with a bakehouse, and no sewer pipe or drain to have an opening within the bakehouse).

These provisions were designed to protect the health not just of the persons employed in bakehouses, but also of their customers. But the task facing the inspectors, particularly in the south of Ireland, was considerable, and their effectiveness was undoubtedly limited by the large number of their other duties. The problem was said to be particularly acute in country towns, where 'the small bakehouses were kept so uncleanly, and the men worked such very long hours, that if the people saw the bread manufactured, they would not eat it'.[49] But even the treasurer of the United Trades Society in Cork, where many bakeries were said to be 'very unhealthy' and the law requiring lime-washing 'a dead letter', testified that 'I do not suppose there is a baker in Cork who knows the factory inspector'.[50] Given the number of prosecutions referred to earlier, this criticism appears to be unfair and exaggerated. But it was echoed in England,[51] and frequently reiterated in Ireland after 1900 as a reason why the sanitary arrangements and ventilation in many bakehouses 'leave much to be desired'.[52]

The inspectors would have denied cause and effect; but they, too, found conditions less than satisfactory in many instances. In the north of Ireland, for example, floors, 'rarely, if ever' reached the required standard of cleanliness:

Dirt of a very undesirable nature is commonly trodden in from streets and yards, and workers do not always refrain from expectoration in the bakehouses. The floors are generally very dry and the risk of clouds of dust arising is not small, particularly in the process of 'cleaning', which commonly consists of a dry brushing, supplemented by scraping. Sugar ... and flour adhere so firmly to the floors that this brushing rarely thoroughly cleanses them, and occasionally where a floor is uneven, or perhaps still worse, where it is a 'dirt' floor, the results are far from satisfactory.[53]

Conditions in some country bakehouses were particularly bad. In one case, for example, baking was carried on in a converted stable:

There had not been any real treatment of the floor or the surface of the walls to render them sanitary. A gulley was in the centre of the floor, said to lead to a disconnected portion of the main drain, and at one part of the floor rats had played

49 *Evidence taken before Group C of the Royal Commission on Labour, 1893*, iii, 329, where Murray Davis claimed that 'even if there was a small army of inspectors they would not find them out ...'. His solution was to give the job of inspection to the police.

50 *Evidence taken before Group C of the Royal Commission on Labour, vol. ii*, pp. 244 and 246 [C. 6795–III], H.C. 1892, xxxvi, 692 and 694 (J. H. Jolley). In 1906, the supervision of bakehouses by inspectors was described as 'patchy' and the inspectors themselves as 'supine': *Report of the Thirteenth Irish Trades Union Congress* (Athlone, 1906), p. 11.

51 See e.g. *Chief insp. ann. rep., 1882*, p. 18 (in London six factory inspectors now did the work previously the responsibility of nearly eighty local authority officers).

52 *Report of the Ninth Irish Trades Union Congress* (Cork, 1902), p 38. Murray Davis had earlier informed congress that 'what consumers required was clean bread, and one third of the bakeries of Ireland were not fit to keep pigs in': *Report of the Fourth Irish Trades Congress* (Waterford, 1897), p 32.

53 *Chief insp. ann. rep., 1906*, pp. 147–48 (Williams). The air of the bakehouse frequently contained sulphurous fumes from the coke-fired ovens and 'fumes from gas engines were occasionally noticed'.

havoc with the ground. Just against one wall was a stable in use and an old opening connecting the two places had been only partly filled up with rough boards which did not fit. Over the top of this room was a partly disused loft with refuse and rubbish on the floor.[54]

In another bakehouse, 'the room was filled with numbers of flies, which thickly covered everything in the place; the excuse given in answer to my remonstrations was that they came from a manure heap close by, and could not be exterminated. The machines, benches, boards, trays, windows and floors of the place were very dirty, and no methodical attempt was made to produce cleanliness'.[55]

Bakeries in Belfast, on the other hand, enjoyed a much better reputation. Indeed, Murray Davis boasted that Belfast had 'the best [bakeries] in the world as far as ventilation and cleanliness were concerned'.[56] In 1908 one of the inspectors more modestly noted that the law was 'generally well observed' in the district;[57] but only one year later came reports of open drains, accumulations of rubbish and unsatisfactory sanitary arrangements.[58] One of the leading firms, Inglis & Co., were found to have neglected to lime-wash parts of their bakehouse. Their defence was that they were installing electric lighting; but Eraut had warned them earlier that the lime-washing was overdue and they were convicted and fined 20s. – even though the court was of the opinion that Inglis generally kept their premises in perfect order.[59]

In the south of Ireland, the larger bakeries in cities such as Dublin, Cork and Waterford were 'on the whole kept in a cleanly condition';[60] but the picture in country areas was again much less satisfactory.[61] A particular problem was the state of workshop bakeries, the sanitary condition of which were the responsibility of local authorities. Criticism of their provision for inspection came from many quarters, not least the factory inspectors themselves.[62] And even when the local authority did act, the results were often disappointing.[63] Nor was the position with regard to underground bakehouses any more

---

54 *Chief insp. ann. rep., 1912*, p. 100 (Eraut) See also *1908*, p. 104 (Brothers).
55 *Chief insp. ann. rep., 1914*, p. 3 (Bennett).
56 *Report of the Seventh Irish Trades Union Congress* (Dublin, 1900), p. 10.
57 *Chief insp. ann. rep., 1908*, p. 104 (Owen).
58 *Chief insp. ann. rep., 1909*, p. 105 (Eraut).
59 *Belfast Newsletter*, 11 Sept. 1909, p. 5.
60 *Chief insp. ann. rep., 1906*, p. 148 (Parker) and *1914*, p. 3 (Allhusen). Cf. 'many' cases were found of drains opening into bakehouses, 'even in the largest towns': *Chief insp. ann. rep., 1905*, p. 190 (Jackson).
61 See e.g. *Chief insp. ann. rep., 1906*, p. 148 (Warren) and *1910*, p. 24 (Allhusen, adding that 'some of the older bakehouses in country parts are unfit for use and should be condemned').
62 'No action is being taken by the local authorities to enforce half-yearly limewashing ...': *Chief insp. ann. rep., 1905*, p. 190 (Jackson) and *1906*, p. 148 (Parker). Concern was also expressed by the ITUC – see e.g. *Report of the Tenth Irish Trades Union Congress* (Newry, 1903), p. 24.
63 'The ceilings [were] frequently forgotten, and very little attention paid to the floor of the bakehouse': *Chief insp. ann. rep., 1906*, p. 148 (Parker).

satisfactory.[64] A number of these were found to be in use without the necessary local authority certificate; in the case of one bakery, which 'was practically a coal cellar', this was not at all surprising, 'considering the sanitary conditions found'.[65]

The law – and the inspectors – may have brought about some changes for the better; but there was clearly still considerable scope for improvement.

CREAMERIES

From the seventeenth century, Irish butter represented an important part of the agriculture industry, particularly in terms of exports to the readily-accessible British market.[66] But even in the early days of the factory acts, butter-making was still undertaken by farmers individually without the aid of machinery – it was, in short, a typical agricultural activity outside the reach of 'industrial' legislation. By 1860 or thereabouts, however, things were beginning to change; imports from Europe, particularly Denmark, Holland and France, became increasingly competitive, and with the invention of the centrifrugal separator in the late 1870s, the new 'creamery' butter quickly became more attractive to consumers than the heavily-salted Irish butter.[67] At first, 'the majority of Irish farmers, who had no one to help or instruct them, and comparatively little contact with the outside world ... paid little heed to the changes',[68] and butter-making in Ireland went into decline. As one inspector later observed, 'the butter trade was in great danger of dying out altogether'.[69] But the Irish response to these developments was not long in coming. The centrifugal separator encouraged the production of butter on a factory basis, a process facilitated by new methods of refrigeration and pasteurisation. A number of 'proprietary' creamery plants were established in Ireland in the early 1880s, and the process was given a further boost with the development of the co-operative movement usually credited to Sir

64 'Underground bakeries were very good for Baden-Powell and General White, but they were not good enough for people in Ireland at the present day': *Report of the Seventh Annual Irish Trades Congress* (Dublin, 1900), p. 11 (Murray Davis).
65 *Chief insp. ann. rep., 1909*, p. 132 (Martindale). Part of the room was still used for storing coal, and 'the only light and air came from the hole through which the coal was shot.... A table had been placed along one wall, and on this the cakes were made.'
66 See e.g. L.M. Cullen, *An economic history of Ireland since 1660* (London, 1972), pp. 8–12 and 52–58.
67 'Heavily salted, often dirty, and relatively unstandardised, the product of the Irish dairy industry was in no condition to meet a challenge': ibid., p. 154.
68 L. Smith-Gordon and L.C. Staples, *Rural reconstruction in Ireland: A record of co-operative organisation* (London, 1917), p. 91.
69 *Chief insp. ann. rep., 1895*, p. 254 (Bellhouse). This is an exaggeration according to C. Ó Gráda, 'The beginnings of the Irish creamery system, 1880–1914' in *Econ. Hist. Rev.*, 30 (1977), 285 stating that exports of Irish butter to Britain in 1904 were only one-third higher than in the early 1870s.

Horace Plunket and George Russell (Æ).[70] The first co-operative creamery, with 50 members, opened in Drumcollogher, Co. Limerick in 1889; by 1900 there were 171 co-operatives with 26,577 members, and by 1914 the total had risen to 350, with 47,086 members. But there were similar increases in the number of creameries in private ownership; by 1900, for example, there were 200 proprietary, and 30 joint-stock, plants,[71] and by 1906, less than one-half of the estimated 800 creameries in Ireland were co-operatives.[72] The net result was that 'the Irish farmer ... quickly made up lost ground':[73] the amount of creamery butter produced rose from two million pounds in 1892 to more than twenty million pounds in 1904 and over thirty-seven million pounds in 1915.[74]

As late as 1883, the official view was that dairies, even those using steam power, 'have always been considered to be agricultural operations and outside the factory acts'. But six years later it was a different story: 'more recently, dairies have been established as commercial undertakings ... [and] are quite as much factories within the meaning of the [1878] act as any of the miscellaneous occupations which are [declared in that act to be] factories or workshops'.[75] This view was shared by the inspectors in Ireland: 'Nearly all the butter factories are worked by steam or gas power, and it has been found necessary to visit them as far as possible in order that the occupiers may be properly instructed as to the necessary guarding of machinery.'[76] The safety of those working in the new creameries was, of course, important; but it soon became clear, at least in Ireland, that the principal issue was the irregular working hours during the summer months, occasioned by the exigencies of the manufacturing process.

70 According to Smith-Gordon and Staples, *Rural reconstruction*, p. x, Sir Horace Plunket was the inspiration, and R.A. Anderson the mainspring of a co-operative movement which was to bring about a general rural regeneration; they were assisted by the foundation of the Irish Agricultural Organisation Society (with Anderson as its secretary) in 1894, and by the setting up of a separate Irish Department of Agriculture and Technical Instruction in 1899. See further C.C. Riddall, *Agricultural co-operation in Ireland: The story of a struggle* (Dublin, 1950). Cf. 'The folk-lore surrounding the birth and early development of Ireland's creamery system is plentiful ...': Ó Gráda, 'Beginnings of the Irish creamery system', p. 284.

71 R.A. Anderson (secretary, IAOS) to Sir Matthew Ridley (home secretary), 14 March 1900, reproduced in *Chief insp. ann. rep., 1899*, p. 109.

72 Ó Gráda, 'Beginnings of the Irish creamery system', p. 289, who adds that 'Well into the [twentieth] century the growth of proprietory creameries rivalled that of co-operatives'. But it was the co-operatives which attracted the particular interest of the inspectors: 'The movement seems to be spreading all over the country.... There is hardly a county now in the whole of Ireland that does not contain at least one factory of this sort': *Chief insp. ann. rep., 1897*, p. 116 (Bellhouse).

73 Ó Gráda, 'Beginnings of the Irish creamery system', p. 285.

74 All these figures are taken from Smith-Gordon and Staples, *Rural reconstruction*, pp. 270–71.

75 A. Redgrave (chief insp.) to Sir Godfrey Lushington (permanent under-sec., home office), 4 Sept. 1889 (PRO HO 45/9657/A40767).

76 *Chief insp. ann. rep., 1890*, p. 24 (Woodgate). See e.g. *Chief insp. ann. rep., 1898*, pt. I, p. 56 (butter manufacturer in Co. Kerry and creamery in Co. Cork convicted of

Insofar as creamery work, such as separating the cream from the milk, was done by men, there was no problem. But the process of churning the cream into butter was in Ireland carried out mainly by women and girls,[77] in respect of whom the 1878 act prescribed permitted hours of work during the week, a half holiday on Saturday and a complete prohibition of Sunday work.[78] With fresh supplies of milk arriving every morning and afternoon, the creameries tended to work irregular hours seven days a week.[79] Some flexibility was possible under section 56 of the 1878 act, which permitted women (but not young persons), on certain strict conditions,[80] to work two hours' overtime daily – but only if the home secretary was satisfied that this was necessary 'by reason of the perishable nature of the articles or materials which are the subject of the manufacturing process ... and that such employment will not injure the health of the women employed'. This relaxation was immediately applied to a number of 'perishable' trades, such as fruit preserving and fish curing;[81] but it was not until August 1893 that it was extended to 'non-textile factories in which are carried on the occupations of preparing cream, and making butter and cheese'.[82] This concession quickly proved to be inadequate.

In July 1894 a proprietary butter manufacturer in Co. Kerry was prosecuted for employing two women on a Sunday; that charge was dismissed, but the defendant was convicted of other offences;[83] the following summer, a creamery in Co. Limerick was fined for employing three women on a Saturday evening,[84] and in the summer of 1897, four more creameries in Co. Kerry (including at least two co-operative creameries) were fined for employing women on a Sunday.[85] Although the fines imposed were small,

---

failure to fence dangerous machinery and fined £1 and 10s. respectively) and *1899*, p. 406 (creamery in Co. Kerry fined 10s. for the same offence).

77　*Chief insp. ann. rep., 1899*, pp. 105 and 109 (Bellhouse).

78　1878 act, s. 13 prescribed for non-textile factories a normal working day from Monday to Friday of 6.00 a.m. to 6.00 p.m., or 7.00 a.m. to 7.00 p.m. (to include at least one and a half hours per day for meals); on Saturdays, a woman or young person could work from 6.00 or 7.00 a.m. to 2.00 p.m. (with not less than half an hour for meals). By s. 21, a young person or woman 'shall not ... be employed on Sunday in a factory or workshop'.

79　The pattern of work tended to differ between north and south. In the north, no work was done on Sundays, when the farmers kept the milk for home use. This was practicable, given that many of the dairy farms were small; there was also 'a very strong religious feeling against Sunday labour, which is not found amongst the Catholics of the south' – where the farms also tended to be larger: *Chief insp. ann. rep., 1899*, p. 106 (Bellhouse).

80　In particular, overtime was not to be worked on more than ninety-six days in any twelve-month period – a limit reduced to sixty days by 1895 act, s. 14(2).

81　1878 act, sch. 3, pt. 5.

82　Order of 22 Aug. 1893 – see *Redgrave's Factory Acts* (7th ed., 1898), p. 159. This provision was effectively continued by 1901 act, s. 49 and Overtime employment of women for press of work order 1903 (No. 1156).

83　Including failure to guard the fly-wheel of an engine: *Chief insp. ann. rep., 1894*, p. 283.

84　*Chief insp. ann. rep., 1895*, p. 83.

85　*Chief insp. ann. rep., 1897*, p. 284.

the situation was clearly unsatisfactory, the essence of the problem being the way in which 'the rigid regulations of factory law' could be 'usefully adapted' to a new industry.[86] From 1897 to 1902, therefore, intensive discussions took place to determine whether the law should yield to the requirements of a particular industrial practice – or whether that practice should change in order to comply with the law. The efforts made to resolve a problem which involved a relatively small number of 'protected' persons indicate the extent to which the government was prepared to accommodate a rare success story in the difficult industrial climate of the south of Ireland.

The negotiations opened with the publication of a special report.[87] The suggestion that a number of creameries might be taken outside the ambit of the factory acts altogether was rejected as 'out of harmony with the general spirit of the factory and workshop legislation'.[88] The inspectors were also opposed to any proposal which would 'deprive workers of all the advantages at present secured to them by factory legislation which are concerned about sanitation, the protection of life and limb, etc.'. They initially accepted as affording 'the basis of a settlement' a proposal for allowing greater flexibility in the hours which could lawfully be worked by women on weekdays and on Sundays during the summer months: 'It seems unreasonable that greatly enlarged privileges should have been granted in the cases of cleaning and preparing fruit, and gutting, salting and packing fish, and not in the present instance.'[89] But on the basis of further investigation of the industry throughout the United Kingdom, they changed their view of the matter. The problem was *not* the law, but old-fashioned working practices; if the creameries moved to a single daily delivery of milk, and made more use of pasteurisation, there would be no need to depart from the factory acts at all:

[Morning-only delivery of milk] has been adopted universally in the north of Ireland and in Scotland; it has also been adopted in many places in England, and where it has been tried in the south of Ireland it is reported to have worked satisfactorily. In creameries carried on on this system the hours of work seldom exceed eight or nine per day.... [Sunday] churning is not necessary, inasmuch as there are many creameries [especially in England] where this part of this process is not carried on. It can be avoided by the adoption of a pasteurizing plant, or by some special arrangement for cooling down the cream....[90]

86 *Chief insp. ann. rep., 1899*, p. 232 (Cooke-Taylor).
87 *Special report on creameries by W. Cooke Taylor (superintending inspector for the Scotland/Ireland division), Inspector Graves (Glasgow) and Inspector Bellhouse (Dublin)*, reproduced in *Chief insp. ann. rep., 1897*, p. 117.
88 Ibid. This proposal, limited to cases where butter-making was 'supplementary' to the whole work of an agricultural establishment, was in any case likely to give rise to 'almost insurmountable' problems in practice.
89 Ibid. Not only was there no less urgency that milk be processed before turning sour, but the concessions already made for fruit-preserving and fish-curing (1878 act, ss. 43 and 100; 1891 act, s. 32) extended to the employment of children and young persons, a 'latitude' not sought for creameries.
90 *Chief insp. ann. rep., 1899*, p. 106 (Bellhouse). Even with IAOS encouragement, however, pasteurisation in 1900 'is the exception rather than the rule', in part because

If the creameries were unwilling to adopt such practices, 'there always remains the alternative of employing only men to do the work'![91]

These 'deductions' were unanimously rejected by the creamery occupiers at a conference of all the interested parties held in Dublin in December 1899.[92] The factory acts had failed to make 'adequate' provision for creameries only because their establishment and rapid development had occurred after 1878, and their special requirements 'were not either understood or sufficiently urged when subsequent ... legislation was enacted'.[93] During the summer, a limited amount of Sunday work by women and young persons *was* necessary, 'owing to the fact that the largest proportion of the milk supply is produced at this period'; if this work was *not* carried out by women and young persons, 'great injury' would result to the dairying industry of Ireland 'as, generally speaking, female labour is found to be more satisfactory and better adapted to the special branch of the industry ...'.[94] Comparison with practice in the north of Ireland or in other parts of the United Kingdom where winter dairying prevailed was 'unfair and misleading', given that in the south and west of Ireland dairying was almost exclusively a summer industry.[95] And, although the number of hours actually worked per day never exceeded the permitted maximum, work after the 'legal' hours on week-days was also necessary, given the 'intermittent character' of the manufacturing process.[96]

The creamery occupiers underlined their point of view by emphasising that 'there is no case on record where either a woman or young person employed in an Irish creamery has suffered injury to health either from disease traceable to their employment or from accident'. What they sought was not in any way contrary to the *spirit* of the factory acts, but merely a reasonable exemption similar to that already granted to other industries involving perishable goods and

of the expense, said to be 'about £100'. But in view of the outbreaks of enteric fever which occurred in Ireland from time to time, 'it is essential ... in the interest of public health' as well as for the benefit of the creamery itself: *Chief insp. ann. rep., 1900*, p. 333 and *1901*, pt. I, pp. 142–43 (Bellhouse). See generally J.J. Welply, *Creameries and infectious diseases* (London, 1895), particularly pp. 30–39, 'On state inspection of creamery dairies', reproduced from *The Lancet*, 10 Nov. 1894.

91   *Chief insp. ann. rep., 1899*, pp. 106–07 (Bellhouse).
92   Ibid., p. 108. A report of the conference is given at p. 110.
93   Ibid., p. 110.
94   Ibid., pp. 110–11. A survey of 82 creameries 'thoroughly representative of the butter-making industry in Ireland' showed that 70 employed women and/or young persons; only 29 had pasteurizing plant, but 67 thought that about four hours of Sunday work could not be avoided without severe loss to the industry. The 'vast majority' considered that the working hours laid down by the factory acts 'were quite unsuitable for the creamery business': ibid., pp. 114–15.
95   Ibid., p. 111. The concentration on summer working was said to give rise to a disadvantage on the British market – see e.g Smith-Gordon and Staples, *Rural reconstruction*, p. 109. But Ó Gráda, 'Beginnings of the Irish creamery system', pp. 289–90 contends that 'the small premium offered by creameries for winter milk probably would not have justified the costly switch from summer dairying'.
96   The creamery survey revealed, however, that forty-five of the 82 creameries were supplied with milk once every day: *Chief insp. ann. rep., 1899*, p. 115.

which would enable a business of great importance to Ireland to be carried on 'without any unnecessarily hampering restriction'.[97] Cooke-Taylor, the superintending inspector who had chaired the Dublin conference, advised the home secretary to take a 'comprehensive' view:

Many of [the creameries] are very small, acting in fact but as feeders to others. They are necessarily situated far apart, each one being the centre, as it were, of its own particular little grazing district. The circumstances of their location are thus exactly the opposite of ordinary factories, which tend to agglomerate and constitute industrial districts, and the labour of inspecting them is proportionately increased. It is even difficult to find them. Every factory is required by law to notify its existence, but the occupiers of these are commonly unaware of this responsibility. The inspector has thus to be constantly asking his way about from one to another, and depending on chance for procuring that uniform administration of the law which is above all things desirable. Further the distinction between a dairy and a creamery has never been authoritatively made, nor the status of a creamery workshop determined; and finally, the economic condition of the south and west of Ireland – where they most abound – makes it of the first importance that nothing should be done to cripple, or even seriously incommode, its one thriving and increasing industry.[98]

All these considerations persuaded Sir Matthew Ridley to accept that some special provision was necessary, and in 1900 a new 'exemption' clause was accordingly included in the new factory bill.[99] But when that bill was temporarily withdrawn, the home secretary took the opportunity to remind the creameries that they could readily comply with the law if they changed their working practices.[100] The creameries, however, stood firm; the practice of supplying milk to the creameries only once daily was *not* increasing in the south and west of Ireland, the rapid development of creameries in Ulster might lead to changes in practice there, and even in Denmark 'Sunday churning is the rule'.[101] In March 1901, R.A. Anderson, the secretary of the Irish Agricultural Organisation Society, had a meeting with Whitelegge, the chief inspector of factories, at which the terms of the ultimate settlement appear to have been agreed. During the summer months, the creameries would be allowed to work on Sundays for no more than three hours, and on weekdays women could work a maximum of 11 hours per day ('so as to compensate for the three hours worked on Sunday'), split into separate morning and evening periods of employment.[102]

97 R.A. Anderson (secretary, IAOS) to Sir Matthew Ridley (home sec.), 14 March 1900, reproduced ibid., p. 109. Anderson emphasised that he was writing on behalf of the whole dairy industry in Ireland.
98 *Chief insp. ann. rep., 1899*, p. 232.
99 Factory and Workshop Bill 1900, clause 36 – see H.C. 1900 (111), ii, 240.
100 'The Secretary of State trusts that before the difficulties .. recur next summer, the available means of meeting them without breach of the Acts will have been generally adopted in the south and west of Ireland as elsewhere': Sir Kenelm Digby (perm. under-sec., home office) to Anderson, 8 Aug. 1900, reproduced in *Chief insp. ann. rep., 1900*, pp. 102–03.
101 Anderson to Digby, 20 Oct. 1900, reproduced ibid., pp. 103–04.
102 Anderson to Sir Henry Cunynghame (legal ass't under-sec., home office), 12 March

In due course section 42 of the 1901 act provided that in the case of creameries in which women and young persons are employed, the home secretary may by special order vary the beginning and end of the working day and allow their employment for not more than three hours on Sundays and holidays – but only on the basis that no woman or young person was required to work in excess of the daily or weekly maximum number of hours allowed by the act. The details were provided in a special order issued in June 1902.[103] During the months of May to October, women and young persons could be employed for any twelve hours (including meal times) on weekdays, beginning at 6 a.m. and, including a break of at least five hours, extending to 9 p.m., and on Sundays from 6 a.m. to 9 a.m., but only on certain conditions.[104] Before adopting such hours, however, the creamery owner had to comply with the general provisions of the 1901 act by exhibiting in the workplace a written notice giving the relevant details and sending a copy to the inspector, and the owner could not change those hours without written notice to his employees and to the inspector.[105] These restrictions reflected the traditional opposition of the inspectors to unduly flexible working hours, which had made the task of inspection and enforcement much more difficult, if not impossible.

Not surprisingly, many creameries took advantage of the new exemption. Indeed, the continuing increase in their numbers and the 'special attention' which they now required led the home office in 1902 to conclude that an additional inspector was required in the south of Ireland.[106] Accordingly, W.J. Neely was transferred to Limerick and given special responsibility for the creameries 'in the more important part of the creamery district'.[107]

It soon became apparent that the provision for Sunday work was too inflexible:

It has been found in practice that the churning operations ... in many cases cannot be commenced so early as 6 a.m., and that therefore the occupiers of such places were precluded from availing themselves of the full period of three hours allowed by the Act. Again, in some of the remoter country districts it may arise that mass is read only at eight o'clock in the morning, and in this case also attendance thereat necessarily reduces the period during which the women may be employed.[108]

On Neely's advice, the home secretary conceded this point, and in 1903 the special order was amended to allow Sunday work for any three consecutive

---

1901; Cunynghame to Anderson, 29 March 1901, both reproduced ibid., pp. 105 and 106.
103 Reproduced in *Chief insp. ann. rep., 1902*, pt. I, p. 341.
104 No woman or young person was to be employed for more than five hours without an interval of at least thirty minutes for a meal, and no overtime was to be worked.
105 1901 act, ss. 32 and 60.
106 *Report of the factory staff committee 1902*, p. 14 (PRO LAB 15/5).
107 *Chief insp. ann. rep., 1904*, pt. I, p. 198. Neely, a graduate of Trinity College, Dublin, had been a junior inspector in the south of Ireland from his appointment in October 1896. In 1900 he had moved to Leeds, but returned in June 1903 to take up his appointment in Limerick.
108 *Chief insp. ann. rep., 1903*, pt. I, p. 150 (Bellhouse).

hours between 6 a.m. and 7 p.m.[109] This change 'resulted in a great improvement in the observance of the conditions laid down in the special exception'.[110]

In spite of all these efforts to resolve the problem, the inspectors were disappointed to find that 'there is still no readiness or apparent inclination on the part of the trade generally ... to make an honest attempt to arrange their work in such a manner as to conform to the [normal] requirements of the law'.[111] The problem was the nature of the industry itself: 'Most of the difficulties arise either from a want of proper "plant", and from a want of a proper system of working.' The standards of the factory acts were best observed in the larger creameries, and Bellhouse took hope from the fact that the industry appeared to be moving in the direction of fewer, but larger, churning factories.[112] Both Bellhouse and Neely were convinced that such a development was in the larger interests of the industry generally,[113] though Neely was concerned about the shortage of capital for such developments.[114] But it is clear that some creamery managers continued to think that they could in the summer make up for the necessarily short hours worked in winter,[115] and there continued to be problems with Sunday work.[116] Many occupiers contended that they could not stop the process of butter making once it had started, or that they had no choice but to break the law if they received a consignment of cream in danger of going sour.[117] The law may have gone much of the way to accommodate the special needs of the

109 Order of 23 Oct. 1903 (1903 No. 893) – see *Redgrave's Factory Acts*, ed. J. Owner (14th ed., London, 1931), pp. 71–72.
110 *Chief insp. ann. rep., 1905*, p. 207 (Neely).
111 *Chief insp. ann. rep., 1903*, pt. I, p. 150. See also *1902*, pt. I, p. 136, where Bellhouse refers to 'a small proportion of malcontents who still are inclined to argue that their trade is being ruined by the application of the acts', but adds that 'on the whole the new provisions are looked upon as perfectly equitable and just'.
112 *Chief insp. ann. rep., 1903*, pt. I, p. 150. As he had earlier explained: '[I]nstead of each creamery doing its own churning ... the cream from each will be sent to one large central dairy where the churning operations will be completed. Should such a scheme be carried out to any large extent ... the problem of the hours of labour will be still further simplified, for it would be necessary to have in such large churning centres proper refrigerating and pasteurizing plant, and it is probable that all the work could be done within the regular factory hours': *Chief insp. ann. rep., 1902*, pt. I, p. 136.
113 'This will have a good effect from a market point of view as well, owing to the greater uniformity of the butter from principal churning stations': *Chief insp. ann. rep., 1903*, pt. I, p. 151 (Neely). According to Ó Gráda, 'Beginnings of the Irish creamery system', p. 295, 'the larger creameries ... operated on a lower unit cost of production'.
114 *Chief insp. ann. rep., 1905*, p. 207. See further the note on capital investment in Ó Gráda, 'Beginnings of the Irish creamery system', p. 301. By 1911, less than one-half of the Irish creameries had pasteurising plant – see *Final report of the vice-regal commission on the Irish milk supply*, pp. 48–49 [Cd. 7129], H.C. 1914, xxxvi, 650–51.
115 *Chief insp. ann. rep., 1906*, pp. 170–71, where Williams reported that he had prosecuted two creameries in the north of Ireland for failure to give a half-holiday on Saturday, in the hope of calling general attention to the matter.
116 See e.g. ibid., p. 171, where Neely reported that the three hours' limit 'is not as strictly adhered to as it should be'.
117 *The Kerry Sentinel*, 9 Sept. 1903, p. 2.

industry; but in the view of some occupiers it had not gone far enough. In a few cases, this led to the replacement of women and girls by men,[118] and it is a matter of some irony that a derogation designed as far as possible to maintain the general standards set by the factory acts in the interests of women and young persons may in the end have cost them their employment.

AERATED WATER WORKS

Although brewing and distilling were more important sectors of the drinks industry in Ireland in terms of employment and production, it was the manufacture of aerated or mineral water which attracted greater attention from the factory inspectors. This branch of the industry expanded during the latter part of the nineteenth century[119] and by 1900 there were more than 150 plants located in cities and towns throughout Ireland, with Belfast and Dublin in particular two of the most important centres for the industry in the United Kingdom.[120] In Belfast, for example, Ross's made a Royal Ginger Ale which was 'a delicious aromatic and refreshing beverage, utterly free from any intoxicating tendency', while the 'Lithia waters' produced by Cantrell and Cochrane were advertised as 'sparkling like champagne, agreeable to the taste as that much lauded and very costly wine, but not leaving ... repentance and self reproach as a heritage of the morrow'.[121] By 1912, such beneficient delights were available throughout the world:

Of the aerated waters exported from Ireland by far the larger proportion is made in Ulster, and particularly in Belfast. These productions have found their way to the most remote and diverse countries, and governments, railways and steamship companies purchase them in enormous quantities. They also figure in the wine lists of all the leading clubs and hotels and the commissariat departments of a number of historic expeditions have included them as part of the necessary stores.[122]

The conditions of employment in aerated water works first came under scrutiny as a result of the Workshop Regulation Act 1867, and so became the

118 See e.g. *Chief insp. ann. rep., 1906*, p. 171, where Neely reported that some creameries were employing men for Sunday work. But he thought that this was only temporary, since the managers believed that dairy maids were more satisfactory. See also *Chief insp. ann. rep., 1909*, p. 33, where Allhusen reported that a good many creameries in the Cork district 'have given up the employment of dairy maids'.
119 For a brief history, see D.L. Armstrong, *The growth of industry in Northern Ireland: The story of the golden age of industrial development 1850–1900* (Long Hanborough, Oxford, 1999), pp. 461–62.
120 See *Chief insp. ann. rep., 1898*, pt. II, p. 15. By 1907 the number had increased to 183: *Chief insp. ann. rep., 1907*, p. 124.
121 *Belfast Directory 1887*, quoted J. Bardon, *A history of Ulster* (Belfast, 1992), p. 391, who says that 'Belfast was rapidly becoming a world centre for the production of aerated waters – an extraordinary achievement considering the water was obtained by boring artesian wells through the foul sleech of Cromac.' See also Plate 20 above.
122 *Belfast Newsletter*, 29 Nov. 1912.

responsibility of the factory inspectors in 1871.[123] From 1878 they would normally have qualified as non-textile factories. Given the seasonal nature of the business, which resulted in a 'press of orders ... regularly recurrent and inevitable'[124] and because 'the article supplied is in its nature perishable',[125] it was quickly accepted that special provision should be made to allow overtime to be worked on certain conditions.[126] In spite of this concession, however, a number of firms were prosecuted for employment, particularly of young persons, outside the permitted hours.[127] As in other cases, the workers should not be required to work excessive hours:

Twelve hours' work, with one and a half hours off for meals, is sufficient strain upon the health of any worker, especially upon the soda-water bottler, whose constant and continuous attention, often in a standing posture, is imperatively demanded by her occupation. The Committee do not consider it to be for the advantage of the trade, or the consuming public, or for the future of our working population, that either women or young girls should be allowed to work for an indefinite period at a harassing occupation, often in ill-ventilated or insanitary workshops, because their employers neglect to pay them for a full day's work on a scale at which they can support themselves in decency and comfort.[128]

Although the hours of employment in aerated water works remained a concern of the inspectors,[129] it was with the question of safety that they became particularly engaged.

The manufacturing of the mineral water itself gave rise to little or no risk of accidental injury; but the water then had to be bottled, stopped, inspected

123 Factory and Workshop Act 1871, s. 3. Within a year, Cramp had visited all the aerated water works in his south of Ireland district: *Chief insp. ann. rep., 1872*, p. 126.
124 *Report of the factory and workshop commissioners 1876*, p. xlii.
125 Ibid., Appendix C, pp. 19–20 (Cameron), adding that 'this is so essentially a seasonal trade that great care has to be observed during the summer months to prevent infractions of the act in the matter of overtime; and as young persons and, frequently, children are employed in considerable numbers, a strict compliance with the provisions laid down is the more essential. The various firms apply for and receive the usual permission to work for an extra two hours per diem, but the limit has always been fixed at 9 p.m.'.
126 1871 act, sch. 1; 1878 act, ss. 42 and 53 and sch. 3, pts I and III; 1901 act, s. 49 and sch. 2.
127 See e.g. *Chief insp. ann. rep., 1876*, pp. 133 (Cantrell & Cochrane of Belfast fined £4 for employing four young persons on Good Friday, a statutory holiday) and 175 (Wright & Co. of Waterford fined 10s. for employing young person after 3 p.m. on Saturday); *Chief insp. ann. rep., 1883*, p. 144 (Moore & Co. of Belfast fined £3 for employing a young person without a fitness certificate, the firm having previously been cautioned on several occasions); *Chief insp. ann. rep., 1888*, p. 223 (Kirker & Co. of Belfast fined £1 10s. for three like offences).
128 *First report of the departmental committee appointed to inquire into and report upon certain miscellaneous dangerous trades*, p. 27 [C. 8149], H.C. 1896, xxxiii, 27. The committee had been informed that some women were keen to work longer hours because they received 3d. an hour for overtime.
129 See e.g. *Chief insp. ann. rep., 1911*, p. 321 (88 of 125 convictions of mineral water factories in the United Kingdom were in respect of employment offences).

and labelled.[130] The bottlers who operated the filling machines were exposed to the greatest danger, since the bottles frequently burst while they were being filled under pressure or when they were being removed from the filling machine. The wirers who put stoppers or corks into the bottles,[131] the sighters who checked the filled bottles for impurities, and finally the labellers were exposed to a lesser risk, although the bottles could burst at any of these stages. In Britain, most of this work was done by women, whereas in Ireland 'all the work, with trifling exceptions, was done by men and boys'.[132]

Many of the workers wore protective face-guards[133] and arm gauntlets, and these undoubtedly reduced the number of accidents. But some employers did not provide such protection – and, even when they did, the workers often failed to wear them, particularly when supervision was lax:

> In the mineral water works (of which there are a large number) scattered over the various towns of Ireland, more particular attention has been paid to induce the masters to enforce the wearing of shields or helmets over the face for protecting those employed in filling the bottles with aerated water.... Further attention has also been given ... to the supplying and wearing of armlets, for the better protection against accidents by those employed in the mineral-water factories, and I am glad to be able to report that numbers of occupiers have already complied with these requirements.[134]

The number of accidents across the United Kingdom, however, gave rise to continuing concern, and the home secretary responded by referring the matter to the dangerous trades committee. In 1896 they concluded that more could be done to safeguard the workers throughout the industry and recommended that the bottling process should be certified as 'dangerous to life or limb' so that special rules could be made under the authority conferred by section 8 of the Factory and Workshop Act 1891.[135] In spite of 'considerable opposition' from a large number of the manufacturers,[136] the home secretary agreed, and in 1897 made an order setting out special safety rules to apply in respect of the bottling of aerated water.[137]

---

130 See generally R. Squire, 'Women's labour in aerated water works', in T. Oliver (ed.), *Dangerous trades: The historical, social and legal aspects of industrial occupations as affecting health* (London, 1902), chap. L. For a detailed analysis of the injuries caused by 'explosions' in such plants in 1900, see *Report by Mr Simeon Snell on the bottling of aerated waters*, in *Chief insp. ann. rep., 1900*, pp. 80–81.
131 Wiring was considerably reduced with the introduction of patent stoppers, such as the 'Crown stopper' – a metal cap squeezed onto the top of the bottle – which was widely used in Ireland: *First report of the dangerous trades committee, 1896*, p. 27.
132 Ibid.
133 Two different sorts of guards were used – goggles and masks – but it was found in practice that goggles which covered only the eyes failed to give sufficient protection to the face.
134 *Chief insp. ann. rep., 1890*, pp. 24–25 and *1891*, p. 6 (Woodgate).
135 *First report of the dangerous trades committee, 1896*, p. 1.
136 *Chief insp. ann. rep., 1897*, p. 60 (Whitelegge).
137 Set out ibid., p. 61.

All occupiers were now required to provide bottlers with face-guards, masks or veils of wire gauze, and with full-length gauntlets for both arms – and the bottlers 'shall' wear them while at work. The occupiers were also to provide wirers, sighters and labellers with face-guards or goggles, and with gauntlets for both arms protecting at least half of the palm and the space between the thumb and forefinger – and, once again, those workers, with the exception of labellers when labelling bottles standing in cases, 'shall' wear them while at work. Finally, the occupiers were to 'cause all machines for bottling to be so constructed, so placed, or so fenced, as to prevent as far as possible, during the operation of filling or corking, a fragment of a bursting bottle from striking any bottler, wirer, sighter, labeller or washer'.[138]

In general, the occupiers appear to have attempted to comply with the new rules; the problem was that 'there has not been the same readiness on the part of the workers to adopt the precautions which are required of them'.[139] As in the linen industry, the inspectors found that many of the workers objected to the wearing of protective safeguards which they claimed were uncomforable or even dangerous. The rules did not require any of the safeguards to be 'suitable' or to be maintained in good condition, and it is clear that some face-masks were more comfortable to wear than others.[140] Some workers even claimed that the masks or guards which they were required to use endangered their eyesight – a claim specifically refuted in 1900 in a special report by an opthalmic surgeon commissioned by the chief inspector.[141] But comfort and safety were not the only considerations: 'The sighters say the faceguard interferes with their proper observation of the bottles, and the labellers dislike the gauntlets, or woollen mittens, because they interfere with the rapid handling of the bottles.'[142]

The inspectors sought to enforce the rules by prosecuting workers rather than employers. In 1899, two wirers and two bottlers in Dublin works were each fined five shillings for failing to observe the safety rules,[143] and in the following year prosecutions were successfully brought against eight wirers

---

138 As Squire, a lady inspector, explained in 'Women's labour in aerated water works', pp. 698–700, the washers were a class of workers not otherwise covered by the rules; like women in wet-spinning mills, they worked in wet conditions which were unhealthy; unlike the spinners, however, they were not required by special rule to be provided with waterproof aprons.

139 See e.g *Chief insp. ann. rep., 1901*, pt. I, p. 136 (Bellhouse). Under 1891 act, s. 9(1), continued by 1901 act, s. 85, an occupier was liable for the breach of any special rule by a worker unless he proved that he had taken all reasonable means by publishing, and to the best of his power enforcing, that rule.

140 'The masks at present in use admit of improvement so as to be worn with more comfort ... they should be as light as possible, and fit without undue pressure': *Report on the bottling of aerated waters, 1900*, p. 80.

141 Ibid., p. 72. Having examined workers in seventeen factories in England, Snell concluded that 'there is no evidence of the protectors causing injury to eyesight'.

142 T. Oliver, *Diseases of occupation from the legislative, social and medical points of view* (London, 1908), p. 375.

143 *Chief insp. ann. rep., 1899*, pp. 407 and 409.

and two bottlers.[144] But the inspectors were not wholly unsympathetic to the workers' concerns: 'Even H.M. Inspectors are sometimes loath to call upon grown men to enclose their heads in wire cages against their will, contrivances which [the men] declare are injurious and offensive to them, or to wear gauntlets on their arms, represented by them to be productive of rheumatism and allied complaints.'[145] Bellhouse, who was 'exceptionally active' in seeking to enforce the new rules in the south of Ireland, agreed: 'The face-guards appear to be specially objected to, and, as it seems to me, not altogether without cause. Long periods of work, during which the eye is being constantly used through a veil of netting with a very close mesh, must, I think, be very trying even to strong eyes.'[146]

Workers who failed to observe the rules did not just expose themselves to the possibility of a small fine; if injury resulted, they risked disqualification from compensation[147] and considerable hardship:

I interviewed one woman aged 20 years, who had been employed in one [Irish mineral water] works from three to four years and had met, during this time, with three accidents, by one of which she had been deprived of almost the entire sight of one eye; in another her arm was severely cut and she had lost most of the power in one finger. Each accident necessitated several weeks of idleness. Her wages were eight shillings a week and it was before the days of National Health Insurance.[148]

The obvious solution to the problem was better machinery,[149] better safety equipment – or stronger bottles.[150] Better supervision by employers also helped: 'from the way in which [the safety rules] are complied with in certain works it is evident that occupiers can enforce them'.[151] Some employers were, however, reluctant to press the issue 'as if they dismissed their hands, they would find difficulty in replacing them'.[152]

144 Six wirers and one bottler working in Newry, Belfast and Ballymena were each fined one shilling; those convicted in Dublin and Cork were each fined five shillings: *Chief insp. ann. rep., 1900*, pp. 659, 664 and 670.

145 Ibid., p. 329 (Cooke-Taylor).

146 Ibid. Bellhouse also acknowledged that 'cold, wet, woollen gauntlets can't be agreeable at any time': *Chief insp. ann. rep., 1901*, pt. I, p. 136.

147 See especially *M'Caffrey v. Great Northern Railway Co.* (1902) 36 ILTR 27, and below, chap. 11.

148 H. Martindale, *From one generation to another, 1839–1944* (London, 1944), p. 121, expanding upon her original report in *Chief insp. ann. rep., 1909*, p. 140.

149 It was, for example, thought that a new rotary bottling machine, which was automatic and completely enclosed, 'should practically do away with accidents while filling': *Chief insp. ann. rep., 1909*, p. 114. Two years later it was reported that 'certain makes of bottle-filling machines have excellent fixed guards to minimise the danger arising from the process': *Chief insp. ann. rep., 1911*, p. 33.

150 Some makers supplied bottles with a 'guarantee' that only three per cent would burst, but some mineral water manufacturers were prepared to pay a higher price for a better bottle; new bottles were more likely to burst than those returned for further use: see *Report on the bottling of aerated waters, 1900*, p. 77.

151 *Chief insp. ann. rep., 1903*, pt. I, p. 148 (Nicholl).

152 *Chief insp. ann. rep., 1905*, p. 205 and *1907*, p. 125 (Warren).

All that the inspectors could do in such circumstances was to exhort all concerned to do better. But they were clearly exasperated by the attitude of many of the workers: 'Not only do such defaulters expose themselves to risk of injury, but too often they set an influential and bad example to new hands. They merit full penalties.'[153] And so the prosecution of 'defaulters' continued. In 1908, for example, Michael Landers of Tralee, who had bottled mineral waters for twenty-four years, was found on several occasions to be working without protective wear. His excuse was that the mask hurt his eyes. The inspector was not entirely unsympathetic – he brought a prosecution, but asked for a nominal fine. The court convicted and fined Landers five shillings; but they warned him that if he appeared before the court for a second offence, the full penalty would be imposed.[154] In 1909, five workers were successfully prosecuted in Belfast,[155] and when, in 1911, an exceptionally hot summer led many workers to put aside their face-guards and arm gauntlets, prosecutions were taken 'in the interests of factory discipline and the workers' own welfare'.[156]

By the end of the period under consideration, the inspectorate were satisfied that they were making some progress, the number of reported accidents in mineral water works across the United Kingdom having declined from 831 in 1901 to 347 in 1910.[157] But the number of 'severe' accidents had increased, and the inspectorate once again pinned their hopes on new technology, since 'the old difficulties and objections to the merely palliative safeguards of masks and gauntlets continue unabated'.[158]

LUCIFER MATCH WORKS

A method of applying phosphorus to a wooden stick was discovered in the early 1830s, and by 1840 'lucifer' or 'strike anywhere' matches, using white or yellow phosphorus,[159] were being extensively manufactured in Great Britain and in many other parts of western Europe. As early as 1843, the industry employed not just women and young persons, but a large number of children from the age of seven or eight, who were required to work long hours, often during the night, in 'unwholesome' conditions.[160] By 1850,

---

153 *Chief insp. ann. rep., 1906*, p. 166 (Knyvett, superintending insp., Scotland/Ireland division).
154 *The Kerry Sentinel*, 10 Aug. 1908, p. 3.
155 *Chief insp. ann. rep., 1909*, p. 113.
156 *Chief insp. ann. rep., 1911*, p. 33 (Lewis, superintending insp., SW division).
157 See *Chief insp. ann. rep., 1910*, pp. 234–35. Separate figures for Ireland are not available.
158 *Chief insp. ann. rep., 1911*, pp. 121 (Eraut) and 143 (Anderson). By 1914 the number of reported accidents had risen to 499: *Chief insp. ann. rep., 1914*, p. 129.
159 'Safety' matches could also be made with red phosphorus or sesquisulphide of phosphorus, which was much less dangerous to health. But relatively few of these matches were made in the United Kingdom before 1900.
160 *Second report of the commissioners for inquiring into the employment and conditions of*

medical experts had identified 'a most painful and loathsome disease' arising from exposure to white or yellow phosphorus, and this disease, which affected adults as well as children, quickly became known as 'necrosis of the jaw', or more colloquially, 'phossy jaw'. The first symptoms of the disease were toothache and inflamed gums; then –

The wound in the gum ... was found not to heal; offensive matter would begin to ooze from it, and ere long a portion of the alveolus [the tooth socket in the jaw bone] became exposed. Occasionally the portion of the bone thus denuded came away, bringing with it, perhaps one or two of the neighbouring teeth, and the disease made no further progress. More frequently, however, the disease continued to spread; and sometimes slowly, sometimes rapidly, more and more of the jaw-bone became denuded, the gums grew spongy ... the teeth got loose and fell out, the fetid suppuration became more and more copious.... And thus the disease continued to progress, till in the course of six months, a year, two years – it might be even five or six years – the patient sank [died] from debility, or from phthisis, or from some other consequence of the local affection; or, having lost piecemeal ... large portions ... of the upper or lower jaw, returned to his original state of health, but the victim of a shocking and permanent deformity.[161]

Four aspects of the manufacturing process exposed the worker to the risk of infection: mixing the phosphorus with other ingredients to form a paste; dipping bundles (or 'frames') of wooden or wax match-sticks in the paste; drying the bundles of matches after dipping, and boxing the dried matches.

In 1862, the dangers to the health of a workforce which consisted largely of 'protected' persons brought lucifer match-making to the attention of another children's employment commission. The commission accepted that there was a serious risk to those who worked in small, inadequately ventilated and generally 'ill-arranged' factories. But 'where ... the places of work are well-arranged and airy, and where the employer is careful to lay down, and to cause to be attended to, sanitary regulations which are the best safeguards against the danger to health attending some of the processes, the liability to the disorder is greatly diminished and, in many cases, seems to have been almost entirely removed'.[162] These conditions could be secured by bringing

children in mines and manufactories: Trades and manufactures, pp. 140–41, H.C. 1843 [430], xiii, 449.

161 Dr G. Cunningham (senior dental surgeon, London Hospital), 'Report to the secretary of state for the home department on the use of phosphorus in the manufacture of lucifer matches, with special reference to the dental aspects of the question', p. 150 in *Reports on the use of phosphorus in lucifer match manufacture* [C. 9188], H.C. 1899, xii, 600. See also Dr T. Oliver, 'Report to the secretary of state for the home department on the use of white and yellow phosphorus', ibid., p. 545 and his chapter on 'Phosphorus and lucifer matches' in Oliver (ed.), *Dangerous trades*, chap. xxvii.

162 *First report of the commissioners on employment of children in trades and manufactures not already regulated by law*, p. xlix [C. 3170], H.C. 1863, xviii, 51. This conclusion was supported not only by the medical evidence given to the commission, but also by an independent medical report prepared for John Simon, the medical officer of the privy council: ibid., p. liv and *Fifth annual report of the medical officer of the committee*

the industry within the provisions of the factory acts, 'detaching' rooms used for the manufacture of lucifer matches from other premises, prohibiting the employment of children and young persons with decayed teeth, and appointing a special medical inspector, on a temporary basis, to draw up special rules designed to protect the health and safety of the workers generally.[163]

Some of these recommendations were implemented by the Factory Acts Extension Act 1864 which, as part of the first general 'extension' of the acts to non-textile factories, specifically applied to 'any place in which persons work for hire in making lucifer matches, or in mixing the chemical materials for making them, or in any process incidental to making lucifer matches, except the cutting of the wood'. In addition to the existing general provisions, it was provided that every factory was to be kept in 'a cleanly state' and properly ventilated and that no child, young person or woman was to take any meals in any part of a factory where lucifer matches were manufactured. But no other restrictions were placed on the employment of children or young persons – and no provision was made for the appointment of a special medical inspector.

The few match factories in Ireland at this time appear to have been so 'ill-arranged' as to have been badly in need of regulation.[164] Thus, Malcomson's of Belfast was described as follows:

A long narrow building of three stories, low and flat ceiled, standing in a street and necessarily confined .... The ground floor is a wood-cutting shop, where four men and three boys work; on the first floor girls make boxes. In this a quantity of matches are stored, and cause a strong smell. The second floor is the match-making shop.... There is no roof ventilation, and only three very small square windows on one side, and small window holes, kept closed by shutters, on the other. At the farther end is a room perfectly dark, heated by a stove, for drying the wood splints before being dipped. The composition is heated at this stove, but is brought out into the lighter room to be stirred, close by some of the boys.... In this workshop the matches are dipped, set on racks to dry, and cut and put into boxes. The smell is strong and oppressive.[165]

The employees included children as young as Margett Hore, age 8: 'Here half a year. Makes boxes. Comes at 6 [a.m.]. Leaves off at 7 [p.m.]. "Nine at your breakfast and two at your dinner." Goes home. Tea after she has done. Works by the piece. Can make 1*s*. 3*d*. a week sometimes, or a 1*s*. .... Cannot read.... Cannot write.... "My da learns me when I go home every evening, except some evening he's late, and does not."'[166]

No evidence has been found as to the enforcement of the 1864 act in Ireland. But although they were told that phossy jaw 'has entirely ceased', the

of council on the state of the public health, pp. 13 and 162–205, H.C. 1863 (161), xxv, 13 and 162–205.

163 *First report of the children's employment commission 1863*, p. liv.
164 A report prepared for the commissioners by J.E. White contains details of three Irish factories – two in Belfast (Malcomson and Osborne) and one in Dublin (Johnson) – which employed about 120 'protected' persons, including 21 children: ibid., pp. 101–05.
165 Ibid., p. 102.
166 Ibid., p. 103. A boy aged six was employed in Johnson's of Dublin.

factory and workshop commissioners in 1876 nevertheless recommended that the employment of children in the dipping of matches should be prohibited as being one of a number of activities 'specially prejudicial to the health of workers of tender years',[167] and the Factory and Workshop Act 1878 so provided.[168] This new provision combined with other factors to bring about improvements in the Irish match factories:

[T]here is a marked social improvement in the class of workers engaged in this trade. In former times the industry was somewhat looked down on, and there was considerable difficulty in securing respectable hands. This was met by employment at an early age, and gradual education, which, in a measure, secured continuance of service, but such difficulties have now disappeared. The employment of children also has ceased owing to improvements in machinery in the factory.[169]

But the act did little to reduce the incidence of 'phossy jaw', and when the hazardous working conditions at Bryant and May's factory in London were exposed to the public during the famous match-girls' strike of 1888,[170] the home secretary called for a further report on the industry. The inquiry, conducted by three factory inspectors, produced evidence which 'proves the necessity for adopting every reasonable means for getting entirely rid of so fearful a malady'.[171]

The 'reasonable' means turned out to be further regulation rather than outright prohibition – a compromise still supported by medical opinion.[172] In June 1892 the home secretary, acting under the general power conferred by section 8 of the 1891 act, certified that the manufacture of lucifer matches, 'except such as are made with red or amorphous phosphorus', was dangerous or injurious to health. As a result, it became unlawful to operate a lucifer match factory unless it was certified by a factory inspector to conform to a number of special rules.[173] The processes of mixing, dipping and drying must be undertaken in departments which were separate from the rest of the

---

167 *Factory and workshop commissioners 1876: Minutes of evidence*, p. 6 (Redgrave) and *Report*, p. lxxxv.

168 Section 38 and sch. 1, para. 4(b), re-enacted as 1901 act, s. 77(4). For the purposes of the general provisions of the act, lucifer match factories were classified as non-textile factories.

169 *Chief insp. ann. rep., 1887*, pp. 21–22 (Cameron). Cf. the children employed in match factories in London were 'the poorest of the poor and the lowest of the low': *Hansard 3*, clxxv, 1718 (14 June 1884)(H.A. Bruce).

170 N. Mackenzie and J. Mackenzie, *The first Fabians* (London, 1977), p. 91. In 1892 the chief inspector (Sprague Oram) explained that his inspectors had not been able to discover the true situation because 'the victims are immediately removed from work and attended by the firms' medical advisers and supported at the expense of the firms': *Chief insp. ann. rep., 1892*, p. 21.

171 Ibid., p. 31 (Sprague Oram).

172 'Match-making is not incompatible with a good share of health, and with life of average duration, provided always the workpeople are sound when they take up the occupation, and that they rigidly attend to cleanliness and work in well-ventilated rooms': J.T. Arlidge, *The hygiene diseases and mortality of occupations* (London, 1892), p. 459.

173 These rules are set out in *Chief insp. ann. rep., 1892*, p. 32.

factory and provided with 'efficient means', both natural and mechanical, for thorough ventilation; washing conveniences of a specified type must be provided and measures taken to ensure that every worker washed his or her hands and face before meals and before leaving the works – a precaution underlined by imposing a reciprocal obligation on the workers themselves. Finally, any worker complaining of toothache or of swelling of the jaw must be immediately examined by a qualified medical practitioner at the occupier's expense and any symptoms of necrosis were to be reported to the factory inspector; no person who had suffered from necrosis or had a tooth extracted was permitted to resume work without a certificate of fitness from a medical practitioner.

The promulgation of these rules was followed by a special inspection, by May Abraham, one of the newly-appointed lady inspectors, of all the lucifer match factories in the United Kingdom.[174] Only two cases of necrosis were found in one factory, but the severe nature of the disease was considered to make it desirable to add a further requirement to the effect that all workers should be medically examined at least once a month.[175] By this time, there were five match works in Ireland – three in Belfast, and one each in Dublin and Cork. Paterson & Co., with factories in Belfast and in Dublin, were the largest employers; the other three firms (Irish Match Co. and Francis Mussen in Belfast and O'Donovan & Sons of Cork) were all small affairs.[176] Altogether they employed no more than 237 persons, out of a total of 4,300 for the United Kingdom.[177] The factories in Dublin and Cork, at least, were found to be 'well ventilated with strong currents of fresh air wherever workers are employed.... No cases of necrosis are reported';[178] both were willing to adopt the extra precautions laid down in the special rules – but 'as there has never been any real case of illness in either factory, it is difficult to say to what extent the hands have benefitted thereby'.[179]

But this was clearly *not* the case elsewhere; in the five years 1894–1898 there were thirty-six recorded cases of necrosis among the 2,000 or so workers exposed to phosphorus in the match factories of the United Kingdom.[180] In 1898, the home secretary instructed the principal lady inspector (Adelaide Anderson) to conduct a 'systematic' enquiry into the observance of the rules 'with a special view ... to detecting unreported cases, if any, of phosphorus

---

174 See *Chief insp. ann. rep., 1893*, pp. 132–33.
175 Ibid., pp. 135–36.
176 *Chief insp. ann. rep., 1898*, pt. II, p. 30.
177 Professor Thorpe, 'Report to the secretary of state for the home department on the use of phosphorus in the manufacture of lucifer matches', pp. 9–10, in *Reports on the use of phosphorus in lucifer match manufacture 1899*, pp. 459–60.
178 *Report by Miss Eliza Orme and Miss May Abraham on the conditions of work in various industries in ... Ireland*, p. 326 [C. 6894–XXIII], H.C. 1893–94, xxxvii (pt. 1), 874.
179 *Chief insp. ann. rep., 1895*, p. 55.
180 See 'Introductory memorandum by the chief inspector', p. vi, in *Reports on the use of phosphorus in lucifer match manufacture 1899*, p. 442. These were the 'reported' cases; it seems likely that many cases were not reported.

necrosis or slighter symptoms of phosphorus poisoning'.[181] 'Several' unreported cases of necrosis were found, as was evidence of 'deliberate and long-continued concealment'. In addition, there were 'many' other cases of ill-health 'possibly partly attributable to the lack of proper nourishment attendant on miserably low wages, but also, no doubt, to the generally unhygienic conditions in workrooms' – although the special rule relating to washing after meals and on leaving work was 'generally and carefully carried out'. The Irish works were on this occasion inspected by Lucy Deane, who reported as follows:

[T]wo points were especially noticeable. First, the fact that medical practitioners (with the exception of certifying surgeons) were almost universally ignorant of the necessity for reporting cases of phosphorus poisoning contracted in factories.... Secondly, that the methods of ventilation were, except in one instance, unsatisfactory; in one or two instances, very much so.... Even where mechanical ventilation was employed, as in Belfast, the position in which one of the firms had placed the fan minimised its usefulness.... The dangerous and non-dangerous departments were in some cases not properly separated so that workers were needlessly subjected to the fumes, and the provision for washing the hands was also in some cases unsatisfactory....[182]

Miss Anderson was not sure what to make of all these reports: 'It is difficult to say which of two results of the whole inquiry appeared to us more impressive, the silent endurance of extraordinary suffering or the general apathy in the factories towards such measures as had been so far prescribed for lessening the risks of the occupation.'[183]

Such findings – and reports of developments in other European countries[184] – made it clear that, although the 1892 rules had improved conditions and lessened the risk of necrosis, further action was required. Accordingly, the home office commissioned further scientific and medical reports, which were then evaluated by the chief inspector of factories.[185] Whitelegge agreed that 'due diligence' has not been generally exercised 'either in observing the letter and spirit of the existing rules, or in introducing the improvements and precautions which have been brought forward, to some extent, in this country, but more extensively abroad, since the rules were framed'.[186] He considered the possibility of outright prohibition,[187] but decided against it. The United Kingdom had an extensive export trade in matches which might

181 *Chief insp. ann. rep., 1898*, pt. II, p. 160.
182 Ibid., p. 161.
183 Ibid., p. 160.
184 Denmark had already prohibited the use of yellow phosphorus for matches and a number of other countries were considering doing so.
185 The reports, by Professor Thorpe, Dr Oliver and Dr Cunningham, are in *Reports on the use of phosphorus in lucifer match manufacture* [C. 9188], H.C. 1899, xii, 437.
186 'Introductory memorandum by the chief inspector', ibid., p. v.
187 Whitelegge was advised by Professor Thorpe, principal chemist of the government laboratory, that 'as yet, no method of using [red or amorphous phosphorus] in a "strike anywhere" match is commercially possible': 'Report on the use of phosphorus', ibid., p. 17.

be lost should the country act unilaterally. He accepted that 'if grave injury to the health of the workpeople were inevitable, the loss of the trade might well be regarded as the smaller sacrifice of the two'; but the expert reports pointed to a different conclusion: 'With due selection of workpeople, strict medical and dental supervision, proper structural and administrative conditions, and substitution of machinery for hand labour in the phosphorus processes, it seems that the dangers hitherto attending the use of yellow phosphorus can be overcome.'[188]

Accordingly 'more stringent' special rules were issued in 1899.[189] These were much more detailed than the earlier rules,[190] and in particular provided for all workers to be examined within one month of first employment and thereafter at least once every three months by the certifying surgeon and by a duly qualified dentist appointed for this purpose by the occupier. The certifying surgeon or the dentist could suspend from work any worker found to be suffering from phosphorus necrosis or to be in such a condition as to incur danger of injury to health if allowed to continue to work in a phosphorus process, and no suspended person could return to work without a certificate of fitness signed by the certifying surgeon or appointed dentist. All relevant details of medical and dental examinations were to be recorded in a 'health register' to be produced at any time when required by a factory inspector.

The new rules were accompanied by a circular from the home secretary:

While the Secretary of State believes that most of the manufacturers will be ready voluntarily to adopt the medical and dental precautions, the improved machinery and ventilation and other methods of precaution recommended by the experts, it will clearly be his duty without delay to take steps to see that the necessary safeguards for the protection of the health of the work people are established and effectively maintained in all factories in which white and yellow phosphorus continue to be used.[191]

This barely disguised warning apparently led to – or at least was shortly followed by – the closure of several of the Irish match factories. In 1907, it was reported that the new rules were being 'well carried out' by Paterson's and

---

188 'Introductory memorandum by the chief inspector', p. viii. Professor Thorpe had advised that 'It has been conclusively established that where such rules are vigorously enforced, phosphorus necrosis has almost entirely disappeared': 'Report on the use of phosphorus', p. 12.

189 See *Chief insp. ann. rep., 1899*, pp. 52–54. The rules were criticised as too weak and an unsuccessful attempt made to annul them when they were presented in parliament – see especially *Hansard 4*, lxxxii, 985 (7 May 1900).

190 Thus, all rooms in which a phosphorus process was carried on were to contain at least 500 cubic feet of air space per worker, and separate ventilation requirements were imposed for each part of the manufacturing process, so that, for example, 'Boxing shall not be done except under a hood provided with an efficient exhaust fan so arranged as to draw the fumes away from the boxer and prevent them from entering the air of the boxing room.'

191 Sir Henry Cunynghame (legal ass't under-sec., home office) to Irish Match Co., 16 March 1899, PRO HO 87/16, 3123930/169 ('Draft for Circulation', p. 99).

that no cases of necrosis had occurred.[192] But enquiries elsewhere produced less satisfactory results – and it was also becoming clear that the obvious advantages of 'safety matches' were leading more and more European countries to prohibit the use of white or yellow phosphorus altogether. In 1905, however, the government refused to support an International Labour Organisation convention designed to bring about an 'absolute' prohibition.[193] In the absence of assurances that most other countries would follow suit, such action 'would destroy the remainder of the industry of match-making with white phosphorus in this country'; in any case, 'it was an open question whether the existing special rules would not satisfactorily deal with the matter'.[194]

But a widely-publicised death from necrosis and continued agitation for reform forced the home office to concede at least that the special rules should be further tightened up.[195] Faced with this 'oppressive' proposal, the manufacturers finally agreed among themselves to prohibition – provided this was coupled with a reciprocal ban on the importation of lucifer matches. The home secretary agreed,[196] and in due course, section 1(1) of the White Phosphorus Matches Prohibition Act 1908 made it illegal for any person to use white phosphorus in the manufacture of matches after 1 January 1910, thus allowing the United Kingdom somewhat belatedly to sign and ratify the Berne Convention of 1906.

CONVENT LAUNDRIES

The regulation of laundries began when those which formed part of a manufacturing process (such as the making of linen) became subject to inspection under the Factory Acts Extension Act 1867, as involving 'manual labour ... incidental to making ... or adapting for sale any article'.[197] The inclusion of the words 'for sale', however, meant that the 1867 act did not apply to the new 'commercial' laundries which, as a result of new technology, were

---

192   *Chief insp. ann. rep., 1906*, p. 170 and *1907*, p. 129 (Jackson).
193   Opposition from other countries, including Sweden and Japan, meant that general agreement could not be reached in 1905 or 1906; the five European countries which had already prohibited the use of white phosphorus – Germany, Denmark, France, Holland and Switzerland – together with Italy and Luxembourg agreed in 1906 to their own convention, which was to come into force in 1912. See *Chief insp. ann. rep., 1908*, p. iv.
194   *Hansard 4*, cl, 1397–99 (2 Aug. 1905) and clxxiii, 179 (25 April 1907). See also *Memorandum on the international conference on labour regulations held at Berne, September 1906*, pp. 5–6 [Cd. 3271], H.C. 1906, cxxi, 283–84.
195   *Chief insp. ann. rep., 1907*, p. xix and *1908*, pp. iv–v (Whitelegge). This was also the view taken by Sir Henry Cunynghame and Whitelegge in their *Report to the secretary of state for the home department ... on the match factory of Messrs Moreland & Sons, Gloucester, with special reference to a recent fatal case of phosphorus necrosis* [Cd. 3373], H.C. 1907, x, 441.
196   See *Hansard 4*, cxcvii, 1746 (3 Dec. 1908).
197   1867 act, s. 3(7).

transforming what had been essentially a domestic operation into a modern industry:

The old-fashioned 'washerwoman' is fast disappearing, and is superseded by the enterprising young 'laundry proprietor' who, turning the tubs out of the back kitchen, fills their place with 'washing-machines' and, connecting them with a little gas-engine … blossoms forth as the owner of a 'factory laundry', ready to deal with six times the amount of work that his predecessor could hope to cope with….[198]

Side by side with this development … is to be found the rapid multiplication of the large laundry companies and syndicates, certain of which own as many as a dozen or more fine well-equipped steam laundries filled with the latest ingenious inventions in labour-saving machinery, and organised into 'departments' in which the division of labour is at least as marked a feature as it is in the majority of non-textile factories. … In place of the elderly married woman or widow 'washer', we find skilled engineers in charge of a shedful of machinery still called the wash-house, while scores of girls and young women, from thirteen years upwards, 'tend' the various kinds of ironing machines, with exactly the same mechanical precision and routine as those in any other factory….[199]

The appalling working conditions in many of these 'commercial' laundries gave rise to widespread and continuing concern.[200] But the apparently simple task of bringing them under the aegis of the factory acts was so intertwined with the political and religious controversy surrounding the inspection of yet another group of laundries – the 'convent' laundries – that it took forty years to complete the process of regulation begun in 1867.

During the nineteenth century, in Great Britain as well as Ireland, religious orders provided work for 'penitents' living in the community or in an institution run by the order.[201] Of particular concern in the present context were the 'Magdalen' or 'refuge' convents,[202] which were established throughout Ireland (and elsewhere in the United Kingdom) for the 'reformation' of prostitutes, unmarried mothers and other 'fallen' women and girls. Many of these institutions undertook, for outside contractors, extensive laundry work which provided not only badly-needed financial support, but also a means of

---

198 These were the so-called 'tenement' laundries.

199 *Chief insp. ann. rep., 1900*, p. 382 (Deane).

200 See especially L. Deane, 'Laundry workers' in Oliver (ed.), *Dangerous trades*, chap. xlvii and P.E. Malcolmson, *English laundresses: A social history 1850–1930* (Urbana, Illinois, 1986).

201 'Amongst the industries started by Sisters in various parts of Ireland are hand-loom linen weaving, power-loom tweed weaving with spinning, hosiery, cooking, baking, dairy farming, poultry farming, embroidery, shirt making, and plain sewing and lace making': *Orme-Abraham report on conditions of work in various industries in Ireland 1893*, p. 328. Most of these endeavours were factories or workshops within the factory acts – see e.g. *Chief insp. ann. rep., 1900*, pp. 399–400 (Squire).

202 See C. Clear, *Nuns in nineteenth-century Ireland* (Dublin, 1987), pp. 105–06; M. Luddy, 'Prostitution and rescue work in nineteenth-century Ireland', in M. Luddy and C. Murphy, *Women surviving* (Dublin, 1990), pp. 51–84 and M.P. Magray, *The transforming power of the nuns: Women, religion and cultural change in Ireland 1750–1900* (Oxford, 1998), chap. 3. See also Plate 21, above.

discipline and 'rehabilitation': 'The penitents should never be allowed to be idle.... Labour should form part of their penance; it should be proportioned to their strength and capacity. They will generally be found disposed to idleness. On the judicious employment of their time their conversion greatly depends, but they ought not to be over-worked or harassed, lest it may deject them. Laundry work is well suited to the generality of them.'[203]

In 1876 the factory and workshop commissioners explained that 'the apparently accidental absence of a word in the ... definition of a manufacturing process implying the various operations of cleaning, washing and furbishing an article, by way of trade, but not in order to its sale, has operated to exclude those employed ... in laundries ... from the protection of the law'.[204] *All* laundries should be subject to inspection, and the new Factory and Workshop Bill so provided.[205] But when an Irish member of parliament proposed an amendment to the effect that the act should not apply to 'any convent, monastery, orphanage or charitable institution',[206] the whole provision was dropped from the bill[207] – a process which was repeated in 1891.[208]

When the Trades Union Congress in 1893 passed a resolution 'strongly' urging the government to bring laundries under the factory acts,[209] the response of the home secretary (Asquith) was to direct the inspectors to make special inquiries throughout the United Kingdom. The commercial[210]

---

203 From *Guide for the religious called Sisters of Mercy* (London, 1866), reproduced in M. Luddy, *Women in Ireland, 1800–1918: A documentary history* (Cork, 1995), p. 60.

204 *Report of the factory and workshop commissioners 1876*, p. xx. The same 'accident' had led to the exclusion of those employed in railway cleaning sheds and in bottle-washing.

205 See H.C. 1878 (3), iii, 1 (clause 88 and sch. 4, pt. 2).

206 *Hansard 3*, ccxxxviii, 351 (25 Feb. 1878)(E.D. Gray, home rule MP for Co. Tipperary).

207 Ibid., col. 891 (7 March 1878). Further inquiry had convinced the home secretary (Cross) that 'there were difficulties in the matter ... which were not placed before the [factory and workshop] commission, and he thought it better to leave the laundries alone'. Accordingly the definition of 'factory' remained unchanged – see 1878 act, s. 93.

208 *Hansard 3*, ccliv, 928–47 (19 June 1891). A number of Irish MPs asserted that the inspection of convent laundries would be very much resented in Ireland, but other speakers could not see why Irish convents should stand in the way of improving conditions in English laundries. However, most agreed with the home secretary (Matthews) that the factory acts 'have, by repeated decisions of parliament, been confined to establishments in which ... articles are manufactured for purposes of gain': ibid., col. 935. The 1891 act, ss. 1 and 2 nevertheless provided a role for the inspectors in the enforcement of public health regulations in laundries.

209 See *Chief insp. ann. rep., 1893*, p. 328. An earlier resolution to the same effect had been supported by the Belfast Trades Council – see *Hansard 3*, ccliv, 932 (19 June 1891). But the Royal Commission on Labour was curiously equivocal, given that 'the women themselves often prefer to work irregular hours, and that ... to bring all laundries under the factory and workshop acts would have the effect of crushing out the small laundries ... and transferring much of the employment from women to men and boys, or to machinery': *Fifth and final report of the Royal Commission on Labour*, pp. 92–93 [C. 7421], H.C. 1894, xxxv, 100–01.

210 The Rathfarnham Laundry in Dublin had, for example, recently reduced the working day from eighteen hours 'on most days of the week' to twelve or thirteen hours – a reduction which had improved both the quantity and the quality of the

and convent[211] laundries in Ireland which were visited for the purposes of this inquiry received a clean bill of health. But the more general findings of the inquiry led the chief inspector to recommend in favour of regulation. The objection to inspection came largely from convent laundries, but these could be visited 'only in case of complaint and under the special instructions of the chief inspector, the nunneries to be inspected only by lady inspectors'.[212] The inclusion of the convent laundries on this basis would meet the concerns of the commercial laundries, which 'complain of the advantages which such laundries would [otherwise] possess; for instance, exemption from the cost of fencing machinery, and exemptions from the regulations affecting child labour.'[213]

Introducing the factory and workshop bill 1895, Asquith declared that the factory inspectors had brought to light 'a state of things almost incompatible with civilisation [and] certainly with the whole spirit of our factory legislation'.[214] In particular, the fencing of dangerous machinery was 'frequently neglected', and women and girls were often required to work in conditions of excessive heat and humidity for up to 85 hours per week.[215] He was prepared to exempt from regulation laundries connected with reformatories, refuges, penitentiaries and industrial homes; but now that there were lady inspectors, he could see no further need to exclude convent laundries: 'The nuns and others who carry on these institutions object, with perhaps good reason, to the intrusion of men into such places, but the inquiries that have been made in Ireland by one of the lady inspectors lead us to believe that the same objection will not be raised with regard to the inspection of these institutions by ladies.' The 'peculiar' character of some of these institutions might require 'somewhat more elastic rules'; but 'they are not entitled without inspection to have machinery which is dangerous ... or to employ persons for a larger number of hours than the factory act allows'.[216]

Issue was joined on the second reading:

work: *Report of H.M. inspectors of factories as to hours of work, dangerous machinery and sanitary conditions in laundries*, p. 7 [C. 7418], H.C.1894, xxi, 715.

211 Two convents run by the Sisters of Charity in Dublin employed most of the child labour; but 'the children are never employed under ten, and rarely under eleven, years of age [and] from that age until about fourteen they are only employed for three or four hours during the day. There is no dangerous machinery, and the sanitation is good': ibid., pp. 7–8 (Abraham). A report on Magdalen homes in Ireland made to the Royal Commission on Labour was equally favourable – see *Orme-Abraham report on conditions of work in various industries in Ireland 1893*, p. 328.

212 *Chief insp. ann. rep., 1893*, p. 330; *Report as to conditions in laundries, 1894*, p. 3.

213 *Report as to conditions in laundries, 1894*, p. 7. Cf. the Royal Commission on Labour was advised that 'the prices charged by convents are generally higher, and in no cases we heard of lower, than those of the other industries': *Orme-Abraham report on conditions of work in various industries in Ireland 1893*, p. 328.

214 *Hansard 4*, xxxii, 1454–55 (22 April 1895).

215 *Hansard 4*, xxxi, 175 (1 March 1895).

216 *Hansard 4*, xxxii, 1455 (22 April 1895).

The [convent laundries] were kept going by ladies whose lives were devoted to works of the noblest charity, and who eked out their want of fortune by the small assistance which they could derive from these laundries. He would take, for instance, the Order of the Good Shepherd, the members of which devoted their efforts to the reformation of fallen women. The ladies of these institutions viewed the intrusion by the government inspector with feelings of pain and almost horror, and he thought they certainly should not to be subjected to such treatment unless some strong case was made out.[217]

In committee, the issue was debated at considerable length. The members of the committee 'were besieged by letters and petitions from convents and homes, clergymen and philanthropists, Anglicans and Roman Catholics. The Irish vote, usually with Mr Asquith, turned solidly against him.'[218] In the event, it was decided by a large majority to exclude from the bill laundries in institutions conducted in good faith for religious or charitable purposes.[219]

The controversy over convents led to the enactment of a hotch-potch provision for the inspection of commercial laundries, which were not brought directly under the factory acts, but made subject to an ad hoc code.[220] The normal safety provisions applied; but special provision was made particularly in relation to the hours of employment on the grounds that laundries came under great pressure of work on particular days of the week: 'while the total weekly number of hours of employment should not exceed sixty [excluding mealtimes], there may be elasticity with respect to the daily distribution of these hours'.[221] This concession was criticised as illustrative of a fundamental flaw: 'In other trades, the practice of parliament has been to take the standard of the good employers, and force the bad ones up to it. With regard to laundries, [the 1895 act] took the standard of the bad employers, with the result that the good ones stand in serious danger of being forced down to it.'[222]

The inspectors in Ireland nevertheless anticipated 'little or no trouble' with the implementation of the 1895 act by commercial laundries.[223] But they were critical of the 'illogical' decision[224] to exempt convent laundries:

---

217 Ibid., col. 1484 (H. Matthews, a former home secretary).
218 H. Bosanquet, L. Creighton and B. Webb, 'Law and the laundry' in *Nineteenth Century*, (1897), 224, 225.
219 See clause as set out in *Hansard 4*, xxxv, 147–48 (3 July 1895) and 1895 act, s. 22(3).
220 1895 act, s. 22.
221 *Hansard 4*, xcv, 113 (11 June 1901). In particular, women could be required to work for up to fourteen hours a day, but only for three days in any week and not more than thirty days in any year.
222 Bosanquet, Creighton and Webb, 'Law and the laundry', p. 226.
223 *Chief insp. ann. rep., 1895*, pp. 19–20 (Bellhouse). The commercial laundry owners did, however, complain of unfair competition derived from unregulated working hours and from the fact that, being charities, 'convent' laundries often automatically received the 'high class' trade: ibid.
224 Enquiries in France and Germany had established that religious, charitable and reformatory workplaces were subject to 'the general hygienic and safety provisions of their industrial laws': Anderson, *Women in the factory*, p. 183.

If all the conditions of work are ideal, acquiescence in the general law (which requires a minimum standard far short of ideal) could not be troublesome, while the example set by a body which holds itself superior to the ordinary commercial public would be of far-reaching value. Where the conditions, however, are in any respect such as fall below the low minimum standard of the law, or such as would not be permitted in other workplaces, the case becomes graver, and from this point of view there is the very natural and just objection raised by the legitimate 'business man' who employs workers also.... Carrying on his business in a law-abiding manner and without making any high-sounding claim to philanthropy, thereby incidentally benefitting his employees, he sees other establishments in which the national standard respecting certain elementary conditions is being ignored with impunity. It certainly offends his sense of justice when he learns that the offenders being 'philanthropists' enjoy immunity from the law.

It is to be regretted that when industries are started for the avowed purpose of ameliorating the lot of the worker there should be any failure to grasp the importance of establishing them on a sound and legitimate basis, of leading the way, indeed, and setting an example by carrying them on under scrupulously law-abiding and healthy conditions.[225]

In any case, visits by inspectors to convent laundries gave rise to no problems in practice:

In every instance I received a courteous welcome from the Reverend Mother Superior, and found both she and the Sisters in charge of the weaving, lacemaking, laundry or whatever industry it might be, most anxious to learn the requirements of the Factory Acts, and where its provisions were explained to them and misconceptions cleared away all acknowledged that they were reasonable and right, and in no case was objection raised to the application of the Acts to that particular convent.... [M]y advice on many points ... was asked, and I anticipate no difficulty in securing compliance in all matters regulated by the Factory Acts in those convents hitherto unaccustomed to outside regulation, nor was any objection raised to inspection, only the hope expressed by some of the Reverend Mothers that the inspector would always be a woman.[226]

Criticism of the 1895 act[227] and the lack of uniformity in its application and enforcement,[228] the continuing danger to health and safety[229] and the

225 *Chief insp. ann. rep., 1899*, p. 274 (Deane). This was said by way of reaction to conditions in some workhouse schools run by the congested districts board, but would appear to be of general application. See also L.C.F. Cavendish, 'Laundries in religious houses' in *Nineteenth Century* (1897), 232, 233: 'We are not without warning ... of the harm that comes of even well-intentioned, ably-conducted and religiously-inspired despotisms.'

226 *Chief insp. ann. rep., 1900*, p. 400, where Squire adds that a 'strong influence for good' had been set by a pioneer in this field, the Reverend Mother Superior of the Foxford Convent, where a successful woollen factory had long been carried on.

227 The 'elasticity' as to permitted hours of work, which meant that the laundry owner could change the work hours from day to day, made the detection of illegal overtime 'exceedingly difficult': *Chief insp. ann. rep., 1895*, p. 121 (Paterson). Indeed, the home secretary in 1901 (Ritchie) conceded that these provisions were 'practically incapable of enforcement': *Hansard 4*, xcv, 113 (11 June 1901).

228 'Next to prosecutions under the Truck Act, prosecutions under section 22 of the 1895 act ... involve perhaps more technical complications and pitfalls than any other the factory inspector has to undertake ...': *Chief insp. ann. rep., 1900*, p. 383 (Deane).

229 'The constant exposure to steam ... and the long hours at exhausting work, amply

need for 'a more rational system of regulation of laundries' continued to come from inspectors in England, especially those with responsibilities in the London area.[230] The Factory and Workshop Bill 1901 accordingly took the obvious and logical step of classifying laundries simply as non-textile factories (if mechanical power was used) or as workshops (if not), and as such subject to all the 'normal' regulations.

Ritchie, the new home secretary, could not 'for the life of me' see why provisions designed to protect laundry workers from being overworked, to ensure that they worked in safe and sanitary conditions, etc. should not apply to laundries in religious and charitable institutions – though he conceded that some modification might be required, given that much of the work was done by 'persons who almost approach the criminal classes – or, at any rate, who are penitents of a character which requires reformation'.[231] This argument attracted considerable support, with some MPs also suggesting that 'a great deal of fault' had been found with some convent laundries and that the desire to be free of inspection meant that they had something to hide.[232]

But the government's proposals were nevertheless vehemently opposed, particularly by Irish MPs. Redmond thought that 'it would be a misfortune, from the point of view of the factory acts as a whole, if by any device they applied nominally a system of inspection to these institutions ... and that this inspection should be a mockery and deliberately made a nullity. It would be far better to exempt the institution from inspection than to apply a system of inspection on the understanding that it would be merely a nominal one.'[233] He explained that he was not seeking exemption for convents as such, but only for Magdalen or refuge laundries. He was supported by many other members, particularly Irish nationalist MPs, who argued that convent laundries should not be subject to state inspection at all. The idea that they had something to hide was 'utterly absurd'; the nuns were not afraid of inspection, but organisations such as the Society of the Good Shepherd did not want unnecessary interference which would weaken their authority and so impede the work of rehabilitation: 'The members of this Society ... are unanimously of opinion that the introduction into their institutions of an outside authority in the shape of government inspectors would completely

explains the tendency to pulmonary disease. The badly arranged floors ... are a constant source of discomfort and probably of ill-health.... One can only feel surprise that accidents are not more numerous when one realises that the slightest carelessness or inattention may result in the fingers or hand being drawn between the hot cylinders [of ironing rollers], and when one considers how easily such inattention may arise in the case of the overtired young workers': ibid., pp. 383–84 (Deane).

230 See generally ibid., pp. 380–88, and M.E. Tennant, *The law relating to factories and workshops, including laundries* (London, 1896).
231 *Hansard 4*, xcv, 114 (11 June 1901).
232 See e.g. *Hansard 4*, xcix, 660–62 (13 Aug. 1901), where H.J. Tennant referred to a newspaper report about two girls who had 'escaped' from a Good Shepherd laundry in England and told stories of starvation, hard work and cruel treatment.
233 *Hansard 4*, xcv, 137–38 (11 June 1901).

destroy the discipline of their institutions,[234] and make their already almost impossible task absolutely impossible.'[235] The issue was *not* a narrow sectarian one; opposition to inclusion came from Protestant as well as Roman Catholic institutions – and was not confined to Ireland.[236] Nor did the convents engage in unfair competition: 'the nuns charge higher prices for the work done in order to avoid as far as possible competing unfairly with ordinary laundries.'[237]

An attempted compromise having 'pleased neither one side nor the other', Ritchie reluctantly decided that if he was to save the other provisions of the bill, he would need to withdraw the whole clause and simply re-enact the existing law.[238] This decision was reluctantly accepted by the house of lords, albeit with government assurances that they would return to the issue 'at the earliest opportunity'.[239]

During the debates, the bishop of Winchester and others associated with laundries run by religious and charitable institutions in England stated that they would welcome visits and advice from factory inspectors, provided suitable modifications could be made in respect of their particular needs.[240] Accordingly, in January 1902, Ritchie issued a circular explaining the principles of the factory acts and asking for an indication of willingness to accept a voluntary system of inspection. The initial replies suggested that the Irish institutions were less willing to agree than their counterparts in England

234 'The penitent was not treated as an adult and had no control over her life in the refuge. The nuns organised her day and took away all the responsibility of decision-making.... Penitents were trained in deference and subordination in isolated refuges which shielded them from the world, the source of possible temptation. The nuns stressed the importance of personal guilt and that only personal discipline could lead to salvation': Luddy, 'Prostitution and rescue work', pp. 76–77.

235 *Hansard 4*, xcix, 135 and 678 (13 Aug. 1901), where Dillon contended that to have the inspection carried out by a female inspector was, if anything, likely to make things worse. Cf. T.L. Corbett (Down N.) could not understand 'the extraordinary opposition' to what seemed a fair proposal: ibid., col. 667.

236 Ritchie acknowledged that he had received 'many more representations upon this matter from religious institutions in this country ...': ibid., col. 651. But the issue did succumb to sectarian politics in south Belfast, where Colonel Saunderson, Unionist MP, was accused by T.H. Sloan of voting against the inspection of convent laundries – see J.W. Boyle, 'The Belfast Protestant Association and the Independent Orange Order 1901–1910' in *IHS*, xiii (1963), 120–21. Sloan went on to win the election in 1902 and, with support from Corbett, continued his campaign in parliament – see e.g. *Hansard 4*, cliii, 133–34 (5 March 1906)(lack of legislation solely the result of opposition from the Roman Catholic Church in Ireland).

237 *Hansard 4*, xcix, 675 (13 Aug. 1901) (Dillon).

238 Ibid., cols. 650–53. It would be 'intolerable' if the law was strengthened in respect of 'outside' laundries, while the 'immunity' for religious and charitable laundries was retained. A.J. Balfour (soon to be prime minister) agreed that this 'great consolidation bill' must not be lost on the basis of a clause on which there was 'a profound, bitter, implacable dissent': ibid., col. 685. The house approved of Ritchie's decision by a large majority – ibid., col. 692, paving the way for 1901 act, s.103.

239 *Hansard 4*, xcix, 869 (15 Aug. 1901). Earl Spencer and several other peers urged the government to restore the original clause, but the government refused to do so.

240 Ibid., col. 878.

and Scotland;[241] but later returns suggested that 44 (out of 51) Roman Catholic, and nine (out of 12) Protestant institutions in Ireland were amenable to this suggestion.[242]

To begin with, the laundries accepting voluntary inspection were, with few exceptions, found to satisfy the factory acts 'in essentials', and any advice offered by the inspectors 'was welcomed by those in charge'.[243] Bellhouse, who visited a number of convent laundries in the south of Ireland, was 'enormously impressed by the excellent arrangements in all of them for the workers'. He then went on to explain:

Much of the opposition to the factory act on the part of these institutions has been due to ignorance of what the law might mean to them. They have been afraid that we might interfere with their religious ceremonies by binding them to certain definite and unalterable hours, but I have always carefully explained matters and pointed out that they were as a matter of fact already complying to the fullest extent with all the provisions of the Act, and that its application to them could make no possible difference in their arrangements. I do not believe that there is any opposition to or feeling against visits by an inspector, male or female. In this district they are already well accustomed to such visits, for there is nearly always attached to the convent either an industrial, national or technical school, to which visits are paid by government officials, or the convent is under the control of the Congested Districts Board, and subject to visits by officials from them.[244]

But Adelaide Anderson, the principal lady inspector, was not convinced: 'in general voluntary inspection yields as regards hours, holidays ... and the like little more than a written statement from the head of the institution'.[245] Two years later, Martindale agreed that 'thorough inspection' was necessary:

Such questions as the means of escape in case of fire, ventilation, screening of the stove used for heating irons, escape of steam from the copper [boilers] have received scant attention. The periods of employment, as far as I was able to ascertain, have been usually less than those allowed by the Factory Act. It was singular to find that even in those institutions where inspection had been invited, there was a rooted objection to the essential methods of efficient inspection. With the exception of one institution ... I found fear exhibited amongst those in authority lest I should speak to the workers and, in fact, care was taken that I should not have the opportunity to do so. In almost every case I have been informed that the needed improvements, which were essential for the health of the workers, were, owing to lack of funds, out of the region of possibility.[246]

241 *Chief insp. ann. rep., 1902*, pt. I, pp. v and xxiv, and *List of religious and charitable institutions in which laundries are carried on* ... [Cd. 2500], H.C. 1905, lxxii, 501, which suggests that only 12 institutions (out of 40) in Ireland accepted inspection, as opposed to 96 (out of 152) in England and 9 (out of 12) in Scotland.
242 *List of religious and charitable institutions in which laundries are carried on* ... [Cd. 2741], H.C. 1906, xcviii, 85.
243 *Chief insp. ann. rep., 1902*, pt. I, p. 147 (Anderson). Indeed, the method of fencing calenders in one convent laundry provided a model which the London commercial laundries would do well to follow: ibid., pp. v and 165.
244 Ibid., p. 137.
245 Ibid., p. 147.
246 *Chief insp. ann. rep., 1904*, pt. I, p. 269. She was not referring specifically to convent laundries in Ireland.

These reservations came at a time of growing anxiety about the number of accidents in laundries of all descriptions, particularly with regard to young girls using irons and calenders.[247]

Accordingly, the lady inspectors set out in 1905 to visit all the convent laundries in the United Kingdom. In Ireland, Deane and Martindale were generally received 'with great civility'; but they were seldom 'met with complete frankness' and found it 'impossible not to remark that in only a few places has any request been received for advice or suggestion'. In the larger convents, 'where there is evidently more capital', the machinery was generally in good condition; but this was not so in the smaller institutions. In general, the fencing of that machinery was 'not good', there was 'extraordinary ignorance' of danger and the information with regard to accidents was 'entirely unreliable'.[248] The inspectors were clearly impressed by the profitable nature of laundry work, and suggested that commercial considerations were often given preference over the physical well-being of young girls, the training of women for domestic service and the reformatory needs of penitents.[249] With regard to the latter in particular, they challenged the underlying philosophy:

The statement ... that laundry work is beneficial for the formation, amelioration and development of character, is one which should not be accepted without grave consideration. We feel that it should be considered whether laundry work exercises the refining influence which is essential for the upraising of those degraded characters so often found in penitentiaries, and whether women, who are many of them inebriates, are best employed in a kind of work which not only induces thirst, but provides them with a trade which is notoriously one in which the temptations to drink are rampant. To anyone who has seen wash-house work in full swing, with its damp, oppressive heat, its heavy odour, it must appear at least questionable how far such work is the most suitable for the reformation and education of the kind of girl committed to a reformatory or penitentiary – whether undue weight is not given to the fact that undisciplined women take readily to this work, and that consequently little effort is made to find other employment for them.[250]

---

247 See e.g. *Chief insp. ann. rep., 1902*, pt. I, pp. 162–67 and *1904*, pp. 248–49. Cf. 'It is surprising to find in North Ireland that accidents on laundry machinery are comparatively few. Considering the large number of smoothing machines ... in use ... and their often unfenced condition, this absence of accidents stands out more prominently. I feel that this can only be accounted for ... by the fact that the hours are shorter and more regular, [and] that there is not the same rush and pressure as in London laundries': *Chief insp. ann. rep., 1906*, p. 206.

248 *Chief insp. ann. rep., 1905*, pp. 258–63; Martindale, *From one generation to another*, pp. 94–96. They were refused admission to five of the 42 Roman Catholic, and two of the 15 Protestant institutions which carried on laundry work.

249 *Chief insp. ann. rep., 1905*, pp. 259–60. Whether laundry work was suitable for growing girls 'has to be carefully weighed', and in so doing, 'it would be well to ask whether [it] would maintain its present important position in institution life were it as unremunerative as, for example, wood-carving or type-writing'. It was noticeable that the Department of Agriculture and Technical Instruction for Ireland 'holds such strong views on this question that it entirely refuses to subsidize any so-called training homes in which the girls are continually employed in laundry work carried on as a commercial enterprise'.

250 Ibid.

Having also criticised the condition of laundries in Houses of Mercy, orphanages and industrial schools run by religious orders, the inspectors concluded their report with the following indictment:

The mischief which has resulted from the acquiescence in a low standard in charitable work is incalculable, and it is deplorable that reproach is seldom attached to sheer incompetence, provided it is cloaked under sufficient good-will and charitable intention. The money spent in maintaining women and children in an institution under circumstances of overcrowding, or of uncleanliness, or of bad ventilation, or of depressing and incessant labour, or an insufficient and unsuitable diet, or under the supervision of ill-paid and incompetent matrons, had better been spent in helping them in another way. The enquiry has impressed on us the value of a minimum standard.... Taking into consideration the amount of commercial enterprise which at present exists in these charitable institutions, and the peculiar training necessary for gauging the conditions under which it is carried on, we believe that the factory inspector can render them that service.[251]

These criticisms were not addressed solely to Irish religious institutions, the conditions in which do not appear to have been significantly worse than those in other parts of the United Kingdom.[252] But it was obvious that the voluntary system of inspection had failed, and the issue of regulation, which had largely lain dormant since 1901, was at once revived.[253] In July 1906, the earl of Lytton claimed that the existing provisions relating to commercial laundries 'have proved altogether unworkable', with the result that less scrupulous employers were now exploiting the 'very large margin' which they were allowed.[254] With regard to convent laundries, the experience of voluntary inspection had shown that the fear that inspection might interfere with the authority of the sisters was 'chimerical' – and that any difficulties in applying the law owing to the character of the 'penitents' could be overcome. Some at least of the convent institutions made large profits and it was unfair to exempt them from the restrictions and limitations imposed on commercial establishments. Last, but not least, there was now evidence that although many convent laundries were well managed, 'there are many accounts ... of conditions which can only be described as far from satisfactory'.[255] The newly-

---

251 Ibid., p. 263. The managers of religious institutions 'have failed to perceive that in essence an inspector merely gauges the compliance of the matter inspected with the minimum standard laid down, not by himself, but by public opinion crystallised in some code [and that] ... those who are inspected often have at their service the advice of an experienced expert, of which not seldom they are glad to avail themselves'.
252 See e.g. *Chief insp. ann. rep., 1906*, p. 187.
253 It appears that the question of tariff reform preoccupied – and divided – the Conservatives for several years; but the election in December 1905 of a Liberal government with a large majority provided the opportunity to make good on earlier pledges: see *Hansard 4*, clxii, 21 (27 July 1906)(earl of Lytton).
254 Ibid., cols. 13–22, referring to the views of the inspectors, laundry employers and employees, and spokesmen of both political parties. The inspectors, in particular, had noted that some benevolent employers were suffering from unscrupulous competition – see e.g *Chief insp. ann. rep., 1903*, pt. I, p. 223 (Anderson).
255 *Hansard 4*, clxii, 19 (27 July 1906).

elected Liberal government conceded the strength of these considerations, and promised to deal with the question 'effectively' in forthcoming legislation.[256]

The home secretary (Herbert Gladstone) accordingly met representatives of the various institutions and their supporters (including Redmond) and negotiated a set of arrangements which would bring about a degree of compulsory inspection without unduly interfering with 'reformatory' work. Having gone 'as far as they think they can fairly go in the direction of meeting the wishes of those who are experienced in the management of these institutions'[257] – while at the same time placating the commercial laundries[258] – the government once again set out to bring all laundries under the factory acts. In spite of a last-ditch attempt to prevent the introduction of a system of 'particular inspection' for convent laundries,[259] the government finally succeeded.

The Factory and Workshop Act 1907 began by declaring that 'laundries carried on by way of trade or for the purpose of gain, or carried on as ancillary to another business [such as an hotel] or incidentally to the purposes of any public institution [such as a hospital]' were now to be considered non-textile factories (if using mechanical power) or workshops (if not) for the purposes of the factory acts.[260] The acts were also to apply to laundries forming part of a charitable or reformatory institution 'notwithstanding that the work carried on therein is not carried on by way of trade or for the purposes of gain ...'. But their application could be modified in respect of any institution which satisfied the home secretary that 'the only persons working therein are persons who are inmates of and supported by the institution, or persons engaged in the supervision of the work or the management of machinery, and that such work ... is carried on in good faith for the purposes of the support, education, training or reformation of persons engaged in it'.[261] In

---

256 Ibid., col. 23 (Earl Beauchamp).
257 *Hansard 4*, clxxiv, 739 (14 May 1907)(Earl Beauchamp). The government received strong support from the Archbishop of Canterbury, who failed to understand the objections to inspection and thought that it should be 'universal and compulsory', albeit with some modifications 'to meet their special and different conditions': ibid, cols. 741–42. One of their most strident critics was T.L. Corbett (Down, N): '[T]he Bill was scarcely worth the paper it was printed on. Clause 5 ... would ... exempt, in the most insidious way, all religious institutions from inspection of any kind whatever. ... For every one of those institutions fifty years ago, there were twenty now, and they were competing most unfairly with other laundries, in wages and hours of labour, and free from all control whatever ...': *Hansard 4*, clxxix, 1999 (6 Aug. 1907).
258 See *Hansard 4*, clxxxi, 921 (21 Aug. 1907), where Gladstone reported that 'a deputation from the Launderers' Association ... expressed themselves as satisfied with clause 5 [which] really gave nine-tenths of what was wanted'.
259 Ibid., cols. 914–923. Gladstone (at col. 921) expressly refuted the allegation that the government had made 'an undue concession to the Catholics', while Redmond (at col. 922) argued that it was the nationalist MPs who had made the greater concession.
260 Section 1. But special conditions still applied – see ss. 2 and 3, and generally A. Hutchinson and T. Taylor, *The factory acts, so far as they apply to commercial laundries* (London, 1908).
261 This provision was *not* intended to apply to institutions such as workhouses, reformatory and industrial schools and inebriate reformatories, already subject to

such cases, the managers of the institution could substitute their own scheme for regulating the hours of employment and the education of children, provided (i) the home secretary was satisfied that the provisions of the scheme 'are not less favourable than the corresponding provisions of the [1901 act]', (ii) the implementation of the scheme was subject to negative resolution by parliament, and (iii) the necessary particulars of the scheme were entered in a register for the information of the inspector.[262] The act further provided that the medical officer of an institution could, on application by the managers, be appointed by the chief inspector of factories to be the certifying surgeon for the institution,[263] and that the managers of a reformatory institution could stipulate that an inspector 'shall not, without [their] consent ... examine an inmate of the institution save in the presence of one of the managers ...'.[264] In return, as it were, the managers were required to make an annual return to the home secretary setting out all the relevant details of the institution.[265]

By 1909, Gladstone was able to report that all 358 convent laundries on the home office registers had been inspected.[266] Although more than one hundred special schemes had been approved, only five of these (three Roman Catholic and two Protestant) were in respect of institutions in Ireland.[267] There was at least one unsuccessful claim for exemption from the act altogether,[268] and a further two schemes were rejected either as exceeding

some other form of government inspection; these were covered by section 6 of the act – see *Chief insp. ann. rep. 1908*, p. viii and H.E. Austin, *The law relating to laundries, charitable, reformatory and public institutions under the factory and workshop acts 1901 and 1907* (London, 1907).

262 The home secretary could 'withdraw these concessions at any time from an institution in the event of any abuse, failure to comply with the provisions of the Act, or the like': *Explanatory statement on the Factory and Workshop Bill, 1907*, p. 3, H.C. 1907 (289), lxviii, 5.

263 This modification was applied for in most cases – see *Chief insp. ann. rep., 1908*, pp. 148 and 149.

264 By 1909, this provision had been invoked in 181 instances: *Hansard 5 (commons)*, ix, 640 (12 Aug. 1909)(Gladstone).

265 The 1909 return showed that nearly 7,000 persons were employed in laundry work: *Chief insp. ann. rep., 1909*, p. vii.

266 *Hansard 5 (commons)*, ix, 640 (12 Aug. 1909), in response to a question from Corbett. For a further exchange between Corbett (and Sloan) and Gladstone, see ibid., cols. 1768–69 (23 Aug. 1909). The matter was then dropped.

267 *Chief insp. ann. rep., 1908*, pp. vii; *Schemes for the regulation of hours of employment, etc. of workers in charitable institutions approved by the Secretary of State in pursuance of the powers conferred on him by section 5(2)(c) of the Factory and Workshops Act 1907*, H.C. 1908 (341), xcvi, 1025 (where details of twenty-three schemes are set out) and *Schemes of hours, holidays, etc. approved for institution factories and workshops to June 1909 under section 5 of the Factory and Workshop Act 1907*, PRO LAB 15/99.

268 Sir Malcolm Delevigne (ass't under-sec., home office) to Superioress, Convent of Mercy, Navan, 15 April 1908 (PRO, HO 87/20, p. 916), explaining that although exemption was 'impossible', an order of modification could be made.

permitted limits or as being too vague.[269] But 'the desire for exceptional treatment in hours' had 'practically died out' by 1910.[270]

There were, however, some serious breaches of the 1907 act. In one 'large and important' convent in the south of Ireland, Martindale found that 'practically no attempt was being made to carry out the requirements of the law', and in another 'the managers were desirous of working the inmates for no less than fourteen hours a day on three days in the week, with two hours for meals'.[271] But these were exceptional cases. Martindale herself admitted that 'in some of the institutions the high standard of cleanliness found has been most satisfactory, and the fear of accidents has resulted in good guards being chosen for the machines',[272] and two other inspectors in the south of Ireland were able to report that conditions in convent laundries now compared favourably with those in ordinary laundries.[273] By 1914, the principal lady inspector could report that 'in the great majority of homes under section 5 of the act of 1907 there continues to be faithful observance of the law'.[274]

269 Delevigne to Superioress, St. Martin's Female Orphanage, Waterford, 26 Feb. 1909 (PRO HO 87/21/174, pp. 909–10)(two hours' instruction after five hours' employment and time spent carrying out various domestic duties *not* a regime to which young girls should be subjected); Delevigne to Messrs O'Keefe and Lynch, Cork, 8 April 1908 (PRO HO 87/20/158, p. 871 ('A provision such as is suggested, Saturdays generally 9.30 a.m. to 5 p.m., could not be allowed').
270 *Chief insp. ann. rep., 1910*, p. 131 (Anderson).
271 *Chief insp. ann. rep., 1908*, p. 149. See also ibid., p. 20, where May (Dublin) reported that section 5 'has been the source of considerable difficulty'.
272 *Chief insp. ann. rep., 1910*, p. 131.
273 *Chief insp. ann. rep., 1908*, p. 20 (Franklin) and *1909*, p. 33 (Allhusen).
274 *Chief insp. ann. rep., 1914*, pp. 46–47 (Anderson).

CHAPTER TEN

The prosecution of offences

INTRODUCTION

Controversy has long raged over the most effective strategy for securing optimum compliance with regulatory standards. 'Private' enforcement, voluntary self-regulation, economic deterrence, moral persuasion and collective bargaining having been rejected or failed to bring about significant improvements in general working conditions in the early stages of the industrial revolution, the government opted in 1833 for a system of 'public' enforcement by a small corps of full-time officials appointed by and responsible to the central government. It was always envisaged that this factory inspectorate would rely primarily on a co-operative strategy, designed to raise standards by means of exhortation supported by sound practical advice and guidance. But failure to comply with the requirements of the factory acts was from the outset an offence punishable in the magistrates' courts, and in the last resort the inspector could take a recalcitrant occupier – or in appropriate cases a defaulting worker – to court with a view to the imposition of a fine. The threat posed by the stigma of conviction for a criminal offence combined with a financial penalty was intended as a form of specific deterrence which would nevertheless operate less as a means of punishing individual failure than as a method of encouraging general compliance. Accordingly, the decision to exercise what was always a discretion to bring proceedings in a magistrates' court frequently involved considerations which went beyond the individual case.

During the period under consideration, extensive changes occurred not only in the scope of the factory acts themselves but also in the political, social and regulatory context in which they operated. There can be no doubt that, as a result, the role of the inspectors in the bringing of prosecutions, and the role of the magistrates' courts, underwent considerable change between 1833 and 1914. Much has been written about the political and social philosophies revealed by the pattern of enforcement of the first factory acts; but there has been noticeably less interest in what seems inevitably to be the much more complex question of their operation in the late nineteenth and early twentieth centuries. From at least 1875 onwards the prosecution of individual employers seems likely to have have had less significance as the regulation of working conditions in factories and workshops increasingly became the object of political activity, trades union agitation and economic considerations on a national and international scale. It is not appropriate in the present context to attempt a general or theoretical analysis of the impact of these changes; we concentrate instead on the much more basic task of attempting to provide an empirical picture of the reception given to the inspectors when they sought to enforce the factory acts in the magistrates' courts in Ireland.

Statistical note

Until 1900, the inspectors' reports contain lists of 'prosecutions in detail' which, as exemplified in Plates 22 and 23 above, ostensibly include information about every individual case in named magistrates' courts throughout Ireland; from 1901 to 1914, the reports contain less detailed information in tabular form. In addition, the annual criminal judicial statistics record the number of factory act cases heard and determined in the magistrates' courts from 1863 onwards. It has to be said at the outset that we have frequently found it impossible to reconcile the data provided by the inspectors with that provided by the clerks of petty sessions; it seems likely, however, that the former are more reliable and we have, accordingly, preferred to rely on them. But it has also to be said that the information provided by the inspectors sometimes comes in different forms which are not easily reconcilable, if at all. Accordingly, the statistics which are given in this chapter must, unfortunately, be regarded as approximate only.

The basic statistical unit employed by the inspectors was the number of 'cases' or 'informations'; if one occupier was, for example, prosecuted for employing three women beyond the permitted hours, for employing four young persons on a Sunday and for failure to report an accident, this was recorded as eight 'cases'. Given that many prosecutions involved two or more cases, the number of firms or persons prosecuted is, therefore, much lower than the number of 'cases'.

INAUGURATING THE NEW REGULATORY SYSTEM

We have already seen in chapter 1 that the power given to the inspectors in 1833 to hear and determine cases themselves does not appear to have been used at all in Ireland. From the outset, cases were brought, if at all, in the magistrates' courts. These courts were at that time still in their infancy in Ireland, having been put on a proper footing only in 1827, when the justices of the peace were, for the first time, required to sit in regular 'petty sessions', in a 'public justice room' and with a paid clerk to keep a written record of the proceedings.[1] What was envisaged was a court consisting of a number of magistrates; but the 1833 act provided that a case could be heard and determined in petty sessions by a single magistrate – who might even be the

---

1 Petty Sessions (Ire.) Act 1827 (7 & 8 Geo. IV, c. 67). One of the first manuals published after 1827 included a lengthy summary of the 1833 act – see J. O'Donoghue, *The summary jurisdiction of magistrates* (Dublin, 1835), pp. 159–67.

occupier of the textile mill or factory in question.[2] Although the court could include a resident magistrate appointed under the Constabulary (Ireland) Act 1836,[3] it seems likely that 'summary' proceedings in Ireland prior to the Famine would still have been a rough and ready affair, from which there was virtually no appeal.

The procedure for bringing a prosecution under the 1833 act was simple and straightforward. Within fourteen days of the commission of an offence, the inspector gave written notice to the offender of his intention to prefer a complaint. The complaint was then lodged with a justice of the peace, who issued a summons giving brief details of the offence(s) and specifying when and where the case would be heard. The justice could also, at the request of the inspector, summon witnesses to give evidence on pain of imprisonment for up to two months for failure to comply. The case, as presented by the inspector, was then heard and determined in the regular petty sessions. On conviction, an occupier could be fined not less than £1 and not more than £20 at the 'discretion' of the court; but the court could mitigate the fine or discharge the offender altogether if of opinion that the offence was 'not wilful nor grossly negligent'.[4] The inspector could, on conviction, be awarded one-half of any fine, in addition to 'all costs of prosecution and conviction'; the court could also order that the other half of the fine – or even the whole fine – be paid 'for the benefit of any school wherein children employed in mills or factories are educated'.[5] Unless the defendant had been convicted of forging a certificate or other document required by the act, there was no appeal against conviction; nor, subject to the same exception, was any conviction removable to a superior court by way of certiorari.[6]

As we have seen, the first factory inspectors in Ireland were satisfied that the standards set by the 1833 act could best be achieved by explanation and persuasion rather than by 'altercation' and prosecution.[7] Viewed in this light, the small number of prosecutions in Ireland during the 1830s and early 1840s is not to be seen as reflecting a particular difficulty in obtaining evidence, a lack of confidence in the impartiality of the magistracy or the furtherance of the interests of a ruling elite, but rather as a result of a preferred method of 'enforcement' which was claimed to be effective in securing general compliance with the law. As a result, we have found details of only four prosecutions prior to 1844.

---

2 Factories Act 1833, s. 34. Cf. Labour in cotton mills act 1831 (Hobhouse's act), ss. 10 and 22 had provided for cases to be heard by 'any two or more justices', none of whom was to be, or even closely related to, a mill owner.

3 Sections 31–33. Special arrangements applied in Dublin, where summary proceedings were heard in the police court by one of the divisional justices appointed under the Dublin Justices Act 1824, s. 7.

4 Section 31.

5 Section 43. If the fine was not paid within the time appointed, the amount could be levied by distress or the offender could be imprisoned for up to two months (ss. 34 and 41).

6 Section 42.

7 See above, pp. 23–25.

The very first case was brought by Inspector Howell in 1835, when James Reilly of Dublin was convicted of an unspecified offence and fined £4 (with £1 costs).[8] Reilly was again prosecuted the following year for over-working a child and allowing him to remain in the mill without the necessary certificate of fitness; on conviction, he was fined £10 (including costs).[9] At the end of 1836 Howell prosecuted Obadiah Willans & Sons – the Hibernia Mills – in Dublin for employing a girl under 13 for more than 48 hours a week, without a fitness or a school certificate. The occupier admitted the facts, but (as he was entitled to do under section 30 of the 1833 act) argued that the child was employed by her father without the occupier's 'consent, concurrence or knowledge'. The court accepted this argument, acquitted the occupier and fined the father 20s.[10] Finally, in October 1841, Frederick Hayes, the owner of a flax-spinning factory near Banbridge, was charged with employing a young person at night, for 12½ hours in one day and without the necessary certificates. The case was heard by a bench of three justices – two uncles and a brother-in-law of the defendant – who dismissed the case 'on the alleged ground of want of evidence'.[11]

For a period in which more than four thousand informations were brought before the courts elsewhere in the United Kingdom, leading to fines totalling almost £7,000,[12] this record tends to support the view that the early inspectors, and particularly Stuart, were unduly complacent or too accommodating to the factory owners.[13] But it is, of course, possible that the working conditions in Ireland were much better than in Great Britain and/or that the owners, either voluntarily or at the behest of the inspectors, were more amenable to bringing their factories and work practices into compliance with the new law without the need for any significant resort to the courts.

THE PROCESS OF FORMALISATION, 1844–1878

The factory act of 1844 subjected the process of prosecution and adjudication of offences to greater legal formality and control, as the inspectors' own rule-making and judicial powers were withdrawn on the grounds that they 'had proved an embarrassment to the inspectors in the exercise of their own proper functions'.[14] This reduction in their discretionary administrative status and power by subjecting the inspectors to more formal and legal

8   *Names of persons fined under the Factory Act*, p. 19, H.C. 1836 (77), xlv, 189.
9   *Number and names of persons summoned for offences against the Factory Act, from 1st May 1836 to 1st January 1837*, pp. 56–57, H.C. 1837 (97), l, 162–63. The fine (less costs) was made over to the National School at 'Blancherstown'.
10 Ibid., pp. 58–59. See also *Insp. rep., Dec. 1836*, p. 58 (Stuart).
11 *Insp. quart. rep., Dec. 1841*, p. 98 (Stuart).
12 'Summary of prosecutions 1834–1843' in *Number and names of persons summoned for offences against the factory acts, etc.*, p. 19, H.C. 1844 (106), xxxix, 293.
13 See above, p. 24.
14 B.L. Hutchins and A. Harrison, *A history of factory legislation* (3rd ed., London, 1926), p. 86.

regulation has been criticised as designed to *reduce* their effectiveness; but other commentators take the view that this process of formalisation assisted the inspectors by increasing their apparent objectivity in the enforcement of positive legal rules.[15]

To begin with, the act sought to clarify the issue of liability as between occupier and worker by making the former primarily responsible for compliance with the law.[16] In the event, most of the proceedings taken in Ireland, as elsewhere in the United Kingdom, were against occupiers, although the power to prosecute individual workers was occasionally invoked. The act then simplified the procedure for issuing a summons, and in particular extended the period within which the inspector was required to lodge a complaint to two (or in certain cases, three) months.[17] An inspector (as well as a magistrate) was given power to summon any person charged with an offence and 'all witnesses who may be needed to give evidence concerning the charge', and the inspector himself was made a competent witness even though the prosecution had been brought by him.[18] The rules of evidence were also modified to facilitate proof of certain offences; with certain exceptions, any person found to be present in a factory during normal working hours was deemed to be employed there 'unless the contrary shall be proved', and a declaration by a certifying surgeon that he had personally examined a person and believed him or her to be under such age as was set forth in the declaration was evidence of that person's age 'until the contrary shall be made to appear'.[19] It may also be noted in this context that the general organisation of, and proceedings in, magistrates' courts in Ireland were re-organised and put on a more modern footing in 1851.[20]

From 1844, all proceedings under the factory acts were to be heard by two or more justices.[21] More significantly, perhaps, 'in reference to the

---

15   See especially H.W. Arthurs, *'Without the law': Administrative justice and legal pluralism in nineteenth-century England* (Toronto, 1985), chap. 4 and S. Field, 'Without the law? Professor Arthurs and the early factory inspectorate', in *J. Law and Society*, 17 (1990), 445, discussed above, pp. 35–37.

16   By s. 41, where an offence had been committed, the occupier was deemed to be responsible unless he could establish that he had used 'due diligence' to ensure compliance with the act and that the offence had been committed 'without his knowledge, consent or connivance'. This presumption was retained in the 1878 act, s. 87 and 1901 act, s. 141.

17   Sections 44, 46–47 and 49–50. No objection was allowed to the information or summons for any defect of substance or form; if the defendant was misled by such defect, the case was simply to be adjourned.

18   Sections 48 and 49. To avoid unfair repetition of the case, however, an inspector who was both prosecutor and principal witness for the prosecution was not to open the case in the usual manner: A. Redgrave (inspector) to Sprague Oram (sub-inspector), 2 Feb. 1870, PRO HO45/9877/B15295.

19   Sections 52–55.

20   See especially Petty Sessions (Ire.) Act 1851, as explained e.g. in C. Molloy, *The justice of the peace for Ireland: A treatise on the powers and duties of magistrates in Ireland* (Dublin, 1890).

21   Section 45 – presumably with the exception of Dublin. Cf. Summary Jurisdiction Act 1857, s. 1 allowed stipendiary magistrates to sit alone in England and Wales; but this

decided opinion expressed by the inspectors, and the very strong feelings entertained on the subject by the operatives',[22] the 1844 act revived, albeit in more limited form, the restriction omitted from the 1833 act, by providing that 'no complaint preferred for any offence against this Act committed in a factory shall be heard by a justice of the peace ... being an occupier of the factory, or being the father, son or brother of the occupier of the factory in which the offence set forth in the complaint shall have been committed'.[23] As also recommended by the select committee, the 1844 act set out a more detailed legislative tariff of penalties by specifying minimum and maximum fines for various offences. At the lower end of this scale, an occupier who employed a child or young person for a period longer than that allowed by law was liable to be fined 'not less than twenty shillings and not more than three pounds for each child or young person so illegally employed'; if the offence was committed at night, the fine was increased to £2-£5. However, the parent of a child employed contrary to the act was liable only to a fine of 5–20s. At the other end of the scale, an occupier who failed to fence any machinery as required by the act, with the result that a person suffered bodily injury, could be fined from £10 to £100, and an occupier who obstructed an inspector in his inspection of a factory at night was liable to a fine 'not less than £20 and not more than £50'. To complete the range of penalties, any person guilty of fraud or wilful falsehood in relation to a certificate or document required by the act might be fined from £5-£20 *or* imprisoned for up to six months.[24] And as a result of abuse which had 'contributed to render nugatory the provisions of the [1833] act',[25] the court lost the power to remit any fine at its discretion.

The 1844 act finally gave an aggrieved defendant a right of appeal against conviction. Under section 69, a person convicted of an offence punishable by fine or imprisonment, or convicted of any offence and fined more than £3, could now appeal to quarter sessions – provided he or she entered into a recognizance, with two sufficient sureties, to appear at the hearing of the appeal, to abide by the judgment of the court and to pay such costs as the court might award. In 1851, this right of appeal was extended to any case in which the defendant had been fined more than 20s.[26] Alternatively, an aggrieved defendant could (under section 70 of the 1844 act) have the

act did not apply in Ireland and it was not until 1878 – and perhaps later – that a similar power was conferred on resident magistrates in Ireland. See further below, p. 311.

22 *Final report from the select committee appointed to inquire into the operation of the [1833] act* ... , p. 22, H.C. 1841 (56), ix, 584.

23 Section 71 (emphasis added). Cf. Hobhouse's act 1831, s. 10 had excluded the owner of *any* cotton mill or factory. But it was the more limited provision which was to be retained in the 1878 act, s. 89 and the 1901 act, s. 144(4) – see below, p. 318.

24 Sections 56–57, 52 and 60, and 63, respectively.

25 *Report on the operation of the 1833 act, 1841*, p. 18. However, the justices in Dublin continued to have a power of remittal under the Dublin Police Act 1842, s. 63, as Howell was to discover to his dismay in 1856 – see below, p. 308.

26 Petty Sessions (Ire.) Act 1851, s. 24, confirmed by 1878 act, s. 106(9) and 1901 act, s. 160(9).

conviction removed by certiorari to the court of queen's bench, something which had been generally forbidden by the 1833 act. But in an attempt to preclude judicial review based on a mere technicality, no proceedings 'shall be quashed or deemed illegal for matter of form ...' which did not affect the 'essence' of the offence or the clear understanding of the person charged.

A factory inspector, on the other hand, had no right of appeal against dismissal of a complaint prior to 1857.[27] But an informal method of challenging an adverse decision was revealed by the case of *Darkin* v. *Francis Ritchie & Sons*.[28] The owner of a felt factory in Belfast was charged with a number of offences when unfenced mill-gearing caused severe bodily injury to one of the workers. A court consisting of a resident magistrate, the lord mayor and a justice of the peace dismissed the case in June 1856 on the grounds that the premises did not constitute a 'factory' because no woman, child or young person was employed there. Unable to appeal, Howell (Darkin's superior) sought the opinion of the Irish law officers,[29] who were of opinion that the court was in error. Howell then sought to set the record straight:

[I]n order that the law which is obeyed elsewhere may be equally obeyed at Belfast, I have transmitted a copy of the opinion of the law officers to the clerk of petty sessions there, in conformity with the Irish Petty Sessions Act [1851], s. 5(4), which directs that the clerk of petty sessions 'shall retain ... all ... opinions of the law officers or advisers of the Crown, addressed or transmitted to the justices'. So that it may be confidently expected that in this respect the law will henceforth be interpreted and enforced at Belfast in the same manner as in all other places.[30]

But this strategy failed, at least on this occasion. When Francis Ritchie & Sons were again prosecuted in February 1857, the court 'adhered to the former decision' and dismissed the case 'in direct opposition to the opinion of the law officers'. Howell 'greatly ... regretted that ... more important engagements elsewhere should have prevented the resident magistrate from attending when the same question was re-argued ...' – but even he let Howell down (or was outvoted) when a third case was dismissed by a strong bench in July 1857.[31]

---

27 As evidenced by *Steen* v. *Dargan & Co.* in *Insp. half-yearly rep.,April 1857*, p. 62, where a defendant 'counselled by astute lawyers ... very unscrupulous in their line of action' secured the dismissal of a charge of obstruction. The home office noted ruefully that there was no power to appeal against a dismissal, even on a point of law on which the law officers had given a contrary opinion: PRO HO 45/6380. See further below, p. 308.

28 *Insp. half-yearly rep., Oct. 1856*, p. 59.

29 A strategy he had employed two years earlier in an attempt to determine whether the Petty Sessions (Ire.) Act 1851 had impliedly repealed section 68 of the 1844 act, which provided that fines could be applied for the benefit of schools providing education for children employed in factories: PRO HO 45/5216 (May 1854). Field, 'Early factory inspectorate', pp. 448–49 suggests that the inspectors regularly used the law officers in an attempt to avoid blatantly biased or restrictive court decisions – a strategy which could, and often did, backfire when the law officers agreed with the magistrates.

30 *Insp. half-yearly rep., Oct. 1856*, pp. 50–52.

31 *Insp. half-yearly rep.,April 1857*, pp. 51 and 60 and *Oct. 1857*, p. 26.

The *Ritchie* case was clearly not an isolated example of magisterial error. Even as it was being decided, parliament was enacting the Summary Jurisdiction Act 1857, sections 2–5 of which provided generally, for England and Wales as well as for Ireland, that a defendant or complainant dissatisfied with the determination of a magistrates' court on any information or complaint as being erroneous in point of law could appeal by way of case stated to any one of the superior courts. The lower court could only refuse to state a case if of opinion that the application 'is merely frivolous'; if the justices erroneously refused to state a case, the superior court could order them to do so.

PROSECUTIONS IN IRELAND UNDER THE 1844 ACT

The coming into force of the 1844 act appears to have had an immediate impact on prosecutorial activity in Ireland, with proceedings involving some 168 informations being brought against 22 factories, predominantly in the north-east, in the period 1845–1849 and resulting in fines totalling £197. But this picture is distorted by an intriguing 'blitz' on ten factories in the Belfast area in 1845 for unlawfully employing 125 young persons on Good Friday, a statutory holiday; all the defendants were convicted and fined at the minimum rate of £1 per young person concerned.[32]

Table 10.1: Factory act prosecutions in Ireland, 1845–64[33]

	1845–49	1850–54	1855–59	1860–64	Total
No. of factories prosecuted	22	23	40	22	107
Total no. of informations	168	215	396	400	1,179
Informations withdrawn	–	16	90	183	289
Informations dismissed	4	33	91	51	179
No. of convictions	164	166	215	166	711
Total amount of fines	£197	£227	£240	£208	£872
Average fine	£1. 4s. 0d.	£1. 7s. 4d.	£1. 2s. 4d.	£1. 5s.1d.	£1. 4s.6d.

The number of prosecutions did, however, gradually increase during the 1850s and early 1860s. But relatively few cases were brought outside the Belfast area and counties Londonderry and Dublin/Meath. Indeed, just over one-half of all prosecutions during this period were in Belfast,[34] where the

32 *Number and names of persons summoned for offences against the factory act … 1845*, pp. 58–59, H.C. 1846 (87), xxxiv, 558–59.
33 Extrapolated from the lists of prosecutions in the inspectors' reports, 1845–1864.
34 The other areas mentioned in the text accounted for most of the remainder, but small numbers of prosecutions were also brought in counties Tyrone, Cork, Laois and Tipperary. This left twenty-three counties without any prosecutions at all.

court often included a resident magistrate and was therefore less likely to be 'confused' by 'singular objections on what are called points of law'.[35] Resident magistrates occasionally sat in cases outside Belfast, but there the court was more generally composed of two or three justices. By the 1850s the magistrates' courts in Ireland were hearing more than 200,000 cases annually, and it is perhaps well to remember that factory act cases represented only a tiny fraction of this work-load – as compared, for example, to cases of drunkenness (seldom less than 60,000 per year) or common assault (about 20,000–25,000 per year). A further complication from the inspectors' point of view was that there were by now 3,000–4,000 justices and some 600 petty sessions districts. A factory inspector in England typically dealt with 30 magistrates' courts; the north of Ireland district generally comprised more than 150, and the south of Ireland more than 400, petty sessions districts. Given the small number of prosecutions, many justices in Ireland seldom, if ever, heard and determined proceedings under the 1844 act.

An inspector normally conducted the prosecution himself.[36] But on occasions the factual or legal complexity of the case led him to seek legal advice and assistance. Here, too, the inspectors in Ireland were at a certain disadvantage as a result of the administrative arrangements under the Act of Union. The factory acts, in Ireland as in England and Wales, were the responsibility of the home office, a central government department. Should an inspector in Ireland require the assistance of the police or a lawyer, this would be provided by the Royal Irish Constabulary or crown lawyers, both of which were 'Irish' services under the control of the lord lieutenant and chief secretary. These services were available to the factory inspectors – but only indirectly, via the home office and Dublin Castle.[37] No doubt the system normally worked smoothly enough; but there must have been occasions when direct access would have produced greater speed and efficiency.

The most common charge against employers during this period (roughly 80 per cent of all informations) was for employing women or young persons outside the permitted hours of work, the normal penalty for which was the minimum fine of £1 per person. Very few employers were charged with safety offences, and few parents or workers were prosecuted for any offence.[38] As

---

35 *Insp. half-yearly rep., April 1857*, p. 51 (Howell). Cf. most resident magistrates were *not* qualified lawyers, but former army or police officers or others whose lack of legal experience frequently gave rise to criticism – see e.g. P. Bonsall, *The Irish RMs: The resident magistrates in the British administration of Ireland* (Dublin, 1998), p. 16. They were also criticised for their lack of independence of Dublin Castle – a trait which, if true, might have led the inspectors to believe that resident magistrates were more likely to be sympathetic to their cause than 'ordinary' justices.

36 The right to do so was subsequently confirmed by the 1901 act, s. 120.

37 R. B. McDowell, *The Irish administration, 1801–1914* (London, 1964), pp. 29–31.

38 See e.g. *Insp. half-yearly rep., Oct. 1854*, p. 48 (James Hall of Belfast charged with altering child's age certificate; 'the defendant being a labourer with a large family, and as the offence could not be fully proved without the evidence of his own child, I withdrew the case, believing that the warning given by the resident magistrate would effect the object I had in view'); *Oct. 1856*, p. 62 (mule spinner carelessly set a

elsewhere, it was not unusual for at least some informations to be withdrawn on payment of costs, at the request – or even 'urgent solicitation' – of the bench. No case has been found in which a defendant was sentenced to imprisonment, and the maximum penalty imposed in a single prosecution appears to be the £80 which Charles Duffin & Co, flax spinners of Belfast, were fined (by W. S. Tracy RM) for employing forty young persons before 6 a.m.[39]

Although the number of cases dismissed was quite high by comparison with the general standard of the magistrates' courts, this does not appear to have given rise to adverse comment by the inspectors. No doubt most of the cases were straightforward; but the difficulties which the inspectors some-times faced may be illustrated by the case of *Johnstone and Beck* v. *Darkin*.[40] Sub-inspector Darkin, accompanied by a police constable, went to the defendants' flax-spinning mill in Belfast at a few minutes after 6.00 p.m. The building was lit up 'as if in full work' and they could hear the noise of machinery in motion. Several young persons were found in the spinning-room 'as if quitting their work'; but as Darkin was taking down their names, 'all the lights were suddenly and simultaneously extinguished'. The defendants were charged with employing 18 young persons after normal hours, and with obstructing the sub-inspector at night in the execution of his duties. The magistrates' court convicted on both counts, and imposed fines of £36 and £20 respectively. When the defendants appealed to Co. Antrim quarter sessions, the 'importance of the case' led the home office to request the lord lieutenant to direct the sessional crown solicitor to instruct counsel to appear on Darkin's behalf. Judge J.H. Otway QC upheld the conviction on the first count; but after a lengthy review of all the factory acts since 1802, con-cluded, with what Karl Marx characterised as 'a quite Talmudic sagacity',[41] that the obstruction had not occurred 'in the night' and accordingly quashed the conviction on the second count. An irate Baker (Darkin's superior) went to considerable lengths to show why the learned judge had erred.[42]

Difficulties of another kind were experienced at the flax-spinning mill of Messrs. Haughton and Dargan at Chapelizod, near Dublin. In 1854 a charge of employing twelve females after 2 p.m. on a Saturday was dismissed on a

machine in motion, killing a young person; fined £2); *Oct. 1857*, p. 26 (gatekeeper fined three guineas for wilfully preventing inspector from entering factory); *April 1864*, p. 46 (overlooker in spinning mill ordered women and young persons to clean machinery during meal time; fined £1 in respect of one case, another five withdrawn on payment of costs of £1.4s. 6d.).

39 *Insp. half-yearly rep.*, Oct 1854, p. 45, where Darkin noted that 'all the hands had commenced work at half-past 5 o'clock a.m. for seven months'. He had offered to withdraw fifteen cases, but 'the presiding magistrate said he had recorded convictions in the whole forty, and no withdrawal could take place'.

40 *Insp. half-yearly rep., April 1860*, pp. 49–52 and 68–78.

41 *Capital: A critical analysis of capitalist production,* trans. from 3rd German edition by S. Moore and E. Aveling (Moscow, 1958), i, 264.

42 According to Otway, whose judgment is reproduced in full, 'night' began at 8.30 p.m., whereas Baker was convinced, on the basis of 'a very high legal opinion', that it included the whole period between 6 p.m. and 6 a.m.

technicality. Dr Kelly RM stated that the merits of the case were clearly with the inspector, but awarded costs to the defendants; in return for a 'proposition' by the defendants to forego these costs, which were 'very heavy', Darkin agreed to withdraw a further charge of obstruction.[43] In August 1856 Steen, the new sub-inspector, secured a conviction for employing 15 young persons and women after 6 p.m. – only to have the fine remitted under the Dublin Police Act 1842 from £15 to 15s., with the warning that 'if the defendant should be again convicted before him, he would impose the heaviest penalties'.[44] A further charge of employing seven women and young persons after 2 p.m. on a Saturday was dismissed, 'the evidence being insufficient to convict'.[45] Further charges of unlawful employment followed in February and March 1857, only to be dismissed 'on technical grounds',[46] and (anticipating the *Johnston and Beck* case) a charge of obstruction at night was dismissed on the grounds that it had occurred at 6.30 p.m. Later that same year Steen obtained convictions on charges of obstruction and unlawful employment; the former resulted in a fine of £6. 6s. 0d. (confirmed on appeal to quarter sessions), but the fine in respect of the latter was once again reduced (from £6 to 6d.), albeit with heavy costs (£6. 6s. 0d.).[47] Steen returned to the fray early in 1858, when he secured convictions resulting in fines amounting to £11 (and costs of £3. 0s. 6d.) for various offences arising from further obstruction and the unlawful employment of children.[48] His persistence was finally rewarded in February 1858, when he secured further convictions for unlawful employment and obstruction, leading to fines totalling £20 (and costs of £4. 3s. 0d.).[49]

In 1864 and 1867 the factory acts were extended to cover a number of non-textile factories, and in 1871 the inspectors took over from local authority officials the responsibility for workshops.[50] Table 10.2 summarises the impact which these developments had on the nature and frequency of prosecutions in Ireland.

---

43 *Insp. half-yearly rep.*, Oct. 1854, pp. 50–51.
44 Insp. *half-yearly rep.*, Oct. 1856, p. 61. '[I]n no other part of the United Kingdom would [these offences] have been visited with a lower penalty than £15, and ... might have been visited with a penalty of £45. The present is the first instance in which the power of reducing fines below the lowest amount fixed by the legislature has ever been applied to any offence against the factory acts ...': ibid., p. 53 (Howell).
45 Ibid., p. 62.
46 *Insp. half-yearly rep., April 1857*, p. 62.
47 *Insp. half-yearly rep.*, Oct. 1857, pp. 26–27. According to Howell, the 'normal' fine for such offences was £6–£18.
48 *Insp. half-yearly rep., April 1858*, pp. 31–32.
49 Ibid., p. 27. It was this factory also which gave rise to *MacCracken* v. *Dargan and Haughton*, which appears to have been the first reported employer's liability claim in Ireland to have succeeded – see further below, p. 340.
50 See above, chap. 2. The first prosecution under the 1864 act, of Robert M'Loughlin, a pipe manufacturer in Dublin, was defended on the basis that 'some indulgence' was to be allowed for a time after the act came into force; he was fined £1 for an offence committed in July 1865: *Insp. half-yearly rep.*, Oct. 1865, p. 144.

Table 10.2: Factory act prosecutions in Ireland, 1865–78[51]

	1865–70	1871–74	1875–78	Total
No. prosecuted	44	67	91	202
No. of informations	275	272	487	1,034
Informations withdrawn	97	60	166	323
dismissed	16	34	16	66
convicted	160	137	297	594
other	2	41	8	51
Amount of fines	£169	£128	£239	£535
Average fine	£1. 1s. 0d	18s. 8d.	16s. 1d.	18s. 0d.

Compared to the period before 1864, there was a continuing rise in the number of firms or persons prosecuted, but (at least until 1875) a reduction in the number of informations[52] – a trend which suggests a tendency to prosecute smaller firms and, after 1871, workshops. It remained the case that the bulk of these prosecutions were for overworking women or young persons in one way or another,[53] but there is a noticeable increase in the number of informations concerning the unlawful employment of children[54] and failure to comply with the administrative requirements concerning the employment of young persons. During the first half of the 1870s the inspectorate were also somewhat more active in charging a parent with 'not causing his [or her] child to attend school'.[55]

51 Extrapolated from the lists of prosecutions in the inspectors' reports, 1865–1878. Statistics on the number of persons proceeded against from 1863 onwards are also available in the criminal judicial statistics, but as already explained, the two sources do not always agree – the criminal statistics, for example, show that 215 prosecutions were brought in the period 1865–1878. We prefer to use the information provided by the factory inspectors.

52 The annual number of prosecutions follows no consistent pattern, but there is a noticeable – and sustained – increase after 1871, when the inspectorate became responsible for workshops. But the large number of prosecutions for the period 1875–1878 is mainly attributable to one 'rogue' year – 1876 – when 46 defendants were charged with a total of 234 informations.

53 Informations charging an employer with the employment of women or young persons after 6 p.m. or before 6 a.m. (Monday to Friday), on Saturday afternoon or evening, or during meal-times represent two-thirds of the informations laid between 1865 and 1878. Ewart & Sons of Belfast (see above, Plate 24) were persistent offenders in this respect; 'what makes the case worse is that Mr Wm. Ewart, junior, is a magistrate and alderman': *Insp. half-yearly rep., April 1871*, pp. 70–71 (Cramp).

54 Cf. in *Insp. half-yearly rep., Oct. 1870*, p. 80, Baker reported that parents were resorting to 'all kinds of devices' in order to mislead the certifying surgeon as to the age of a child. He was so exasperated with 'constant' falsification that he directed his sub-inspectors 'simply to tear them up' and not to prosecute the parents 'since there is not only a considerable difficulty in proving a guilty knowledge, but there is the additional danger of setting parents' evidence against children, which was to be deplored'.

55 Ten such cases were brought between 1872 and 1874. The usual fine was five shillings (and 1s. 6d. costs); but on some occasions the case was withdrawn on payment of the costs, no doubt on account of the poverty of the parent in question.

Table 10.2 also reveals a relatively high rate of dismissals and of cases withdrawn on payment of costs by the defendant. Many of the latter reflect the attitude of both inspectors and justices to defaulting workshop occupiers, particularly in cities and towns with little or no previous experience of factory act prosecutions. Many of these prosecutions were brought against small businesses, particularly milliners and dressmakers, and this may also help to explain the reduction in the average fine which occurred in the 1870s.[56] It was this development, too, which was probably responsible for the bringing of prosecutions in eight counties which hitherto had not experienced such cases. Increased prosecutorial activity is also to be seen in the cities of Dublin, Cork and Limerick; but the Belfast area still provides the venue for almost 60 per cent of prosecutions and informations. The depleted level of industrial activity in the south and west of Ireland is reflected in the fact that by 1878 out of the twenty-three counties of Leinster, Connaught and Munster, eleven had still not experienced a single factories act prosecution – and many of the others had witnessed only one or two such cases.[57]

Enforcement of the acts could still pose problems, if the case of *Cramp* v. *Trimble*[58] in 1869 is anything to go by. In November 1868, Trimble, the occupier of the *Fermanagh Reporter* printing office, was fined £6 for unlawfully employing five young persons. A few months later, he was again prosecuted on two charges of unlawful employment, and the case came before Enniskillen petty sessions in March 1869. Cramp was opening the case when Trimble's solicitor asked what authority he had to appear as prosecutor. Cramp had been appointed to the new north of Ireland district and he produced his warrant of appointment by the home secretary; but it was contended that this did not authorise Cramp to act outside his district (Fermanagh now being in the Central district). In spite of Cramp's insistence that a factory inspector could enter any factory in the United Kingdom, the districts being only an 'arbitrary arrangement', the chairman (Mr G. Brackenridge) held that the act, being penal, must be strictly construed. Cramp reported that 'it was apparent to everyone in court that the Chairman was only too glad of any loophole by which to allow the defendant to escape'. The following month, Cramp tried again – this time

56 The first prosecutions of dressmakers' workshops in Dublin resulted in fines of ten shillings, since 'the magistrates wished to deal leniently with the defendants': *Insp. half-yearly rep., April 1873*, p. 81. For the same reason, the first workshop case in Omagh resulted in a fine of six shillings: *Insp. half-yearly rep., Oct. 1875*, p. 206.

57 In Leinster, counties Carlow, Kildare, Kilkenny, Longford, Louth, Offaly, Westmeath and Wicklow; in Connaught, Leitrim, Mayo and Roscommon – to which may be added the Ulster counties of Cavan, Donegal and Monaghan. According to the criminal statistics, 72% of factory act cases were in Ulster, 14% in Leinster, 13% in Munster and only just over 1% in Connaught.

58 *Insp. half-yearly rep., April 1869*, pp. 127 and 129–30; PRO HO 45/8254. Letterpress printers and newspaper offices were 'as a rule, more opposed to the operation of the [1867] act than any other class of manufacturers', and they were frequently prosecuted in this period for ignoring the restrictions on hours of employment when under pressure to meet a deadline: see especially *Insp. half-yearly rep., Oct. 1868*, pp. 139–58 (Baker) and 259 (Cramp).

being represented by a solicitor. Brackenridge was once again in the chair – and this time the case, which was not reached until 3.15 p.m., was talked out of court by means of 'a lot of technical objections' raised by Trimble's solicitor. Undaunted, Cramp saw to it that Captain Butler, a resident magistrate, was directed to attend the petty sessions in April 'to assist in the investigation of the case in question'. The third hearing of the case was much more satisfactory; Trimble was convicted on both counts, and given the maximum fine of £5 on each.

MAGISTERIAL SHORTCOMINGS, 1878–1914

No major changes in the procedure for bringing prosecutions in respect of offences under the factory acts occurred in 1878 or thereafter.[59] But the opportunity was taken to declare that a magistrates' court dealing with such a case in Ireland 'shall be constituted within the police district of Dublin metropolis of one of the divisional justices of that district sitting at a police court ... and elsewhere of a stipendiary magistrate sitting alone, or with others, or of two or more justices of the peace sitting in petty sessions ...'.[60] This use of the term 'stipendiary magistrate', however, was taken to mean that a case could not be heard and determined by a single *resident* magistrate, an oversight which led to frequent adjournments resulting in 'considerable waste of time and money'.[61] In 1896, the government introduced a bill to remedy the situation, but for some unexplained reason this was withdrawn after the second reading.[62] Accordingly the matter was only resolved by section 160(8) of the Factory and Workshop Act 1901, which substituted the term 'resident magistrate appointed under the Constabulary (Ireland) Act 1836'.

The increasing complexity of the work undertaken by the magistrates' courts generally led to calls for their reform. It was suggested that more of the work should be undertaken by resident or stipendiary magistrates – and that those magistrates should be qualified barristers or solicitors.[63] Neither

59 Some minor changes were made. Thus, the time limit for making a complaint was increased from two to three months by the 1891 act, s. 29.
60 1878 act, s. 106(8).
61 *R. (Jackson)* v. *Tipperary JJ.* (1894) 28 ILTR 107 held that a resident magistrate was not a 'stipendiary magistrate' for the purposes of the Licensing Act 1872, and the resident magistrates took the view that this decision was equally applicable to the 1878 act: G. Bellhouse to W. Cooke-Taylor, 8 May 1896 (PRO HO 45/9910/B21238) and *Chief insp. ann. rep., 1899*, p. 223, where Bellhouse reported that 'many resident magistrates ... refuse to hear [factory act] cases when sitting alone'.
62 Stipendiary Magistrates (Ire.) Bill, H.C. 1896 (196), vii, 277 – see *Hansard 4*, xl, 525 (4 May 1896) and xliii, 242 (20 July 1896).
63 See e.g. W.F. Bailey, 'Magisterial reform; being some considerations on the present voluntary system, and suggestions for the substitution of an independent paid magistracy', in *JSSISI*, 8 (1879–85), 595 and *Statement of the Council of the Irish Bar with respect to the qualifications and appointments of Irish resident magistrates*, reproduced in *ILT & SJ*, 42 (1908), 107 (all new resident magistrates should be practising barristers or solicitors of at least five years' standing).

of these proposals was formally adopted until after 1914; but the number of
qualified lawyers appointed as resident magistrates gradually increased.[64]
This was particularly the case in Belfast, where, after the riots of 1886, it
became customary to have two resident magistrates, usually a protestant and
a roman catholic, with legal qualifications[65] – a custom largely confirmed by
section 2 of the Resident Magistrates (Belfast) Act 1911.

Outside Belfast and Dublin, however, justices of the peace continued, at
least in theory, to predominate at petty sessions.[66] But they, too, underwent
change in terms of their composition. Until 1890 or thereabouts, they remained
as a body predominantly protestant and upper-class. In 1886, for example,
three-quarters of the 5,065 justices were protestant, and more than half were
landed proprietors, only 631 were 'merchants or manufacturers', although the
proportion was higher in some counties, particularly in Down and Antrim.[67] In
1892, however, a significant change, both in religious and social terms, was set
in train by the Liberal chief secretary, John Morley, whose nominations for
appointment caused controversy not only because they were predominantly
catholic, but also on account of their allegedly inferior quality: 'They were, for
the most part, men dependent on the people for their living – shopkeepers,
farmers, publicans and the like – and independent action was well-nigh
impossible for these with the shadow of boycotting hanging over them on the
one hand, and the shadow of bribery and corruption on the other.'[68] By
1912, 40 per cent of the magistrates were catholic, and the proportion of
landed gentry had declined in favour of farmers, merchants and others.[69]

Another possible reform, supported by some inspectors but more enthusiastically taken up by trades unions, was the appointment of 'working-men'
magistrates, to counterbalance 'the evident bias of those who are now administering justice in our provincial and county police courts'.[70] In 1901, the Irish

64 In 1888, for example, 50 of the 75 resident magistrates were former army or police
    officers; only 12 were barristers or solicitors: by 1912 there were 26 barristers or
    solicitors, as compared to 27 former police or army officers: see e.g. Bonsall, *The Irish
    RMs*, pp. 50–55.
65 Ibid., pp. 34–35.
66 Any number of magistrates could sit in petty sessions – a principle frequently relied
    upon in an important or controversial case. When, for example, Martindale
    prosecuted two large firms in the north of Ireland in 1908, a bench of eleven
    magistrates dismissed one of the cases – and a bench of twelve convicted in the other:
    From one generation to another, pp. 103–06.
67 *Return for each county, city and borough in Ireland of the names of the persons holding the
    commission of the peace, and ... so far as can be ascertained, the designation, profession or
    occupation of each such person at the time of his appointment ...* , H.C.1886 (20 – sess. II),
    liii, 417.
68 C.P. Crane, *Memoirs of a resident magistrate, 1880–1920* (Edinburgh, 1938), pp.
    191–92. See also L.W. MacBride, *The greening of Dublin Castle: The transformation of
    bureaucratic and judicial personnel in Ireland, 1892–1922* (Washington, D.C., 1991), pp.
    47–50 and 191, and L. Ó Broin, *The chief secretary: Augustine Birrell in Ireland*
    (London, 1970), pp. 158–59.
69 See *Return showing the names and addresses and occupations or descriptions of the persons
    appointed to the commission of the peace ...* , p. 28, H.C. 1912–13 (396), lxix, 720.
70 *Chief insp. ann. rep., 1894*, p. 223 (Bowling, inspector for Southampton).

Congress of Trades Unions unanimously resolved that all 'labour' cases, and not just cases under the factory acts, 'ought to be decided by duly qualified stipendiary magistrates'; but if not, then at least 'working men' magistrates should be appointed.[71] Limited success was reported in 1908, with appointments 'from the ranks of labour' having been made in Dublin and Belfast.[72]

The increasingly heterogeneous composition of the magistracy makes it difficult to generalise about their attitude to factory act cases. It is evident that much could depend not just on the composition of the bench in a particular case, but also on the identity of the defendant – and even on the nature of the offence charged. Successive chief inspectors maintained the policy of prosecuting cases only as a last resort: 'Most of the irregularities which are discovered are dealt with by instruction or warning to the offender. The few brought into court are those in which a mere caution is thought to be inadequate ...'.[73] Just how few of the known 'irregularities' were brought into court came to be revealed by the practice of publishing the number of informal 'contravention notices' issued by the inspectors; in 1907, for example, 87,567 of these notices were issued in the United Kingdom as a whole, including 7,125 in Ireland, in a year when 4,474 and 319 informations respectively were prosecuted in the courts.[74]

These large numbers emphasised the need for consistency in prosecution policy. In an attempt to resolve the ever-present tension between centralised decision-making and operational efficiency, control over the decision to prosecute lay with the superintending inspector, acting on the strength of a 'prosecution report' forwarded by the district inspector: 'The larger experience of the controlling officer [is] very valuable.... The personal feelings of the [local inspector] may be advantageously checked by the interpretation of a superior, who, unmoved by the irritating circumstances which may have accompanied the offence, has yet enough personal and local knowledge to form a fair judgment of the case.'[75] If there was any doubt about a prosecution the superintending inspector could refer the case to the chief inspector, who in turn could consult the home secretary.[76] Prosecutions conducted by lady inspectors after 1893 were subject to the approval of the principal lady inspector.[77]

---

71   *Eighth Annual Report of the Irish TUC* (Sligo, 1901), pp. 44–45. Similar motions were passed in 1902, 1903 and 1905 – see *Ninth Annual Report* (Cork, 1902), pp. 46 and 52, *Tenth Annual Report* (Newry, 1903), p. 33 and *Twelfth Annual Report* (Wexford, 1905), p. 48. The issue was also raised by J.P. Nannetti, MP for Dublin (College Green) in the house of commons on several occasions – see e.g. *Hansard 4*, xcvi, 435 (1 July 1901) and cxix, 91 (9 March 1903), only to be met with a straight bat – such matters were the responsibility of the lord lieutenant and the lord chancellor, who were 'always desirous of making suitable appointments'.

72   *Fifteenth Annual Report of the Irish TUC* (Belfast, 1908), p. 5.

73   *Chief insp. ann. rep., 1898*, pt. II, p. 79 (Whitelegge).

74   *Chief insp. ann. rep., 1907*, pp. xxix, 112–13 and 316.

75   *Report of the factory and workshop commissioners 1876*, p. xc.

76   See especially *Departmental committee on the truck acts, vol. ii: Minutes of evidence* (days 1–37), p. 28 [Cd. 4443], H.C. 1908, lix, 178 (Whitelegge).

77   Ibid., p. 65 (Anderson). But the practice seems to have varied. When Abraham was

So far as Ireland is concerned, the first point to note in this period is the considerable increase in the number of prosecutions after 1880:

Table 10.3: Factory act prosecutions in Ireland, 1880–1914[78]

	1880–89	1890–99	1900–09	1910–14	Total
No. of informations	618	1,990	2,497	927	6,032
Informations withdrawn	14	61	135	13	223
Informations dismissed	10	51	105	24	190
No. of convictions	594	1,878	2,257	890	5,619

Bearing in mind that, on average, two to three informations were included in each prosecution, it would appear that during the 1880s, the number of factory or workshop occupiers being prosecuted each year was in the region of 25. Between 1890 and 1910, however, that number rose dramatically, only to fall again in the years immediately preceding the great war. As might be expected, the bulk of these prosecutions were once again brought in Ulster and Leinster; indeed, in 1887 a resident inspector was even withdrawn from the south and south-west of Ireland on the grounds that he was no longer needed there.[79]

The number of prosecutions in Ireland appears to have been relatively higher than in the rest of the United Kingdom:

Table 10.4: Incidence of informations per 1,000 workers, 1895–1909[80]

	Ireland		England and Wales		Scotland	
	Average no. of cases per year	*No. of cases per 1,000 workers*	*Average no. of cases per year*	*No. of cases per 1,000 workers*	*Average no. of cases per year*	*No. of cases per 1,000 workers*
1895–1899	250	1.15	2,784	0.78	87	0.63
1900–1904	250	1.10	2,783	0.70	193	0.30
1905–1909	250	1.04	3,450	0.82	248	0.38

appointed superintending lady inspector in 1896, she was authorised to make prosecutorial decisions. In 1898, however, it seems that the chief inspector was given the final say: 'The slight loss of time which this involves is immaterial compared with the importance of securing carefully considered and properly co-ordinated action': *Report of the factory staff committee 1898*, PRO LAB 15/5, pp 31–32. In 1903, however, the decision was once again left to the judgment of the principal lady inspector alone.

78 Source: *Chief inspector's annual reports 1880–1914*. The figures for 1880–1894 are extrapolated from the lists of prosecutions in detail, while those for 1895 onwards are taken from the tables of prosecutions by district and offence.

79 *Chief insp. ann. rep., 1887*, p. 5.

80 The numbers of informations or cases have been extrapolated from the tables of prosecutions by districts in *Chief insp. ann. rep., 1895–1909*, and the number of workers from *Chief insp. ann. rep., 1898*, pt. I, p. 208 (for 1897), *1907*, p. 300 (for 1904) and *1911*, p. 289 (for 1907).

This greater rate of prosecutions in Ireland may, of course, be a consequence of lower managerial standards – part of the explanation offered at the time:

This is a test … not merely of the activity of the inspectors, though of that too; not wholly of the criminality of employers, though this, of course; it is related to two other circumstances which have to be borne in mind in apportioning its proper value. One of these is the wide and scattered nature of the area of operations, together with the character of the industries pursued there,[81] and of those directing them…. In many of the remoter parts of Scotland and Ireland, an inspector's visits are comparatively infrequent; compared, that is, with closely packed industrial districts; the industries are small, the employers illiterate, stubborn, careless. To such apprehensions, and amid such surroundings, a prosecution is generally the most efficient, is often the only way of inspiring a proper respect for the law…. In this way, an occasional prosecution acts both as a means of advertising the law and securing respect for it…. Argument is thrown away, the most painstaking instruction neglected or ignored. What alone is fully understood, regarded, feared is the appearance of the offender before a local court of summary jurisdiction….The other circumstance … is the paltry character of the penalties commonly inflicted on conviction. These are sometimes so low as to be not merely altogether disproportionate to the magnitude of the offence, but often an indirect incitement to its continuance, nay, even to tend, in some cases, towards the scandalous imputation of a sympathy on the part of the magistrates with it.[82]

But just who in Ireland were brought to court? The information provided in the annual reports between 1880 and 1900 enables us to suggest the following:

Table 10.5: Number of prosecutions in Ireland, 1880–1900, by industry[83]

	No. of firms or persons prosecuted	No. of prosecutions per 1,000 workers		No. of firms or persons prosecuted	No. of prosecutions per 1,000 workers
Linen	351	4	Saw mills	35	7
Wool	16	4	Engineering/		
Clothing	564	13	metal works	26	1
Food and drink	132	5	Other/not known	191	13
Letterpress printing	67	7			
Brick works	31	10	TOTAL	1,413	6.5

81 Cf. in 1896 the ratio of prosecutions per 1,000 workers in the textile industry in the United Kingdom was estimated to be 0.39 for flax, as compared to 0.82 for cotton – much lower than the comparable rate for food and drink (1.34) and the clothing industry (2.14): *Chief insp. ann. rep., 1896*, p. 51.

82 *Chief insp. ann. rep., 1899*, p. 222. Cf. 'It is only by unceasing vigilance and firmness, combined no doubt with a courteous bearing and, above all things, inflexible justice, that laws alien in many respects to the habits and modes of thought of the Irish people can be imposed on them with any permanent success. Any paltering with these, any pusillanimity in enforcing them, anything in the nature of a retreat from the position once taken up, is fatal': *Chief insp. ann. rep., 1900*, p. 342 (Cooke-Taylor, superintending inspector, Scotland/Ireland division).

83 In this Table, we refer to the number of persons prosecuted rather than the number

This table suggests that the number of prosecutions of firms and persons engaged in various aspects of the linen industry and in engineering and metal works was *lower* than average, while those engaged in the clothing industry (and in brick works) were more frequently brought to court.[84] These findings, coupled with the preponderance of smaller trades and industries, might be taken to suggest that the inspectors were too timid to tackle the major industrial entrepreneurs in the north of Ireland. This, indeed, might be the case; but it may equally be the case that it was the smaller employers who were most frequently – and most blatantly – in breach of the acts. Commenting on the large number of prosecutions in the south of Ireland in 1900, for example, Bellhouse observed:

I do not ... attribute this to increased irregularity; it is due rather to our having been obliged to adopt stronger measures when we have failed to obtain compliance by mere instruction and cautions. Most of the prosecutions have been for employment after legal hours, and for the most part in workshops. There is an utter want of system in the carrying on of businesses in the country towns. Work begins very late in the morning ... and there is consequently often necessity of keeping [workers] in late in the evenings after legal hours.[85]

On some occasions at least, the inspectors did show themselves willing to pursue a major employer, whatever the consequences:

A report had been spread through the town that if I won the case ... the factory would be closed; and as the factory was one of the principal means of support for the inhabitants of the town, the report was calculated to counteract my efforts. I provided a popular subject of discussion at tea parties; and on paying a visit one morning to one of the principal clergy of the town, I was ushered into a drawing-room where I found a small conclave of people discussing ... what they called the 'crusade against the factory'. Needless to say I did not get much assistance from that quarter! Astonishing fear was exhibited, not only by workers but by people in positions which were such as one would imagine would make them entirely independent.[86]

The defendant in the case was 'a prominent man in the City of London', and Martindale went to great lengths to establish the case against him, by calling six expert witnesses, another factory inspector, Dr Legge (the medical inspector of factories), two certifying surgeons, a government chemist and a professor of pathology – in addition to the mother of two girls who had died from working in the factory. Not unsurprisingly, she secured a conviction![87]

One obvious factor which influenced the decision whether or not to prosecute was the sufficiency of the evidence. This was a matter of particular

---

of informations. The number of workers in each category is derived from the returns set out in *Chief insp. ann. rep.*, *1896*, pp. 208, 214–15 and 224–25.

84 See further below, p. 327.
85 *Chief insp. ann. rep.*, *1900*, p. 342.
86 Martindale, *From one generation to another*, pp 104–06.
87 Ibid.

comment by the lady inspectors, who often encountered difficulties in obtaining witnesses in the first instance – or, having done so, found that they changed their story before or at the hearing:

In every way it is excessively difficult to collect evidence in Ireland. One's arrival at a town or in a village is at once noted, and the news spread quickly. Many of the factories in country places stand in isolated positions, so that one's approach is easily watched. Added to the fear of answering the inspector's questions so often exhibited by the worker, the custom is somewhat prevalent among foremen and forewomen of going to a worker soon after I have left her, and enquiring as to my questions and the replies given.[88]

There can be little doubt that many workers were in fear of losing their employment if they gave evidence against their employer, and that intimidation of one kind or another was quite widespread. In 1898 an indemnity fund was set up by the Industrial Law Committee to assist women and girls who had been sacked for giving evidence, and this fund was to prove useful in a number of Irish cases, particularly in relation to the suppression of truck practices. After a difficult case in Donegal, for example, Deane observed that 'it is not too much to say that the action of the fund committee which ... undertook to indemnify the witnesses, thus dismissed, against the actual loss of employment and to find work for them, alone made proceedings for the enforcement of the law possible'.[89]

But not all was doom and gloom:

The increase in the number of complaints which have reached me has been one of the most noteworthy results of my residence in Ireland. In several cases, workers have found their way to my office and poured out their grievances, while in other instances their parents or friends have called or written to me regarding the matters of which they had to complain. I have received considerable help in my work from the priests, clergy and ministers, from certifying surgeons, and women sanitary inspectors, as well as trade union officials, and I am glad that an Irish branch of the Industrial Law Committee has been started in Dublin, from which I am sure the workers in factories and workshops will reap great benefit, and by means of which public opinion in Ireland will be roused on industrial matters.[90]

When they appeared in court, the inspectors in Ireland – as in England and Wales[91] – preferred to have their cases heard by a resident or stipendiary magistrate.[92] As we have seen, a justice of the peace who was the occupier of

---

88 *Chief insp. ann. rep., 1908*, p. 163 (Martindale).
89 *Chief insp. ann. rep., 1899*, p. 250.
90 *Chief insp. ann. rep., 1909*, p. 126 (Martindale).
91 See e.g. *Chief insp. ann. rep., 1894*, p. 223 and *1897*, p. 119.
92 There are a number of cases in which the home office, through the Irish administration, sought to ensure the attendance of one, or even two, RMs for the hearing of a controversial case – see especially D. Greer, '*Middling hard on coin': Truck in Donegal in the 1890s* (ILHS, Dublin, 2000). Cf. 'Governments found it useful to have a core of reliable magistrates in the service of the state. ... They were always regarded and treated as members of the civil service, but this did not ameliorate the

the factory or workshop, or the father, son or brother of the occupier, was expressly excluded from a court hearing a case arising out of an offence committed in or with reference to that establishment.[93] In 1901, this restriction was considerably extended: 'a person engaged in, or being an officer of any association of persons engaged in, the same trade or occupation as a person charged with any offence under this Act shall not act as a justice of the peace in hearing and determining the charge'.[94] The inspectors in Ireland nonetheless felt that many of the justices of the peace who were eligible to hear their cases were too sympathetic to occupiers, either out of friendship or notions of social cohesion,[95] or on account of political or other antipathy to the factory acts.[96] In this respect the lady inspectors were particularly critical of 'the vagaries' of summary justice in Ireland:

The Bench retired to consider their decision. On their return the Resident Magistrate made a long speech. He said the case was one which, if proved to their satisfaction, would lead to the highest penalty the law allowed. They had the evidence of the young lady, Miss Martindale, who seemed to have behaved with great pluck and activity, and His Majesty was to be congratulated upon the possession of a lady inspector who did her duty so conscientiously and well. But it had not been proved to the satisfaction of the magistrates that Miss Martindale had seen any person whom they could consider to be held accountable for the actions of the firm.... They regretted that the people at the factory on this particular day did not behave with more common sense and give the information asked for by the young lady.... [But] taking all the circumstances into consideration, and desiring as they did to see the law carried out, they agreed on dismissing the case.[97]

Martindale 'became accustomed to such verdicts coupled with Irish blarney'.[98] No doubt there were some unmerited acquittals – though Martindale's case may *not* be one of them. In general terms, however, the overall conviction rate remained consistently high, seldom falling below 95 per cent and, at least until 1905, not noticeably out of line with that in the other two jurisdictions.[99]

suspicions of those who saw them as "Castlemen" and believed that, far from being impartial law officers, they were influenced in their judicial functions by political instructions from Dublin': Bonsall, *The Irish RMs*, p. 13.

93 1844 act, s. 71, re-enacted as 1878 act, s. 89 and 1901 act, s. 144(4).

94 1901 act, s. 144(5), as anticipated by Truck Act 1887, s. 15 and as recommended in *Chief insp. ann. rep., 1894*, p. 223 (by the chief inspector).

95 See e.g. the magistrate who advised Squire that 'we all know that the defendant would not do anything that was unfair or unreasonable': *Chief insp. ann. rep., 1904*, pt. I, p. 282. This view was shared by others: 'If a person of any local influence should fall into trouble, he endeavours to get all the neighbouring justices who may be friends to attend at the petty sessions, and fight his battle': Bailey, 'Magisterial reform', p. 599.

96 'One constantly feels that the bench [in the south of Ireland] ... look upon the Acts as being unnecessary in their small factories and workshops, and as being merely a hindrance to their businesses, and convictions are given therefore with reluctance, and the penalties are put at the lowest possible sum': *Chief insp. ann. rep., 1901*, pt. I, p. 129 (Bellhouse).

97 *From one generation to another*, pp. 101–02.

98 Ibid., p. 102.

99 Between 1900 and 1904, for example, the dismissal rate in Ireland was just over 2 per

But the aspect of the magistrates' courts which most concerned the inspectors was the low level of fines which they frequently imposed in what were considered to be serious cases. Part of the responsibility for this situation rested with parliament. As we have seen, the 1844 act imposed *minimum* as well as *maximum* fines in respect of various offences. This practice was not followed when the acts were extended to workshops in 1867, a decision which attracted the criticism of the factory and workshop commissioners in 1876.[100] But the 1878 act contained no provision for minimum fines. It appears that the government then and later took the view that *minimum* penalties discouraged some magistrates from convicting some offenders,[101] and the act accordingly prescribed only *maximum* fines. This approach, which was in general replicated in the 1901 act,[102] attracted the criticism of the inspectors:

I am convinced that such a [minimum fine] provision would be of the greatest service. Occupiers do not mind running the risk of being caught when they know that they will only be fined a nominal penalty of from 1*s*. to 2*s*. 6*d*., even if proceedings are taken against them; but they are very much more careful when they know that there is a minimum penalty of 20*s*. in each case. There might be individual cases of hardship when the defendant is some poor struggling employer, but I think an inspector could always use his discretion in such cases, and not take more cases into court than appeared necessary to meet each individual offence.[103]

From time to time, the government acknowledged that low fines presented 'some difficulty'; but they were reluctant to interfere, in part because the magistrates were 'extremely jealous' of their independence and in part because the government was, in effect, the prosecuting authority: 'It would be a delicate and difficult matter for the prosecutor to press upon the ... magistrates the fact that they were not punishing adequately the offences which the department was prosecuting before them.'[104] All that could properly be done was to issue a circular, 'couched in moderate and

cent, as was also the case in Scotland and England and Wales. But in the period 1905–1910, just over 5 per cent of cases in Ireland were dismissed, as compared to 3 per cent in Scotland and 2.5 per cent in England and Wales. The most notable discrepancy is to be found in 1908, when just over 14 per cent of cases in Ireland were dismissed, as compared to 4 per cent in Scotland and 2 per cent in England and Wales. The dismissal of 27 of the 139 cases brought that year in the north of Ireland was primarily responsible for this outcome – see *Chief insp. ann. rep., 1908*, p. 231.

100 *Report of the factory and workshop commissioners, 1876*, p. lxxxvii.
101 See e.g. *Hansard 4*, cxxxix, 1044 (4 Aug. 1904)(A. Akers-Douglas, home sec.).
102 Cf. 1901 act, ss. 135(1), 136 and 137(1), re-enacting 1891 act, s. 28, provided for a minimum fine of £1 where a factory occupier was convicted of the same offence within two years. The rare application of this provision in Ireland was singled out for special mention in 1911; but in the following year, a defendant in Sligo was fined only 2*d*. for a second offence: *Chief insp. ann. rep., 1911*, p. 39 and *1912*, p. 31.
103 *Chief insp. ann. rep., 1899*, p. 223 (Bellhouse). For the view that minimum penalties would also suit magistrates, 'who in a large proportion of cases have thrust upon them the unpleasant duty of sitting in judgment on fellow manufacturers and friends', see *Chief insp. ann. rep., 1898*, pt. II, p. 80 (Commander Smith, Sheffield).
104 *Hansard 4*, cviii, 1034 (30 May 1902) (Ritchie, home sec.).

reasonable language', drawing to the attention of the magistrates the need to impose an 'adequate' fine when a case was clearly proved.[105]

The majority of offences committed by factory or workshop occupiers attracted a maximum fine ranging from £2 to £10; higher penalties (up to £100) were payable for truck offences, for breaches of safety provisions which resulted in death or injury and for forgery or fraud.[106] Where an offence was committed by a servant or workman employed by the occupier, he or she 'shall be liable to the same fine as if he were the occupier'; but a parent who allowed his or her child to be unlawfully employed or to fail to attend school risked a maximum penalty only of £1.[107] The general abolition of minimum fines, however, led throughout the United Kingdom to the imposition of *lower* fines after 1878, a development which was criticised by the chief inspector:

In cases which are important enough to call for more than a caution and instruction, and in which the evidence is sufficient to satisfy the court that conviction ought to follow, the inspector may reasonably expect that substantial penalties will be imposed. Unfortunately the tendency has of late years been in the opposite direction.... The average penalty for proved offences ... in 1897 was 13s. 1d.... If the average be thus inadequate, individual instances must be far more so, and many examples of this will be found....[108]

It would appear that the average fine in Ireland in 1897 was even lower, at 10s. 7d.[109] As the average penalty per information across the United Kingdom rose after 1897, reaching 19s. 6d. in 1903, before falling again to just over fifteen shillings in 1909,[110] the fines imposed in Ireland tended to *decrease*, the average fine having fallen by 1906 to 9s. 6d.[111]

All these figures are, of course, in respect of informations, and it should be remembered that many cases would have involved two or more informations. This means that a typical factory act fine would have been higher than the average fine imposed in respect of all offences tried in the magistrates' courts; in Ireland in 1900 this would appear to have been less than 5s. It should also

---

105 See e.g. *Hansard 4*, cxxxix, 1006 (4 Aug. 1904) (Sir Charles Dilke).
106 See especially 1878 act, ss. 68, 77–78, 81–83, 85 and 88; 1901 act, ss. 135–137 and 139; Truck Act 1831, s. 9, as applied by Truck Amendment Acts 1887, s. 11 and 1896, s. 4 (one of the few cases in which a minimum fine (£5) remained in force – see above, p. 199).
107 1878 act, ss. 84 and 86; 1901 act, ss. 138 and 140.
108 *Chief insp. ann. rep., 1897*, p. 119.
109 This figure has been extrapolated from the list of prosecutions in detail in *Chief insp. ann. rep., 1897*, pp. 280–84. This list suggests that the average fine in the north of Ireland was 13s., as compared to 6s. in the south. The earlier annual reports suggest that during the 1880s the average fine imposed by the Irish courts was only 9s.
110 See *Chief insp. ann. rep., 1903*, pt. II, p. xiii and *1911*, p. xv.
111 See *Chief insp. ann. rep., 1906*, pp. 174–75 – where, however, the average which is given is per prosecution, not per information; the figure given in the text is an attempt to calculate the latter from the former. The average fine in the north now appears to be *lower* than that in the south, a change which was already evident in 1900 (when the average fine appears to have fallen below 6s.).

be pointed out that a substantial fine could be imposed in a case regarded by the court as involving a serious breach of the law. In June 1895, for example, the Henry St. Warehouse, a firm of dressmakers and tailors in Dublin, were fined £21 for employing seven women after hours on a half-day,[112] and in December 1897, Teresa Boyle of Ardara was fined £40 in respect of four truck offences.[113] But these are exceptional cases and it was rare for a firm to be fined more than £5 or £10.

The inspectors in Ireland were consistently – and outspokenly – critical of the fact that fines in general were considerably lower than those which would have been imposed in respect of the same offence had it been committed elsewhere.[114] In 1900, for example, the superintending inspector for the Scotland-Ireland division, having noted that the penalties imposed in Scotland 'are of a deterrent character', continued:

There is a somewhat painful consensus of opinion on the subject as regards ... the north of Ireland. All the inspectors there [refer to] the want of adequate support afforded them by the courts of summary jurisdiction. The penalties inflicted for breaches of the law are often ridiculously low; sometimes even the magistrates seem to side with the offenders; not seldom they manage, whether designedly or not, to leave that impression on the public mind, whatever their formal judgment may be.[115]

Offences which in Scotland resulted in the imposition of a 'substantial' penalty received fines of 6*d.* or 1*s.*, with the result that 'prosecutions are more abundant here, and have far less effect'.[116] Nine years later, nothing had changed: 'such contraventions as employing females until 11 p.m., and using a steam boiler in such an unsafe condition that it eventually blew up, are met with a fine of one penny'.[117]

112 *Chief insp. ann. rep., 1895*, p. 83 – reduced to £5. 0*s.* 5*d.* on appeal.
113 *Chief insp. ann. rep., 1897*, p. 282. But this fine was subsequently annulled – see Greer, *Truck in Donegal in the 1890s*, p. 33.
114 And not just the inspectors. In 1905 the Irish TUC called for all serious breaches of the factory acts to be made punishable by imprisonment – and were immediately brought to earth by a delegate from the flaxdressers' union: 'What would they say if the employers passed a resolution that trades unionists should be imprisoned for infringement of the law?': *Report of the Twelfth Irish Trades Union Congress* (Wexford, 1905), p. 45.
115 *Chief insp. ann. rep., 1900*, p. 340 (Cooke-Taylor). Inspector Snape added that 'magistrates, especially in the country, do not view the administration of the factory acts in at all a favourable light'. They had in mind two particular cases. A letterpress printer in Enniskillen had employed two young persons at illegal hours; 'for a grave and obvious breach ... the local magistrates at first refused to convict, and [then] ... inflicted a fine of *one penny!!!*': *Chief insp. ann. rep., 1899*, pp. 213 (emphasis in original) and 404, and a dressmaker in Monaghan who failed to give three women a statutory holiday (St Patrick's Day) was fined fourpence on each charge, on the basis that 'the factory act was never intended for places like Monaghan': *Chief insp. ann. rep., 1900*, pp. 341 and 659.
116 *Chief insp. ann. rep., 1900*, p. 340 (Kirkwood). In 1905, the average fine in Scotland was 17*s.*, in Ireland 8*s.* – and in the north of Ireland closer to 6*s.* – see *Chief insp. ann. rep., 1905*, p. 211.
117 *Chief insp. ann. rep., 1909*, p. 119 (Graves, superintending inspector).

The stipendiary magistrates in Dublin did tend to impose fines 'properly commensurate with the offence', with the result 'most certainly' that there was a 'large' reduction in the incidence of illegal over-work in the city.[118] But elsewhere in the south things were just as bad as in the north. In 1901, for example, Bellhouse attributed his 'very little success' in preventing illegal employment in workshops 'entirely to the miserable penalties that are inflicted in such cases.... If these cases are to attain a proper degree of usefulness, the penalty must ... have a really deterring effect. As things are, employers are quick to recognise that the most flimsy excuse will be accepted by the bench, and that the profits derived from the late hours will more than pay for the small penalty that may be inflicted.'[119] In 1908, his successor complained of 'totally inadequate penalties' of 6d. and 1s. being imposed in cases of illegal overtime – 'and the Treasury often being mulcted more heavily in costs than the convicted employer'.[120] Four years later, yet another inspector complained that throughout the south of Ireland 'the acts receive no judicial support and are treated with hostility by nearly all the magistrates except the resident magistrates, who are, of course, generally over-ruled by the remainder of the bench'.[121]

And yet, for all that, one frequently finds cases in which low fines have been imposed for reasons which would nowadays be considered valid, and which even the inspectors themselves acknowledged at the time – previous good record,[122] a first offence,[123] the first prosecution in the neighbourhood,[124] a solemn promise to comply with the law,[125] poverty[126] – and even a 'once-in-a-lifetime' predicament.[127]

THREE CASE STUDIES

Most of the prosecutions conducted by the inspectors in Ireland were simple and straightforward affairs – they were, after all, heard and determined by a

---

118 *Chief insp. ann. rep., 1901*, pt. I, p. 129.
119 Ibid., citing examples of low fines imposed in Limerick, Ballinasloe, Borris, Mullingar, Longford, Youghal and Newcastle West. In *Chief insp. ann. rep., 1904*, pt. I, p. 201, he referred again to 'the continued prevalence of small and utterly inadequate fines'.
120 *Chief insp. ann. rep., 1908*, p. 30 (May).
121 *Chief insp. ann. rep., 1912*, p. 31 (Allhusen).
122 E.g. *Cameron* v. *Springfield Spinning Co.*, *Chief insp. ann. rep., 1882*, p. 114; *Cameron* v. *Wallace*, *Chief insp. ann. rep., 1888*, p. 225.
123 E.g. *Cameron* v. *Ulster Woollen Co.*, *Chief insp. ann. rep., 1890*, p. 127; *Woodgate* v. *Power*, *Chief insp. ann. rep., 1894*, p. 283.
124 E.g. *Woodgate* v. *Watters*, *Chief insp. ann. rep., 1890*, p. 133 (Dundalk); *Woodgate* v. *Lynch*, *Chief insp. ann. rep., 1884*, p. 148 (Bailieborough, Co. Cavan).
125 E.g. *Cameron* v. *Ligoniel Steam Brick Works*, *Chief insp. ann. rep., 1882*, p. 114; *Woodgate* v. *McAdam*, *Chief insp. ann. rep., 1891*, p. 93.
126 E.g. *Cameron* v. *Sinton & Co.*, *Chief insp. ann. rep., 1883*, p. 360 (Irish manufacturers not as rich as those in Lancashire); *Cameron* v. *McGurk*, *Chief insp. ann. rep., 1887*, p. 195.
127 *Snape* v. *Matier & Co.*, *Chief insp. ann. rep., 1890*, p. 216 (rush to complete orders for USA before imposition of McKinley tariff).

court of 'summary' jurisdiction. But on a small number of occasions, the proceedings became extremely convoluted, as the inspectors, either by design or by lack of an adequate appreciation of local sensitivities, stirred up a degree of local controversy which gave rise to tactical forensic manoeuvres. We have dealt elsewhere with one such case;[128] three further cases are now examined briefly by way of further illustrating the tensions which sometimes arose between the Irish magistracy and the enforcement of the factory acts.

Snape v. Young (1898–99)

In spite of its importance as an integral part of the production of fine linen, the traditional method of scutching flax in Ireland was crude and inefficient – and virtually immune from improvement.[129] Having reached its peak in the 1860s, it was by the end of the century an industry in decline, finding it difficult to compete with the more modern methods adopted in other countries, and in particular Belgium. A major part of the problem was that scutching took place in a large number of small mills, which were not only 'ill-built and ill-kept', but run on a part-time basis by owners who generally had little capital or technical expertise. The working conditions in these mills were both dangerous and unhealthy and, in spite of objections from the owners, they were brought under the aegis of the factory acts in 1878. The provision which particularly concerns us here is the following:

If in a factory ... where ... any process is carried on, by which dust ... or other impurity is generated and inhaled by the workers to an injurious extent, it appears to an inspector that such inhalation could be to a great extent prevented by the use of a fan or other mechanical means, the inspector may direct a fan or other mechanical means of a proper construction for preventing such inhalation to be provided within a reasonable time....[130]

During the 1880s the inspectors tended to the view that the nature of the work and the poverty of most scutch mill owners made the strict application of this provision impracticable. Part of the problem was the lack of a suitable, but inexpensive, fan – a shortcoming which seemed to be resolved when John Stewart, a scutch mill owner near Coleraine, installed a fan designed by Blackman Ventilation Co. of Belfast with good results.[131] In any event, by 1897 or so, Inspector Snape[132] and his superiors clearly felt that the time had

---

128 Greer, *Truck in Donegal in the 1890s*.
129 See above, pp. 142–51 and 166–69.
130 Section 36, as amended by 1895 act, s. 33.
131 The local inspector (Snape) made a particular point of referring to this development, which had been reported in the *Belfast Newsletter*, 14 Dec. 1895: *Chief insp. ann. rep., 1895*, p. 134.
132 Gerald Snape had been the occupier of a cotton factory in England before his appointment as an inspector in 1883. After working for a time in England, he was appointed inspector for the north of Ireland district in 1890, and served in that capacity until 1905, when he returned to England.

come for a more positive approach. A circular was sent to all scutch mill owners
in the north of Ireland advising them of the need for proper ventilation; some
of the owners acted on the circular, but many did not. Having visited a
scutch mill at Blackhill, near Coleraine, and found it in a particularly poor
condition, Snape then invoked the 1878 act to direct James Young, the
owner, to install a fan or other suitable mechanical means to provide proper
ventilation. When he refused to do so, Young was summoned to appear at
Garvagh petty sessions in October 1898.

The proceedings were seen on both sides as a crucial test case.[133] The
home office requested the assistance of the local crown solicitor,[134] and
Snape set about securing the evidence of expert medical witnesses; Young
appointed his own solicitor and a number of other scutch mill owners rallied
to his support. As a result, the hearing of the case took on some unusual
features. Of the four local justices who turned up for the hearing, two were
scutch mill owners themselves. In anticipation of the express prohibition
introduced in 1901,[135] they took a 'discreet and proper course'[136] and retired
from the bench. The first decision taken by the two remaining justices was to
allow a third solicitor, 'who appeared to watch the interests of certain other
millowners who would be affected by the decision in the case' to have a
limited role in the proceedings.[137] They then acquiesced in a special request
by the prosecution to have the material part of the evidence of the witnesses
taken down in writing.[138] The stage was now set for the presentation of the
prosecution case.

Snape began by describing the dusty conditions in Young's mill and, in
response to a question from the bench as to whether he had received any
complaints from the workers, stated that he would be calling them as
witnesses. He then gave evidence of the beneficial effect of proper ventilation

---

133   The account which follows is derived from *Chief insp. ann. rep., 1898*, pt. II, p. 136
       and *1899*, pp. 34–37, and from the home office file at PRO HO 45/9939/B28084.
134   The need for an indirect approach to Dublin Castle via the home office caused an
       'accidental' delay which led Snape to have a consultation with a local solicitor 'in
       order to avoid any risk of being left entirely without legal advice on the difficult
       questions which had arisen'; the home secretary sought payment for the solicitor on
       the grounds that 'there was an emergency of sufficient importance to excuse, if not
       to justify, the inspector's action': Sir Henry Cunynghame (legal ass't under-sec.,
       home office) to Secretary to the Treasury, 4 March 1899 (PRO HO87/16, p. 86).
135   'A person engaged in ... the same trade or occupation as a person charged with an
       offence under this act shall not act as a justice ... in hearing and determining the
       charge': 1901 act, s. 144(5).
136   As Crampton J had advised in *R. v. Cork Justices* (1857) 7 ICLR 244, 248.
137   The solicitor in question (Warke) stated that 'This prosecution is not aimed at this
       mere defendant, it is aimed at mills in general.... [Inspector Snape] means to set a
       precedent for other mills, and why is he to shut out other mills from taking an
       interest in this case?' The chairman of the court 'cannot see that it will do any harm'.
       Warke's role appears to have been limited to the cross-examination of prosecution
       witnesses.
138   As provided by Petty Sessions (Ire.) Act 1851, s. 20(4), but rarely done in factory act
       cases. A short-hand transcript of the hearing was also taken for the home office.

by suitable fans in two local scutch mills and pointed out that there was not a single mill without fans in the neighbourhood of Courtrai, with the result that 'the atmosphere in the [Belgian] mill ... on the day of his visit was as clear as that of the court house in Garvagh'.[139] In response to the bench he said that the cost of a suitable fan was 'about £7 to £10'. The cross-examination by Young's solicitor seems to have been designed to show that the conditions in the mill were not so bad as to be 'injurious' to health; further cross-examination by the solicitor acting for other mill owners was directed at Snape's competence to give 'scientific' evidence and attempted to show that he lacked a proper understanding as to the different methods of scutching adopted in Ulster and Belgium.

The prosecution then called three scutch workers to give evidence of the effect of inhaling the flax dust[140] – and two workers from Stewart's mill, where a fan had made the atmosphere 'a great deal better'. Medical evidence was provided by two local doctors and by Dr Legge, the newly-appointed medical inspector of factories. Dr Morrison, medical officer for health for Aghadowey, testified that many scutch workers suffered from asthma; but 'before they have asthma, they take bronchitis and cough, or irritation of the pipes leading to the lungs which goes on to produce heart disease and probably kidney disease and destroys the whole system'. Dr Steele, medical officer of health for Articlave, thought it unlikely that any man could remain healthy in a scutch mill. Dr Legge's evidence as to the harmful effects of flax dust was based on scientific tests which he had conducted at Young's mill: 'His microscopic examination of the particulars of dust and impurities in that flax mill went to show that such are particles which, when they get into the lungs, cannot be got rid of, and are therefore injurious to the health of the man who inhales them.'[141]

The defence began by putting the case in a broader context:

There are two interests involved here – one the interest of the workman who has to depend on this industry as his means of livelihood and the other the gigantic interest of the whole of the flax owners in Ireland. We are fast losing our hold of the flax trade in this country and are being ousted out, one place after another, by foreign competition.... If we and the flax mill owners in this country are to be tied down by these little petty rules, it will absolutely cease to be an industry that can be carried on with any profit and it will cease to be an industry that can be carried on at all....

The answer to the particular charge was a classic example of legal pleading. The 1878 act did not apply, and was never intended to apply, to scutch mills;

---

139 *Ballymoney Free Press*, 3 Nov. 1898, p. 3.
140 Snape was later to explain that Dr Morrison had spent 'a great deal of time ... in visiting the workers and inducing them to given evidence, which as a class they are very reluctant to do, for fear of offending their employers.... Had it not been for Dr Morrison's zeal, interest in the case and influence with the workers, the evidence given would have been of far less value, if indeed it would have been possible to procure any evidence at all.'
141 *Chief insp. ann. rep., 1899*, p. 36 (Judge Overend QC).

if it did apply, Young's mill was properly ventilated by means of doors and windows; if it was not properly ventilated, the dust was not inhaled by the workers to an injurious extent. Three workers with long experience of working in scutch mills testified that they were in good health and did not know of other workers who were unwell as a result of their working conditions. Two scutch mill owners, including one of the justices who had excused himself from sitting on the bench, gave evidence that their workers had never complained about the absence of a fan, and explained that the exposure to dust was limited to a short period of the year – and that workers could, and often did, go outside for a breath of fresh air. A doctor testified that on the basis of his experience the atmosphere in a scutch mill was not such as would harm a healthy worker.

Finally, Young himself gave evidence on his own behalf. This is of particular legal interest, since the Criminal Evidence Act enacted earlier that year to replace the old common law rule that a defendant in a criminal case was not a competent witness, did not apply to Ireland. However, section 49 of the Factory and Workshop Act 1895, which *did* apply to Ireland, had expressly provided that 'a person charged with an offence under the factory acts may, if he thinks fit, tender himself to be examined on his own behalf, and thereupon may give evidence in the same manner and with the like effect and consequences as any other witness'. Young accordingly testified that he had owned the mill since 1871, and that he had never in all that time had any complaints from his workers. The mill was normally worked only three months of the year and, when working, rarely exceeded five hours per day.

Somewhat surprisingly, there were no closing speeches, and the bench quickly announced their verdict: 'We are satisfied that working in the mill under existing circumstances is injurious to health, and we will convict the defendant.' At the request of his solicitor, Young was fined £1. 1s. 0d. to enable him to lodge an appeal[142] – and he was ordered to pay the same amount in costs.[143]

The appeal to Coleraine quarter sessions, which was by way of rehearing, lasted two days in January 1899.[144] The prosecution case was much as before, but 'a very large number of millowners and scutchers' appeared on Young's behalf – to no avail. Upholding the decision of the court below, Judge Overend QC first extolled the virtues of the factory acts, which 'form one of the brightest pages in the history of the United Kingdom'. He emphasised the wider importance of the case, 'seeing that there are in Ireland alone about 900 flax scutching mills ... and but very few provided ... with anything in the nature of a fan or other mechanical means of ventilation ...'; but he acknowledged that 'this particular decision relates to James Young's

142   See above, p. 303. The maximum fine for this offence was £10: 1878 act, s. 81.
143   The cost of the case to the home office in respect of witness expenses and shorthand notes alone exceeded £20.
144   The composition of the court is not without interest. It was presided over by the recorder of Londonderry (Judge Overend QC), who sat with a resident magistrate and two justices, one of whom had heard the case at petty sessions.

mill only', and that it was possible for that mill to be properly ventilated by a variety of methods. But he was satisfied on the evidence that the dust generated in the mill was inhaled by the workers to an injurious extent. In contrast to the impressive medical evidence adduced by the prosecution, 'a strange thing about the evidence for the defence was that it was all practical, and not backed up by that of a single scientific witness ... who will say that the inhalation of flax dust ... is not injurious to health'.[145] Accordingly the conviction and fine were affirmed – and a further order made that Young's mill was not to be worked in the next season without a fan or other suitable mechanical means of ventilation having first been installed.

Snape may have been disappointed at the level of the fine imposed on Young, but otherwise both he and the home office must have been satisfied with the outcome of this test case, which provided a useful precedent for future prosecutions. But although they won the battle, they largely lost the war, for the efforts of the inspectorate over the next ten years or so produced little in the way of a general improvement in the ventilation of scutch mills.[146]

Snape v. *Alexander et al.: The 'Coleraine prosecutions' (1900)*

The poor conditions in which large numbers of women and girls were employed in millinery and dress-making establishments brought them to the attention of the Children's Employment Commission in 1864. Rejecting the contention that the work was 'private' or 'domestic', the commission regarded these undertakings as essentially 'industrial and commercial', and as such properly liable to legislative regulation.[147] Accordingly, many millinery and dress-making establishments became subject to the Workshop Regulation Act 1867 and then to the Factory and Workshop Act 1878, which applied to any 'premises, room or place' in which manual labour 'is exercised by way of trade or for the purposes of gain in or incidental to' the making, altering, ornamenting or finishing of any article or 'the adapting for sale' of any article.[148] The occupier of any such establishment was required to comply with all the provisions relating to workshops, including formal requirements as to displaying certain notices[149] and the more substantive provisions regulating the permitted hours of employment. Women and young persons were normally to cease work at 8.00 p.m. on a weekday and 4.00 p.m. on a Saturday; but, being employed in a

---

145 Judge Overend noted that a doctor had been called as a defence witness at petty sessions, but not on the appeal, 'perhaps for the reason that his evidence would not have favoured the defence'.
146 See above, pp. 167–69.
147 *Second report of the commissioners on the employment of children in trades and manufactures not already regulated by law*, pp. xlvi–lxvi [C. 3414], H.C. 1864, xxii, 48–68, discussed above, p. 46. See also M. Neill, 'Women at work in Ulster, 1845–1911' (unpublished Ph.D. thesis, Queen's University Belfast, 1996), chap. 5.
148 Section 93(2).
149 By s. 78, an abstract of the 1878 act and various statutory notices were to be affixed at the entrance to a workshop 'in such position as to be easily read by the persons employed'.

trade liable to a 'sudden press of orders arising from unforeseen events', women (and until 1895 young persons) could be required to work on a week-day until 10.00 p.m., provided certain conditions were satisfied.[150]

Social conventions and the customary working practices designed to accommodate them brought many Irish milliners and dress-makers into conflict with the new law: 'One has only to pass second or third-rate millinery [or] dress-making ... establishments in the large towns of Belfast and Derry, late on Saturday nights, and similar establishments ... in the county towns at 10 p.m. or 11 p.m. on market days and Saturdays, to get ample evidence of infringements of the law.'[151] Old habits died hard, however, and during the 1880s the inspectors regularly brought prosecutions in an attempt to enforce the law.[152] But it was in the period 1894–1900 that they were exceptionally active in this respect, with almost 350 prosecutions in every corner of the island.[153] In 1894 alone, more than 60 prosecutions were brought in courts as far apart as Gorey and Ballina, Skibbereen and Dungiven – including three in Coleraine.[154] Another case in Coleraine was among the 60 or so prosecutions brought in 1899,[155] and the following year was to see a determined effort to bring unlawful employment practices to an end throughout the island, and more particularly in Belfast, Londonderry, Lisburn, Lurgan, Portadown, Dublin and Cork.[156] On the sixth of July 1900, Inspector Snape attended Coleraine petty sessions intent on adding Coleraine to that list.

The particular problem which he faced arose from the practice of drapers to buy in untrimmed bonnets and hats and employ a shop-assistant with 'a knowledge of millinery' to work on them when not attending to customers in the shop. Such work was often undertaken on a Saturday evening long after the normal 4.00 p.m. limit. The work was usually done in the shop itself, and the question, therefore, was whether the work done by the assistant, who was paid a higher salary than an ordinary shop-assistant,

150　1878 act, ss. 13, 15 and 53 and sch. 3, pt. 3; 1895 act, ss. 14(1) and 36.

151　*Chief insp. ann. rep., Oct. 1869*, pp. 230–31 (Cramp).

152　In 1883, for example, seven prosecutions were brought in Belfast, Dublin, Londonderry and Sligo, resulting in fines amounting to £16: *Chief insp. ann. rep., 1883*, pp. 145–48 and 159.

153　Leading a trades union delegate to complain that 'the present factory inspectors were confining their attention to dress and mantle-making warerooms in the south to the neglect of the factories and workshops': *Report of the Fourth Irish Trades Congress* (Waterford, 1897), p. 28.

154　*Chief insp. ann. rep., 1894*, pp. 265–84. In Coleraine, one milliner was fined 5s. for employing a woman after 4 p.m. on a Saturday and a dressmaker was fined 3s. for employing a young person and two women without proper arrangements for mealtimes; the case against another milliner for failing to display an abstract of the 1878 act in his workshop was dismissed.

155　*Chief insp. ann. rep., 1899*, pp. 402–09. A Coleraine dressmaker was fined two shillings for failing to maintain the necessary registers.

156　*Chief insp. ann. rep., 1900*, pp. 656–64. Magisterial opinion as to the appropriate fine varied considerably; the average fine for an 'employment' offence in Portadown was 16s., in Belfast and Lurgan, 10s., in Londonderry, Lisburn and Dublin, 5s. and in Cork, 1s.

amounted to 'adapting' an article for sale, thus making the shop a 'workshop' for legal purposes.[157] Snape was satisfied that it did and he acted accordingly.

The proceedings which he brought against four Coleraine firms were all essentially on the same facts.[158] In *Snape* v. *Alexander*, for example, he had found a woman trimming a bonnet at 8.55 p.m. one Saturday evening. As it happened, she was a niece of the occupier, and if a prosecution in such circumstances is somewhat surprising, this feeling is compounded by the fact that she gave evidence against her aunt. The defence was that she voluntarily 'helped out' with pressing orders from time to time. In *Snape* v. *Porter & Co.*, on the other hand, the prosecution case was that a woman who had started work at 9 a.m. was still engaged in millinery work at 9 p.m.; the defence in this case appears to have been to challenge the veracity of the evidence.[159] In all four cases, the bench[160] clearly considered Snape's contention that millinery work converted a shop into a workshop was unrealistic: 'It would appear to me that if there are people employed in a shop, it is [according to your argument] a crime for them to do anything except waiting behind the counter.'

Accordingly, all four cases were dismissed.[161] Snape thereupon requested the court to state a case; but the chairman of the bench, adroitly advised by the resident magistrate, replied that the application was 'frivolous', and – as provided by section 4 of the Summary Jurisdiction Act 1857 – refused to do so.[162]

Given that 'fully 75 per cent of the places where millinery is sold in my district, partial trimming and altering or ornamenting ... is done in a retail shop',[163] both Snape and his superintending inspector (Cooke-Taylor) were dismayed. Citing the decision as an example of how the magistracy in the north of Ireland 'do not view the administration of the factory acts in at all a favourable light', Snape added that 'the effect of this decision has had a very bad effect in my district, as many shopkeepers are continually referring [me] to these cases'.[164] Cooke-Taylor was even more outspoken about this 'serious miscarriage of justice':

157 In particular, 'If a young person or woman is employed by the same employer on the same day both in a ... workshop and in a shop, the whole period of employment ... shall not exceed the number of hours permitted ... for his or her employment in the ... workshop': 1895 act, s. 16(4).

158 The account which follows is based on *Chief insp. ann. rep., 1900*, pp. 340–42, the home office file at PRO HO 45/9990/X79535 and *Coleraine Chronicle*, 14 July 1900.

159 'Do you believe there is intelligence in Ireland? I believe you are from Scotland': *Coleraine Chronicle*, 14 July 1900, p. 8. For a further report of the case, see *The Constitution*, 14 July 1900.

160 Sir Hervey Bruce (chairman), Captain Welch RM and five local justices.

161 Three of the defendants were also charged with failing to exhibit an abstract of the 1878 act; these charges, too, were all dismissed: *Chief insp. ann. rep., 1900*, p. 341.

162 According to the *Coleraine Chronicle*, 14 July 1900, he added: 'I have heard from an eminent lawyer that it is dangerous for magistrates to write down specific reasons for their actions [laughter]'.

163 *Chief insp. ann. rep., 1900*, p. 342.

164 Ibid., pp. 342–43. When Snape later returned to the defendants' premises, he found that 'precautions had been taken against surprise visits' and work suspended:

I have no hesitation in saying that the factory acts are systematically violated and defied in that neighbourhood on account of it, and that the evil is spreading. They are notoriously and openly so defied; to the detriment of the workers, thus deprived of their protection; to the weakening of the authority of H.M. officers in those parts, who have their administration in charge; and to the general demoralisation of a community only too prone to treat all legally constituted authority with contempt.... Finally, it is unjust to other employers more regardful of the interests of their workers and the laws of their country and who are thus placed at a trade disadvantage by the misconduct of competitors.[165]

Fortunately, one might think, a more considered review of the case was carried out at a higher level. Whitelegge, the chief inspector, advised the home office that 'it seems clear that the magistrates were wrong, and that their decision ... will hamper further action in that locality'.[166] But the home office was not convinced[167] – and not only refused to countenance any further prosecutions, but declined to take the opportunity to change the wording of the legislation.[168] However, Snape was quickly vindicated. In *Fullers Ltd.* v. *Squire*[169] a conviction based on the decision that packing and arranging sweetmeats in ornamental boxes with ornamental ribbons amounted to 'adapting' them for sale was upheld on appeal. And any remaining doubts were put to rest in 1907, when it was held in *Hoare* v. *Robert Green Ltd.*[170] that shop assistants in a florist's shop who also made up flowers into bouquets or wreaths were thereby adapting them for sale.

Paterson v. Donegal Fish Curing Co. (1899)

The depressed economic condition of much of the western seaboard of Ireland led in 1891 to the establishment of the Congested Districts Board to reform the system of landholding and to foster industrial development.[171]

Whitelegge (chief insp.) to Sir Kenelm Digby (perm. under-sec., home office), 27 July 1900 (PRO, HO 45/9990/X79535/2).

165 *Chief insp. ann. rep., 1901*, pt. I, p. 128. He had earlier suggested that 'the proprietors of workshops in that neighbourhood refuse to conform with the well-known principles of the law in view of what had occurred, and threaten to remove all their workers from the workshop proper to the shop, that they might be wholly independent of it. This too after they had up till then willingly conformed': *Chief insp. ann. rep., 1900*, p. 341.

166 Whitelegge to Digby, 11 July 1900 (PRO HO 45/9990/X79535/1).

167 'I don't think the changing of a hat-band or replacing a flower in a bonnet is adapting an article for sale. Would the affixing of a string to a pair of eye-glasses make the optician's shop into a workshop?': Digby to Whitelegge, 27 July 1900, ibid.

168 This part of the definition of 'workshop' was not amended by Factory and Workshop Act 1901, s. 149.

169 [1901] 2 KB 209.

170 [1907] 2 KB 315.

171 Purchase of Land (Ire.) Act 1891. A 'congested' district was one in which more than one-fifth of the population lived in electoral divisions where the average rateable value was less than £1 10s. 0d. per head. See generally W.L. Micks, *An account ... of the congested districts board for Ireland from 1891 to 1923* (Dublin, 1925). For a useful

The board took an active interest in the development of the fishing industry by means of expert advice, the building of curing stations, assistance with marketing, etc., to such effect that 'the value of fish landed on the congested districts coast in 1891 was estimated at £51,000, and in 1913 at £167,000'.[172] As part of this development, the duke of Abercorn and others, as a philanthropic endeavour, established a fish-curing company in Burtonport, Co. Donegal.[173]

On the return of the fishing fleet, much of the work of preparing the fish for curing was undertaken by women. It was not an easy job:

The chief causes of injury to health in the industry are two: (1) long and irregular hours of work; (2) exposure ....The curer's object is to have the fish dealt with as soon as possible after they are landed, both to prevent deterioration and in order to be ready for the next supply. Hence the long hours, the night work, the absence of regular hours or of intervals sufficient for meals .... Rheumatism, bronchitis and the pulmonary troubles from which so many of them suffer, are consequent upon exposure to inclement weather .... [T]he tendency to contract ... epidemic diseases ... is the result of their generally lowered physical condition, due to their unhealthy mode of living.[174]

It was 'small wonder' that 'strong and healthy as the women are at the commencement of the fishing season, they are towards the end of it frequently crippled in health'.[175]

In principle, fish-curing establishments were workshops subject to the normal restrictions as to hours of work, safety, etc. But in 1871, and again in 1878, it had been accepted that the work had to be done at whatever time necessary to prevent a catch from being spoiled and, accordingly, 'nothing in this act shall extend ... to the process of gutting, salting and packing fish immediately upon its arrival in the fishing boats'.[176] Although this exemption is limited both in point of time and as regards the nature of the work, the inspectors for many years took a broad view and ignored virtually all aspects of fish-curing. In 1895, however, the chief inspector temporarily decided that curing was distinguishable from 'gutting, salting and packing' and therefore came within the 1878 act; but he changed his mind in the face of con-

summary in the present context, see H.D. Gribbon, 'Economic and social history' in W.E. Vaughan (ed.), *A new history of Ireland, VI: Ireland under the Union II, 1870–1921* (Oxford, 1996), pp. 283–92.

172 Gribbon, 'Economic and social history', p. 284. The industry prospered during the first world war, but declined thereafter.

173 The company was reported to have been set up at a cost of £10,000, and to have contributed an annual sum of £8,000 to the local economy: PRO HO45/9944/B29311/8, citing *Freeman's Journal*, 29 July 1899.

174 M.M. Paterson, 'Fish curing and fruit preserving' in T. Oliver (ed.), *Dangerous trades: The historical, social and legal aspects of industrial occupations as affecting health, by a number of experts* (London, 1902), pp. 675–76.

175 T. Oliver, *Diseases of occupation from the legislative, social and medical points of view* (2nd ed., London, 1908), p. 369.

176 Factory and Workshop Act 1871, s. 4; Factory and Workshop Act 1878, s. 100(2).

siderable opposition.[177] There the matter stood until February 1898, when a special report prepared for the home secretary concluded that the exemption conferred by the 1878 act went too far; fish-curing *should* be generally subject to the provisions of the factory acts.[178] It was, however, conceded that 'considerable relaxation as to hours of labour is absolutely essential'; but this relaxation should be confined to the employment of women and young persons 'according to the exigencies of the trade, in the immediate and continuous processes necessary to prevent the fish from spoiling on the day or night of its arrival'.[179]

Into the middle of an uncertain legal scenario replete with fine distinctions came the prosecution by Inspector Paterson of the Donegal Fish Curing Co.[180] The company engaged in kippering and also made the boxes in which the kippers were packed, and Paterson took the view that this work went beyond 'gutting, salting and packing' and was therefore subject to the protection of the 1878 act. She inspected the premises in December 1898 and found them in an unsatisfactory state.[181] Repeated inspections and representations having achieved nothing 'beyond a defiantly expressed determination to work outside the limits of the factory acts', it was decided to prosecute the company.[182] To keep the case simple and straightforward, she relied on a single representative information – failure to affix at the entrance to the premises the prescribed abstract of the factory acts, contrary to section 78(1) of the 1878 act.

The case was heard at Dungloe petty sessions on 7 March 1898, by a bench consisting of a resident magistrate (Butler) and three local justices, all of whom were local tradesmen 'in the same way of business' as the defendants.[183] The facts were not in issue; the only question for the court was whether the kippering came within the exemption in respect of 'gutting, salting and packing' and whether the box-making was such a minor part of the business as not to be carried on 'by way of trade or for purposes of gain' as required by section 93(3) of the act. The defence categorised the prosecution as

---

177 See especially *Report to the secretary of state for the home department by two of HM inspectors of factories appointed to enquire into the conditions of work of the fish-curing trade of the United Kingdom*, pp. 5–7 [C. 8753], H.C. 1898, xiv, 389–91.

178 In Ireland at this time there were some 130 factories and workshops engaged in fish curing and employing 3,574 persons, almost three-quarters of whom were women or young persons: ibid., p. 16. The inspectors drew special attention (at p. 13) to the 'wretched conditions' under which mackerel curing was carried on in south-west Ireland.

179 Ibid., pp. 14–15.

180 This account is based on the report in *Chief insp. ann. rep., 1899*, pp. 247–48 and the home office file at PRO HO 45/9944/B29311 [hereafter '*Home office file*'].

181 *Chief. insp. ann. rep., 1898*, pt. II, p. 179.

182 At the hearing of the case in March 1899, Paterson was asked whether the prosecution was brought under instruction from the home office; she replied that she was not at liberty to say, since this was a matter between herself and her superiors: *Home office file*, p. 3. But it seems highly unlikely that the principal lady inspector and chief inspector would have made the decision on their own.

183 *Chief insp. ann. rep., 1899*, p. 247.

'vindictive' and 'an attempt to strangle a new industry in Ireland by putting restrictions on it that the home office does not care to impose in England'. The principal lady inspector considered the court to be 'still far from the influences and training of the factory system'. But the draftsman had clearly obscured the ambit of section 100(2) by inserting a marginal note which reads 'Saving for person employed ... in process of *curing* fish'.[184] The impact on the court of such legal niceties – as opposed to broader political considerations – is not known; but in the event the bench was evenly divided. The chairman thereupon announced that the case was being dismissed 'without prejudice'.[185]

Paterson's first reaction was to ask the court to state a case. But she was then advised by the sessional crown solicitor (Mackey) that the form of the dismissal 'left it open to us to begin afresh and have the same case tried by the same court with an increase in the number of magistrates so as to secure a majority' one way or the other.[186] Although the defendants would, no doubt, object to being charged a second time with the same offence, and there would be 'objections to my referring to examining or cross-examining on evidence given at a previous trial', Paterson was given authority by the home office to bring a second prosecution. When this became known to the defendants, they immediately contacted the chief secretary:

The efforts of the company are being frustrated by a government prosecution at the instance of Miss Paterson.... Miss Paterson is bringing the case forward again and should she succeed in obtaining a conviction a very serious injury will be done to the whole of the British fish curers to whom at present the law does not apply, for if its regulations are to be observed it will simply be impossible to utilize the herrings which the poor fishermen bring ashore to preserve them in the form of kippers and bloaters. May I ask you to be good enough to give the matter your careful consideration and if possible, to use your powerful influence in staying this second prosecution.[187]

When this letter was forwarded to the home secretary, he was advised by the chief inspector (Whitelegge) *not* to stay the proceedings, on account of the wider implications of the case: 'If we cannot compass this in Ireland we must exempt completely all the fish-curing places.'[188]

---

184 Judges differ as to the value of marginal notes as an aid to the interpretation of a statute. On one view, they should be ignored, as being inserted 'not by Parliament nor under the authority of Parliament, but by irresponsible persons': *Re Woking UDC (Basingstoke Canal) Act 1911* [1914] 1 Ch. 300, 322, *per* Phillimore LJ; but in *Stephens* v. *Cuckfield RDC* [1960] 2 QB 373, 383, Upjohn LJ observed that 'it is at least permissible to approach a consideration of [the section's] general purpose and the mischief at which it is aimed with the note in mind'.

185 *Chief insp. ann. rep., 1899*, p. 247.

186 Ibid.

187 John Sager (treasurer, Donegal Fish Curing Co.) to Gerald Balfour, 28 March 1899: *Home office file*, p. 5.

188 Whitelegge to Sir Matthew Ridley, 2 April 1899: *Home office file*, p. 6.

Paterson was accordingly authorised to prosecute the company a second time. The hearing took place in May 1899 before an enlarged bench consisting of a resident magistrate and four local justices. Although Paterson was on this occasion represented by Mackey, and had the support of the resident magistrate, the court, by a majority of three to two, dismissed the case on the merits:

[T]he resident magistrate wished to convict, and the point on which the case turned was fully proved. ... It would be interesting to know exactly what knotty legal point was in the minds of the magistrates who were so strongly convinced that all the work was 'exempted by the act'. The whole of the incidents surrounding the case, and the proceedings themselves, were full of the humour, conscious and unconscious, which makes an Irish court seem like part of a play and difficult to treat altogether seriously, and the appeals to the bench by the defending solicitor to dismiss the case on the grounds of 'injustice to Ireland', my own nationality, were curious to listen to in what purports to be a court of law.

The evidence necessary to prove the case did not occupy very much time, but the case lasted about an hour, most of which was occupied by the elaborate speech of the solicitor for the defence, in which he called on the magistrates to follow the example of the Bishops in their revolt against authority, quoting at some length from Macaulay's *History*. ... The climax of his oration was reached when he appealed to the magistrates not 'to allow Miss Paterson to hie herself back to the Home Office bedecked with plumes of victory'.[189]

This dismissal paved the way for an appeal by way of case stated, which was duly lodged. The involvement of the sessional crown solicitor meant that the Irish 'Crown authorities', rather than the home office, were responsible for carriage of the appeal – and a lack of co-operation, to put it at its lowest, quickly became apparent. The home office expressed concern that the statement of the case had been drawn up without consulting Paterson, and that no consultation had been arranged with crown counsel even though 'the points involved are important and somewhat intricate, [and] it seems very desirable that counsel should be fully informed of the views of the Home Office upon the subject before the appeal is heard'.[190]

Through his Dublin agents, Mackey lodged the appeal with the queen's bench division of the high court on 13 June 1899 and on the following day gave notice of the appeal to the defendant's solicitors. Unfortunately, section 2 of the Summary Jurisdiction Act 1857 provides that 'the appellant shall, within three days after receiving [the case stated], transmit [it] to the court ... *first* giving notice in writing of such appeal, with a copy of the case ... stated ... to the other party to the proceeding ...' (emphasis added). Compliance with this provision was 'a condition precedent to the court hearing the appeal'.[191] When the case came on for hearing on 28 June 1899, T.M. Healy QC, MP,

189 *Chief insp. ann. rep., 1899*, p. 248 (Paterson).
190 Whitelegge to Sir Kenelm Digby (perm. under-sec., home office), 25 June 1899: *Home office file*, p. 11. It was, however, conceded that the case stated 'seems sufficiently clear for the main purposes of the appeal'.
191 C. Molloy, *The justice of the peace for Ireland* (Dublin, 1890), p. 295, citing *Guardians of South Dublin Union* v. *Jones* (1883) 12 LR Ir 358.

representing Donegal Fish, drew this procedural irregularity to the attention of the court, which duly ordered the case to be struck out and directed Paterson to pay to the defendants 'any costs properly and necessarily incurred by them'.[192]

The home office – and no doubt Paterson – were furious: 'This important case would seem to have been mismanaged from first to last',[193] and they were hardly placated when the chief secretary wrote 'to express His Excellency's regret at this unfortunate termination of the case'. The attorney general for Ireland demanded an explanation from Mackey, who blamed his Dublin agents for failing to carry out his instructions.[194] This 'defence' appears to have succeeded: 'while Mr Mackey's explanation by no means excuses his neglect, the circumstances do not call for anything further than a reprimand and a caution, and Mr Mackey has been so informed.'[195]

The manner in which the appeal was (mis)conducted may suggest that the proceedings were 'sabotaged' by an Irish administration reluctant to allow the factory acts to become an impediment to economic development in the congested districts.[196] This view of the case tends to be supported by the fact that one of the chief 'complaints' of the home office was that newspaper reports of the hearing in the queen's bench division had failed to emphasise that Paterson's counsel 'publicly repudiated the implication made by the respondent's counsel that an important philanthropic effort was being hampered by the actions of the Home Office'.[197]

The broader issue was quickly resolved. In 1901, legislation gave effect to the compromise recommended in 1898; exemption from the provisions of the factories acts was now restricted to the hours of employment of women and young persons engaged in 'processes in the preserving and curing of fish which must be carried out immediately on the arrival of the fishing boats in order to prevent the fish from being destroyed or spoiled'.[198] All such processes were now made subject to other protective provisions, such as those relating to sanitation and safety – and non-'immediate' curing had to be undertaken during normal working hours. But the new law had little impact in Co. Donegal: when Martindale inspected the working conditions in fish-curing establishments in the county in 1907, she found that little had changed.[199]

192 *Freeman's Journal*, 29 June 1899.
193 Whitelegge to Digby, 3 July 1899, *Home office file*, p. 13. To make matters worse, the home office claimed to have learned of the outcome of the case only 'accidentally' by reading the *Freeman's Journal*. The court's decision was made on 29 June, but it was not until 5 July that the home office received word from Dublin Castle: ibid.
194 Sir David Harrel (under-sec., chief sec.'s office) to Digby, 5 July 1899: *Home office file*, p. 17.
195 Harrel to Digby, 17 July 1899: *Home office file*, p. 24.
196 In 1903, Bellhouse acknowledged that 'there can be no doubt but that [fish-curing] is the greatest god-send, financially, to the poor districts where it is carried on': *Chief insp. ann. rep., 1903*, pt. I, p. 152.
197 Cunynghame to Harrel, 4 July 1899: *Home office file*, p. 16.
198 1901 act, s. 41.
199 *Chief insp. ann. rep., 1907*, pp. 149 and 176.

CHAPTER ELEVEN

Civil proceedings

INTRODUCTION

Prosecution by a factory inspector may have been the principal method of enforcing the law, but it was not the only one. As time went on, factory and workshop owners who fell below the statutory standards became increasingly subject to pressures of one kind or another to improve working conditions. It is not possible or appropriate in the present context to examine these alternative 'remedies' in any detail; but given the close connection between the factory acts and the prevention of accidents, it is proposed in this chapter to look at the role played by civil proceedings as a supplementary method of encouraging factory and workshop occupiers to comply with the safety provisions of the acts.[1]

THE EARLY HISTORY OF EMPLOYERS' LIABILITY[2]

The limited role which inspectors could be expected to play in the achievement of minimum safety standards was, as we have seen, acknowledged from the outset by the factory commissioners in 1833: 'we apprehend that no inspector would probably be so fully conversant with all the uses of every variety of machinery as to be acquainted with all the dangers which may be provided against.' The power to prosecute should, therefore, be supported by means of 'pecuniary consequences' imposed through a system of strict liability imposed 'on those who have the best means of preventing the mischief' and in this way 'combine interest with duty, and add to the efficiency of both'.[3]

This early example of general deterrence theory found no support from a government which took the view that this supplementary role could be

---

1 A similar study could be conducted in relation to the role played by actions for breach of contract. Many of the issues in this context are examined by P.S. Atiyah, *The rise and fall of freedom of contract* (Oxford, 1979).

2 For a fuller treatment of this subject, see D.S.Greer, '"A false, mawkish and mongrel humanity"? The early history of employers' liability in Ireland' in O. Breen, J. Casey and A. Kerr (ed.), *Liber memorialis Professor James C. Brady* (Dublin, 2001), p. 227. See also J. White, *Civil liability for industrial accidents* (Dublin, 1993), i, 2–23. For England and Wales, see especially P.W.J. Bartrip and S.B. Burman, *The wounded soldiers of industry: Industrial compensation policy 1833–1897* (Oxford, 1983), chaps. 1, 3 and 4 and W.R. Cornish and G. deN. Clark, *Law and society in England 1750–1950* (London, 1989), pp. 520–28.

3 *First report of the central board of H.M. commissioners appointed to collect information in the manufacturing districts as to the employment of children in factories …* , p. 31, H.C. 1833 (450), xx, 31, adding that 'if the pecuniary consequences from unavoidable accidents

---

adequately fulfilled by the existing common law, under which compensation was, in theory, paid to those injured as the result of the negligence of the occupier.[4] But the underlying problem with common law liability was the acceptance by the judges for much of the nineteenth century of a philosophy expressly rejected by the factory commissioners – that the workers themselves should have 'the obligation of perpetual care and apprehension of danger'.[5] Not only was this the best method of securing the safety of the workman, but it was what he had contracted for.[6] It was this philosophy which brought about judicial recognition of three 'defences' – contributory negligence, *volenti non fit injuria* and common employment – any one of which normally defeated a worker's claim, even when he or she could establish negligence on the part of the employer or someone for whom he was vicariously liable. Some judges, it is true, were willing to accept that 'it is, in most cases, impossible that a workman can judge of the condition of a complex and dangerous machine, wielding irresistible mechanical power, and, if he could, he is quite incapable of estimating the degree of risk involved in different conditions of the machine; but the master may be able, and generally is able, to estimate both ...'.[7] But even these judges drew the line at strict liability: 'To hold that the master warrants the safety and proper condition of the machine, is ... unjust to the master, for no degree of care can insure perfect safety; and it is equally inconvenient to the public, for who would employ such machines if he were an insurer?'[8] There could be no alternative to liability based on fault.

Nevertheless, some injured workers did manage to obtain damages by bringing civil proceedings in the courts.[9] But the weakness of this supplementary method of enforcing the factory acts was recognised as early as 1841, when it was recommended that 'inspectors should be empowered to

were considerable, the imposition of the proposed responsibility may be met by the master, or by a deduction from wages ...'.

4 See *e.g. Hansard 3*, xix, 221–22 (5 July 1833).

5 In the well-known words of Lord Abinger: 'The servant is not bound to risk his safety in the service of his master, and may, if he thinks fit, decline any service in which he reasonably apprehends injury to himself': *Priestley* v. *Fowler* (1837) 3 M & W 1, 6, 150 Eng Rep 1030, 1034. Equally (in)famous is the observation of Lord Cranworth in *Bartonshill Coal Co.* v. *Reid* (1858) 3 Macq 265, 272: 'If men engaged for certain wages in a work of great risk, it is to be supposed that the risk forms an element in their contemplation in agreeing to accept the stipulated remuneration.'

6 See e.g. *Potts* v. *Plunkett* (1859) 9 ICLR 290, 298, where Lefroy CJ stated that, subject to limited exceptions, 'if the cause producing the injury is equally known and equally palpable to the servant as to the master, the servant cannot complain, for it may be said that he went into the danger with his eyes open'.

7 *Clarke* v. *Holmes* (1862) 7 H & N 937, 948, 158 Eng Rep 751, 755, per Byles J.

8 Ibid.

9 See especially *Cotterrell* v. *Samuel Stocks & Co., Insp. quart. rep., Sept. 1840*, pp. 7–8 (Howell). It would seem that Ashley made the case, which excited a good deal of interest, a test case: 'if it were found that the law gave no protection to suffering individuals in the situation of this plaintiff, then it would be high time to call upon the legislature to provide by enactment for such cases.' For Ireland see *MacCracken* v. *Dargan and Haughton*, below, p. 340.

direct proceedings to be instituted, whenever dangerous machinery shall have been left exposed, contrary to [the] order [of an inspector] ... and bodily mutilation or suffering shall in consequence have occurred'.[10] The Factory Act 1844 in due course provided that the home secretary could, on the report and recommendation of an inspector, authorise him to bring an action for damages against an employer in breach of the act where a textile worker had been injured by dangerous machinery; any damages so recovered were to be paid to or for the benefit of the worker in question.[11]

But this provision was singularly ignored by the authorities from the outset; no instance of its use has been found in Ireland or in Great Britain. It seems highly unlikely that resort to formal proceedings was unnecessary 'inasmuch as the occupiers of the factories who were liable, have provided readily ... that which the law required to be obtained from them, viz., reasonable compensation for the injured person'.[12] No doubt voluntary compensation payments were made in some cases; but the need for some compulsory mechanism was recognised in an alternative procedure, also dependent on the inspectors, provided by the 1844 act. Where an occupier, on prosecution by an inspector, was found guilty of an unlawful failure to fence dangerous machinery which had resulted in injury to a worker, the occupier became liable to a fine of not less than £10 and not more than £100, 'the whole or any part of [which] may be applied for the benefit of the injured person, or otherwise as the Secretary of State shall determine'.[13] This procedure was for some time used to benefit a number of factory accident victims in Great Britain.[14] But its impact in Ireland was minimal; we have found only one case in which section 60 was invoked – and that was ultimately unsuccessful.[15] By the early 1860s, indeed, the section had virtually fallen into disuse throughout the whole of the United Kingdom.[16]

---

10 *Report from the select committee appointed to inquire into the operation of the act for the regulation of mills and factories*, p. 28, H.C. 1841 (56), ix, 585. Any costs involved would be borne by the state.

11 Sections 24 and 25. Bartrip and Burman, *Wounded soldiers of industry*, p. 55 suggest that as a result, it was not until *Caswell* v. *Worth* (1856) 5 El & Bl 849, 25 LJQB 121, 119 Eng Rep 697 that it was settled that a worker could sue a factory occupier independently of the home office. That point was certainly argued in that case; but it seems preferable to limit its application to the question, not then clearly answered, whether a defendant could be civilly liable for breach of a safety provision of the 1844 act, a point which the court found it unnecessary to decide. See further below, p. 339.

12 *Insp. half-yearly rep., April 1853*, p. 55 (Redgrave).

13 1844 act, s. 60.

14 Bartrip and Burman, *Wounded soldiers of industry*, p.57, referring to a case in 1848 in which £40 was paid over to an injured girl. For another example, see *Insp. half-yearly rep., Oct. 1855*, p. 36 (£10 fine paid over to 'a poor Irish woman' working in England who lost her left hand as a result of her employer's failure to fence a blowing machine).

15 *Darkin* v. *Herdmans of Sion Mills, Insp. half-yearly rep., Oct. 1854*, p. 29 (fine of £10 reversed on appeal), discussed Greer, 'Early history of employers' liability', pp. 241–42.

16 Bartrip and Burman, *Wounded soldiers of industry*, p. 58; Greer, 'Early history of employers' liability', pp. 235–36. See also R.L. Howells, '*Priestley* v. *Fowler* and the factory acts', in *Modern L. Rev.*, 26 (1963), 394, noting that the greatest need for

In short, legislative attempts to ameliorate the weakness of the common law as a secondary method of enforcing the factory acts failed to make a significant impact at a time when the factory inspectors themselves do not appear to have considered that the incidence of accidental death and injury required strong action in the form of criminal prosecutions. During the 1850s, however, it seemed for a time that there might be scope for greater private initiative as the judges appeared to accept that the safety provisions of the 1844 act imposed duties on occupiers which should be recognised and enforced in civil as well as criminal proceedings. The notion of common law liability for breach of statutory duty first arose in *Coe* v. *Platt*,[17] where the plaintiff's case was that an occupier, who had not been negligent, was nevertheless liable in tort on the grounds that he was in breach of section 21 of the 1844 act. The court decided that the occupier had not acted unlawfully; but it suggested quite clearly that failure to comply with the section would *per se* entitle the injured worker to recover damages.[18] Support for this view can be found in *Couch* v. *Steel*[19] and *Schofield* v. *Schunck*.[20] But an attempt to free the 'action upon the statute'[21] from one of the shackles of common law liability was rejected in *Caswell* v. *Worth*,[22] where the defendants claimed that the accident was the result of wilful misconduct on the part of the plaintiff. Rejecting the argument that this was not a good defence to an action based on breach of section 21, Lord Campbell CJ stated that 'The Factory Acts ... have had a very salutary effect, but they would have a most unjust and oppressive operation if this action could be maintained ... . [I]t would be contrary to all principle to hold that the plaintiff, having himself, by his own misconduct, wilfully caused the injury to himself, may maintain an action for compensation.'[23]

penal compensation was in the period 1844–1880, 'when the conventional legal remedies proved most ineffective'.

17 (1851) 6 Exch 752, (1852) 7 Exch 460 and 923, 155 Eng Rep 1030 and 1226.

18 'Though its main object may have been to afford security to children and young persons, who are more likely to sustain injury than others, yet there is a positive enactment [in the 1844 act] that, in all factories ... when any part of the machinery is used for any manufacturing process, it shall be securely fenced. Consequently if any person sustains an injury through the violation of the enactment, he has a right to bring an action': 6 Exch 757, *per* Parke B. Cf. the court of exchequer chamber in *Clarke* v. *Holmes* (1862) 7 H & N 937, 158 Eng Rep 751 expressly doubted whether Parke B was correct, but found it unnecessary to decide.

19 (1854) 3 El & Bl 402, 118 Eng Rep 1193. Lord Campbell CJ held that the defendant was in breach of statutory duty under the Merchant Seamen Act 1844 and awarded the plaintiff damages, notwithstanding that the act provided for the imposition of a £20 fine, part of which could be paid over to the informer.

20 (1855) 24 LT (QB) 253.

21 As Crampton J called this cause of action in *MacCracken* v. *Dargan* (1856) 1 Ir Jur (ns) 404, 406.

22 (1856) 5 El & Bl 849, 25 LJQB 121, 119 Eng Rep 697, immediately followed and applied in *MacCracken* v. *Dargan* (1856) 1 Ir Jur (ns) 404.

23 (1856) 25 LJQB 121, 123. Coleridge J did, however, suggest (at p. 124) that 'if it had appeared that this was the case of a young person shewn to be within the policy of the Act ... a different principle may prevail from that which applies in the case of an adult person ...'.

But the whole basis of the new tort was put in doubt as the courts began
to resile from the broad principle implicit in the early cases.[24] By the 1870s,
it was being said that a common law action would lie only where the statute
creating the duty in question failed expressly to provide a remedy for its
breach.[25] Although none of these cases involved the 1844 act, it seems[26] that
their cumulative effect cast some doubt on the legitimacy of decisions such
as *Coe* v. *Platt*, a doubt which was not to be put at rest until 1898.[27]

In any event, the inspectors themselves helped to undermine this new
form of action, ironically in the context of the first recorded case in which a
person injured in a factory accident in Ireland succeeded in obtaining common law damages. In *MacCracken* v. *Dargan and Haughton*[28] the plaintiff, a
spinning master aged 22, lost an arm when he was putting a belt onto a
revolving horizontal shaft situated some nine feet above the floor. Acting on his
own behalf, 'and not on the report and recommendation of the inspector',[29] he
brought a claim for damages alleging failure by his employers to fence the
shaft securely. A special jury in the court of queen's bench awarded the
plaintiff damages of £200.

The case was heard just before the passing of the Factory Act 1856, which
limited the occupier's duty to fence mill-gearing to those parts with which
women, young persons and children were 'liable to come into contact'.[30] The
act also enabled an inspector to require other transmission machinery to be
fenced; but in these cases, the occupier could take the matter to arbitration.
The inspectors immediately became concerned about the impact of any such
arbitration on the right of an injured worker to claim damages:

If the inspector should unwarily give rise to an arbitration ... and if the arbitrators,
looking at such machinery, should ... adjudge that it need not be fenced, and if a
young person should afterwards, in the course of his 'ordinary occupation' suffer a
similar injury to that of the plaintiff MacCracken ... from such machinery remaining
unfenced ... we apprehend that the formal though extra-judicial award of two
arbitrators, appointed under the authority of an Act of Parliament, and acting in
pursuance of its provisions ... would materially damage the plaintiff's case before a
jury, if not destroy his right of action altogether.[31]

---

24 K.M. Stanton, *Breach of statutory duty in tort* (London, 1986), pp. 3 and 34.
25 *Atkinson* v. *Newcastle & Gateshead Waterworks Co.* (1877) 2 Ex D 441; *Norton* v.
    Kearon (1871) IR 6 CL 126; *Hildige* v. *O'Farrell* (1880) 6 LR Ir 493.
26 According to Cornish and Clark, *Law and society in England*, p. 519, the changed
    judicial attitude in the 1870s and 1880s 'was bound to wash against the industrial
    accident claim based on breach of statute'.
27 *Groves* v. *Lord Wimborne* [1898] 2 QB 402.
28 *Insp. half-yearly rep.*, Oct. 1856, p. 3.
29 A rare reference to section 24 of the 1844 act.
30 1856 act, s 4. Section 21 of the 1844 act had always applied this qualification to
    steam-engines, water wheels, hoists and teagles. For the background to the 1856 act,
    see Bartrip and Burman, *Wounded soldiers of industry*, pp. 63–66 and R. Dickson,
    'Legal aspects of the factory act of 1856', in *J. Legal Hist.*, 2 (1981), 276.
31 *Insp. half-yearly rep.*, Oct. 1856, p. 4 (Howell).

Accordingly, the inspectors 'refrained' from requiring occupiers to fence dangerous machinery by issuing a notice 'which would call into action the imperfect extrajudicial kind of arbitration' provided by the 1856 act.[32] It did not take the home secretary long to spot the flaw in his inspectors' reasoning:

It appears to Sir George Grey that if an action were brought by any person for damages on account of an injury received from machinery or mill gearing of any kind, with regard to which the inspector ... was authorized by law to give notice to the occupier of the factory that he deemed it to be dangerous, but had purposely abstained from doing so, it might be not unreasonably argued on behalf of the defendant that it was not deemed to be dangerous by the inspector....[33]

No doubt the inspectors took this advice to heart. But the superior courts in Ireland continued to hear very few employers' liability claims. Precise information is not available; but we do know that in 1870, for example, only thirty-one personal injury or fatal accident claims arising out of *all* kinds of accidents were tried in Dublin or on assizes – and that only nine of these resulted in judgment for the plaintiff.[34] It seems that the position in England and Wales was much the same.[35] But the inspectors nevertheless continued to believe that civil litigation could function as an aid to enforcement. When the scope of the factory acts was extended to a wide variety of non-textile factories in 1867, for example, both Redgrave and Baker (the 'chief' inspectors of the day) concluded that inspection could have only a limited impact in terms of safety:

The accidents caused in the works under the Act of 1867 are of such a different nature from those caused in textile factories that the same regulations are ... inapplicable, and I do not see how those statutory regulations could be enlarged to render employment less liable to accidents. The only way to cause employers to keep their attention fixed upon the prevention of accidents would be to give an injured person a ready and inexpensive mode by which he could obtain compensation without being compelled to go through the cumbersome process of an action at law in a superior court.[36]

The failure of the common law – and of parliament – to provide a 'ready and inexpensive mode' of obtaining compensation had not, apparently, destroyed

---

32 Ibid., p. 7. Since the arbitrators had to be 'skilled in the construction of the kind of machinery' in question, they were liable to be closely associated with the factory occupiers; they might not be familiar with the investigation of accidents and they had no power to summon witnesses.

33 H. Waddington (perm. under-sec., home office) to H.M inspectors of factories, 31 Jan. 1857, PRO LAB 15/4.

34 *Judicial statistics (Ireland) 1870, Part II: Civil statistics*, pp. 199, 201, 204–04 and 208 [C. 443], H.C. 1871, lxiv, 429–38. These cases represented a small proportion (less than 10 per cent) of all cases entered for trial in the superior courts in 1870.

35 In 1870, 239 actions for death or personal injury were tried, with 148 resulting in judgment for the plaintiff: *Judicial statistics, England and Wales, part II: Civil proceedings*, pp. 3, 6, 9 and 11–12 [C. 442], H.C. 1871, lxiv, 195–203.

36 *Insp. half-yearly rep., April 1869*, pp. 473–74 (Redgrave).

the belief originally professed by the factory commissioners in 1833 in the beneficial effects of the 'pecuniary consequences' principle.

THE ATTEMPT TO FIND A COMMON LAW SOLUTION

Notwithstanding the reforms in practice and procedure brought about by the Common Law Procedure Act (Ireland) 1853 and the Supreme Court of Judicature (Ireland) Act 1877,[37] the bringing of a claim in the superior courts (queen's bench, common pleas and exchequer) remained a lengthy and complex business,[38] which could be particularly expensive if the claim was unsuccessful.[39] Such proceedings would clearly have been out of the question for most factory workers unless they received financial assistance of some kind. Some workers presumably qualified for free legal representation under the *in forma pauperis* procedure,[40] while others may have secured private or charitable benefaction or found solicitors willing to engage in 'speculative' actions.[41] Workers with relatively minor injuries could, of course, resort to the county courts, where the 'civil bill' procedure had for long provided in Ireland a speedy and inexpensive form of litigation in respect of small claims.[42]

By 1870, the principles on which damages for personal injury or death were assessed by the jury had essentially been settled in their modern form. In a case of personal injury, damages were awarded for (i) loss of earnings, both actual and projected; (ii) medical and other expenses, and (iii) pain and suffering and loss of amenities.[43] The amount of the award was intended to

---

37 See especially J.O. Wylie, *The Irish Judicature Acts* (Dublin, 1895).

38 See e.g. *Smyly* v. *Glasgow & Londonderry Steam Packet Co.* (1867) IR 2 CL 24.

39 As a general rule the successful party was entitled to recover the full costs of the suit from the losing party. A figure frequently quoted is the estimated costs of £600 incurred in *Cotterrell* v. *Samuel Stocks & Co*, the case brought with Lord Ashley's help in 1840 – see e.g. Bartrip and Burman, *Wounded soldiers of industry*, p. 27.

40 This early form of legal aid was available only to a person (a) with 'a good cause of action' and (b) who was 'not worth £5 in the world' – see e.g. W.D. Ferguson, *Practice of the Courts of Queen's Bench, Common Pleas and Exchequer of Pleas in Ireland, in personal actions and ejectments* (Dublin, 1841–42), ii, 730. Figures do not appear to be available for Ireland; but in England and Wales only five persons per year benefited from this procedure before 1883, when the financial limit was raised to £25; thereafter the annual average rose to twenty: Bartrip and Burman, *Wounded soldiers of industry*, pp. 26–27.

41 A solicitor could properly agree to make no charge if the claim failed, but to recoup his normal fees (either from the defendant or from the claimant's damages) if the claim succeeded; what he was not allowed to do was to charge a 'contingent fee' higher than normal in the event of the claim succeeding. This subtle distinction continued to be made well into the 20th century – see especially *Report of the committee on legal aid and advice in Northern Ireland* (Cmd. 417, 1960), paras. 29–33.

42 Civil bill jurisdiction in personal injury actions was limited to £40 by the Civil Bill Courts (Ire.) Act 1851, s. 35, but was raised to £50 by the County Officers and Courts (Ire.) Act 1877, ss. 50 and 52, which also gave unlimited jurisdiction in cases remitted from a superior court.

43 *Phillips* v. *L & SWR Co.* (1879) 4 QBD 406, 5 QBD 78 (first trial); 5 CPD 280 (second trial). See in particular the method of assessing damages in 'the common case of a labourer', as explained by Bramwell LJ at 5 CPD 287.

reflect the plaintiff's personal 'loss', and therefore depended in particular on the length of time the plaintiff was unable to work as a result of the injury, his or her normal wages or salary and the severity of the injury and its impact on his or her ability to enjoy life. In theory, there was no financial limit to the size of an award; in one well-known English case, for example, the plaintiff was awarded £16,000.[44] There was already some evidence of the apparent inconsistency of juries;[45] but in practice 'the general expectation of a humbler person rendered totally unfit for work was thought to be some three years' wages'.[46] Irish juries may on occasion have been more generous;[47] but in general damages of £300 or less were awarded in the great majority of personal injury claims determined by a jury.[48]

Where a person was killed in a factory (or any other) accident, a successful claim under the Fatal Accidents Act 1846 entitled the deceased's family to recover damages for their financial loss resulting from the death, based on a reasonable and just expectation of the pecuniary benefit which they would have derived from the deceased's earnings had he or she not been killed.[49] But damages were *not* payable in respect of the grief or mental suffering occasioned by the death[50] – though juries could be tempted to circumvent this rule.[51]

As a result of the legal and practical difficulties in securing damages for personal injury or death, some workers had begun to make 'mutual benefit' arrangements in the form of friendly societies, widows' protection funds and the like, which made financial payments to members in various circumstances,

---

44 Ibid. The plaintiff, a successful physician earning £5,000 per year, was badly injured and permanently incapacitated; the initial jury award of £7,000 was set aside by the court of appeal as wholly inadequate, and the case was heard by another jury.

45 See e.g. *Egan* v. *Freeman's Journal Ltd.* (1901) 1 NIJR 214 (award of £2,000 to married woman for pain and suffering arising from permanent back and leg injuries which required seven weeks in hospital upheld by court of appeal); *Beattie* v. *Moore* (1878) 2 LR Ir 28 (award of 1s. to plaintiff 'laid up' for six weeks set aside); *Blanchfield* v. *Murphy* (1912) 47 ILTR 24 (damages of £5 so low as to be 'wholly out of proportion' to injuries suffered by plaintiff).

46 Cornish and Clark, *Law and society in England*, p. 494, noting that it was this practice which provided 'the justification ... for introducing such a limit into the Employers' Liability Act 1880'. See further below, p. 349.

47 The spinning master aged 22 who lost an arm was awarded £200 by the (special) jury in *MacCracken* v. *Dargan and Haughton, Insp. half-yearly rep., Oct. 1856*, p. 3. Cf. *Scott* v. *Brookfield Linen Co.* [1910] 2 IR 509 (award of £450 to weaver who lost one eye and suffered serious injuries to the other); *Williams* v. *Morrissey* (1903) 3 NIJR 136 (woman deprived of sight of one eye in road accident awarded £200).

48 An analysis of jury awards in all personal injury and death cases in Ireland (they are not separately distinguished in the annual judicial statistics) suggests that the average award gradually rose from £206 in 1866–70 to £360 in 1906–10; two-fifths of these awards were for sums of less than £100.

49 See e.g. *Barnett* v. *Lucas and others* (1872) IR 6 CL 247 (widow of flax mill owner awarded damages of £500); *Murphy* v. *Pollock and Pollock* (1864) 15 ICLR 224 (father awarded £30 in respect of death of son killed in the course of his employment).

50 See especially *Blake* v. *Midland Rly. Co.* (1852) 18 QB 93, 118 Eng Rep 35.

51 See e.g. *Wolfe* v. *GNR Co.* (1890) 26 LR Ir 540, where the parents of a 10-year old girl killed in a railway accident were awarded damages of £150 by a special jury. Reducing the award to £50, Porter MR commented (at p. 563) that 'the element of

including injury or death arising from an accident at work.[52] Although these funds were primarily underwritten by the workers themselves, they sometimes benefited from contributions from sympathetic employers which, in exceptional cases, matched or even exceeded the amounts paid in by their employees.[53] In other cases, employers were willing to make some payment directly to the injured worker or his or her family:

> We do all we can to dissuade persons who have been injured from 'going to law' against the employers. Our experience has shown that in nearly every instance in which the case of a sufferer has been placed before the manufacturer in a fair spirit, he seldom refuses compensation, and the injured person is in the end better off by accepting moderate compensation at once than trusting to the chances of a verdict which, if in his favour, is always reduced by the unestimated amount of costs.[54]

But, of course, not all employers were so benevolent, and the struggle continued to improve the *right* to compensation. In terms of the common law, this took two principal forms – the extension of the employer's liability for negligence and his liability for breach of statutory duty.

1. Employers' liability

The main stumbling block facing a worker whose claim was based on negligence was the doctrine of common employment, which reached its peak during the 1860s and 1870s.[55] Employers were not vicariously liable to one worker for any injury caused by the negligence of a 'fellow servant':

> [B]y contracting to enter into a service and do a particular kind of work, the workman impliedly takes upon himself to run such personal risks as are incidental to the nature of the employment .... He is taken to know that, with the greatest possible care, machinery will go wrong or break down from latent defects, and that workmen, however carefully selected, will sometimes be careless.... He must be taken to know that workmen are prone to be careless of themselves, and of other people in the course of their work. Unless this were so, the master would be practically an insurer of the workman's safety.[56]

---

solatium [was not] altogether absent from the minds of the jury when they estimated the loss at £150 ...'. See to the same effect *Holleran* v. *Bagnell* (1880) 6 LR Ir 333 (jury award of £110 in respect of death of child aged 7 'reversed' by full court).

52 Cornish and Clark, *Law and society in England*, p. 522. For details of the Mayfield Provident Society established at Malcomson's factory, see Hunt, *Portlaw, Co. Waterford, 1825–1876*, p. 29. See also D.G. Hanes, *The first British workmen's compensation act, 1897* (New Haven and London, 1968), pp. 22–23.

53 Bartrip and Burman, *Wounded soldiers of industry*, p. 159, stating that the more general level of employer contribution was 10–25 per cent of the fund.

54 *Chief insp. ann. rep., 1879*, pp. 63–64 (Redgrave).

55 See especially *Bartonshill Coal Co.* v. *Reid* (1858) 3 Macq 266 and *Wilson* v. *Merry and Cunningham* (1868) LR 1 Sc & Div 326. *Bartonshill* was immediately followed in *M'Eniry* v. *Waterford & Kilkenny Rly. Co.* (1858) 8 ICLR 312, albeit with some misgiving; in particular, Perrin J (at p. 320) 'cannot see the reason, the principle or justice of the authorities which have been cited ...'.

56 H. Hanna, *The Workmen's Compensation Act 1897, as applied to Ireland* (1st ed., Dublin, 1898), pp. 10–11.

There were two principal means of avoiding the defence. The first was to establish some *personal* negligence on the part of the employer himself. Given that it was rare indeed for employers to be directly involved in the manufacturing process, this was a difficult, if not impossible, task in most cases.[57] In the case of an injury caused by another worker, however, the plaintiff could argue that the employer himself had been negligent in employing an *incompetent* 'fellow servant'[58] – but this allegation could pose considerable evidential problems for the injured worker.[59]

The alternative was to argue that the plaintiff and the person who caused the injury were not in 'common' employment because of the difference in their status. Some judicial support was forthcoming for such a distinction,[60] but it had to be abandoned when the house of lords held that a labourer and a senior manager could be in common employment – the manager being in law simply a servant having greater authority.[61] This ruling meant that an employer 'might delegate to a competent engineer or foreman the duty of taking reasonable and proper precautions against accidents to their workmen ... [and then] rely on the doctrine of common employment as a defence to an action founded on the negligence of the person to whom he has delegated his duties'.[62] For this reason, 'common employment operated with peculiar hardship on those workmen whose employers took little or no share in the conduct and management of their own business'.[63]

---

57 See e.g. *Ashworth* v. *Stanwix and Walker* (1861) 3 El & El 701, 121 Eng Rep 606; *Mellors* v. *Shaw and Unwin* (1861) 1 B & S 437, 121 Eng Rep 778.

58 See e.g. *Skerritt* v. *Scallan* (1877) IR 11 CL 389, 401, where Palles CB stated: 'When it is shown that a servant is incompetent, and that through his incompetency injury results to his fellow-servant, the mere fact of his incompetency throws the onus on the master of showing that he exercised due and reasonable care in selecting him ...'.

59 See especially *Murphy* v. *Pollock and Pollock* (1864) 15 ICLR 224 (no evidence of incompetence or even negligence on part of worker, and in any case no evidence that the employer kept him on knowing him to be incompetent). Cf. Deasy B's unsuccessful attempt (at pp. 230–31) to shift the burden of proof of competence to the employer, on the grounds that he 'can always explain the circumstances under which the employment arose, the knowledge which he had, and the reason which induced the employment of the person complained of'. See also *M'Carthy* v. *British Shipowners' Co.* (1883) 10 LR Ir 384 (a negligent act or default by a fellow-servant is, in general, *not* in itself evidence of incompetence).

60 In *Clarke* v. *Holmes* (1862) 7 H & N 937, 949, 158 Eng Rep 751, 752, Byles J asked: 'Why may not the master be guilty of negligence by his manager ... whose employment may be so distinct from that of the injured servant, that they cannot with propriety be deemed fellow servants?'

61 See *Wilson* v. *Merry and Cunningham* (1868) LR 1 Sc & Div 326 and *Allen* v. *New Gas Co.* (1876) 1 Ex D 251 – unless the person in question was a deputy or *alter ego* entrusted by the master with entire control of the business. These cases were followed in Ireland – see e.g. *Waldron* v. *Junior Army & Navy Stores Ltd* [1910] 2 IR 381.

62 *Carlos* v. *Congested Districts Board* [1908] 2 IR 91, 95, *per* Wright J. The traffic manager of a railway company and a milesman employed by the company were held to be fellow-servants in *Conway* v. *Belfast and Northern Counties Rly. Co.* (1877) IR 11 CL 345. Cf. *Ramsay* v. *Quinn* (1874) IR 8 CL 322, where the captain and an ordinary seaman on a ship were *not* fellow-servants, the captain being the agent or representative of the owners of the vessel during the voyage.

63 S.C. Porter, *The law relating to employers' liability and workmen's compensation* (Dublin,

The extent of the protection thus afforded to large and wealthy employers, and the adverse effect of virtual immunity from common law liability on the enforcement of safety provisions and the prevention of accidents, led to agitation in parliament from 1862 for the abolition of the defence of common employment.[64] Although consistently and vehemently opposed on the basis that 'unrestricted' common law liability would be too burdensome for employers, the movement for reform had by the late 1870s gained such momentum that the only question was how, rather than if, the law should be amended. In practical and political terms, the choice lay between a modest limitation of the scope of the defence and its virtual abolition. The argument for the former was, as before, that the greatest safety in factories was to be achieved by relying on fellow-workers to enforce safety provisions, a strategy which was consistent with the 'true principle of law ... that no man is responsible except for his own acts and defaults'; in addition, to abolish common employment 'would effect a serious disturbance in the industrial arrangements of the country. Sooner or later the position of master and workman would find its level by a readjustment of the rate of wages, but in the meantime great alarm would be occasioned, and the investment of capital in industrial undertakings would be discouraged'.[65] But there was *some* room for manoeuvre, given that many businesses were now run on behalf of employers by 'chief managers'; in such cases (but no others), 'the acts or defaults of the agents who thus discharge the duties and fulfil the functions of master, should be considered as the personal acts or defaults of the principals and employers' for the purposes of common law liability.

The case for a more substantial reform in the changed industrial conditions of the time was ably stated by Charles Meldon, an Irish barrister and MP:

At that time [when *Priestley* v. *Fowler* was decided], machinery was comparatively unused, and industrial and manufacturing operations were carried on by a small number of workmen who were under the immediate supervision of their employers. Now we have dangerous and complicated machinery in every possible industrial operation; the labourers are numbered by legions, and instead of being under the immediate eye of their employer, they are superintended by middle-men of a superior grade, whom the constantly increasing scale on which mining and manufacturing establishments are conducted ... has called into existence; there are more gradations of servants, more separation or distribution of duties, and more delegation of authority....[66]

Employers should, therefore, be liable to their workers for injuries arising from the negligence not just of general managers, but also of *any* servant in a superior grade or employed in a different department of the business.

1908), p. 20. The many small employers in Ireland may not have benefited from this application of the doctrine – but in the absence of employers' liability insurance would seldom have been worth suing.

64 Bartrip and Burman, *Wounded soldiers of industry*, pp. 111–30.
65 *Report from the select committee appointed to inquire whether it may be expedient to render masters liable for injuries occasioned to their servants, etc.*, p. iv, H.C. 1877 (285), x, 554.
66 Ibid., p. 132 – a separate report received too late to be considered by the committee,

Such was the pressure for something to be done that reform of common employment became an election issue (at least in Great Britain) in 1880, and the new Liberal home secretary (Sir William Harcourt) acted promptly to honour a campaign promise to 'abolish' the defence. But he appears to have done so precipitately, by adopting a private member's bill which took the form of 'a rather muddleheaded compromise',[67] albeit along the lines recommended by Meldon, but 'paid for' by a limit on the amount of compensation which could be obtained. After a lengthy debate (in which Irish members, as the land war reached its height, took little part), the bill received the royal assent in September 1880.[68]

The Employers' Liability Act[69] 'is not by any means a sweeping enactment. ... Parliament went slowly and warily...'.[70] A 'workman'[71] could now elect to sue his or her employer under the act rather than at common law; if the case was brought under the act, the employer was prevented from raising common employment as a defence in five specified cases. According to F. H. Pollock, writing not long after the act was passed: 'So far as [it] has any principle, it is that of holding the employer answerable for the conduct of those who are in delegated authority under him.'[72] In particular, section 1(1)

but republished as an article in *ILT & SJ*, 11 (1877), 357. Meldon, a graduate of Trinity College Dublin, had been called to the Irish bar in 1863, and became a QC in 1877. As MP for Co. Kildare from 1874 to 1885, he supported Butt rather than Parnell – see *The Times*, 19 Sept. 1892, p. 9. The case for reform was also supported, by reference to cases from the United States and Scotland, in two articles which appeared in *ILT & SJ*, 14 (1880), 293 and 303.

67 Hanes, *First British workmen's compensation act*, p. 19. See generally Bartrip and Burman, *Wounded soldiers of industry*, pp. 130–55.

68 The act was originally intended to remain in force only for seven years (s. 10), but it was regularly continued in force by Expiring Law Continuance Acts and only formally repealed in Northern Ireland by the Law Reform (Miscellaneous Provisions) Act (N.I.) 1948, s. 1(2) and in the Republic by the Law Reform (Personal Injuries) Act 1958, s. 1.

69 43 & 44 Vict., c. 42. For the application of the act in Ireland, see S.C. Porter, *The law relating to employers' liability and workmen's compensation* (Dublin, 1908), pp. 19–32, H. Hanna, *The Workmen's Compensation Act 1897, as applied to Ireland* (1st ed., Dublin, 1898), pp. 15–21 (section not repeated in second edition) and T.J. Campbell, *Workmen's compensation under the Workmen's Compensation Act 1906 and the Employers' Liability Act 1880* (5th ed., Dublin, 1908), pp. 17–27.

70 Campbell, *Workmen's compensation*, p. 17. *The Irish Law Times* 'do not anticipate that the act will have a widespread consequence either in provoking antagonism between employer and employee or in handicapping industry in meeting foreign competition': *ILT & SJ*, 14 (1880), 521. The journal provided a detailed analysis of the act – ibid., pp. 521, 531, 555, 567, 577, 589, 611 and 621.

71 As widely defined in the Employers and Workmen Act 1875, s. 10, namely, 'a railway servant' and 'any person [other than a domestic or menial servant] who, being a labourer ... or otherwise engaged in manual labour, has entered into or works under a contract with an employer, whether the contract be ... express or implied, oral or in writing, and be a contract of service or a contract personally to execute any work or labour'. This definition nevertheless gave rise to a certain amount of litigation – see e.g. Campbell, *Workmen's compensation*, pp. 19–25.

72 *The law of torts* (1st ed., London, 1887), p. 90. He was later to say that 'the law as it stands under the act of 1880 appears ... anything but satisfactory. The act is not

provided that an employer was liable for 'any defect in the condition of the ways, works, machinery or plant connected with or used in [his] business ..., provided the defect arose from, or had not been discovered or remedied owing to, the negligence of the employer or of some person in the service of the employer entrusted with the duty of seeing that the ways, etc. were in proper condition'.[73]

The injured worker had still, of course, to prove that the employer or 'supervisor' had been negligent[74] – and the employer could still rely on the defences of contributory negligence[75] and *volenti*.[76] More specifically, section 2(3) of the act provided that the employer was *not* liable 'in any case where the workman knew of the defect or negligence which caused his injury, and failed within a reasonable time to give ... information thereof to the employer or some person superior to himself in the service of the employer ...'.[77] The combined effect of these provisions was considered in *Campbell* v. *Brennan*,[78] where a painter fell from scaffolding and was killed. The court held that the scaffolding was defective and, following *Yarmouth* v. *France*,[79] rejected the defence that the deceased had voluntarily accepted the risk:

There are many circumstances in which a man might place himself outside the power of recovery under the old maxim that the whole thing was entirely the man's own fault.... [But] in order to enable a defence to be taken on that principle it must be shown that not only was there knowledge of danger, but an adequate appreciation of the risk that was about to be experienced by bringing a man into contact with that danger.[80]

In the present case, the deceased *did* know of the danger; but did not have an 'adequate appreciation' of the risk. Two years later, this view of the effect of the 1880 act was confirmed by the house of lords in *Smith* v. *Baker & Sons*.[81]

adequate in redressing the injustice brought into the law by the quite modern doctrine of "common employment"; and the measure of redress which it does give is given in a cumbrous and intricate form, so that to the persons most concerned the law must seem even less just than it really is': *Fifth and final report of the royal commission on labour*, p. 126 [C.7421], H.C. 1894, xxxv, 134.

73 See further 'Employers' liability for defective ways, means, works, machinery or plant' in *ILT & SJ*, 21 (1887), 453 and 467 and 'Employers' liability for defective "works"' in *ILT & SJ*, 26 (1892), 177 and 201.

74 See e.g. *Noonan* v. *Dublin Distillery Co.* (1893) 32 LR Ir 399.

75 So held in *M'Evoy* v. *Waterford SS. Co. (No. 2)* (1886) 18 LR Ir 159, 168, *per* Andrews J: 'In my opinion this defence is just as open and unrestricted in cases within the act as in cases outside it.'

76 As to which see *Campbell* v. *Brennan* (1889) 23 ILTR 84, below.

77 According to Hanna, *Workmen's Compensation Act 1897*, p. 18: 'The effect of this [provision] was to give to the employer a new statutory defence. Before the Employers' Liability Act, it would not have been a defence for the employer to say that the workman knew of the defect and had not told about it.'

78 (1889) 23 ILTR 84.

79 (1887) 19 QBD 647.

80 (1889) 23 ILTR 84, 85, *per* Andrews J.

81 [1891] AC 325.

The *quid pro quo* for the restriction of common employment was that in cases brought under the act the maximum amount of compensation payable to an injured worker (or to his dependants in case of death) was limited to 'such sum as may be found to be equivalent to the estimated earnings, during the three years preceding the injury, of a person in the same grade employed during those years in the like employment and in the district in which the workman is employed at the time of the injury' – less any sum already recovered by way of penal compensation.[82] Subject to this limit, the compensation was apparently to be assessed on the same basis as common law damages.[83] There was no maximum sum imposed in cash terms; but it is generally accepted that awards under the act seldom, if ever, exceeded £150.[84]

To simplify the procedure for making a claim, an action under the act had to be brought in the civil bill court, whose jurisdiction in such cases was not subject to the normal financial limit of £50. A case was removable to a superior court on application by the plaintiff or defendant on the usual grounds;[85] but the fact that a plaintiff was likely to obtain damages in excess of £50 was not a ground for removal, and indeed it seems that few cases were removed for any reason.[86] As in other civil bill cases, trial could be by judge and jury;[87] alternatively, the judge could sit with assessors 'appointed for the purpose of ascertaining the amount of compensation'.

One of the most controversial aspects of the 1880 act, as confirmed by *Griffiths* v. *Earl Dudley*,[88] was that it contained nothing to prevent a workman

---

82 Sections 3 and 5.
83 Or under the Fatal Accidents Act – see e.g. *Thompson* v. *Belfast Harbour Commissioners* (1889) 23 ILTR 48 (compensation based on pecuniary loss to dependants as a result of the death).
84 For example, the average wage of a rougher in the linen industry in 1886 was 18*s*. 6*d*. per week; by 1906 it had increased to 21*s*. 8*d*., yielding maximum compensation under the act of £144 and £169 respectively. The earnings of women were much lower – a spinner in 1886 averaged 8*s*. 5*d*. per week, rising to 10*s*. 5*d*. in 1906; such earnings would have entitled them to maximum compensation of £66 in 1886 and £82 in 1906: *Report of an inquiry by the Board of Trade into the earnings and hours of labour of workpeople of the United Kingdom, I: Textile trades in 1906*, pp. xlix–liii [Cd. 4545], H.C. 1909, lxxx, 49–53. Cf. in *Campbell* v. *Brennan* (1889) 23 ILTR 84, 86, the court considered £1 per week to be fair compensation for the painter's widow and two children and therefore awarded damages of £156; the family had claimed £219.
85 County Officers and Courts (Ire.) Act 1877, s. 57. Cf. *M'Menamin* v. *M'Elwee ILT & SJ*, 17 (1883), 545, where removal was refused on the grounds that the county court was the proper forum for claims under the 1880 act, unless there were very exceptional circumstances or the case gave rise to a complex question of law.
86 See especially *M'Evoy* v. *Waterford Steamship Co. (No. 1)* (1885) 16 LR Ir 291, 297, where Dowse B stated that 'it would be to defeat the object of the legislature in conferring this great benefit upon workmen to remove an action from the inferior court, with all the expenses consequent upon that proceeding, in a case like this, which presents no difficulties in point of law, and in which no special circumstances have been shown to exist'.
87 As, for example, in *Noonan* v. *Dublin Distillery* (1893) 32 LR Ir 399.
88 (1882) 9 QBD 357. According to Field J (at p. 363): 'It is said that the intention of the legislation to protect workmen against imprudent bargains will be frustrated if

from 'contracting out' of the new right of action. On one interpretation, this was a *benevolent* provision. Faced with the uncertain impact of the act, some employers increased their contributions to a workers' injury fund as a *quid pro quo* for contracting out by the workers: 'A workman may agree with the employer to look solely to a benefit society for compensation and forego his statutory remedy ...'.[89] But in many cases contracting out conferred no such benefits, and was simply a condition of employment – or continued employment. Moreover, 'the threat of litigation ... tends to make employers more careful and responsible; whenever contracting out occurs, the employer, no longer threatened, tends to negligence and the incidence of accidents goes up'.[90]

In December 1880 (before the act came into force) the *Irish Law Times* reported that '[A]n extensive movement [is being] made with a view to procuring the workmen to contract themselves out of the advantages conferred by the legislature.'[91] Systematic information on this particular aspect of the act does not appear to be available; but we do know that, at least in terms of the number of cases tried in court, the act was for a time used quite extensively in Ireland, at any rate in comparison with England and Wales:

Table 11.1: *Employers' Liability Act: Number of cases tried in county courts, 1881–96*[92]

	No. of cases tried		Total amount claimed		Total amount awarded	
	E/W	Ireland	E/W	Ireland	E/W	Ireland
1881–85	882	124	£153,648	£12,660	£34,362	£2,345
1886–91	1,042	92	£166,552	£11,429	£44,509	£1,574
1892–96	1,138	91	£164,083	£12,582	£50,409	£2,442

This Table suggests that, in the period to 1896, there were on average 20 cases tried per year in Ireland, as compared to 200 or so in England and Wales; this ratio may be contrasted with the comparable ratio of one to 40 in the number of reported factory accidents resulting in death or injury.[93] The high point for claims in Ireland appears to have been 1885, when 57 cases were

---

contracts like this one are allowed to stand. I should say that workmen as a rule are perfectly competent to make reasonable bargains for themselves.' For Irish cases see e.g. *Magee v. Martin* (1882) 16 ILTR 5 and *O'Callaghan v. Martin* (1904) 38 ILTR 152.

89 Campbell, *Workmen's compensation*, p. 26.

90 Hanes, *First British Workmen's Compensation Act*, p. 23, where the arguments for and against are fully summarised.

91 *ILT & SJ*, 14 (1880), 521 (referring to English examples only). See also 'Contracts in ouster of the Employers' Liability Act, 1880', in *ILT & SJ*, 16 (1882), 303.

92 *Return of the total number of cases tried in county courts under the Employers' Liability Act 1880* (published periodically). In addition to the cases tried, there were a number of cases settled and a number struck out; but such information is not given with regard to Ireland.

93 According to *Chief insp. ann. rep., 1900*, p. 548, the number of recorded factory accidents in England and Wales resulting in death or injury (68,506) was roughly forty times that in Ireland (1,588). For a commentary on the working of the act in England and

tried, as compared to 340 in England and Wales. Never again was the act to reach such heights in Ireland. And Table 11.1 also reveals the small amount of compensation paid under the act – an average in Ireland of £20 per case tried, as compared to £42 in England and Wales.[94]

The decline in the use made of the 1880 act in Ireland accelerated after the enactment of the Workmen's Compensation Act in 1897.[95] By 1900, the number of cases of all kinds tried under the 1880 act had declined to an annual average of fifteen or thereabouts, of which less than half arose from factory accidents. Table 11.2, which does not reflect the (unknown) number of cases settled out of court, suggests that Irish factory workers were more likely to be successful than their counterparts in England and Wales; but unless they suffered total incapacity (where the average award in Ireland of £95 was slightly higher than that in England and Wales (£84)), they were likely to receive less compensation – £69 (as compared to £152) in respect of a death, and £31 (as compared to £61) for partial incapacity. On the other hand, the cost of litigation was much lower in Ireland; while the solicitors' costs allowed in England and Wales were typically £20–£25, in Ireland they seldom exceeded £5.

Table 11.2: Employers' Liability Act 1880: Total number of cases tried, 1899–1908[96]

	No. of cases tried		Judgment for plaintiff		Total damages awarded by court	
	Ireland	E/W	Ireland	E/W	Ireland	E/W
Factory cases						
Death	4	110	–	41	–	£7,003
Total incapacity	11	688	5	195	£474	£16,416
Partial incapacity	42	2,065	21	514	£644	£31,195
All other cases						
Death	18	148	5	40	£344	£5,288
Total incapacity	8	593	6	156	£557	£13,942
Partial incapacity	71	1,271	38	349	£1,262	£23,602

Wales, see Wilson and Levy, *Workmen's compensation*, i, 37–50 and Cornish and Clark, *Law and society in England*, pp. 525–27.

94 John Murphy, a member of Belfast Trades Council, commented that the 1880 act was carried out by the Irish judges 'in the most contradictory and inconsistent manner', although he allowed that some were 'fair and honourable': *Report of the Third Irish Trades Congress* (Limerick, 1895), p 39.

95 Cf. Campbell, *Workmen's compensation*, p. 26 explains that 'injured workmen prefer, in some instances, to proceed under the Employers' Liability Act than to proceed under the Workmen's Compensation Act', particularly if the injury was 'slight' or did not give rise to permanent disability. This assumes, of course, that the worker could establish negligence on the part of the employer.

96 Derived from *Statistics of proceedings in England and Wales, in Scotland, and in Ireland, under the Workmen's Compensation Act and the Employers' Liability Act*, published annually from 1899.

By 1908 contested claims under the 1880 act in respect of factory accidents had virtually died out in Ireland. In that year, there were only two claims for partial incapacity tried in the county courts; one was successful, resulting in an award of 8s. 6d.; no factory claims at all were lodged in 1909, but one claimant suffering partial incapacity recovered £30 in 1910.[97]

It is generally agreed that the 1880 act had a very limited impact on employers' liability. Not only did it effect only a modest increase in the scope of liability, but it also made little difference to the practical difficulties facing an injured worker:

Even those whose case fell within its ambit found themselves obliged to bring a personal action against their own employer – something which for many was put beyond possibility by a long habit of dependence, if not by fear of dismissal. Only slowly were the unions organising themselves to provide the moral and financial support that such an undertaking required. Moreover, the man audacious enough to claim might be met with a denial of liability, and before long he would find himself facing the hazards of negligence litigation – proving that he was a 'workman' as defined by the Act, proving the negligence of a supervisory fellow-servant or that a 'defect in the ways, works, machinery or plant' had gone unremedied by the appropriate supervisor, warding off counter-assertions of contributory negligence, *volenti*, or failure to give the employer the notice required by the Act.[98]

Even the 'official' verdict on the act was dismissive: 'Compared with the number of accidents, the number of actions brought was exceedingly small, and in a large proportion of them the workman failed. Regarded ... as a means of obtaining compensation for injury with a reasonable degree of certainty, the Employers' Liability Act of 1880 must be considered to have been a failure.'[99]

The low number of successful court claims does not, however, appear to have dampened the factory inspectors' enthusiastic support for the act as strengthening their hand when they sought to persuade employers to fence dangerous machinery. In 1881, Cameron reported from the north of Ireland: '[U]ndoubtedly, the provisions of the ... act are of service in illustrating the importance of fencing and of *keeping efficient* the guards which have been put up. I think that the penalties [sic] under the act may probably secure a more perfect system of general supervision, and a more prompt replacement of any guard which has broken or become inefficient.'[100] Many of the other inspectors based in other parts of the United Kingdom agreed with this assessment, and

---

97   Ibid., *1908*, pp. 66–67 [Cd. 4894], H.C. 1909, lxxx, 1014–15; *1909*, pp. 66–67 [Cd. 5386], H.C. 1910, lxxii, 1022–23; *1910*, p. 64 [Cd. 5896], H.C. 1911, lxxv, 806. During these three years there were a further six claims arising from non-factory accidents; three of these succeeded and total compensation of £47. 14s. 6d. was awarded.

98   Cornish and Clark, *Law and society in England*, pp. 525–26.

99   *Report of the departmental committee appointed by the home secretary to inquire into the law relating to compensation for injuries to workmen*, p. 11 [Cd. 2208], H.C. 1904, lxxxviii, 754 [hereafter referred to as '*Report of committee on workmen's compensation, 1904*'].

100 *Chief insp. ann. rep., 1881*, p. 12 (emphasis in original). As part of their campaign against injuries from flying shuttles, for example, they reported a number of cases in which damages had been awarded – see e.g. *Chief insp. ann. rep., 1884*, pp. 12–13

Redgrave, the chief inspector, observed that after their 'very considerable apprehension' at the effect of the act, employers 'are now feeling that by taking all reasonable and possible precautions for the safety of their workpeople, they will not be held to be unfairly responsible for all kinds of accidents'.[101] Ten years later the inspectors were still positive: 'The Employers' Liability Act, by making employers feel their responsibilities more fully, has certainly been of use in ... making them more ready to adopt suggestions for obviating danger.'[102] But by this time the low number of court cases must have made them doubt the impact of an act to which the employers had quickly adjusted: 'Employers who had been worried about the disastrous effects of the act soon realised that their fears were unwarranted. Business was able to settle down and continue, little affected by the new liability rules.'[103]

The most important achievement of the act may well have been the fillip which it gave to the development of employers' liability insurance[104] – and the added pressure brought by insurance companies requiring employers to take greater safety precautions in order to keep premiums as low as possible. There were still those who thought that liability insurance undermined accident prevention by relieving employers of their responsibilities.[105] But as one factory inspector pointed out in 1893, the greatest problem with employers' liability insurance was that it did nothing for the large number of workers whose injuries were caused 'by purely accidental circumstances or the carelessness of the sufferer'.[106]

2. Breach of statutory duty

Notwithstanding its virtual demise in the 1860s and 1870s, the notion of 'penal' compensation was revived by the Factory and Workshop Act 1878[107] and then further extended in 1895 to cover any case of death, bodily injury or *injury to health* caused by the occupier's neglect to observe any provision of the factory acts.[108] But an injured worker who had commenced proceedings under the Employers' Liability Act *before* the prosecution for breach

(damages of £225 awarded to overlooker of weavers for loss of eye) and *1889*, pp. 39–40 (damages of £172 awarded to woman who lost sight of one eye and injury to the other).

101 *Chief insp. ann. rep., 1881*, p. 3. As a result, Redgrave thought that the practice of contracting out, though much discussed, had not been extensively adopted.
102 *Chief insp. ann. rep., 1892*, p. 1 (Whymper, chief insp.).
103 Bartrip and Burman, *Wounded soldiers of industry*, p. 189.
104 Ibid., pp. 165–69. See also H.E. Raynes, *A history of British insurance* (2nd ed., London, 1964), chap. xiv.
105 See e.g. the unsuccessful attempt to introduce an Employers' Liability (Insurance Prohibition) Bill, H.C. 1890 (101), v, 37 (not printed).
106 *Chief insp. ann. rep., 1893*, p. 224 (Johnston).
107 Section 82. Similar provisions are to be found in the Coal Mines Regulation Act 1887, s. 70 and the Metalliferous Mines Regulation Act 1872, s. 38, both of which applied to Ireland.
108 Factory and Workshop Act 1895, s. 13, continued by Factory and Workshop Act 1901, s. 136. An injury to health had to be caused 'directly' by the breach.

of the factory acts came before the magistrates' court was not entitled to any such compensation, whether the action under the 1880 act was ultimately successful or not.[109]

The relationship between penal compensation and common law liability was considered in *Blenkinsopp* v. *Ogden*.[110] Through his own carelessness and wilful disobedience of his foreman's orders, a boy aged 13 was injured when he caught his hand in an unfenced printing machine. Although the boy's conduct would have defeated a common law claim, the court held that he had suffered the injury 'in consequence of' a breach of the factories acts and that the employer was, therefore, liable to a penal compensation fine:

[W]e are dealing with a section the primary object of which is not to compensate the injured person, but to provide safe machinery. It is to the interest of the state that the machinery should be safe for negligent as well as for careful people, and it is reasonable that the state should impose a penalty upon the party omitting to fence even under circumstances under which the person injured by the omission could not recover damages.[111]

The employer was fined £25, which was then paid over to the injured boy.[112]

Nevertheless, it appears that relatively little use was made of this extended provision.[113] Detailed information is available only for 1898–1903;[114] in this six-year period, penal compensation was sought in 210 cases throughout the United Kingdom, and resulted in fines of just over £2,000, roughly one-half of which was paid over to the relatives of the deceased or to the injured person.[115] Only five of these cases arose in Ireland. The sole claim in respect of death concerned a 15-year-old boy killed by a gas engine in Wexford Sawmills; this case was dismissed, and a civil action was also unsuccessful.[116] Sawmill accidents also gave rise to two injury cases. A saw-mill owner in Newcastle West was fined 5*s.* when a man suffered eye injuries from flying wood; 'the injured man was compensated', presumably by his employer;[117] and a sawmill owner in Dublin was fined one shilling when a man lost his

---

109 Employers' Liability Act 1880, s. 5. If he commenced proceedings *after* receiving penal compensation, that amount was deducted from any damages awarded under the 1880 act.

110 [1898] 1 QB 783.

111 Ibid., p. 786, *per* Kennedy J.

112 *Chief insp. ann. rep., 1898*, pt. II, pp. 84–85. Grantham J. had pointed out that it was 'entirely' a matter of discretion whether penal compensation was paid to an injured worker; but it seems that, in the exercise of that discretion, the home secretary was not guided by common law principles.

113 See generally R.L. Howells, '*Priestley* v. *Fowler* and the factory acts', in *Modern L. Rev.*, 26 (1963), 367.

114 See 'Table of penal compensation cases' in *Chief insp. ann. rep., 1898*, pt. I, pp. 82–85; *1899*, pp. 38–41; *1900*, pp. 42–45; *1901*, pt. II, pp. 48–51; *1902*, pt. II, pp. 52–53 and *1903*, pt. II, pp. 34–37. Publication of this table ceased in 1903.

115 The maximum fine of £100 was imposed in just two fatal cases and one injury case; the average fine in case of death was £21, and in case of injury £9. But on average only one-half of the fine was paid over by way of compensation.

116 *Chief insp. ann. rep., 1902*, pt. II, pp. 52–53.

117 *Chief insp. ann. rep., 1901*, pt. II, pp. 50–51.

hand and part of his arm in a planing-machine accident, the employers having paid him compensation of £300.[118] Dublin City Distillery were fined £25 when a man suffered neck and shoulder injuries in a steam engine accident; £20 of the fine was applied to the injured man.[119] And the Metropole Southern Hotel in Cork was fined £1 when a 26-year-old woman caught and fractured her arm in the rollers of a wringer.[120]

The small number of cases in which workers benefited from penal compensation may reflect the fact that the magistrates normally took into account any other compensation which the victim had received, or was likely to receive, from his or her employer.[121] But it also reflects the relatively small number of prosecutions for breach of the safety provisions of the factory acts in a period when the ambit of those provisions was being extended to meet the concern over the rising number of reported accidents. The inspectors may have been assiduous in seeking to achieve safe working conditions – though this in itself was doubted;[122] but they did not, apparently, attach great importance to securing compensation for injured workers. This was primarily a matter for the workers themselves.[123]

In this respect, we have already seen that, in the absence of negligence, common law liability for the breach *per se* of a safety provision of the 1844 act was imposed in some cases during the 1850s. A reaction then set in, as doubts arose as to whether such liability was intended where a statute, such as the 1844 act, expressly provided its own penalty for breach. These doubts were finally set to rest by two decisions at the end of the century. In *Baddeley v. Earl Granville*,[124] the plaintiff's claim was based on the breach by her deceased husband's employer of a statutory rule governing safety in mines. The court not only upheld the claim, but went on to hold that the defence of *volenti* was not available in such a case on the grounds that 'it would be against public policy to recognise an implied agreement whereby an employee would exempt an employer from fulfilling his strict statutory obligations'.[125]

---

118 *Chief insp. ann. rep., 1903*, pt. II, pp. 36–37.
119 *Chief insp. ann. rep., 1901*, pt. II, pp. 50–51.
120 *Chief insp. ann. rep., 1903*, pt. II, pp. 36–37 (no other details are given).
121 Cf. penal compensation paid to an injured worker *was* apparently deducted from common law damages, since (unlike the similar provision in the Coal Mines Regulation Act 1887, s. 70), the factory acts did not expressly provide that payment of such compensation should not affect any civil proceedings arising out of the injury. This was also the position with regard to workmen's compensation until 1906 – see Workmen's Compensation Act 1897, s. 1(5), reversed by Workmen's Compensation Act 1906, s. 1(5).
122 According to Miss Galway, secretary of the Textile Operatives Society of Ireland, 'the machinery would be better looked after if there were more prosecutions and efficient inspection': *Report of the departmental committee on accidents in places under the Factory and Workshop Acts: Minutes of evidence*, p. 249 [Cd. 5535], H.C. 1911, xxiii, 325.
123 Cf. penal compensation was not formally abolished in Northern Ireland until the Factories Act (N.I.) 1965 and still remains on the statute book in the Republic – see Factories Act 1955, s. 103.
124 (1887) 19 QBD 423.
125 Stanton, *Breach of statutory duty*, p. 121.

Of greater importance, at least in the present context, was *Groves* v. *Lord Wimborne*,[126] where a boy was injured by a steam winch which was not properly fenced in accordance with section 5 of the 1878 act. The uncertain state of the law may be shown by the fact that the trial judge (Grantham J) held that the employer was *not* liable in tort for breach of his statutory duty.[127] But the court of appeal strongly disagreed. Breach of the 'absolute and unqualified' statutory duty imposed by the 1878 act *prima facie* gave the plaintiff a cause of action which was not taken away by the fact that the act contained an express provision for an award of penal compensation in such a case. For a start, 'It seems monstrous to suppose that it was intended that in the case of death or severe mutilation arising through a breach of the statutory duty, the compensation to the workman or his family should never exceed £100.'[128] But in any case, the fine is inflicted by way of punishment and was proportionate not to the severity of the injury but to the character of the offence – and it could be imposed on a worker rather than an employer, thus reducing the 'semblance' of compensation 'to a mere shadow'.[129] And even if a more substantial fine was imposed, the discretionary nature of penal compensation meant that 'not a penny of the fine necessarily goes to the person injured or his family'.[130] For these reasons, parliament cannot have intended penal compensation to have been the only remedy in the event of a breach of the act, and the plaintiff therefore did have a right of action upon the statute for injury caused by breach of the statutory duty thereby imposed.

Furthermore, in an action for breach of statutory duty, the defendant was *not* entitled to rely on the defence of common employment:

The defence of common employment only applies where the action is by a servant against the master and is founded upon the negligence or misconduct of his fellow-servant. In the present case ... there is no resort to negligence on the part of a fellow-servant or of any one else.... The defendant cannot shift his responsibility for the performance of the statutory duty on to the shoulders of another person.[131]

When viewed in the context of the expanding scope of the safety provisions in the factories acts after 1878, as consolidated in the act of 1901,[132] the decisions in *Baddeley* v. *Earl Granville* and *Groves* v. *Lord Wimborne* should have enabled many injured workers to obtain compensation whether or not criminal proceedings in respect of the breach of the act were brought

---

126 [1898] 2 QB 402, followed in *Bermingham* v. *O'Reilly* (1903) 3 NIJR 116.
127 However, he apparently anticipated that the case would be appealed, for he asked the jury to assess the damages payable to the plaintiff in the event of the defendant being held liable; they awarded the plaintiff £150.
128 [1898] 2 QB 402, 414, *per* Rigby LJ.
129 Ibid., p. 415.
130 Ibid., p. 408, *per* A.L. Smith LJ.
131 Ibid., p. 410, a statement of the law applied in *Scott* v. *Brookfield Linen Co.* [1910] 2 IR 509.
132 Sections 10–18. Damages were, for example, awarded in *Scott* v. *Brookfield Linen Co.* (above) for a breach of section 10(1)(c).

by the inspectors. Even if no breach of the factory acts could be established, the law of negligence was also beginning to move in the worker's favour. In *Smith* v. *Baker & Sons*[133] the house of lords all but eliminated the defence of *volenti* from factory accident claims. Mere knowledge of the danger alone no longer implied consent, but was only one factor to be taken into account when determining whether the plaintiff had knowledge *and appreciation* of the risk – and consented to take the risk upon himself. In the words of Lord Watson: 'The question ... to be considered is not whether he voluntarily and rashly exposed himself to injury, but whether he agreed that, if injury should befall him, the risk was to be his and not his master's.'[134]

There was also some evidence that judges and juries, influenced by the sentiments of the legislature reflected in the Employers' Liability Act and the Workmen's Compensation Act, were taking a broader view of what constituted negligence on the part of the employer:

Numbers of cases show that the courts are becoming increasingly strict in their view of what amounts to negligence by a master.... [What is required is] what Mr. Justice Willes called 'the absence of care according to the circumstances', and the care in this phrase simply is the ordinary care of a prudent man towards another to whom he owes the duty of observing such care. It is not unfair that the master should be bound to guard in a reasonable way against danger to the safety of his workmen. He is bound to have his machinery and tackle in good order and condition.... If the machinery is anywise dangerous, then the employer must be particularly on his guard against the more imminent risk of accident. Very slight circumstances will, under such conditions, tell strongly, and, it may be, irresistibly, against him on the score of negligence.[135]

If we add to this the first murmurings of judicial opposition to the doctrine of common employment in cases not falling within the act of 1880,[136] it would seem that the time was ripe for civil proceedings for compensation to begin to play a much more significant role in relation to industrial safety. But these doctrinal developments were slow to have a practical effect,[137] and failed to compensate for the inability of the Employers' Liability Act to satisfy the demand for a greater right to compensation in the event of accidental death or injury.

133 [1891] AC 325. A change of judicial attitude had begun to appear in cases such as *Thomas* v. *Quartermaine* (1887) 18 QBD 685, *Yarmouth* v. *France* (1887) 19 QBD 647 and *Campbell* v. *Brennan* (1889) 23 ILTR 84 – see above, p. 348.
134 [1891] AC 325, 355.
135 Campbell, *Workmen's compensation*, pp. 25–26. See also Bartrip and Burman, *Wounded soldiers of industry*, pp. 182–84.
136 See e.g. *Johnson* v. *W.H. Lindsay & Co.* [1891] AC 371, as followed in *M'Cartan* v. *Belfast Harbour Comm'rs* [1911] 2 IR 143 (injured worker and negligent servant not in *common* employment).
137 In 1900, only 25 of the 330 cases tried in the superior courts arose from personal injury or death arising from *all* accidents, with 17 resulting in a verdict for the plaintiff; by 1910, the number of these cases had risen to 47 out of a total of 346, of which 29 resulted in a verdict for the plaintiff: *Judicial Statistics (Ireland), part II: Civil statistics, 1900*, pp. 42–43 and 64–67 [Cd. 682], H.C. 1901, lxxxix, 722–23 and 744–47, and *1910*, pp. 40–41 and 64–67 [Cd. 5848], H.C. 1911, cii, 592–93 and 616–19.

WORKMEN'S COMPENSATION

By 1893 disappointment with the working of the Employers' Liability Act 1880 had reached a stage where both the main political parties had committed themselves to further reform of the law.[138] In broad terms, there were two competing strategies.[139] The first was to expand the ambit of the fault principle enshrined in the common law and in the 1880 act by completely depriving employers of their principal defence of common employment, coupled with a total prohibition on contracting out. This strategy, strongly supported by the Trades Union Congress and ably articulated by Asquith on behalf of the Liberal government, was founded on the notion that the optimum means of preventing factory accidents was to make the employer directly liable for his own negligence and vicariously liable for that of his workers. Making accidents more costly to employers, it was once again argued, would make them more safety conscious – but only if they were required to pay for accidents which could have been avoided by taking reasonable care. Workers, too, should 'pay' for injuries caused by their own negligence by allowing employers to continue to rely, where appropriate, on the defence of contributory negligence. A bill based on these principles was adopted by the house of commons in 1893,[140] but the contracting-out provision was amended by the house of lords in ways which proved unacceptable.[141]

But there was in any case a major problem with this strategy – many, if not most, factory accidents were not attributable to negligence on the part of employer or worker. For this reason, there was growing support for more radical reform, pioneered in Germany and attracting widespread interest throughout Europe, which would make employers liable to pay compensation, irrespective of fault, for *all* accidental death or injury sustained by workers in the course of their employment. On this view, articulated by Chamberlain on behalf of the Conservatives in 1893,[142] the costs of accidents were a necessary

---

138　See generally Bartrip and Burman, *Wounded soldiers of industry*, pp. 173–85; Cornish and Clark, *Law and society in England*, pp. 520–28; Hanes, *First British Workmen's Compensation Act*, chaps. 3–5; A. Wilson and H. Levy, *Workmen's compensation* (London, 1939), i, chap. III.

139　The political background to the act is examined at some length by Hanes, *First British Workmen's Compensation Act*, chaps. 3 and 4.

140　For a detailed analysis of the bill, see ibid., chap. 5.

141　Contracting out would be allowed, but only where certain conditions, such as a ballot of the workforce, were satisfied – see especially ibid., p. 80. But at its inaugural meeting in Dublin in 1894, the Irish Trades [Union] Congress condemned the house for 'destroying' the bill, and called for a total prohibition of contracting out – and a new provision putting on employers the onus of proving that they had not been negligent: *Report of the First Irish Trades Congress* (Dublin, 1894), p 17. This motion was repeated two years later – see *Report of the Third Irish Trades Congress* (Limerick, 1895), p 39.

142　In Chamberlain's words: 'No amendment of the law ... will be final or satisfactory which does not provide compensation to workmen for all injuries sustained in the ordinary course of their employment, and not caused by their own acts or default' – see Hanes, *First British Workmen's Compensation Act*, p. 61, where the debate is discussed in detail.

consequence of industry and should be borne by the trade and ultimately by the consumer. Unlike Chadwick's 'pecuniary consequences' principle,[143] however, the primary goal of this approach was now compensation rather than accident prevention – and to make such a system 'affordable', that compensation would have to be considerably lower than the 'full' compensation payable at common law.

Chamberlain may have lost the battle in 1893, but he won the war; by the time of the general election in 1895, there was widespread support for his campaign promise of 'a compensation Act for workmen, irrespective of the cause of accident'.[144] Returned to power with a sizable majority, Chamberlain successfully steered through parliament a Workmen's Compensation Bill based on three main principles. First, it was 'just and right' that workmen in 'dangerous' employments in which accidents inevitably occurred should be entitled to compensation of a moderate and limited amount upon proof of injury or death, irrespective of fault. Secondly, the obligation of providing such compensation was to be on the employer, since he was the person most fit to bear it. And thirdly, there was to be a simple procedure, entailing little expense, for the adjudication of any disputed claims. Hanna, writing in 1898, summarised these principles as follows:

The Act of 1897 proceeds on the fundamental principle, that, where a person, on his own responsibility, and for his own profit, sets in motion agencies which create risks for others, he ought to be civilly responsible for the consequences of what he does. This principle from another aspect may be stated thus, that it is in the public interest of the community, as a matter of public policy, that a workman who sustains an injury in the course of his employment, should have a right to be indemnified.... A further principle which seems to have been acted upon in the framing of the measure is, that the compensation ... shall be a charge upon the trade or employment in which the accident occurs. It is not the principle of the bill that the employer should be punished, or that any new moral responsibility should be created, for the compensation is not intended as a fine upon the employer, but, as a recognition of the just claims of the workman.[145]

The essence of the act was set out in section 1(1): 'If in any employment to which this Act applies personal injury by accident arising out of and in the course of the employment is caused to a workman, his employer shall ... be liable to pay compensation in accordance with ... this Act.' We select the following provisions, as amended in 1906 following a review by a select committee of the house of commons in 1904,[146] as appropriate for more detailed examination in the present context.

143 See above p. 336 and Bartrip and Burman, *Wounded soldiers of industry*, pp. 68–73.
144 Hanes, *First British Workmen's Compensation Act*, p. 90.
145 *Workmen's compensation* (1st ed.), pp. 21–22. For a detailed analysis of the act, see *Hanna's law of workmen's compensation*, ed. H. Hanna and T.D. Kingan (2nd ed., Dublin, 1907), S.C. Porter, *The law relating to employer's liability and workmen's compensation* (Dublin, 1908) and T.J. Campbell, *Workmen's compensation under the Workmen's Compensation Act 1906* (5th ed., Dublin, 1908).
146 *Report of the departmental committee appointed by the home secretary to inquire into the*

(i) Relationship with the common law　The injured workman was not bound to proceed under the act; he could still claim damages at common law or under the Employers' Liability Act – but he was required by the 1897 act to opt for one or the other, at least at the outset. If he opted to pursue a common law claim and the court held in favour of the defendant, the plaintiff was nonetheless entitled to ask the court, if satisfied as to entitlement, to assess the compensation payable under the 1897 act;[147] but he could not otherwise claim such compensation.[148] Conversely, an injured worker who made an unsuccessful claim under the 1897 act was *not* thereby debarred from bringing a common law action for damages;[149] this restriction applied only if the workmen's compensation claim was successful.[150]

(ii) Workers covered by the act　The 1897 act applied to a number of 'dangerous' employments, including all 'factories', but not workshops, covered by the factory acts. A concession made during the passage of the bill also brought laundries and dock labourers within the scheme, a development welcomed by the Irish Trades Congress.[151] Coverage was extended by the Workmen's Compensation Act 1900 to include all persons in agricultural occupations,

---

law relating to compensation for injuries to workmen [Cd. 2208], H.C. 1904, lxxxviii, 743. Cf. 'Taken as a whole, the act of 1906 did no more than extend, amend, and improve earlier legislation and provide some further protection for injured workmen. The basic principles of the law were, as a matter of policy, retained intact ...': Wilson and Levy, *Workmen's compensation*, i, 118.

147　1897 act, s. 1(4), as applied e.g. in *Clemenger* v. *Jacob* (1903) 3 NIJR 243. The act provided that the defendant's costs in the common law claim could be deducted from the compensation payable under the 1897 act.

148　So held in *Edwards* v. *Godfrey* [1899] 2 QB 333. See also *M'Allister* v. *Jones* (1902) 36 ILTR 215 (unsuccessful action under Employers' Liability Act estopped proceedings under the 1897 act in respect of same injury).

149　*Beckley* v. *Scott & Co.* [1902] 2 IR 504. The question divided both the king's bench division and the court of appeal. In the latter, FitzGibbon LJ (at p. 526) thought that refusing the injured worker the right to sue would impose 'a punishment [which] does not fit the crime' and he declined to do so 'by elaborate implication from confused and complicated clauses'. But Holmes LJ (at pp. 534–35) considered that it was 'not unreasonable' to guard an employer from being subjected to two law-suits in respect of the same injury, and 'not too much to ask' a worker 'to choose between two modes of procedure each having the same object'. Walker LJ, with considerable misgivings, agreed with FitzGibbon LJ – but the English courts tended to agree with Holmes LJ – see e.g. *Cribb* v. *Kynock (No. 2) Ltd.* [1908] 2 KB 551 and *Harrison* v. *Wythe Moor Colliery Co.* [1922] 2 KB 674.

150　*Mehaffey* v. *Collen Bros.* (1902) 36 ILTR 216 (injured boy who had received half-wages from employer for several weeks after accident held to have exercised option and not entitled to bring common law claim). But in *O'Callaghan* v. *Martin* (1904) 38 ILTR 152 the court of appeal emphasised that before a workman is to be barred from legal proceedings by receipt of wages 'in full settlement of all claims', there should be clear evidence that he knew what he was doing and the nature of the rights he was giving up.

151　*Report of the Fourth Irish Trades Congress* (Waterford, 1897), pp. 24 and 27–28. Congress resolved, however, that the bill should be further extended to cover all workers. Although disappointed with the eventual scope of the act, they were optimistic that 'with a little more agitation, its provisions will eventually be extended to other industries': *Report of the Fifth Irish Trades Union Congress* (Belfast, 1898), p. 37.

and by the 1906 Act to include workshops and virtually all kinds of workers, including domestic servants, shop assistants, teachers and 'sailors'.[152] The extended coverage provided by this amending legislation meant that the number of workers in the United Kingdom covered by the act doubled, from 7.25 million to 15 million.[153] But outworkers still remained outside the act,[154] an omission of particular concern to the Irish TUC:

Surely it was not the intention of Parliament to place a premium on out-working by exempting from all responsibility employers who sweat these poor wretches? As most people are aware, the sweaters' victims, especially in the tailoring trade, work under the most insanitary conditions, where germs of typhoid and many other diseases abound. In fact, many of the so-called workshops are veritable death-traps, yet no protection is vouchsafed to those who are compelled to work in dens of this description.[155]

(iii) The definition of work accidents   An employer was liable to pay compensation where personal injury or death was caused to any worker 'by accident arising out of and in the course of employment'. Although intended to be simple and straightforward, these eleven words provoked 'many a wordy war', as Hanna had predicted as early as 1898.[156] There was no need to prove negligence or breach of statutory duty on the part of the employer. But a worker proved to have caused his own injury by 'serious and wilful misconduct' was at first wholly disqualified from obtaining compensation.[157] The 1906 act, however, provided that this disqualification was no longer to apply where the injury resulted in death or in serious and permanent disablement.

Accidents resulting in minor injuries were excluded by section 1(2)(a) of the 1897 act, which provided that no compensation was payable in respect of any injury 'which does not disable the workman for a period of at least two weeks from earning full wages' – a provision which appears to have excluded about one-quarter of all accidental injuries.[158] The intention was to provide an incentive to workers to get back to work as quickly as possible – and to weed out small claims:

152   Provided they were 'workmen' within the meaning of the act and 'members of the crew of any ship'. These requirements meant, as Wilson and Levy, *Workmen's compensation*, i, 182 point out, that the dependants of the bandsmen who played on while the *Titanic* sank did not qualify for compensation under the 1906 act.
153   Ibid., p. 102.
154   See 1906 act, s. 13.
155   *Report of the Fourteenth Irish Trades Union Congress* (Dublin, 1907), p. 20.
156   Hanna, *Workmen's compensation* (1st ed.), p. 25. By 1907 he was able to record that 'these words ... have been the subject of a good deal of judicial interpretation': (2nd ed.), p. 9.
157   1897 act, s. 1(2)(c), as applied e.g. in *M'Caffrey* v. *Great Northern Rly. Co.* (1902) 36 ILTR 27. See also *Quinn* v. *Langley* (1901) 1 NIJR 88 (workman, though frequently warned of the danger, persistently refused to wear protector when working with a steam-saw; death in accident held attributable to his 'serious and wilful default').
158   Hanna, *Workmen's compensation* (1st ed.), p. 40.

[I]f this incentive were removed or weakened, workmen even of a better class would be apt, unconsciously and without any intent to malinger, to exaggerate the effects of the injury and to stay off longer than necessary.... Again, any alteration in favour of the workman of the two weeks' limit, whether it was abolished or only reduced, would undoubtedly be followed by a large increase in the number of claims, and it seems more than probable that this increase would be so large as to make it impossible for the employers to check each claim properly, or, except at great disproportionate expense, to exercise an effective supervision over the case in which compensation was being paid.[159]

In 1906, this 'waiting' period was reduced to one week; but if a worker was off work as a result of the injury for less than two weeks, he or she was not paid for the first week. At least one major Irish employer – Harland & Wolff Ltd. – considered this two-week requirement 'ridiculous' on the grounds that it merely encouraged workers to stay off work for the extra days in order to qualify for compensation from the date of the accident: 'For years my firm have waived this proviso and paid compensation in all cases where incapacity lasted for one week or more.'[160]

(iv) The definition of personal injury   Compensation was payable for 'personal injury' and death. The 1897 act made no explicit provision for any industrial disease which might arise out of a person's employment, and this general policy was endorsed in 1904.[161] By then, however, the courts had begun to accept that some industrial diseases amounted to 'personal injury' and were already covered by the act.[162] The opportunity was therefore taken in 1906 to make a more definite (and exceedingly complex) provision for compensation to be paid in respect of certain prescribed diseases which disabled the worker *and* arose from the particular nature of his or her employment.

The initial list of prescribed diseases had little application in Ireland;[163] but there was considerable interest in the proposal to add phthisis to the list in 1907.[164] James Lindsay, a professor of medicine, and Robert Hall, a consultant surgeon, explained that this disease was indeed common among flax workers; but although it was a disease to which working in the industry

159 *Report of the departmental committee on compensation for injuries to workmen, 1904,* pp. 71–72.
160 *Departmental committee on the system of compensation for injuries to workmen: Minutes of evidence,* i, 298 [Cmd. 908], H.C. 1920, xxvi, 384 (James Robertson, accident and compensation department, Harland & Wolff Ltd.).
161 *Report of the departmental committee on compensation for injuries to workmen, 1904,* pp. 45–46, agreeing with Dr Legge (medical inspector of factories) that there was a clear distinction between 'accidental injury' and 'disease' and going on to recommend a separate system of 'sick insurance' in respect of the latter.
162 See especially *Harrisons Ltd. and Turvey* v. *Brintons Ltd.* [1904] 1 KB 328 (anthrax).
163 1906 act, s.8 and sch. III. Between 1908 and 1913 fifty–eight claims for industrial disease were recorded in Ireland (including sixteen where death had resulted), as compared to 2,609 (including 295 resulting in death) in England and Wales.
164 *Report of the departmental committee on compensation for industrial diseases,* pp. 12–19 [Cd. 3495], H.C. 1907, xxxiv, 1062–69.

conduced 'to a certain extent', its incidence in the population as a whole meant that it could not be said to be 'peculiar to the trade'.[165] The committee nevertheless accepted that phthisis was 'a specific and sufficiently distinguishable trade disease' in some industries at least; but the question of the flax industry ultimately did not arise in light of their recommendation that the disease should *not* be added to the schedule on account of the practical difficulties involved, arising from the 'long preliminary period during which there are symptoms which may, on the one hand, be arrested or disappear, or which may, on the other hand, become graver and ultimately declare themselves as the disease for which compensation is payable'.[166]

The 'peculiar to the trade' test could give rise to hardship and a sense of injustice, and it therefore comes as no surprise that various attempts were made to extend the scope of the 1906 act. The view of the Irish TUC, for example, was that compensation should be payable whenever a worker contracted a prescribed disease through his or her employment, whether or not that disease was particular to that kind of work. It might be difficult to prove that the disease arose 'out of and in the course of employment' and not from other causes; but the necessary connection could be made in a significant number of cases.[167] But even though this argument was supported by the principal lady inspector, Dame Adelaide Anderson, amongst others, it was rejected on the grounds that 'the extension of the act to cover any disease or injury which is not specific to the employment, would ... give rise to constant and irritating disputes and involve employers and workers in a great deal of costly and fruitless litigation and would not, except in rare instances, secure any benefit to the disabled workman.'[168]

(v) The assessment of compensation The *quid pro quo* for the extended right to compensation was a reduction in the level of compensation payable at common law:

The Act did not ... contemplate the grant of a statutory right to anything approaching full pecuniary indemnity, but merely provided that a fair proportion of the loss sustained was to be borne by the employer, who had to make such provision as would, in ordinary circumstances, suffice to save the injured person (but not his family) from suffering actual destitution as a consequence of his misfortune....[169]

---

165 Ibid., *Minutes of evidence*, pp. 229–235. Professor Lindsay was of opinion that the incidence of the disease had been 'greatly diminished' by better ventilation (p. 230) and that 'the flax trade is not so deadly as the steel trade of Sheffield' (p. 229).

166 *Report*, pp. 15–19. As a result, employers would have 'a strong inducement' to avoid possible liability by opting 'to dismiss or refuse to engage any workmen who show these symptoms', with unacceptable consequences for all 'innocent' workers.

167 *Departmental committee on compensation for injuries to workmen, 1920: Minutes of evidence*, i, 382 (Patrick Daly, secretary, Dublin United Trades Council).

168 *Report of the departmental committee on the system of compensation for injuries to workmen*, p. 26 [Cmd. 816], H.C. 1920, xxvi, 26.

169 Wilson and Levy, *Workmen's compensation*, i, 66.

The compensation was limited to financial loss; nothing was payable in respect of medical expenses, pain and suffering or loss of amenities.

In the case of an injury causing total or partial incapacity, the injured worker was entitled to one-half of his or her average weekly earnings up to a maximum of £1 per week. The amount of the weekly payment was reviewable at the request of either party, and could at any time be commuted for a lump sum by agreement. When a weekly payment had been made for six months or more, the employer could insist on commutation. Both of these provisions gave rise to considerable controversy. Employers who considered that the condition of an injured worker had improved often stopped the payment altogether, leaving it to the worker to persuade an arbitrator or the court that he or she was still entitled to some level of compensation.[170] But it was the practices resorted to by many employers (or their insurance companies) to induce workers to accept unfairly low lump sums by way of commutation of their weekly payments which gave rise to the greatest criticism and controversy. In an attempt to deal with such practices, the 1906 act provided that the lump sum in any case of permanent total incapacity should be such an amount as would purchase an annuity for the workman equal to 75 per cent of the annual value of the weekly payment. But this guideline does not appear to have been particularly successful in practice.[171]

Analysis of the data published in the annual reports of the working of the Workmen's Compensation Acts suggests that the average lump sum paid in respect of total incapacity was £20–£30 in Ireland (as opposed to £30–£50 in England and Wales), and in the case of partial incapacity, £15–£30 (much the same as in England and Wales); weekly payments in Ireland for incapacity of either kind were in the region of ten or eleven shillings, slightly lower than in England and Wales.

Where an accidental injury resulted in the worker's death, the compensation payable depended on the circumstances of the deceased. If he or she left persons who were wholly dependent on him or her financially, they were entitled to a sum equal to three years' earnings or £150, whichever was the larger – but in no case to exceed £300. If those persons were only partially dependent on the deceased, then they were (subject to the £300 limit) entitled to such sum as was 'reasonable and proportionate' to their loss. If there were no dependants at all, compensation limited to £10 was payable for reasonable expenses of medical attendance and burial. In Ireland, the average award in respect of death appears to have been in the region of £130–£150 (as opposed to £160–£180 in England and Wales).

Criticism of the level of workmen's compensation was not long in coming.[172] Miss Galway, secretary of the Textile Operatives Society of Ireland, argued

---

170   Ibid., p. 205.
171   *Departmental committee on compensation for injuries to workmen, 1920: Minutes of evidence*, i, 383–84 (Daly).
172   A particular complaint was that no compensation was payable to a worker, especially a woman or young person, badly disfigured by an accident which did not impair her

that 'half the average of the wage in Belfast is very little for a woman to live on when she is injured. She would require more nourishment than that money would bring her.'[173] The Irish TUC agreed,[174] and later proposed that the employer should bear the whole cost of the accident by paying compensation on a common law basis, rather than sharing it with the injured worker.[175] But all such arguments were rejected, generally on the grounds that any increase would 'act oppressively upon the employer'.[176]

(vi) The procedure for dealing with claims   Mindful of the complexity and expense of common law proceedings in the superior courts, Chamberlain set out to provide a simple and straightforward procedure for dealing with disputed workmen's compensation claims, with legal representation kept to a minimum and costs constrained by a scale of maximum fees. And the workers' representatives in Ireland were at first satisfied that he had achieved his ambition: 'The Act ... does away with ... nine-tenths of the technicalities which have disappointed the just hopes of the injured workman.'[177] But as is well known, both were quickly shown to be wildly optimistic.

It was hoped that most claims for compensation would be settled by agreement between employer and worker; if they could not agree, the claim would be settled informally by an arbitrator agreed upon by the parties. In the absence of such an agreement, the claim would be determined by a county court judge sitting without a jury[178] but with the assistance of a medical referee.[179] An appeal on a point of law only lay from the decision of the county court judge to the court of appeal and thence to the house of lords.

earning capacity. Cf. *Ball* v. *William Hunt & Sons Ltd.* [1912] AC 496 (compensation payable where disfigurement such as to leave worker physically able to work but which prevented him from getting such work).

173 *Departmental committee on accidents in places under the factory and workshop acts: Minutes of evidence*, p. 247 [Cd. 5535], H.C. 1911, xxiii, 323. In some cases, a worker was subjected to unfavourable treatment by her employer after a successful claim; but the more usual practice was simply to move to another job: 'They do not seem to like remaining with the firm after having claimed compensation.' It was easy enough for a woman injured in an accident in one factory to get employment in another – but only if she was 'a competent worker ... fit for the work': ibid.

174 Congress had resolved that half wages should be the *minimum* compensation for injury and £300 the minimum for death: *Report of the Fourth Irish Trades Congress* (Waterford, 1897), pp. 27–28. A resolution in favour of higher levels of compensation was also adopted in 1904 – see *Report of the Eleventh Irish Trades Union Congress* (Kilkenny, 1904), p. 21.

175 *Departmental committee on compensation for injuries to workmen, 1920: Minutes of evidence*, i, 381 (Daly).

176 *Report of the departmental committee on compensation for injuries to workmen, 1904*, p. 92.

177 Richard Wortley, President of the Belfast Trades Council, in *Report of the Fifth Irish Trades Union Congress* (Belfast, 1898), p. 37.

178 1897 act, ss. 1(3) and 2(1) and sch. II; Workmen's Compensation Rules (Ire.) 1898, r. 22.

179 1898 Rules, r. 23 – a power frequently exercised by the recorder of Dublin: *Departmental committee on compensation for injuries to workmen, 1920: Minutes of evidence*, ii, 446 (T.L.

In practice, however, many cases were not settled by agreement and arbitrators were seldom appointed; as a result, in Ireland as in the rest of the United Kingdom, many cases went to the county court[180] – and beyond. In 1904 it was acknowledged that the act had given rise to 'an excessive amount of litigation'; in an attempt to reverse this trend, the appointment of more 'arbitration committees' representative of employers and workers was recommended, to follow the 'excellent example set by the coal owners and miners in the county of Durham'.[181] Although the 1906 act sought to encourage the creation of such committees,[182] it seems that in Ireland, as in most of Great Britain, 'the requisite mutual confidence and co-operation between employers and workmen was generally lacking'.[183] Disputed cases therefore continued to go to the courts, where they were treated with a certain degree of inconsistency, both in judicial attitude and in judicial practice.[184]

Where claims were settled by agreement between the parties, the position appears to have been equally unsatisfactory. Employers (or more frequently their insurers) often drove a very hard or even oppressive bargain, particularly when the injured worker did not belong to a trade union.[185] The safeguard in the 1897 act designed to obviate unfair agreements was the provision that a written memorandum of the agreement should be recorded in a county court register and thereby made enforceable as a county court judgment.[186] But the enforcing of agreements made out of court was regarded as the great weakness of the 1897 act, and these provisions 'were practically disregarded'.[187] In 1904 the departmental committee set out to ensure 'that advantages may

---

O'Shaughnessy KC). Cf. *Quinn* v. *Flynn* (1910) 44 ILTR 183 (county court judge not bound by medical referee's report, but should form an independent judgment).

180   Most of the cases were heard by the judge sitting alone. Between 1899 and 1913, only five cases (out of more than 5,000) in Ireland were heard by an arbitrator, and the number of such cases was only slightly higher in England and Wales.

181   *Report of the departmental committee on compensation for injuries to workmen, 1904*, p. 42.

182   1906 act, sch. II, para. 1.

183   Wilson and Levy, *Workmen's compensation*, i, 218.

184   While some Irish workers' representatives were prepared to accept that some of the judges were 'fair', most were critical. Thus, 'one judge contradicts the decision of another': *Report of the Eleventh Irish Trades Union Congress* (Kilkenny, 1904), p. 21 (McManus); 'there is apparently no sympathy for the workman for his sufferings when it comes to the court': *Departmental committee on compensation for injuries to workmen, 1920: Minutes of evidence*, i, 388–89 (Daly). The recorder of Dublin admitted that he did not confer with his judicial colleagues in Belfast and elsewhere, and that county court judges in Ireland did not make any attempt to secure 'uniformity of decisions': ibid., ii, 446 (O'Shaughnessy).

185   Wilson and Levy, *Workmen's compensation*, i, 93. Patrick Daly, secretary of Dublin United Trades Council, claimed that 'agents of insurance companies invariably approach the worker when he is at his lowest ebb, for the purpose of getting him to consent to an amount that is considerably less than that which he ought to receive': *Departmental committee on compensation for injuries to workmen, 1920: Minutes of evidence*, i, 385.

186   1897 act, sch. II, para. 8.

187   Hanna, *Workmen's compensation* (2nd ed.), p. 120.

not be taken of workmen or dependants to obtain from them acknowledgments in full discharge without adequate compensation having been given, and ... that workmen ... may be bound by proper agreements definitely entered into ... [which should not be capable of being] reopened without good cause'.[188] All agreements were to be registered in the county court, and the court could refuse registration where it appeared that the compensation was inadequate or that the agreement had been obtained by fraud, undue influence or other improper means.[189]

Swannick v. Trustees of the Congested Districts Board for Ireland[190] provides a good example of how this system worked. A stonemason earning 30*s.* per week was injured when a splinter of stone struck his right eye, and was awarded compensation of 15*s.* per week. Two years later, the weekly payment was by agreement commuted to a lump sum of £30 and a memorandum of the agreement was presented to the county court for registration. Registration was refused on the grounds that the lump sum was inadequate; the plaintiff's right eye was 'useless' to him and he could no longer work as a mason; he had been 'hard up in Liverpool' when he signed the agreement, and the statutory guideline suggested that in his case a lump sum in excess of £500 was required to purchase an annuity equal to 75 per cent of the annual value of the weekly payment. But at this point the system failed the claimant. The employers appealed, and the court of appeal held that the statutory guideline did not apply in the absence of a finding that the plaintiff was permanently incapacitated. The case was remitted to the county court for reconsideration – but unfortunately the outcome of that reconsideration is not recorded.

In the event, the new safeguard proved to be a failure, since few agreements were in fact registered with the county courts.[191]

(vii) Contracting out   Given the prolonged controversy over the employer's right to contract out of the Employers' Liability Act, it is somewhat surprising to find that contracting out of the Workmen's Compensation Act was not just permitted, but even encouraged[192] – but only on the strict condition that a workman could not lose thereby. The employer was, therefore, required to put in place an alternative compensation scheme approved by the

---

188   Ibid., p. 120. It is therefore strange to find (p. 123) that it was not necessary for the agreement to be in writing.

189   'In many cases, when the case is brought up in this way, the parties ask me to say what in my opinion the agreed sum ought to be, and I frequently do so': *Departmental committee on compensation for injuries to workmen, 1920: Minutes of evidence*, ii, 445 (O'Shaughnessy).

190   (1912) 46 ILTR 253.

191   The number of agreements registered 'is still only a small proportion of the cases in which compensation is settled by agreement': *Statistics of compensation and of proceedings under the Workmen's Compensation Act ... for 1910*, p. 15 [Cd. 5896], H.C. 1911, lxxv, 757.

192   Hanna, *Workmen's compensation* (1st ed.), pp. 22–23. Cf. 'The obnoxious principle of "contracting-out" is rendered nugatory ...': *Report of the Fifth Irish Trades Union Congress* (Belfast, 1898), p. 37 (Wortley).

registrar of friendly societies. Such approval could only be given if the registrar, after consulting the workers themselves, considered that the scheme was 'on the whole not less favourable to the general body of workmen and their dependants than the provisions of this Act'. No scheme was to be certified 'which contains an obligation upon the workmen to join the scheme as a condition of their hiring'. In addition, the workers were given the right to require the registrar to examine the working of the scheme at any time to determine whether it was still at least as favourable as the act, whether the provisions of the scheme were being violated and whether the scheme was being fairly administered. If the registrar was satisfied that good cause existed for the workers' complaint, he was required to revoke his certificate, unless or until the cause of complaint had been removed.

It appears that these provisions, which were tightened up even further by the 1906 act,[193] were seldom invoked – for the obvious reason that employers rarely wished to enter into an agreement more favourable to the workers than the act.[194] By 1900, when some seven million workers were covered by the act, only 46 schemes with 123,000 members had been registered; in 1908, when the act applied to some fifteen million workers, there were only 32 schemes with 65,000 members.[195] No evidence has been found of any alternative scheme of this kind in Ireland.[196]

THE WORKMEN'S COMPENSATION ACTS IN IRELAND

As in England and Wales workmen's compensation immediately supplanted the Employers' Liability Act as the source of compensation for most injured workers.[197] The number of claims rose fairly steadily from 1899, and increased spectacularly when the 1906 act came into force. Some of this increase arose

193 The 1906 act, s. 3(1) added various conditions, including the requirement that the scheme be approved by a majority of the workmen to whom it was applicable, to be ascertained by ballot.

194 *Report of the departmental committee on workmen's compensation, 1920*, pp. 63–64 found that the power of contracting out was 'very little' used. The committee nonetheless recommended that the power be retained: 'We feel that now it is more desirable than ever that no opportunity should be lost of fostering any scheme which brings employers and workmen together in the joint management of affairs in which both have material concern': ibid.

195 *Departmental committee on compensation for injuries to workmen, 1920: Minutes of evidence*, ii, 413 (Stuart Robertson, chief registrar of friendly societies). Most of the workers involved worked on the railways or in mines; in 1911, for example, factory workers represented only 30 per cent of the 74,000 workers covered by schemes: *Report of the chief registrar of friendly societies for the year ending 31st Dec. 1911 (part A)*, p. 23, H.C. 1912–13 (123), lxxxi, 23.

196 Ibid., pp. 23–24 gives details of 31 schemes then in active operation – 29 in England and Wales and 2 in Scotland.

197 In 1899, there were only 9 recorded claims under the 1880 act, as opposed to 72 under the 1897 act: *Statistics of proceedings ... under the Workmen's Compensation Act and the Employers' Liability Act during 1899*, pp. 33–35 [Cd. 281], H.C. 1900, lxix,

from factory accidents; but by 1908 such claims had been overtaken by 'other' claims arising from accidents, for example, in agricultural employment, domestic service, road transport and building operations.

Table 11.3: No. of recorded workmen's compensation claims for injury or death, 1899–1913[198]

	Ireland			England and Wales		
	Factory	Other	Total	Factory	Other	Total
1899						
County court	37	22	59	686	661	1,347
Memoranda	12	1	13	227	536	763
Total	49	23	72	913	1,197	2,110
1903						
County court	101	111	212	953	1,080	2,033
Memoranda	48	35	83	1,286	1,709	2,995
Total	149	146	295	2,239	2,789	5,028
1908[199]						
County court	143	520	663	1,440	3,822	5,262
Memoranda	216	555	771	7,756	12,716	20,472
Total	359	1,075	1,434	9,196	16,538	25,734
1913						
County Court	211	917	1,128	2,381	4,878	7,259
Memoranda	154	683	837	7,046	11,652	18,698
Total	365	1,600	1,965	9,427	16,530	25,957

Assisted by the fact that workshops were brought under the Workmen's Compensation Act 1906, there was, nevertheless, a seven-fold increase between 1899 and 1913 in the the number of claims arising from accidents in establishments coming under the factory acts in Ireland – a rate of increase which was slighly *lower* than that in England and Wales.

In Ireland, as in England and Wales, a number of these 'recorded' claims were settled out of court, as indeed were many cases which never came to the notice of the court at all. Those which were heard and determined by the

481–83. But the number of claims under the 1880 act rose to 19 in 1900 and remained at that level for some years – see above, p. 351. It would appear, therefore, that it was the 1906 act, rather than that of 1897, which brought about the effective demise of the 1880 act.

198 Derived from the annual *Statistics of proceedings in England and Wales ... and in Ireland under the Workmen's Compensation Act.* 'County court' refers to judicial 'arbitration', while 'memoranda' connotes claims settled out of court (by agreement or otherwise) and formally registered in the county court.

199 The figures given here are for claims under 1906 act; there were also a small number of 'old' claims under the 1897 and 1900 acts.

court were normally decided in the claimant's favour; but for most of the period up to 1914, the Irish courts seem to have been somewhat less favourable to claimants than those in England and Wales.[200] Table 11.4 is intended to provide a summary of those cases which were either subject to a formal memorandum of agreement or were decided by the court:

Table 11.4: Workmen's compensation in the Irish
county courts, 1903 and 1913[201]

	Lump sum		Weekly payments	
	No. of cases	Amount	No. of cases	Amount
1903				
Death	17	£2,682	–	–
Incapacity	30	£1,510	48	£19
Total factory	47	£4,191	48	£19
Other workers	39	£2,140	43	£13
Grand total	86	£6,331	91	£32
1913				
Death	35	£4,613	–	–
Incapacity	65	£2,666	35	£15
Total factory	100	£7,279	35	£15
Other workers	604	£33,091	178	£80
Grand total	704	£40,370	213	£95

A comparison with England and Wales suggests that, while the vast bulk of the compensation was paid by way of a lump sum in both jurisdictions, the proportion of the compensation paid in this way was even higher in Ireland.[202]

But a more accurate impression of the overall cost of workmen's compensation is to be obtained from the annual returns which every employer was required to send to the home office. In 1908, these returns suggested that the total compensation paid in respect of factory and workshop accidents in the

200 In 1900, for example, just over 80 per cent of claimants in England and Wales were successful, as compared to 60 per cent in Ireland. Cf. in 1908, all but eleven of 427 Irish cases were decided in the claimant's favour. It should also be noted that solicitors' costs were lower in Ireland – an average of £5, as compared to £11-£12 in England and Wales.
201 Derived from *Statistics of proceedings in England and Wales ... and in Ireland, under the Workmen's Compensation Act 1897 ... during 1903*, pp. 36–37 [Cd. 2269], H.C. 1905, lxxv, 480–81; *Statistics of compensation and of proceedings under the Workmen's Compensation Act 1906 ... during the year 1913*, pp. 54–58 [Cd. 7669], H.C. 1914–16, lxi, 1044–48. The figures are for county court arbitrations and registered memoranda combined, but do not include claims and compensation in respect of prescribed industrial diseases.
202 In 1913, for example, lump sum compensation in England and Wales amounted to just over £700,000, while the weekly payments came to nearly £4,000.

United Kingdom as a whole was just over £800,000; the cost of compensation per person employed was roughly three shillings per year, ranging from 9*d*. per head in the woollen industry and 1*s*. 6*d*. in cotton, to 6*s*. 3*d*. in the metal industry and 12*s*. 0*d*. in engineering and shipbuilding. Put another way, the cost of workmen's compensation per £100 wages paid was 2*s*. 2*d*. in the woollen industry, 3*s*. 5*d*. in cotton and 2*s*. 2*d*. for all other textile trades.[203] By 1911, the total cost of workmen's compensation in respect of just over five million workers in factories and workshops throughout the United Kingdom was almost £1.2 million, the average cost per annum per person having increased to 4*s*. 6*d*., ranging from 1*s*. 7*d*. in textiles other than cotton (2*s*. 3^{1}/2*d*.) and wool (1*s*. 11^{1}/2*d*.) to 15*s*. 0^{1}/2*d*. in engineering and shipbuilding and £1. 1*s*. 9*d*. in respect of dock labour.[204]

The potential cost of workmen's compensation raised the question whether employers should be obliged to be insured against liability under the act. With one possible exception,[205] neither the 1897 act nor the 1906 act made insurance compulsory. In this respect the United Kingdom legislation departed from similar schemes in other countries, particularly Germany, where insurance was not only compulsory but also state controlled. It appears that many 'small' employers in Ireland did not in practice take out insurance[206] – and that their failure to do so could put injured workers at a disadvantage, especially when business was poor.[207] Nor was it just a question of compensation; some of the factory inspectors were in favour of compulsory state insurance on the grounds that it would strengthen their hand in the enforcement of safety legislation.[208]

The absence of insurance may for a time have given rise to problems in Ireland; in 1907, for example, the Irish TUC criticised the absence of compulsory insurance for small employers.[209] But the position appears to

---

203 *Statistics of compensation and of proceedings under the Workmen's Compensation Act during the year 1908*, pp. 7–8 [Cd. 4894], H.C. 1909, lxxx, 955–56. Unfortunately, a separate figure is not given for the linen industry.

204 *Statistics of compensation and of proceedings under the Workmen's Compensation Act during the year 1911*, p. 17 [Cd. 6493], H.C. 1912–13, lxxv, 793.

205 By 1906 act, s. 8(7) the home secretary was given power, under certain circumstances, to require all the employers in a particular industry to insure against liability to pay compensation in respect of prescribed industrial diseases. But it appears that this power was not exercised before 1914 – if at all.

206 See e.g. *Departmental committee appointed to consider whether the post office should provide facilities for insurance under the Workmen's Compensation Act: Minutes of evidence*, p. 151 [Cd. 3569], H.C. 1907, lxviii, 329, where the factory inspectors in Ireland reported that small employers were generally not insured because of 'want of foresight', 'cost of insurance' or 'indifference to bankruptcy'.

207 *Report of the departmental committee on compensation for injuries to workmen, 1904*, pp. 112–14. If an employer went into bankruptcy, an injured worker entitled to compensation was not a preferential creditor; even if the employer was insured, a worker had no claim against the insurance company itself.

208 Wilson and Levy, *Workmen's compensation*, i, 127.

209 *Report of the Fourteenth Irish Trades Union Congress* (Dublin, 1907), p 4. The home secretary took the view that this question could not be dealt with 'until further experience has been gained of the working of the act of 1906': *Fifteenth report* (Belfast, 1908), p. 14. Cf. 'It is necessary for the protection of workmen, and is not

have improved by 1909, when Miss Galway reported that insurance had become 'more general these last few years', and that this had had a good effect on the willingness of the employers to pay compensation properly.[210] But there continued to be evidence of cases where an uninsured employer had not been in a position to pay compensation.[211]

A special case study

Between 1907 and 1914, Harland & Wolff Ltd. employed some 11,410 workers per annum, the average wages bill coming to £878,702 per annum.[212] On average there were 740 accidents per year, resulting in 529 claims for compensation. The compensation paid each year averaged £7,802, representing 0.89 per cent of the total wages bill – or 13s. 9d. per worker per year.

Table 11.6: Workmen's compensation payments in Harland &
Wolff Ltd. (selected years)[213]

Year	Average no. of workers	Total wages paid	No. of 'lost time' accidents	No. of W.C. claims	Total compensation paid	Compensation as % of wages	Cost of compensation per worker
1907	10,043	£740,320	559	322	£8,254	1.1%	16s. 5d.
1910	10,275	£754,753	758	536	£7,410	1.0%	14s. 5d.
1913	12,822	£1,056,744	905	663	£7,268	0.7%	11s. 4d.

Harland & Wolff Ltd. were self-insurers, and dealt with claims through their own accident and compensation department, which (according to the head of the department) had worked 'with gratifying smoothness' to the satisfaction of the workers and 'at a cost to the firm of an annual outlay considerably less than the price of an insurance premium'.[214] The company took the view that self-insurance 'encourages the avoidance of accidents and the taking of precautions' – but did not lead to 'economy' in the settlement of claims:

> contrary to the interests of the employers themselves, that those who are unable safely to carry the risk should be compelled to insure': *Report of the departmental committee on workmen's compensation, 1920*, p. 19.

210 *Departmental committee on accidents in places under the factory and workshop acts: Minutes of evidence*, p. 247.
211 *Departmental committee on compensation for injuries to workmen, 1920: Minutes of evidence*, i, 385 (Daly).
212 Much of the account which follows is based on evidence given in 1919 by James Robertson, who was in charge of the accident and compensation department of Harland & Wolff: see ibid., ii, 288–300.
213 Ibid., p. 289.
214 Ibid., p. 290. They had been quoted a premium of 2% of the wages bill by one insurance company anxious to get the business, as opposed to the average cost of 0.9% for self-insurance. The latter figure did not, apparently, include the firm's administrative costs of approximately £800 per year; but this would have added no more than 0.1% to the average cost.

The manner in which the firm deals with its injured workmen has frequently been the subject of appreciative comment by people well-qualified to judge. Trade union delegates ... our local County Court Judge and his Registrar ... solicitors and medical gentlemen who advise injured workpeople, have all testified on many occasions to the spirit of fairness and generosity in which my firm administers its liability.[215]

The number of claims varied from year to year,[216] but nearly all were settled out of court: 'When it comes to a borderline case ... we generally give the injured workman the benefit of the doubt. It is only in cases where we are perfectly satisfied that we are not liable that we defend in the county court.'[217]

Where a workman was killed, his widow was often employed as a charwoman. If there were no children, the widow often remarried: 'The fact that they have a sum of £300 is an attraction.' If there were children, one-third of the award was generally paid to the widow immediately, and the remainder paid quarterly for the maintenance and education of the children. It was usually found that such payments lasted until the children reached the age of 15 or 16, 'when they would be going into some form of employment'.

Where a workman was injured, compensation usually took the form of a lump sum, rather than a weekly payment; on receipt of the lump sum, the worker usually left Harland & Wolff for other employment:

In some cases where we have practically compelled them to come back and take other employment, we have found their services very unsatisfactory; they would not carry out the orders of the foreman and the managers, and really would not make an effort honestly to fulfil their new duties. So long as there is a possibility of getting a lump sum we find the workmen use every endeavour to get it, because in Belfast they can always get employment elsewhere.

Accordingly, the firm's practice was not to re-employ a worker who had been paid compensation by way of a lump sum. This could obviously be disadvantageous if other employment was not available – as was the firm's practice *not* to re-employ a worker who had been permanently partially disabled 'in case he should meet with another accident, and then we might be faced with a total disability claim'.[218]

215 Ibid., p. 290.
216 The building of large vessels such as the *Titanic* raised the number of accidents because 'when they are in skeleton form there is a larger percentage of risk, particularly of serious accidents ...'. When the *Titanic* sank, with eleven shipyard workers on board, compensation was payable to their dependants: ibid., p. 289.
217 Ibid., p. 292. Mr Robertson had earlier confirmed that the firm did not have a joint committee of management and employees to decide disputed cases.
218 Ibid., p. 298 – or at the least be less productive, as the plaintiff in *M'Bey* v. *Edenderry Spinning Co.* (1883) 17 ILTR 78 gave as the reason for her dismissal, when she went back to work after losing a finger in an allegedly unguarded spinning frame.

The impact of the act on the safety of workers

Whether or not workmen's compensation would operate in favour of increased safety was much discussed when the 1897 bill was going through parliament. When the act had been in force for five years, the evidence was found to be inconclusive: '[We cannot say whether the act] has had any marked or ascertainable effect one way or the other upon the safety of the workmen.'[219] But a number of the inspectors appeared to take the view that the practice of insuring against liability under the act did make employers more careless.[220] On the other hand, the experience in Germany led the home office to conclude that 'it is usually found that the more completely the system of compulsory insurance is developed the more thorough-going and effective is that portion of the legislation which deals with the prevention of accidents'.[221] But the German experience was ignored when the 1906 bill was being drafted.

The apparent increase in the number of reported factory accidents gave rise to such concern that in June 1908 the home secretary agreed to appoint a departmental committee to consider the question.[222] As we have already seen,[223] the committee concluded that there had been little real increase in the accident rate. The Workmen's Compensation Acts had reduced the accident risk, but led to some increase in the number of reported accidents. The evidence from factory inspectors, workers and employers was generally to the effect that the acts had had 'a beneficial effect in directing the attention of occupiers to the occurrence of accidents and to the importance of finding methods for their prevention'.[224] The committee could not accept the view that insurance relieved employers of their responsibility for preventing accidents, since (a) the premiums payable by employers increased with the number of accidents, and (b) insurance companies were induced by competition to take steps (such as inspection, clauses in policies requiring the insured to take reasonable precautions and differential rates of premium for more or less dangerous factories) to keep the accident rate as low as possible. The committee also rejected the view that the acts had tended to make workers themselves less careful: 'The bulk of the evidence ... is against this

219 *Report of the departmental committee on compensation for injuries to workmen, 1904*, p. 23.
220 See especially ibid., *Minutes of evidence*, p. 487 (Commander Smith, superintending inspector of factories). In 1900, the Irish TUC called for 'more efficient inspection' of premises where the employer was insured: *Report of the Seventh Annual Irish Trades Congress* (Dublin, 1900), pp. 36–37. Cf. several inspectors referred to the value of the act in promoting the fencing of dangerous machinery, and considered that the pressure brought to bear by insurance companies was important in this respect: *Chief insp. ann. rep., 1898*, pt. II, p. 8.
221 'Memorandum on foreign and colonial laws relating to compensation for injuries to workmen', quoted *Report of the departmental committee on compensation for injuries to workmen, 1904*, p. 33.
222 *Report of the departmental committee on accidents in places under the factory and workshop acts* [Cd. 5535], H.C. 1911, xxiii, 1.
223 Above, pp. 141–42.
224 *Report of the departmental committee on accidents*, p. 17.

view, and no evidence has been produced to render credible to the committee the idea that workmen will let themselves be injured for the purpose of getting compensation.' Witnesses 'of all classes', however, were agreed that the acts had both a good and a bad effect on injured workers:

Workpeople are now in a better position to stay away from work for the legitimate purpose of giving proper attention by rest and treatment to injuries which formerly they often neglected ... [but] the requirement of fourteen days' absence as a condition of receiving compensation ... undoubtedly offers a considerable inducement to injured persons not to return to work before the end of a fortnight....[225]

But cases of malingering 'account only for a very small proportion of the compensation cases'.

The general conclusion seems to be that the cost of workmen's compensation to industry either directly or through the payment of insurance premiums was not unbearable: 'the gloomy apprehensions of employers were not realised.'[226] From the workers' point of view, the acts were a mixed blessing. It is undoubtedly the case that they provided injured workers in Ireland with an aggregate amount of compensation which exceeded that recovered at common law. On the other hand, the level of compensation in individual cases was inadequate, the law increasingly technical and complex and the procedure for dealing with claims highly unsatisfactory:

Between the two sides of industry, an atmosphere of antagonism built up over the settlement of claims; and among the exacerbating factors lay the fact that claims were in the end handled by lawyers following ordinary court procedures.... Private insurers already had, by 1897, considerable experience of compromising their liability under various forms of policy by direct approaches to the victim. Cheap and quick settlements were to be secured from men who had rarely possessed any capital sum before and who in any case feared a dispute involving their employers.... [There was considerable evidence of] plausible approaches to men still sick in hospital and the persistent visiting and even the bullying that [injured men] might suffer at home.... Improvident or oppressive settlements for lump sums were 'much too frequent'.[227]

Chamberlain's objective of a simple and straightforward procedure for resolving disputed cases was quickly undermined: '[N]o act has ever brought more grist to the legal mill. An act, which was meant to be a paragon of simplicity, has been found a cloudland of obscurity.'[228] We can do no better than leave the final word to the leading authority on the act:

From the moment of the accident or injury ... to the final settlement of his claim to compensation is generally a long, and sometimes a crooked, path, beset with almost as many dangers and temptations as Bunyan's Pilgrim encountered. The path is

225 Ibid.
226 Wilson and Levy, *Workmen's compensation*, i, 83.
227 Cornish and Clark, *Law and society in England*, p. 531.
228 Campbell, *Workmen's compensation*, p. 2.

broad till it reaches the wicket-gate marked Claim, the keepers of which are men skilled in the law; it grows narrower and more tortuous till it ends at the portals called Settlement, which is manned by officers of justice. It may take the pilgrims a few months, or several years, to traverse the distance between the entrance gate of Claim and the exit of Settlement; the path is flanked by legal quagmires and judicial fences, guarded by predatory creatures which often deter men who have not a trustworthy guide from going farther on their journey, though their welfare and that of their family depends upon their reaching the other end.[229]

229 Wilson and Levy, *Workmen's compensation*, i, 198.

CHAPTER TWELVE

Epilogue

The legal history of the factory acts in Ireland in the nineteenth and early twentieth centuries provides another chapter in the study of the response of the government and parliament of the United Kingdom to local economic and social conditions. That chapter is informed by a rich diet of legislation, both primary and secondary, by an extensive case law and by a multitude of official reports which deal with many matters in great detail, all of which we have endeavoured to take into account. But we accept that what we have provided is largely an *official* history; the views of employers and workers are much less accessible and a more comprehensive study of the acts from their perspective must await further research. Nevertheless, we have attempted to trace the development of legislation which, by 1914, applied to one quarter of a million workers employed in some twelve thousand industrial establishments throughout Ireland.

In general terms, the legal response to industrial working conditions in Ireland was largely governed by a 'parity' principle which dictated that, notwithstanding any distinctive features which they might possess, the factories and workshops throughout the island should essentially be subject to the same regulatory regime as was, at any given time, in place in England, Wales and Scotland. Given that Irish manufacturing industry never represented anything more than a small percentage of the gross national product, and that industrial conditions (as opposed to industrial development) in Ireland never became a major political issue, this approach is readily understandable. But as time went on the application of regulatory provisions designed primarily for British (even English) industrial conditions gave rise to some particular difficulties and tensions. In a number of instances, a sympathetic response demonstrated that the authorities in London were able and willing to make allowances for local conditions and circumstances; in others, the 'national' rules were more strictly applied and enforced, not necessarily to the detriment of Irish workers. In our examination of the general development of the law and its practical application to selected industries, we have sought to identify the extent to which special provision was made with a view to dealing with those working conditions which differed from those to be found elsewhere in the United Kingdom.

During the first three decades of the nineteenth century, a period in which there was much concern about the prospects for industrial development in Ireland, there was little or no public interest in working conditions, even in the textile industry which was bringing to the island the factory system already developed in Great Britain. On the contrary, it was public concern about the plight of child workers in the cotton mills and factories of the north of England which led to the first attempts to regulate their working conditions, and the inclusion of Ireland in this legislation was made without any investigation, with little discussion and virtually without effect. Given that the various statutes enacted between 1802 and 1831 had little impact anywhere in the United Kingdom, their significance is primarily symbolic, in that they went some way to establishing the *principle* of regulation, as well as suggesting the limited form which that regulation should take.

It was the heightened public interest in the condition of child and other workers in the north of England which led in the early 1830s to a national survey which included the first official report on working conditions in the textile factories of the north of Ireland. The findings of this limited inquiry, and of a further survey conducted in the early 1840s, tend to corroborate Black's assertion (above, p. 9) that its later development in Ireland meant that the worst excesses of the factory system were avoided, at least in the first half of the nineteenth century. Nevertheless, there was considerable scope for improvement, even by the limited standards set by the first 'real' factory act of 1833. Setting a precedent which became much more significant later in the century, Ireland was initially divided into two districts for administration and enforcement purposes. But the reorganisation of inspectorial duties in 1836–1837 led to the whole of the island being 'united' under the elderly – and controversial – inspector Stuart, who was also responsible for the whole of Scotland. Even allowing for the relatively small number of Irish textile factories for which Stuart and his assistant inspector were responsible, their assertion that the 1833 act was being generally observed throughout the island seems somewhat optimistic. Given, however, a policy of prosecuting only in cases involving 'decided disobedience' of the law, a strategy which may well have been justified in the circumstances, it is difficult at this distance to make an informed evaluation of the immediate impact of the 1833 act.

But two general points may be made. It was the English cotton industry which provoked the early factory acts; the inclusion in those acts from 1833 onwards of *all* textile factories led to the regulation of the Irish linen, as well as cotton, industry. The principal application of the acts to Ireland was, therefore, somewhat incidental to their main purpose, and it may well have taken some time for the need for legislative regulation to have become readily accepted here. On the other hand, given the increasing importance of linen in the Irish industrial sector of the mid-Victorian period, the *fact* of regulation should have meant that the need for minimum standards in respect of working conditions was transparently obvious to other industrial entrepreneurs, to an extent which may not have been so pronounced in Great Britain. Accordingly, if – as the inspectors lead us to believe – the legal requirements were generally observed in Ireland, there may have been a 'filtering down' process to other industries, making them more amenable to regulation when the ambit of the acts was extended in the 1860s. Unfortunately, further evidence which might support this or any other theory is not readily available. But it is the case that when the factory acts came to be reviewed in the 1870s, one of the major issues for the commissioners was the extent to which the legislative regulation of non-textile factories and of workshops should be brought up to the standards already applicable to textile factories, given the difficulties which the inspectors had encountered in this regard during the previous decade.

The factory acts of 1833–1856 regulated the textile industry primarily with regard to the hours of employment of children, young persons and (from 1844) adult women, the education of child workers and (also from 1844) the safety precautions to be taken for the benefit of all workers in respect of the fencing and cleaning of machinery. The first attempt to broaden the scope of this legislation in the early 1840s succeeded only in relation to coal-mines; but it was that extension which led in 1844 to the inclusion of adult women within the category of 'protected' factory workers. These early factory acts, which have no provisions peculiar to Ireland, have attracted considerable interest among more modern commentators, as a prime example of state regulation enacted during an era supposedly dominated by *laissez faire* principles. But even classical economists could accept the need for *some* state intervention in appropriate areas, and the protection of child and women workers could be justified as an exception to the general rule on the basis that they were not capable of perceiving their own best interests – a view shared by O'Connell, and not vehemently opposed by Irish industrialists. On the other hand, the parlous state of much of Irish industry led O'Connell to oppose further state intervention in the manner in which wages were paid, with the result that the additional protection for workers provided by the Truck Act 1831 was *not* extended to Ireland.

These early factory acts have also sparked controversy in other directions. Were they simply the product of benevolent paternalism – or a device for safeguarding the upper echelons of industry from 'unfair' competition? Were they designed solely to protect those considered unable to look after their own interests or as a bridgehead for improving the working conditions of adult males who had full capacity but were unable to achieve their goal of a shorter working day by other means? Or were they 'really' designed to keep women at home as much as possible in order to enhance the role of the male breadwinner? Unfortunately, what is known about the operation of these early acts in Ireland in mid-century does not add greatly to this debate. But the Irish evidence does tend to portray the acts as operating in practice to afford some protection to the women, young persons and children forced by economic necessity to seek paid employment in order to sustain the family, with the result that there was, in the words of Isabella Tod (above, p. 63), no support for 'any serious modification of their restrictive provisions'. The fact that many defendants were smaller firms or businesses may mean that they were the worst offenders, and that the acts, as enforced, operated for the benefit of the upper echelons of the textile industry; but the evidence is too equivocal to allow such an assertion to be made with any degree of confidence.

In any case, the influence of the factory inspectors, and of the factory acts, should not be overestimated. The small number of factory inspectors appointed for the whole of the United Kingdom inevitably meant that there were limits to what they could realistically achieve. This was a common phenomenon of the time; the apparently broad scope of legislative regulation suggested by the fact that twenty-two inspectorates of one kind or another had been created in the United Kingdom by 1875 is offset by the fact that the total number of inspectors came to less than five hundred.[1] In addition, the 1844 act significantly reduced the status of the factory inspectors by formally depriving them of legislative and judicial authority. No doubt it was constitutionally more appropriate for these powers to lie elsewhere. But a 'modest' administrative structure meant that there were limits, too, to the managerial capacity of the home office, which was entrusted with ultimate responsibility for the due administration of the acts and the further development of the law.[2] In the case of Ireland, this bureaucratic limitation was further complicated by the need for co-operation between the home office in London and the chief secretary's office in Dublin. And there were from the start doubts and misgivings about the appropriateness of the magistrates' courts as the judicial mechanism for enforcing the law against recalcitrant employers. Accordingly, much was left to the initiative and moral authority of the individual inspectors, but in a way which makes it difficult to assess their real effectiveness – or otherwise.

By the 1850s, when there were in Ireland some 30,000 workers under the aegis of the factory acts, we can begin to see more clearly an active Irish contribution to the development of the law, at least on behalf of the employers. Linen magnates were, for example, openly involved in the campaign to secure the fencing concession embodied in the factory act of 1856 (above, pp. 126–27), and a few years later they secured the exemption from regulation of open-air bleach works (pp. 43–44). In the former instance they merely reiterated the common cause of owners throughout the United Kingdom by repeating the dangers of over-regulation and in particular the dire effects which it would have for an industry increasingly in competition with mainland Europe and the United States. Fortunately, successive governments tended to give little credence to gloomy prognostications of 'a forest of smokeless chimneys' in Belfast. In respect of bleachworks, however, the owners relied successfully on the difference between the practice in Ireland and the rest of the United Kingdom, thereby establishing a precedent which was to be frequently pressed into service in later years.

The third phase of the factory acts in Ireland began in the mid–1860s and may be said to have continued until the late 1880s. This period began with

1 K.T. Hoppen, *The mid-Victorian generation, 1846*–1886 (Oxford, 1998), p. 109.
2 See e.g. J. Tomlinson, *Government and the enterprise since 1900* (Oxford, 1994), pp. 32–33.

the extension of the acts to non-textile factories and to many kinds of textile and non-textile workshops. A nationwide experiment initially devolved responsibility for the inspection of workshops to local authorities; but this failed generally, and spectacularly so in Ireland, and the workshops, too, came under the supervision of the factory inspectors from 1871 onwards. These radical extensions of the ambit of the acts were significant in Ireland in two particular respects. The much wider range of establishments to be inspected meant that the factory acts for the first time had a significant impact throughout the island as a whole, and not just to those limited areas in which the textile industry flourished. Secondly, the much larger number of establishments, and the related increase in the number of workers – to at least 125,000 by 1870 – meant that a system of inspection, which had already begun to creak, quickly proved to be inadequate. But although the organisation of the inspectorate, as well as the law, was reformed in 1878, relatively little change was noticeable before 1890. The inspectorate, under its first chief inspector (Redgrave), was slow to adjust to the radical change brought about in the 1860s, and in particular their numbers and expertise failed to keep pace with their growing responsibilities.

By this time Ireland consisted of two widely differing industrial 'districts'. The north (roughly coterminous with the province of Ulster) was a typical manufacturing area much the same as those to be found throughout Great Britain. By the 1890s it had embarked upon its golden era, which may be said to have reached its peak in the years immediately before the first world war. Here were to be found most of the larger factories in Ireland, providing work for a large part of the island's industrial workforce. The south, consisting of the other three provinces, was roughly three times the size in geographical terms – but much smaller in terms of industrial development, characterised by typically small enterprises widely dispersed and, in aggregate, providing employment for only one half of the number of industrial workers to be found in the north. The nature of this district caused at least one inspector (Martindale – see p. 111) openly to wonder whether legislation drawn up to deal with the conditions of employment in Lancashire cotton mills 'quite fitted a little woollen mill in the west of Ireland'. Indeed, it would be mistaken to think of the large mill or factory (linen or otherwise) as the archetypal focus for the factory acts in Ireland. By 1907, textile mills and factories accounted for just under one-third of the industrial workforce in Ireland (albeit a rather higher percentage of 'protected' workers), a statistic which also reflected the relative decline in the significance of the linen industry in the context of more general industrial development. Almost as many 'protected' workers were to be found in non-textile factories, many of which were comparatively small. If we add to these both the large number of small workshops and a significant number of linen and other outworkers, we can readily see that comparatively little of the inspectors' time and effort would have been spent in the supervision of the great mills and factories.

Nevertheless it was the declaration by the home secretary in 1894 that those linen mills and factories were 'dangerous and injurious to health' as a result of the excessive dust and humidity generated in the manufacturing process which may be said to have confirmed a new departure in the history of the factory acts in Ireland prior to 1914. The home secretary's declaration was the result of the first of the four official inquiries into working conditions in the linen industry to be conducted within a twenty-year period. The upshot was a series of special regulations which made increasingly detailed provision for the ventilation and general running of these mills and factories, as the linen industry learned from the experience of the cotton industry in Great Britain: on a few occasions, even, this process was reversed. From 1890 onwards, too, numerous committees of inquiry – and an increasing number of more highly qualified inspectors – actively investigated 'Irish' problems – in creameries, convent laundries, out-working, scutch mills, dress-making and millinery, and so on. Their findings frequently attracted the support of the home office, and not inconsiderable steps were taken to create special exceptions or to enforce the existing law in an attempt to resolve these particular problems. A good example of special treatment – in respect of only a small number of protected workers – is provided by the enactment of special regulations for Irish creameries (see pp. 267–71). By way of contrast we may cite the failure to make the kind of special provision which might have enabled the inspectors to solve the problems caused by the excessive dust found in Irish scutch mills (see p. 147). In other cases it was through the application of undifferentiated legal provisions that attempts were made to deal with problems which were found in, but were not peculiar to, Ireland.

All these references to special provisions relating to specific industries reflect the particularistic nature of the factory acts. In 1876 the factory and workshop commissioners had taken support from the fact that the law was designed primarily to meet 'proved abuses' and to rectify 'particular evils', and they explained that 'it has never been sought to prescribe one invariable rule ... merely for the sake of elegance in the statute book ...'. This refusal to take 'a general view of the subject', and to focus instead on 'remedying a single ascertained evil'[3] continued to inform the drafting of legislation generally, as may be seen from the great consolidations of 1878 and 1901. In many instances, the solution to a particular 'evil' was simply to adopt existing best practice; on a few occasions, indeed, Irish manufacturers were held up as exemplars for the rest of the United Kingdom. In terms of regulatory theory, however, there is a question as to the extent to which the administrative process may have been 'captured' by powerful manufacturing interests who shaped the law in ways which suited them, rather than their workers – or the broader public interest.[4] This broader question goes beyond the ambit of our study. But as we have seen, it *was* the case that the consultative process which preceded the making of many

---

3 Sydney Webb, in the preface to B.L. Hutchins and A. Harrison, *A history of factory legislation* (3rd ed., London, 1926), p. viii – adding that 'with the nineteenth-century House of Commons no other method would have secured any progress at all'.

4 See e.g. R. Baldwin and M. Cave, *Understanding regulation: Theory, strategy and practice* (Oxford, 1999).

special provisions allowed both employers and workers a significant say, and there were certainly some occasions at least when the views of one or more of the interested parties (more usually, but not invariably, the employers) influenced the form and substance of legislation. It also appears to have been generally accepted that the level of regulation should not be such as to stifle industrial competitiveness, to inhibit technological development or to restrict adaptation to changing economic conditions. Accordingly, the official verdict in 1876 (see p. 62) – that the factory acts had improved working conditions without 'serious loss' to the employers – no doubt remained true in 1914. But as we have seen, there were those in Ireland who believed that the cost of adopting the standards laid down by the acts could have a detrimental effect on economic development in the poorer parts of Ireland – a difficult conflict of interest *not* confined to the nineteenth-century.

Another factor limiting the impact of the factory acts was the general perception, at least of the inspectors, that it would be undesirable for 'external' inspection to relieve employers of the primary responsibility for the proper management of factories and workshops, which the employers alone were capable of fulfilling. This principle, still being openly expressed at the end of the century in respect of the regulation of steam boilers (see p. 246), was in our view rightly designed to prevent employers from 'sheltering' behind the inspectors. But it was also an honest recognition of the practical limits of a system of inspection which continued to permit an average of only one visit per annum to a particular factory or workshop. In the early part of the nineteenth century the 'primacy' principle was undermined by common law judges in both jurisdictions who took the view that, at least in the area of safety, the responsibility was at least as much that of the workers as of the employers. But by the end of the period under consideration, even the judges, cautiously prompted by Parliament, were beginning to develop the concept of employers' liability, an additional form of 'enforcement' of safety standards which was welcomed by the inspectors.

But although the factory acts were, from the outset, aimed primarily at employers, they also recognised that workers, too, must play their part. This was particularly the case with regard to the employment of children and matters of health and safety. In the absence of any systematic form of social welfare, the attitude of poorer parents towards putting their children to work, paid or unpaid, remained virtually unchanged throughout the century. As a matter of economic necessity, children were expected to be wage earners from an early age – to such an extent that a leading lady inspector regarded their illegal employment as 'one of the most pressing problems in Ireland'. On this subject, public opinion in Ireland continued, according to Martindale (see p. 115), to lag 'far behind' that in Great Britain. On the question of health and safety also, the inspectors could – and sometimes did – direct their attention to the 'prejudice' of the workers against the use of protective devices and their failure to exercise reasonable care. While not unsympathetic to claims that many safety devices were not just inconvenient and uncomfortable, but also adversely affected earnings (particularly in the case of piece-work), the inspectors drew attention to the 'excessive zeal', carelessness and even rashness of some workers – and in some cases even resorted to the prosecution of individual workers, such as machine hacklers and aerated water bottlers. As a result, many of the special regulations expressly imposed duties on workers as well as employers.

The formal mechanism for enforcing the factory acts was a criminal prosecution in the magistrates' courts. Although regarded by many commentators as 'the Achilles heel' of the system of regulation, these summary proceedings may well have had a significant impact in some areas of industrial practice. While it is true that the level of fines imposed by the magistrates' courts was even lower in Ireland than elsewhere in the United Kingdom, it was the prospect of conviction which seems to have weighed more heavily, at least with those defendants known to have made strenuous efforts to secure an acquittal. The inspectors, too, attached considerable store to a successful outcome to court proceedings, not least in terms of the resulting publicity, and they were prepared in cases regarded as particularly important to go to great lengths to secure a conviction. In this regard these home office officials were generally – but not invariably – supported by the Irish administration.

But in the end the 'enforcement' of the factory acts turned upon the quality and motivation of the inspectors and their preference for proceeding by way of advice, guidance and persuasion: 'What could not be gained by adjudication had to be secured by informal discussion, guidance, compromise, publicity, exhortation, bluff and co-operation.'[5] It is here that the work of the inspectors is least visible, although much evidence is available from their reports and from their contributions to official inquiries and their part in the shaping of new statutory provisions and secondary regulations. It is our view that Ireland was in general well served by the inspectors who were from time to time given responsibility for administering the acts in this country. No doubt some were better than others; but a significant number went on to the higher echelons of the inspectorate. It is clear that they had not a few failures and disappointments with respect to a number of problems which they sought to resolve. But they also had some notable successes, and we believe that, taken in general, the factory acts and the inspectors who administered them in Ireland *did* make a positive contribution to the improvement of working conditions in Irish industry during the eighty or so years culminating in the outbreak of the first world war. In so doing, they also set a commendably high standard for those who continued their work, north and south, during the later years of the twentieth century.

5   H.W. Arthurs, *'Without the law': Administrative justice and legal pluralism in nineteenth-century England* (Toronto, 1985), p. 112.

Biographical notes on the principal factory inspectors who served in Ireland 1833–1914

ABRAHAM, May
Born in Dublin in 1869, the daughter of George Abraham, registrar in lunacy. Moved to London in 1887 to work with Emilia Dilke and the Women's Trade Union League. In 1892 appointed an assistant commissioner for the Royal Commission on Labour. One of the first two lady inspectors appointed in 1893, she became superintending lady inspector in 1895, when she was also appointed to serve on the committee on dangerous trades. Resigned from the inspectorate in 1897 following marriage to H.J. Tennant MP, but remained active in women's labour matters, serving e.g. as chairman of the Industrial Law Committee, director of the women's division of the National Service Department during the first world war and as a member of the Central Committee on Women's Employment. Appointed C.H. in 1917. Died in 1946. Publication: *The law relating to factories and workshops (including laundries and docks* (London, 1896). See further V.R. Markham, *May Tennant, a portrait* (London, 1949).

ALLHUSEN, Ernest Lionel
Born 1875. B.Sc. Chemist and geologist. First appointed in April 1900. Served as junior inspector in North London (1900–1903), Leeds (1903–1904) and Newcastle-upon-Tyne (1904–1908). Transferred to Cork as inspector in 1908 and stayed there until 1922, when he moved to Edinburgh. Retired from inspectorate in 1935.

ANDERSON, Dame Adelaide Mary
Born 1863. M.A. Moral Sciences (Cantab.), 1887. Lecturer to Women's Co-operative Guild, 1889. Clerk and précis writer for the Royal Commission on Labour, 1892–1894. Appointed inspector in 1894, and served as Principal Lady Inspector from 1897–1921. Appointed DBE, 1921. Retired from inspectorate at time of amalgamation of men's and women's branches (which she opposed) in 1921. Engaged in study of labour conditions, with particular reference to China, and in 1931 served on an ILO mission regarding a factory inspectorate for China. Died 1936. Publications: *Women in the factory: An administrative adventure, 1893–1921* (London, 1922); *Humanity and labour in China* (1928).

BAKER, Dr. Robert
Born 1803. A surgeon in Leeds until appointed a sub-inspector in 1834. Promoted to inspector in 1858, when he took over responsibility for Ireland (as well as Wales and the west of England) from Howell. Remained in charge until 1878, when he

retired. Died in 1880. Publications: *The factory acts made easy, or How to work the law without the risk of penalties* (London, 1851, 1860 and 1868) and (less optimistically) *The Workshops Regulation Act 1867, made as easy as possible for the use of masters, workpeople and parents* (London, 1867). See further W.R. Lee, 'Robert Baker: The first doctor in the factory department' in *Br. J. Industrial Medicine*, 21 (1964), 85 and 167.

BELLHOUSE, Sir Gerald
Born 1867. Father in cotton spinning business in Manchester. BA (Cantab) 1888. Became cotton spinner (master). Appointed inspector in 1891. Moved to Ireland in 1895 as district inspector for South Ireland district. In 1905 returned to England (East London). Promoted to superintending inspector in 1908 for North Western Division (until 1912), then South Eastern Division (1912–1917). Appointed deputy chief inspector in 1917, and chief inspector in 1922. Member of numerous departmental committees. Knighted in 1924. Retired in 1932, and died in 1946.

CAMERON, Henry James
Born 1844. Private secretary to Lieutenant Governor of Honduras before appointment as junior inspector in 1872. Served in East London (for only a couple of months) and Bolton (1872–1874). Came to Ireland in March 1874 as district inspector for the North Ireland district. Stayed until 1890, when he returned to East London. Transferred to Central Metropolitan district in 1895. Remained in London until he retired in 1898.

COOKE-TAYLOR, Richard Whately
Born 1842. Educated Kilkenny College and TCD. In 1859 entered office of paymaster of civil service in Dublin Castle. In 1861 moved to paymaster-general's office in London. First appointed factory inspector in 1869, and served as a junior inspector, based in Cork, from 1869 to 1874. Transferred to Preston, and later moved to Coventry. Promoted to superintending inspector for the Scotland/Ireland Division in 1895. Appointed senior superintending inspector in 1902 and transferred to the Southern Division, based in London, until retirement in 1905. Died 1918. Publications: *Introduction to a history of the factory system* (London, 1886); *The modern factory system* (1891); *The factory system and the factory acts* (London, 1894 and 1912). Contributor to many journals – and also wrote several plays.

CRAMP, Sir William Dawkins
Born 1840. Assistant Master at Guilsborough Grammar School, 1860, then clerk in Examiner's Office, Customs House, London, 1861–1868. Appointed inspector in 1868, and served in North Ireland district from 1869 to 1875, when he returned to England. Inspector in various districts in England (Mid-Lancashire, North Staffs. and South Midlands) until 1891, when promoted to superintending inspector for the Birmingham division. Transferred to London in 1899 as superintending inspector for the Southern Division, and acted as deputy chief inspector from 1902 until 1907, when he retired. Knighted in 1908. Died 1927.

DARKIN, William Straker
Born 1810. First appointed in 1855 and sent to the north of Ireland, where he served until 1867. Transferred to Wolverhampton, but almost immediately resigned on grounds of ill-health.

DEANE, Lucy Anne Evelyn
Sanitary inspector in London, lecturer in public health and member of the Women's Trade Union League. First appointed inspector in April 1894 with peripatetic duties which brought her to Ireland on a number of occasions, principally before 1901. Given special responsibilities for West London district in 1900–1905, when she returned to peripatetic duties. Seconded to South Africa during the Boer War as a member of the War Office Commission of Enquiry into concentration camps. Promoted a senior lady inspector in 1903 and served until 1908 when she resigned on health grounds. Married Granville Streatfield in 1911, but continued to maintain an active interest in women's work. Appointed CBE in 1918 and became one of the first women magistrates. Died 1950.

ERAUT, Sydney
Engineer (Whitworth Exhibitioner). First appointed in 1895. Served in London, Liverpool, Bristol, Norwich, Newcastle-upon-Tyne and Preston before coming to Ireland in 1908 as district inspector for the North Ireland district. Remained in Belfast until 1922, when appointed 'chief inspector' in the Ministry of Labour for Northern Ireland, and served in that capacity until retirement in 1927.

HORNER, Leonard
Born 1785 (Edinburgh), the son of a linen merchant. Horner was a distinguished geologist and scientist, and a successful businessman, who had played a leading role in Whig politics in Edinburgh before his appointment (at the age of 48) as one of the first inspectors. From 1833 until 1836 he was responsible for the north of Ireland (together with Scotland and the north of England). Thereafter served as an inspector in the north of England until his death in 1859. Generally regarded as the most able and vigorous of the early inspectors. See especially B. Martin, 'Leonard Horner: A portrait of an inspector of factories' in *Int'l Rev of Social History*, xiv, (1969) 412 and P. Wusteman, 'Leonard Horner' in *HM inspectors of factories 1833–1983: Essays to commemorate 150 years of health and safety inspection* (London, 1983), pp. 9–13. See also K.M. Lyell, *Memoir of Leonard Horner* (London, 1890).

HOWELL, Thomas Jones
Formerly Judge Advocate of Gibraltar and Commissioner for West Indian Islands relief, Howell is something of a nonentity who has attracted none of the attention paid to Horner. Responsible for Division B (which included the south of Ireland) from 1833–1837, when replaced by Stuart. From 1837 until 1849, he was in charge of Wales and the west of England. On Stuart's death in 1849, he also became responsible for the whole of Ireland, and remained in charge of this Division until his death in 1858.

HUDSON, John Percival
First appointed in March 1837, and served for a few months under Horner in the north of England. Appointed sub-inspector for Ireland under Stuart in August 1837, and served mainly in Ireland (and occasionally in Scotland) until his death in 1855.

JACKSON, Sir John
Born 1865 (Manchester). Cotton doubler (master). First appointed an inspector in 1892. Served in Walsall and South Staffordshire as junior inspector before appointment as inspector for South Ireland district in 1905. Stayed there until 1908 when

transferred to Liverpool. In 1912 appointed superintending inspector for the North Western Division, and later became deputy chief inspector until retirement in 1930. Knighted in 1929. Died in 1933.

McCAGHEY, William John

Confidential clerk in linen factory before appointment as junior inspector at Bradford in July 1903. Transferred to Ireland in 1906, and based in Belfast until 1912, when he moved to Manchester. In 1922 he returned to serve as a district inspector in Northern Ireland, and in 1927 succeeded Eraut as 'chief inspector'. Retired in 1931.

MARTINDALE, Hilda

Born 1875. Educated at Royal Holloway College and Bedford College for Women, where she studied hygiene and sanitary science. Travelled extensively enquiring into methods for dealing with children in State care. Appointed inspector in 1901, she was based in London until appointed one of the first 'resident' lady inspectors, for the Potteries, in 1904. In 1905 transferred as 'resident' lady inspector for the whole of Ireland, based in Belfast (though still spending one-third of her time in Staffordshire). In 1907 given full-time appointment in Ireland, still based in Belfast. Promoted a senior lady inspector in 1908, and remained in Ireland until 1912, when she returned to England as senior lady inspector for the Midlands and later for the South Eastern Division. Following amalgamation of the two branches of the inspectorate in 1921, she became superintending inspector for the Southern Division. Returned to Northern Ireland briefly in 1924 to report to the Minister of Labour on factory conditions for women workers. Served as deputy chief inspector 1925–1933 with responsibilities for the whole of England and Scotland. Left the inspectorate in 1933 to become director of Women Establishments at the Treasury. Retired in 1937, and died in 1952. Publications: *Women servants of the state, 1870–1938: A history of women in the civil service* (London, 1938); *From one generation to another, 1839–1944* (London, 1944); *Some Victorian portraits and others* (London, 1948).

MAY, Eliot Francis

Worsted spinner (apprentice). First appointed inspector in 1895, and served as junior inspector in Birmingham, Stafford and North Staffordshire. In 1900 moved to Bristol as inspector, and then to Worcester. In 1908 transferred to Dublin as inspector for the South Ireland district and served in this capacity until 1918. He then spent four years in Scotland before being appointed superintending inspector for the Liverpool, and later the Manchester, districts. Retired in 1935.

MONSELL, William Thomas

First appointed 1872, and served as junior inspector in Leeds District until 1874. Transferred to South West Ireland district in 1874 and served as district inspector, based in Limerick, until February 1880, when he resigned from the inspectorate.

NEELY, William John

BA from Trinity College Dublin in 1895. First appointed inspector in Oct 1896, and sent as junior inspector to Dublin. Stayed in Dublin until August 1900, when transferred to Leeds. Returned to Dublin in 1903 and stayed until 1908, when transferred to Inverness. Remained there until 1915, when transferred to London. In 1918 returned to Dublin as district inspector for the South Ireland district. Died in post shortly after transfer to Monmouthshire in 1922.

PATERSON, Mary Muirhead
Born in Glasgow c. 1862. Studied at Queen Margaret College, and travelled to North America with her uncle, a member of the independent labour party. On her return became active in social work with working women and girls. Appointed (with Abraham) as one of the first lady inspectors in 1893, assigned to Scotland but made frequent visits to Ireland. Promoted to a senior lady inspector in 1903. In 1908 transferred to London and promoted to deputy principal lady inspector, and senior inspector in charge of the South Eastern and South Western divisions. Resigned from inspectorate in 1911 to accept appointment as National Health Insurance Commissioner for Scotland 1912–1919. Died 1941.

SNAPE, Gerald Birch
Cotton weaver (employer). Appointed junior inspector in 1883, and served in the north of England until 1887, when attached to the Home Office in London. Came to Ireland in 1890 as district inspector for the North Ireland district, and stayed until 1905. Served as inspector in Bristol until 1908, when transferred to West London. Retired from inspectorate in 1909.

SQUIRE, Rose Elizabeth
Born 1861, daughter of Harley St. doctor. Public health inspector before her appointment as a factory inspector in 1896. While a peripatetic inspector, spent a considerable part of her time in Ireland, until promoted to senior lady inspector in 1903. In 1906–1907 seconded to the Royal Commission on the Poor Law as a special investigator. In 1908 moved to Manchester as resident senior lady inspector for the Northern Division. Appointed Deputy Principal Lady Inspector, based in London, in 1912. Served on Health of Munitions Workers Committee, 1915–1918 and acted as Director of Women's Welfare in the Ministry of Munitions and later in the Ministry of Labour in 1918–1919. Returned to factory inspectorate in 1920, but the following year transferred to the Home Office as a principal officer in the industrial division. Retired in 1926. Died 1938. Publication: *Thirty years in the public service: An industrial retrospect* (London, 1927).

STUART, James
The son of a Church of Scotland minister, Stuart qualified as a writer to the signet, but never practised law. His chequered career included management of the family estates and involvement in Scottish politics as a Whig. He went bankrupt in 1825 and left the country. Returning to England in 1831, he became editor of *The Courier*, a London evening paper. Through his friend Lord Brougham, Stuart was appointed an assistant commissioner for Scotland and Ireland to make inquiries on behalf of the factory commissioners in 1833. In 1836, he was appointed a factory inspector at the age of 61. Took over north of Ireland (and Scotland) from Horner in 1836, and became inspector responsible for whole of Ireland (and Scotland) in 1837. Served in that capacity until his death in 1849. See further U. Henriques, 'An early factory inspector: James Stuart of Dunearn' in *Sc. Hist. Rev.*, 50 (1971), 18.

WILLIAMS, William
Home Office clerk. Appointed inspector in March 1892. Became inspector for cotton cloth factories in 1894 and served in this capacity until 1906. Transferred to the North Ireland district in 1906 and stayed there until moved to East London in 1908. Promoted to superintending inspector for the Northern Division in 1912.

WOODGATE, Arthur George Kennedy
Foreign Office clerk. First appointed May 1872. Started in South West Scotland (1872–74), then in Huddersfield (1874–75). Came to Ireland in July 1875 as district inspector for the Central District. Remained in Ireland until 1895, when transferred to Northampton. In 1900 went to South London, where he stayed until he retired in 1908.

Bibliography

MANUSCRIPT SOURCES

Public Record Office (Kew)
Home Office
HO 45   Registered papers, 1839–[1914]
HO 87   Factory and mines entry books, 1873–1914
HO 152   Domestic and industrial entry books, 1899–1921

Ministry of Labour
LAB 14   Safety, health and welfare registered files, 1878–[1914]
LAB 15   Factory department and inspectorate: registered files and other records,
         1836–[1914]
Treasury
T1   Treasury papers, [1830]–1920

Public Record Office of Northern Ireland
D   Private business and commercial papers

National Archives of Ireland
Chief Secretary's Office
CSOLB   Letter books,
CSORP   Registered papers.

PARLIAMENTARY PAPERS AND REPORTS

1. Factory inspectors reports
*Note: The reports to the Home Secretary which the factory inspectors were required to make under
section 45 of the 1833 act were at first published at somewhat irregular intervals. From 1837 until
1844 the reports were made on a regular quarterly basis, but published only every six months. In 1845
the reports became half–yearly, and were published on this basis until 1877. Thereafter (as required by
section 67 of the 1878 act and section 118(7) of the 1901 act) the report of the chief inspector was
published annually, at first for the year ending 31 October and then for each calendar year.*

Reports of the factory inspectors for the period to –

July 1834	H.C. 1834 (596), xliii, 423	*July 1835*	H.C. 1835 (342), xl, 689
Aug. 1835	H.C. 1836 (78), xlv, 155	*Feb. 1836*	H.C. 1836 (78), xlv, 163
Dec. 1836	H.C. 1837 (73), xxxi, 53		

Reports of the factory inspectors for the quarter ending

31 Mar. 1837	[119], H.C. 1837–38, xxviii, 81	30 June 1837	[119], H.C. 1837–38, xxviii, 94
30 Sept. 1837	[119], H.C. 1837–38, xxviii, 105	31 Dec. 1837	[119], H.C. 1837–38, xxviii,116
31 Mar. 1838	[131], H.C. 1837–38, xxviii, 133	30 June 1838	[612], H.C. 1837–38, xlv, 55
30 Sept. 1838	[159], H.C. 1839, xix, 433	31 Dec. 1838	[159], H.C. 1839, xix, 447
31 Mar. 1839	[201], H.C. 1839, xix, 539	30 June 1839	[201], H.C. 1839, xix, 550
30 Sept. 1839	[218], H.C. 1840, xxiii, 1	31 Dec. 1839	[218], H.C. 1840, xxiii, 9
31 Mar. 1840	[261], H.C. 1840, xxiii, 27	30 June 1840	[261], H.C. 1840, xxiii, 37
30 Sept. 1840	[294], H.C. 1841, x, 161	31 Dec. 1840	[294], H.C. 1841, x, 174
31 Mar. 1841	[342 – sess. 2], H.C. 1841, vi, 213	30 June 1841	[342 – sess. 2], H.C. 1841, vi, 224

30 Sept. 1841	[31], H.C. 1842, xxii, 337	31 Dec. 1841	[31], H.C. 1842, xxii, 353
31 Mar. 1842	[410], H.C. 1842, xxii, 441	30 June 1842	[410], H.C. 1842, xxii, 466
30 Sept. 1842	[429], H.C. 1843, xxvii, 289	31 Dec. 1842	[429], H.C. 1843, xxvii, 306
31 Mar. 1843	[523], H.C. 1843, xxvii, 335	30 June 1843	[523], H.C. 1843, xxvii, 346
30 Sept. 1843	[524], H.C. 1844, xxviii, 533	31 Dec. 1843	[524], H.C. 1844, xxviii, 544
31 Mar. 1844	[583], H.C. 1844, xxviii, 565	30 June 1844	[583], H.C. 1844, xxviii, 575
30 Sept. 1844	[639], H.C. 1845, xxv, 431		

Reports of the factory inspectors for the half-year ending –

30 April 1845	[639], H.C. 1845, xxv, 443	31 Oct. 1845	[681], H.C. 1846, xx, 565
1846	[721], H.C. 1846, xx, 611	1846	[779], H.C. 1847, xv, 441
1847	[828], H.C. 1847, xv, 489	1847	[900], H.C. 1847–48, xxvi, 105
1848	[957], H.C. 1847–48, xxvi, 149	1848	[1017], H.C. 1849, xxii, 131
1849	[1084], H.C. 1849, xxii, 283	1849	[1141], H.C. 1850, xxiii, 181
1850	[1239], H.C. 1850, xxiii, 261	1850	[1304], H.C. 1851, xxiii, 217
1851	[1396], H.C. 1851, xxiii, 293	1851	[1439], H.C. 1852, xxi, 353
1852	[1500], H.C. 1852, xxi, 377	1852	[1580], H.C.1852–53, xl, 461
1853	[1642], H.C.1852–53, xl, 533	1853	[1712], H.C. 1854, xix, 257
1854	[1796], H.C. 1854, xix, 373	1854	[1881], H.C. 1854–55, xv, 275
1855	[1947], H.C.1854–55, xv, 367	1855	[2031], H.C. 1856, xviii, 211
1856	[2090], H.C. 1856, xviii, 335	1856	[2153, sess. 1], H.C.1857, iii, 559
1857	[2247, sess. 2], H.C. 1857, xvi, 201	1857	[2314], H.C. 1857–58, xxiv, 661
1858	[2391], H.C.1857–58, xxiv, 721	1858	[2463, sess. 1], H.C. 1859, xii, 149
1859	[2538, sess. 2], H.C. 1859, xiv, 403	1859	[2594], H.C. 1860, xxxiv, 407
1860	[2689], H.C. 1860, xxxiv, 471	1860	[2765], H.C. 1861, xxii, 353
1861	[2854], H.C. 1861, xxii, 409	1861	[2923], H.C. 1862, xxii, 221
1862	[3029], H.C. 1862, xxii, 269	1862	[3076], H.C. 1863, xviii, 437
1863	[3206], H.C. 1863, xviii, 587	1863	[3309], H.C. 1864, xxii, 555
1864	[3390], H.C. 1864, xxii, 721	1864	[3473], H.C. 1865, xx, 429
1865	[3557], H.C. 1865, xx, 573	1865	[3622], H.C. 1866, xxiv, 251
1866	[3751], H.C. 1866, xxiv, 403	1866	[3794], H.C. 1867, xvi, 327
1867	[3914], H.C. 1867, xvi, 475	1867	[4010], H.C. 1867–68, xviii, 143
1868	[4093], H.C. 1868–69, xiv, 75	1868	[4093–I], H.C. 1869, xiv, 123
1869	[4093–II], H.C. 1869, xiv, 465	1869	[C. 77], H.C. 1870, xv, 75
1870	[C. 215], H.C. 1870, xv, 363	1870	[C. 348], H.C. 1871, xiv, 525
1871	[C. 446], H.C. 1871, xiv, 625	1871	[C. 543], H.C. 1872, xvi, 87
1872	[C. 602], H.C. 1872, xvi, 37	1872	[C. 745], H.C. 1873, xix, 41
1873	[C. 849], H.C. 1873, xix, 223	1873	[C. 937], H.C. 1874, xiii, 1
1874	[C. 1086], H.C. 1874, xiii, 189	1874	[C. 1184], H.C. 1875, xvi, 63
1875	[C. 1345], H.C. 1875, xvi, 251	1875	[C. 1434], H.C. 1876, xvi, 17
1876	[C. 1572], H.C. 1876, xvi, 237	1876	[C. 1693], H. C. 1877, xxiii, 1
1877	[C. 1794], H.C. 1877, xxiii, 181	1877	[C. 2001], H.C. 1878, xx, 1

Report of the chief inspector of factories for the year ending 31st October –

1878	[C. 2274], H.C. 1878–79, xvi, 439	1879	[C. 2489], H.C. 1880, xiv, 93
1880	[C. 2825], H.C. 1881, xxiii, 101	1881	[C. 3183], H.C. 1882, xviii, 1
1882	[C. 3488], H.C. 1883, xviii, 269	1883	[C. 3945], H.C. 1884, xviii, 181
1884	[C. 4369], H.C. 1884–85, xv, 93	1885	[C. 4702], H.C. 1886, xiv, 797
1886	[C. 5002], H.C. 1887, xvii, 539	1887	[C. 5328], H.C. 1888, xxvi, 395
1888	[C. 5697], H.C. 1889, xviii, 359	1889	[C. 6060], H.C. 1890, xx, 579
1890	[C. 6630], H.C. 1890–91, xix, 443	1891	[C. 6720], H.C. 1892, xx, 463
1892	[C. 6978], H.C. 1893–94, xvii, 65		

Report of the chief inspector of factories for the year ending 31st December –

1893 [C. 7368], H.C. 1894, xxi, 1	1894 [C. 7745], H.C. 1895, xix, 1
1895 [C. 8067, 8068], H.C. 1896, xix, 89	1896 [C. 8561], H.C. 1897, xvii, 215
1897 [C. 8965], H.C. 1898, xiv, 1	
1898 (Pt. 1) [C. 9281], H.C. 1899, xii, 1	1898 (Pt. 1I) [Cd. 27], H.C. 1900, xi, 1
1899 [Cd. 223], H.C. 1900, xi, 249	1900 [Cd. 668], H.C.1901, x, 1
1901 (Pt. 1) [Cd. 1112], H.C. 1902, xii, 45	1901 (Pt. II) [Cd. 1300], H.C. 1902, xii, 391
1902 (Pt. 1) [Cd. 1610], H.C. 1903, xii, 1	1902 (Pt. I1) [Cd. 1816], H.C. 1904, x, 1
1903 (Pt. 1) [Cd. 2139], H.C. 1904, x, 119	1903 (Pt. II) [Cd. 2324], H.C. 1904, x, 665
1904 (Pt. 1) [Cd. 2569], H.C. 1905, x, 291	1904 (Pt. II) [Cd. 2848], H.C. 1906, xv, 873
1905 [Cd. 3036], H.C. 1906, xv, 405	1906 [Cd. 3586], H.C. 1907, x, 1
1907 [Cd. 4166], H.C. 1908, xii, 367	1908 [Cd. 4664], H.C. 1909, xxi, 343
1909 [Cd. 5191], H.C. 1910, xxviii, 589	1910 [Cd. 5693], H.C. 1911, xxii, 407
1911 [Cd. 6239], H.C. 1912–13, xxv, 565	1912 [Cd. 6852], H.C. 1913, xxiii, 283
1913 [Cd. 7491], H.C. 1914, xxix, 541	1914 [Cd. 8051], H.C. 1914–16, xxi, 399

2. General reports and papers

Report from the committee appointed to inquire into the state of the laws which regulate the manufacture and sale of bread, H.C. 1814–15 (186), v, 1341

Minutes of evidence taken before the select committee on the state of the children employed in the manufactories of the United Kingdom, H.C. 1816 (397), iii, 235

Minutes of evidence taken before the lords committee appointed to inquire into the state and condition of children employed in cotton factories, H.L. 1819 (24), cx, 1

Report from the select committee to whom the bill to regulate the labour of children in mills and factories of the United Kingdom was referred, H.C. 1831–32 (706), xv, 1

Central board of His Majesty's commissioners appointed to collect information in the manufacturing districts, as to the employment of children in factories, and as to the propriety and means of curtailing the hours of their labour, with minutes of evidence and reports of district commissioners:

    First report, H.C. 1833 (450), xx, 1

    Second report, H.C. 1833 (519), xxi, 1

    Supplementary reports, H.C. 1834 (167), xix, 253 and xx, 1

Return of the number of persons employed in the cotton, woollen, worsted, flax and silk mills and factories of the United Kingdom, distinguishing ages, H.C. 1836 (138), xlv, 51

Names of persons fined under the Factory Act, etc., H.C. 1836 (77), xlv, 171

Number of children employed under 14 years, etc., H.C. 1836 (254), xlv, 203

Return of the number of mills and factories in each district, visited by the inspectors ... between 1st August 1836 and 1st February 1837, H.C. 1837 (122), L, 199

Directions to factory inspectors relative to the regulation of factories, H.C. 1837 [74], xxxi, 123

Rules and regulations issued by the factory inspectors since May 1836, etc., H.C. 1837 (67), l, 35

Number and names of persons summoned for offences against the factory act, etc.,

H.C. 1836 (278), xlv, 193	H.C. 1837 (97), L, 107
H.C. 1837–38 (120), xlv, 87	H.C. 1839 (43), xlii, 429
H.C. 1840 (171), xxxviii, 577	H.C. 1841 (99), xviii, 657
H.C. 1842 (40) xxxii, 547	H.C. 1843 (66), xlii, 283
H.C. 1844 (106), xxxix, 275	H.C. 1845 (121), xxxvii, 267
H.C. 1846 (87), xxxiv, 501	H.C. 1847 (106), xlvi, 559

Return of mills and factories, specifying ... the numbers of persons employed in cotton, woollen, worsted, flax and silk factories of the United Kingdom, etc. H.C. 1839 (41), xlii, 1

Numbers of factories within the district of each inspector, the number of mills visited, etc., H.C. 1839 (135), xlii, 499

Return of the number of days in 1838–1839, during which the different inspectors of factories have been in their various districts, H.C. 1839 (390), xlii, 509

Number of penalties, sums that were inflicted, from the lowest sum to the highest, with which any offence was punished, H.C. 1840 (227), x. 284

Select committee appointed to inquire into the operation of the act for the regulation of mills and factories:

> First report: Minutes of evidence, H.C. 1840 (203), x, 1
> Second report: Minutes of evidence, H.C. 1840 (227), x, 161
> Third report: Minutes of evidence: H.C. 1840 (314), x, 295
> Fourth report: Minutes of evidence, H.C. 1840 (334), x, 363
> Fifth report: Minutes of evidence, H.C. 1840 (419), x, 505
> Sixth report: H.C. 1840 (504), x, 687

Report from the select committee appointed to inquire into the operation of the act for the regulation of mills and factories, H.C. 1841 (56), ix, 557

Special reports of inspectors of factories on the practicability of legislative interference to diminish the frequency of accidents to children and young persons employed in factories, arising from machinery being cleaned when in motion, and from being left unguarded: H.C. 1841 (311), x, 199

Commissioners for inquiring into the employment and condition of children in mines and manufactories:

> First report: Mines [380], H.C. 1842, xv, 1
> Second report: Trades and manufactures [430], H.C. 1843, xiii, 307
> Appendix to second report, with reports and evidence from sub-commissioners [431], H.C. 1843, xiv, 1; [432], H.C. 1843, xv, 1

Number of days ... during which the inspectors of factories have been engaged in the discharge of their duties, etc., H.C. 1844 (77), xxxix, 267

Return of the total numbers of persons employed in cotton, woollen, worsted, flax and silk factories respectively, in the United Kingdom, etc., H.C. 1847 (294), xlvi, 609

Return of the number of cotton, woollen, worsted, flax and silk factories subject to the Factories Acts in each county, etc., H.C. 1850 (745), xlii, 455

Sixth annual report of the commissioners for administering the laws for the relief of the poor in Ireland [1645], H.C. 1852–53, L, 159

Numbers reported by the inspectors to have been killed or injured in the factory districts from 30th April 1845 to 30th May 1854, etc., H.C. 1854 (409), lxv, 497

Report of the commissioner appointed to enquire into the expediency of extending the acts for the better regulation of mills and factories to bleaching works ..., with minutes of evidence and appendix [1943], H.C. 1854–55, xviii, 1

Instructions issued by the inspectors of factories to the sub-inspectors, with regard to the fencing of mill-gearing or machinery, H.C. 1856 (121), l, 149

Returns of the number of cotton, woollen, worsted, flax and silk factories subject to the factories acts in each county ...,

> H.C. 1857 (7 – sess. 1), xiv, 173
> H.C. 1862 (23), lv, 629
> H.C. 1867–68 (453), lxiv, 811

Report of the select committee appointed to inquire into the circumstances connected with the employment of women and children in the bleaching and dyeing establishments in England, Scotland and Ireland, and to consider how far it may be necessary or expedient to extend to these establishments provisions regulating such employment:

> First report, with minutes of evidence, H.C. 1857 (151 – Sess. 2), xi, 1
> Second report, with the proceedings, minutes of evidence, appendix and index, H.C. 1857 (211 – sess. 2), xi, 259

Report from the select committee on bleaching and dyeing works, with the proceedings and minutes of evidence, H.C. 1857–58 (270), xi, 685

Report to the home secretary upon the expediency of subjecting the lace manufacture to the regulation of the Factory Acts, [2797], H.C. 1861, xxii, 461

Annual report of the medical officer of the committee of council on the state of the public health:

> First report, [2512 – sess. 1], H.C. 1859, xii, 257
> Second report, [2736], H.C. 1860, xxix, 201
> Third report, H.C. 1861 (161), xvi, 339
> Fourth report, H.C. 1862 (179), xxii, 465
> Fifth report, H.C. 1863 (163), xxv, 1

Report to the home secretary relative to the grievances complained of by the journeymen bakers:
    First report, with appendix of evidence [3027], H.C. 1862, xlvii, 1
    Second report [3091], H.C. 1863, xxviii, 323
Reports of the commissioners on the employment of children and young persons in trades and manufactures not already regulated by law:
    First report: Pottery, lucifer matches, etc. [3170], H.C. 1863, xviii, 1
    Second report: Lace, hosiery, wearing apparel, etc. [3414], H.C. 1864, xxii, 1
    Third report: Metal manufactures [3414–I], H.C. 1864, xxix, 319
    Fourth report: Metal and other trades, tobacco, etc. [3548], H.C. 1865, xx, 103
    Fifth report: Printing, bookbinding, warehouses, scutch mills, etc. [3678], H.C. 1866, xxiv, 1
    Sixth report: Agriculture gangs, [3796], H.C. 1867, xvi, 67
Return of the name, salaries, etc. of the inspectors and sub-inspectors of factories, etc., H.C. 1864 (318), lviii, 147
Reports made to the secretary of state by Mr Tremenheere on the operation of the Bakehouses Regulation Act, H.C. 1866 (394), lxvi, 373
Report by Mr Tremenheere and Mr Tufnell on the Print Works Act, and on the Bleaching and Dyeing Works Act, with appendix [4149], H.C. 1868–69, xiv, 777
Select committee appointed to inquire into the cause of steam boiler explosions, and as to the best means of preventing them, etc:
    First report, H.C. 1870 (370), x, 459
    Second report, H.C. 1871 (298), xii, 267
Return of the number of manufacturing establishments in which the hours of work are regulated by act of parliament in each county of the United Kingdom, etc., H.C. 1871 (440), lxii, 105
Commissioners appointed by the Truck Commission Act 1870 for the purpose of inquiring into the operation of the [Truck Act 1831] and upon the operation of all other acts or provisions of acts prohibiting the truck system:
    Report, schedules and supplement [C. 326], H.C. 1871, xxxvi, 1
    Minutes of evidence [C. 327], H.C. 1871, xxxvi, 281
Return of all fatal and other accidents reported in the reports of the inspectors of factories ... for 1869–1870, H.C. 1873 (355), lxi, 39
Report to the local government board on proposed changes in hours and ages of employment in textile factories by J.H. Bridges, MD and T Holmes [C. 754], H.C. 1873, lv, 803
Report from the select committee appointed to inquire whether it may be expedient to render masters liable for injuries occasioned to their servants by the negligent acts of certificated managers ... to whom the control of workshops, etc, is committed, H.C. 1876 (372), ix, 609
Report of the commissioners appointed to inquire into the working of the factory and workshop acts with a view to their consolidation and amendment:
    I: Report, appendix and index [C. 1443], H.C. 1876, xxix, 1
    II: Minutes of evidence [C. 1443–I], H.C. 1876, xxx, 1
Return of all fatal accidents from boiler explosions in the United Kingdom in the years 1875 and 1876, etc., H.C. 1877 (361), lxviii, 373
Report from the select committee appointed to inquire whether it may be expedient to render masters liable for injuries occasioned to their servants, etc., H.C. 1877 (285), x, 551
Return of the number of factories authorized to be inspected under the factory and workshop acts, with number of persons employed in each industry, etc., H.C. 1878–79 (324), lxv, 201
Return of the names, ages and previous occupations or professions of the inspectors ... appointed since 1 Jan. 1867, H.C. 1880 (371), xl, 335
Report to the secretary of the board of trade upon the working of the Boiler Explosions Act 1882, etc. (published annually):
    1881–82, [C. 3903], H.C. 1884, xvii, 319
    1888–89, [C. 5855], H.C. 1889, xviii, 119
    1900–01, [Cd. 733], H.C. 1901, ix, 567
    1903–04, [Cd. 2513], H.C. 1905, ix, 891
    1909–10, [Cd. 5730], H.C. 1911, xxii, 139
    1913–1914, [Cd. 7797], H.C. 1914–16, xxi, 113
Report from the select committee on industries (Ireland), with the proceedings, evidence, appendix and index, H.C. 1884–85 (288), ix. 1

Return of the total number of cases tried in the county courts under the Employers' Liability Act 1880, etc.
　　H.C. 1884 (151), lxiii, 139
　　H.C. 1884–85 (320), lxiv, 195
　　H.C. 1886 (226 – sess. 1), liii, 99
　　H.C. 1888 (290), lxxxii, 147
Return showing the names, dates of appointment, and present salaries of Her Majesty's inspectors of factories, etc., H.C. 1887 (305), lxvi, 459
Memoranda ... on the registry and inspection of land boilers prepared for the consideration of the right honourable the president of the Board of Trade [C. 5375], H.C. 1888, lxxx, 519
Fifth report from the select committee of the house of lords on the sweating system in the United Kingdom, H.L. 1890 (169), xvii, 257
Return of the number of accidents to men, women, young persons and children by shuttles flying from power looms, which have occurred in the cotton, woollen, worsted, flax and silk trades in ... 1879, 1885 and 1890, H.C. 1890–91 (197), lxxvii, 343
Reports made ... by E.H. Osborn, esq., one of H.M. inspectors of factories, upon the conditions of work, etc. in flax mills and linen factories in the United Kingdom [C. 7287], H.C. 1893–94, xvii, 537
Royal commission on labour:
　　Fifth and final report [Cd. 7421], H.C. 1894, xxxv, 9
　　Secretary's report on the work of the office, and summaries of evidence, with index thereto [Cd. 7421–I], H.C. 1894, xxxv, 263
　　Report by Miss Eliza Orme and Miss May Abraham on the conditions of work in various industries in ... Ireland [C. 6894–XXIII], H.C. 1893–94, xxxvii (pt. 1), 545
　　Evidence taken before Group C, vol. ii [C. 6795–VI], H.C. 1892, xxxvi (pt. 2), 441
Report on the wages of the manual labour class in the United Kingdom, with tables of the average rate of wages and hours of labour of persons employed in several of the principal trades in 1886 and 1891 [C. 6889], H.C. 1893–4, lxxxiii (pt. II), 1
Report of H.M. inspectors of factories as to hours of work, dangerous machinery and sanitary conditions in laundries, [C. 7418], H.C.1894, xxi, 709
Departmental committee appointed to inquire into and report upon certain miscellaneous dangerous trades:
　　First report [C. 8149], H.C. 1896, xxxiii, 1
　　Second report [C. 8522], H.C. 1897, xvii, 45
　　Third report [C. 9073], H.C. 1899, xii, 143
　　Fourth report [C. 9420], H.C. 1899, xii, 197
　　Final report [C. 9509], H.C. 1899, xii, 231
Report of the departmental committee on factory statistics [C. 7608], H.C. 1895, xix, 583
Report of a committee appointed to inquire into the working of the Cotton Cloth Factories Act 1889 [C. 8348 and 8349], H.C. 1897, xvii, 61,
Report to the secretary of state for the home department by two of HM inspectors of factories appointed to enquire into the conditions of work of the fish-curing trade of the United Kingdom [C. 8753], H.C. 1898, xiv, 385
Reports on the use of phosphorus in the manufacture of lucifer matches [C. 9188], H.C. 1899, xii, 437
Report from the select committee appointed to inquire into and report on the advisability of legislation to insure the systematic and regular inspection of boilers, with the object of diminishing the risk to life and property arising from boiler explosions, H.C. 1900 (294), vi, 285.
Report from the select committee to whom the steam engines and boilers (persons in charge) bill was referred, H.C. 1901 (278), viii, 1
First report of the departmental committee appointed to inquire into the ventilation of factories and workshops, with appendices [Cd. 1302], H.C. 1902, xii, 467
Report upon the conditions of work in flax and linen mills as affecting the health of operatives employed therein [Cd. 1997], H.C. 1904, x, 465
Report to His Majesty's secretary of state for the home department on the draft regulations relating to docks, wharves and quays [Cd. 2284], H.C. 1904, lxxii, 515

Report of the departmental committee appointed by the home secretary to inquire into the law relating to compensation for injuries to workmen [Cd. 2208], H.C. 1904, lxxxviii, 743

Report of the inter-departmental committee on physical deterioration [Cd. 2175], H.C. 1904, xxxii, 1

Statistics of proceedings in England and Wales, in Scotland, and in Ireland, under the Workmen's Compensation Act and the Employers' Liability Act (published annually from 1898):
      1898, [C. 9251], H.C. 1899, lxxix, 383
      1903, [Cd. 2269], H.C. 1905, lxxv, 445
      1908, [Cd. 4894], H.C. 1909, lxxx, 949
      1909, [Cd. 5386], H.C. 1910, lxxii, 958
      1910, [Cd. 5896], H.C. 1911, lxxv, 743
      1911, [Cd. 6493], H.C. 1912–13, lxxv, 777
      1913, [Cd. 7669], H.C. 1914–16, lxi, 991

List of religious and charitable institutions in which laundries are carried on:
      [Cd. 2500], H.C. 1905, lxxii, 501,
      [Cd. 2741], H.C. 1906, xcviii, 85

Report to His Majesty's secretary of state for the home department on the draft regulations ... for the processes of spinning and weaving flax and tow, and the processes incidental thereto, by G.A. Bonner, barrister-at-law [Cd. 2851], H.C. 1906, xv, 943

Illustrations of methods of dust extraction in factories and workshops compiled by Commander Sir Hamilton P. Freer-Smith RN [Cd. 3223], H.C. 1906, cx, 125.

Memorandum on the international conference on labour regulations held at Berne, September 1906 [Cd. 3271], H.C. 1906, cxxi, 279

Second report of the departmental committee appointed to enquire into the ventilation of factories and workshops [Cd. 3552], H.C. 1907, x, 449

Report of the departmental committee on compensation for industrial diseases [Cd. 3495], H.C. 1907, xxxiv, 1045

Return of the names and previous occupations or professions of the inspectors, the inspectors' assistants and the lady inspectors, who are now serving, etc., H.C. 1907 (172), lxxvi, 319

Departmental committee appointed to consider whether the post office should provide facilities for insurance under the Workmen's Compensation Act: Minutes of evidence [Cd. 3568], H.C. 1907, lxviii, 163

Report of the departmental committee on the checking of piecework wages in dock labour [Cd. 4380], H.C. 1908, xxxiv, 467

Schemes for the regulation of hours of employment, etc. of workers in charitable institutions approved by the Secretary of State in pursuance of the powers conferred on him by section 5(2)(a) of the Factory and Workshops Act 1907, H.C. 1908 (341), xcvi, 1025

Departmental committee on the truck acts:
      vol. i: Report, and appendices [Cd. 4442], H.C. 1908, lix, 1
      vol. ii: Minutes of evidence (days 1–37) [Cd. 4443], H.C. 1908, lix, 147
      vol. iii: Minutes of evidence (days 38–66) [Cd. 4444], H.C. 1908, lix, 533
      vol iv: Precis and appendices [Cd. 4568], H.C. 1909, xlix, 177

Belfast Health Commission, Report to the local government board for Ireland [Cd. 4128], H.C. 1908, xxxi, 699

Report of an inquiry by the Board of Trade into the earnings and hours of labour of workpeople of the United Kingdom, I: Textile trades in 1906 [Cd. 4545], H.C. 1909, lxxx, 1

Report of the departmental committee on humidity and ventilation in cotton weaving sheds [Cd. 4484], H.C. 1909, xv, 635

Report by Sir Ernest Hatch as to the methods of applying the 'particulars' section of the Factory and Workshop Act 1901 to sundry industries [Cd. 4842], H.C. 1909, xxi, 709

Summary of returns ... of persons employed in 1907:
      Textile factories   [Cd. 4692], H.C. 1909, lxxix, 851
      Non-textile factories   [Cd. 5398], H.C. 1910, lxxxiii, 789
      Workshops   [Cd. 5883], H.C. 1911, lxxxix, 1.

Departmental committee on accidents in places under the factory and workshop acts:
      Report [Cd. 5535], H.C. 1911, xxiii, 1.
      Minutes of evidence, etc. [Cd. 5540], H.C. 1911, xxiii, 71

Second report of the departmental committee on humidity and ventilation in cotton weaving sheds [Cd. 5566], H.C. 1911, xxiii, 807

Royal commission on the civil service:

Second report: Minutes of evidence [Cd. 6535], H.C. 1912–13, xv, 259

Fourth report Minutes of evidence [Cd. 7338], H.C. 1914, xvi, 1

Report of the committee of enquiry into the conditions of employment in the linen and other making-up trades of the north of Ireland, with evidence [Cd. 6509], H.C. 1912–1913, xxxiv, 365

Report to the secretary of state for the home department on accidents occurring in shipbuilding yards, by H.M. Robinson (HM deputy chief inspector of factories) and H.J. Wilson (HM inspector of factories, Glasgow) [Cd. 7046], H.C. 1913, lx, 115.

Departmental committee on humidity and ventilation in flax mills and linen factories (mainly in Ireland):

Report [Cd. 7433], H.C. 1914, xxxvi, 1

Minutes of evidence [Cd. 7446], H.C. 1914, xxxvi, 107

Report of the departmental committee on agricultural credit in Ireland [Cd. 7375], H.C. 1914, xiii, 1.

Report of the committee of inquiry into night work in the bread-baking and flour confectionery trade [Cmd. 246], H.C. 1919, xxvi, 485

Departmental committee on the system of compensation for injuries to workmen:

Report [Cmd. 816], H.C. 1920, xxvi, 1

Minutes of evidence, vol. i [Cmd. 908], H.C. 1920, xxvi, 87

Minutes of evidence, vol. ii [Cmd. 909], H.C. 1920, xxvi, 605

LIST OF CASES

Clemenger v. *Jacob* (1903) 3 NIJR 243 — 360n

Coe v. *Platt* (1851) 6 Exch 752, (1852) 7 Exch 460
and 923, 155 Eng Rep 1030 and 1226 — 339, 340

Conway v. *Belfast & Northern Counties Rly. Co.* (1875) IR 9 CL 498,
(1877) IR 11 CL 345 — 345n

Corry v. *Lucas* (1868) IR 3 CL 208 — 244

Cotterrell v. *Samuel Stocks & Co., Insp. quart. rep., Sept. 1840*, p. 7 — 337n, 342n

Couch v. *Steel* (1854) 3 El & Bl 402, 118 Eng Rep 1193 — 339

Cramp v. *Ewart (William) & Sons, Insp. half-yearly rep., April 1871*, p. 70 — 309

Cramp v. *Robert Rowan & Co., Insp. half-yearly rep., Oct. 1873*, p. 146 — 130n

Cramp v. *Trimble, Insp. half-yearly rep., April 1869*, pp. 127, 129 — 310–11

Cribb v. *Kynock (No. 2) Ltd.* [1908] 2 KB 551 — 360n

Darkin v. *Brookfield & Doagh Spinning Co., Insp. half-yearly rep., Oct 1858*, p. 73 — 130n

Darkin v. *Foster Connor, Insp. half-yearly rep., Apr. 1857*, p. 59 — 130n

Darkin v. *Charles Duffin & Co., Insp. half-yearly rep., Oct. 1854*, p. 45 — 307

Darkin v. *Francis Ritchie & Sons, Insp. half-yearly rep., Oct. 1856*, p. 59 — 130n, 304, 305

Darkin v. *Francis Ritchie & Sons, Insp. half-yearly rep., Apr. 1857*, p. 60 — 130n, 304

Darkin v. *Herdman's of Sion Mills Insp. half-yearly rep.,*
Oct. 1854, p. 29 — 126, 130n, 131, 338n

Darkin v. *James Kennedy & Son, Insp. half-yearly rep., Apr. 1856*, p. 28 — 130n

Darkin v. *James Kennedy & Son, Insp. half-yearly rep., Apr. 1858*, p. 31 — 130

Deane v. *Boyle, Chief insp. ann. rep., 1897*, pp. 90 and 108 — 202–03, 321

Deane v. *Wilson* [1906] 2 IR 405 — 217–18

Doel v. *Sheppard and Others* (1856) 5 El & Bl 856, 119 Eng Rep 700 — 126, 127

Edwards v. *Godfrey* [1899] 2 QB 333 — 360n

Egan v. *Freeman's Journal Ltd.* (1901) 1 NIJR 214 — 343n

Eraut v. *Inglis & Co., Belfast Newsletter*, 11 Sept. 1909 — 263

Eraut v. *McCaughey, Northern Whig*, 1 Aug. 1911 — 242n

Eraut v. *Ross Bros. Ltd.* [1910] 2 IR 591 — 187

Fogarty v. *Wallis & Co.* [1903] 2 IR 522 — 238n

Fullers Ltd. v. *Squire* [1901] 2 KB 209 — 330

Glasgow v. *Irish Independent Printing Co.* [1901] 2 IR 278 — 199n

Griffiths v. *Earl Dudley* (1882) 9 QBD 357 — 349–50

Groves v. *Lord Wimborne* [1898] 2 QB 402 — 340n, 356

Hanlon v. *North City Milling Co.* [1903] 2 IR 163 — 238n

Harrison v. *Wythe Moor Colliery Co.* [1922] 2 KB 674 — 360n

Harrisons Ltd. and Turvey v. *Brintons Ltd.* [1904] 1 KB 328 — 362n

Hewlett v. *Allen & Sons* [1892] 2 QB 662 — 212n

Hildige v. *O'Farrell* (1880) 6 LR Ir 493 — 340n

Hindle v. *Birtwhistle* [1897] 1 QB 192 — 70n, 132, 155

Hoare v. *Ritchie* [1901] 1 QB 434 — 166n

Hoare v. *Robert Green* [1907] 2 KB 315 — 205n, 330

Holleran v. *Bagnell* (1880) 6 LR Ir 333 — 344n

Ingram v. *Barnes* (1857) 7 El & Bl 115, 119 Eng Rep 1190 — 204n

Johnson v. *W.H. Lindsay & Co.* [1891] AC 371 — 357n

Johnstone & Beck v. *Darkin, Insp. half-yearly rep., April 1860*, pp. 49, 68 — 307, 308

Langridge v. *Levy* (1837) 3 M & W 519, 150 Eng Rep 863 — 244

Le Fanu v. *Malcomson* (1848) 1 HL Cas 637, 9 Eng Rep 910 — 26–27

Leech v. *J.H. Gartside & Co., Chief insp. ann. rep., 1884*, pp. 11–12 — 154

M'Allister v. *Jones* (1902) 36 ILTR 215 — 360n

M'Bey v. *Edenderry Spinning Co.* (1883) 17 ILTR 78 — 373n

McCaffrey v. *Great Northern Rly. Co.* (1902) 36 ILTR 27 — 276n, 361n

McCartan v. *Belfast Harbour Commissioners* [1910] 2 IR 470,
[1911] 2 IR 143 — 242n, 357n

M'Carthy v. *British Shipowners' Co.* (1883) 10 LR Ir 384 — 345n

MacCracken v. *Dargan* (1856) 1 Ir Jur (ns) 404 — 339n

TABLE OF STATUTES

Acts of the Parliament of Ireland

Acts of the Parliament of England/Great Britain

Acts of the Parliament of the United Kingdom

1901	Factory and Workshop Act (*cont.*)	
	s. 115	74n
	s. 116	76, 209–11, 234
	s. 118	86n
	s. 119	78
	s. 120	306n
	s. 122	115n
	s. 135	140–41, 319n, 320
	s. 136	319n, 320, 353
	s. 137	319n, 320
	ss. 138–140	320
	s. 141	302
	s. 144	303, 318, 324
	s. 149	67, 148, 230, 259, 330n
	s. 156	73
	s. 160	303, 311
	sch. 2	259n, 273
	sch. 6	67n, 148, 230, 258
1906	Notice of Accidents Act (6 Edw. VII, c. 53)	70n, 137, 141
	Workmen's Compensation Act (6 Edw. VII, c. 58)	236, 359–76
	s. 1	355n
	s. 3	368
	s. 8	371n
	s. 13	361
	sch. II	366
1907	Employment of Women Act (7 Edw. VII, c. 10)	148, 168
	Factory and Workshop Act (7 Edw. VII, c. 39)	295–97
	Notification of Births Act (7 Edw. VII, c. 40)	121n
1908	White Phosphorus Matches Prohibition Act (8 Edw. VII, c. 42)	284
1909	Trade Boards Act (9 Edw. VII, c. 22)	224–26
1911	Factory and Workshop (Cotton Cloth Factories) Act (1 & 2 Geo. V, c. 21)	165n, 185n
	National Insurance Act (1 & 2 Geo. V., c. 55)	121
	Resident Magistrates (Belfast) Act (1 & 2 Geo. V, c. 58), s. 2	312
1914	Government of Ireland Act (4 & 5 Geo. V, c. 90), s. 4(6)	95n
1918	Trade Boards Act (8 & 9 Geo. V, c. 32)	226
1919	Sex Disqualification (Removal) Act (9 & 10 Geo. V, c. 71)	104n
1920	Employment of women, young persons and children act (10 & 11 Geo. V, c. 65), s. 1(1)	67n, 118
1938	Baking Industry (Hours of Work) Act (1 & 2 Geo. VI, c. 41)	261n

Statutes of the Oireachtas

1936	Night-Work (Bakeries) Act (c. 42)	261n
1955	Factories Act (c. 10), s. 103	355n
1958	Law Reform (Personal Injuries) Act (c. 38), s. 1	347n

Statutes of the Parliament of Northern Ireland

1948	Law Reform (Miscellaneous Provisions) Act (c. 23), s. 1(2)	347n
1965	Factories Act (c. 20)	355n

Statutory Rules and Orders

SECONDARY SOURCES: BOOKS

Abraham, M.E., *The law relating to factories and workshops*. London. 1896.

Anderson, A.M. *Women in the factory: An administrative adventure, 1893 to 1921*. London. 1922.

Arlidge, J.T. *The hygiene, diseases and mortality of occupations*. London. 1892.

Armstrong, D.L. *The growth of industry in Northern Ireland: The story of the golden age of industrial development, 1850–1900*. Long Hanborough, Oxford. 1999.

Arthurs, H.W. *'Without the law': Administrative justice and legal pluralism in nineteenth-century England*. Toronto. 1985.

Ashton, T.S., *The industrial revolution, 1760–1830*. Oxford. 1976.

Atiyah, P.S. *Accidents, compensation and the law*. ed. P. Cane. 6th ed. London. 1999.

—— *The rise and fall of freedom of contract*. Oxford. 1979.

Austin, H.E. *The law relating to laundries, charitable, reformatory and public institutions under the factory and workshop acts 1901 and 1907*. London. 1907.

Baines, E., *A history of the cotton manufactures in Great Britain*. London. 1835.
Baker, R., *The factory acts made easy, or How to work the law without the risk of penalties*. London. 1851, 1860, 1868.
—— *The Workshops Regulation Act made as easy as possible*. London. 1867.
Baldwin, R. and Cave, M. *Understanding regulation: Theory, strategy and practice*. Oxford. 1999.
Bardon, J. *A history of Ulster*. Belfast. 1992.
Bartrip, P.W.J. *Workmen's compensation in twentieth-century Britain*. Oxford. 1987.
—— and Burman, S.B. *The wounded soldiers of industry: Industrial compensation policy 1833–1897*. Oxford. 1983.
Beckett, J.C. and Glasscock, R.E. (ed.). *Belfast*. London. 1967.
Berg, M. (ed.) *Markets and manufacture in early industrial Europe*. London. 1991.
Beven, T. *The law of employers' liability for the negligence of servants*. London. 1881.
—— *Principles of the law of negligence*. 2nd ed.. London. 1895.
Black, R.D.C. *Economic thought and the Irish question*. Cambridge. 1960.
Bolger, P. *The Irish cooperative movement: its history and development*. Dublin. 1977.
Bonsall, P. *The Irish RMs: The resident magistrates in the British administration of Ireland*. Dublin. 1998.
Boston, S. *Women workers and the trade unions*. London. 1980.
Bowley, A.L. *Wages in the United Kingdom in the nineteenth century*. Cambridge. 1900.
Bowstead, W. *The law relating to factories and workshops, as amended and consolidated by the Factory and Workshop Act 1901*. London. 1901.
Boyle, E. *The Irish flowerers*. Holywood, Co. Down. 1971.
Boyle, J.W. *The Irish labor movement in the nineteenth century*. Washington, DC. 1988.
Brooke, E. *A tabulation of the factory laws of European countries*. London. 1898.
Brooke, P. (ed.). *Problems of a growing city: Belfast 1780–1870*. Belfast. 1973.
Byers, J.W. *Public health problems*. Belfast. 1906.
Calder, J. *The prevention of factory accidents*. London. 1899.
Campbell, T.J. *Workmen's compensation under the Workmen's Compensation Act 1906 and the Employers' Liability Act 1880*. 5th ed. Dublin. 1908.
Carson, W.G., 'The institutionalisation of ambiguity: The early factory acts', in G. Geis and E. Stotland (ed.). *White collar crime*. London. 1980.
Cawthon, E.A. *Job accidents and the law in England's early railway age: Origins of employers' liability and workers' compensation*. Lampeter, NY. 1997.
Clark, G. and Ó Gráda, C. *Cheap labour and Irish industrialisation*. Dublin. 1991.
Clark, W. *Linen on the green: An Irish mill village, 1730–1982*. Belfast. 1983.
Clark, W.A.G. *Linen, jute and hemp industries in the United Kingdom*. London. 1913.
Clarke, A. *The effects of the factory system*. London. 1899.
Clarkson, L.A. (ed.). *The industrial revolution: A compendium*. Basingstoke. 1990.
Coe, W.E. *The engineering industry of the north of Ireland*. Newton Abbot. 1969.
Cohen, M. *Linen, family and community in Tullylish, Co. Down, 1690–1914*. Dublin. 1997.
—— (ed.). *The warp of Ulster's past*. London. 1997.
Cole, G.D.H., *A short history of the British working class movement, 1789–1947*. London. 1960.
Collins, B., 'The organisation of sewing outwork in late nineteenth-century Ulster', in M. Berg (ed.), *Markets and manufacture in early industrial Europe*. London. 1991.
Cooke-Taylor, R.W. *Introduction to a history of the factory system*. London. 1886.
—— *The factory system and the factory acts*. London. 1894.
Cornish, W.R. and Clark, G. de N. *Law and society in England 1750–1950*. London. 1989.
Coyne, W.P. (ed.). *Ireland: Industrial and agricultural*. 2nd ed. Dublin. 1902.
Crawford, W.H. *The hand-loom weavers and the Ulster linen industry*. Belfast. 1994.
Crawford, Sir William. *Irish linen and some features of its production*. Belfast. 1910.
Cullen, M. and Luddy, M. (ed.). *Women, power and consciousness in 19th century Ireland*. Dublin. 1995.
Cullen, L.M. *An economic history of Ireland since 1660*. London. 1972.
Daly, M.E. *Social and economic history of Ireland since 1800*. Dublin. 1981.
Dickson, D., 'Aspects of the rise and decline of the Irish cotton industry', in L.M. Cullen and T.C. Smout (ed.), *Comparative aspects of Scottish and Irish economic and social history, 1600–1900*. Edinburgh. 1977

Djang, T.K. *Factory inspection in Great Britain.* London. 1942.

Gaskell, P. *The manufacturing population of England, its moral, social and physical condition.* London. 1833.

Gill, C. *The rise of the Irish linen industry.* Oxford. 1925.

Graham, B.J. and Proudfoot, L.J. (ed.). *An historical geography of Ireland.* London. 1993.

Gray, R. *The factory question and industrial England, 1830–1860.* Cambridge. 1996.

Greaves, C.D. *The life and times of James Connolly.* London. 1961.

Green, E.R.R. *The industrial archaeology of Co. Down.* Belfast. 1963.

—— *The Lagan valley, 1800–1850: A local history of the industrial revolution.* London. 1949.

Greer, D.S. 'Middling hard on coin': Truck in Donegal in the 1890s. Dublin. 2000.

Greer, D.S. '"A false, mawkish and mongrel humanity"? The early history of employers' liability in Ireland', in O. Breen, J. Casey and A. Kerr (ed.), *Liber memorialis Professor James C. Brady.* Dublin. 2001.

Gribbon, H.D. 'Economic and social history', in W.E. Vaughan (ed.), *A new history of Ireland, VI: Ireland under the Union II, 1870–1921.* Oxford. 1996.

Gribbon, H.D. *The history of water power in Ulster.* Newton Abbot. 1969.

Hanes, D.G. *The first British workmen's compensation act, 1897.* New Haven and London. 1968.

Hanna, H. *The Workmen's Compensation Act 1897, as applied to Ireland.* 1st ed.. Dublin. 1898.

Hanna's law of workmen's compensation. ed. H. Hanna and T.D. Kingan. 2nd ed. Dublin. 1907.

Henriques, U.R.Q. *Before the welfare state: Social administration in early industrial Britain.* London. 1979.

HM inspectors of factories. *1833–1983: Essays to commemorate 150 years of health and safety inspection.* London. 1983.

Hilton, H.W. *The truck system.* Cambridge. 1960.

Hobsbawm, E. *The age of capital 1848–1875.* London. 1975.

Holmes, J. and Urquhart, D. *Coming into the light: The work, politics and religion of women in Ulster, 1840–1940.* Belfast. 1994.

Horn, P. *Children's work and welfare, 1780–1880s.* Basingstoke. 1994.

Hunt, T. *Portlaw, County Waterford 1825–1876: Portrait of an industrial village and its cotton industry.* Dublin. 2000.

Hutchins, B.L. and Harrison, A. *A history of factory legislation.* 3rd ed. London. 1926.

Hutchinson, A. and Taylor, T. *The factory acts, so far as they apply to commercial laundries.* London. 1908.

Irwin, M.H., *The conditions of women's work in laundries.* Glasgow. 1893.

—— *Home work in Ireland: Report of an inquiry.* 2nd ed., Glasgow. 1913.

Jevons, W.S., *The state in relation to labour.* London. 1910.

Jones, E., *A social geography of Belfast.* London. 1965.

Kay, J.P. *The moral and physical condition of the working classes employed in the cotton manufacture in Manchester.* London. 1832.

Kennedy, L. and Ollerenshaw, P. (ed.). *An economic history of Ulster, 1820–1939.* Manchester. 1985.

Kirby, R.G. and Musson, A.E. *The voice of the people: John Doherty, 1785–1854, Trade unionist, radical and factory reformer.* Manchester. 1975.

Lubenow, W.C. *The politics of government growth: Early Victorian attitudes to state intervention, 1833–1848.* Hamden, Conn. 1971.

Luddy, M. *Women in Ireland, 1800–1918: A documentary history.* Cork. 1995.

—— *Women and philanthropy in nineteenth-century Ireland.* Cambridge. 1995.

—— and Murphy, C., *Women surviving: Studies in Irish women's history in the nineteenth and twentieth centuries.* Dublin. 1990.

Lyell, K.M. *Memoir of Leonard Horner.* London. 1890.

McCall, H. *Ireland – her staple manufactures: being sketches of the history and progress of the linen and cotton trades.* 3rd ed. Belfast. 1870.

McCarthy, C., *Trade unionism in Ireland, 1894–1960.* Dublin. 1977.

McCutcheon, W.A. *The industrial archaeology of Northern Ireland.* Belfast. 1980.

MacDonagh, O. *Early Victorian government, 1830–1870.* London. 1977.

McDowell, R.B. *The Irish administration, 1801–1914.* London. 1964.

McFeely, M.D. *Lady inspectors: The campaign for a better workplace 1893–1921.* New York and Oxford. 1988.

Markham, V.R. *May Tennant: A portrait.* London. 1949.

Marshall, L.C. *The practical flax spinner.* London. 1885.

Martindale, H. *Women servants of the state, 1870–1938: A history of women in the civil service.* London. 1938.

—— *From one generation to another, 1839–1944.* London. 1944

—— *Some Victorian portraits and others.* London. 1948.

Martineau, H. *The factory controversy.* Manchester. 1855.

Mess, H.A. *Factory legislation and its administration 1891–1924.* London. 1926.

Messenger, B. *Picking up the linen threads.* Belfast. 1982.

Micks, W.L. *An account ... of the congested districts board for Ireland from 1891 to 1923.* Dublin. 1925.

Mokyr, J. (ed.). *The British industrial revolution: An economic perspective.* Oxford. 1993.

Molloy, C. *The justice of the peace for Ireland: A treatise on the powers and duties of magistrates in Ireland.* Dublin. 1890.

Moody, T.W. and Beckett, J.C. (ed.). *Ulster since 1800: A political and economic survey.* London. 1955.

Morgan, A. *Labour and partition: The Belfast working class 1905–1923.* London. 1991.

Moss, M. 'Shipbuilding in Ireland in the nineteenth century', in S. Ville (ed.), *Shipbuilding in the United Kingdom in the nineteenth century: A regional approach.* St. John's, Newfoundland. 1993.

Moss, M. and Hume, J. *Shipbuilders to the world: 125 years of Harland and Wolff, 1861–1986.* Belfast. 1986.

Nardinelli, C. *Child labor and the industrial revolution.* Indianapolis. 1990.

Ó Broin, L. *The chief secretary: Augustine Birrell in Ireland.* London. 1970.

O'Connor, E. *A labour history of Ireland 1824–1960.* Dublin. 1992.

—— and T. Parkhill (ed.). *A life in Linenopolis: The memoirs of William Topping, Belfast damask weaver, 1903–1956.* Belfast. 1992.

Ó Gráda, C. *Ireland: A new economic history 1780–1939.* Oxford. 1994.

Oliver, T. (ed.). *Dangerous trades: The historical, social and legal aspects of industrial occupations as affecting health, by a number of experts.* London. 1902.

—— *Diseases of occupation from the legislative, social and medical points of view.* 2nd ed. London. 1908.

Patterson, H. *Class conflict and sectarianism.* Belfast. 1980.

Pellew, J. *The Home Office 1848–1914: From clerks to bureaucrats.* London. 1982.

Pollard, S. and Robertson, P. *The British shipbuilding industry, 1870–1914.* London. 1979.

Peirson, J.G. *Great shipbuilders: The rise of Harland and Wolff.* Belfast. 1935.

Perkin, H., *The origins of modern English society.* Toronto. 1969.

Pollock, F. *The law of torts.* 1st ed. London. 1887.

Porter, S.C. *The law relating to employers' liability and workmen's compensation.* Dublin. 1908.

Purdon, C.D., *On the influence of flax spinning on the health of the mill workers of Belfast.* Belfast. 1875.

—— *Longevity of flax mill and factory operatives.* Belfast. 1875.

—— *The sanitary state of the Belfast factory district during ten years (1864 to 1873 inclusive) under various aspects.* Belfast. 1877.

—— *The mortality of flax mill and factory workers as compared with other classes of the community, the diseases they labour under and the causes that render the death-rate from phthisis, etc. so high.* Belfast. 1873.

Reid, A. 'Skilled workers in the shipbuilding industry, 1880–1920', in A. Morgan and B. Purdie (ed.). *Ireland: Divided nation, divided class.* London. 1980.

Redgrave's Factory Acts. ed. J.A. Redgrave and H.S. Scrivener. 7th ed. London. 1898.

Redgrave's factory, truck and shop acts. ed. C.F. Lloyd. 12th ed. London. 1916.

Redgrave's Factory Acts. ed. J. Owner. 14th ed. London. 1931.

Rhodes, G., *Inspectorates in British government.* London. 1981.

Riddall, C.C. *Agricultural co-operation in Ireland: The story of a struggle.* Dublin. 1950.

Robson, A.P. *On higher than commercial grounds: The factory controversy 1850–1853.* New York and London. 1985.

Rubin, G.R. and Sugarman, D. (ed.). *Law, economy and society, 1750–1914: Essays in the history of English law.* Abingdon. 1984.

Ruegg, A.H. and Mossop, L. *The law of factories and workshops.* London. 1902.

Smith-Gordon, L. and Staples, L.C. *Rural reconstruction in Ireland: A record of co-operative organisation.* London. 1917

Soldon, N.C. *Women in British trades unions, 1874–1976.* Dublin. 1978.

Squire, R.E. *Thirty years in the public service: An industrial retrospect.* London. 1927.

Stanton, K.M. *Breach of statutory duty in tort.* London. 1986.

Steinfeld, R. *Coercion, contract and free labour in the nineteenth century.* Cambridge. 2001.

Steinmetz, W. (ed.). *Private law and social inequality in the industrial age.* Oxford. 2000.

Swift, J. *A history of the Dublin bakers.* Dublin. 1948.

Taplin, E. *The dockers' union.* Leicester. 1985.

Tennant, M.E. *The law relating to factories and workshops, including laundries and docks.* 6th ed. London. 1908.

—— *Women in industry from seven points of view.* London. 1908.

Thackrah, C.T. *The effects of the principal arts, trades and professions, and of civic states and habits of living, on health and longevity.* London. 1831.

Thomas, M.W. *The early factory legislation: A study in legislative and administrative evolution.* Leigh-on-Sea, Essex. 1948.

Tucker, E. *Administering danger in the workplace: The law and politics of occupational health and safety regulation in Ontario, 1850–1914.* Toronto. 1990.

Tuckwell, G.M. *A short life of Sir Charles W. Dilke.* London. 1925.

Vynne, N. and Blackburn, H. *Women under the Factory Act.* Oxford. 1903.

'K.W.', *Sketches of the Merino factory, descriptive of its origin and progress and of its system of discipline and moral government.* Dublin. 1816–1818.

Ward, J.T. *The factory movement 1830–1855.* 2 vols. London. 1962.

Webb, B 'Women and the factory acts', in S. and B. Webb (ed.). *Problems in modern industry.* London. 1902.

—— and Webb, S. *History of trade unionism, 1666–1920.* London. 1920.

—— *Industrial democracy.* London. 1902.

Webb, S. (ed.). *The case for the Factory Acts.* London. 1901.

White, J. *Civil liability for industrial accidents.* Dublin. 1993.

Wilson, A. and Levy, H. *Workmen's compensation.* 2 vols. London. 1939.

Wilson, M. *Our industrial laws.* London. 1899.

Wohl, A.S. *Endangered lives: Public health in Victorian Britain.* London. 1983.

Woodward, E.L., *The age of reform, 1815–1870.* Oxford. 1971.

Yeandle, S. *Women of courage: 100 years of lady factory inspectors.* London. 1993.

SECONDARY SOURCES: ARTICLES

Abraham, M., 'The women's factory department', in *Fortnightly Review* (July 1898), 151.

Almquist, E.L., 'Labour specialisation and the Irish economy in 1848 – an aggregate occupational analysis', in *Econ. Hist. Rev.*, xxxvi (1983), 506.

Armstrong, D.L., 'Social and economic conditions in the Belfast linen industry 1850–1900', in *IHS*, vii (1950–51), 235

Babington, T.H., 'Flax mills – their machinery: accidents occurring therein, with suggestions for their prevention', in *Dublin Q.J. of Med. Science*, 43 (1866), 392.

Bailey, W.F., 'Magisterial reform; being some considerations on the present voluntary system, and suggestions for the substitution of an independent paid magistracy', in *JSSISI*, 9 (1879–85), 595

Bartrip, P.W.J., 'Success or failure? The prosecution of the early factory acts', in *Econ. Hist. Rev.*, xxxviii (1985), 423

—— 'State intervention in mid-19th century Britain', in *J. Brit. Stud.*, 23 (1983), 63

—— 'British government inspection 1832–1875', in *Hist. J.*, 25 (1982), 605

—— and P.T. Fenn, 'The evolution of regulatory style in the nineteenth-century British factory inspectorate', in *J. Law & Society*, 10 (1983), 201

—— 'The administration of safety: The enforcement policy of the early factory inspectorate 1844–1864', in *Public Admin.*, 58 (1980), 87

Bosanquet, H., Creighton, L. and Webb, B., 'Law and the laundry', in *Nineteenth Century* (1897), 224.

Carson, W.G., 'The conventionalization of early factory crime', in *Int'l J. Sociology of Law*, 7 (1979), 37

Cavendish, L.C.F., 'Laundries in religious houses', in *Nineteenth Century*, 41 (1897), 224

'Contracts in ouster of the Employers' Liability Act, 1880', in *ILT & SJ*, 16 (1882), 303.

Crawford, W.H., 'The evolution of the linen trade in Ulster before industrialization', in *Ir. Econ. & Soc. Hist.*, 15 (1988), 32

Cromwell, V., 'Interpretations of nineteenth-century administration: An analysis', in *Victorian Stud.*, ix (1966), 245

Dickson, R., 'Legal aspects of the factory act of 1856', in *J. Legal Hist.*, 2 (1981), 276.

'Employers Liability Act 1881', in *ILT & SJ*, 14 (1880), 521, 531, 555, 567, 577, 589, 611 and 621.

'Employers' liability for defective ways, means, works, machinery or plant', in *ILT & SJ*, 21 (1887), 453 and 467

'Employers' liability for defective "works"', in *ILT & SJ*, 26 (1892), 177 and 201.

Editorial, 'The factory act 1901', in *ILT & SJ*, 36 (1902), 393.

Field, S., 'Without the law? Professor Arthurs and the early factory inspectorate', in *J. Law & Society*, 17 (1990), 445

Froggatt, P., 'Industrialization and health in Belfast in the early nineteenth century', in *Hist. Stud.*, 13 (1981)

Geary, F., 'Deindustrialization in Ireland to 1851: some evidence from the census' in *Econ. Hist. Rev.*, li (1998), 512.

—— 'The rise and fall of the Belfast cotton industry: some problems', in *Ir. Econ. & Soc. Hist.*, 8 (1981), 30

—— 'The Belfast cotton industry revisited', in *IHS*, 26 (1988–89), 250.

—— 'Regional industrial structure and labour force decline in Ireland between 1841 and 1851', in *IHS*, 30 (1996), 167

Glynn, J.A., 'Irish convent industries', in *New Ireland Rev.*, 1 (1894), 236

Harrison, B. 'Suffer the working day: Women in the "dangerous trades", 1880–1914', in *Women's Studies Int'l Forum*, 13 (1990), 79.

Harrison, J.B., 'On the injurious effects arising from the manufacture of lucifer matches, as observed in the neighbourhood of Manchester', in *Dublin Q.J. of Med. Science*, xiv (1852), 10

Hart, J., 'Nineteenth-century social reform: A Tory interpretation of history', in *Past and Present*, xxxi (1965), 39

Henriques, U. 'An early factory inspector: James Stuart of Dunearn', in *Sc. Hist. Rev.*, 50 (1971), 18.

Hinsley, A. 'The hours of labour', in *Ir. Eccles. Rec.*, xiii (1892), 911.

Howells, R.L. '*Priestley* v. *Fowler* and the factory acts', in *Modern L. Rev.*, 26 (1963), 367.

Jones, H. 'Women health workers: The case of the first women factory inspectors in Britain', in *Social History of Medicine*, 1(2) (1988), 165

Lee, W.R. 'Robert Baker: The first doctor in the factory department', in *Br. J. Ind. Med.*, 21 (1964), 85 and 167

Longfield, A.K. 'Prosperous, 1776–1798' in *J. Kildare Arch. Soc.*, xiv (1966–67), 25.

Maconchy, J.K. 'A comparison between the accidents which have occurred in scutch mills, and in factories subject to government inspection, as they have come to my notice during the eight years of my connexion with the county Down infirmary', in *Dublin Q.J. of Med. Science*, 43 (1867), 65

McCutcheon, W.A. 'Water-powered corn and flax-scutching mills in Ulster', in *Ulster Folklife*, xii (1966), 41

MacDonagh, O. 'The nineteenth-century revolution in government: a reappraisal' in *Hist. J.*, 1 (1958), 51

Mandler, P. 'Cain and Abel: Two aristocrats and the early Victorian factory acts' in *Hist. J.*, 27 (1984), 83.

Martin, B. 'Leonard Horner: A portrait of an inspector of factories' in *Int'l Rev. Social History*, xiv, (1969) 412

Marvel, H.P. 'Factory regulation: A reinterpretation of early English experience' in *J. Law & Econ.* (1977), 379

'Match manufacture in Cork', in *Ir. Builder*, xxv (1883), 264

'Match manufacture in Dublin', in *Ir. Builder*, xiv (1872), 285

Monaghan, J.J. 'The rise and fall of the Belfast cotton industry', in *IHS*, 3 (1942–43), 1

Moore, Dr. J. 'On the influence of flax spinning on the health of the mill workers of Belfast', in *Transactions of the National Association for the Promotion of Social Sciences meeting in Belfast, 1867* (Linenhall Lib., N 13668)

Moore, W., 'A notice of some cases of injuries produced by the machinery of flax scutch mills', in *Dublin Q.J. of Med. Science*, xvii (1854), 60

Nardinelli, C. 'The successful prosecution of the factory acts: A suggested explanation', in *Econ. Hist. Rev.*, xxxviii (1985), 428

—— 'Child labor and the factory acts', in *J. Econ. Hist.*, 40 (1980), 739

Ó Gráda, C. 'The beginnings of the Irish creamery system, 1880–1914', in *Econ. Hist. Rev.*, 30 (1977), 284

Parris, H., 'The nineteenth-century revolution in government: A reappraisal reappraised', in *Hist. J.*, 3 (1960), 17

Peacock, A.E. 'The successful prosecution of the factory acts, 1833–1855' in *Econ. Hist. Rev.*, xxxvii (1984), 197

Purdon, C.D., 'The diseases which prevail among workers in flax', in *Dublin Q.J. of Med. Science*, lxii (1876), 370

Seaby, W.A. 'Employers' truck tickets and food vouchers issued in Ulster during the latter half of the 19th century and the early part of the 20th century', in *Numismatic Society of Ireland Occasional Papers*, nos. 5–9 (1969), 11

Smith, H. 'Judges and the lagging law of compensation for personal injuries in the nineteenth century', in *J. Legal Hist.*, 2 (1981), 258

Takei, A. 'The first Irish linen mills, 1800–1824', in *Ir. Econ. & Soc. Hist.*, xxi (1994), 28

Thompson, . 'Social control in Victorian Britain', in *Econ. Hist. Rev.*, 34 (1981), 189

Welply, J.J. 'On state inspection of creamery dairies', in *The Lancet*, 10 Nov. 1894.

THESES

Bleakley, D.W., 'Trade union beginnings in Belfast and district' (unpublished MA thesis, Queen's University Belfast, 1955).

Boyle, E.J., 'The economic development of the Irish linen industry 1825–1913' (unpublished PhD thesis, Queen's University Belfast, 1979)

Browne, B.M. , 'Trade boards in Northern Ireland, 1909–1945' (unpublished PhD thesis, Queen's University Belfast, 1989)

D'Arcy, F.A., 'Dublin artisan activity, opinion and organisation, 1820–1850' (unpublished MA thesis, National University of Ireland, 1968).

Hamill, J.P., 'A study of female textile operatives in the Belfast linen industry, 1890–1939' (unpublished PhD thesis, Queen's University Belfast, 1999)

Harris, J., 'Working and effects of trade boards in the linen industry' (unpublished PhD thesis, Queen's University Belfast, 1924)

Jordan, A., ' Voluntary societies in Victorian and Edwardian Belfast' (unpublished PhD thesis, Queen's University, Belfast, 1989)

McDermott, M., 'Domestic industry in post-famine rural Ireland' (unpublished MA thesis, National University of Ireland, 1996)

Monaghan, J., 'A social and economic history of Belfast in the first half of the nineteenth century' (unpublished PhD thesis, Queen's University Belfast, 1940)

Neill, M. 'Women at work in Ulster, 1845–1911' (unpublished PhD thesis, Queen's University Belfast, 1996)

D. Rebbeck,, 'The history of iron shipbuilding on Queen's Island up to 1874' (unpublished PhD thesis, Queen's University Belfast, 1950)

A. Takei, 'The early mechanization of the Irish linen industry, 1800–1840' (unpublished MLitt thesis, University of Dublin, 1990).

NEWSPAPERS

Ballymena Weekly Telegraph

Ballymoney Free Press

Belfast Directory

Belfast Evening Telegraph

Belfast Newsletter

Brotherhood

Coleraine Chronicle

Derry Standard

Donegal Vindicator

Down Recorder

Dublin Evening Telegraph

Freeman's Journal

Impartial Reporter and Farmers' Journal

Irish Times.

Irish Worker

Kerry Sentinel

London Gazette

Londonderry Sentinel

Lurgan Times

Northern Whig

Index

NB: The names of factory inspectors are given in italics.

The Irish Legal History Society

Established in 1988 to encourage the study and advance the knowledge of the history of Irish law, especially by the publication of original documents and of works relating to the history of Irish law, including its institutions, doctrines and personalities, and the reprinting or editing of works of sufficient rarity or importance.

PATRONS

The Hon. Mr. Justice Keane
Chief Justice of Ireland

Rt. Hon. Sir Robert Carswell
Lord Chief Justice of
Northern Ireland

COUNCIL, 2001–2002

PRESIDENT
Professor W.N. Osborough

VICE-PRESIDENTS
J.I. McGuire, esq.

His Honour Judge Martin QC

HONORARY SECRETARIES
Kevin Costello, esq. BL

Ms. Sheena Grattan

HONORARY TREASURERS
R.D. Marshall, esq.

John Gordon, esq.

COUNCIL MEMBERS
The Hon. Mr. Justice Geoghegan
His Honour Judge Hart QC
Roderick O'Hanlon, esq. BL

Professor G.J. Hand
Daire Hogan, esq.
Professor D.S. Greer

Professor Norma Dawson